CHURCH AND STATE IN CZECHOSLOVAKIA

Historically, Juridically, and Theologically Documented

by

LUDVÍK NĚMEC

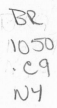

VANTAGE PRESS, INC., NEW YORK

Nihil Obstat: John M. A. Fearns, S.T.D.
Censor Librorum

Imprimatur: ✠ Francis Cardinal Spellman
Archbishop of New York

October 12, 1954

The nihil obstat and imprimatur are official declarations that a book or pamphlet is free of doctrinal or moral error. No implication is contained therein that those who have granted the nihil obstat and imprimatur agree with the contents, opinions or statements expressed.

Library of Congress Catalog Card Number: 54-7406
MANUFACTURED IN THE UNITED STATES OF AMERICA

Devoutly Dedicated

to

OUR LADY OF FATIMA

the Hope

of the Church of Silence

ACKNOWLEDGMENTS

I take this opportunity to express my sincere gratitude to the following persons:

His Excellency John Francis Dearden, Bishop of Pittsburgh, for his interest in the painful fate of the Church in Czechoslovakia;

Right Reverend Ambrose Ondrák, Abbot of St. Procopius in Lisle, Illinois, for his inspiring preface;

Very Reverend Francis Dvorník, Ph.D., S.T.D., LL.D., Professor at Harvard University and Dumbarton Oaks, Washington, D.C., for his valuable advice;

Dr. Vladimir Gsovski, head of the legal section of the Library of Congress, Washington, D.C., for his aid in securing legal source material;

Very Reverend Raphael M. Huber, O.F.M. Conv., S.T.M., S.T.D., Professor Emeritus of the Catholic University of America for his assistance and encouragement;

Reverend John Gallagher, C.S.Sp., Ph.D., of Duquesne University, Pittsburgh, Penna., for reading the manuscript;

Reverend John Lang, S.J., and Reverend Jaroslav Popelka, S.J., for procuring documents from the CML archives at the headquarters of the Sts. Cyril and Methodius League in London;

Mr. Frank A. Hall, head of the NCWC News Department, for documentary service from NCWC archives;

Dr. Roy Deferrari, secretary-general of the Catholic University Press, for permission to reprint Chapter XII from the author's book *Episcopal and Vatican Reaction* . . ., published by the Catholic University of America Press, 1953;

Monsignor Francis Planner, for documentary material from the *Veritas* archives in Rome;

Reverend Karel Kolek, O.S.B., director of the Bohemian Press in Chicago, and his editorial staff, for their assistance;

Reverend Bonaventure Buc, O.F.M., Ph.D., of Pittsburgh, and Dr. Jaroslav Navrátil of New York, for their help;

Miss Eleanora A. Bevil, B.S., M.Ed., of Pittsburgh, for reading a copy;

Miss Edith Kukurin, of East McKeesport, Penna., for typing the manuscript;

Sister M. Adele Whaley, M.A., of the Sisters of St. Joseph of Baden, for reading galley and page proofs, and helping to index;

The National Committee For Free Europe, New York, for furnishing current news material;

Vantage Press, Inc., New York.

To these persons, and others I may have unintentionally overlooked, I feel deeply grateful for help and encouragement. Furthermore, I hereby make a general and public acknowledgment to all the authors and the publishing houses that are cited in the Bibliography of my book.

PREFACE

THIS VOLUME MAKES AVAILABLE TO THE ENGLISH-SPEAKING world a well-documented record of anti-Christian persecution and heroic martyrdom which the historians of the future will have to rank at least with the persecution of the early Christians. This book of the Reverend Dr. Ludvík Němec, well-known Catholic priest refugee and professor from Czechoslovakia who now lives among us in the free world, takes us into the small, but beautiful and highly cultural country of Czechoslovakia. Bohemia, Moravia, Silesia, Slovakia, Carpatho-Ruthenia—all these provinces of Czechoslovakia have a Catholic culture and tradition that is more than a thousand years old. All of them have abundant architectural treasures consecrated to the honor and glory of God. There one finds hundreds of churches and Marian shrines, thousands of little chapels and crosses placed in the fields and at crossroads—all of them erected during past centuries, a profession of Catholic faith throughout the country to which this book is dedicated. There too in the provinces are many famous places of pilgrimages marked in the past by miracles or apparitions of the Blessed Mother of God.

As one walks through Prague, the splendid capital of Czechoslovakia, he is overwhelmed by the great number of churches. Especially impressive is the royal Hradčany, the massive residential castle of Czech kings, in the center of which is located the cathedral of St. Vitus. This huge Gothic structure is over five hundred feet long, and shelters the tombs of Saints Wenceslaus, Adalbert, John Nepomucene, and of kings and Roman emperors. Inside the courtyard of the cathedral are two other ancient churches—the thousand-year-old church of St. George, with the grave of St. Ludmila, grandmother of the Prince, St. Wenceslaus, and also All Saints' Church, where lie the remains of St. Procopius. Nearby is the historical abbey of Strahov, called the "Sion" of Prague, with the remains of St. Norbert. In other cities, also, are to be found monumental churches which are a rich treasure of Catholic culture.

Such churches are eloquent testimony of the fervent piety of the people in the past. But what about their descendants? Formerly they were deeply pious and faithful to the Church. Unbelievers among them were extremely few. It used to be said of them that they were a *Marian* nation. For their countryside was dotted with numerous Marian shrines, and people thought nothing of undertaking several days' pilgrimage on foot to reach the shrines. This fact may account for the many Marian songs written in the Bohemian and Slovakian languages. In the matter of Marian hymnology, these languages have no equal. Furthermore, the people of these countries were firm in their loyalty to the Church, even when waves of German Protestantism threatened them from the North. Heresy made only short-lived gains among them while Central Europe was exposed over and over again to the devastating powers of darkness. The first to tempt the faith of the people were the impact of the heresies of John Hus and the waves of Protestant pressure that resulted therefrom. But each time the people were successful in regaining their former status, and re-activated Catholicism was victorious.

During the last century, when the heart of Europe was poisoned by pseudo-philosophies and anti-Christian propaganda, which culminated in the French Revolution and which the spirit of Liberalism carried into all corners of Europe, the provinces comprising present Czechoslovakia were invaded by waves of rationalism, deism, modernism, religious indifferentism, and finally atheism. The infiltration came by way of the universities and among the intelligentsia, and thence spread to the masses.

The first to accept these progressive ideas was Bohemia; and once the traditional religious spirit was undermined there, a deplorable change was noticeable among its people. Many Czechs not only disregarded the things their forefathers had treasured and defended with their blood, but even gave evidence of a contempt for them that culminated in the lowest type of vandalism. For example: the first week after their liberation from the Austrian yoke in 1918, a mob of Prague citizens razed a pillar ornamented with an historic statue of the Blessed Virgin. Climbing to the top of the pillar, a young man tied a rope to the neck of the image and pulled until it crashed into fragments on the ground, while civil authorities stood nearby without objecting to such sacrilege, their silence seeming to condone it.

Excesses like these, some of them even inspired by persons in public life, were indications that materialistic liberalism had penetrated the Czech mind. Many good people, of course, were shocked at such abuses, but fearing reprisal and punishment, found themselves helpless. There were, however, sufficient good and courageous Catholics to demonstrate their disapproval of the forces of materialism on the march. Catholics awoke, and by 1935 had erected on the main square in Prague, named for St. Wenceslaus, a massive Cross of Christ, and there a million people paid homage to their Eucharistic King. The Czechoslovak National Church, which was established during the turbulent days following World War I, began to lose its glamor and prestige. Since the time of the famous National Eucharistic Congress in 1935 the Catholic Church has consistently re-enforced her position and prevailed in her attempt to recover her vigor.

But another blow fell. During the Nazi occupation, priests were thrown into prison, many to die there. Hundreds of them suffered unspeakable hardships, but not a single one submitted to the godless intruder. Then came the 1945 "liberation" of Czechoslovakia from Nazi occupation. The previous Away-from-Rome trend was seized and supported by Communists, and people fallen from the Faith became their easy prey. With the advent of the unhappy February 25, 1948, persecution of faithful Catholics began to make rapid strides.

All these periods of Church-State affairs in Czechoslovakia are adequately discussed from an historical point of view in this study. It is difficult, of course, to expose fully the glory and sacrifices of martyrdom in the Church, especially of recent times. There can be stressed only the trends and the tendencies by which the persecution is being led; there can be explained the defense which Catholics are making under the leadership of their bishops. But the shrewdness of Communist methods, and the unbelievable courage of bishops, priests, religious, nuns and the faithful—these the author has treated in much detail.

I know personally many representatives in this drama of

martyrdom now being portrayed in Czechoslovakia. I know Archbishop Beran—the small man with the mighty mind, most courageous among the Czech and Slovak bishops in the defense of divine rights and the rights of his nation. I know Bishop Trochta, Salesian, who worked tirelessly for laborers and youth (for whom he built a remarkable home in the suburbs of Prague), and was finally imprisoned by the Nazis in the same concentration camp as Archbishop Beran. Both these men have been spared to lead their people back to God.

I am acquainted with the activities of Bishop Hlouch in České Budějovice, who formerly labored among workmen in Hodolany, and was later a professor in the University of Olomouc, and finally a bishop well-known for his oratorical ability and pastoral zeal. Also remarkable is the firmness of the very old Bishop Mořic Pícha of Hradec Králové, who said from the altar: "I shall now read the pastoral letter of the Czechoslovak hierarchy, which the government has forbidden us to read. I do it because God, rather than man, should be obeyed. I am now eighty years old—I am prepared to die. They can come and arrest me. I am prepared for it." Instead of arresting him, policemen in the church disappeared, and the people sang *Te Deum.*

I know Monsignor Karel Skoupý, Bishop of Brno, who on December 8, 1953, as he entered the cathedral to proclaim the pastoral letter concerning the Marian Year, was arrested and deported to parts unknown. I also know young Abbot Anastasius Opasek from Břevnov, who worked zealously to spread the Benedictine spirit throughout the country.

These and others are the heroes we shall meet when reading Father Němec's book. One fact is of outstanding interest: Czechoslovak resistance to the Communist oppression was general and exemplary, firm among the hierarchy and the people. Many bishops have been condemned; others are deprived of their jurisdiction; not one among them has remained free. Such an heroic stand on the part of bishops, abbots, priests, nuns, and the faithful in general is a source of inspiration to all Catholics throughout the world. This is the hour of martyrdom for Czechoslovakia, the time for shedding innocent blood, and sealing faith with martyrdom. This period of heroism will furnish the basis for a renaissance of Christian and national tradition. We who preach the kingdom of Christ in the free world are encouraged also, as this glorious martyrdom of the Church of Silence is unfolded in *Church and State in Czechoslovakia.* In this contact with modern martyrs, with their example and inspiration, lies the value of the book now and for future times.

✠Ambrose Leo Ondrak
President, St. Procopius College
Abbot, St. Procopius Abbey

Lisle, Illinois
Easter 1954

CONTENTS

Page

Preface by Ambrose Leo Ondrák vii

PART ONE

Theological Bases for the Position of the Catholic Church

Chapter

1 An Introduction to Two Conflicting Ideologies 3
2 The Church as a Perfect Society 17
3 The Jurisdiction of the Pope 31
4 The Ecclesiastical Hierarchy as a Divine Institution 47

PART TWO

The Catholic Church and the Czechoslovak State

5 John Hus and the Reformation 65
6 The "Away from Rome" Movement 96
7 World War II and Religion in Czechoslovakia 146

PART THREE

The Catholic Church and the Communist State

8 The Communist Infiltration 177
9 The Communist Constitution and Its Effect on Ecclesiastical Affairs 221
10 The Calvary of the Catholic Church 259
11 The Attack on the Vatican 366
12 The Reaction of the Vatican (according to the documents issued in: *Acta Apostolicae Sedis*) 400
13 Czechoslovakia in Exile 436

Epilogue 447
Appendix 451
Footnotes 459
Bibliography 527
Index 563

LIST OF ILLUSTRATIONS

St. Vitus Cathedral in Prague

Panoramic view of Prague

Monsignor Joseph Beran being welcomed in Prague after his return from the Nazi concentration camp at Dachau

Archbishop Josef Beran
Right Reverend Abbot Vít Tajovský

Archbishop Beran carrying the reliquary containing the head of St. Adalbert, patron of Czechoslovakia

Archbishop Beran granting blessings

Nepomucenum, the papal college in Rome

Right Reverend Jan Opasek at procession in honor of St. Adalbert

Pavol Gojdič, Bishop of Prěsov, Slovakia

Greek Catholic Bishop Gojdič of Prěsov, with Basil Hopko

His Excellency Štěpán Trochta after his consecration

His Excellency Josef Hlouch, Bishop of Budějovice

His Excellency Josef Karel Matocha, Archbishop of Olomouc in Moravia

Auxiliary Bishop of Prague, Monsignor Kajetán Matoušek

Scene at the consecration of Bishop Josef Hlouch

His Excellency Bishop Karel Skoupý, Bishop of Brno
Official picture of Bishop Trochta

Most Reverend Josef Carsky
Most Reverend Karol Kmetko

PART ONE

THEOLOGICAL BASES FOR THE POSITION OF THE CATHOLIC CHURCH

CHAPTER ONE

AN INTRODUCTION TO TWO CONFLICTING IDEOLOGIES

TO UNDERSTAND THE HOSTILITY OF CZECHOSLOVAK COMmunists toward the Catholic Church one must have some knowledge of the theological principles which are basic to the present conflict. Inherent in the situation of the Czechoslovak Communists—which is the same in all of the other satellite countries behind the Iron Curtain—was the attack on some of the fundamental tenets of the Catholic Church; primarily, an attack on the doctrine that holds that the Church is a perfect society, and, in particular, a perfect society of the public order.[1] Because of the nature of the principles involved, it is understandable that this struggle was to be a bitter one.

The Czechoslovak Catholic bishops indicated the principles involved in this struggle to maintain the rights of the Church in their letter of June 15, 1949. The following is a paraphrase of a section of the letter:

1) The Christian world viewpoint must be recognized and respected in public life and education, both in word and deed.

2) The government must recognize the spiritual authority of the Pope of Rome as the supreme head of the Church in all religious and ecclesiastical matters. This arrangement is a natural consequence of recognized basic human rights and especially of the freedom of religion, since these matters, according to recognized authority, do not come within the compass of the sovereignty of the state.

3) Before the beginning of negotiations, all measures restricting and threatening religious freedom of Catholics of the Czechoslovak Republic, especially those referring to

the religious freedom and education of youth, must be repealed. [2]

These minimum conditions were also stressed in a memorandum sent to the Czechoslovak government by the Catholic bishops assembled in conference at Trnava, August 14, 1949.[3]

The theological concepts which form the basis for these points are as follows:

1. The Church is a perfect society.[4] 2. The Pope has legitimate jurisdiction over the whole Church.[5] 3. The hierarchy is a divine institution.[6] 4. The Church is a public society or a society of the public order.[7]

Furthermore, that these tenets constitute the basis for the proper relationship between the Church and state is further upheld by the statements in the decree of the Sacred Congregation of the Council, dated June 29, 1950: "The Catholic Church by the institution of Christ himself is a hierarchically constituted perfect society, over which supreme government and jurisdiction rest with the Roman Pontiff, successor of St. Peter in the primacy."[8]

It appears unnecessary to explain and prove here these fundamental truths about the Church, as they are evident from the many quotations from Holy Scripture;[9] they are the foundation of the dogmas of the faith; they are confirmed by the declarations of the councils.[10] Furthermore, they are necessary properties of the Church of Christ, both as a work of God and as an historical institution. Even though the well-known theological tracts concerning these truths exclude every doubt concerning their meaning and implications, it is most important to stress the point that the Catholic Church is a public society or, to use legal terminology, a society of public order. It necessarily follows, therefore, that the state must recognize the Church's rights. This must be stressed all the more if that state has diplomatic relations with the Holy See, particularly since Professor Antonín Hobza of Charles University in Prague, who is recognized as a law expert by the Communists, has tried to deny the rights of ecclesiastical law at the trials of the Church.[11]

A society must be called public which, by virtue of its

own institution, organization, and purpose, as also by its scope of action, goes far beyond the limits of any private society of men—especially if it has been formed to produce social, external, and general effects. That the Church is such a society is easily seen from:

1) Its end, or purpose and mission: the Church was instituted and so ordained that it might lead men, both as individuals and as members of domestic and civil society, to the perfection of Christian life and thereby to eternal life.

2) Its universality: because of the nature of its purpose, it extends itself to embrace the whole of mankind.

3) Its origin, institution, and hierarchy, and also from its necessity: its juridical activity is of such efficacy in the excellence of the external and social effects it produces that it cannot be subordinate to any other society.

Moreover, the Church is of such a nature that, judged solely by human criteria, that is, not taking into consideration its supernatural character and the rights and prerogatives divinely conferred upon it, and therefore considered simply as it actually exists in the social external order, it can claim for itself the character of an institution of public order. There are three things to be considered here, and these can be recognized as sufficient to establish the public nature of any human institution, namely: its juridical status, which has been recognized as belonging to the Catholic Church for centuries; its extension, either numerical or territorial; and finally, the social force and efficacy of its influence in the external order, which belong to it because of the innate power of the means it uses and the organized activity it employs to achieve its ends. Since all these characteristics are found united in the Church, she suffers great injury when any civil society treats her as being on the same level as institutions of a merely private nature.[12]

The juridical foundations of this argument were attacked by Professor Hobza, whose erroneous assertions became official theses of the Czechoslovak Communist government. A legal, internationally recognized basis for an appropriate Catholic Church-state relationship was limited by juridical conditions in which the exclusive supremacy of the state, detrimental to the supremacy of the Catholic Church, was stressed, regardless of canon law. Hobza's juridical interpretation was used many times[13] at the trials of Church representatives as the official attitude of the Czechoslovak government:

> The proper function of a law expert in a trial is to clarify the facts in the matter under consideration from different viewpoints, in order to reach a right and just decision. Such a thorough juridical clarification is necessary especially in the questions which have to be judged not only according to one juridical system, but according to different systems.
>
> The modern state, with certain exceptions, constitutes a uniform juridical sphere, which places precise limitations on foreign countries, and which, according to international law, excludes any interference from abroad. This held good for the bourgeois concept of the state, and also holds good for the people's democratic state and the socialistic state, whose juridical order is but the expression of the sovereign will of the people.
>
> Since the agreement with Italy in 1929, the Pope is the sovereign head of the little state of Vatican City, but principally he is the spiritual head of all faithful Catholics. This function, however, is being pushed further into the background, and another function is being stressed more emphatically; namely, the political function. However, since the Vatican is an important international factor, various governments still maintain diplomatic relations with it through nuncios and internuncios. These enjoy, according to the generally accepted practice, all the privileges of secular diplomatic representatives, and therefore also have the obligation not to interfere in the internal affairs of the state.
>
> However, the relation of the nuncios and the internuncios with the Pope is not based on international law but upon the so-called canon law, which, in the eyes of the modern state, is not considered a law at all.
>
> This opposition between the state law and canon law, as well as the Pope's political aspirations, based upon this canon law, in the past centuries had already caused many conflicts between the Vatican and various states. The governments of the people's democratic and socialistic states deny basically and consistently even the concept that any foreign functionary could follow, in the respective countries, a law originating neither in the will of the people nor in the will of the sovereign nation. Finally, after a long, wavering, and confused historic development, the

principle of the territoriality of the law is here carried out to its ultimate consequences. Today the juridical life in a state is not divided any more into the state sphere and the canon law sphere but is exclusively and uniformly based upon the state law.

All matters with which state law is concerned are considered to be the internal affairs of the state, and according to international law, no diplomatic representative is allowed to interfere in them. This also includes any state laws that set the norms for questions concerning the ecclesiastical life in the state territory.

From the preceding it follows that any direct contact of the internuncios with the Czechoslovak bishops has no official standing, nor can it be considered as official either in the sense of Czechoslovak law or international law. The internuncio in Czechoslovakia is simply a political representative who is entitled to act officially only with and through the government.

Consequently, the internuncio, in the Czechoslovak Republic, has no right to bring to the bishops any papal decrees which do not agree with the law, and he has no right to tell the people how they must act concerning the law or the ordinances of civil authority. If he does this notwithstanding, then he infringes upon international law since he interferes in the internal affairs of the state, and at the same time, according to Czechoslovak law, also commits a crime. If the court discovers that the perpetration of such a crime has been proved during the process, then the matter takes on the aspect of a major crime in the sphere of international law.

It is well known to all of us that the enemies of the Czechoslovak Republic are putting forth every effort to destroy it by inciting and encouraging treacherous actions and by organizing spying, and the Vatican collaborates with them toward the same end. The spying of the Vatican, compared to that of other states, has a greater advantage. This is because of the institution of canonical obedience of the lower church organizations to the higher ecclesiastical organs.

Therefore the state that does not recognize canon law does not, as a matter of fact, in any way recognize canonical obedience. A Czechoslovak Church representative who gives priority to canonical obedience to any foreign power without regard to the state laws becomes a traitor.

The case which is under the consideration of this honorable court charges nine ecclesiastical functionaries with grand treason, spying, and war preparations against the Czechoslovak Republic. They are further charged with participating in the abuse of the so-called faculties, that is, using their full powers in subversive activities in this country.

The faculties, according to canon law, are delegated and subdelegated forms. The faculty gives to a lower ecclesiastical functionary authority which otherwise pertains to a higher functionary. This institution of delegation and subdelegation is of extraordinary importance in periods of political revolution. These secret papal faculties are the well-established proof of the Vatican's fight against this country.

Since the Czechoslovak Republic does not recognize canon law, the episcopal and papal faculties have no efficacy within this country. Following the express ordinance of the Law #7 No. 218/49, only persons who have received permission from the state and who have made the pledge are allowed to perform spiritual functions in the ecclesiastical and religious societies.

The ecclesiastical functionary who, because of delegated faculties, performs the actions of a higher organ in the realm of administration, which may not be of a purely spiritual and sacramental nature, finds himself in conflict with the laws of the state and may be called by the administrative authorities as well as by the court to give an account of himself.

If, however, he abuses papal and other ecclesiastical faculties in order to further secretly his anti-state activities, to complete the net of spies and to organize an underground ecclesiastical hierarchy, then the state must deal with an organized plot whose director in the state territory is the internuncio, and whose highest authority is the Pope—both foreigners who can not be tried in the internal court.

The net of secret ecclesiastical faculties, which are to be delegated and subdelegated in this country to persons substituting for all ecclesiastical functionaries, proves that the Vatican considers that the fight against the state will flare into the open in the near future.

As a matter of fact, that is the view of the papal curia on the present situation in the Czechoslovak Republic. I discovered this by studying the secret faculty granted, at the order of the Vatican, to the Vicar-General and the auxiliary bishop, Dr. Stanislaus Zela, by the Archbishop of Olomouc.

This attitude of the Vatican towards the Czechoslovak Republic, which promulgated the Law No. 218/1949 and necessitated the governmental decree No. 219/1949 to assure the economy of the Roman Catholic Church, is certainly characteristic.

In judging the crimes committed against the state, obviously the hierarchical position and subordination of the ecclesiastical functionaries must be taken into consideration, and the appropriate principle applied: the higher the functionary, the greater the crime and the greater the punishment.

If this court discovers from the results of the procedure that any diplomatic representative of the Vatican in the Czechoslovak Republic interfered, no matter how, in the internal affairs of this state, that representative will be viewed as having seriously infringed upon the international law and the laws of the Czechoslovak Republic, and as having abused his diplomatic position. [14]

Because there are those who do not recognize the Church as a society of public order and as a moral person of the perfect society, we find a clash in the relations between the Church and the state. The Catholic opinion concerning the relative positions of two perfect societies[15] does not detract from the state, either in its own competence or in its sovereignty, but on the contrary, assists it in obtaining the complete fulfillment of its mission. The Church makes, of course, a precise distinction between the boundaries of the natural and supernatural orders and their mutual relations. As a perfect society she reserves exclusively to herself competency in her own sphere and missions originating in the supernatural order. But, as Jacques Maritain says:

> The pagan city, which claimed to be an absolute whole of the human being, absorbed the spiritual in the temporal power and at the same time apotheosized the State. Its ultimate worship of the Emperors was the sure consequence of an infallible internal logic. Even the Christian Emperors and Constantine, the first of them, did not immediately repudiate certain divine honors, such as the building of temples and the celebration of games in their honor.

The iconoclasts destroyed the images of Christ and the Saints at Byzantium, but respected the images of the Emperor. It was not until the fourth century that the Emperor Gratian gave up using the title of Pontifex Maximus. And, to avoid running down the whole subsequent course of history, it will be sufficient to observe that by the blasphemous beast "come up out of the sea" and the other beasts "come up out of the earth" that "see great signs," both securing the adoration denied to the Lamb, the Apocalypse intends to symbolize the profaning and usurping civilization of all times and all countries.

The Lord Christ said, "Render therefore to Caesar the things that are Caesar's and to God the things that are God's." He thereby distinguished the two powers and by so doing emancipated the souls of men. [16]

The indirect subordination[17] of the state to the Church is the necessary result of the objective competency of both these orders: their mutual positions do not depend on the will of the people. Their relations or positions arise ontologically, that is, from their very being, and they must be recognized as such. In order that a clash between the Church and the state may be avoided, it is logically necessary that there be mutual cooperation.[18]

The theological problem is not new. It has frequently recurred in history. Caesaro-papism with its principle of *imperator est episcopus rerum externarum,* as we already read in the Codex Encyclius[19] (and the medieval idea of *rex sacerdos*[20]), was the measure of the relations between Church and state in Central Europe, and finally the foundation of the feudal system. This was taken over by the Communists and added to the hostility toward the Church which ever since the time of John Hus has plagued this Bohemian land. Dvorník has well said:

> Let me explain by the same historical and comparative method why the new regimes in Central Europe are everywhere concentrating their fiercest attacks on the Vatican. This can not be explained only by the traditional dislike of the Czechs for Rome, a dislike which has its roots in the Czech Reformation—the Hussite period—and which was artificially fermented in the nineteenth century by the progressive Czech intelligentsia. [21]

There can be no doubt that the errors of Hus concerning

the Church,[22] the Pope,[23] and the bishops[24] caused a crisis that manifested itself throughout the Reformation and Counter-Reformation. In these, the central point is the struggle between the forces hostile to Rome and those in favor thereof. Complications were introduced and multiplied by the pre-Reformation and Reformation activities of Wyclif,[25] Hus, Luther,[26] and Zwingli[27] which sought to eliminate the Church as a visible society.[28] All these influences had their effect on the relations between the Church and the state. The principle formulated at Augsburg in 1555—*Cujus regio, ejus religio* (the ruler's religion is the religion of his subjects)—which was accepted by Protestants and forced on Catholics at the time of the Reformation, was only an odd and perverted survival of the old *rex sacerdos* theory.[29]

The servile position of the Church with respect to the state was further influenced by Gallicanism through the principle of the royal *placet* or *exsequatur*. Febronianism further abetted this opinion by its recognition of the power of the state to direct the external affairs of the Church; and Josephinism invented the concept of a national church subject to the state: "The Church is a department of the police which must serve the aims of the State, until such time as the enlightenment of the people permits its release by the secular police."[30]

Liberalism[31] and Modernism[32] had already declared that the Church had only the function of a private society. The spreading atheism of the nineteenth century destroyed the internal bond between the faithful and the Church and consequently also had an influence on the Church-state relationship. A classical example is Austria, where, although the reigning dynasty was that of the Catholic Hapsburgs, the relation between the Church and the state had to be governed by a concordat,[33] which was violated not only by the constitution of December 21, 1867, but also by the public laws of May 25, 1868,[34] up to the suspension of the Vatican Council in 1871. The *Los von Rom* movement,[35] which sprang from political principles and the *Kultusministerium* of Vienna also had an effect on Church affairs. Naturally, all these doctrines and movements had their echo in the lands of Bohemia and Slovakia which at that time were parts of the Austro-Hungarian monarchy.

The Bohemian national movement at the end of the nineteenth and the beginning of the twentieth century was infected with ideas inimical to the Catholic Church. Fostered by the Austrian *Los von Rom* movement, it brought about widespread defection from the Church of Rome. The struggle for liberty of the national groups under the Austro-Hungarian monarchy was slowed up by the central government at Vienna. This was the real reason for their aversion to the Catholic Church, although they were also subject to the same central power through the influence of the *Kultusministerium*, the Ministry of Culture, which regulated matters of religion. At the same time, this was also the reason why the movement under the leadership of T. G. Masaryk (1850-1937) accepted the antithesis "Reformation—Counter-Reformation," and why the Catholic Church was the object of radical attacks by the "progressive movement," the excesses of which were characterized by the Bohemian poet, Victor Dyk, in the words, "It is progress to the point of stupidity."[36]

Moreover, the juxtaposition "Vienna-Prague" further complicated the situation in which the Church found herself. Her servile position was passed on to the newly formed Czechoslovak Republic (1918) and, until the time of the *modus vivendi* (February 2, 1928),[37] the Church was treated according to the provisions of the former Austrian laws.[38]

Under the influence of the Czechoslovak bishops and of the political leader, Monsignor John Šrámek, the Church passed from its despised position to one of respectability, so that in 1935 it was able to demonstrate in the first Catholic congress in Prague its venerable and honorable status.[39] During the time of the Nazi occupation, the people were able to experience pragmatically that the Catholic Church in Czechoslovakia was an institution worthy of trust,[40] and thus she gained a further measure of respect. After World War II (1939-45) the Czechoslovak Communists once more tried to place the Church in a state of servitude. After the *coup d'état* of February, 1948, the Communists began their attempts to bring the Church into subjection, but they encountered the opposition of the bishops. The Archbishop of Prague, Joseph Beran, in his last public address in a church of Strahov, solemnly stated on June 18, 1949: "But I declare before God and before the nation that I shall never conclude an agreement against the rights of the Church or the bishops."[41] By these words the Archbishop made it clear that the recognition of the fundamental truths was necessary to the Church if she was to have true freedom and fulfill her mission. After this address of the Archbishop, the attack against the Church became more vehement.

The Communists of Czechoslovakia, influenced by Russia, also made use of the historical antipathy of the Orthodox East to Rome and tried to use the servile status of Orthodoxy in Russia[42] as a pattern for placing the Catholic Church in a similar position. The Orthodox idea of independence from Rome especially pleased them, and they deliberately fostered this notion through an appeal to Pan-Slavism. Only in this way can we explain why, in the beginning, many political leaders in Czechoslovakia did not see the great danger hidden in this appeal.

The insincerity of the Communists in their appeal to Pan-Slavism is best seen in the cruel fate of the Greek Catholic Church, although this Church drew its ideals from the unity founded on the sacred traditions of the old Slavonic liturgy from the time of Sts. Cyril and Methodius, and fostered harmonious relations between the Slavic groups.[43] The persecution of the Greek Church is further evidence of how the infiltration into Czechoslovakia of the Orthodox Church tended to weaken the Catholic Church.[44] Herein is also evidence that the Communists did not intend to recognize the Catholic Church as a public society nor the liberty of the Catholic Church and her manifest rights. They borrowed from history all the ideologies hostile to the Church, especially the concept of Josephinism, and the attitude of the Austrian *Kultusministerium* in the legislation they promoted. These ideas not only aided them in subjecting the Church to inspection, but also furnished them with means to enslave her—a step toward the complete destruction of the Church. Toward this objective the Communists seem to have aimed their various political and tactical programs. It is a historical fact that the Catholic Church endures terrible agonies behind the Iron Curtain, for there she cannot live in liberty, either as a society of public order (*publici juris*) or even as a private society in her own right, despite the declarations and assurances to the contrary put forth by the Czechoslovak Communists.

The principles by which the state seeks a relationship with the Church are utterly untenable. The struggle between the Catholic Church and the Czechoslovak democratic people's regime does not consist simply in a battle on the part of the Church to protect her full rights; it is an effort merely to maintain the exercise of those inalienable rights which are the necessary minimum if she is to survive at all.

This state of affairs in Czechoslovakia is most instructive. The Czechoslovak bishops, when setting forth this bare minimum which should have been recognized and accepted, not only fulfilled their own obligations as guardians and pastors of the Church but also manifested their willingness to formulate an agreement and their sincere desire to reach some measure of cooperation with the state. Their stand was expressed in a pastoral letter of June 15, 1949, which read in part as follows:

> We declare that we have been and that we always are in favor of a just accord with the State in all politico-ecclesiastical questions, because such an accord forms the basis of any fruitful cooperation for the tasks of the two parties. It will, however, only be possible if the state refrains from interfering in ecclesiastical and religious affairs, just as the Church refrains from interfering in political affairs. [45]

In the same pastoral letter the bishops suggested that in the eyes of the regime it was a question not so much of an agreement between church and state as of the subordination of the Church to an anti-Christian ideology, which sought to replace religion with Marxism and to attribute to the state the right of intervening in matters of conscience, of faith and of morals—something no Christian can accept.[46]

The Catholic Church did not attempt to encroach[47] upon the rights of the state, but she did insist on defending her religious freedom.[48] In regard to this, the Archbishop of Prague, on April 26, 1948, gave this statement to the Minister of Justice, Dr. Čepička:[49]

> We shall not betray either the state or the people, but neither shall we betray God or the Church. [50]
>
> And if the Church does not think it right to interfere without just reason in such earthly and purely political

> affairs, still, it cannot rightfully tolerate that political power shall take excuse therefrom either to oppose the good of the higher order, on which depends the salvation of souls, or to harass it by unjust laws or decrees, or to violate the Divine constitution of the Church itself, or to trample on the laws of God Himself in civil society. [51]

That the stand of the Catholic bishops remained firm is clearly shown in their pastoral letter of August 26, 1948:

> The negotiations broke down and all the blame was put on the Church. We have been criticized on the ground that we did not endorse unconditionally all that was being done, as other churches did. We expressly announced that we would not betray our duties towards the state and its government, but we added that, in accordance with Christ's teaching, we would give to Caesar only that which is Caesar's, and that above all we must give to God what belongs to God. We were unable to endorse everything unconditionally because, unfortunately, we had too much evidence of a hidden anti-church and anti-religious struggle that has started in our country. This has been carried on according to a pattern used in other countries against the Church and religion. We would like to emphasize more particularly such breaches of religious law as the circumstance that leaders of the Church have been prevented from carrying out their functions for the sole reason that they had not participated in political demonstrations and public addresses. [52]

According to this statement, a relationship between state and church would be regulated from the side of the Church only to the extent that it would make it possible for the Catholic Church to obtain the minimum conditions for observing her independence, according to canon law and to Vatican instructions. It was Pius XI, of course, who in discussing his negotiations with Mussolini, remarked that he would negotiate with Satan himself[53] in the interest of mankind's salvation. With this in mind, Czechoslovak bishops negotiated with the Communists in the interest of Catholics, but with no success.

Defending the Church against subjugation to the state, by laws of October 14, 1949, and against open persecution during the last years, especially since 1950, the Czechoslovak bishops were extremely conscious of the advice which had been given by Pope Benedict XV[54] and repeated by Pius XI:[55]

> But we declare once again to you, Venerable Brethren, that never will we allow that in such agreements anything shall find place that is contrary to the liberty and dignity of the Church; for it is most distinctly necessary in the interests of civil society itself, especially in such times as these, that the liberty and dignity of the Church should be secure and intact. For it is undeniable that harmony between the civil and religious society is most necessary for the tranquillity of public order, the foundation of well-being in every sense.

From this point of view all addresses, memorandums, and pastoral letters of Czechoslovak bishops from 1948 to 1951 were drawn up[56] in such a way that they stressed the full guilt of the Czechoslovak government in the failure of all negotiations and of the creation of an impossible church-state relationship.

Against Czechoslovak Communists it is possible to use the words of Pius XII: "A new danger has arisen—the subordination of everything to politics and the heresy of a national state which subordinates all to human law."[57] This is in substance the reason why the relationship between church and state in Czechoslovakia is so pitiful, because Communists do not recognize cooperation *suo modo*[58] between church and state, but only *communistico modo,* i.e., using the enslaved Church for purposes of state in the sense of entire subordination of everything to Communist politics. This principle, of course, was not accepted by Czechoslovak bishops and consequently the friction began and was glorified by the heroic sufferings of those who defended the basic rights of an independent Church. This state of affairs in Czechoslovakia was bound to lead to their calvary all who insisted that those rights be respected.

CHAPTER TWO

THE CHURCH AS A PERFECT SOCIETY

THE INDIVIDUAL IS THE BASIC FACTOR IN SOCIETY. WHILE INDIVIDUALS have constant qualities of their own peculiar kind, all remain different from one another.[1] Individuals who live in society and the world of things are bound by rules which regulate all of their relations.[2] These relationships arise in proportion to the number of individuals involved. King among creatures is man, for whom, by the decision of Almighty God, all other creatures were made before his arrival, as a proof of his dignity. Human beings, having perfect bodies and immortal souls,[3] are the kings of all creatures and beings, because they were created in the eternal image and likeness of God.[4] God himself stated that the result was good.[5]

God, in creating Eve, illustrated his decision that Adam should live in society. And by this he indicated that a human being, in his relationship with others,[6] has social attributes.[7] Society itself is a necessary result of human relationship, the basis of which is the human individual. From this follow the logical prerogatives for human society, and its order, functions, and relations. According to Jacques Maritain:[8]

> A man is born to live in society, for Providence has intended him, who cannot acquire in isolation either the resources necessary for the maintenance of life or perfection of mind and heart, to associate with his fellows in a society, not only domestic but also civil . . . *ad vitae sufficientiam perfectam.*[9]

The purpose of the existence and establishment of a society is to help man to satisfy his needs and to improve himself. The needs of a human being are both material and spiritual, and logically so, because every human being consists of a body and a soul. If society is to fulfill its twofold mission, it must constantly respect the human as its basic unit, taking regard of its own duty to improve in its being and in its members. There are no other reasons for the existence of society; thereby also its order is defined.[10] This order depends on the relative importance of the body and the soul. The immortal soul should be preferred before the body. The same should be the rule in proceedings of society, when dealing with human problems.

Society is an association of persons with a common goal which is to be attained[11] by united efforts.[12] In establishing a society, four factors are necessary: (a) human beings as members, who form the body of the society; (b) a consciousness of a uniting force; (c) a purpose; (d) the means necessary for carrying out the aim of the society.[13]

The *purpose* of society is the main factor in the definition of a society, because *in ordine ad societatis constitutionem est prima ratio cohesionis socialis.*[14] As to the means which are needed to reach the aim, St. Thomas[15] lays down the following principle: *non tanto aliquid fit melius quanto maius est instrumentum, sed quanto est magis fini proportionatum.* Here, end and means are in contact. The moral bond of the people is the result of society's existence and activities.

Established society inherently evokes respect and high esteem.[16] This respectability allows the moral power to regulate and arrange whatever is necessary and propitious to the public interest. In fact, a society with such qualities[17] is a necessary condition of civilization. The human being alone can satisfy only a few of his needs. Isolated, he may be able merely to exist, but only in society can he attain the optimum mental and moral advancement that is implied in the concept of public welfare.

A society is perfect which by its nature is independent in its own order. Not absolute but relative independence is recognized as satisfactory; for example, the human body—a perfect organism—is independent, yet it needs sunshine, air, food, etc. The condition is that such a society have some manner of functioning satisfactorily, and a perfect aim, which is the welfare of all.

As only that society is perfect which has all the means necessary to obtain its purpose, it is logical that such perfect societies cannot be numerous. Actually there are only two orders established by God: the natural and the supernatural.

The natural order comprises all that applies to human life, and it forms the secular society of human beings; the supernatural order comprises all those elements which are intended to bring about the redemption of man for eternal life. Ecclesiastical society has been established in this latter order. It follows, therefore, that there are only two perfect societies: the Church and the state. As only these two societies are distinguished as principal types, and only these are perfect, other societies belong or are subordinated to either the Church or the state, according to the character of the end they propose.[18] The essential right to existence is inherent in these perfect societies, because perfect good, either spiritual or secular, is independent of the human will. Thus, perfect societies are governed by law and order, not by voluntary decision and enlistment.[19]

Since a perfect society must have some aims and purposes, the attainment of which brings with it indirect advantages for individuals who are members of the society, and because in carrying out such aims certain rights and duties must be met, every perfect society has a personal status,[20] being subject as a person is to rights and liabilities. This characteristic of behaving as an individual is inherent in the nature of a perfect society and is a fundamental factor in the legal formation and theological character of the society in reference to the order, either natural or supernatural, of which the perfect society is a representative organ.

The nature of a society's purpose determines: (a) the nature of the society; (b) its legal status; (c) its internal construction; (d) its external form; (e) its authorization to use necessary and useful means.[21] As the end distinguishes the kinds of societies, only such a society is perfect which aims at reaching the universal good.[22] That society is imperfect whose purpose it is to attain some other good even though conceived of by that society as the supreme good.

By natural goodness is generally meant any imperfect happiness of earthly life. By supernatural goodness is meant imperfect happiness, even though supernatural in this life, e.g., the blessing of people by grace.[23] Natural happiness is the highest aim in the natural order, and supernatural satisfaction is the uppermost aim in the order of the supernatural. Every human being seeks happiness. Saint Augustine says: "The heart of man is restless until it rests in Thee, O God."[24]

It is certain and beyond dispute that the Catholic Church does follow and has always followed these prerequisites for universal goodness, insisting only on the foremost aim of a perfect society. It is evident that the Church is a perfect society, because perfection is an inherent attribute of those things of which God is the author. The beauty of her doctrines, the harmony of her principles, her exalted goals seen throughout her history, were cherished by the devoted interest of Christians and all men of good will. It is a matter of fact, too, that the enemies of the perfect Church have continually sought reasons for hatred in her "Achilles' heel"—the weaker members and servants. This proves also the perfection of the Church.

It is evident even from the secular point of view, that the Church is a society comprised of members intent on the devotional worshiping of God for their own eternal welfare.[25] When we keep in mind the philosophical dictum[26] that perfection connotes "the best manner of being and existing," i.e., any good which is complete, without the possibility of being improved, there is seen in evidence this *modum essendi optimum* in all the workings of a perfect society. From the relation of the Church to Christ as her head, and from her relation to God the Father and the Holy Ghost, we deduce the nature and essence of the Church.[27] Here should be mentioned the usual definition of the Church as the "body of Christ"[28] for the explanation of which, we can cite the words of Saint Thomas. As the relation of the Church to Christ is as close as that of the head to the body, and since Christ is perfect, it is evident that the Church, established by him, must be perfect.

Consulting Sacred Scripture we will find that the Church exists as an ontological and historical fact, having attributes of a perfect society, established and blessed by Jesus Christ. In her history we will find the description of all the activities of the Church, fully complying with the intention of Christ, who founded and established her, thus proving her beauty. We will find varied accounts of her persecution, repeated and woven throughout her history like a scarlet thread, the glory of her long years.

The Church is defined by theologians as a society of people of the same faith, who accept the same sacraments, are guided by lawful priests and are ruled by the representative of Christ, the Holy Father, in Rome.[29] This definition of the Church and her mission comprises all the essential factors of which the Church consists as a society:[30] (a) members, i.e., the material make-up of a society; (b) unifying bonds, bringing all believers into closest relation—faith, love, authority;[31] (c) sacraments as a means to an end; (d) supernatural purpose of the society.

It is evident that the Church is a society with an external system and government. We pointed out before that the Church does not exist only by reason of some legislative decree, as a society rooted in any law system, but because Jesus Christ, who established her, was divine and he himself has given her his divine authority and jurisdiction.[32]

The establishment of the Church by Christ is a certain and a proved historical fact,[33] regardless of how critical the enemies of the Church may be in their expositions of the Bible. Even the word church is derived from Christ, the Lord, as its author.[34]

The truth and the strength of the evidence given in the Scriptures will remain unshaken by her doubters and opponents: (a) the Rationalists and liberal Protestants, who repudiate the Church as a visible society;[35] (b) the Deists and Rationalists, who deny the divine origin of the Church and admit only that Christ was a teacher of mankind; (c) the modernists, who assert that Christ wanted to establish a kingdom of an internal and eschatological nature; (d) the liberals, who admit the Church as a society but deny her legal public nature;[36] (e) the heretics, who attack her fundamental theological doctrines and expositions; (f) the Communists in their atheistic aversion to any religion at all.[37]

It is a matter of fact that Christ, in authorizing the teaching office of the apostles, founded his Church in the form of a society.[38] It is clear in this authorization that Christ wanted to determine the nature and authority of the apostolic college as a society, not only in relation to these individual groups of Christians, but also to stress that his Church as a whole does exist as a society in the fullest meaning of the word. It is a dogma of the Catholic faith that the Church has been established by Christ as a society, and it is theologically certain that this foundation is to be seen in Christ's authorization of the jurisdiction of the apostles as teachers.[39]

The obvious meaning of the Gospels shows that Christ, having all power on earth and in heaven, gave precise instructions to the apostles and authorized them to teach all nations the revealed truth, to sanctify them by certain sacred acts, to lead all who, by being baptized, became disciples of Christ and bound themselves by his commandments. The faithful are required to obey, to believe, to confess the Gospels as revealed by God, to accept the sacraments and to give evidence in their lives of the discipline of Catholic moral principles.[40]

Through their work the apostles fulfilled their mission and authorization by teaching, sanctifying, and guiding the faithful who proved their willingness to be disciplined; and this the apostles did, not only by preaching the doctrines of Christ, but also by establishing the Christian society, i.e., the Church.

Everything developed in good order: first, Christ came with full jurisdiction;[41] then Christ chose from his followers certain ones as apostles,[42] and gave them the authority[43] to preach, to baptize, and to judge.[44] After that Christ gave Peter the authority to rule the Church and gave to that Church his blessing and the promise of eternal existence.[45]

The apostles, from this explicit authorization, received their jurisdiction: to teach all over the world, to consecrate, govern, convoke and maintain religious congregations. These units were managed by bishops and priests, until they were fused into one divine Church. Saint Paul speaks of this authority in the following words: "Let a man so account us as the servants of Christ, and the stewards of the mysteries of God."[46] This power did not die with the apostles; they transferred it to their successors, giving them the command to use the same power.[47]

The Church, established and authorized by Christ himself, is a true society, because in addition to all its organic factors, it has the fundamental asset of the perfect society, which is the power to attain its purposes. Herein is fulfilled the definition of the perfect society. That the Church is a perfect society is proved:[48]

1) By the words of Christ himself. The Church was

founded by him; not borrowing authority from a secular power, the Church was thus established as an independent society. Before his Ascension, Christ reasserted the authority delegated by God and not by men, and said: "All power in heaven and on earth has been given to me."[49] With this power, independent of any other, he said to his apostles: "Go and teach. . . ." He subordinated this power to no one, but claimed it as his own. The apostles obeyed Christ, and as his subordinates, they taught all nations, baptized, and ruled, even against the will and power of secular societies, as had been prophesied by Christ: "But before all these things they will arrest you and persecute you, delivering you up to the synagogues and prisons, dragging you before kings and governors for My Name's sake."[50]

2) By the activities of the apostles. The apostles, independent of any other society, by their Christ-given authority, even against the secular power of that time, proclaimed the kingdom of God, founded religious associations, convoked meetings, managed the affairs of the Church, and obeyed the orders of God. The apostles told the Jewish priests in Jerusalem: "Whether it is right in the sight of God to listen to you rather than to God, decide for yourselves. . . .[51] We must obey God rather than men."[52]

3) By the practice and doctrine of the Church. It is generally known from history, that although under persecution, the Church spread immensely during three centuries—a proof of her independence of any secular power. It is known, too, that under Christian rulers, the Church preserved and protected her independence. It is known from the works of the older theologians[53] how attention was constantly called to the independence of the Church. Positive proof of this is the bull of Boniface VIII,[54] a document of supreme importance.

4) By the constitution and the purpose of the Church. The Church, by her very nature, is independent of any other society because her supernatural end is paramount. She can therefore never be subordinate to any other society since all others must be of a lower grade. The purpose of the Church is universal, i.e., the redemption of all people. She can therefore never be only a part of another society. No other society extends to all mankind. The constitution of the Church is, by

divine authorization, hierarchical and supernatural. It would be a contradiction for divine matters to be subordinate to human and natural powers.

The Church alone was established directly by Christ himself and it would be illogical to subordinate the kingdom of God to secular power. It is known how strongly Jesus Christ opposed the rulers in his time by his divine spiritual doctrine, and how the order taught by him was different from the concept of that time. Independently of the concepts of states and societies, he founded his Church—a new type of society in aim and conception. The controversies between the state authorities and the Church came about because the states could not conceive of the Church's being independent. When sovereignty was recognized as a substantial attribute of a society, the Church by her nature declared her independence *par excellence*.

That the Church is a perfect society is indicated by the idea that a society which is supreme, and not subordinate to another society—complete—is perfect. The Church is such a society. This is evident in regard to the Church in an outstanding way when one considers her aim, authority, and the nature of her mission. Proof of this can be seen in another way: societies are distinguished by their type of power, which is an attribute of any form of life. When this power is independent, the society in its essence is independent as well. The power of the Church is independent of any other society.

In this connection is to be mentioned the text of Holy Scripture which gives Christ's words in establishing his Church: "Amen I say to you: whatever you bind on earth shall be bound also in heaven; and whatever you loose on earth shall be loosed also in heaven.[55] By these words, the Church, which was established by Christ, was empowered and given authority. Proved and explained thus, this perfection of the Church cannot be challenged by such theories as the following:

1) Modern law students[56] assert: *"A perfect society has territory, but the Church has none."* This theory overlooks the fact that the territory of the Church is the whole world, as derived from the words of Christ: "Teach ye all nations." In spite of this, however, the Church in reality not

only has her territory, but besides that, the Church exercises her jurisdiction all over the world. This is apparent from the title of her spiritual power which is to lead all people, to sanctify them and to bring them to eternal salvation.

2) *The Church needs secular power for reaching her aim and therefore she is not complete in her jurisdiction.* It is evident that the Church needs material things. For instance, she cannot administer the sacraments without water, bread, oil; she needs churches and sacred vestments; she needs people who, although members of the Church, are also subject to state power. But the Church uses all these things by her own right and thereby her independence is sustained. The perfection of the Church is not disproved because she is dependent either on necessary materials, or on the secular order, or on the goodness of the other powers. The human organism, in essence perfect, needs food and other things too. It is in keeping with the attributes of a perfect being to secure these things by his own authority and to dispose of them by his own right. The Church is entitled by her divine authority to ask for necessary things from her followers, and to dispose of these things as she sees fit.[57]

3) *The Church has no effective power to defend her own right and jurisdiction or to defend her own freedom. She is therefore not perfect.* The Church has no *material* power but she has *spiritual* power. Even though the right of the Church is not respected, and her freedom is oppressed, nevertheless the authority of the Church is recognized and respected by her faithful. The Church has always defended her freedom and she is doing that especially at the present time. Even though she is oppressed and persecuted and with all her material treasures confiscated, she persistently continues to fulfill her mission, as is proper for the perfect society.

The foregoing objections do not disprove the perfection of the Church. On the contrary, they are an indictment of all usurpers, oppressors, and tyrants. It is no wonder that the Church is persecuted, since she has always opposed the intentions and practices of tyrants. It is difficult to understand the persecution of the Church as she leads people only toward the good things. But the greater the persecution, the more proof there is of the perfection of the Church.

There are many reasons for the necessity of declaring the

Church a vital society.[58] According to the theologians there are two main reasons: her teaching and the means she employs.[59] The necessity of teaching is taken from the divine order by reason of which a man is commanded to do certain things in certain ways determined by the positive order of God, under penalty of losing eternal salvation.

It is clearly the will of Christ that all people should be members of the Church, because eternal salvation can be attained only through her.[60] That the Church is necessary is proved further by the existence of an immortal soul as an object of salvation.

The degree of respect for the human soul corresponds with the degree of respect for the Church. Thus it is understandable why the attitude of the Communists toward the Church is so cruel and reckless. They do not admit and recognize the existence of the immortal soul at all.

The Church is a visible society. This attribute is proved not only by the fact that she is comprised of and joins together human beings, but also by reason of the fact of her existence in a visible appearance and for visible purposes.[61] The visibility of the Church has been accurately defined by Saint Robert Bellarmine in the following words:

> The Church is not formed by angels or by souls, but by human beings. She could be a society of these, when being without external and visible appearances; there is no society if members do not know the others; these would not know one another, if they were not bound by visible and external appearance and nature. [62]

Material visibility is not necessary; visibility of a formal nature is sufficient. This means that members of the society are known as being members of this society.[63] The two kinds of visibility, according to the theologians, are seen in the Church by reason of her doctrine and work among men.[64] The Church must be conceived according to two forms: first, as a religious society and second, as a true society of the faithful, in which are implied all principles of supernatural life and of eternal salvation.[65] When considering the Church as a religious society, Catholics say the Church is visible because of the order of Christ and according to her internal existence. To this extent is the external form of this society conceivable by human senses. Viewing the Church as a supernatural society, Catholics prove the Church is visible from revelation[66] because the entity of the Church, the hierarchy by which she is regulated, and the faithful associated with her have been given by God the promise of the kingdom of heaven and the keys of eternal life.

There is no doubt that the right to these visible proofs has been given only to the Catholic Church, for even as far back as the Nicea-Constantinople Synod the Church was called one, holy, catholic, apostolic.[67] These marks correspond to all the attributes of visibility in which all authority was given in a visible way to teach, govern, and consecrate. Its members are associated by visible bonds, i.e., by the Creed, obedience to priests and bishops, and participation in the Sacraments. But the Church cannot be conceived as a visible society without admitting human membership. This would only be nonsense and against the nature of things.[68] The fact that Christ appeared in flesh as the God-Man, i.e., assumed a human appearance to become better recognized by men, also shows the necessity of conceiving of the Church as a visible society. Wherefore, all heresies asserting that the Church is an invisible society must be resolutely rejected.[69]

It is very important that the Church preserve the right to be recognized as a society by public law, as expressed in legal terminology. From this recognition, for which the Church is authorized by her very nature and by right, it also follows that the rights of the Church in public affairs must be recognized by others, i.e., by the organizations and authorities of states.

A society is called public when by the nature of its purpose, organization, mission, and activities, it infringes on the private life of its subjects, and is able to carry out all social functions, external and general. There can be no doubt that the Church is really such a society because of her purpose, mission, and institution, her universality, and her establishment and hierarchical administration. The Church is thus proved to be a public society even according to human judgment and concept, even without regard to her divine authorization. In addition, the Church has legal order, legal jurisdiction, and effective power.

By her character as a public society, the Church must be recognized as a legal and moral power by the same right as all other societies which are characterized by having a general aim. As regards her internal administration and government in her own sovereignty, the Church works naturally in the supernatural order, and solves all differences with the secular power by agreement or by separation, according to the given circumstances of the case. The relation between the Church and the state depends on the relation of the state authorities to the Church, and their appreciation of the Church as a society of public law.

But these relations exist practically only in principle since the Church is fully sovereign as a result of the authorization given to her by her divine founder. The Church is a legal society. The legal order comprises the whole sphere of regulations,[70] which are measures to judge acts, and by these rules man is induced to perform some acts, or he is kept from performing others.[71] Because of our recognition of God, our highest acts cannot be judged by human principles, but solely in relation to the divine wisdom, by which all happenings are regulated;[72] this is true because God is the supreme lawgiver. From this it follows that God's commands are the supreme law; that mankind, which exists by the will of God, cannot be regulated and governed exclusively by human principles of law; and that, in compliance with the nature of this society, law be recognized in theory and practice by principles of positive legal systems.[73]

The Church is a legislative society everywhere, because the divine order extends its power to all parts. The law concerns all for whom it was enacted. Therefore the Church is a lawmaker everywhere, as appears from the words of Christ: "Go into the whole world and preach the gospel to every creature."[74] Legislative competence can be judged by either earthly or heavenly goodness. Under both aspects, the legal competence of the Church must be defended because the Church is destined as a means for eternal salvation, and temporal good is subordinated to the eternal good.

The Church therefore as a divine society, by the very expression of her purpose and mission, exists legally and demands respect and recognition as a result of the necessity of the existence of goodness, which can be obtained only by herself.

Finally, the Church professes unity of faith and of life.[75]

It is logical that Christ wanted to order and establish his Church spiritually and figuratively as the sole-authorized Church. Otherwise his orders would not be carried out. Unity, figuratively speaking, is an expression of the Scriptures concerning the tradition and nature of the Church. Numerous heretical ecclesiastical societies were established as a result of a misunderstanding concerning the Scriptures, as well as for other reasons. It is the mark of perfection of the Church that the bonds among its members should be as close as possible.

Owing to all these attributes, the Church should be defined in the following way: the Church is a society of the public order, appointed and authorized by Christ, by which people alone can reach the supernatural aim. Upon this definition rests the very nature of the Church.[76] Her perfection as a legislative body is beyond doubt. This can be seen from what has already been said regarding the Church as the highest society.

The sovereignty of a complete legal society is derived from its purpose and aim; this is an undeniable principle. Societies are distinguished according to their aims, and that society which has the highest aim is supreme. Such a society is the Church. The purpose of her existence is both general and important; hence she is the highest. She was established to make it possible for men to reach eternal salvation. Such a legal society is also legally perfect since she has in her order the perfect and highest goal as her aim; she is self-sufficient as to her means; and she is independent and seeks to obtain the highest good.

The perfection of the Church is evident by the fact that she is a spiritual and supernatural society. It would be antithetical to the quality of a supernatural society if the Church were subject to a natural society.

Her perfection as a legal society is evident from the fact that the Church is one and universal, established by the will of Christ, who is the highest lawmaker. Christ is the way of faith, of truth, and of life, being the Son of God. From the point of view of her power,[77] the Church must be accepted as a society, and because the Church is a perfect society, her power is unlimited. Within her God-given rights, her power must be independent[78] in all the prerogatives of governmental power; the same is true of jurisdiction and the extent of the competence of her courts.

Having been authorized in the way mentioned above, the jurisdiction of the Church is doubtless a proof of her perfection.[79] Thus, the power bestowed on the Church is the strongest proof of her independence and perfection;[80] and it is proof of her sovereignty[81] according to the following statement: the Holy Father, the visible head of the Church, possesses universal jurisdiction over the whole Church.[82] This is the thesis of the following chapter. In it the perfection of the Church will be made still more evident.

CHAPTER THREE

THE JURISDICTION OF THE POPE

THERE IS A NECESSARY CORRELATION BETWEEN THE FORM of a society and its authoritative head. Authority is a necessity for every society for the regulation of the acts and conduct of its members and in order to bring them into closer mutual cooperation. This is, in the main, the moral power of any society.[1] This is also necessary for the welfare and success of the society. The necessity for such an authority is derived by reason of the *principium directivum et coactivum.*[2] By a regulating principle we mean that the members of a society need restrictions for their mutual cooperation, which restrictions should be respected; by a coercing principle we mean that authority is needed to oppose selfish trends and all attempts to disintegrate the good purpose of the society.

The characteristics of authority correspond to this need. Authority should be one, a symbol of unity, effective and visible according to the visibility and the effectiveness of the society. It may be either a physical person or a corporation. Usually, to limit authority, we indicate its right to issue regulations for members of a society, to establish order, and to fulfill the purpose of the society.[3]

As authority is necessary for the existence of any society, it appears that the main purpose and legal reason for a society is the legal reason for the authority. It means that adequate and necessary authority was established by the same right by which the society was established.

Accordingly, it is inevitable that the ruling authority comes from the same source from which the society was established.[4] A perfect society is entitled to require all that is necessary and useful to attain its aim. And whoever is subject to the purpose is also bound to the means. If members of a society are subject to the use of the means for attaining its aim, there is a correlative right to demand these means.

Authority is generally limited thus: by reason of a main executor as proper and vicarious, according as the power is exerted by one's own name or by authorization; by the source of the power which is by order and by delegation if the power is exerted by authorization of public office, or by designation of a person; by the characteristics of a society, in which the power is used as domination and jurisdiction, whether the society in which the power is used is perfect or imperfect. Jurisdiction is the authority in a perfect society,[5] the moral power by which all members and organs are subject to the attainment of the aim.

The three aspects of power—legislative, executive, and judicial—are apparent by their nature. According to the hierarchical order, upon which the Church, as a perfect society, is constituted, the hierarchy is divided between *ordinis* and *jurisdictionis.* Hierarchy of ruling is inherent in the ecclesiastical office and priesthood. It establishes an order of priests. By it, the difference between priests and laymen is established.[6]

Hierarchy of jurisdiction is a power in religious matters. It applies to the spiritual society. Hierarchy of order and jurisdiction are mutually related because the Church is a spiritual society. St. Thomas Aquinas states this in the following definition: *Potestas spiritualis datur cum aliqua consecratione. Et ideo clavis cum ordine datur. Sed executio clavis indiget materia debita, quae est plebs subdita per jurisdictionem. Et ideo, antequam jurisdictionem habeat, habet claves, sed non habet actum clavium. Et quia clavis per actum definitur, ideo in definitione clavis ponitur aliquid ad jurisdictionem pertinens.*[7] Both are inherent. The main and noblest task of the priesthood is to act as mediator between God and man[8] when the sacraments are administered, but this work depends on jurisdiction. Therefore God has given to the Christian priesthood the power of jurisdiction, because Christ founded the Church not only as a religion, but as a society, legally perfect. *Potestatem jurisdictionis dicimus esse potestatem publicam legitimi superioris a Christo, ut ab Ecclesia per canonicam missionem, concessam, regendi baptisatos in ordine ad salutem aeternam. Baptisatorum directio autem fieri debet ipsorum cooperationem gratiae Dei promovendo, tum per rectae fidei professionem, tum per actuam conformationem bonis moni-*

bus: hinc duplex obiectum circa quod potestas jurisdictionis exercetur, pro regimine hominum: hoc est fides et mores, ideoque duplex, pro obiecti diversitate, potestatis huius ratio seu functio; magisterium videlicet et imperium.[9]

From this it is evident that the hierarchy of order and jurisdiction applies internally.[10] According to canon law, only ordained priests are entitled to jurisdiction; laymen are empowered only by special permission granted by the Holy Father.[11] In its execution, the power of order depends upon that of jurisdiction. The object of the hierarchical jurisdiction is religious acts in the name of the Church as a society, carried out by members of the religious society for reaching the given aim. Both types of power have a common source because both are given by God, a common substance because both are supernatural by origin, by aim and by object, and a common purpose, which is ultimately the glory of God and the salvation of souls.

These two types of power are distinguished by the manner by which they are executed and by their attributes. The power of order is enacted by ordination; jurisdiction is performed by canonical constitution or appointment. The power of order is sacred by nature and does not depend on human beings. Jurisdiction can be granted by canonical mission; it can cease when the conditions for it are absent.[12]

The two hierarchies (*ordinis* and *jurisdictionis*) are divided by the order of God (*juris divini*) and by the regulations of the Church (*juris ecclesiastici*). This division in the hierarchy of jurisdiction is certain[13] because there is no doubt that only the authorization of Saint Peter and his legitimate successors[14] and the mission of bishops as successors of the apostles[15] are of divine order. The other degrees of the hierarchy of jurisdiction which have been set up, are regulations of the Church. Ecclesiastical jurisdiction is divided as to the form (legislative, judicial, executive), the subordination (direct and indirect), and the relation (general and universal). Universal relation is limited neither as to the object nor to the place, and this is really only the jurisdiction of the Pope of Rome. On the other hand particular jurisdiction applies only to some persons and to certain places.

This brings us to the point of our problem, the reasons for which are indicated in the fact that the Pope is endowed with general (universal) jurisdiction over the whole Church. Since the Communists look upon this indisputable fact in a cynical way and do not recognize it, it is necessary to expose the problem in its essence and substance by fundamental argument. In line with this, the following facts must be explained:

1) The apostle Saint Peter[16] was appointed by Jesus Christ as the leader of all the apostles and as the visible head of the whole militant Church; thus he received directly and without mediation from Jesus Christ not only the honor, but mainly the power of jurisdiction.

2) Saint Peter was appointed by Jesus Christ, through divine order. His power is confined by no limits and must have successors until the end of time.

3) The Popes of Rome are the successors of the leader of the apostles; therefore these too have their supreme jurisdiction over the whole Church by divine order. This power embraces not only the authority to supervise and rule, but also includes true jurisdiction, full and direct, over all churches and over all priests and believers.

As it is necessary that the authority of Peter must remain eternal in the institution of Popes, the same applies to the bishops who are successors of the apostles. Since they have direct power which is inherent, it follows that the institution of bishops forms the constitution of the Church. This fundamental concept is basic for our understanding of the Roman pontificate. In logical reference to its constitution we will expound our whole thesis.

There are two instances in the Holy Scriptures where the words of Jesus Christ treat this question: "And I will give thee the keys of the kingdom of heaven. And whatever thou shalt bind upon earth, shall be bound in heaven; and whatever thou shalt loose on earth, shall be loosed also in heaven."[17] The second evidence was given to all the apostles: "And if he refuses to hear them, appeal to the Church, but if he refuse to hear even the Church, let him be to thee as the heathen and the publican. Amen I say to you: whatever you bind on earth shall be bound also in heaven; and whatever you loose on earth shall be loosed also in heaven."[18]

By these words the Church is granted true ruling power and endowed with all the attributes of a public society.

Furthermore, this power is independent of all supremacy of man; it belongs only to the Church and may not be confined by any limits.[19]

The words "keys of the kingdom of heaven" describe the power of jurisdiction or the power to rule in this kingdom of heaven, as granted by Christ, and indicated by the parable of Holy Scripture.[20] The words "bind and loose" can be explained only by the right to enact rules and regulations, to impose penal verdicts, to loose and to judge; that is, all that is necessary for a society to be administered and governed. This wide power of the keys given by Christ himself comprises a twofold jurisdiction: the first is a privilege of the Church; the second is laid in her hands as a commission of divine authorization. The first is the authorization to bind, and although it applies to all who aim to attain the kingdom of heaven, it really pertains to the members of the Church only.

The loosening does not mean the right to evade any regulations or rules given by God nor those issued either by natural or secular power, but it does mean the right to loose persons from bonds which they placed on themselves by delinquencies against the divine order.

This indicates that the Church has its separate forum which is external and public, but besides this, there is also the internal forum of the Church, instituted by divine law. The jurisdiction of the Church embraces also the forum of divine law, and it is clear that the jurisdiction which was given to the Church must be of the same sort as that within the divine forum preserved for her.[21]

It is a fact of the greatest importance that Christ, when authorizing power, speaks exclusively and always to Peter, by which fact the priority he had among the apostles is proved. Since this priority can be judged in many ways,[22] there is no doubt that Christ gave Saint Peter the priority of jurisdiction, not only of administering, but especially of ruling and reigning. By reason of this priority, Saint Peter's authority extends to lawmaking; the issuance of regulations and instructions; and legislative, judicial, and executive power.

This priority and supremacy was first promised by Christ to Peter and then granted to him after the Resurrection. In this jurisdiction, the types of power are twofold. One is moral, which binds and determines limits to the freedom of the spirit; the other is sociological, which, by its essence, concerns the mutual relation among members and their relation to the power to which they are subject.

Regarding the Church as a society having a hierarchical order, primacy is uppermost in the degree of this hierarchical jurisdiction. It is necessary to explain this fact, stated in Holy Scripture, to make the ontological significance of Saint Peter's primacy the more evident.

1) *Promise of the primacy*: In Caesarea Philippi, Christ surprised the apostles by asking: "Who do men say the Son of Man is?"[23] Many answers were given. Some said John the Baptist; others, Elias;[24] and others, Jeremias,[25] or one of the prophets. No one admitted that Jesus was the Messias. Christ continued his questioning by asking: "But who do you say that I am?"[26] This question, very difficult to answer if taken by itself, assumes a strict expression of the internal conviction of the apostles. Simon Peter himself answered: "Thou art the Christ, the Son of the living God."

This answer expresses not only the truth of Christ's Messianic mission, but also comprises the full confession of Christ's divine dignity and recognition that he is truly the Son of God. Christ himself gave evidence that this statement is true by proclaiming: "Blessed art thou, Simon Bar-Jona, because flesh and blood hath not revealed it to thee, but my Father in heaven." And in this connection, Christ, using the metaphor of the rock and keys, promises the primacy to Peter in the following words:

"I say to thee, thou art Peter, and upon this rock I will build my Church, and the gates of hell shall not prevail against it." He thereby proclaims the establishment of a religious society, firm on an unshakeable base, and everlasting, despite all the diabolical elements of hell itself.

"And I will give thee the keys of the kingdom of heaven." He thereby constitutes the jurisdiction and establishes the relation of Peter to the Church. By these words Christ gives Peter the power over the Church, full and supreme.

"And whatever thou shalt bind on earth, shall be bound also in heaven, and whatever thou shalt loose on earth, shall be loosed in heaven." This declaration constituted the nature of Peter's authorization and described the plan of it.

From the point of view of these three statements, this authorization is to be viewed as a power over a society: *hierarchically* organized because Christ himself endowed the power to the authorization of the Holy rule, and gave it over to Peter; *monarchical,* because this authorization is full, supreme, and was given only to Peter. That these aforementioned words were spoken to Peter himself is evident and excludes all doubts.

2) This promise of the primacy was renewed by Christ after his resurrection, when he said to Peter: "Feed my lambs; feed my sheep."[27] These words are quoted by Matthew, too.[28] It is necessary to clarify the meaning and sense of these words not only because they are used so often in Holy Scripture but also because Christ called himself the Good Shepherd.[29]

This historical fact becomes an ontological phenomenon of everlasting nature by the sanction: "And the gates of hell shall not prevail against it." These words of Christ are of great importance, not only by reason of their everlasting significance, but also because despite all persecutions the identity of the Church is guaranteed forever. The Church is a kingdom with God present in her, and this will be so under all conditions and during all centuries.[30] The Church of Christ is immune to any damage which could be caused by time, especially with regard to her authorization to teach all nations, to be "the light of the world" and to be "the city set on a mountain,"[31] in its everlasting, unchangeable appearance.

In wonderful comparisons, Christ predicted all the worries, problems, and troubles which would confront the Church and her development in various periods of time. In addition, this ontological fact of the existence of the Church is evidenced by the message of Christ: "All power in heaven and on earth has been given to me. Go therefore and make disciples of all nations, baptizing them in the name of the Father and of the Son and of the Holy Spirit, teaching them to observe all things that I have commanded you; and behold I am with you all days, even unto the consummation of the world."[32] By these words the primacy of Peter, derived from divine constitution, has an unchangeable stability in all things which belong to its very substance. The evidence of primacy deduced from the words of Holy Scripture holds for all times.

The primacy of Peter presupposes the supreme rule of Christ. Saint Thomas[33] states that Christ, who is the invisible and supreme head of the Church, surpasses on three points the dignity of the Pope, who is the visible head of the Church: Christ is superior in virtue of the internal influence of grace which comes exclusively from him; Christ is the supreme head of all the faithful adhering to the Church during all ages. The Pope is the head of the Church only for those of the faithful who are on the way to eternity during his pontificate; Christ is the head of the Church by his own power and authority. The Pope is the substitute for Christ, for Peter is called the "vicar" of Christ, and not his successor, since succession occurs when the predecessor loses his power. Christ did not lose his authority, but he gave it over and left that authority to the Church.

The relation of Peter toward the other apostles was regulated by reason of apostolic and supreme authorization. As regards apostolic authorization, Peter was equal to the other apostles.[34] As to the supreme authorization, Peter is first in rank among the other apostles by virtue of the dignity of being the head of the whole Church.

This is so because the power of ruling was given exclusively to Peter. Therefore Peter alone, and not the apostles either individually or collectively, was entitled to issue regulations. In addition, this power to rule over the Church was given by special grace according to the quality of delegates, but to Peter it was granted as being included in the delegation of papal authority.[35] Further, the extraordinary power of the apostles came to an end at their deaths, but the authorization of Peter as a substitute for Christ was to remain forever.[36]

From wrong conceptions of the relation between Peter and the apostles there arose some erroneous doctrines regarding the primacy of the Pope. Thus the followers of Photius did not fully recognize that Peter was the head of the apostles; Marsilius of Padua did not admit the primacy of Peter at all; Melanchthon, Isaac Barrow, August Meyer, and Germanus recognized only a primacy of honor. Febronians admitted that primacy concerned only the authority to control and supervise. The basic reason for establishing various churches is caused by the wrong conception of Peter's relation to the apostles. Beyond any doubt, this question was clarified by the

Vatican Council, which decided: *Si quis igitur dixerit, beatum Petrum Apostolum non esse a Christo Domino constitutum Apostolorum omnium principem et totius ecclesiae militantis visible caput; vel eundem honoris tantum, non autem verae propriaeque jurisdictionis primatum ab eodem Domino nostro Jesu Christo directe et immediate accepisse; anathema sit.*[37]

The fact of primacy is proved beyond a doubt by the words of Holy Scripture. Christ, after his resurrection, appearing to the apostles at the Sea of Tiberias, said to Peter, "Simon, son of John, dost thou love me more than these do?" Peter said to him, "Yes, Lord, thou knowest that I love thee." Christ said to him, "Feed my lambs." Again he asked, "Simon, son of John, dost thou love me?" When Peter repeated his first answer, Christ spoke again, "Feed my lambs." When Christ asked his question the third time, Peter was grieved and said, "Lord, thou knowest all things; thou knowest that I love thee." Then Christ said again, "Feed my sheep."[38]

By this command, Christ gave the extraordinary and supreme power of jurisdiction exclusively to Peter, and intended it to extend over the entire Church. This fact is proved by the special circumstances[39] identifying Peter.

Christ changed the name of Simon to Peter.[40] This double name denotes a special choice and mission. Saint Paul says:[41] "The rock was Christ," indicating a special relation between the apostle Peter and Christ. This changing of names did not take place with the other apostles. Besides this, the first rank was given to Peter. Although Andrew met Christ earlier, nevertheless Peter is always mentioned as first among the apostles. Moreover, a special honor was conferred on Peter by Christ when, preaching from his boat,[42] he promised to make him a "fisher of men." At the last supper, he washed Peter's feet;[43] after the Resurrection it was Peter who received a special message.[44]

The final proof is in the acts of Peter after the death of Christ: Peter presided at diverse meetings; Peter took care to fill the number of apostles after the treason of Judas; Peter was the first to preach to the Jews on Pentecost;[45] Peter first proclaimed the decision of the council in Jerusalem. Straub describes and explains all these preferences in a very definite way.[46]

Not only does biblical history give satisfactory proof of

Peter's primacy; tradition proves the same. This is evident in the way all the Fathers expound the texts of Holy Scripture which relate to the primacy of Peter.[47] Protestants either do not mention the explanations of the Fathers when discussing the primacy of Peter, or they distort the explanations that have been given. Some Protestants do not deny that Peter was honored in a significant way, but add that Catholics esteem the explanations of the Fathers rather than the words of Holy Scripture. Some endeavor to see the primacy at Jerusalem in James. Also, while some are compelled to admit the primacy of Peter, others object on the ground that this was the personal privilege of Peter and did not cover his successors.[48]

This argument is evidently contradictory because the substance of the Church remains unchanged. Primacy belongs to this substance and essence, and for that reason primacy is eternal and includes all the successors of Saint Peter. The necessity of an everlasting primacy is a prerequisite to a unified leadership of the Church. Saint Thomas says: *Optimum autem regimen multitudinis est ut regatur per unum; quod patet ex fine regiminis, qui est pax; pax enim et unitas subditorum est finis regentis; unitatis autem congruentior causa, est unus quam multi. Manifestum est igitur regimen Ecclesiae sic esse dispositum ut unus toti Ecclesiae praesit.*[49]

It is impossible to deny that the primacy descends to the successors of Saint Peter, in the face of the logic of Christ who established the Church, and constituted her thus. It is logical that he wanted all this to last forever and not only for the lifetime of Peter. The words of Christ about eternal existence of the Church give full proof of this.

Peter was given jurisdiction over the whole Church, universal and full in the true meaning of the word.[50] Peter was authorized with general extensive jurisdiction by the words: "Feed my lambs, feed my sheep." It cannot be doubted that this indicates the whole sheepfold of Christ. Further, the jurisdiction of full extent was given to Peter by the words: "Whatsoever thou shalt bind, whatsover thou shalt loose." The "lambs and sheep" which were bestowed on Peter doubtlessly included also the apostles, whom Christ eliminated when authorizing Peter by the words: "Dost thou love me more than all these?" By these words, in a symbolic way, the primacy of Peter was constituted.

The same power and authorization applies to his successors. This authority was constituted by Christ; no limits or instructions can be made concerning it. Such restrictions would be illegal and unlawful, because this authorization has been given by the highest laws given by the Church, of which Jesus Christ is the invisible head. Thus the jurisdiction of the Pope of Rome as the successor of Peter is proved.

Former disputes as to whether Peter came to Rome, whether he lived and died there—a point of difference between Catholic[51] and Protestant theologians—were solved when Pope Pius XII announced[52] on Christmas Day of the Holy Year 1950 that the grave of Saint Peter had been found. History thus proved the tradition—a tradition nearly two thousand years old. The discovery dissipated all doubts.

The historical fact of the life and death of Peter in Rome affected the primacy of Peter in Rome. The enemies of the Church concentrated their efforts on the question as to whether the Roman Popes were really the successors in Peter's primacy, given them by divine constitution, with Peter as the first of them, irrespective of any ecclesiastical law or any other historical institution. A distinction is to be made between papal power itself and the use of this authority. Power remains the same, even when in its exercise it is adjusted to the aims of a respective time period. Although this fact is evident, various enemies rose up against papal jurisdiction, the best known among whom are Photius, Wyclif and Hus, Calvin and Luther. The schismatic Photius recognized the extent and authority of the primacy, but asserted that this was transferred to Constantinople in virtue of the transfer of the Emperor's power thereto.[53] Wyclif and Hus, condemned among others by the Council of Constance, proclaimed the Church to be the synagogue of the devil. The Council also repudiated the doctrine of Calvin, who abused Paul's expression about the Antichrist,[54] saying that this applied to the Roman Pope. Luther's *Adversus Execrabilem Antichristum Bullam* appeared in 1520. There were those also who *veritamen factorum evidentia nonnumquam quoque modernorum animum intendit, ut primatum primis ecclesiae temporibus in agendo, sed nondum in theoretica, adfuisse fateantur.*[55]

The thesis that the popes are the successors to the primacy of Peter is proved beyond a doubt. In whatever has been done for God and Jesus Christ, the Pope of Rome has been the originator and the leader. Therefore, the Pope of Rome cannot be the Antichrist that Wyclif and Hus have named him, but a man of God. It would not make sense in terms of divine Providence with regard to the rule of the Church that the authority of God and Christ, from the beginning until today, should be in the care of the Antichrist. From this it follows that the Pope of Rome is really the successor of Peter.

The nature and extent of the Pope's primacy has been fully defined by the Vatican Council.[56] The Pope has been endowed not only with the authority to be supervisor and ruler, but with the full right of jurisdiction. This jurisdiction is universal, which means that it is to be exerted over the whole Church, not only in matters of faith and morals, but also in things relating to the discipline and ruling of the Church, spread throughout the world. This jurisdiction is therefore universal as to place, matter, and persons. In addition, this jurisdiction is complete. This means that the Pope of Rome not only has power of the highest degree, but that this power is also full and complete—that is to say, complete jurisdiction has been given over to the Church by Christ.

The Pope of Rome is therefore authorized, without bishops and without any supposed consent of the Church, to perform all affairs within the framework of jurisdiction in the Church. No recourse can be made against any decision of the Pope; nobody is entitled to criticize or to make an appeal against any decision of his. All ecclesiastical officers are subject to the power of the Pope since this power covers all ecclesiastical matters.

The Pope can exert direct power over all churches, ecclesiastics, and believers. He is therefore head, father, and teacher of all Christians so that all ecclesiastics and faithful are individually and in their entirety subject to him and bound in obedience to him. The power of the Pope of Rome is immediately endowed by Christ. This means that the Pope receives his power not by consent of the faithful, but he exerts it as the successor of Peter, on whom Christ himself, by virtue of the first constitution, conferred the primacy.

These expositions concerning the limitations of papal power given by the Vatican Council thus repudiated a number of opposing opinions. In the Councils of Pisa (1409),

Constance (1414-1418), and Basle, some of the Fathers approved placing higher power in the Councils than in the Pope. Richerianism[57] denied full and complete jurisdiction and admitted only the primacy *inspectionis* and *directionis*. This error asserted that the power of the Pope was given by the universal Church as a whole. Febronianism and Josephinism really only modified Gallicanism, the errors of which were condemned. The former endeavored to distinguish between fundamental and auxiliary rights of the primacy.[58]

By the characteristics of papal power as defined by the Vatican Council the theory of the Czechoslovak Communists is *a priori* repudiated and denied, since they would place limitations on the universal jurisdiction of the Pope of Rome by extending it only to matters of faith and morals. Especially do "patriotic priests" deny his jurisdiction as to discipline and governing power. But in every well-administered society, the power of the head has an extent commensurate with the complete well-being of a society. Maintenance of the unity of the Church and support of its spiritual welfare, which is the aim and purpose of the Roman Pontiff's primacy, requires that he should have full and supreme power, because it would otherwise be impossible to maintain unity and serve and support the spiritual welfare. Saint Thomas Aquinas expressed this concept when he said: *Ad unitatem Ecclesiae requiritur quod omnes fideles in fide conveniant. Circa vero ea quae fidei sunt, contingit quaestiones moveri; per diversitatem autem sententiarum divideretur Ecclesia, nisi in unitate per unius sententiam conserveretur. Exigitur igitur ad unitatem Ecclesiae conservandum quod sit unus qui toti Ecclesiae praesit. Manifestum est autem quod Christus Ecclesiae in necessariis non deficit quam dilexit et pro ea sanguinem suum fuerit. Non est igitur dubitandum quia ex ordinatione Christi unus toti Ecclesiae praesit.*[59]

Scheeben further elucidates this by saying:

> Therefore the unity of the Church in its social life depends in a special way on the unity of the pastoral power. This unity of the pastoral power must be a clear sign that the Spirit of the Church operating in many organs is a single Spirit, who brings all these organs together in one whole, and causes them to exercise their activity in an order-

ly manner conformable with the unity of the whole.

This unity of pastoral power in the Church is guaranteed by the revealed doctrine that the entire plenitude of such power is in one supreme pontiff. Moreover, this power is so vested that the whole flock of the Church and even the priests and high priests are entrusted to his care and are subject to him, and that all these high priests and priests can obtain and exercise their pastoral office in the Church only in dependence on him and in union with him. The entire social structure of the Church rests on him as its foundation. The pastoral power passes from him to the other pastors of the Church as rays proceed from the sun, brooks from their source, branches from the tree. Owing to the fact that the plenitude of the pastoral power resides in him, and that no such power can be envisaged in the Church as independent of him, the Church is made truly and perfectly one, not only in its summit, but in its deepest base—and from the base up; not only in its topmost branch, but in its roots—and from the root up. Any other, lesser unity in the Church is unthinkable; unless the structure of its social organization is to be quite at odds with its inner nature.[60]

Such is the sovereign concept of papal power. Nevertheless it is attacked by all enemies of the Church. But Christ warned these enemies: "I will smite the shepherd and the sheep of the flock will be scattered."[61]

History has shown many attacks against the Holy See. The persecution under diabolical communism is the latest example. Of course, the "scattering of the sheep" mentioned above is dependent on the indifferent attitude of many Catholics toward their shepherd. Roving sheep will always follow their shepherd. Indifferent Catholics in various countries often do great harm to the Church and its shepherd through their inactivity and lack of a true spiritual bond with the Supreme Pontiff.

Apropos of this, Jacques Maritain has written:

With such a programme of unqualified adhesion to every pontifical direction, Catholics, if they so desire and whatever their difference in other spheres, can usefully unite in accordance with the constantly reiterated desire of the Sovereign Pontiffs and work in harmony. Such a union is possible in the first place in the order of knowledge. The desire to become better acquainted with the doctrine of the Church, of which so many baptized persons are so lamentably ignorant, is apparent on all sides and ought to be fortified against hydra-headed error by serious philosophical and theological training. Fierce assaults are in preparation against the Church at the moment, while many minds are threatened by a sort of syncretism, indulgent to every kind of error. Recourse to arms brooks no delay.

The union mentioned is equally practicable in the sphere of action, on condition that the proximate ends of the action contemplated are sufficiently universal. Whether it be a question of cooperating in such a spiritual restoration of Christendom—and this would seem to be the great task of today—or assisting in the work of evangelization, in the immense labor of the missions at home and abroad; or rediscovering the principles of Christian politica and combating laicism and its laws; or preparing for the establishment of a Christian social order and opposing social conditions contrary to the justice and the spirit of the Gospel; or practicing works of spiritual and corporal mercy, or bringing succor to all the suffering members of Christ, not only to the poor and sick, but also to so many ardent hearts enervated by the error of false doctrines, the iniquity of this godless world, the aridity and egoism of orthodoxy for cooperation of Catholics because they are Catholics. It would be sufficient if all who have been working for years in separate teams in a multitude of admirably various and necessarily independent tasks got to know one another. The new forms which might arise would take their place in that concert, whose supreme rule would be the integral teaching imparted by the Papacy. A harmonized activity so proceeding from the spirit of faith, the love of Christ, in His Church and a great devotion to His word unreasoningly transmitted by His Vicar, far from diverting souls from the life of union with God, would rather impel them the other way.[62]

We should be sorry for Churches which are separated from the Pope; they have nobody to defend them against the power of the world. There is no man raised above all the kings to interpose his hand and the hand of God between them and the instinct of tyranny natural to the civil power. The Russian Church had never accepted, as is too commonly thought in the West, the oppression she suffered at the hands of the Imperial Government; she prayed in secret for her liberty. Lenin and martyrdom were required to set her free—in a terrible persecution.

We should be sorry also for nations that know not the Church and the Pope. They cannot adjust the spiritual and the temporal in a proper harmony. We should be sorry above all for nations which, gathered by a signal favor of grace around the Pope and having in their midst the voice of Christ, indefatigably reminding them of all that Truth requires, have persisted for centuries in stopping up their ears.[63]

CHAPTER FOUR

THE ECCLESIASTICAL HIERARCHY AS A DIVINE INSTITUTION

WE KNOW THAT THE CHURCH WAS FOUNDED BY CHRIST AS A visible, everlasting, and honorable society. The first distinguishing feature of the Church is its hierarchical constitution, which is monarchically administered. This hierarchical structure is not only a basis for the purity of the Catholic Church, but also a dividing line between Catholic and other churches such as Lutheran, Baptist, Reformist, Congregationalist, Episcopalian, and Anglican, or so-called national churches, since all are organized democratically. Etymologically, hierarchy means a "holy rule";[1] in an abstract sense it means sacred power. Considered concretely, it means a person or corporation of persons who possess and exert this power. It is called *sacred* because of the source of its constitution, which is Jesus Christ; because of the purpose for which it was instituted, the glorification of God and the salvation of souls; and finally because of the persons exerting this power, since they are baptized, ordained, and devoted to the service of God.[2] We can thus define hierarchy as a body or entity of superiors, divinely authorized and accredited by sacred power to rule over the faithful and servants of divine cult.[3]

In the Church, there are three kinds of sacred or hierarchical power: the power of order, the pastoral power, and the power of jurisdiction. The power of order (*potestas ordinis*) is concerned exclusively with the divine rite and consecration of men. It is constituted by ordination; its character cannot be wiped out; it is efficient *ex opere operato*. There are three degrees of this power, based on divine authorization: episcopate, priesthood, and ministers. In addition, there are lower degrees of this power which will be mentioned later.

Pastoral power (*magisterii*) has as its task the protection of the holy legacy of revelation, and the explanation and maintenance of it, not only as a teacher, but as one who expands it authentically and authoritatively, being accredited by a divine mission.

The power of jurisdiction (*potestas iurisdictionis*), which relates to a perfect society, has a moral character, binding the members of a society to attain by their acts the well-being of all. This power is based upon the mission of Christ and of his Church, and has two degrees: bishopric and papacy. As it is not possible in practice to separate the pastoral power and the power of jurisdiction, these are usually mentioned as the power of order and power of jurisdiction.[4]

The latter power is represented by a council or order of superiors who are part of the faithful and members of the Church. It is called a council since its leaders are federated by a certain order (Pope, bishops, priests, ministers).[5] This council is the essential element of the hierarchy as is shown formally in its power by the divine authority given directly by God. This feature of constituted power is a basic characteristic because in the Church there would be no hierarchy,[6] but a democracy, if people alone should exert all power either directly or by delegates. This is the aim of Calvinist Presbyterians who assert that the power of the priest is delegated by the people themselves; similarly, of the so-called modernists who wish to reform the Church by giving to it a more democratic organization.[7] Such ideas obviously are opposed to the strict will and orders of Christ himself. Thus also the attempts of Czechoslovak Communists to eliminate the hierarchy from any influence to regulate and decide the affairs of the Church, by infiltration of so-called "patriotic" priests or "lay commissioners" of the episcopal offices, oppose the nature and constitution of the Church.

These attempts are in opposition to the will of Christ because a hierarchically organized Church is undeniably the will of God himself. "These twelve Jesus sent forth having instructed them thus: 'Do not go in the direction of the Gentiles, nor enter the towns of Samaritans; but go rather to the lost sheep of the house of Israel. And as you go, preach the message, The kingdom of heaven is at hand. Cure the sick, raise the dead, cleanse the lepers, cast out devils. *Freely you have received, freely give.*' "[8]

In this manner Peter and the apostles received the power

of Christ and were authorized to pass it on to others. This is evidently the hierarchical form of organization: a council of men who by virtue of sacred power and by the right to administrate the Church are distinguished from the faithful by divine power.[9]

In the possession of the council of superiors are contained: (*a*) the power of orders regarding sacred acts; and (*b*) the power of jurisdiction regulating Christians. All who are in leading positions are called clerics;[10] all who do not belong to the hierarchy are called laymen as the term was used by Peter.[11] The clerical state forms a separate section and by the nature of its construction and constitution, certain facts become evident: the Holy Rule appointed by Christ has been constituted to be transferred from predecessors to successors, thus to exist forever; clerics are divided by degrees; the power of the hierarchy cannot be gained either by people or by secular power or by any office, not even by private persons, but only by legal succession and the rite which was constituted by Christ; the Church is not a society in which all are of equal rank. This is by divine constitution.[12]

This superior position of clerics over the faithful laymen is made reasonable by the relation of the hierarchy to the highest priest, Christ, who, because of his everlasting life, possesses everlasting priesthood.[13] To him alone pertains the most elevated power, merited by his sufferings and death and effective in all the sacraments, which are conferred and administered in his name. Truly do "the sufferings of Christ unite him to human nature; he is the essence of our redemption, merited and effective not directly because of his authority, but by virtue of his humanity as the means of his divinity. And since these are connected with divinity in his person, his being has dignity and effective ability regarding external means. These are the servants of the Church. . . ."[14]

Accordingly then, the hierarchy is endowed with the authority of influence over all the faithful of the Church, as to external administration, and activity to attain the external effect of sacraments as ministers: *eadem ratio est ministri et instrumenti; utriusque enim actio exterius adhibetur, sed sortitur effectum interiorem et virtute principalis agentis quod est Deus.*[15]

Christ himself possesses the primacy of the priesthood.[16]

The hierarchy is viewed as being made up of the stewards of the mysteries of God.[17] It participates in the eternal priesthood of Christ, as both the tool and the intermediator of his power. By this intermediacy, the hierarchy is a substantial factor of the Church; its significance is proven by ontological fact. The priesthood of Christ is a reality, the hierarchy a necessity for the Church's purpose. Therefore, all assertions by those who desire to have the Church without any ministers or intermediators, suffer either from ignorance or from malice. This view, nevertheless, is expressed today by so-called "progressive" people. The existence of the Church requires the existence of her ministers. Hence it is evident that the Founder has the right to his ministers, appointing them for the society constituted by him. Billot says well that the hierarchy is a necessary requirement of the Church.[18] From the nature of things we cannot say that there is no man who should be the head of others, or who could be entitled to claim to be this head. But Jesus Christ is ruler over the whole Church. He it is who gave himself for us that he might redeem us from all iniquity and cleanse for himself an acceptable people, pursuing good works.[19] He it is who loved the Church so much "that (he) delivered himself up for her that he might sanctify her, cleansing her in the bath of water by means of the word; in order that he might present to himself the Church in all her glory, not having spot or wrinkle or any such thing, but that she might be holy and without blemish."[20] God proclaimed himself head of the Church "who is his body who gives all to all."[21] The relation between the Church and her head is quite different from that between a society and its superior. It follows in the nature of things that the relation of the Church to Christ is as Jesus Christ authorized it by his power and by her constitution.

Hierarchy, which means the power of Christ's authorized ministers, exists in the constitution given by Christ for the well-being of the Church. Hierarchical power entails the exercise of all duties of the office, both those pertaining to the glorification of God and the salvation of souls. Thus the Pope of Rome, viewed from this aspect of power, is "the servant of the servants of God."

Hierarchy is necessarily, by its origin, of a supernatural nature[22] because it has been authorized by Christ himself, either by reason of the subject (revelation of God, sacraments, way of life for believers) or by reason of the purpose which is the sanctification of the faithful.

The Church is called a hierarchical society, since a council of superiors is a feature of the constitution of such a Church, this constitution having been given by God for all times. It is well known that there is no society that has a hierarchical constitution or an organization like that of the Church. In other religious societies the power is not transferred and the power in such churches is not supernatural and given directly by God. This uniqueness is proof of the special and extraordinary character of the Catholic Church which also has special organization in virtue of its hierarchical constitution.

Even in the order of grace, the hierarchical order in the Church is suitable for its members. Something can be suitable when it does not damage anyone, even though it does not contribute to making him perfect. Something can be suitable for someone to the extent that it makes him perfect, or is necessarily required for his perfection. The hierarchical constitution of the Church is suitable in both these aspects; it does not oppose the order of grace and human nature. It aims at the perfect order of grace and of man, and under some conditions it is necessary.

The Dominican theologians, Schultes[23] and De Groot,[24] both present arguments which prove the suitability of the hierarchical constitution of the Church. It is an evident conclusion that Christ, establishing the Church, built a perfect work. It would not follow that this work would be perfect if the multitude and entity of all believers could not be arranged and regulated in some way, since he endowed the Church with certain tasks and accredited her with certain powers. In such a way must things be arranged by every founder who establishes any kind of society. In the kingdom of Christ, more than in any other kind of society, the power depends only on Christ.

Furthermore, God himself, preserving the world in its existence, acts through suitable and natural causes. The same method is preserved in the order of grace, because grace does not exclude the natural order. Thus God assigned sacred power to some people. As in the natural order there is a multiplicity of causes and consequences, so also in the order of grace there is the order of sacred and hierarchical power.

It is known from experience that people federated in a society can more easily attain the purpose and aims of all. This is basic in founding any society. It would not be prudent to deprive a man of such significant purposes of a society as the consecration and care of souls. Therefore Christ, by constituting the Church and her hierarchical organization, established her suitability and her necessity for all men. It is a fact that believers federated in the Church attain their aim more easily and in a more perfect way than they would if they should remain as individuals and unfederated. The faithful, by the pastoral activity of the Church, are better instructed about the truths of the faith; they have certitude concerning the sacraments and absolution; and they are led and informed by the ruling power of the Church to the way of a good life.

Since by the will of God sinners achieve grace and salvation in Jesus Christ, the Church is a continuation of his mission. It follows the order of grace and the authority of the Church that people are sanctified by other men through visible means. To quote Saint Thomas: "Now the minister is compared to his master as an instrument to the principal agent; for, just as the instrument is moved by the agent in order to produce an effect, so a minister is moved by his master to execute his will. Again, the instrument should be proportionate to the agent. Therefore Christ's ministers should be conformed to him. Now Christ wrought our salvation, as master, by his own authority and power, inasmuch as he is God and man: in that, his sufferings were made efficacious for our salvation. Consequently Christ's ministers needed to be new, and to share in his Godhead by a kind of spiritual power."[25]

These theological expositions about the necessity of existence of servants are reasons for the need of a hierarchy, which should not be looked upon as a matter of a *social specialty,* but as the *substantial element of ecclesiastical society* which has been built by the Church to exert her jurisdiction on the basis of orders given by Christ himself. A hierarchy which would not be constituted by Christ would not be necessary; by this fact its suitability and necessity are evident.

It is an indisputable fact based on the testimony of Holy Scripture and the history of the Church that the apostles were the first council of the hierarchy. They formed the basis upon which the ecclesiastical hierarchy was constituted. This thesis is evident from the words of Holy Scripture, where we learn of the authority given to the apostles. The apostles first obtained the promise of a hierarchical power; thereafter they received that power itself; and finally, they exerted it. The solemn and general mission of the apostles and the granting of hierarchical power were expressed in the words of Christ, who granted hierarchical power to the apostles alone.

The substance of the mission is given through the hierarchical power. Saint John[26] positively mentions the power to forgive and retain sins, which is sacred power, and also the power of jurisdiction for the internal forum of the Church. Saint Matthew[27] describes in a stricter way the extent of hierarchical authorization. Christ himself possesses full pontifical jurisdiction. Thereafter he lets the apostles participate in his own pastoral power, and sends them into the whole world to continue the work of salvation. "Go, make disciples of all nations" is what Christ said when he granted full pastoral jurisdiction, adding the severe sanction, "He who believes and is baptized shall be saved, but he who does not believe shall be condemned."[28]

As full power is included in the pastoral authorization, there is proof that the apostles are representatives of it. Apostles should teach all believers, baptize them, and instruct them to preserve all orders and commandments of Christ. It is evident too that when the apostles were solemnly sent to exert their mission, all the power which had appeared necessary for founding, organizing, and administering to Christian communities was granted to them.

It is clear from the instructions given by Christ that the hierarchical constitution was instituted by him.[29] This thesis is proved by the words of Christ himself in Holy Scripture, where he describes the Church as a society hierarchically organized,[30] calling it the "kingdom of God." The name "kingdom of God" represents the Church as a society instituted, and having various offices, tasks, and power. In the kingdom of Christ, all power has its source in Christ and in his name, and only by the virtue of his authority has it been exerted. Furthermore, the word "church" does not mean a society without a constitution but, on the contrary, one duly constituted and organized. The constitution of the Church depends upon the will of her Founder, who appointed Peter as her head and conferred on him all power to act. So too, the titles "house of God," "Church of God," "community of God," and similar expressions presuppose a hierarchical society.

Christ subsequently appointed apostles as superiors of the Church. He chose twelve apostles who had followed him from the beginning, and he reminded them: "You have not chosen me, but I have chosen you, and have appointed you that you should go and bear fruit. . . ."[31] They were called apostles by Christ himself[32] to indicate that they were sent by him, thus becoming servants of the kingdom of God by the authority of Christ. "He who hears you, hears me; and he who rejects you, rejects me. . . ."[33] He granted them full power: "Go therefore make disciples of all nations (pastoral jurisdiction), baptizing them in the name of the Father, of the Son, and of the Holy Spirit (authorization to sanctify), teaching them to observe all that I have commanded you (ruling power)." In addition, he gave the apostles the divine character of their executive power: "I am with you all days even unto the consummation of the world." Besides, Christ promises to perpetuate the kingdom of God—namely, the Church forever.[34] Thus it is evident that the hierarchy will be the everlasting constitution of the Church.[35] In the eternal Church, no substantial change is possible. The hierarchical organization of the Church is proved by the apostolic administration of Christ's Church and by the appointment of other ministers by the apostles,[36] which is logically a hierarchical decision.

Since Christ built the Church by giving authority to the apostles, logically, then, this authority has been made part of the essence of the Church, and will endure until the will of the Founder is changed. This apostolic authorization has been transferred to bishops by the rite and manner constituted by Christ.[37] This rite is ordination.

A question arises as to who are the real successors to the power of the apostles, and who are the other members. Regarding this question, the bishops should be viewed not only as individuals, but as a corporate whole, including the

Pope of Rome. The proof of the proper successors appears from the following argument: the apostles in their threefold authority must have successors, because this authority is forever, as the Church also was established to be perpetual. No one except bishops can be considered as successors. Therefore, apostolic authority has been transferred to bishops.[38] In comparing the activities of bishops with those granted exclusively to the apostles, we find that the apostles had been teaching by the highest authority, preserving discipline, judging and condemning even priests themselves, and that these are the tasks bishops have carried on since the time of the apostles. The bishops, in accepting these tasks, must be viewed as the apostles' successors. And the priests, in participating in this power, have been subject to bishops and authorized by them.[39] And the fact that there is no higher ordination in the Church than that of bishops is indicative that only bishops, having full power, are true successors of the apostles.

These facts are significant because they are proof that the episcopal power is not a result of any historical development,[40] but rather prove that this institution of bishops is a true confirmation of the delegation of apostolic authority.

It is certain that the institution of bishops was effective in the second if not the first century and was gradually introduced into the whole Church. In the first century there existed many special churches having episcopal and monarchical constitution. An example is the community at Jerusalem, which is described in the Acts of the Apostles. Considering this and the fact that all sources prove the authority of the apostles, one can conclude that the beginning of episcopal constitution is derived from the apostles, and is of divine origin because they too acted as apostles of Christ,[41] and knew only Jesus Christ, his doctrine, his will, his authority, upon which they thereafter built and founded their churches. Tertullian (A.D. 200) used the fact of the apostles' delegated authority as the strongest proof against heretics of his time.

To be true successors of apostolic power, it is necessary that bishops have as full an extent of power as the apostles had, because hierarchy, from the very meaning of the word, necessarily requires an order. By order we mean: . . . *dispositio superiorum et inferiorum rerum, quae inter se ita aptae sunt, ut una ad alteram referatur. Quum itaque in hoc ministro (ecclesiastico) multi sunt gradus et variae functiones, omnia vero certa ratione distributa sint et collocata, recte et commende ordinis nomen ei impositum videtur.*[42]

Beginning with the lowest, the seven orders in the Church are: porter, lector, exorcist, acolyte; and the higher: subdeacon, deacon, priest. In the order of priesthood, the first degree of dignity and power is the priest; the second degree is the bishop. Diaconate, priesthood, and bishopric are of divine law.[43] The different degrees of bishops, archbishops, metropolitans, and patriarchs are of ecclesiastical right. Bishops, by the authorization of Christ, are the highest of the orders. This conclusion is proven by Holy Scripture, by tradition and by the hierarchical constitution of society.

Christ appointed seventy-two[44] who were of a lower degree of power and dignity than the apostles. The bishops as successors of apostles are the priests' superiors. Bishops place their hands, and priests are ordained by them.[45]

The Church Fathers, since the time of Clement and Ignatius of Antioch, distinguish bishops from priests by giving the names of bishops, and by giving reasons for the superiority of bishops as instituted by Christ.[46]

In any society there is a need for higher and lower degrees, since in that way these lower degrees are subject to their superiors and the superiors to their head. In the hierarchical Church, bishops are superiors of higher degree. This is according to the constitution authorized by Christ.[47] This applies to the construction of the Church; in this regard, bishops are true successors of the apostles in their authority to organize. They form the true sacred government commissioned to "take heed to yourselves and to the whole flock in which the Holy Spirit has placed you as bishops, to rule the Church of God, which He has purchased with His own blood."[48]

By means of this hierarchical constitution of the Church, the influence of laymen in the Church is eliminated. When Christ appointed a certain council to rule over the Church, it became the first duty of laymen to subject themselves to these superiors and to abstain from any interference in ecclesiastical affairs. Consequently it is spiritually beneficial for them to respect all instructions from their ecclesiastical superiors in public as well as in private life.[49] The help and grace of God could not be expected if the faithful either in public or in private life were considered to be in opposition to, or ignorant of, the orders and regulations of the Church. Nor should they act without the cooperation of their ecclesiastical superiors. Any such work could not achieve the blessing of God, since it was he who constructed the hierarchical Church.[50] That should be kept in mind especially by those who as public officials are using Christianity as the ensign of their work, and who claim to be working for Christian culture and Christian democracy. Such individuals have no regard for the endeavors of Catholic action, but instead look only for the attainment of momentary political gains. They neglect to cooperate after consulting with and obtaining the consent of the Church. This is a sad and precarious abuse which is prevalent today. Yet this is not the worst of the matter. Some so-called Christian public officials, in disfavor with the interests and intentions of the Church, make all kinds of compromises. They follow tactics that advance their own personal aims and for "thirty pieces of silver" collaborate even with the enemies of the Church. This is immoral in every sense. All public officials should respect the position of the Church as a society of the public law. The Church should be respected accordingly, and all laymen should realize that, when exerting their public activities, they are subject to the hierarchy of the Church, because even in this exercise of public affairs they are members of the militant Church. It is not the proper thing for them to make unfavorable compromises concerning matters which are beyond their sphere of activity. It belongs to the pastoral authority to instruct laymen in public affairs;[51] all laymen are subject to show respect and to have regard for these instructions. Only the ecclesiastical hierarchy possesses pastoral authority.

Special exposition is needed to explain the theory concerning charismatic characteristics of the original Church. Adherents of this theory think that the bond of the disciples of Christ was only love and respect for Christ. The same is asserted by modern Protestants, who think the first Christians were bound together by love, enthusiasm, and charisms,[52] by which individuals were told what they should do. As a factor in regulating, unifying, and consecrating the power of the Church, certain persons stood out as possessing special charisms. This can be proved by the Epistles of Saint Paul or of Didaché. According to this doctrine, in the societies established by Paul there was authority and jurisdiction given to certain men, because there was a direct influence of the Holy Spirit by charisms. The first constitution of the Church was charismatic, but in later development it has been changed to a hierarchical one.[53] Following this argument, Harnack[54] concludes: (*a*) charismatics ruled in a hegemonic manner; (*b*) bishops had in the early Church no pastoral authority, but administered the society from an economical point of view. By this, Harnack evades the reality and the existence of the hierarchy. From Saint Paul we know that in the societies which he established there were some charismatic phenomena. Many of the leaders were appointed directly by Christ and accredited with various special ecclesiastical aims, as were the apostles themselves. With apostolic authorization they were endowed with many graces, as it appears from Paul himself.[55]

The charismatic constitution does not exclude, however, the hierarchical constitution of the Church; on the contrary, it aims at that, and confirms it. Neither direct appointment by Christ nor designation by ministers excludes full power. No power of ministers hinders other believers from obtaining any other consecration or authorization given by God, which they could use in favor of the Church. The hierarchy is responsible for regulating the use of these gifts, as Paul dedicated his instructions regarding the same.[56] On the contrary, charismatic institution aims at the hierarchical because *spiritualia* are intended to help the authorization of the hierarchy. Thus many spiritual gifts evident in Saint Paul's communities brought special and particular help "in order to perfect the saints for a work of ministry for building up the body of Christ."[57] As the Church in general has her charisms of sanctity and infallibility, which are visible, so also the ecclesiastical communities of Saint Paul had evident charisms of the Holy Spirit to help and give testimony to the apostle of nations.

Adherents of this charismatic doctrine and adversaries of hierarchical constitution are wrong as to exposition of the *charismata* and *spiritualia*. They confuse freely given charisms with *charismata* which are given by the grace of God. Graces are not divided hierarchically. *Spiritualia* or *pneumatica* comprise also hierarchical power as far as this power has been freely given. Appointment as an apostle was obtained by Paul as a spiritual gift, given freely in favor of the Church. In this sense, Paul said in Ephesus: "And he himself gave some men as apostles, and some as prophets, others again as evangelists and others as pastors and teachers."[58] Besides the above-named theological error, there is the endeavor of adherents of this theory to explain the purity of the Church by elements of psychological and sociological character, as is often done by Protestant theologians. They do this to evade the necessity of admitting the hierarchical constitution of the Church. Over all these theories and concepts remains the everlasting existence of the Church under her ensign of ontological stability.

Charisms in the original Church are only symptoms of divine Providence, so that the Church could more easily come through the countless frontiers of her enemies and that the holy council of apostles could hold more easily the scepter of the kingdom of God on earth. Hence to explain this charism as a most important factor in the societies of Paul is against his own instructions; for he, as is known, established societies constructed hierarchically. This proves that the charismatic theory aimed to support the hierarchy.[59]

It is therefore evident that in the Church there is not only the power of God, but also a definite form and constitution as well; and it follows that all changes are inadmissible because the Church is a society constituted by God and built "according to the example of the heavenly Jerusalem, which remains forever without change."[60]

This hierarchical institution in the Church is explained in the Sacred Scriptures and therefore is *de fide divina*. The Church constitutes the holy council of apostles, as the Vatican Council has stated positively.[61]

Thus condemned were all the errors aiming against hierarchical constitution, namely: (*a*) the theory of Marsilius, condemned already by Pope John XXIII;[62] (*b*) the theory of the Pistorian Synod, condemned by Pope Pius VI;[63] (*c*) the theory of the reformers, condemned by the Council of Trent.[64] Condemnation of all theories attacking the hierarchical constitution of the Church indicates that this belongs to the essence of the Church. The whole theory in regard to the hierarchical constitution of the Church is explained by Leo XIII in his famous encyclical, *Satis Cognitum* June 24, 1896:

At vero quomodo doctrina . . . sic etiam non singulis e populo Christiano, verum delectis quibusdam data divinitus facultas est perficiendi atque administrandi divina mysteria, una cum regendi gubernandique potestate. Neque enim nisi ad Apostolos legitimosque eorum successores ea pertinent a Jesu Christo dicta: "Euntes in nundum universum, praedicate Evangelium . . ." Similique ratione non nisi apostolis, quique eis iure successissent, mandavit, ut pascerent, hoc est cum potestate regerent universitatem Christianorum, quos hoc ipso eis subesse debere atque obtemperare est consequens.[65]

Therefore the character of the Church, the texts of the Holy Scriptures, and the doctrine of the Church all prove that the ecclesiastical hierarchy is constituted by God and that this eternal hierarchy is authorized by divine law.

Whatever form the society has been given by the founder must be respected, because only the will of the founder can change it. Christ gave to his Church by power of consecration, pastoral power, power to rule, doing all this through the apostles appointed by him. He himself expressed his will that the Church should exist for ever. There is nowhere any indication that Christ changed his will. So also Christ expressed his will that the Church should have a hierarchical constitution. In this respect we have the texts of Holy Scripture, which admit of no doubts;[66] furthermore we have the proof of tradition.[67]

By divine law, bishops, priests, and deacons form the hierarchy so often mentioned in Holy Scripture.[68] Successors in the hierarchy are appointed by divine law and given sacred power. Men become members of this hierarchy by the assignment of the authorization to confer the sacraments, to instruct and teach the faithful. This authorization is granted to deacons in the lowest degree, to priests in a higher degree, and fully to bishops. This is assigned in the consecration of the bishop, and thus is independent of any secular power or of any layman or of any human jurisdiction.[69]

This attitude has been followed by the practice of the

Church; never were ministers named by the people, never appointed, removed, punished, nor judged by them. Never has the appeal of the people been admissible or exerted against the verdict of the ecclesiastical court; never have the people issued any ecclesiastical regulation or enforced the issuance of such a law. In short, the will of the people is not able to give sacred power to anyone, because it has none.

For this reason, the Council of Trent has taken an uncompromising view in the following exposition:

a) Docet insuper sacrosancta synodus, in ordinatione episcoporum, sacerdotum et ceterorum ordinum, nec populi, nec cujusvis saecularis potestatis et magistratus consensum, sive vocationem, sive autoritatem ita requiri, ut sine ea irrita sit ordinatio: quin potius decernit, eos, qui tantummodo a populo, aut saeculari potestate ac magistratu vocati et instituti, ad haec ministeria exercenda ascendunt, et qui ea propria temeritate sibi sumunt, omnes non ecclesiae ministros sed fures et latrones per ostium non ingressos habendos esse.[70]
b) Si quis dixerit, episcopos non esse presbyteris superiores, vel non habere potestatem confirmandi et ordinandi; vel eam, quam habent, illis esse cum presbyteris communem; vel ordines ab ipsis collatos sine populi vel potestatis saecularis consensu aut vocatione irritos esse, aut eos, qui nec ab ecclesiastica et canonica potestate rite ordinati, nec missi sunt, sed aliunde veniunt, legitimos esse verbi et sacramentorum ministros, anathema sit.[71]
c) Si quis dixerit, episcopos, qui auctoritate Romani Pontificis assumuntur, non esse legitimos et veros episcopos, sed figmentum humanum, anathema sit.[72]

From this it is clear and logical that only the hierarchy, by its consecration and accredited power of rule over the Church, can rule legally, independently, and in sovereign manner. This jurisdiction is exercised by bishops in their dioceses and by the Pope of Rome in the universal Church of Christ, which is a perfect society established by God—the Catholic Church.

It was well said by Saint Thomas Aquinas that there can be no doubt that the government of the Church as constituted by Christ is the best government possible.[73]

PART TWO

THE CATHOLIC CHURCH AND THE CZECHOSLOVAK STATE

CHAPTER FIVE

JOHN HUS AND THE REFORMATION

BEFORE ANY IDEA BECOMES ESTABLISHED, A LONG PERIOD OF development is always necessary. The seed must first be sown; then follows its growth during a long period. Thereafter come the fruits, good or bad. This is the natural law, but it also has its application to the history of nations as we can see in the development of the provinces of Bohemia, Moravia, Silesia, Slovakia and Carpatho-Ruthenia. In their one thousand years' history, the seed has yielded a rich crop in terms of religion, culture, and politics.

The relation between seed and fruit, expressed so many times in the Holy Scripture,[1] is one of similarity—from good seed we gather good fruit. But when we look to the land of Bohemia, an unusual and astonishing contrast presents itself. The seed was good; indeed the sowing of these lands has been carried out exclusively by Catholic missionaries. Yet the fruit has been disappointing in that evidences of antipathy to the Catholic Church have appeared where one might well expect a filial, loving devotion. For all historical analyses show that the political and cultural developments of Bohemia, Moravia, and Slovakia, from the very beginnings of their history, are but the reflection and result of the Catholic missions.

Accompanied by the special blessings of God, the word of God was preached in these lands by such great representatives of Christianity as Saints Cyril and Methodius,[2] Adalbert,[3] Procopius,[4] Andrej-Svorad,[5] and others, coming from both East and West.[6] Their sowing was on fertile soil, and has yielded good fruit; few nations in all Europe can boast of a national history as brilliantly adorned by saints and martyrs, heroes and noble personalities.[7] This characteristic tradition has been markedly advantageous[8] to the whole nation. Proof lies in the political emergence of the great Moravian Empire (830-906),[9] the period of Saint Wenceslaus

(920-929),[10] the period of the Czech dukes (900-1200), the dynasty of the kings of Przemyslide (thirteenth century), the period of kings from the Luxemburg dynasty (fourteenth century), and especially the reign of Charles IV (1346-1378). Historical analysis of these periods from the ninth through the fourteenth century brings out the importance of all the events of those times in which Bohemia, Moravia, and Slovakia played major roles, being thus in competition with other European nations and participating in the expansion of the Christian culture and way of life.

This growth developed through the efforts of the Catholic Church, whose spiritual and cultural resources are a fountain used by all nations. As all heathen countries shared in receiving the beams of sunlight emanating from Rome's cultural endeavors in this period, so did the lands of Bohemia and Slovakia participate in the careful work of the Catholic Church. It is easy to perceive how progressive these lands appeared at the beginning of the Middle Ages. Yet, despite all this indebtedness to the Church, there is to be found a strong attitude of hostility to the Catholic Church, from whose spiritual and intellectual wealth this territory had enjoyed such evident benefit. That the careful hand and effort of the Church is to be seen in the history of these lands at this period cannot be denied: The establishment of a bishopric at Prague (973), its promotion to an archbishopric (1344), the Church's interest in the Slavic rite in the time of Cyril and Methodius, the use of the Slavic rite in the monastery "Na Slovanech," the efforts of Saint Adalbert, etc., are not to be overlooked. But, like almost every family, the Christian family has also had its ungrateful children. This appears very often in the history of the Church, and in many analogous situations it reappears in the history of many nations.

The changing of special characteristics in the lands of Saint Wenceslaus—which was symbolized by Hussitism and its aims and concepts—is often proclaimed as changes of development, since the intentions of those adversaries of Rome was to decry all aims of so-called movements of advancement. There have even been some for whom these endeavors served as a replacement for the generous mother of all nations, the Catholic Church. There were some who tried to expel her from the nation, in the spirit of the catchword originated by T. G. Masaryk: "Rome must be brought to trial and convicted."[11]

For the most part, spiritual dissension originated in the provinces of the lands of Saint Wenceslaus. What was done in the name of Hus was accepted, even when it had nothing in common with the intentions and aims of John Hus. On the other hand, all that was Catholic was condemned or was grudgingly received because of the hostile reactions fostered especially by wide and uncritical reading of the novels and sagas of the Czech writer, Alois Jirásek, whose malicious and censorious treatment of the whole Baroque period and of the Counter-Reformation implanted many erroneous ideas in the minds of his impressionable countrymen. Although scientists and historians later corrected a considerable portion of these misconceptions, the resultant damage was very great.

The real division of spiritual development, however, became apparent mainly in the period after World War I (1914-1918) following the establishment and proclamation of the Czechoslovak Republic, in the period during which the antithesis "Hus-Church" was nearly the exclusive program of public life, with the intent of accentuating the expression of opposition to the destroyed Austro-Hungarian monarchy of the past. Many events and speeches at this time can be excused as arousing the nationalism of Czechs and Slovaks, even though the awakening nationalism resulting from the endeavors of Catholic priests and laymen cannot be overlooked. This tendency had become the main impulse behind all activities at the end of the nineteenth and at the beginning of the twentieth century, especially in the time before the Czechoslovak state had been proclaimed. Flaunting the slogan, "Away from Rome," and using the help of all non-Catholic Churches, the so-called "advanced" orators, both leftists and rightists, delivered their speeches. From non-Catholic, atheist, and political platforms indictments of the Catholic Church were raised and detraction plagued her throughout the period of the early years of the new Czechoslovak Republic. The same development was to be found in education.

We state as historical fact that it has been utterly unjust to lay such a proportion of crime and injustice at the door of the Catholic Church. To trace this historic struggle we present the story as follows: (a) psychological aversion to the Catholic Church incited by the period of John Hus (1415); (b) development of the negative attitude of the Czechoslovak state toward the Church under the influence of the *"Los von Rom Bewegung"*; (c) World War II (1939-45) and its influence on the religious conditions in Czechoslovakia.

After the acceptance of Christianity the provinces of the Czech crown and Slovakia were almost undisturbed from the ninth to the fourteenth century, in the closest accord with the Catholic idea. But after the proclamation of the teachings of John Hus and his interferences had started, relations with Rome began to change. The spiritual revolution caused by John Hus was reflected very significantly among Czech believers, and the movement incited by the Hus doctrine had its consequences not only from the legal and ecclesiastical, but also from the cultural and sociological point of view. This incitement evoked a movement of the nation to a more radical doctrine which was accepted in a thoughtless way without consideration of the consequences. This new doctrine was spread with fanaticism and enthusiasm. This made it difficult to solve the problem, not only in the internal life of the nation, but also in Rome.

It is interesting to note that the whole Hussite movement was organized by a foreigner, John Wyclif, a well-educated but reckless heretic.[12] Wyclif (1324-82), first active as a preacher, developed into a dogmatic reformer whose doctrines could not but undermine even the basic constitution of the Church. These doctrines spread into the lands of the Czech crown, and, blocking reformation efforts originating there, gave content to the religious movement of the Hussites by their formulation and principles.[13] It is doubtful whether the heretical ideas of Wyclif would have had such significance if they had not been strengthened by the enthusiasm of the nation itself.

Czech professors and students were a minority at Charles University in Prague where Germans of Bavarian and Saxon origin and Poles prevailed.[14] Czechs were a minority also in the population of towns and cities, especially in Prague. The same was true among clerics and the hierarchy. The endeavor to prevail against the Germans and thus to gain leadership in the country, unwittingly caused the Czechs to become ardent fellow travelers with the English and local reformers. In this way, a Czech whose conscience was backed by a subjective conviction of "moral prevalence" became a "fighter of God," thus adding to the incipient struggle a revolutionary and elementary virulence. Thus it happened that the teaching of a foreigner, Wyclif, became strong in practice.

It must be mentioned, too, that Wyclif was a heretic of an extraordinary nature, since all the errors of the Apocalyptists, the Waldensians, Marsilius of Padua, etc.,[15] as well as the problem of nominalism and realism, were within his doctrinal sphere and caused heated disputes in Bohemia as well as in the rest of the world. It has been well said of Wyclif by Cardinal Hergenrother: "All that had been spun by fraudulent philosophy and false theology, as can be read in Waldeus, the Apocalyptists, Occam, Marsilius of Padua, John Janduno, we may find concentrated in the doctrine of the sect established by John Wyclif, so that all of his doctrines center around old and new heretics and heresies."[16]

The basis of his doctrine is pantheistic realism and predestinarianism (the latter, it should be mentioned, is a menace to human liberty and freedom), and on this basis he established his church as a society of chosen men. The Pope, according to him, is the Antichrist. The Church may have no property nor jurisdiction. The Bible is the sole source of faith; no sacraments are necessary; and even the most Holy Eucharist must be conceived only in terms of impanation.[17] This doctrine was a very strong attack against the Church and her whole structure was threatened by it.[18] No one before had dared to make such an attack, although in previous centuries the Church had defended herself against many heretics, as is known from history. This accentuated cynicism of Wyclif appeared, no doubt, to be very ardent. In Wyclif everyone found all that he himself wanted to find there. John Hus accepted nearly all of his doctrines. The comparison of Wyclif and Hus seems surprising, considering the great extent to which John Hus was the imitator of Wyclif.[19] It is enough for argument to compare the condemned articles of Wyclif with those of Hus, as was done during the Council of Constance. Not only the similarity but even the identity of the majority of them becomes evident.[20]

It is surprising that John Hus chose such an irresponsible

and remorseless heretic as Wyclif for his teacher. Some historians explain this in the light of the state of affairs in the Church at the time and think that the extent of the abuse required radical reforms and learned reformers. This explanation can hardly be accepted for the period of the reign of Charles IV, which is generally looked upon as a golden era because of the flourishing condition of religious life, culture, morality, and the emperor's successes in internal and external policy, economy and building up of the country. This was actually the most suitable time for the development of the Church and her institutions.[21] The Church was fostering education and reforms through which the first Archbishop of Prague, Ernest of Pardubice (1344-1364), noted for his famous provincial synods,[22] became an example of a successful ecclesiastical reformer. His successors, Cardinal John Očko of Vlaším (1364-1380), and Archbishop John of Jenštein (1380-1396) continued these efforts,[23] and formulated in Czech and German the so-called *devotio moderna*,[24] in which Konrad Waldhauser and Milič of Kroměříž especially excelled as reformers. The reform movement was being carried out judiciously and had among its adherents both priests and laymen. This movement was a part of prudent activities on the part of the Church and the hierarchy and started before Hus's time. Spiritual reform is an inherent part of the pastoral authority of the Church, forming its base and substance. John Hus, being a Catholic priest, had an opportunity to continue in this endeavor without Wyclif, but through his introduction of the latter's doctrine, his Czech country was stamped with the unhealthy radicalism of Hussitism, which caused many complications in ecclesiastical and in public life. Hus was not the originator of reforms, because they had been begun before him under the supervision of the ecclesiastical hierarchy; but being under the influence of Wyclif's doctrine and inspired by it, he caused this reform to be emancipated from ecclesiastical supervision and to be developed against the Church.

There were certain specific circumstances which induced Hus to rise up against the Church: the struggle between Czech and German nations for supremacy;[25] the existence of a philosophical struggle between nominalism and realism;[26] the papal schism; the unstable character of King Wenceslaus IV (1378-

1419) who, unlike Charles IV with his magnanimous policy and dignified life, was constantly in discord with the ecclesiastical authorities.

Under those circumstances John Hus appeared as a radical type of Wyclifite, fighting against all and risking all. His abilities, average in themselves, were exalted and inspired by these conditions[27] and the movement characterized by his name was dominated by his opinion. In this movement were concentrated almost all the problems of the nation and all its social questions, so that the dynamic determination of the Czech people took no account of authority, and in a revolutionary spirit accepted utopian ideas which were premature for that time. Accordingly, the ideas of the Czech people seemed to be in opposition to the ideals of the Middle Ages. Every new idea was accepted by the people and carried out with the aim of returning to the practices of the early Church. All this found approval by assistance from Hus. But his revolutionary doctrine was examined and condemned by the Council of Constance (1414-18) in a most critical and deliberate manner.

John Hus (1369-1415) was born in Husinec near Prague (not Husinec in South Bohemia).[28] He studied in the parochial school and continued his education at Charles University. In the year 1393 he obtained the degree of bachelor of science, and in 1396, the degree of master of philosophy.[29] In the list of candidates ranked according to the results of their examinations, Hus is mentioned as sixth among twenty-two bachelors and tenth among sixteen masters.[30] Obviously he was a student of just average talents. He then studied theology. By 1398 he had copied four theological tracts of Wyclif, (now in Stockholm). He was ordained a priest in 1400. In 1401 he became dean of the philosophical faculty, and in 1402 the rector of the university for one year. At the university in Prague, not too much interest was given to the problem of nominalism and realism. At this time, John Hus and his teacher, Stanislav of Znojmo, a very clever Czech theologian and the famous leader of Czech Wyclifites, became adherents of the Wyclif doctrine.[31] But Stanislav of Znojmo recanted his participation; John Hus continued.

Nominalism[32] either in extreme or in moderate form meant a decadence of the great scholastic thesis, impoverishment of thought, and an endeavor to weaken the whole structure of Christianity. Harmony between the material, the sensual, and the supernatural was being destroyed. Nominalism preferred and admitted only sensualism on one side, intellectualism and radicalism on the other side. This rationalism looked upon reason not only as a function, but as an exclusive source of the truth. Hobbes, Locke, Hume, Descartes, Leibnitz, and Kant were later followers of nominalism. The Protestant revolt against the Catholic Church is an indirect result of nominalism, as is frankly admitted by the Protestants themselves. At Charles University in Prague, there were no nominalists in the time of Hus, but there is no doubt that nominalism was studied by the masters at Prague.[33] In Prague there was a conflict between moderate realists as defined by Saint Thomas Aquinas, and the definition and degree taught by the German masters and the radical realists. These latter were headed by John Hus, and numbered among their followers such masters as Mikuláš of Litomyšl, Stanislav of Znojmo, Štěpán Páleč, the astronomer Christian of Prachatice, and Jeroným of Prague.[34] It was a fateful decision for John Hus and the Czech masters when they refused to emancipate themselves from their philosophical errors.[35]

In May, 1403, all the masters of the four nations were invited into the great hall at Charles University to express their opinions concerning forty-five articles of Wyclif which were found to be in opposition to the principles of the Church. Great quarreling and turmoil resulted and thereafter occurred more and more frequently. The German masters, being in the majority, condemned the articles and forbade the teaching of them.

The theory of Wyclif that after the transubstantiation there remains in the Eucharist, besides the body of Christ, also the substance of bread, found temporary corroboration in the doctrine of Stanislav of Znojmo, who published in 1404 a dissertation concerning the Eucharist in which he agreed with the Wyclif theory. However, he later repudiated this heresy. The defying of those forty-five articles and the dissension of Stanislav threw very heavy suspicion on the reform suggestions and aims[36] proclaimed by the Czech Wyclifites.

But in spite of the suspicion cast upon them, Archbishop

Zbyněk trusted these masters and gave them various reform tasks. In 1402 John Hus was appointed preacher in the Bethlehem Chapel, so he now had three areas of activity—the university, the synods, and the chapel with which was associated the largest Czech community in Prague. He thereby received a substantial income, but since this was not proper for a reformer,[37] historians are inclined to believe that Hus neglected to reveal this fact.

All of Hus's attacks against papal authority, the hierarchy, and the Church herself originated in the Bethlehem Chapel. By such actions, Hus lost the confidence of the Archbishop of Prague, whom Hus attacked when, according to his duty, the Archbishop condemned Master Jakoubek for his dissertation denying transubstantiation. By the fact that Hus did not speak officially[38] in favor of transubstantiation, it is evident that Hus favored the theory that the substance of the bread and wine remained in the Eucharist even after transubstantiation.

From Bethlehem Chapel there developed a national feeling which was awakened and incited by Hus's Czech sermons. This development became apparent at Charles University when the Kutná Hora decree[39] given by King Wenceslaus IV in 1409 was issued, giving the Czechs absolute majority in the university. Up to that time, the university had had a strictly European character and significance, as a result of tradition and the numbers of its members. Palacký[40] notes that in 1408 the University of Prague had two hundred doctors and masters, five hundred bachelors, and more than thirty thousand students. The Germans and others left for the newly established University of Leipzig. From 1409, the influence and significance of Charles University gradually decreased, so that in the end it had only a faculty of philosophy. However, conditions improved later. Also the local and public administration had more Czech officials. In 1413, besides nine German members of the town council, nine Czech members were elected to the council. Under the reign of King Wenceslas IV, the use of the Czech language for official purposes began; even various official documents were issued in the Czech language.

The intention, started under the new reign of Charles IV, to support and strengthen nationalism was growing, and the Czechs increased their numbers also in the towns. In this respect, Hus did his best as a patriot,[41] writing his works not only in Latin, but also in Czech, thus supporting the growing national consciousness. This manner of things was the main reason why this movement was supported by the rural Czechs, and it can be said that without the help and assistance of Czech peasantry, it would never have grown to such proportions.[42] It can be said, too, that this was the most important factor in the movement, supported by King Wenceslaus IV and used by John Hus himself.

In the year 1409 in Pisa, Alexander V was elected Pope. Since the other two claimants refused to accept the decision of Pisa, the Church now had three popes. This central problem of Christian leadership interested nearly all the nations. Very severe complications followed from this development, since each pope wanted to be generally recognized, and friends and sources of revenue were sought to cover expenses. Many unworthy features appeared. Ecclesiastical offices were bestowed in a business-like manner; simony and favors were frequently used to obtain allegiance.

The jurisdiction of the individual Popes crossed each other's boundaries and the dignity of the papal throne decreased. This condition, which was closely related to the Czech problem, was attacked by many reformers and influenced the relation between the king and the Archbishop of Prague.

Archbishop Zbyněk, in common with all ecclesiastics, recognized the legitimate Pope, Gregory XII; the king and Charles University of Prague declared themselves in favor of Alexander V. The situation grew worse. The Archbishop of Prague issued an interdict and excoriated John Hus and prohibited him from preaching in the Bethlehem Chapel. The king was angered, and the Archbishop fled to Roudnice Castle which was used as a vacation residence by the Archbishop of Prague. Finally the Archbishop was forced to recant, and in September of the same year he also recognized Alexander V (1410), who was later succeeded by John XXIII. Before his death, Alexander V, to stamp out the heresy in Bohemia, sent a bull asking that all of Wyclif's books be located and burned.[43] Many books were burned in the yard of the Archbishop's residence.

In 1410, Rome forbade any preaching in private chapels; this affected John Hus in his preaching at Bethlehem. Hus disobeyed and preached nevertheless; his feelings of resistance were now strengthened. Thinking of the various circumstances in which he found himself, he emancipated himself from ecclesiastical and clerical obedience. Archbishop of Prague, Zbyněk, pronounced an ecclesiastical censure against him (July 8, 1410) and in the course of its proclamation in some districts, turmoil arose.

But the same John Hus who had calumniated the Pope, now appealed to John XXIII, who is not favorably regarded by historians.[44] The sophisms of Wyclif had taken a hold on Hus. In September, 1410, a bull was sent to Prague, summoning John Hus before the papal court on suspicion of heresy. Using the protection of King Wenceslaus and of sympathetic nobles, he did not appear. In 1411, Hus, although excommunicated by the Pope, continued to preach under the protection of King Wenceslaus IV. It is therfore easily conceivable how difficult the position of the Archbishop of Prague had become, since he had been indulgent to John Hus before to such a great extent when Hus had made use of the king's protection.

Hus sent a letter to Pope John XXIII, asking him to cancel and nullify the summons and censure (1411). He also sent letters to many cardinals, apologizing very humbly for his past actions.

In 1411, the very capable and devout Archbishop of Prague, Zbyněk Zajíc of Hassenburg, died, and Albík of Uničov (1411-1412), having been elected by the chapter, became his successor. After the death of this Archbishop of Prague in 1412, King Wenceslaus IV appointed, without taking into account the existence of the chapter, the Bishop of Olomouc, Konrad of Vechta, who later, in 1421, apostatized from the Church.

Hus, having experienced Konrad's leniency, edited his main work, *De Ecclesia,* in which he propounded his doctrines. This work and another book of his, the *Trialogus,* incriminated him at Constance. These books became the most damning evidence against him.

There were fiery disputes caused by the sermons of Hus, repeatedly delivered in Bethlehem Chapel where he expounded his theological heresies. Baltazar Cossa, who as Pope took the name John XXIII, wanted to expel Gregory XII from Rome. Therefore, he proclaimed indulgences in the countries which took his side[45] and used their contributions to assemble a proposed drive against Ladislav of Naples, who protected Pope Gregory XII.

John Hus and other Wyclifites in Bethlehem Chapel decided to attack and oppose this abuse of indulgences. Hus wanted the university to support his intention, but the masters led by Štěpán Páleč decided to respect the orders given by the Pope and the king. This time, Hus also started to attack the king's measures, although up to that time the king had protected the Wyclifites. In this struggle, Hus was helped by Jerome of Prague who delivered many speeches containing attacks and reproaches against the king. In public places, indulgences were promised to people who would receive the sacraments and offer a voluntary contribution and fee. But the indulgences were abused although Archbishop of Prague Albík did not permit the faithful to subscribe to any given sum, and if such cases occurred in the country areas, it was done against the positive instructions which he had laid down. In some places, however, there were individual cases in which it was stressed as a duty to give contributions.

Taking no account of the prohibition of the university and of the Archbishop, Hus, on June 7, 1412, arranged in Charles Hall at the University a discussion in which he attacked the doctrine of indulgences. He said that the Pope did not know whether a sinner was predestined for salvation, that indulgences were doing away with the penances of the faithful who were inclined to sin, that the people were being robbed by all, that the Pope was emptying all purgatory.[46] Jerome of Prague spoke still more passionately. On his initiative, a masquerade procession was arranged to put to shame the papal power.

Soon thereafter, Prague was placed under a papal interdict (September, 1412), and Hus was again excommunicated. John XXIII ordered Hus arrested, and Bethlehem Chapel destroyed. For this reason, Hus left Prague for Kozi Hrádek, delivered speeches in the country, and henceforth wrote exclusively in Czech to draw the nation away from the Catholic Church. At this time, he wrote his *Postila, Simony, Explana-*

tion of the Faith, Exposition of the Ten Commandments, and *Explanation of the Our Father.*

The internal union with Rome had by now been thoroughly broken; at the same time an external symbol of this heresy appeared.[47] The two Masters, Nicholas and Peter, having been expelled from Dresden for being Waldenses, drew the attention of Jakoubek of Stříbro to the fact that both species of the Eucharist were not being given to the faithful. After long study and consultation, it was decided to introduce the partaking of communion under both species. Master Jakoubek proclaimed this as necessary for salvation, and obligatory also for children. Thus was introduced again what the Church for practical reasons had stopped before in the twelfth century. In the year 1414, the distribution of Holy Communion under both kinds for the Hus adherents appeared in these churches of Prague: Saint Michael, Saint Nicolas, Saint Adalbert, Saint Martin-within-the-Wall. Hus himself did not give Communion under both species; only in Constance was this doctrine of Jakoubek accepted by Hus.[48] The originators of this measure however were excommunicated. Thus, the chalice eventually became the visible distinguishing rite of the Wyclif-Hussites, since it appeared to differentiate them from the rest of the Catholic Church.

As Pope John XXIII was not able to remain in Rome and offer further resistance to Pope Gregory XII, he left for northern Italy, and in Lod, on the advice of King Sigismund, made up his mind to convoke a general council to unify the Church and to prevent further schisms in the various countries. On this occasion, Sigismund wrote Wenceslaus IV to call Hus before the Council. King Wenceslaus IV himself asked Hus to stand before the Council, to defend the Czech name. Even Konrad, Archbishop of Prague, testified in writing that he knew of no heresy against Hus.[49] Sigismund assured Hus of safe-conduct.[50] Hus, having been thus assured, started his trip. But if Hus thought that he would be able to preach to the Council as he had in his Bethlehem Chapel, he was greatly mistaken.

In view of the great problem of rectifying the papal schism, the Council of Constance became one of the most important councils of the Middle Ages,[51] not only because of the number of participants, but also for its intrinsic importance. The greatest credit for its convocation and procedure belongs to King Sigismund. Hus was being treated according to the regulations of ecclesiastical law. At the request of Sigismund, Hus was allowed to plead for himself before the whole council. This was a very significant concession, differing from the regular procedures of earlier councils.

The safe-conduct was violated, but Sigismund did all in his power to fulfill what he had promised. The safe-conduct did not unconditionally promise the return of John Hus to Bohemia, and this was not even asked by Hus. He wrote to Sigismund that he would not refuse to suffer as a heretic if he should be found guilty of any heresy.[52]

Because many heresies were found in his teachings, he was charged, tried, and condemned. The whole trial against Hus was in reality a dispute among the Czechs themselves and was exclusively a Czech matter. Even in a foreign country, the attorney and the public prosecutor against Hus were Bishop Jan Železný, a Czech noble, and Štěpán Páleč, a Czech theologian; Emperor Sigismund, heir to the Czech throne, himself acted as chairman.[53] After Hus was found guilty, he was turned over to the secular power and his condemnation followed.

Hus had three public hearings on the fifth, seventh, and eighth of June, 1415. One article after another was read, and he was asked whether he acknowledged it, insisted upon it, or recanted it. When Hus asserted that some articles from the indictment were not in accord with the text of his books, one of the Cardinals read all articles from the indictment and another English bishop read the respective section in the book. It appeared thus that the text of John Hus's books was stronger than the extract in the indictment. Despite this fact, in some historical books it is maintained that Hus was not tried justly.[54] Against all these insinuations, it will suffice to read the letter of Jerome of Prague, who was Hus's closest friend. In it he says that he ". . . found among his articles, some that were heretical, some that were erroneous, others that were scandalous . . . all were detrimental . . . I compared them with his manuscripts . . . and I found all these same tenets within his own books."[55] There is no doubt that the articles condemned are articles contained in Hus's doctrine, and that in the judgment of the Church they are heretical.

The court was humane and kind to Hus.[56] It proved to

be broad-minded, endeavoring to make it easier for Hus to return to the Church. Hus could have recanted the articles in the indictment by the summary sentence: *Illos articulos nec tenui, nec praedicavi, et si fecissem, male fecissem.*

It cannot be denied that the Council did everything possible to avoid severity.[57] Only after the Council had exhausted all its patience and all possibilities to rescue him did it proclaim Hus a heretic, on July 6, 1415. According to the existing law concerning heretics issued by Emperor Frederick II (1212-1250) and promulgated to the whole empire, John Hus, having been found guilty, in consequence of this secular bill, was burned. It was the secular sovereigns who burned the heretics; they were not burned by the Church. The Church only asserted herself against error. She is not only entitled, but obliged to do so. The death of Hus was the only logical consequence of his doctrine.

By his death, he impressed on his work the seal of disobedience and resistance. His verdict was felt as a nation's shame. His spirit has given to many generations the contents of their orientation. His legacy has been used not only as propaganda, but it is abused to disfavor truth and to split the nation and bring it into everlasting disputes. Why should the Catholic Church be reproached and made to suffer for having proclaimed Hus a heretic, when he really was that? It is senseless to charge the Church with that, because the council was bound to judge his doctrine. And the Council would be judged on the manner of its judgment.

Psychological reflection on this event was confused by the joining of national and religious ideas. The religious side of the affair has been decided. In Constance, John Hus was condemned not in his capacity as a Czech, but as John Hus, the heretic. The national movement did not, however, differentiate between these two features and therefore there was a strong tendency for this reflection. Wherefore the historical aversion to Rome has remained in Hussitism since its very beginnings.

This tendency has appeared in the controversial opinions of T. G. Masaryk[58] and Pekař[59] concerning the philosophy of Czech history; its existence dates back to Hus. Czech historian Joseph Pekař exposes this period in a nationalistic, not in a religious way, as does T. G. Masaryk. Also at the time of the Reformation, radicalism—for which a heretic was condemned—did not lose its contacts and relation to the Church, but a Czech led only by nationalistic feelings identifies himself with a Czech heretic, to the disfavor of the Church. This was the reaction to Hus's death. There were more reactions like that in Czech history. The fact that the Church condemned heretical citizens of other nations, too, indicates that in Constance only the religious point of view was considered; and this point of view called for the condemnation of heretics. In Hus's case, it was a heretic who menaced the structure of the Church and of secular society as well. Considering that Hus provoked attacks against the Church and these of a very cynical nature, it is natural that the Church should judge these attacks since she was not only being menaced by them, but also because she found the source of this cynicism in his works and doctrine. The Church never refused to make reforms when they were needed; the best proof of that is her history. She sought to carry out reforms and accepted them when they were presented in an endeavor to assist improvement.

Besides this exposition of the historical development of the matter, a summary of Hussitism and its spirit and doctrine must also be made. The main error of Hus concerns the substance of the Church. This is indicated in the following four articles:

1) There is but one holy and universal Church, and that is the society of the predestined. [60]
2) That the Church is the society of the predestined, whether they be actually in the state of grace or prescinding from their present state of justification, is an article of faith. [61]
3) The foredoomed are not members of the Church since no part of the Church is at any time cut off from her, insofar as the bond of predestination which holds her together is never broken. [62]
4) Although the foredoomed may on occasion actually be in the state of grace under the present dispensation, they nevertheless never constitute part of the Holy Church; the predestined always remain members of the Church, for even though they may at times fall away from occasional grace, they do not fall from the grace of predestination. [63]

By these articles Hus hoped to destroy entirely the concept of the Church as a society of the faithful, a society visible, perfect, and public. He integrated falsely the exposition of Saint Augustine, endeavoring to strengthen his own doctrine by means of Augustine's theses.[64] He interpreted Holy Scripture wrongly (Matt. 16:18; John 21:15), using it to prove his own doctrine and accepting it as the exclusive source of faith. The Church appeared in his words as a society of predestined people, instead of a perfect society hierarchically instituted by Christ.

In additional articles Hus stated his views concerning the measures and jurisdiction of the Roman Pope:

1) Peter is not and never was head of the Holy Catholic Church.[65]
2) Papal prestige stems from Caesar, and the dignity and elevation of the Pope emanates from the power of Caesar. [66]
3) It is wrong to believe that he who happens to be the Roman Pontiff is the head of any particular sanctified Church unless God has predestined him.[67]
4) No one, without a special revelation, can reasonably maintain in his own case or in that of another that he is the head of a particular Church or that the Roman Pontiff is the head of a particular Church. [68]

This senseless and unreasonable concept of predestination brought Hus to the idea of contesting the divine institution of the primacy of Peter; the papacy was for him an institution of human origin. He contested in a cynical way the fundamental principle of the Catholic Church and of its existence. The Pope was to him an Antichrist,[69] and he considered the Church as an institution of the devil.[70] He aimed many attacks against the Pope.[71]

In other articles, Hus indicated his belief that the power of the Pope was dependent on grace and life:

1) No one takes the place of Christ or Peter unless he imitates him in his moral life; no other requisite is more relevant nor can one otherwise receive delegated power from God. For the function of vicar are required both similar moral rectitude and proper delegation. [72]

2) The Pope is not the true and certified successor of Peter, the Prince of the Apostles, if his morals are not in harmony with those of Peter; and if he cultivates avariciousness, then he is the vicar of Judas Iscariot. And likewise the Cardinals are clearly not true and certified successors of the band of Christ's other apostles unless their lives are like those of the apostles and they follow the commandments and injunctions of Our Lord Jesus Christ. [73]
3) The Pope or a bishop who is evil and foredoomed is only deceptively a pastor; he is in fact a thief and a robber. [74]
4) If the Pope is evil and particularly if he is foredoomed, then he is, like Judas, a disciple of the devil, a thief and a son of perdition, and he is definitely not the head of the holy militant Church, since he is not even a member of it. [75]

Explaining the jurisdiction of the Pope as dependent on grace, he contested the jurisdiction of the whole hierarchy as well: "By the ecclesiastical censures of excommunication, suspension and interdict, the cleric governs the laity for his own interests, fosters his avariciousness, protects his evil ways and prepares the reign of the Antichrist. Those censures, which they in their law courts call denunciations, obviously emanate from the Antichrist; by them the cleric particularly takes measures against those who expose the wickedness of the Antichrist, who will for his purposes gain special control of the cleric."[76]

Hus also attacked and nullified obedience to superiors: *Obedientia ecclesiastica est obedientia secundum adinventionem sacerdotum Ecclesiae praeter expressam auctoritatem Scripturae.*[77]

According to him, the relation between superiors and subordinates should be nullified; nevertheless, a right relationship is a fundamental and intrinsic part of the hierarchical government of the Church. Moreover, John Hus made secular power dependent on grace: *Nullus est dominus civilis, nullus est praelatus nullus est episcopus, dum est in peccato mortali.*[78] In this, Hus followed Wyclif exactly.

Hus denied tradition and recognized Holy Scripture as the exclusive norm for Christian life. Effectiveness of the

The centuries-old St. Vitus Cathedral in Prague. In the foreground is the historic castle of former emperors and kings, now the residence of the presidents of the Republic of Czechoslovakia. To the left is the palace of the Archbishop of Prague.

Panoramic view of Prague, the capital of Czechoslovakia on the river Vltava, showing the Castle Hradčany in the background.

Monsignor Josef Beran being welcomed on the steps of St. Adalbert Church of the major seminary in Prague. The scene took place in May, 1945, after his return from the Nazi concentration camp at Dachau in Germany. Behind the archbishop is the Reverend Doctor Felix Mikula, now in exile.

Left: Archbishop Josef Beran of Prague, shown on his episcopal throne after his consecration. *Right*: Right Reverend Abbot Vít Tajovský, who was sentenced with ten other superiors of various religious orders at a notorious trial by the Communists in 1950.

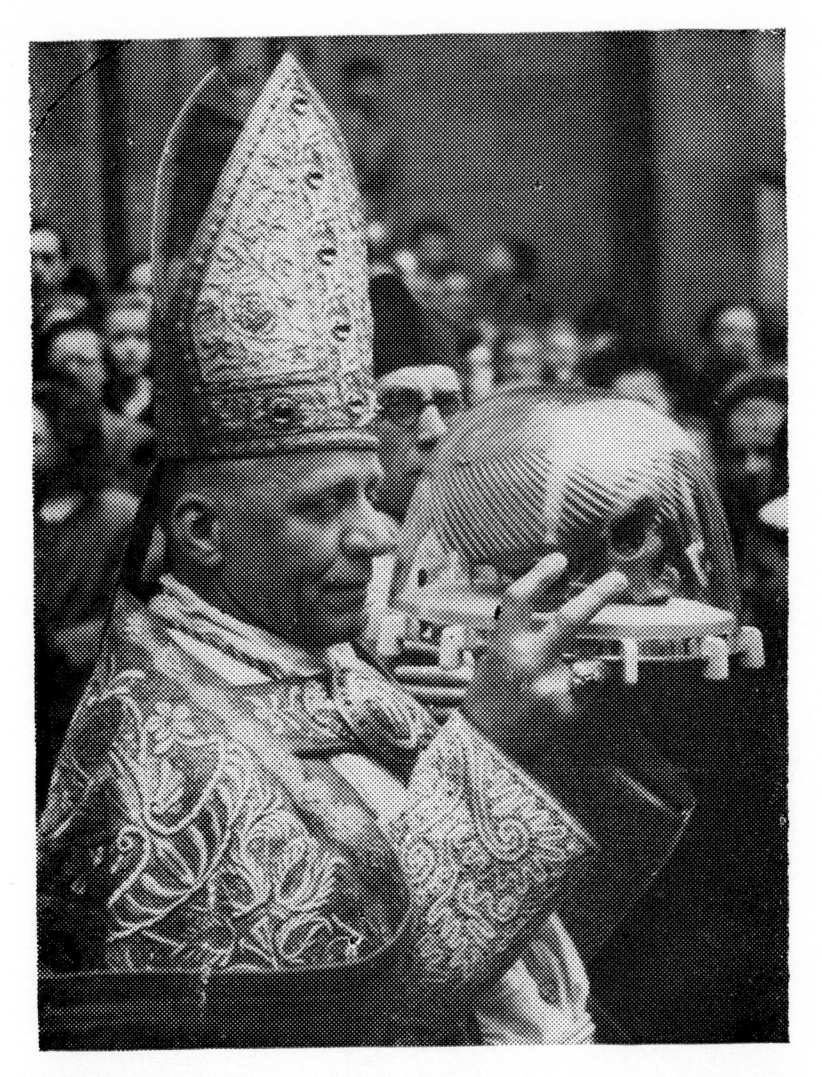

Archbishop Beran of Prague carrying the reliquary which contains the head of St. Adalbert, patron of Czechoslovakia, at the opening of the national celebration in honor of the saint in 1947.

Archbishop of Prague, Josef Beran, granting blessings with the remains of St. Adalbert at the closing of the national celebration in 1947.

Nepomucenum, the papal college in Rome, where Czech and Slovak priests are trained.

Right Reverend Jan Opasek, Benedictine Abbot of the centuries-old monastery in Břevnov, Prague. The occasion is a procession in honor of St. Adalbert. Since 1950 Abbot Opasek has been serving time as a Communist prisoner in Prague.

The heroic leader of the Greek Catholics, his Excellency Pavol Gojdič, Bishop of Prešov, Slovakia, received a life sentence at his trial by the Communists in January, 1951.

Greek Catholic Bishop Gojdič of Prešov, with his Auxiliary, Basil Hopko. This picture was the last before both prelates were jailed in July, 1950.

His Excellency Štěpán Trochta, Bishop of Litoměřice, greeting the people from the balcony of the palace of the Archbishop of Prague after his consecration, October, 1947. To his left is Archbishop Beran.

His Excellency Josef Hlouch, Bishop of Budějovice, capable and courageous leader of resistance against the Communists, who was banished from his see in 1952.

His Excellency Josef Karel Matocha, Archbishop of Olomouc in Moravia, well-known philosopher and scholar, and a determined defender of the Faith and the rights of the Catholic Church against Communism.

Auxiliary Bishop of Prague, Monsignor Kajetán Matoušek, who was secretly consecrated. Never recognized by the Communist regime as a bishop, he worked as an assistant pastor at several churches in Prague.

Scene at the consecration of Bishop Josef Hlouch, Bishop of Budějovice. At his right is Archbishop Beran; at left is Auxiliary Bishop Stanislav Zela.

His Excellency Bishop Karel Skoupý, Bishop of Brno, who was banished from his see by Communists in 1953.

Official picture of Bishop Trochta, who was the moderator of all negotiations between the bishops of Czechoslovakia and the Communist regime in Prague. Silenced in 1951 and later banished from his see, he received a sentence of twenty-five years at hard labor in 1954.

Most Reverend Josef Carsky

Most Reverend Karol Kmeťko

sacraments, he maintained, was dependent on the individual extent of grace, and the Church was dependent on grace exclusively for official power and authorization.

Hus took over all of Wyclif's teachings and, in addition, defended him: "The doctors' condemnation of the forty-five articles of John Wyclif is unreasonable and malicious and improperly drawn up; the charge alleged by them is false, namely that none of the articles is Catholic and that every last one of them is either heretical or erroneous or scandalous."[79]

The thirty articles of Hus condemned by the Council formed the framework for all his heresies, and it is surprising that Hus, since he was a trained theologian, did not seem to realize what the consequences of his actions would be. To plead for a reform which contains a contest is to plead for destruction. Pleading for reform, Hus should have regulated his relationship to the Church in accordance with principles of faith and of the nation. What was the point of Hus's reform, if the Church instituted by Jesus Christ was not recognized by him as existent, if the Pope too was not recognized and his own jurisdiction was thus denied as well? Why did Hus go before the Council of the "gathering of the devil"? His going there was proof of his pride and defiance by daring to bring his articles to be discussed.[80] By going there, he was compelled to discover the true contradiction of his articles. It is incredible and inadmissible that John Hus as a theologian did not realize this. Even the learned Master Jerome of Prague, Hus's friend, was incapable of defending his articles,[81] although he too impressed the council by his eloquence.[82] It was impossible to evade the critical revision and judgment of the Council which had been established to serve truth. Truth was impartial toward personal conviction of character. No exception could be made for Hus.

The doctrines of Hus, as subsequent history proves, were a strategic link in a complicated chain of events. Hus at the stake was the victim of collision between simple truth and personal conviction. It was the collision between individual freedom of religious conviction and revealed truth, a collision which in later centuries was brought into philosophy and did not leave theology untouched, so that the Church was forced to defend her doctrines by a formulation of articles of faith. The Catholic Church has done that and can be certain of the result. She has done so even at the cost of many apostates, because being authorized and commissioned by Jesus Christ to teach religion, she is obliged to do so. Therein lie her strength and the reason for her everlasting existence. Psychological reflection on this collision between freedom of thought and revealed truth has given it the appearance of a fight for individual freedom and freedom of thought, all against the authority of the Church. This fight became greatly extended when the spirit of the Gothic period[83] supplied this struggle with enthusiasm, being strengthened by the general conviction that Hus was unjustly condemned. And the nation in time was incited to revolution.

The consequences of Hus's errors soon appeared. People did not stop to weigh the principle of individual freedom but adopted also the stand of Hus concerning the poverty of the Church. In this point of view were united not only fellow travelers of the nobility, but the peasant class as well. Formulating his aims as to the original Church, Hus proved to be very efficient in procedure. In proclaiming his theory about the dependence of everything on grace, he was attempting to destroy the jurisdiction not only of spiritual power, but of secular power as well. He also threatened the principle of private ownership. When a bad Christian was declared by Hus to be one who is not in grace, unworthy to rule, and unworthy to hold property,[84] the gates to all social changes were ostensibly opened. Under this pretense of religious ideals were also united revolutionary principles of national and social character. This was the opening of the fifteenth century in which the Gothic school of thought clashed with Humanism.

The national problem, because of the significant position of German nationality, was more urgent, but the whole Hussite movement derived its impetus from social aims. The participation of peasants in this period can be explained according to the historian, Pekař, who wrote: "The participation of peasantry in Hussitism should be conceived as a proof of their relative richness, well-being, and freedom, not as a proof of their economic and social poverty."[85]

Only by expounding the national and social factors before the religious can one understand the strength of the conviction with which these fanatic religious doctrines were received in a period that was controlled by scholastic education after the end of Charles's reign.

Under these conditions, it is conceivable that the announcement of Hus's death was received with feelings of excitement. In Prague and in the rural districts, priests were attacked and expelled from the churches, and in their place were established priests who would give communion under both species of the Eucharist. Four hundred and fifty-two Czech and Moravian nobles held a meeting in Prague in which they protested the verdict of the Council[86] in condemning a priest to death, and railed against the shame brought upon the whole country. These nobles decided to defy all preachers of the word of God even to the sacrifice of their blood. This was really a union against the supreme authority of the Church. Catholic nobles gathered in October, 1415, in the Archbishop's town, Český Brod, and sent to Constance their letter promising obedience to the Council and faithfulness to the Church. These Catholic nobles, although only fourteen in number, included the famous Wenceslaus of Dubá, who had defended Hus at Constance but after Hus's death remained faithful to the Catholic Church. The odds of four hundred and fifty-two to fourteen are indicative of the strength with which the Hussites started their drive against Rome.

Free preaching of the word of God and partaking of Communion under both species of the Eucharist were the principal aims of the reform movement, and began to be carried out throughout the country. Ecclesiastical property began to be confiscated. The same state of affairs prevailed in the royal domain: churches were destroyed; priests were expelled; believers true to the old order were persecuted. Even King Wenceslaus IV did not dare to stop this wave, although he began to oppose it on the insistence of his brother Sigismund. Wenceslaus met the resistance in Prague, and in the southern part of Bohemia in a village called Tábor, which had been established by enthusiastic adherents of the new doctrine. The leader of these adherents was an experienced fighter, born of a small noble family, one-eyed Jan Žižka of Trocnov (1380-1424), under whose leadership the revolutionaries adopted radicalism, causing bloodshed throughout the country. But through Žižka's efforts, all of Hus's aims were achieved: The Church was poor; it prohibited solemn worship and advocated annihilation of the hierarchy; Holy Mass was very simple and without sacred vestments; bishops were elected by the people and the faithful themselves explained Holy Scripture.

Aiming to punish what they considered mortal sins, these Taborites used force against priests, monks, and others whom they thought of as adversaries, usually in fanatic ways. They went so far that after a wave of vandalism, Bohemia, which had been rich in art treasures and buildings, was culturally bereft.[87] All this was performed under the ensign of the chalice and to the singing of "You Fighters for God," reputedly composed by Žižka himself.[88] This ruthless destruction of historical buildings had its roots in the doctrine of Valdes, which had been adopted by the Taborites. About 1420, the Taborites' ministers started to preach chiliasm. This error stirred the emotions of this revolutionary movement; Žižka himself was affected. He felt himself to be chosen by God to correct the entire institution of the Church and to stop all "idolatry."[89] This was the reason he ordered all who qualified in his eyes as heretics to be executed. This cruelty is expressed in the well-known song of the Taborites, "Kill, Slaughter, Let No One Live." The country was thus reduced to chaos. The movement had no unified order.[90]

Once the Bible had been proclaimed as the sole source of faith, all kinds of heretics appeared in the country. The university defended its authority only among nobles, inasfar as these were adherents to Hussitism, and among the citizens of Prague. Their principles were compiled in the so-called "Prague Articles" (free teaching of the word of God, partaking of Communion in both forms, interdiction against the participation of priests in the secular government, punishing of mortal sins). The Prague Articles (1420) were the first formulation of the mixture of doctrines at that time. They became famous throughout the world.[91] However, the existence of extremes was eliminated (*adamits*). The differences and disputes between Prague and Tábor were not over. The Prague group still respected the Church and maintained some relations with it, while the Taborites opposed her in principle. The disputes as they developed and later appeared were diminished and somewhat extinguished only by the common danger, but the disputes continued, nevertheless.

Sigismund, seeing that the disturbances were prevalent everywhere, decided to use military force, but was unsuccessful. In some battles which he undertook (Vyšehrad, Hradčany, Žatec, Kutná Hora, Německý Brod) he was defeated. The Taborites, called "Orphans" after the death of Žižka, conquered several towns (Ústí on the Elbe, Tachov) and carried out a military expedition to Slovakia (in 1428 and again in 1430), to Moravia where they besieged the capital Brno, and in 1431, they penetrated to the Bavarian frontier; they were also successful in the battle near Domažlice. It appeared that the Hussites could not be made loyal by force. The whole Christian world looked toward the Czech frontier with fear; their arms frightened others from making incursions against them; and the Church decided to open negotiations with them. The Prague group accepted the opportunity for negotiations, while the "Orphans" at first refused. But at last they agreed because of the exhaustion of the people and the chaos in the country. The Church convoked the Council of Basle (1431) and invited the Hussites. Before that, a meeting was arranged in Cheb, and it was granted that the Czechs would not be merely tried, but a discussion with them would be opened in which Holy Scripture would be taken as arbiter, together with the practice of it by the early Church.[92] The Czechs agreed to this and were satisfied for the time being.

In 1432, a great delegation led by Rokycana and Prokop Holý came, and the discussions opened with the question of partaking of Communion under both species. The delegation returned, and the general Council approved the use of the chalice for Czechs, provided allegiance to the Church would be restored. In the meantime, the Hussites' military forces were unsuccessful: in 1433 they failed even after encircling the city of Plzeň which was defended by Catholics, and in 1434, they lost the battle near Lipan because the Prague group and nobles of all confessions federated to form the so-called "nobles' agreement." This association was proof of the extent of the country's exhaustion. Some historians have expressed the opinion that Czech democracy died in the battle of Lipan. Palacký's view[93] that Žižka was a democrat is entirely erroneous. The Tábor group was democratic neither in theory nor in practice.[94] As for the social point of view, the revolution did not attain the idea of equality of citizens.[95] Although the Taborites were defeated in the battle of Lipan, it was not the defeat of democracy. The Hussite revolution was indicative of an endeavor to strengthen the significance and the political rights of town groups and of lower-grade nobles. The democratic attitude appears in the religious statement denying allegiance to an ecclesiastical superior[96] when the order given by the superior does not conform to the Bible. This should be taken as an attack and campaign against the Pope and hierarchy as a result of the erroneous doctrine of Hus concerning grace. The proof against the assertion that the Tábor group was democratic is given by the book of Peter Chelčický (concerning the three categories of people) written in the year 1424-25 and addressed to Taborites. There is no talk about democracy, but only of Christian anarchy. The doctrine of Chelčický that the Bible is satisfactory for the regulation of civic life spread very quickly. Anarchy was a general phenomenon of this period; and it came as a practical consequence of the doctrine of Hus.[97] Some historians[98] characterize this anarchism as a republic with a socialistic-communistic program.

After the battle of Lipan, the general council in Basle started to resume negotiations. In 1436, the Czech assembly was convoked at Jihlava, where Emperor Sigismund was also present. The commissioners of the Council also appeared. During the solemn session in the town square, *compactata* were proclaimed and the legates canceled the censure formerly placed upon the Hussites. The substance of these *compactata* is known from the Prague Articles. Affairs were settled by the necessity for conciliation. When the view of the Church concerning the partaking of Communion under both species[99] became critical, the chalice was granted. The compromise had many defects, because it granted no hierarchy to the Hussites. The approval of the Pope was not given.[100] This happened at the time when the Council adopted for itself highest jurisdiction.[101] The consequence of this appeared during negotiations between King George of Poděbrady (1458-1471) and Pope Pius II, who in 1462 studied this compromise, because George was interested in and acted for both sides.[102] Because of this development, the question remained unsolved and the possibility of a solution was eliminated by the death of King George. His intention had been to unify both parties, but he failed. If the problem had been solved, it would have prevented the spread of Lutheranism in Bohemia, which happened afterward.

So the development of Hussitism was able to proceed in its own way, symbolized by the defiance of Hus. It was in the period of negotiations between the Church and Hussites that Peter Chelčický (1460) proclaimed that only the Bible was the norm regulating secular life. In this spirit was founded the Unity of Brethren, led first by Řehoř. They appointed their own priests and separated themselves from the universal Church, and also from the Utraquists in 1467.[103] It was a new doctrine, rooted indeed in Hus doctrines, but substantially distinguished from that of the Taborites.

An attitude of irreconcilability with the Church was a major idea with this group for centuries. But they were not consistent in their dogma, since they accentuated Christian practice.[104] Although the Unity of Brethren developed as a Czech reform movement, a reflection of the Hus defiance transformed it into a bridge to the German reformation of Martin Luther which was eventually the new attack and resistance against unity, loyalty, and discipline in the Church. The nationalistic factor in Hussitism was weakened by the idea of defiance to Rome, whereas the assembly of the "United Brethren" opened the way to the German reformation, notwithstanding the fact that Germans were called by Hussites, "enemies of the law of God." Recalling that in the beginning, missions in Czech lands were handicapped by the German origin of Lutheranism and induced the citizens of Prague to stop all efforts to spread Lutheranism,[105] we can realize the effectiveness of the "United Brethren" in spreading Protestantism, regardless of national development. The national attitude in this matter was first pointed out later by Jan Blahoslav, Comenius, and Charles of Žerotín, who saw that they were being encircled by Germanism. This historical fact should always be taken into account when too much credit is given the Reformation.

In the time of the Jagellons (1471-1526),[106] there was an apparent relaxation of the religious point of view. The two wise kings, Vladislav (1471-1516) and Ludvík (1516-1526), were very tolerant of Hussites who claimed the settlements at the Basle Council were valid although these had been repudiated by the Pope. Although the Hussites had considered themselves faithful sons of the Church, the latter did not accept this view, because between them and the Church there were great differences. By the agreement of the Kutná Hora in 1485, a conciliation was effected. It was agreed that for both sides—that is, for Utraquists (Hussites) and for the group communicating under one kind—special churches should be reserved. This agreement was really a document of great religious tolerance. Both groups, communicating under one or both species, were considered equal under secular law. The Hussites (Utraquists) had their own chapters, their own administrators who were not recognized by the Pope, and who, on their part, did not respect the orders issued by the Pope. Catholics respected all regulations issued by the Pope, tolerating Hussites for the sake of peace.

The Unity of Brethren was not recognized by law. It deviated more and more from its original doctrine, while the ideas of Chelčický increasingly permeated the cultural and political life of the group; they seemed to be gradually imbibing the Hussite attitude of defiance toward Rome.

In 1526, the Hapsburgs ascended the Czech throne; for the next four hundred years the strength of Hussitism was gradually minimized by this Catholic dynasty. Differences between the Catholic dynasty and the Czech population furthered the increased penetration of Lutheranism into Bohemia and the countries federated with it. As a result, the tolerant relation between Utraquists and Catholics began to wane. Lutherans infiltrated into the Utraquist groups and seized control, forming the "neo-Utraquists," so called by the old Utraquists who felt themselves to be regulated by the agreement of Kutná Hora. These neo-Utraquists reiterated and spread defiance of Rome and prepared to separate themselves from the Church.

King Ferdinand (1526-1564) continued the opposition. He defended both the Catholics and the old Utraquists. In 1556, he introduced Jesuits to Bohemia, restored the archbishopric of Prague in the year 1561, and sought to carry out the regulations of the Council of Trent. A new era was ushered in through Lutheranism now because the Lutherans, Czech

Brethren, and neo-Utraquists were united against the Catholics. Belligerence developed on both sides. Czech Brethren and neo-Utraquists met decisive resistance from the Catholics who were supported by the ruling dynasty. The inflexible definitions and formulations issued by the Council of Trent made certain that agreement would be impossible.[107] A new wave of German immigrants flooded the towns and the villages. The strength of the Lutherans reinforced religious antagonism. Open conflict seemed to be unavoidable. In 1575, the Czech Brethren and the neo-Utraquists united in the so-called "Czech Confession."

In 1609, Emperor Rudolf issued the so-called "Majestas," granting freedom of religion. This royal gift and indication of anti-Catholic strength served to rearouse religious antagonism; and hatred of the Hapsburg dynasty increased. This fight for religious freedom and the rights of nobles united the German nobles of Bohemia, Moravia, Silesia, and Lužice with the Czech nobles, and the German and Czech town citizens. By this arrangement they achieved a substantial measure of pressure. During the reign of Matyáš (1612-1619) some strong Counter-Reformation measures were issued, so that disharmony became general and attained full growth before the zealous Catholic, Ferdinand II, ascended the throne. The whole matter was resolved on White Mountain (November 8, 1620) by Ferdinand's victory, the initial step in the Counter-Reformation.

History provides a proverb: Action provokes reaction. This was dramatically proved in the Counter-Reformation. The Holy See, according to the rule accepted in 1555 in Augsburg, decided for the nobles of both religions that secular power has the right to enforce its subjects to accept its religion —*ius reformandi; cujus regio, eius religio.*

The apostolic legate, Garaffe,[108] influenced all actions performed by Ferdinand II (1620-1637). Charles University of Prague was united with the Academy of the Jesuits in the institute called Caroloferdinandea Universitas. The president, always a Jesuit, controlled all schools in Bohemia and Moravia, and controlled the censorship of books.[109] The attempt to re-Catholicize Bohemia was continued in the tradition of Charles IV, and was the main reason for many new regulations issued at that time. In 1624, all non-Catholics were banished from the country; included were all Lutheran nobles, since they refused to receive the Catholic faith. Both Czechs and Germans were affected. The historian Pekař[110] mentions that, paradoxically, the battle of White Mountain banished not only defiant Czechs, but great numbers of Germans. About three hundred or three hundred and fifty noble families and thirty thousand other families left the country; into exile went such prominent persons as Comenius, the last bishop of the Czech Brethren, the painter John Kupecký, and others. Most of the Czech Brethren went to Slovakia, Silesia, and Poland; the Lutherans to Lužice, Saxony, and Brandenburg. Expropriation of property was a not unexpected sequel to this emigration.

It should be mentioned that the revision of the Constitution of the country in 1627 must be taken as Ferdinand's revenge against the nobles, who in 1618 had resisted his election as king of Bohemia. By this Constitution, he secured the hereditary right to the Czech crown for the dynasty of the Hapsburgs.[111] By the Pragmatic Sanction of 1713, this hereditary succession was extended to include female descendants. Not only religious but also political factors were the background for these measures. After the battle of White Mountain the lands of the Czech crown remained a self-ruling and independent state unit.[112] A symbol of this was the so-called Czech Council with an office in Vienna. The Czech and German languages had been granted full rights in all the courts and were in official use. This was in reaction to the tendencies toward centralized administration of all countries which were federated by the personal union of the sovereign. The troublesome state of nobles and peasants was caused by conditions which should be viewed as consequences of the Thirty Years' War (1614-1648), and by emigration. The result of this development attained its highest point by the issuance of patents about bondsmen in the years 1717 and 1738. Under these conditions a counter-reformation developed in the period from 1620 to 1740. The following period of the enlightened absolutism of Maria Theresa (1740-80) and Joseph II (1780-90) brought a change of policy, which was until that time substantially Catholic. By the time that enlightened absolutism seemed to be the leading idea of the state, oppression of Catholics had ushered in an era that ended with the vandalism of Joseph's reforms. The collision of faith and reason became a phenomenon of the eighteenth century. The Patent of Tolerance canceled not only the serfdom of subjects, but made them free to accept the religion of Lutherans and reformists. To these sects there were enrolled at that time forty-five thousand persons, in Moravia fewer, but almost the whole population remained Catholic.[113] The Jesuits were expelled, and in the universities as well as in the high schools they were replaced by secular teachers. Thus begins the period of separation of the national, educational, cultural, and social problems from religious influence.

The Counter-Reformation lost its significance because of indifference to religion and lack of respect for Rome which was being made dependent on its power. Assertions of the state since the time of Joseph II were of formal character given by Catholics of the reigning dynasty. Misuses of the power caused by this dynasty as to cultural and national points of view were taken as a sign of aversion to the Church. This aversion increased during the Enlightenment (eighteenth century) and Liberalism (nineteenth century). This development could not be evaded by reactionary absolutism (1790-1848) under the rule of Leopold II (1790-1792), Francis (1792-1835), and Ferdinand V (1835-1848). At this time the Catholic Church renewed her strength after the reforms of Joseph. The year 1848 is a landmark of the influence of the Catholic idea; the second half of this century is full of struggles to minimize her influence. The leading factor, nationalism, having been started in the time of the Counter-Reformation, separated itself, aiming to be fully independent of the Germanizing Hapsburg dynasty which was formally Catholic.

So started the aversion of nationalism not only to the dynasty, but also the Catholic Church herself. The Church pleaded guilty to all mistakes of the dynasty. All the merits of the priests Bohuslav Balbín, Peřina, Beckovský, and others, remained fully overlooked. The Church, which always supported national consciousness, came to be taken as an opposing force to timely nationalism. The spirit of defiance, as in the Unity of the Czech Brethren, reasoned by the emigration after the battle of White Mountain, was being expressed by the works of Alois Jirasek who wished to unify all enemies of the Church. In its exaggerated form, the Counter-Reformation was being called a "darkness." The spirit of Hussitism revived.

These were the conditions that prevailed in the second half of the last century, a period which suffered from the Germanizing tendencies of Joseph II. No substantial change occurred until the year 1860, when the so-called "October" decree was issued proclaiming the renewal of land parliaments. As a result of it came the February Constitution of 1861, which regulated the relation between the state parliament and the self-rule organs of the provinces. This solution was enforced by nationalities federated in the Austrian monarchy. The Czech nation was led by Josef Dobrovský, Gelasius Dobner, Josef Jungman, and Francis Palacký (1798-1876) who stressed the history of the nation. In Slovakia there were nationalist indications, led by John Kollar, Bernolák, and Ludovit Štur.

This national awakening was intensified by the Frankfurt Council (1848) and its pan-Germanic tendencies, which were treated ironically by a young journalist, Karel Havlíček Borovský (1856). This national movement, becoming general, had Catholic participants too. After the Vatican Council (1870) religious struggles started again, incited by Bismarck's *Kulturkampf* (1870-1878), and the violation of the Concordat of 1855 by the Austrian monarchy through issuance of the bills of 1868 and 1874,[114] which made the Church subject to the state. Liberalism like this influenced members of the dynasty even more. In Austria and Sudeten a movement against Rome began, led by Austrian nationalists and liberals, having as its slogan and catchword: *"Los von Rom."* This was the signal for the Czech *"Pryč od Říma,"* which influenced the end of the nineteenth and the beginning of the twentieth century. Czechs found inspiration in the Hungarians who had achieved the recognition of their national aims and establishment of their state in the Austro-Hungarian monarchy. This strengthened their endeavors but also prepared their separation from Austria. World War I was a welcome occasion for their purpose.[115]

It can be seen by this exposition that Hussitism is never far from the scene whenever the Church comes into any collision with the state of the Czech nation. Her "Achilles' heel" is always being watched by her enemies. This circumstance has been thus well commented on by the Czech historian in discussing the roles of Wyclif and Hus in relation to the Czech nation:

> The nest of snakes (books of Wyclif) was burned, but the poisonous snake favored by Czechs was already out. It crept into the country, hissed, pinched and poisoned, infiltrating into the veins of Czech nations the hatred of Rome. Since that time, this snake has not been expelled from our country. Its checkered body is going through our whole history, taking on various colors in different centuries. The first was Wyclifism, then Hussitism, Taboritism, Czech Brethren, Lutheranism, Calvinism, Voltairism, or Enlightenment, until the last one sent after the revolution. Every one of these sects and opinions is only another stripe on the body of the same snake, which by flattery deceived Eve, inspired her to sin, and expelled her from paradise. By establishing sects, a new substantial formulation enters our history. Only part of our nation was incited by it to military success. This collapsed early and our history was embittered by it, as if covered by gall and wormwood. [116]

These changes were too many for such a small nation. The more critical they become of Hussitism, the more historians search into the archives of the nations. But propaganda has its own principles. Its barriers of criticism and defiance of the Catholic Church in favor of Hussitism have required much work and effort of historians. The radicalism of Hussitism is necessarily found wherever there is chaos, criticism and revolution. But order is more necessary everywhere. Order, not chaos, should be the general program. In the words of the historian Krofta: "We may be proud to have had Hussitism, but if it had missed us we should not be sorry."[117]

CHAPTER SIX

THE "AWAY FROM ROME" MOVEMENT

THE "AWAY FROM ROME" MOVEMENT (LOS VON ROM BEWEGUNG) appears to have been caused by a number of different factors, among them movements and philosophical doctrines aimed at solving the difficulties between faith and reason, which culminated in the struggle between Church and state. The Counter-Reformation was defeated by Josephinism; the movement known as the Enlightenment deprived the Church of her majesty; Liberalism brought on religious indifferentism, the consequence of which was mass apostasy. This development was accentuated by nationalistic feelings, which these individual proceedings changed into a movement and people, educated by enlightenment, found their senses in it. Political liberalism exaggerated the discord, and the enemies of the Church participated in the development.

The eighteenth and nineteenth centuries under the Hapsburg dynasty comprised a period of struggle between the Church and these discordant factors. This was the time of appeasement and concordats, full of understanding for differently formulated freedoms. This was also the time of conflicts which the Church could not evade, being forced to defend herself. The state strengthened its own power and increased its extent by utilizing a policy of absolutism. This minimized the jurisdiction of the Church which, having been attacked from all sides, lost much of its strength so that at the end of this period it was unable to surmount many of these influences.

It must be mentioned that the Catholic dynasty of the Hapsburgs did not fulfill many of its duties in the Czech provinces; it did not give any blessing or advantage to the development of the Catholic Church. On the contrary, the Germanizing tendencies of this dynasty closed for the Church the way to the hearts of non-Germans who were in an awakening period.

The movement "Away from Rome" was a phenomenon typical of the chaotic situation which was rather general in the Hapsburg Empire, but it is also a proof of the resistance and defiance of Catholicism. The movement of Enlightenment had as its principal catchword, "Away from the clerical tradition."[1] This was supported by non-Catholics who accepted the movement as a daughter of Protestantism.[2] The drive to liquidate the Catholic Church was thus opened. The Church was forced to defend herself against any infiltration of Protestantism as well as against absolutist state power. Unfortunately Enlightenment also affected some priests, particularly in Bohemia. Typical for this period is the case of Rev. Josef Dobrovský (1829), patriarch of Slavic sciences, who, while he was a Catholic priest, received into his work and life not only the Enlightenment, but also Freemasonry.[3] It was, of course, according to the concept of the time[4] and the national awakening, that all conform to the official attitude of the state in such matters. Winter[5] calls him a "slavishing German." Through his initiative the monastery of the Augustinians in old Brno in Moravia was affected, and a center for the Enlightenment movement developed there. There was in that period an eminently successful author, Abbot E. F. Napp; his successor was the Right Reverend Gregor Mendel, famous for having discovered the principles of heredity. Later, there came the philosophers Father Bratránek and Father Francis Matthew Klácel (1808-1880), who was arrested for preaching the doctrine of Hegel and for defending the rights of the Czechs.[6] Great influence was exerted by a Bernard Bolzano (1781-1848), not only among the Germans, but among the Czechs as well.[7] Using the doctrines of Immanuel Kant, Leibnitz, and Wolf as a basis, Bolzano taught the theological sciences at the philosophical faculty in Prague (1805-1820). Bolzano educated a whole generation and achieved great popularity. In his honor, in the theological seminary at Litoměřice, the "Federation of Christian Friendship" was established, against the will of Bolzano himself. The founders of this association were Michael Fesl and Bishop Hurdálek. Litoměřice, like Prague, was a center for Bolzano's adherents. Abbot Salesius Krugner of Osek and Abbot Benedict Pfeiffer of Strahov were Bolzano's protectors. The main principle of Bolzano's teaching was "In education, after humanity, the love for country is most important." He influenced many men, among them the priest-philosopher, Father Zahradník of Mladá Boleslav, who in 1829 founded a magazine for priests; the Reverend Karel Al. Vinařický, aide to Monsignor Chlumčanský, the Archbishop of Prague; Father Jablonský, author and poet of the Czech people, and monk of Abbey Strahov; and finally Karel Havlíček,[8] who came in contact with Bolzano through the Reverend Schneider. Havlíček later gave full stress to the nationalist concept.

Prominent among the friends of Bolzano were Václav Štulc and Valerian Jirsík. The former became a provost of the Vyšehrad Chapter after 1848; the latter became a bishop in Č. Budějovice. All bishops and archbishops in Bohemia until 1848, excepting Bishops Hille and Molde of Litoměřice, were adherents of the Catholic Enlightenment, or had friends among its adherents.[9] Germans in official places disapproved of this idea and refused to support it. Therefore Michael Fesl was condemned for treason and the Czech Bishop Hurdálek was forced to abandon the Litoměřice bishopric.

However, in an attempt to gain greater freedom, the Enlightenment was finally surmounted by political and religious Liberalism. Liberalism was a general idea in the Hapsburg monarchy in the second half of the nineteenth century, and the situation of the Church became precarious.[10] Kirsch-Veit says of it:

> As an aspect of its political attitudes Liberalism opposed the introduction of philosophic and religious considerations into the affairs of the constitutional state, as dogmatic Christianity held proper. It further assailed the practice of granting legal recognition to religious denominations as granting privileged status. In national politics, it sought broader rights of representation for the people. In the sphere of business and social welfare, it advocated practically unlimited freedom of opportunity and movement for the individual and almost unrestricted liberty of competition, contracts, profits and use of private property. [11]

All was set in motion, and the year 1848 witnessed the

first indications of freedom for the whole society of nations and individuals. Their cry became the catchword of the time. Some measures were being attempted also against the central government in Vienna. The new Emperor Francis Joseph tried to control the revolutionary movement, but even the so-called absolutism of Bach (1851) was a complete failure. Set in motion by the Emperor's directives in 1855, concordats with the Holy See were made. The concordats became the pattern by which relationship between Church and state[12] were regulated. The full validity and power of canon law was recognized by the Hapsburg dynasty, and the Church was given extensive jurisdiction and influence in education.[13] The Church thus should have become the central point of the whole empire which was practically disintegrating, and should have been the main support for the authority of the dynasty. Although it was thought this would necessarily follow, the real psychological reaction was evident in increased defiance toward the dynasty.

All national groups began expressing their claims and demands, especially after 1867, when dualism was introduced into Austria-Hungary.[14] Czechs were represented by the movement of the old Czech party (Frant. Palacký, Frant. Brauner, Fr. L. Rieger) which wanted trialism.[15] The Prime Minister of that time, Count Karel Sigismund of Hohenvart, by his federalistic concept of nations in Austria-Hungary, was inclined to favor the demands of the national groups. But he was succeeded by Count Adolf of Auersperg and the attitude of centralism prevailed. Later, Minister Beust confirmed this policy.

After dualism was settled, the relation between Church and state suddenly changed. Austria opened its attack on the concordats.[16] The constitution of December 21, 1867, and the bills of May 25, 1868, which regulated laws about marriage, education, and interdenominational affairs, were formulated as ammunition against the concordats. Rome turned its attention toward them, and Pope Pius IX called these bills *leges abominabiles, vehementer reprobandae et damnandae* in an allocution that was characteristic of the times. It was delivered in private consistory, June 22, 1868, and is as follows:

VENERABLE BRETHREN:

We certainly never thought that hardly thirteen years after entering upon the widely acclaimed Concordat with the Austrian Emperor and the Apostolic King we would now have to deplore the difficulties and adversities by which, through the machinations of hostile men, the Catholic Church in the Austrian Empire is so sadly oppressed and disrupted. But the enemies of our divine Faith have worked unremittingly to balk that Concordat and inflict grievous wrongs upon the Church, ourselves and this Apostolic See. For, as a foundation stone of its political structure, the Austrian government passed, on December 21st last, a really vicious law, affecting and binding, in all corners of the Empire, even in those which are totally Catholic. By this law complete freedom of opinion and of the press, freedom of faith and conscience, and freedom of expression is granted; permission is given to all subjects, whatsoever be their beliefs, to establish works of education and propaganda; and all religious denominations of whatsoever kind are placed on equal footing and given recognition by the State. When we first sorrowfully learned of this we wanted to express our position immediately, but in the spirit of forbearance we decided that at the moment we should remain silent, particularly since we hoped that the Austrian government would give attentive consideration to the protestations of our venerable brother bishops in Austria and might adopt a more sensible attitude and take more acceptable measures. But our hope was in vain. For on May 25th of this year that same government passed a law binding all groups within the Empire, including Catholics, stipulating that children of a mixed marriage are to follow the religion of the father in the case of boys and of the mother in the case of girls, and further that those under seven years of age should follow their parents in case of defection from the true faith. By this same law all force is taken from the promises which the Catholic Church properly and rightfully exacts and prescribes before the performance of mixed marriages; apostasy, whether from Catholicity or from Christianity, is elevated to civil status; furthermore, all ecclesiastical control of consecrated ground is totally abolished and Catholics are compelled to inter in their own cemeteries the bodies of heretics whenever these heretics do not have their own burial ground.

On that same date, May 25th of this year, the government went so far as to issue a law concerning matrimony in which it completely overrode the laws enacted in conformity with the aforementioned Concordat and brought back into force those previous legislations which were utterly incompatible with Church law; it even confirmed civil matrimony, and in case any Church denied a celebration of it, it held the denial to be invalid and not legal. By this same law the government completely wipes out all authority and jurisdiction of the Church in matrimonial cases and sets aside its tribunals. In the matter of schools it promulgated a law by which all power of the Church is destroyed and determined that the ultimate management of all curricula and teaching, as well as inspection and supervision of the schools, is within the compass of the jurisdiction of each denomination and that various groups of each faith may each open their own school for the young who follow that particular system of belief; such schools are subjected to the over-all inspection of the State and textbooks are to be approved by the civil authority, except for those books which are to be used in the teaching of religion; these latter are to be approved by the proper authorities of the denomination involved.

You immediately see, venerable brethren, that this abominable legislation of the Austrian government cannot be too strongly denounced and rejected; it is incompatible with the natural law itself and with the teaching of the Catholic Church, its judicious laws, its authority and its divine constitution; it spurns the prestige of this Apostolic See and the aforementioned Concordat. Hence we, charged as we are by our Lord himself with the care of all churches, speak out in this your plenary session and with all the weight of our Apostolic authority denounce and reject those laws as well as each and every act, decree and like attempt of the Austrian government or any lower court in these or other matters to the jurisdiction of the Church; we declare that those decrees and their codicils infringing on our authority never had and never will have any validity. And we urge and insist that those professed Catholics who have dared to formulate, foster, approve and accept those laws and legislations keep in mind the censures and spiritual penalties which the Apostolic Constitutions and the decrees of the Ecumenical Councils have defined as ipso facto incurred by those who infringe on the rights of the Church.

At the same time, however, we also heartily congratulate

in the Lord and fittingly commend our respected brothers, the archbishops and bishops of the Austrian Empire, who, in the fullness of their episcopacy, have fearlessly defended and upheld in speeches and writings the cause of the Church and the said Concordat and have not been remiss in warning the faithful under their charge. We sincerely hope that the venerable brothers, the archbishops and bishops of Hungary, will follow the admirable example of their fellow bishops and will be similarly alert and zealous in defending the rights of the Church and in adopting measures to preserve the Concordat.

Amid the calamities which in these troubled times so beset the Church on every side, we, in deep humility, venerable brethren, and with renewed fervor, ceaselessly implore that God will in His omnipotence foil the evil designs of His enemies and the enemies of His Church and will turn back their wicked assaults, crush their attacks, and in His mercy bring them back to the paths of justice and salvation. [17]

The document indicates that the validity of the Concordat was short-lived. By this it can be seen that the Hapsburg dynasty was not consistent in its relationships with the Church. The dynasty formed attitudes according to her needs and used the Church as a means to her ends. In the meantime, anti-Catholic groups were exerting greater pressure. Czech Protestants, supported by the so-called "Protestant Patent" of 1861, and led by Pastor F. W. Kossuth of Prague and the Protestant minister, Rev. Ružička,[18] tried to unify Czech Lutherans and Czech-Moravian Brethren. Their model was the work of John Amos Comenius. Kossuth, extracting ideas from the history of Palacký, proclaimed a doctrine based on the program of John Hus, formulating it as a unifying factor for all Czechs. The trend was marked by the *Kutná Hora* Epistles of Karel Havlíček and by the excommunicated priest, Augustin Smetana (1814-1850),[19] who wrote many pamphlets against the Church.

The ecclesiastical magazine, *Časopis katolického duchovenstva,* which had been edited since 1848 by Bishop V. Jirsík, and the review, *Blahověst,* which had been edited since 1846 by Vyšehrad Canon Václav Štulc, strove to face the movement of mass apostasy.

Nationalism, at that time the governmental policy, claimed the right of countries to establish national churches. In France, Ferdinand Fr. Chatel (b. 1795), Capitular-Vicar in Moulino,[20] supported these tendencies. In Germany, John Ronge (1872) began misusing German nationalism to oppose and attack the Church, as Luther had done.[21] The Congress of Leipzig (1845) established the so-called "German Catholic Church," which, not having fulfilled the expectation of unification of all Germans, collapsed. Ronge himself died as "Essighaus-Apostel" (Apostle of Vinegar House). In Austria-Hungary, this "Away from Rome" movement, assisted in its development by the favorable conditions in the period after 1870, organized mass apostasies, of which the Pan-Germanic movement was the main factor.

The Vatican Council (1870) with dramatic procedure[22] made clear the attitude of the Church concerning Enlightenment in the impending struggle; it also showed its attitude towards Gallicanism, Febronianism, and Josephinism[23] by proclaiming the dogma of the infallibility of the Pope,[24] thus strengthening the authority of the Holy See. Among later nations and among Catholics throughout the world, this dogma found acceptance. But in Germany and Austria-Hungary, opposition to it was strong. Even during the council sessions the following very ardently expressed their opinions against the dogma: Cardinal Schwarzenberg of Prague, Cardinal Rauscher of Vienna, Archbishop Haynald of Kolscza, Hungary, and Bishop Strossmayer of Diakovar.[25] They were known as "non-opportunists."[26] They were influenced by the Guntherians who were against the proclaimed dogma on principle. The Cistercian priest, Salesius Majer of Osek, a Gunther adherent, was an adviser to Cardinal Schwarzenberg and exerted great influence everywhere.[27]

The wave of resistance against the proclaimed dogma began to spread throughout all Germany. Chief representatives of this group of dissenters were Professor Schulte of Prague and the well-known ecclesiastical historian, Ignatz Doellinger. They counted among their adherents such educated men as Fridrich, Reischl of Munich; Langen, Rensch, Kroodt of Bonn; Reinkens, Baltzer, Weber of Breslau; Michelis of Braunsberg; and others.[28] They arranged a meeting in Nuremberg on August 27, 1870, and called themselves "Old Catholics." Having been asked by the Archbishop of Munich to express their attitude toward the position of the general council, Doellinger, Fridrich, and Huber gave a negative statement. Fridrich and Huber were excommunicated, and Doellinger had resigned all priestly dignities when he was elected a rector of Munich University. Under the honorary chairmanship of Schulte, a general congress was arranged in Munich for the year 1871; adopted a strong attitude against the Pope and against "ultramontanism." There was a suggestion that an independent church be proclaimed, but Doellinger frustrated the move. Due to the strong opposition of local bishops, the influence of the "Old Catholics" was attacked; nevertheless, through the aid of state power, the "Old Catholic Church" was established in certain districts, especially in Sudeten. In Warnsdorf in 1873, the center of this church was established and the first bishop was Pašek, a relative of Anton Gunther. In Aussig on the Elbe in Bohemia, there were about two thousand "Old Catholics." In some other areas they started up but disappeared quickly. Exasperated pupils of a German priest from Sudeten, Anton Gunther, actually became the founders of the "Old Catholic Church," but Anton Gunther must be considered the father of this idea.[29] The priest Rittel, a supporter of the *"Los von Rom"* movement, was Gunther's friend. Under the protection of the king of Germany, some "Old Catholic" churches were established in Bavaria, Baden, and Prussia in 1873. Professor Reinkens, having been elected Bishop, was ordained by Jansenists.[30]

But at the grave of Saint Boniface in Fulda, loyal priests and the faithful gathered on October 12, 1870, to send to the Pope their pledge of loyalty, designating themselves as Neo-Catholics. The Church in Germany, therefore, would have passed through this period without any serious disturbances[31] had not the antagonism of Bismarck intervened.[32] Actually, this became the Church's fight for existence and independence in Germany.[33] The main figure and cause of this *Kulturkampf* was Minister Falk,[34] noted Freemason, who by the May bills concerning education[35] and by the so-called "pulpit bill" menaced the freedom of the Church. The Church happily was led by the wise diplomacy of Leo XIII, and the policy of the Center party in Bavaria was being managed by the courageous Ludwig Windthorst,[36] whom even Bismarck respected.[37] The dramatic struggle was ended by an agreement which meant the defeat of Bismarck. But the spirit of Prussian Pan-Germanism also influenced the central government in Vienna. Thus the Constitution of May 7, 1874, complicated the relation between Church and state. The Church's freedom was being restricted by state intervention. A significant section from the Constitution stated that "every legally recognized church and religious organization arranges and conducts its internal affairs independently" but like all other organizations they were "subject to state law."

The Church remained in this critical position in Austria-Hungary until World War I. Out of regard for the Emperor, the execution of the acts was moderated by the instruction of the Ministry for Education on May 22, 1874.[38] Regulations issued by the Vatican Council were unfavorably received by the Austro-Hungarian monarchy. "Old Catholics" were considered fully equal to Catholics after 1875.[39] Nevertheless, Catholics as a whole remained loyal.

Catholics of the Alpine provinces and those of other national groups established the People's party,[40] hotly opposing liberals and German nationalists. The more German aggression against the Church increased, the more favorable were the official statements of Prime Ministers Taaffe[41] and Badeni toward non-German nations. Germans from Sudeten were especially menaced when Badeni decided to endow the Czech language with the same rights as the German, and to admit the Czech language to official use.[42] This was possible because German nationalism was being backed by the All-German Federation,[43] established in the year 1893 with the aim of unifying all Germans. The most favorable means of attaining this aim was to support the Protestantization of Austria, because the Hohenzollerns were protectors of Lutheranism. Chief leaders in this movement were George von Schoenerer (1842-1921), the poet Peter Rosegger (1843-1918), V. Einsenkolb, and Ferdinand Meyer from Zwickau.[44]

George von Schoenerer, a farmer, became a member of parliament in Austria in 1873, and after 1879 was the most radical of all Germans. He originated the Linz Program (1882) and as a leader of the radical wing, he established anti-Semitism,[45] in addition to working against the Hapsburgs for the unification of Austria and Germany.

Schoenerer began his political life on the Left, and cooperated with future Socialists like Viktor Adler and Pernerstorfer in working out the Linz Program of September 1, 1882. According to this, the 1879 alliance with Germany was to be strengthened and developed into a grand Middle Europe unity. Within the monarchy, Dalmatia (together with Bosnia and Herzegovina), Galicia, and Bukovina were to be cut away from Austria. In the Austria which remained, the German language was to be officially enforced as the national tongue. On this basis, Schoenerer founded his *Deutschnationaler Verein.* The indignation against Schoenerer on the part of Czechs and Slovaks who were thus cut off from their fellow Slavs, to become a minority and to lose everything they had gained, can well be imagined. To Schoenerer, of course, the Germans in Austria were cut off and kept at a disadvantage in just the same way by the existent state of affairs. It is the tragedy of Central Europe that every administrative demarcation appears arbitrary to those whom it reduces to a minority. And in old Austria, it was the same with every school law or new language regulation; it seemed impossible to legislate so that one nation's gain was not the other's loss.

George von Schoenerer was turbulent and quarrelsome. To the tune of his slogan, *"Durch Reinheit zur Einheit,"* he repeatedly purged his party, while his enemies whispered, *"Durch Reinheit zur Kleinheit."*

Schoenerer was also the author of the anti-Semitic phrase, *"In der Rasse liegt die Schweinerei."*[46] In 1888 he forced an entrance to the offices of *Neues Wiener Tagblatt,* and propagated false views about the death of Emperor William I. He was arrested for his action, and lost his membership in parliament and his knighthood. Later he returned to parliament as a member from 1897 to 1907; he fought there bitterly. He became a leader in the *Los von Rom* movement, and apostatized, becoming a Protestant. His articles were published mainly in newspapers and magazines: *Unverfälschte deutsche Worte* (1890-1912), *Alldeutsches Tagblatt,* and *Grazer Wochenblatt.*

Another leader of the "Away from Rome" movement was Peter Rosegger,[47] son of a farmer, born in Krieglach, in Steiern. He attended an academy in Graz (1865-1869) and traveled in Holland, Switzerland, and Italy. He wrote a novel, *Der Gottsucher* (1883), by which he excited all clergymen. In this and his other novels, *Mein Himmelreich, Das ewige Licht* (1896), *Erdsegen* (1900), *Weltgift* (1903), and *Christusbuch* (1905), he propagandized the "Away from Rome" movement.[48] Innsbruck was the center of the movement, and there the *Ulrich Hutten Bund* was established, and the newspapers *Der Scherer* and *Pfeile aus der Ehrenburg* were published. This movement grew and spread until by 1899 it had circulated over two million pamphlets. The main organ after 1905 was *Die Wartburg*.[49] All expenses entailed in propaganda favoring mass apostasies were paid by the Protestant associations *Evangelischer Bund* and *Gustav Adolf Verein*. These were so interested in the movement that special institutes in Bielitz and Halle were established to support apostatized Catholic priests.

Thus equipped by Pan-Germanic nationalism[50] and supported by Protestantism and George von Schoenerer, the adherents of the movement arranged a German Day in Vienna on December 12, 1897, with a demonstration against the policy of Prime Minister Badeni in favor of national groups. In April, 1897, a great congress was arranged of the German Catholics who were in the People's party. The People's parties of the Slavic nations also participated in this congress. Badeni himself delivered the main speech in which he solemnly proclaimed equality of rights for the Czech language.[51] The attendance of German Catholics at this congress aroused liberals and German nationalists. For this reason, on German Day, many orators calumniated them and a fanatical student named Rakus initiated the catchword *Los von Rom*. That catchword expressed the program of the "Away from Rome" movement, and by it were propagated the mass apostasies in Austria-Hungary. It is therefore evident that the German liberals had observed[52] that the Austro-Hungarian monarchy had to resolve the problem of national groups and that the liberals were not inclined to agree with a solution in favor of these groups.[53] Influenced by the Bismarck policy, the Schoenerer movement[54] attempted to save the situation by amalgamation of Austria with Germany.[55] The strong support of Protestants[56] approved this effort to attain Prussian uniformity; Bismarck's *Kulturkampf* gave it an orientation.

This whole endeavor was the reaction of liberals against the demands of national groups. Austrian Catholics conceived the need for a solution of the problems in the spirit of the policy of the great Pope Leo XIII (1878-1903), who in the Czech problem was inclined to support Czech demands. As early as 1890, he had sent his *Breve*[57] to the Archbishop of Prague, concerning the establishment and maintenance of the Czech College Nepomucenum in Rome, in favor of which a special papal endowment was set aside. In the fight for equality of rights of the Czech language, he supported the attitude of the Czechs. In his speech of February 11, 1889,[58] he justified these demands, and, in 1901, he stressed in his letter to the episcopate:[59] "Everyone is entitled to defend his mother language; a higher position belongs to the faithful and to the religious in whose care the clergy are educated; therefore, they should set a good example; this means also that they should not interfere in any nationalist struggles." In 1902, Pope Leo asked all bishops[60] to confer often and thus to moderate all national excesses, to evade splitting the strength of ecclesiastics and to prevent apostasies.

This favorable attitude was known to the Czechs, and the leader of the conservative Czech party, Dr. F. L. Rieger, maintained direct contact with the Holy See.[61] He tried to support the idea of establishing new bishoprics in Plzeň and Kutná Hora. But the solution to this question was not reached.

Leo XIII had also taken a stand on social problems in his encyclical *Rerum Novarum*.[62] The development concerning Austria made the necessity for a solution urgent. The converts of Mecklenburg, Franz of Florencourt and Karl Knight of Vogelsang, established a conservative movement called Christian-Social.[63] The main magazine for it was *Vaterland*, which was supported by Count Egbert Belcredi and Prince Liechtenstein. Thus the Conservative-Catholic party was established.

These attitudes of meeting national and social demands were stressed by Austrian Catholics led by the devoted and capable Dr. Karl Lueger (1844-1910)[64] who was a personal friend of Pope Leo XIII. In his practical view of social problems, Dr. Lueger was an adherent of the ideas of the Catholic priest Ambrosius Opik who as early as the second half of the nineteenth century was proclaiming in Warnsdorf the urgent necessity for social change, arranging so-called "Catholic Days" (*Katholiken Tage*). Opik edited the newspapers *Oesterreichische Volkszeitung* in Warnsdorf, and the *Reichspost* in

Vienna.[65] For this reason, Austrian liberals and nationalists set up a strong opposition to the Catholic journals, holding that Catholic views on social and national conciliation were contrary to the spirit of liberalism and extreme nationalism.[66]

Thus the movement "Away from Rome" was typically political[67] in character, and there is no reason for viewing it as a movement of a religious character, though it was considered and expounded as such by T. G. Masaryk.[68]

The program of Austrian Catholics concerning social conciliation could have been accepted by non-Catholics, but their rudimentary participation in the "Away from Rome" movement is indication that Austrian nationalism[69] had been infiltrated at that time by the idea of Pan-Germanism, the practical application of which was employed later by Adolf Hitler.[70] "Thus, the first theoretical foundation for a struggle of the Pan-German movement against Catholicism as such was lacking."[71] This is the result of national philosophy as expressed by Paul de Lagarde (1827-1891), whose ideas prepared conditions for this movement.

The "Away from Rome" movement also had religious aims.[72] The failure of its activities awakened Catholics to stronger activity in the opposite direction.[73] According to statistics, there were until 1914 in all Austria a total of fifty-five thousand apostasies to Protestantism and about fifteen thousand to "Old Catholicism."[74] In Sudeten, however, in the period from 1898 to 1908, there were forty thousand apostasies to Protestantism and fifteen thousand to "Old Catholicism."[75] The newspaper *Neue Freie Presse* in Vienna exerted its influence among intellectuals by its anti-clerical attitude in favor of apostasies.

There were fewer apostasies in Austria.[76] Schindler established the *Leo Verein* and endeavored to establish Catholic universities in Innsbruck and Graz and also to build up a new free Catholic university in Salzburg. The *Bonifatius Verein* was cautious and opposed apostasies everywhere. The center of this association was in Prague, in the Emauzy monastery, under the leadership of Abbot Albanus Schlatleiter.[77] This helped to stem the wave of apostasies.

Among intellectuals, Archdean Josef Gross of Falknov was doing his best for the Catholic cause. He was appointed Bishop in Litoměřice in 1910, and fulfilled all expectations.

Otto Willman, a devout Catholic and professor of philosophy, was active at Prague University and as adviser to Bishop Gross. The center of Catholic Action since 1907, the Catholic Central Committee (*Katholisches Central Kommittee*) was in Vienna. Instructions for organizations working with them included material for programs on Catholic Days (*Katholikentage*). Thus, by united efforts, Austro-Hungarian Catholics fought all anti-Catholic trends.

In 1892, on the third Catholic Day, August 8-11, in Linz, Count Sylva Taroneca, president for that day, proclaimed, "The time is past for them to rule against us and without us. Without us they cannot bring their program of social reform to successful completion. For us, religion is not merely a private affair; it is a matter of importance to our very existence, a matter regulating our exercise of power, a matter of national civilization, and of the preservation of our society."[78]

This was also the attitude of all Catholics toward the end of the nineteenth century, including their bishops and archbishops, under whose leadership all Catholic Action proceeded. At the beginning of the twentieth century, the Social Democratic party propagated apostasies by recommending Marxian principles of atheism; this was done especially in industrial districts.[79] The aim of this party thus enlarged the number of the enemies of the Church. Liberalism gave rise to a new concept without the Church.[80] The fight against the Church arose on many fronts: Liberalism, extreme nationalism, Protestantism, Freemasonry,[81] "Old Catholicism," Social Democracy, and the "Away from Rome" movement, with the result that the Catholic Church was menaced from many sides. T. G. Masaryk characterized all these attacks of the enemies of the Church in these words: "The *Los von Rom* movement in Austria is a very complicated movement, shared by the Germans, Bohemians, the Ruthenians, and the Hungarians. It is the natural action against the reactionary anti-reformatory spirit of official Austria. I am aware of the fact that many find in this movement a sign of sickness, and often Austria is spoken of as a sick man. I should think there were now in Europe several sick men and we might soon have a great political hospital there."[82]

It is no wonder that with so many enemies the position of the Catholic Church caused the revival of the Hus tradition in Bohemia. Political life, represented by the Old Czech party under the leadership of Frant Palacký and F. L. Rieger, was being regulated by the conditions already mentioned and was continuing without any substantial changes. When the "Young Czech" movement appeared, it was the first essential change since 1889. Before that time, leading conservative Old Czechs were replaced by freethinking radical Young Czechs under the leadership of the brothers Edward and Julius Gregr. In 1891, the Young Czechs seized full leadership of the national policy. On this party's program were elected T. G. Masaryk, Josef Kaiel, and Dr. Karel Kramář, who formed a group of so-called realists. But these men soon became enemies. Masaryk left the party to establish his own party, having been elected to the central parliament in 1907 as an independent. Kaizl, having been Minister of Finance (1907), died early. There remained Dr. K. Kramář, president of the party. These three men separated because of differences which Masaryk explained as follows: "Both the Old and Young Czech parties were originally of liberal character. Liberalism is now old-fashioned; it is plutocratic and autocratic. It is not progressive. Old Czechs resigned their liberal ideas and the views of Palacký, but until this time, they remained liberals in regard to economics. The same can be said for the Young Czechs. But the Young Czechs preserved some liberal progressive ideas, whereas these also are not fully respected."[83] Thus Masaryk became a leader of the progressives who influenced the whole period after 1883 with cries for progress, with strong stress on Hussitism.

This revolutionary and anti-Catholic Thomas Garrigue Masaryk (1850-1937) was born of Catholic parents and became a Greek Catholic in 1870,[84] and a Protestant after 1885.[85] During his studies at the *Gymnasium* in Brno, an educated and generous Catholic priest, Matěj Procházka, rescued Masaryk from liberalism, and taught him to analyze the greater problems: social injustice and lack of freedom.[86] Thus Masaryk learned his first lessons in social problems.

At Vienna University, the apostate priest, Franz Brentano,[87] a great philosopher, influenced Masaryk, as he himself said: "When I was a student in Vienna, it was Brentano who, as teacher and man, influenced me most."[88] Brentano was substantially different from the usual adherents of Herbart, who were most numerous in Austrian universities.[89] In his methods of thinking, he was an ardent adherent of empirical and natural scientific methods; as to his ideas, he was a metaphysician and adherent of Aristotle. He taught Masaryk to admire not only Plato, but also Socrates and Aristotle. His knowledge of Aristotle helped Masaryk to understand many philosophical complexes, especially Immanuel Kant's criticism and David Hume's skepticism, but he accepted Comte without resigning methods and aims of positivism. The difference between the two men was that for Brentano, philosophy was both a means and an aim; but for Masaryk, who was a politician, too, philosophy was mostly a means. That is why Masaryk did not attain great philosophical stature. His realism,[90] which he called his doctrine, is not free from the influence of metaphysical eclecticism based on Comte's positivism. His realism made him free to regard the present and to act on its problems. He was a sociologist, too, and therefore made analyses by synergism.[91] His philosophy was coming closer and closer to pragmatism,[92] but without its subjective and utilitarian noesis, especially in regard to practical life. By this method he brought into public and cultural life new views and tasks, thus proving his initiative, criticism, and courage. He claimed to be a moralist representing humanitarian ideas, a zealot of national revival, criticizing the whole development of the Czech nation and making philosophical conclusions as a politician, leader of progressive conceptions, and fighter for democracy. He included in his activities all phases of cultural and public life, directly or indirectly, and he solved them according to their urgency.

This disciple of Brentano was appointed to a professorship at the Czech Charles University, which before its separation from the German institution had been part of Carolo-Ferdinandea Universitas in Prague. Here he made a thorough analysis of conditions prevailing in the Austro-Hungarian monarchy, after the defeat of Badeni's government, and believing that the Czechs were being menaced by increasing German nationalism, he proclaimed a cultural and political program against the Catholic Church and against the Viennese government. He said:

> We are the nation of Hus and we like to call ourselves this. . . .[93] Freethinking in Bohemia has its source in the

Czech Reformation, and in the tradition of the Czech Brethren and of Hussites. Our national leaders of the nineteenth century continued its development which had begun to disintegrate because of reaction. It is not a coincidence that the greatest leaders of the new liberty movement, except for the freethinking priest Dobrovský, were descendants of Czech Brethren and their Protestant successors: Kollar, Šafařik, and Palacký. Against the Catholicism of the Counter-Reformation, such men as Dobrovský and these others were defenders of freedom of thought and a noble tradition of Czech reformation. [94]

Every Czech, knowing his nation's history, must make up his mind in favor of either Reformation or Counter-Reformation.[95] I am not making any appeal that we all should be Czech Brethren or Hussites—that we should go back. No, we have to go forward, but the ideas and development which began by our Reformation, we must preserve. It means we must loose ourselves from Rome, spiritually and actually.

I say, and it is true as Palacký said, that in the Czech Reformation and the attainment of ideals of the Brethren were the culminating points of the development of the Czech nation and of mankind. In this we must continue; we must go by way of reformation and feel congenially toward what was of a Czech character in the Reformation.[96] As soon as we attain political freedom, our first task will be the separation of Church and state. Religion must be, as it was for Hus, a problem of conscience and not a question of a political character. Therefore, we must try in the political fight which seems to be anticlericalism, to overcome Rome in ourselves. . . .[97] When mentioning Hus, Žižka, Chelčický, Comenius, we have as many programs as names, but in substance there is only one program for us.[98] In Žižka and the Taborites, there is no doubt that we have a Czech type. Žižka is blood of our blood, bone of our bone—yes, we are all of Žižka. It is not the Polish exaggeration, which is being admired by Mickiewicz, but it is enthusiasm of a special kind, proceeding blindly toward its goal. It is fatalistic, "either all or nothing," but in our case it is an unbreakable courage, awful against the enemy but horrible for a victor because in the depths of his soul it evokes doubts and knowledge and recognition of a crime. It is true because Hus, Comenius, and the Brethren are Czech types, and they are, as appears from history, types numerous and of ever-

> lasting existence. We are therefore the nation of Žižka and Prokop, or of Hus and Comenius.[99]

These opinions of T. G. Masaryk express the whole attitude which is aimed *ex professo* against the Catholic Church. His activities as teacher and politician were regulated and controlled by this attitude, and they were unjustly severe toward Czech Catholics. It is therefore surprising when John Herben writes: "In my opinion, nobody proved in the nineteenth century that he favored the Catholic Church as did Masaryk."[100] To refute that it would suffice to mention some of the writings of T. G. Masaryk: *Ein Katechetenspiegel,*[101] his conflict with Czech-national clergymen;[102] and his unjust review of Catholic political, cultural, and national programs (in *Česká Otázka, Naše nynější krise. Jan Hus, Socialní Otázka*),[103] in which the historical merits of Catholics are underestimated or even overlooked. In them Masaryk criticizes severely all that is of Catholic origin, thus proving that just the opposite of Herben's assertion is true.

Even more, the negative attitude of Masaryk toward the Catholic Church was not only of a tactical character or of national origin,[104] but it appears to have been mainly a matter of principle. The Counter-Reformation is generally mentioned as a reason for his negative attitude toward Catholicism. Such an attitude was similar to that of Otakar Machotka, who writes an account of the Church as follows: "Loyola using immoral means for the benefits of the Church also made use of lies—a dry kind of violence."[105] Similarly, Jan Papánek asserts: "The period of the Czech Reformation was one of the greatest spiritual ferment in Bohemia, while the Counter-Reformation which followed was one of the greatest decline."[106] It was under this aspect, that Masaryk educated a whole new generation and, by his lectures, brought Rome to the people. The time was opportune to ascertain that "in Czech political terminology, the condition resulting from Hapsburg rule is 'Temno,' or darkness."[107]

As a result, the Austrian liberal nationalists forced the government in Vienna to cancel many concessions granted in favor of national groups by the government of Badeni, and German demands took precedence. So also the regulation by Count Gautsch, issued in 1898, which divided Bohemia into an area with an official language exclusively either German or Czech, was repealed by the implacable resistance of the Germans. Especially in Sudeten, the Czechs felt this practice drastic. Therefore Germans decried any appointment of Czech priests in German rectories. The rector of the seminary in Litoměřice at that time, Monsignor Francis Kordač, often attacked in German newspapers, was even tried by the law court in Česká Lipa[108] for so-called efforts to "Czechosize." As early as 1902, on the initiative of Professor Dr. Karl Hilgenreiner, attempts were made to detach the part of Bohemia inhabited by Germans of the archdiocese of Prague, and to establish a new bishopric in Cheb. Bishop Brynych of Hradec Kralové, however, drew the attention of Rome to these intentions in 1902.

Besides these national problems, social questions also increased in urgency. At the same time, workers' attempts to carry their demand for general voting rights[109] made this group an important factor when they fought for their political and social rights. In 1878, the Social Democratic party was established in Austria, based on the principles of Karl Marx. After that, the united front of the Czech Social Democrats against Vienna collapsed. Dr. Francis Soukup became leader of the Czech Social Democrats. Since 1897 the National Socialists had been organizing their own political party under the leadership of Václav Klofač, advocating at the same time the need for solving social and national demands. Czech and Moravian Catholics, after the example of Austrian Catholics, and because of undue influence of the important book, *Otázka Dělnická* (*Social Problem of Workers*), written by Father Matěj Procházka of Brno, established a Christian Social party under the leadership of Monsignor Jan Šrámek. This party endeavored to reconcile social demands with Christianity. Masaryk himself took arguments for his *Otázka Socialní* from Procházka's *Otázka Dělnická*.[110] The Agrarian party was being organized in 1890 on a state basis by Alfons Šťástný, first as a part of the Young Czech party, but after 1899 as an independent party under the wise leadership of the capable Antonín Švehla. Finally there were the Realistic party of Masaryk and the Radical Progressive party. Thus the Czechs were divided when Czech deputies in the central parliament in Vienna proclaimed their program, in which the greatest enemies of the nation were cited as selfish bourgeoisie and domineering feudal nobles.[111] This declaration of the Socialists, while inciting a very strong denial and scandal among the Czechs, was accepted with joy by the Germans. Thus at their first opportunity Social Democrats showed their true colors from a political, religious and national point of view.

Following the example set by the German Social Democrats in industrial districts, their Czech counterparts propagated mass apostasies from Rome in favor of atheism under the Marxist motto: "Religion is the opium of the people." After 1907 when general and equal voting was introduced into Austria-Hungary, political disunity increased. In the last Austrian parliament, of 553 deputies following the general election of 1911, there were over thirty parties represented. The 144 Czech deputies were divided into eleven parties and factions. For this reason, they did not succeed in their demands. The strongest parties were socialistic (a total of thirty-nine deputies); there were fourteen Young Czechs, one Old Czech, and only seven Catholics as compared with seventeen in 1907.[112] These seven deputies were elected in Moravia. There were no Catholic deputies from Bohemia, which in 1907 had sent seven. Besides this, the Agrarian and Workers parties united in this general election of 1911 against the Catholics.[113]

From this short statistical review it is apparent what the situation of the Church was in Bohemia and Moravia toward the end of the nineteenth and the beginning of the twentieth century. It was a path of great decline. The Catholic branch started to break as a result of the liberalism of the Young Czechs. Due to the realists and progressives, supported by the Socialists, it continued to decline; there is no doubt that the Czech Brethren had contributed to this aim. In his program of progress, T. G. Masaryk concentrated on the use of the symbols: Hus, Tábor, Chelčický, Jan Amos Komenský, Dobrovský; the all-inclusive synthesis against the Catholic Church; and on the antithesis, "Reformation—Counter-Reformation." It is not conceivable that all the efforts of Austrian Catholics, except those from Sudeten, were favorable to the demands of the national groups or were not appreciated by those of the Czechs.[114] On the contrary, German nationals and liberals were assisted in their efforts by Czech progressives.

The result was an anomaly. But both groups had the same program of attack on the Catholic Church. As the Austrian Catholics remained aloof, so did the Catholics in Bohemia and Moravia. Nevertheless, Catholics did fight and work on religious and national problems relentlessly.

Meanwhile, in Germany, after the Vatican Council, all apostasies to the "Old Catholic Church" were favored through the influence of the "Away from Rome" movement on Lutherans, the sympathies of Czech liberals aimed at an oriental Orthodox Church, and the ideals of Hussites. As a reaction, Czech and Moravian Catholics sought to unify Slovanic Catholics from all the Slavic nations. In Bohemia, Václav Štulc worked on this plan, and Bishop Jirsík lent his cooperation. In Moravia, the pre-eminently learned priest and patriot, Father Francis Šušil[115] labored strenuously along these lines.

At the twelfth Catholic Day celebration of German Catholics in Prague in 1860, Štulc, the honored guest, announced the establishment of the association of Saint Cyril and Saint Methodius to work for the unity of all Slavic nations. This religious organization was behind the movement led by Father Francis Šušil to celebrate the thousandth anniversary of the arrival of these saints in Moravia. This proved to be a very popular step toward the movement of unionism, with the center in Velehrad, under the care of the Jesuits and the Archbishop of Olomouc, Fuerstenberg. Later the idea was taken over and supported by Fathers Matěj Procházka and Karel Šmídek, and again by Antonin Cyril Stojan, zealous priest and politician. All these priests were educated, generous, and famous, but Father Antonin Stojan became particularly[116] prominent. He so aroused Moravia that Brno and Olomouc became centers for Catholic activities. Catholic political parties arose as a result of this movement. It was the scholarly Dr. Horský who led the National Catholic party in Bohemia. The president-elect of the second party—the Christian Social party—was Monsignor Jan Šrámek. These organizations achieved some measure of success in 1900, and again, but for the last time, in 1907.

Besides these political parties, an association of Czech Catholic intellectuals was established to educate the Czechs for participation in public life. T. G. Masaryk observed a substantial danger to progress in the Cyril-Methodius movement, and in keeping with his revision of the political program, he fought it. "Those who are in favor of the Cyril-Methodius idea are holding the line against progress and are advocating an idea that is not of Czech character."[117] "The proclamation of the Cyril and Methodius idea by Young Czechs, who have no regard for its outlined characteristics, is a resignation and a retreat from our freethinking Czech program.[118] As to the methodological point of view, this idea is a reference to the exaggerated history of the very distant past. . . ."[119] "The idea finds support among the clerics; especially, that man of such high education and devotion, Matěj Procházka, . . ."[120] But not satisfied with the influence of this idea among liberals, he writes: "The idea of Cyril and Methodius is being proclaimed. The formulation of this concept by its authors, as is apparent to the reader of the newspaper *Národní Listy* (of July 28, 1894), insists that only through the realization of the Cyril-Methodius idea will the Czech nation accomplish its revival. We would welcome it, even though we consider it wrong. But it is intolerable for us to write about religious problems with liberal ink and to be zealous for religion and drink national lousy drink.[121] However, the idea of Cyril and Methodius as advanced by convinced Catholics must be viewed in another light."[122]

The magazine *Athenaeum*[123] carried these opinions of Masaryk, while the *Sborník Velehradský,* with its center in Brno, and various periodicals of Czech clerics published the Catholic point of view. Through this Cyril-Methodius idea, Catholics tried to win over the Czech liberals. The latter favored the Orthodox Church, for the benefit of which propaganda was being spread in Bohemia, specifically through the publication of the Orthodox catechism[124] and the introduction of the Orthodox liturgy into Bohemia by Mr. Valečka. Catholics successfully retaliated by introducing the Greek Catholic liturgy and advancing ideas of unionism. In this way they proved themselves staunch supporters of national Slavic solidarity. As a result, the wave of apostasies retreated.

Meanwhile the movement for progress was increasing in strength; the loyalty of Catholics was diminishing; nationalism became the exclusive program. Catholic priests were willing to make any satisfactory arrangement. Some, like Třebízký, wrote novels urging reforms appropriate to the times. Novels from foreign literature were translated, and national motives prevailed in Czech literature. Jindřich Baar, Xavier Dvořák, and K. Dostál-Lutinov, who excelled in producing such literature, were called the "Catholic Moderna."[125] At a congress in 1897 reports were made concerning certain misunderstandings with ecclesiastical authorities. However, the magazine published and issued under the same name as this organization was compelled to change its name to receive ecclesiastical approval.[126] When Pope Pius X in 1907 condemned modernism,[127] and repeated his condemnation in 1910,[128] the Catholic modernists' group was dissolved, for the last time. About one hundred fifty priests and laymen attended the last meeting in Přerov in Moravia. The members of this group, having been followers of progressivism, failed in its original aims, but all but thirteen of them remained loyal to the Church.

This Catholic modernist movement was a typical product and development of the time. It was liberal and emphasized the personal adjustment of the individual, thus accounting for the great decline of religious beliefs and increase of religious indifferentism. The very existence of Catholic modernists was an indication that their attitude was being received favorably and hailed as progressive. But this "progress," to use the words of the poet Victor Dyk, was "progress to the point of stupidity."[129]

Meanwhile progress was being advanced according to the plan of the antithesis "Reformation—Counter-Reformation." The indifferentism of Czech Catholics, supported by another catchword, "Prague-Vienna," aimed to achieve the stand called *"Religio depopulata."*[130] Herein lay the roots of the Czech movement, "Away from Rome." Meanwhile, the Austrian *Los von Rom* movement was being politically organized. This sought to prove that the Catholic Church had committed "crimes" against the Czech nation throughout its history. Admittedly, a motive of retribution can be taken for granted, since the Church in her attempt to re-Catholicize Bohemia was being supported in these efforts by the Hapsburg dynasty. It is sad, however, that all the merits of the Catholic Church recorded in various histories were being willfully forgotten and overlooked. This was the result of the relentless work of those Czech priests who had adapted themselves to progressivism. The propaganda for the movement was spread in the name of national demands.

Such was the stand of the Czech people toward the Catholic Church at the time of the decline of the Austro-Hungarian monarchy. The conditions in Slovakia since 1867 were catastrophic for Slovaks. Whereas Czechs enforced some national demands in their favor, the brother branch of the Czech nation in Slovakia was willing to remain arid under the rule of the Hungarian government. When unfavorable agrarian conditions induced Slovaks to emigrate to the United States, Hungarians were pleased.

The Budapest government found a way to reduce the demands of national groups. Statistics show that out of 3,599 elementary schools in the territory of Slovakia, paid for by church, state, and private Slovak funds, only 340 used the Slovak language. These were Catholic and Lutheran schools where, since 1907, half the subjects were taught in the Hungarian language.[131] In other schools, only the Hungarian language was used. Organs of public service and education, military administrators, and ecclesiastical authorities neglected and calumniated the Slovaks. The only place where the Slovak language found use was in the churches. Some associations were established, as for instance, the Musealní Slovanská Společnost in Turě-Sv. Martin in 1895, the Spolok Sv. Vojtěcha in 1870 in Trnava. Leaders in national life were, it is true, Catholic priests and Protestant ministers, but the majority of other Slovak intellectuals accepted the Hungarian language. Thus it came about that Slovaks understood and appreciated the Church's protests for Slovak national life. The poets Hurban-Vajanský and Hviezdoslav also lent support to such protests. And as a reaction to Hungarian pressures, Pan-Slavism, influenced by Kollar, was proclaimed with no national repercussions. Hlasists, so called from the name of their magazine *Hlas,* were followers of T. G. Masaryk,[132] and advocated cooperation with the Czechs.

The question of the day became this: how could Catholic priests be induced to win the struggle with the Hungarian government through Slovak demands? Much was expected as a result of the introduction of general, direct, and secret voting rights, brought in over the resistance of the Hungarians. Before this type of voting began, Slovaks had only two or three deputies, although having the right, by proportional representation, to forty-five. Happily, World War I took away the intolerably extended burden of Hungarian pressure and persecution. The cooperation between the Church and Slovak people, based upon the internal convictions of the past, was the reason why Slovaks remained immune to almost all anti-Catholic tendencies. Any kind of cultural struggle against the Catholic Church, no matter by whom proclaimed, failed in Slovakia. The antithesis "Reformation—Counter-Reformation" was not successful in Slovakia.

Meanwhile, conditions prevailing in Austria-Hungary were bringing European states into two groups, the Triple Alliance (Germany, Austria-Hungary, Italy), and the Allies (France, Russia, Great Britain). Germany, having succeeded in Pan-German efforts, was led by Emperor William II, who wanted to finish the work of King Frederick II, of Bismarck, and of Moltke. These exaggerated endeavors were opposed by France and Great Britain. The annexation of Bosnia and Herzegovina by the Austro-Hungarian monarchy in 1908 became a substantial victory for Pan-Germanism. The Czechs opposed the annexation because they were enjoying good relations with the Serbs and Croats, and these relations were strengthened thereby. The Balkan arena was the center for Austro-Hungarian expansion, because there could be compensated the defeats suffered by loss of territory in 1859 in Italy and in 1866 in Germany.

It will be remembered that at the beginning of the war of 1914, the Czechs were in an unusual situation. They were forced to fight for Austria, despite their sympathies for Russia, Serbia, and the Western Allies.[133] This was the critical point in the relation of the Czechs with Austria. The tactful stand of Palacký[134] ceased, and under T. G. Masaryk an open fight began. An all-out persecution of Czech traditions, the introduction of the German language into schools, the arrest of Czech and Slovak patriots even in the Czech districts, the arrest of the Young Czech leaders Karel Kramář and Rašín (1915)—all accelerated the decision of the Czechs to raise the flag in the fight for national freedom, with the aim to destroy Austria-Hungary. Resistance, both external and internal, was thus given further opportunity to develop, as Masaryk himself testifies:

> In the country itself, it was not possible for armed resistance or radical opposition to originate. Any *coup d'état* could

> not possibly be arranged. We were forced to go abroad and from there to initiate our fight against Austria.[135]

Enthusiasm was spontaneous, and was supported by all Czechs and Slovaks, without regard to religion or parties. In the country, the so-called Mafia[136] was active; abroad the resistance was led by T. G. Masaryk, Eduard Beneš, and Josef Durich, as the first Czech committee (1915) representing the nation before the world forum. In Russia, France, and Italy, Czechoslovak legions were organized[137] under the co-operation of the Slovak brothers led by Milan Rostislav Stěfaník (1880-1919), who was very famous abroad. Through the united efforts of the nation, a dream was fulfilled when on October 28, 1918, the Czechoslovak Republic was proclaimed. On October 30, 1918, the Sv. Martin Declaration was issued, in which three hundred Slovak representatives asserted Slovakia's freedom from Hungary and declared it a part of Czechoslovakia. [138] President Wilson's famous declaration of January 18, 1918, containing his Fourteen Points, was really a royal gift to small nations, and, in accordance with it, the map of Europe has been greatly changed. Czechoslovakia also benefited by these Fourteen Points.

When the Czech deputies proclaimed their program in 1917, Catholic clerics expressed their consent and in their meetings openly avowed that they were in unanimous agreement with the efforts of the nation to achieve its freedom.[139] Catholics participated in all phases of the activity to achieve national independence. This was true even of Catholic emigrants to the United States; for instance, in their Chicago meeting of November 18, 1917, they drew up a resolution addressed to Pope Benedict XV (1914-1922), asking him to use his influence in favor of the Czech and Slovak nations devoted to the Holy See. This resolution was sent through the Apostolic Delegate in Washington directly to Rome. When President Wilson arrived in France a year later to take part in the Peace Conferences, the Pope asked him to assist the small nations of what was formerly Austria, especially the Czechs.[140] The Pope wrote a letter to Vienna in favor of Dr. Karel Kramář.[141] The share of Catholics in the resistance movement had been really extensive. T. G. Masaryk himself wrote about the American Czechs with expressions of truly great praise, and proclaimed that these had proceeded in full concord with the other groups.[142] It would seem that his antithesis "Reformation—Counter-Reformation" was abandoned, when he no longer had reason to doubt the trustful national character of the Czech and Slovak Catholics. Unity of resistance was doubtless very impressive proof of it and the stands of Pope Pius X and Benedict XV were certainly known to him. Despite all this, T. G. Masaryk brought this antithesis as a program in his fight for freedom before the Allies. At Geneva, Switzerland, in 1915,[143] activities of a resistance movement abroad had opened with a celebration in honor of Hus, and in his name the fight for freedom began. In this spirit all garrisons of the legions were trained and regiments were called exclusively by names common in the Hussite period. For instance, the name of the Saint Wenceslaus regiment was changed to John Hus; the name of the regiment of Saint Cyril and Saint Methodius to the name of George of Poděbrady.[144] This was undeniable evidence that "Reformation—Counter-Reformation" retained its full significance. The fact that the majority of the legions was Catholic made no difference. Surely Catholics had become the victims of progress. During World War I, it was already decided that in liberated Czechoslovakia, Hussitism would be introduced. No regard was taken of the fact that the Catholic associations like Orel and Catholic army chaplains in the legions had taken part in the fight; unrespected remained also the aims of Catholics in the mass meetings.

The antithesis "Reformation—Counter-Reformation" was put forth by T. G. Masaryk as a program of national culture, revival, and policy. But instead of a peaceful establishment of the state's organism, a new fight was evoked, in which *am staerksten ergoss sich eine ausgesprochene Rom- und kirchenfeindliche Bewegung ueber die um das widerwillige slovakische und deutsche Element vermehrte Tschechoslowakei, wo unter Kramář und Masaryk Kloester und Kirchengueter unterdrueckt, Bilder und Gottesdienst gestuermt, die Religion aus den Schulen verbannt und der Huskult wiederaufgefrischt wurde.*[145]

The appearance of this fight was evident when, on November 3, 1918, the revolutionists brutally removed the beautiful statue of the Blessed Virgin in the Old Town

Square, and destroyed it[146] with a crowd of Socialists in attendance.[147] In 1919, teachers in the Prague schools began to remove the Cross from classrooms. About five hundred of these school Crosses were deposited in the city court of the Valdštejn palace. The Order of Christian Brothers and the association of Catholic teachers bought them for 10,000 crowns and deposited them in the Institut Johaneum. Also in the countryside this wave began, so that the Cross was removed from 1,600 schools in all. The statues of the Blessed Virgin, Saint John Nepomucene, Saint Wenceslaus, and monuments in cemeteries were destroyed; pictures were removed and desecrated. Some hundreds of such monuments were completely ruined. Moreover, this iconoclasm was being performed cynically; not even historical monuments were respected. In the same year, about three hundred churches, including their sacred furnishings,[148] were expropriated. In all, about five hundred shrines were robbed and dishonored. In Slovakia, the Slovaks abstained from these acts, but the Czechs carried them out even there, actions which later impeded mutual understanding.

Unfortunately too, among the clergy there were some who let themselves be influenced by such developments. Priests were frequently attacked and calumniated at the meetings of progressives. In Moravia, people remained loyal and exercised their religious duties; in Slovakia, religious life flourished. To be Catholic in those times involved a real risk, especially in Bohemia where churches remained empty. People were frightened, fearful of reproaches by their neighbors. In the schools, matters became intolerable for priests because the majority of teachers were hostile to them. There were many and frequent cases where the teacher attacked the priest and taught the very opposite of what the priest maintained, engendering a decline of respect for priests in the minds of children and students. Priests, to avoid all this unpleasantness, refrained from going into the schools or into society at all. Priests were not spared the weight of slanders and libels even on necessary journeys.

Some priests were willing to adjust themselves to the state of affairs by accepting the tenets of modernists; joined by others they established the Jednota of Catholic clerics (*Jednota katolického duchovenstva*).[149] Leaders in this organization were former Catholic modernists and priests who shared other than thorough Catholic principles. The attention of the whole world[150] became focused on this association headed by Father Xavier Dvořák, and Father Bohuslav Zahradnik, a priest and famous author of light novels.[151] The executive committee decided to formulate the following demands: (*a*) removal of patronage rights; (*b*) election of bishops by priests; (*c*) constitution of a patriarchate for Czechoslovakia; (*d*) social security and adequate wages for priests; (*e*) introduction of a Czech liturgy, with reform of breviary; (*f*) introduction of a democratic constitution for bishoprics; (*g*) facultative use of the clerical garb; and (*h*) abolition of celibacy.

Demands like these were typical of this association, about one-third of the priests supported them. However, the resolution as accepted was signed by only ninety priests, and a delegation was elected to bring the matter to the attention of Rome. The delegation was refused an audience by the papal nuncio in Vienna. Among others in the delegation of June, 1919, was Professor Adalbert Šanda. The Pope's reaction was that "all legitimate demands will be fulfilled (as for instance, the recall of Archbishop Huyn from Prague, and Hungarian bishops from Slovakia); illegitimate demands cannot be fulfilled nor accepted."[152] That is how the matter eventually turned out. Appointment as Archbishop of Prague on September 16, 1919, came to Professor Francis Kordač, a well-known philosopher of Charles University.[153] Without regarding the wishes of the Jednota, the Pope had chosen a very capable and radical person. To solve the problem of Jednota was the task of the day. On January 3, 1920, Pope Benedict XV[154] sent a letter to the Archbishop of Prague, asking him to convoke all bishops of Moravia and Bohemia to hear their suggestions. In this letter, the Pope designated the demands of the Jednota as unwise[155] and gave the following directives: It is impossible to cancel regulations and provisions concerning celibacy; demands of a democratic constitution and appointment of bishops by election do not accord with the principles of canon law, since these depend only on papal jurisdiction. Thus was the position of the Vatican clarified.

When the bishops held their meeting they suggested that

the Jednota be disbanded. Some hesitation was apparent in the priests themselves; some left the Jednota and only the radicals remained. Convoking a meeting on January 8, 1920, in the National House of Smíchov,[156] these priests proclaimed a Czechoslovak schism under the name of a Czechoslovak Church. After a noisy meeting and with the assistance of progressives present at the meeting, the motion carried by 140 votes. Other priests left the meeting; some who had voted in the affirmative revoked their consent; in the end only sixty-six priests remained defiant.[157] This open attack was launched under the slogan "We are settling our score with Rome." Rome responded by a decree of the Congregation of the Holy Office under date of January 15, 1920, in virtue of which *schismatica nonnulorum e clero Bohemo sacerdotum coalitio damnatur*. All priests taking part in it were excommunicated under provisions of Canon 2384. The text of this decree reads as follows:

> It has been brought to the attention of the Holy See that certain priests of the Bohemian clergy, whose actions have even before this caused protests to be presented to the same Holy See, have lately assembled in defiance of law and in an attempt at schism have announced their separation from the Roman Church, the mother and teacher of all other churches and the center of Catholic unity, and have banded together in what they call a "national" church. This august body of the Sacred Congregation of the Holy Office, to whom is entrusted the task of guarding faith and morals, now deeply scorned though it be, recognizes that the said church or schismatic group falls within the scope of its jurisdiction and forthwith reproves, condemns, and anathematizes this monstrous crime, and by this present decree, in the name of and by the authority of His Holiness Benedict XV, reproves, condemns, and anathematizes the aforementioned priests, adjudicating them, whatsoever be their status, position, and condition, to have already incurred ipso facto excommunication reserved by Cannon 2384 *speciali modo* to the Holy See, and sentencing them to be subjected without delay to all attendant penalties and restrictions laid down in the Sacred Canons if—which God forbid!—they persist contumaciously in this state of excommunication. The venerable bishops of the Bohemians shall as part of their duty take

steps in as effective a manner as they in God's sight see fit to make this decree known to the faithful under their charge and to restrain them from in any way associating with this schismatic group lest they also incur the same condemnation.

Issued at Rome from the chambers of the Holy Office, January 15, 1920.

ALOYSIUS CASTELLANO
Secretary
Under the Seal of the Sacred
Congregation of the Holy Office[158]

Thereby the Priests' League (*Kněžská Liga*) was proclaimed schismatic and the priests in it were excommunicated. Catholic bishops made up their minds to disband the Jednota. Sokols and Protestants opened propaganda for mass apostasies.[159] Some of their leading members held the concepts Sokol and Catholic to be incompatible. Former members of the Jednota convoked a general meeting in Prague on October 26, 1920, under the direction of Rev. Krojher. As priests had been ordered by the bishop to leave the Jednota on November 30, 1920, a vote was taken. Three hundred and forty-five priests voted for liquidation of the Jednota. When only sixty of them voted for continuation of its activities, the Jednota was proclaimed liquidated.[160] In the private session of Cardinals on December 16, 1920, the Pope delivered a speech, in which he approved the liquidation of the Jednota, at the same time expressing deep sorrow over the apostasies of priests[161] and the decline in discipline. This done, the activities of the Jednota exerted diminishing influence.

However, the League of Priests continued in the national organization of the Czechoslovak Church. Adherents of this sect had seized thirty-six churches by force, expelling loyal Catholic priests from them. By order of the government on September 15, 1920, this new sect was recognized and established in forty-one parishes in Bohemia, seven in Moravia, and five in Silesia, having 150,000 adherents, mostly former members of socialistic and freethinking organizations. This national Church had no liturgy, and the first congress was arranged on January 8 and 9, 1921,[162] in the hotel Albergo dell'Oca in Prague. The attendance numbered 376 delegates, with only 71 priests and 912 guests. The teacher Vaněk was elected president of the congress. All schismatic Churches sent their delegates. The Serbian Orthodox was represented by Grovanin; the Anglican Church of the United States by the Reverend Gollier; the Russian Orthodox by the university professor Jastrebov; the Czech Brethren by Doctor Stěhule. All these representatives addressed the congress, calling for unification in the fight against Rome. The telegram of the Serbian Bishop Dositej was read, containing the answer to the suggestion of amalgamation of these two Churches. One of the founders of this Czechoslovak Church, Zahradník-Brodský, read this memorandum, and explained the plan for unification with the Serbian Church which had its basis in the conclusions of the Nicean Council and the Nicene Creed. The national Church asked for freedom of conscience, the Czech liturgical language, the possibility of priests' and bishops' marriages, and ordination by Serbian bishops. Zahradník-Brodský and the Reverend Doctor Farský, who spoke after him, did not approve of this unification with the Serbian Church. The apostate priest Dlouhý-Pokorný attacked Rome and the authority of all bishops of the monstrous "sect," as he called the Catholic Church. Some resolutions and outlines of liturgy were accepted and the catechism of the new sect was issued.

The outstanding theologian Monsignor Cinek called this catechism a "unique feature in Czech literature." But the Serbian bishop Dositej himself condemned it for its theological absurdity.[163] Nevertheless, its defiance of Rome increased its circulation. Apostate priests, the number of whom had increased to 288, supported by Socialists, opened a great propaganda drive before the census of the population, set for February 15, 1921. In Plzeň 15,000 apostasies of workers were recorded.[164] The census was being carried out under control and supervision of Professor Boháč, a Protestant and an enemy of the Catholic Church. Anti-clerical teachers assisted the newspaper *Prager Tagblatt,* which informed the public that the governmental commission had decided that civil weddings henceforth would be obligatory, Catholic holidays suppressed, and all records taken from the rectories and handed over to the state chanceries.

News like this intimidated priests. A group of them under the leadership of Fathers Xavier Dvořák and Ludvik Svatoš now began to issue the newspaper *Jednota,* and subsequently incurred excommunication. The text of this decree reads:

> Since, not without deep regret, this august Sacred Congregation of the Holy Office, which is charged with the preservation of integrity of faith and morals, has become aware that the censures pronounced by local bishops since as far back as 1920 and approved and affirmed by the Holy See (cf. *Acta Apostolicae Sedis,* v. XII, p. 57, no. I, and p. 585, no. II) against the schismatic society of certain Czechoslovak priests known as the Jednota have been ineffective in the case of certain individuals, it now, lest in a matter of such importance it should appear delinquent in its duty and functions, is compelled to repeat more emphatically and again affirm those pronouncements in which it denounced and dissolved that society, as is herewith done by this present decree. Therefore let all those priests who in any manner whatsoever are associated with that condemned society know that, unless they shall have retracted their schismatic stand within fifteen days after the bishops' promulgation of this decree and shall have submitted fully and without reserve to the commands of their bishops and of the Holy See, they shall have incurred, ipso facto, without need of further juridical action, excommunication reserved to the Holy See; and further, that those four priests who make up the so-called praesidium shall in a separate decree be punished by excommunication nominatim with all its attendant consequences.
>
> The same august Sacred Congregation takes this opportunity to denounce, condemn and forbid without reserve the news publication which likewise bears the name *Jednota,* and herewith formally pronounces that the excommunication reserved *speciali modo* to the Holy See as determined by Canon 2318, paragraph I extends to all those who edit, defend, read, or keep this publication.
>
> The venerable Czechoslovak bishops will see to it that this decree, which bears the weight of the authority of His Holiness Pope Pius XI, is forthwith promulgated to the priests concerned and to the faithful under their charge, in as effective a manner as they see fit in God's sight, and will inform the Sacred Congregation concerning the outcome as soon as possible.[165]

The sum of 1,200,000 crowns donated to the new Czechoslovak Church by the government was gratefully accepted by the first congress. Despite all endeavor to influence the result of the census, it failed because all the adherents of the Czechoslovak Church numbered 1,388,000. The majority of these were in Bohemia; in Moravia, there were only 150,000 apostasies.[166] Although propaganda made use of terror, asserting that the new sect was really the Czech Catholic Church, many apostates, after having learned that they were victims of deceit, returned to the Catholic Church. Workers, inspired by Social Democratic leaders, after their apostasies either entered the Czechoslovak Church or remained without any confession whatsoever. Thus by 1930 there were 853,000 of them, whereas adherents to the Czechoslovak Church at the same time were only 793,000.[167] Catholics decreased in percentage from 95 per cent to 75 per cent. The nation remained prevailingly Catholic, but progress was delayed.[168]

This statistical exposition is the best indication that many people viewed the Czechoslovak Church as a way to atheism. Undoubtedly it had its analogue in the Austrian *Los von Rom* movement.

After the census had been taken, the leaders of the Czechoslovak Church called in the Archbishop of Prague, Francis Kordač,[169] asking him for the use of Catholic churches. He answered: "As a guardian of the Church, I cannot give any such approval and I repudiate the suggestion." The leader of the delegation replied: "We will look for another way to reach these churches." They approached the government requesting their use. Their suggestions, supported by Mr. Francis Krejčí, were strongly opposed in Parliament by Monsignor Šrámek and Rev. Krojher. Leaders of the Czechoslovak Church used all available means to justify their excesses by law.

Under such conditions, the Catholic Church after 1918 suffered severely. She was robbed of all; believers either apostatized or were intimidated or became indifferent; churches were being seized; priests, calumniated, slandered or libeled; Crosses and monuments were destroyed. The warnings of educated scientists and excellent Czech historians, such as Josef Pekař and Josef Šusta, who repeated their warnings on every occasion, went unheeded. Even Professor Ernest Denis[170] on the occasion of his last visit to Czechoslovakia, on November 30, 1920, while speaking at Charles University in Prague, in the presence of the rector of the university, the French Minister Conget, and the historian Josef Šusta, Minister of Education, condemned the absurdities of Czech progressives and advised them, for the sake of the nation, to moderate the religious fight.

Such happenings were the outcome of Masaryk's antithesis "Reformation—Counter-Reformation." Unchecked, these activities would have brought the country to the desolate state of affairs it had experienced after the Reformation and the time of John Hus.

But Catholics awakened. The irresolute policy of Monsignor Šrámek (for lack of a better way out) attempted to moderate the excesses of the progressive movement. In Bohemia, the zealous priest Chlumský, secretary of the association of Catholic youth there, started his praiseworthy work. Within two years he organized 27,000 young people into 500 groups. The magazine *Dorost* was published in 12,000 copies. By 1921 the Czech Academic League had achieved a membership of 150. The Welfare Association for Students reached 1300 members and planned a congress for 1921. The Catholic athletic association, Orel, with a membership of 70,000, strengthened its activities, defended the churches before they were seized, and faced the propaganda organization of Sokol. The Holy See appointed ecclesiastics for all the bishoprics, choosing them from among the people. In Olomouc the very popular Antonin Cyril Stojan was appointed Archbishop.[171] In Slovakia, Pavol Jantausch and Josef Čarský were appointed bishops;[172] in Prague, the scientist Antonín Podlaha was named auxiliary bishop. A college for young men of the archbishopric of Prague, begun under Cardinal Skrbenský, was finished; the Nepomucenum College was established in Rome; in Moravia the Cyril-Methodius movement gained strength; Catholic associations increased their numbers. After the liquidation of the Jednota the Holy Father sent all the bishops in Czechoslovakia a letter dated November 30, 1921,[173] in which he gave instructions for the resumption of activities of Catholic life in Czechoslovakia. He urged a more thorough education of young priests, revival of discipline in Catholic associations, and recommended the apostolate of Saints Cyril and Methodius.

Such was the reaction of Czech and Moravian Catholics to unfavorable conditions. In Slovakia, people were spared all that. From the very beginning of the Czechoslovak republic the Catholic Church stood alone, with no practical protection from the government.

The government itself was in process of revision: a provisional one under Prime Ministers Karel Kramář (1918) and Vlastimil Tusar, together with President T. G. Masaryk, prepared the Constitution of the Czechoslovak Republic. With its acceptance on February 29, 1920, the constitutional assembly ceased to function.[174]

The Constitution was accepted by the Slovak deputies, and the Slovak People's party, under the leadership of zealous patriot Monsignor Andrej Hlinka, demanded self-rule for Slovakia within the frame of the Czechoslovak Republic, insisting on the so-called agreement of Pittsburgh.[175] After 1921, this fact became the cause of Slovak opposition.

By legislative jurisdiction and in accordance with the aforementioned Constitution, the National Assembly of two chambers was authorized. Members were elected according to a system of proportional representation.

According to the new Constitution of February 29, 1920, No. 121 Coll., the rights of religion were in the main protected by certain provisions. And by it Czechoslovak legislation advanced the principle of freedom of conscience and tolerance. In regard to religion the constitution provided as follows:

Section 117

1) Every person may within the limits of the law express his or her opinion on religious matters by word, in writing, in print, by picture, etc.

2) The same applies to legal entities within the limits of their competence.

3) No one shall suffer in the sphere of his work or employment for exercising this right.

Section 121

Liberty of conscience and religious creed is guaranteed.

Section 122

All inhabitants of the Czechoslovak Republic enjoy to the

same degree as citizens of the Republic the right to profess and exercise publicly and privately any creed, religion, or faith whatsoever, so far as the exercise of the same is not in conflict with public law and order or with morality.

Section 123
No one shall be compelled either directly or indirectly to take part in any religious rite or ceremony whatsoever, rights pertaining to paternal or guardian authority being nevertheless respected.

Section 124
All religious confessions (denominations) shall be equal before the law.

Section 125
The performance of specific religious rights may be prohibited if they are in conflict with public order or public morals.

As an additional protection to the Church's position, there were added later these following Laws:

Law of April 15, 1920, n. 277 Coll.
Sec. 1, art. 1. Parents shall be entitled to specify, within 14 days from birth, the religion of the child or to leave the child without denomination.

Law of April 23, 1925, n. 96 Coll.
Sec. 15. The status "without denomination" shall also be considered a religious denomination within the meaning of the present law. [176]

Finally the Czechoslovak laws declared the right of every citizen not only to choose a denomination but also to be registered officially as having no religious denomination (*bezvyznání*).

Actually, the only essential change that took place dealt with marriage and divorce. In this respect a difference that had existed between the law of the Czech lands and that of Slovakia was eliminated by the Czechoslovak legislation. But still a particular situation in Slovakia called for special legislation there. This situation was concerned with the question of the administration of Church property located in Slovakia but subject to the jurisdiction of authorities now situated across the border. These problems, together with some others, were regulated by the law of December 10, 1918 (No. 64 Coll.). Under its provisions the officials of the central and local government and the officials and dignitaries of the Church were temporarily allowed to continue holding their offices provided they made a pledge of loyalty to the Czechoslovak government. Appeals of the decisions of authorities or courts in Slovakia filed with them were to be held up pending further orders if they were subject to decision by the appellate authorities located across the new border. For the management of Church property located in Czechoslovakia a central board was established by the decree of August 11, 1919, of the Minister for the Administration of Slovakia. These problems were settled in 1928 by an agreement with the Holy See in a so-called *modus vivendi.*

Czech and Moravian Catholics expected to have some legal protection to make possible their defense against any excesses of the progressive movement. Constitutional life and unceasing attacks against the Church evoked in the government certain efforts to regulate the relationship between Church and state. The government of T. G. Masaryk and Eduard Beneš tried to solve the situation in some way.[177] Wherefore, in February, 1921, after the census had proved that the nation would remain predominantly Catholic despite the antithesis Reformation—Counter-Reformation, the Minister of Foreign Affairs, Doctor Beneš,[178] went to Rome to learn more about the situation from a Catholic viewpoint and to prepare a concordat. After his discussion with the Secretary of State, Monsignor Cerreti, concerning all possibilities, he learned that his trip was only of an informational character. The Vatican, however, wanted to make an honest agreement. The problem of ecclesiastical properties, of bishops and their appointment, were of basic importance to the position of the Church. The right of veto for bishops was tolerated by the Vatican. Substantially, these affairs had already been settled between the government and the apostolic auditor, Monsignor Clemens Micara, who already from October, 1919, was in Prague by special authorization of Benedict XV. On May 3, 1922, Václav Pallier was sent by the Czechoslovak government as Minister Extraordinary to the Holy See. In the fall of 1923 the new nuncio, Monsignor Francis Marmaggi, came to Prague and presented his credentials to President Masaryk. During the talk, the President explained that the life of nations, as of individuals, must be based on moral religious principles.

Doctor Beneš tried to regulate the relations between Church and state with especial reference to international considerations. For that reason he went to Rome three different times. These negotiations resulted in the institution of the full right of diplomatic representation. During the negotiations, Beneš was advised by Monsignor Borgongini-Duca[179] that the Holy See would be insulted if a national holiday to honor John Hus were proclaimed. It is apparent that all these efforts of Beneš were based only on motives of political prestige; meanwhile, in internal policy, the government tolerated all forms of attacks and disturbances.[180]

Great excitement in education was caused by the so-called "small bill about education," enacted on June 15, 1922. Religious education was made relatively obligatory; that is to say, education was made dependent on the decision of parents.

The Socialist press campaigned strongly to convince parents that they should repudiate religious education for their children. But Catholics protested against this illegal propaganda, and a delegation of Catholics asked Minister Haberman to admit separate schools. He replied: "Rather will this state perish than approve separate schools." The Archbishop of Prague, Kordač, in the name of all bishops, protested at the beginning of the school year 1923-1924.

In April, 1925, a bill concerning holidays was accepted. Three holidays of the Blessed Virgin Mary were canceled (February 2, March 25, September 8), likewise the holiday of John Nepomucene. For Slovakia only, a provincial holiday of Saint Cyril and Saint Methodius was proclaimed. In lieu of holidays, there were introduced so-called Commemoration Days: October 28 (Independence Day), July 6 (burning of John Hus), and Labor Day, May 1.

The anniversary of Hus's death was celebrated very solemnly that year with official attendance by members of the government.[181] The Vatican took action. The nuncio, Monsignor Francis Marmaggi, sent a protesting note, and the Vatican recalled the nuncio from Prague on May 18, 1925.[182] After that, the government at the demand of Socialists and Communists issued new bills which were inimical to the life and rights of the Church.

Catholics arranged mass meetings in Velehrad from July 31 through August 4, 1924, to demonstrate unionism under the leadership of Archbishop Leopold Prečan, who was authorized by special credentials from the nuncio Marmaggi. Hundreds of thousands of people attended, including more than four hundred bishops. Velehrad became the center of the revival of Catholicism. The bishops of Slovakia even issued a pastoral letter against the Socialists.

The tension between Catholics and the government increased, supported by the activities of Socialists. The general election of November, 1925, caused a great change in internal policy; the result was a warning for the socialistic parties. The People's Catholic party was successful, obtaining three seats in the cabinet. In 1925, Francis Nosek became the Minister of Interior; Monsignor Šrámek, Minister of Mail; and John Dolanský, Minister of Food. In 1926, the cabinet of non-Socialist parties was established under the leadership of Prime Minister Antonin Švehla. The reflection of this development was apparent in moderated relations with the Church, and it was evident that Catholics could not now be overlooked. The Ministry of Foreign Affairs began its negotiation with the Holy See, acting under the influence of Kamil Krofta. The Vatican was temperate; State Secretary Monsignor Ciriaci[183] patiently maintained the Vatican policy of fairness toward Czechoslovakia. In 1927 negotiations were continued when Pius XI (1922-1939) sent a letter to all Czechoslovak bishops on February 13, 1927.[184] He sent the same letter to the bishops of Yugoslavia, giving instructions in favor of the work of unionism as preached by Saint Cyril and Saint Methodius, with due appreciation for the importance of the congresses in Velehrad.

At the end of the year 1927 the government was successful in conciliating the struggle concerning the holiday in honor of Hus. The Vatican mitigated its stand, and the Pope stressed the importance of the work of Saint Cyril and Saint

Methodius in the encyclical, *Rerum Orientalium* of September 7, 1928,[185] recalling the participation of Slavs in this work. Thus was clarified the stand of ecclesiastical policy. The Vatican was very much interested in good relations. And once the *modus vivendi* was settled between the Holy See and the Czechoslovak Republic, normal and friendly relations were established.[186] The *modus vivendi,* signed by Cardinal Gasparri and Dr. Eduard Beneš at the Vatican on February 2, 1928, read as follows:[187]

I—The Holy See and the Czechoslovakian government have agreed on the policy that no part of the Czechoslovakian Republic shall depend upon an Ordinary whose see is located beyond the boundaries of the Czechoslovakian state, and, that likewise, no diocese of Czechoslovakia shall extend beyond those boundaries. The Holy See and the Czechoslovakian government shall agree upon the subject of new boundaries and allotments for the dioceses. In order to prepare such an agreement, two commissions shall be formed within the space of two months, independent of each other: the first, formed by the Holy See and composed of delegates from all dioceses concerned, under the presidency of the representative of the Holy See at Prague; the second, formed by the Czechoslovakian government and composed of representatives of the dioceses concerned and of experts.

II—The administration of ecclesiastical properties and funds in Czechoslovakia, presently under confiscation, is temporary until such time as the agreement mentioned in the preceding article shall be accomplished, and it is confided to a commission under the presidency of the Episcopate of the region in question.

III—The religious Orders and Congregations, whose establishments are located in Czechoslovakia, shall not depend upon the Superior of Provincial Houses of said Orders and Congregations in other countries. If the creation of a province in Czechoslovakia is impossible, said establishments shall be directly subordinate to the General House. Provincial Superiors and local Superiors of religious houses directly dependent upon the General House shall be Czechoslovakian subjects.

IV—The Holy See shall, before proceeding to the nomination of Archbishops and diocesan bishops, of coadjutors *cum iure successionis*, and of the military Ordinary, communicate to the Czechoslovakian government the name of the candidate, in order to be assured that the government has no reason of a political nature to object to such a choice. The above-mentioned prelates shall be Czechoslovakian subjects.
By objections of a political nature are meant all objections which the government would be able to substantiate with reasons which touch upon the security of the State, for example, that the candidate chosen has been guilty of subversive or separatist political activity, or activity directed against the Constitution or the general order of the country. The name of the candidate indicated by the Holy See to the government, as well as the conferences concerning him, shall remain secret.
The dispositions regarding the military Ordinary do not apply except in the case in which the system of exempt religious care is maintained. In this case, besides the objections of a political nature, those also which concern the candidate's position in the army shall be considered.

V—The dignitaries mentioned in the preceding article shall, after nomination and before assuming their functions, swear allegiance to the Czechoslovakian State according to the following formula: *Iuro et promitto sicuti decet Episcopum, fidelitatem Reipublicae Cecoslovachae necnon me non facturum quod sit contra salutem, securitatem, integritatem Reipublicae.*

VI—The government shall, as soon as possible, conform to the legal dispositions contained in the present agreement.[188]

The nunciature in Prague had been restored in 1927, and Archbishop Peter Ciriaci accredited as nuncio on March 12, 1928. Before the time of the *modus vivendi*, there was appointed from the Czechoslovak government to the Holy See only a chargé d'affaires. Those appointed in this capacity were Václav Pallier, followed by Mr. Kober, then by Mr. Jelen, who merited a great deal of praise for preserving good relationships on both sides. After the agreement of the *modus vivendi,* in May, 1928, the first ambassador from the Czechoslovak government to the Holy See, Vladimír Radimský, was appointed. On June 10, 1928, he was received in solemn audience by Pope Pius XI on the occasion of the presentation of his credentials.[189] Consul of the legation was Dr. J. Nepustil, and, after 1931, Mr. Messani and the ecclesiastical counsel were only unofficially appointed.

Catholic life was again regulated; religious revival was appointed in education and the press; associations and orders were renewed; so also were processions and celebrations. All efforts were dedicated to filling the sorely felt need for priests. The Pope was very much interested in the progress of Catholicism in Czechoslovakia, as is evident from his letter to the Czechoslovak bishops on February 20, 1927.[190] Following the suggestion to this letter the work of Catholic Action was undertaken.

On March 4, the thousandth anniversary of Saint Wenceslaus in 1929, Pope Pius XI sent to all the archbishops and bishops of the Czechoslovak Republic, *De Millenaria Celebritate Sancti Wenceslai Ducis, Martyris.* In this solemn apostolic letter the Pope pointed out the significance of the occasion for the whole nation, and the present necessity of following this great saint.[191]

On the occasion of the Oriental Congress, Pope Pius XI sent a letter dated August 2, 1929.[192] Later he addressed another letter to Archbishop Kordač on the occasion of his resignation from the archbishopric.[193] On October 21, 1931, he sent all the bishops a reply concerning the common council;[194] finally, on June 5, 1930, he issued the apostolic Constitution concerning the papal Czechoslovak College Nepomucenum in Rome.[195] At that time, he expressed his concern for the education of Czech and Slovak priests, in whose training the college at Rome would assist.

The *modus vivendi* brought feelings of certainty into the situation and ecclesiastical conditions. Only visitations of the generals of Orders remained unsettled. Some tension was created between the nuncio Ciriaci and the Archbishop of Prague, Kordač, who consequently was forced to resign. This evoked great excitement in the press and throughout the Czechoslovak Republic. Archbishop Kordač was held in high honor by the whole nation as a social-minded, democratic philosopher, highly esteemed also by Masaryk. The period of Kordač's episcopacy had been a real blessing for Catholics. On January 29, 1934, nuncio Ciriaci was sent to Lisbon, Portugal, and the issue was closed. Monsignor Panico succeeded to the administration of the nunciature.

The year 1935 was very important for Czechoslovak Catholics. A Catholic congress was arranged in Prague; for the first time, the strength of the Catholic people was to be seen on Saint Wenceslaus Square. Catholics came from all parts of the Republic to honor Jesus Christ, with one million persons in attendance. When the Holy See appointed Cardinal John Verdier of Paris its special apostolic delegate, the political importance of the congress became evident. The result was a breakdown of the anti-Catholic policy and the Masaryk "Reformation—Counter-Reformation" antithesis was shown to be ineffective. Catholics of the whole republic were thus reincorporated into the life of their nation and state. Masaryk himself, perceiving this dynamic Catholicism in the nation, indirectly expressed the resignation of his antithesis "Reformation—Counter-Reformation" by a new aphorism, "Catholics will have as many rights as they will be able to defend." Although the aphorism was surprising, due to the prevailing majority of Catholics in Czechoslovakia, it does not express such a drastic antithesis as before. Religious antithesis in the life of a nation can have fatal consequences; it is contradictory to the national program.

On August 26, 1935, the Holy See appointed as nuncio in Prague, Archbishop F. X. Ritter, well known for his love of Czechoslovakia, which he called his second home.[196] Nuncio Ritter carried out the agreement contained in the *modus vivendi* and in virtue of a papal bull dated September 2, 1937,[197] fixed the limits of the dioceses in accordance with the frontiers of the Republic. It read as follows:

> For the good and welfare of the Church government it is advantageous to have the boundaries of dioceses so

defined that they correspond with the boundaries of civil divisions, for in this way the faithful are enabled to communicate more quickly and easily with their proper ordinaries at any time.

Since, therefore, as a result of recent events in Central Europe, a number of dioceses now embrace areas falling within different neighboring states, we, after careful consideration and thorough study, and in addition, where necessary, with the consent of those whose interests are obviously or presumably involved, now in authoritative exercise of our apostolic jurisdiction order and direct as follows:

The territory commonly called Vitoraz is to be separated from the diocese of Saint Hippolyt to which it hitherto belonged and is to be added to the diocese of Budějovice.

Similarly the territory known as Valtice is to be taken from the diocese of Vienna and incorporated into the diocese of Brno.

Those parts of the dioceses of Rožnava and Košice (Cassau) which lie south of the republic of Czechoslovakia within the civil boundaries of the kingdom of Hungary are taken from those dioceses and for the time being constituted two Apostolic Administrations directly subject to the Holy See.

The territory which is now the Apostolic Administration of Trnava in the archdiocese of Strigoniensis is separated from that archdiocese and is to remain, until other arrangements are made, an Apostolic Administration directly subject to the Holy See.

The forty-five parishes of the diocese of Satmariensis which lie within the boundaries of Czechoslovakia are taken from that diocese and are to continue in their present status of Apostolic Administrations until other arrangements are made.

As the determination of ecclesiastical boundaries to the north of the republic of Czechoslovakia is still under consideration, decisions will be announced in due time regarding two areas now in German territory: the district of Glacense, now under the jurisdiction of the archdiocese of Prague, and the district of Katscher, now part of the archdiocese of Olomouc. In proper time, too, the decisions of the Holy See will be announced regarding the other parts of these which still lie within the boundaries of the republic of Czechoslovakia and are being administered by the archdiocese of Breslaw.

As regards the status of the dioceses Cassoviensis, Rosnaviensis, and Scipusiensis, which were until now suffragan dioceses of the ecclesiastical province of Agriensis, we are taking them from that province and placing them directly under the Holy See; their bishops are herewith, too, withdrawn from the metropolitan jurisdiction of the Archbishop of Agriensis.

We are likewise separating the dioceses of Neosoliensis, Nitriensis, Mukačevensis, and Presovensis from the metropolitan church of Strigoniensis to which they were heretofore suffragan and we withdraw their bishops from the metropolitan jurisdiction of the Archbishop of Strigoniensis and place them directly under the Holy See.

As soon as feasible the Holy See will establish two new metropolitan sees in the republic of Czechoslovakia, one for the Latin rite in Slovakia and one for the oriental rite in Subcarpathia.

We also lay down that all parishes and affiliates of the Byzantine rite, now scattered through various ecclesiastical districts and existing by approval of the Sacred Congregation in charge, are each withdrawn from their respective diocese and placed under the jurisdiction of the Ruthenian diocese of Mukačevensi.

In line with these decisions, we appoint our venerable brother Xaverius Ritter, titular Archbishop of Aeginensis and Apostolic Nuncio to the Republic of Czechoslovakia, in charge of the execution of those directions which affect areas under the government of that republic. To this end we grant him all proper and necessary faculties, including the power to subdelegate in any particular matter anyone holding ecclesiastical rank. We enjoin him, furthermore, to furnish the Sacred Congregation with a documentary report on the fulfillment of these orders within six months after the promulgation of this letter.

We order and decree that this letter and its contents shall at no time be opposed, questioned or thwarted by subreption, obreption, disregard, perversion of our intention or any other misinterpretation, even though such be defensible and unprovided for. This holds even though some of those whose interests are obviously or presumably involved were not consulted or refused consent to these determinations; all are bound and it is not necessary to give each one specific and individual mention. These determinations are formulated and promulgated after thorough study and with authoritative force and are to be accepted and followed through as valid in perpetuity. They are to be carried out and realized fully and completely in every detail and are to be strictly adhered to by all involved. Should it be that contravening action is wittingly or unwittingly taken by anyone, no matter what his position, we order and rule that such action is null and void.

It is our desire that the same acceptance which would be tendered this letter if the original were received, be given two copies of this letter, even printed ones, provided they are authenticated by a notary public and stamped with the seal of someone holding ecclesiastical rank or office.

Insofar as applicable, this holds in spite of determinations made in synodal, provincial, general or universal councils, in special or general apostolic constitutions, or in decrees or decisions of preceding Roman Pontiffs.

It is permitted to no one to infringe upon or contravene this letter as ordering divisions, unifications or establishments of jurisdiction or as expressing our will and decree. Should anyone rashly attempt to do so let him know that he will incur the wrath of God Almighty and of the blessed Apostles Peter and Paul.

Issued at Castle Gandulfo, in the year of Our Lord nineteen hundred and thirty seven, on the second day of September, in the sixteenth year of our Pontificate.

EUGENE CARDINAL PACELLI
Secretary of State

FR. RAPHAEL C. CARDINAL ROSSI
S.C. Consistorial of State

JOSEPH WILPERT
Dean of the College of Prothonotaries Apostolic

ALPHONSUS CARINCI
Prothonotary Apostolic

Since 1935, President Beneš had enjoyed a very pleasant relationship with nuncio Monsignor Ritter. The proof of their friendly attitude came on June 6, 1938, when Monsignor Saverio Ritter and the auditor of the nunciature, Monsignor Josef Burzio, were presented with the Czechoslovak medal.

In the period from 1918 to 1938, Rome was very severely tried by the actions of the Czech people who were unwitting instruments of progressive factions. Uniting themselves under T. G. Masaryk's slogans—Hussites, Žiška, Táborites, Prokop Holý, Jan Amos Comenius, Peter Chelčický, liberals, Socialists, freethinkers, Freemasons, Lutherans, and Czech Brethren[198]—they strove to seize key positions in the state.

Even though they remained a minority against the Catholic majority,[199] their doctrines infiltrated the body of the Church, and under the slogan of reformation, they established a national Czechoslovak Church, which without their help could never have existed. They influenced the faithful also with their demands for progress, and weakened thereby the strength of Catholics. They were seeking to reign over a majority of Catholics. This condition furnishes an obvious analogy to the Austrian movement, *Los von Rom,* through which, notwithstanding the Hapsburg dynasty, liberals held power and attempted to lead public life away from the influence of the Church. The case of Brentano who continued to teach in the university in spite of the protests by the Viennese Archbishop is proof of this. The Czech movement "Away from Rome" was led in the same way. It was a movement of awakened national feelings; the fight itself, a real fight against religion. The aim of this fight was to weaken the Church.

Hussitism was apparent in the means of deciding with force according to personal conviction. Modern progress brought enough apostles who were actually proceeding energetically. Rome was being tried, but was not being condemned. Gradually was the real face of "progress" being revealed. Catholic truth, however, will always triumph with patience and time. So it proved in the Czech case. Meanwhile, progress triumphed; but Catholics showed themselves to be exemplary national patriots. They placed necessary sacrifices on the altar of the nation and proved to be more courageous than those who in better times had brought pressure for selfishly patriotic reasons.

"Catholics will have as many rights as belong to them" was the unanimous slogan at the first Catholic congress in Prague in 1935. This motto, acceptable for the benefit of the nation, is a right reply only to all tendencies of the revision of history under the aspect of antithesis, actions, or reactions.

Time has given Catholics the opportunity to prove their stand toward their country. This will be analyzed in the next chapter. The influence of World War II (1939-1945) brought a psychological reaction against all preoccupations and prejudices against Catholics; even Masaryk himself said, "Even Protestant 'Gram' prefers rather the Catholic Church."[200]

For the religious, national, and cultural development of a nation, the proven principle of Saint Augustine is: *Justitia, regnorum fundamentum; remota justitia, quid sunt Regna, nisi magna latrocinia?*[201] Only justice toward Catholics was needed to wipe out the disturbances and struggles from which the nation suffered. Saint Augustine's principle was repeated many times by the Czech historians Francis Palacký and Josef Šusta (†1945), who stressed it constantly. There should be engraved on the heart of every Czech, especially of Czech politicians, the need to view history with proper regard for truth and justice. Hus's slogan "Grant truth to everybody" is binding also on Hus adherents in their attitude towards Catholics. Reciprocal appreciation, without exaggeration and insults, is needed.

It was not necessary to spread propaganda to insult Catholics. But when we read, for instance, "In our time T. G. Masaryk was the truest interpreter of the spiritual meaning of Czechoslovak history,"[202] it is necessary to state that Catholics were not recognized by T. G. Masaryk, who did not even refer to the fact that Catholics were a majority of the nation, and that this majority had always given the nation Catholic characteristics. Despite this, all Catholics recognized T. G. Masaryk as a very capable politician for the Czechoslovak Republic and they also honored him as first president of the republic because of their sincere love for their country. This is a proof of the noble and loyal stand of the Czechoslovak Catholics in their sincere relations with the republic. There was no need for anyone to give them a moral lecture on love for their country.

CHAPTER SEVEN

WORLD WAR II AND RELIGION IN CZECHOSLOVAKIA

THE POLITICAL STATE OF EUROPE IN THE FIRST HALF OF THE twentieth century was influenced by Germany in a very significant manner. Germany had incited two wars by the end of the second decade of this century: the first in the years 1870 and 1871; the second from 1914 through 1918, during which the program of Pan-Germanism faced great obstacles in its progress. Humiliation after humiliation between 1914 and 1918 brought on a general depression in the spiritual life of every German. This depression in turn produced a desire for revenge against all who helped to bring about the defeat of Germany. Austria, after its former territory was split, united its aims with Pan-Germanism. Conditions for this union had been prepared by the *Los von Rom* movement.[1] It embraced anti-Semitism, and stress on national culture and religion as prerequisites for the systematic unification of all Germans. George Schoenerer, not Adolf Hitler or Julius Streicher, proclaimed the racist catchword in German policy: "By purity to unity" (*Durch Reinheit zur Einheit*).[2] Against this ideology, the Catholic Church with her principles of equality for all nations was understandably a great obstacle. Efforts to establish a just policy for all national groups in Austria was, for Pan-Germans, inconceivable and inacceptable. Josef Pekař, Czech historian, characterized this development in the following manner: "The Pan-German catchword, 'Away from Rome,' is conceived by them to mean not only, 'Away from Austria,' but at the same time it means, 'Hurra against Czechs.' "[3] The crown prince of Austria, Duke Franz Ferdinand, accentuated this theme in his speech on the occasion of his election as protector of Catholic schools when he said: "I recognized this patriotic and religious agitation for what it was, even in the days of the 'Away from Rome' movement—a movement which was at the same time an 'Away from Austria' movement—and which could not be opposed too strongly."[4]

Under such tension rose the spirit of defiance against the situation in which Germans found themselves after World War I. All the strength of German nationalism was being accentuated, eliminating all religious factors and political indifferentism. The focal point of interest now was nazism, of which Adolf Hitler, who was born and educated in Austria, became the leader.[5]

In 1921-1922, only a few years after the signing of the Treaty of Versailles,[6] the fight for revision of this treaty began. It became the central point of German policy. The tension in Europe, caused by this change in German policy, presaged no happy ending. Trouble came after the May, 1921, decision on the amount of reparations Germany was to pay. The agitation thus engendered did not end until July 2, 1932, when the reparation debt was liquidated at the conference in Lausanne. German reparations were reduced from 132 billion marks to only three billion marks. The German Chancellor, Von Papen, had declared several times during the conference that Germany would pay none of these liabilities. Understandably, the courage of the Germans was strengthened by this victory.

The problem of disarmament ended in the same way. The Locarno agreement was signed on October 16, 1925, and solemnly proclaimed in London on December 1, 1925. At Locarno it was decided to convoke a special conference at Geneva which would formulate the extent and method of general disarmament. Germany left the League of Nations on October 14, 1933, on the occasion of the handling of this problem, but even before that date she had restored her army through compulsory military conscription.[7]

Finally came the revision of territorial boundaries. It began with the agreement offered by Mussolini to four great powers under date of March 18, 1933, in Rome. This was followed by the war between Italy and Ethiopia, then by Hitler's annexation of Austria in 1938, and then by the Munich Conference of 1938 which culminated in the declaration of World War II.

A change in Europe was inevitable; it was regulated now by victorious states which had been defeated in World War I, namely, Germany, where nazism was in power, and

Italy, where fascism held forth. The fate of small nations was soon decided: Czechoslovakia became the victim of the Munich Conference, in which Great Britain and France were defeated by the dictatorial demands of Germany and Italy. Whatever had been agreed upon at Versailles was destroyed by the totalitarian regimes of both these states. Nazism began to spread throughout Europe. Thereupon began a struggle between life and death, a struggle against democracy as a product of the period after World War I, lest anything should remind the Germans of their defeat. An inevitable gap widened between Germany and democratic Czechoslovakia.

Besides this, one more factor helped to precipitate the European crisis. Since its formulation by Karl Marx,[8] communism had taken on many appearances other than the official face of the Russian sphinx. Communism, however, cannot be considered solely as an economic theory, nor as the mere antithesis of bolshevism versus individualism. It is a complete philosophy of life, integral, international in its outlook, and different from all other secular systems.[9] Communism involves both theory and practice. It claims to be the state as well as the church. It teaches a doctrine which controls man's body and soul, and in this respect it is really totalitarian. Communism is a combination of Hegel's (1770-1831) dialectical idealism[10] and Feuerbach's materialism; it appeared as a composite known as dialectical materialism which, through the influence of the French sociologist Proudhon,[11] was applied to economic life. It is also called economic determinism, and, with reference to its history, historical materialism. Against the Christian concept of a human having an immortal soul, this ideology bases itself on Feuerbach's doctrine, "He is human, so far as he is eating." Hegel's theory proclaims that all that is legislated by the state is just and correct. Thus the state is entitled to whatever it wants. Marx thus concluded that "religion is the opium of the people." Marx is not the original author of this motto; it was used and proclaimed for the first time by Charles Kingsley (1819-1875).[12]

By these philosophical theories, diametrically different from the Christian attitude, the human being is deprived of soul, nation, and church, and serves only for material production. Conflict between this theory and Christianity called for revolutionary methods. Not strong enough to cope with these, socialism adopted other "evolutionary" methods. These consisted of education, propaganda, establishment of workers' organizations, formulation of social programs, and increase of the political and cultural pressure against existing conditions.

Accordingly, the end of the nineteenth and the beginning of the twentieth century were witnesses of increasing socialism, formulated under the programs and names of various political parties, especially under the names of social democracy and national socialism. These were to furnish liaison with the nation. Finally there were Christian Socialist parties, which should have been a bridge toward the Church. A moral problem of special nature was thus becoming a political question, and the moral character of social development was thus being changed into a political problem concerning the power of the state. This was understood very well by T. G. Masaryk when he said, "I am not a social democrat; since the early beginnings of my public activities I had taken it as my duty to overarch the abyss between social democracy and other strata of the nation and to work in a positive way toward social reform."[13]

Marxism was repudiated by Masaryk in a positive way, for metaphysical reasons.[14] "If social democracy takes Marx as a prominent authority, I can conceive that, but I am not delighted by that."[15] This stand T. G. Masaryk took on principle.

The mutual exclusiveness of Marxism and Christianity was obvious. The Church, preserving for herself the religious and spiritual sphere, took the social problem as a moral stigma to Christian perfection and solved it by improvement of moral culture of employees and employers, accentuating the need for social justice. Christian democratic parties became the means for carrying out this solution.

Socialism solves social problems in a political manner. In the light of such tactics, it is easy to understand why Marxism was repudiated by the Church,[16] and how socialistic parties can change their procedures according to the situation, time and support of communism, establishing so-called "socialist blocs," sometimes even amalgamating with Communists. Social democracy was always in the vanguard of this fight.

National socialism, whatever country it dominated, established socialism in that country only. This idea, however, began to spread throughout all Europe. In Czechoslovakia, there was a rapid development, because after preparation of the situation by socialism, communism was able to rally the whole country—this too against the will of Catholics and conservatives. In this development lies the tragedy of the matter.

In Germany and Austria, things were much worse, because the economic depression was misused by communism. In both these countries, communism met Pan-German egoism and strong reaction was thus evoked in the form of nazism.[17] Hitler, psychologically manipulating the fear and chaos which existed in Germany, seized power in the state, repulsed efforts to plan revolutions by the same tactics, and used force and fraud to attain the aims of Pan-Germanism. Horror spread in and around Germany. Czechoslovakia, being the closest neighbor, was drinking the chalice of plagues to the last drop: in the whole period from 1938 to 1945 she continued in this way under the Communists who came after the Nazis. It is almost fatally true that Czechoslovakia has suffered under every "ism."

Indications of the danger to Czechoslovakia were already apparent in 1938. The majority of the population in some parts of the provinces of Bohemia and Moravia was German. Despite the fact that Germans in Czechoslovakia were participating in all democratic rights granted to other citizens,[18] they embraced Pan-Germanism. Hitler had inspired them. In his speech of February 20, 1938, he stated: "Over ten million Germans are living in two states neighboring on Germany. It is our duty to protect these Germans and to secure for them their personal, political and ideological freedom."[19]

The Germans in Czechoslovakia took this as a signal. Events moved quickly forward. On March 13, 1938, the annexation of Austria was accomplished.[20] The formulation of Henlein's demands, asking self-rule for the Sudeten, was proclaimed on April 24;[21] mobilization of part of the Czechoslovak Army was effected on May 21; negotiations between the Henlein party and the Czechoslovak government began on May 17; on May 28, Adolf Hitler, in a meeting with his advisers, gave instructions for attacking Czechoslovakia.[22] On

July 26, Mr. Chamberlain announced to the House of Commons that the mission of Lord Runciman in Prague was to assist in the negotiations; on July 12, French Premier Daladier declared sacred and unshakable the loyalty of France toward Czechoslovakia; on August 3, Von Ribbentrop announced to the Italian ambassador that Germany would undertake anything against Czechoslovakia; on September 4, the Czechoslovak government announced to the Sudeten German party its fourth and last proposal, which was meeting its demands for the most part, so that Mr. Runciman himself and even the British government declared[23] that the Germans, incited by Berlin, had rejected any possibility for agreement and really were refusing to accept any proposal. Finally, on October 12, Hitler delivered a very strong speech in Nuremberg,[24] and the crisis came.[25]

On September 15, Prime Minister Chamberlain prepared to call on Hitler in Berchtesgaden, to find out the stand of the Germans. On September 18, statesmen of France and Great Britain arranged a meeting, sending a note from it to President Beneš, recommending the detachment of districts in Sudeten, if such districts had a majority of Germans in the population. The Czechoslovak government did not accept these proposals, and suggested direct negotiation between Czechoslovakia and Germany, according to the arbitrary agreement of 1925. On September 21, the governments of France and Great Britain threatened that in case of military conflict, they would deny any help to Czechoslovakia. Thus forced and menaced, the Czechoslovak government accepted these ultimate demands.

On September 22, in Prague, the government of Dr. Hodža resigned and the new government of General Jan Syrový was formed. That same day, Prime Minister Chamberlain was on his way to Hitler in Godesberg by plane, having already received the reply of the Czechoslovak government. But Hitler made new demands. On September 23, France and Great Britain advised Czechoslovakia to be prepared for self-defense in case of necessity, and the general mobilization of the Czechoslovak Army was proclaimed. On September 24, Chamberlain announced Hitler's new demands to the Czechoslovak government, and Czechoslovakia refused to accept them. That same day Hitler delivered a speech, declaring that Germans would never turn back from their plan to liberate Germans in the Sudeten, and his demands grew in another speech, on September 26, in which he attacked President Beneš.[26]

On September 29, the meeting at Munich was arranged; there, Hitler, Mussolini, Chamberlain, and Daladier decided the fate of Czechoslovakia, without consulting her. On September 30, the result was made known to the Czechoslovak minister, with the remark that the consent of Czechoslovakia was not needed to make this act valid.[27] Czechoslovakia was forced to hand over four zones by October 7, and a plebiscite was to decide the fate of other territories. Thus it came about that Germany got not only territories with a high percentage of German people, but it even gained whole districts with exclusively Czech population.[28] On October 5, President Beneš resigned, and left for London on October 22, after pressure from the Germans, and under threat.[29] Dr. Emil Hácha was elected President;[30] before that, he had been president of the Supreme Court. The new President, Hácha, appointed the governing body headed by the former chairman of the Agrarian party, Rudolf Beran.

Meanwhile, changes were taking place in the internal life of the Czechoslovak Republic. On October 6 in Žilina, all parties of Slovakia demanded self-rule for Slovakia, and on October 7, the autonomous government for Slovakia, headed by Monsignor Josef Tiso, was proclaimed.[31] The Carpatho-Ruthenians were forced to proclaim their self-rule too, with the government headed by Monsignor A. Vološín. Thus did Czechoslovakia change into a federative state which had as a common denominator only foreign policy, an army, and the administration of state debts.[32]

The rest of the territory of the Republic had a Polish minority. In consequence of Poland's note of September 30, 1938, Czechoslovakia was forced to turn over its districts: Těšín, Bohumín, Fryštát, Jablunkov, as well as the territory around Čadca and Javorina. Thus 120,000 Czechs went over into Poland.

From the time of the Munich conference, Czechs and Slovaks ceased to be masters over their homes. They began to exist by the grace of the Germans who changed the Czechoslovak Republic into the Protectorate of Bohemia and Moravia,[33] March 16, 1939. The day before, under dramatic conditions, President Dr. Hácha was forced to turn over those provinces to the protection of Adolf Hitler. Even before Hácha could act, Germans began to occupy those provinces of Czechoslovakia. Slovaks proclaimed an independent state of Slovakia[34] when Dr. Tiso was accepted by Adolf Hitler.[35] By this chain of events were Pan-Germanic policies carried out against Czechoslovakia, following the principle *divide and conquer*.

For convinced democrats like the Czechs, their establishment as a Protectorate of Bohemia and Moravia[36] was a great humiliation. Depression caused by it, as well as the reaction to the Germans, was a necessary consequence of this state of affairs and gave rise to a very strong underground movement. Czech army officers, soldiers, and especially military pilots began to escape through the Balkans to join the Allies and fight for democracy. During all of World War II, Czech pilots especially, as members of the Royal Air Force of Great Britain, made a glorious reputation in the fatal air battle over London in the fall of 1940. Meanwhile, the Germans were unable to maintain order in this Protectorate because of the hatred of the people. They reigned by terror, force, fear, arrests of hundreds of thousands, sentences to concentration camps, and executions. Resistance began to increase. Relations between the Czechs and the Germans were marked by collaboration of some and resistance by the rest, the stand being decided by the drastic circumstances of each individual case.

The Germans were aware of the situation. Dr. Goebbels himself said, "The Germans know how to be terrible enemies, but they also know how to be very good friends. We know how to stretch out our hand to a friend and to collaborate with him in true loyalty. But we also know how to destroy our enemies."[37] The government of the Protectorate was helpless and powerless, serving only as a mediator between the German Reichsprotector and the Czech population. The Reichsprotector was the real sovereign in the Protectorate, and reigned as Hitler's plenipotentiary. The Gestapo was used as a police force for the protection of German interests only. State Secretary K. H. Frank terrorized the whole Protectorate.

In a short time, the truth of Bismarck's dictum was proven: "Whoever is the ruler over Bohemia is also ruler of

Europe."[38] Germans looked upon the occupation of Bohemia as a great triumph. On the occasion of a meeting between Goering, Mussolini, and Ciano, on April 15, 1939, Goering said: "The heavy armament of Czechoslovakia shows, in any case, how dangerous it could have been, even after Munich, in the event of a serious conflict."[39] Germans occupied the Memel territory on April 23, 1939, and in September of the same year, Poland. France and Great Britain declared war on Germany in the first days of September, 1939, as a reply to the invasion of Poland. In the spring of 1940, Germans occupied Belgium, Luxemburg, and Holland, and in May and June, 1940, they defeated France, occupying the greater part of it.[40] The rest of France had as Prime Minister of the Vichy government, Henri Pétain.

Odd were the tactics of Russia, despite all her agreements with, and debts to, Czechoslovakia. Russia not only refused to help according to its treaty with Czechoslovakia, but on August 23, 1939, signed a nonaggression pact with Germany,[41] through the instigation of Russia herself.[42] "This violent and unnatural reversal of Russian policy was a transmogrification of which only totalitarian states are capable,"[43] remarked Churchill. A similar instance of Russia's astonishing behavior came in her relation toward Poland. When Poland was being invaded by Nazis, Russia invaded there too, fighting against the Poles. But in the Warsaw rebellion, the Russians halted their drive, to let the Polish patriots alone fight against the Germans. Thus Russia proved how she really viewed the brotherhood of Slavic nations. These two events are satisfactory proof that Communist Russia follows her own aims exclusively, regardless of the cost to others. Polish distrust of Russia thus became a historic reality and this state of affairs complicated the whole European situation. In the spring of 1941, Germans invaded Yugoslavia and Greece, and feeling that they were strong enough, even attacked Russia on June 22, 1941, thrusting deep into Soviet territory. Reversing Russia's former position, Stalin declared the conflict a "holy war" against the Germans.

This was the state of affairs from 1939 through 1945. Ostensibly the fight was between communism and nazism, but democracy was falling, their victim. In the middle of the war, the two totalitarian regimes attacked each other, but eventually, democracy, using the help of Russia, defeated nazism. After the war, democracy faced communism, and the struggle between them for supremacy was anxiously awaited.

The Catholic Church correctly prognosticated the development of all spiritual doctrines connected with the new political theories, and even before the war, the Pope proclaimed her stand. He observed that under the influence of Austrian and German Protestants, the Pan-Germanic movement aspired to deify all that was of German origin and nature, proclaiming: "One nation, one state, one church."[44] The state was usurping sovereign control over churches and their doctrines;[45] the principles of nazism[46] and the spirit of anti-Semitism were menacing even the revealed truths of Holy Scripture; the spirit of exaggerated nationalism was ruining the family and its influence over the education of children.[47] The Pope resorted to radical measures, so that German Catholics would survive the horrible nazism which was of a completely anti-Christian nature. Nazism was dogmatic, and its aim was to eliminate all that was non-German. Purity of blood, race, and ideas were inherent parts of Nietzsche's *Uebermensch*[48] and Bismarck's *Herrenvolk* and people's *Deutschland ueber alles.*

Adolf Hitler himself was regarded as a prophet of Pan-Germanism, a revengeful and implacable executor of the will of the Pan-German gods. Having been accepted as the redeemer of the German nation, he completely fascinated the crowds. The majority of the nation supported him. Despite all this, the Catholic Church preserved her stand on principle. On November 10, 1932, she settled her *"Inter sanctam sedem et badensem rem publicam solemnis conventio,"*[49] and on July 10, 1933, the *"Inter sanctam sedem et germanicam rem publicam solemnis conventio,"* thirty-four articles of which touched on the extent of Church activities in Germany, and the impossibility of settlement.[50] Strict formulation of the demands granted to the Church is proof of the pressure which was being exerted during the negotiations between Church and state. Franz von Papen and Eugenio Pacelli signed this agreement, thus showing their diplomatic abilities. As this agreement was being attacked by many groups of Nazis,[51] and because the cultural fight of 1936 had been renewed,[52] Pope Pius XI addressed his encyclical *Mit Brennender Sorge* to all bishops and to the German people,[53] showing his determined stand against nazism. This encyclical of March 14, 1937, evoked the interest of official and cultural circles, and it became basic in formulating the relations of the whole world toward nazism and German neopaganism. (His encyclical *Abbiamo Bisogno,* on June 29, 1931,[54] had been directed against Italian fascism. In this he applied for a reinforcement of Catholic action.) About the same time, March 19, 1937, the Pope issued *Divini Redemptoris,*[55] in which he exposed the whole substance of materialistic communism in doctrine, and proposed the resolution of social questions by means of encyclicals.[56] This stand against communism was stressed by the Pope in another encyclical, *Firmissimam Constantiam,* on March 28, 1937, addressed to all ordinaries in Mexico,[57] as a reflection on the former persecution of the Church, which was begun on impulses of the Communists and Freemasons. Thereby, the stand of all Catholics against all forms of totalitarian regimes became absolutely clear. The position of Catholics under all these regimes was really precarious because, until 1941, all these totalitarian ideas—nazism, communism, and fascism—flourished in their states and conquered areas.

The general stand of the Church against all totalitarian ideas was very much appreciated in Czechoslovakia, because there one could see its effect in reinforcing national resistance against nazism. The result was a changed reaction of the Czechs toward the Church which had hitherto been attacked by all progressive factions. Czech archbishops and bishops were determined patriots, standing boldly on their principles. The Archbishop of Prague, Karel Kašpar, created a Cardinal by Pius XI on December 16, 1935,[58] courageously solved the problem between Czech and German occupants after March 15, 1939, in the Protectorate of Bohemia and Moravia: "The credit must also be given to the Catholic Church itself and to the Vatican, both of which from the very beginning took an extremely loyal attitude toward the Czechoslovak Republic, as well as to the Catholics and clergy of the country itself who, headed by Monsignor Šrámek, adopted a policy of class collaboration, with all the other elements of the new State."[59] Those who had attacked the Church before were brought to give such evidence as this:

> In later years, the more the Nazi danger increased, the

more the Catholic Church rallied to the side of threatened Czechoslovakia.[60] The Catholic Church, by its Christian and human spirit, represents one of the greatest forces that have risen against the Nazi doctrine and in consequence Catholicism in Czechoslovakia became doubly the enemy of Hitlerism. National reasons were added to human and religious ones. Hitler, therefore, had a double motive to rage from the very beginning against the representatives of the Catholic world in Czechoslovakia.[61]

The Czechoslovak people opened their eyes, and the mask of "progress" began to be exposed for what is was. While the many adherents of "progress," who proclaimed themselves patriots, bowed their backs before the new German authorities, Catholic priests with their bishops proved to be exceedingly patriotic and faithful, remaining in this stand through all World War II. Nor were collaborators to be found among Czech and Moravian Catholic priests. "Immediately after the German invasion, the churches were filled with believers who came to seek there the spiritual consolations which were the only ones that remained to them."[62] The people felt that Catholic priests were trustworthy protectors of national affairs, despite all former insidious attacks by the progressives of the first Czechoslovak Republic.

Impressive historically is the fact that Cardinal Kašpar never called on the Reichsprotector, although representatives of all the non-Catholic churches visited him. When reproached for this by German officials, he replied: "An ecclesiastical Duke, Cardinal of the Church, accepts visits of foreigners in his palace." While proceeding cautiously, he nevertheless gave no approval to German occupants. The differences between the people and the priests was disappearing and the Catholic priest was being included, *via facti,* among the patriots.

The real expression of this change of heart was given by the resistance movement abroad, when Monsignor Jan Šrámek became Prime Minister of the government in exile in London.[63] This evoked a strong response in the subjugated country. Šrámek remained in this position until 1945. The fact that so many priests, nuns, and Catholic laymen had become victims of the general persecution while the Protectorate of Bohemia and Moravia existed inspired general confidence in their spiritual leaders. Fulfilling their national and pastoral duties, Catholic priests regained the nation for the Church; the number of apostasies diminished. In lieu of the former catchword, "Away from Rome," the cry was actually, "Nearer to Rome." The change came about spontaneously, and was the product of experience, of persecution, and of national humiliation. The heroic stand of the Pope, the hierarchy, priests and the faithful exerted this change in the mind of all toward the Church, a very important indication of what was to come. The Church, along with her leader in the Vatican, was being harmonized with national development, and the existence of a national Czechoslovak Church lost its *raison d'être,* especially when the Czechoslovak Church changed its political constellation, and its name, at the suggestion of the Germans, became the Czecho-Moravian Church.[64]

Furthermore, the stability of the Catholic Church emphasized the changeability of other sects. All the traditions of Saint Wenceslaus, Saint Adalbert, Saint John Nepomucene, Saints Cyril and Methodius, of Sušil, Stojan, of *devotio moderna,* came to be evaluated as a source of national hope and fundamental strength. Places of pilgrimage were visited even by those who formerly despised them or who destroyed Catholic monuments. The people unified their hopes in "knights of the mountain Blaník, under the flag of Saint Wenceslaus," and at the nation's worst time there could be heard in homes, in churches, and in societies, the song, "Saint Wenceslaus, Save Us and Our Children."[65] This song expressed the same courage as the Hussites' "Who Are Fighters for God?"[66]

One more characteristic became evident: Czech Catholics did not recriminate for the past in which they suffered, but they began to work in the underground movement, and they cooperated with every one who was willing to help the subjugated nation, even with those who had despised them. This event is historically important, and it was proof that the nation could rely upon Catholics.

The whole nation was in resistance—both those at home and those in exile. Persecution struck all states, churches, professions, and was becoming general in the Protectorate. Every anti-German move was punished brutally. Economic and cultural motives made persecution especially severe. The underground movement had many victims. Germans were handling Czechs with an iron hand. For listening to London broadcasts, many lost their lives. On every radio set there was a slip of paper with the printed official inscription: "Listening to broadcasting from abroad is punishable by death." Nevertheless, almost all Czechs and Slovaks listened. But because of the tense situation, everyone began to distrust everybody else. People grew frightened. Every Czech and Moravian had two faces: with one he thought, and with the other he acted. But this turned out to be a psychological factor in this uncertainty and chaos, influencing people to put unlimited trust in their Catholic priests.

In the Protectorate, the Germans' first attack on the people was directed against the students. University students of Prague experienced their brutal baptism by German hate on November 17, 1939. This was the Nazis' reply to the demonstration for the celebration of the anniversary of October 28, 1939.[67] Students all over the world paid homage to the courageous resoluteness of students in Prague, by proclaiming November 17 as International Student Day. All Czech universities were closed and many students from colleges, and demonstrators, were deported to concentration camps, especially to Camp Oranienburg. When the sources of culture and education were closed, the worst day in Czechoslovakia's cultural life had dawned. The Nazis also closed theological faculties, thereby endangering the education of new priests.

Even worse, the Germans attempted to weaken the influence of all denominations, especially that of the Catholic Church. They realized early the psychological inclination of the people to their religion, and therefore they devised a plan: the general headquarters of the churches from time to time received from the Czech Ministry of Education instructions which had their origin in the Reichsprotector's office in Prague, ordering the clergy to demonstrate their loyalty to the reigning overlord. The central church boards were asked to publish these orders as if on their own initiative. The local priest was asked to announce it from the pulpit of his church to his flock. In this address there was included the thanksgiving to Fuehrer Hitler for protection, and an appeal to pray for the victory of the German Army and for support of collections for the benefit of the German Red Cross. Reaction was contrary to German intentions. Priests avoided reading these notes or they did not respect them at all. People were bitter about this and the Germans found that things were not going according to their plan.

Shrines such as Stará Boleslav, Hostýn, Velehrad, Svatá Hora, Vavřineček, Klokoty, Loreta, and others, became centers for all Czechs and Moravians who went there to manifest their loyalty to their faith and nation. Velehrad was visited by hundreds of thousands. Hostýn, in the days of the celebrations of the Catholic organization Orel, received many tens of thousands; Stará Boleslav and Holy Mountain drew pilgrims nearly every Sunday. Zealous preachers preached at these places; priests and people left with their hopes enforced and satisfied. After mass demonstrations of Orels in Hostýn in August, 1939, the Nazis forbade all pilgrimages. On this occasion, all organizers and superiors of the holy places were arrested. All functionaries of the Orel association, after the aforementioned pilgrimage, were arrested and deported to concentration camps. Among the first deported and executed was the chairman of the Orel association, Dr. Jílek. This order forbidding any pilgrimage inspired among the people a wave of resistance and instead of organized pilgrimages, people went individually without processions, on Sundays. Others, who usually spent their weekends walking in the forests, very often visited these places of pilgrimage and the churches. On holydays, churches and chapels were decorated in a solemn manner, and despite the orders of the German authorities, attendance at celebrations was consistently high.

The publication of Catholic magazines and weekly and daily newspapers stopped as early as 1939, allegedly because of lack of paper. Editors of these periodicals were arrested. By this measure, the main artery of Catholic life was struck. *Neděle* in Bohemia and *Rozsevač* in Moravia printed many copies, and they were effective helpers in pastoral activities of the Church. The organ of Catholic youth, *Dorost,* was also forbidden to be published. Pamphlets edited in the Retreat House at Hlučín and later during the occupation in Frýdek under the editorship of Father Schikora, a Redemptorist, did not escape the Germans' attention and were prohibited. Different books edited at a Dominican center, and the periodical *Philosophical Review,* with the Reverend Methodius Habáň as chief editor-philosopher, were put to an end under the pressure of the Nazis. The religious review, *Na Hlubinu,* under the leadership of the capable theologians, Dr. Sylvester Braito and Dr. Reginald Dacik, resisted persecution for a long time. Vyšehrad, the Catholic publishing firm in Prague, put out a cultural review called *Řád* (Order) which included the writings of many Catholic authors. In 1942 the Catholic Club in Prague edited, among others, a historical novel by Karel Schulz entitled *Kámen a bolest* (Stone and Plague), which evoked controversy with the Dominicans. Despite severe censorship by the authorities during the war, the Dominican Fathers from Olomouc arranged for "Religious Courses of Higher Grade" in Olomouc, Brno, Prague, Zlín, and Mladá Boleslav. It was very difficult to get government authorities to approve of every lecture. After periodicals were forbidden to be edited, the interest in preaching in the churches grew, and *tridua* (three-day missions) and other devotions became very popular.

At the beginning of September, 1940, nearly all Catholic organizations in the Protectorate were disbanded. Among them were included the Apostolate of Saint Cyril and Saint Methodius, which was very effective in the struggle for Unionism and the Stojan movement. All Legions of Blessed Virgin Mary for laymen and clergy and the Association of Catholic Youth with its center in Prague (as was the Legions'), were disbanded. On September 23, 1942, the Orel gymnastic association of Catholic men, women, and youth was also disbanded. All properties of this last-mentioned association were confiscated by order of the Reichsprotector. At the time of its disbanding, the Orel had more than 80,000 members. The reason for the disbanding was its anti-Nazi activities. The same fate also struck the Catholic Orel in the Czech colony of Vienna.[68] On this occasion, many priests, spiritual advisers of the Orel association, and leading functionaries were arrested. After this purge, members of Orel held their meetings in rectories and dedicated their efforts to Catholic action.

A further act of persecution by the Nazis intended to weaken the position of the Catholic Church, was the illegal confiscation and seizure of Church land. For example, all land properties of the Brno bishopric were seized for the purposes of the German Empire.[69] The Benedictine monastery in Rajhrad, and the Augustinian monastery in Brno were put under German administration. In other monasteries, some German administrators were appointed. The Savings Institute of Saints Cyril and Methodius in Brno and the Czechoslovak Catholic Bank in Prague also fell victims to these German measures. Catholics lost their economic independence because their activities were placed under German control.

The strongest attack against the Church was the stopping of activities of the diocesan consistories, cathedral chapters, and all prominent ecclesiastical offices. Liquidation of these organs was carried out by arrests of the highest officials, made under various pretensions. Czech canons, provosts, and secretaries were in concentration camps in Germany, while Germans were appointed to their offices. In some instances, these offices remained vacant during World War II. The disaster culminated in the deaths of Karel Cardinal Kašpar and Bishop Josef Kupka (1941) in Brno, and their sees remained vacant until the end of the war. Monsignor Stašek of the chapter of Vyšehrad was arrested in February, 1940, because of a sermon he preached at Saint Vavřineček near Domažlice. He was deported to Dachau, and Monsignor Tenora, eighty-year-old dean of the cathedral chapter in Brno, was imprisoned in Špilberg. Also arrested were Monsignor Kratochvíl, capitular vicar of Brno; Monsignor Martinů, vicar-general of Olomouc; Canon Světlík; Monsignor Jemelka, manager of the Apostolate of Saint Cyril and Saint Methodius; Monsignor Stanislav Zela, secretary to the Archbishop of Olomouc; theologian Father Cinek; Monsignor John Lochman, provost of Saint Maurice Rectory in Olomouc; Canon Stanovský and Canon Dohalský from the Prague chapter; Canons Černý and Finda from the chapter in Hradec Králové. Besides, all Catholic political leaders were arrested. Father Karel Fanfrdla from Brno and the famous orator, Monsignor Tylínek, were among them. Many priests were jailed. In all, the Nazis arrested 371 Czech and Moravian priests, of whom seventy-three died in jail.[70] Of priests from various dioceses, 260 were sent to concentration camps in Dachau, Buchenwald, Terezín, and elsewhere. Eight priests were executed; fifty-eight died in concentration camps; seven died as a result of torture; and two died of unknown causes. Such statistics serve to outline the story of how severely the Catholic Church was persecuted by nazism. Other priests were put under control and investigated by the Gestapo. Some scores of priests were deported to forced-labor camps in Germany. Taking into account the shortage of priests even before World War II, the time of German occupation spelled disaster for the Catholic hierarchy in Bohemia and Moravia.

The heroic character and behavior of Catholic priests won people back to the Catholic Church, just as the heroic bearing of priests in concentration camps influenced their fellow-prisoners favorably. The position of the clergy was really difficult, but they surmounted all obstacles in a dignified manner. They refused to be frightened by torture and humiliation, sacrifice and threat. "The Bohemian and Moravian clergy did not fail," was the general consensus among all groups in the nation.

In line with the same program, the Nazis persecuted some other denominations. The Church of the Czech Brethren and the Bohemian Orthodox Church were struck at the time of the assassination of Reichsprotector Heydrich (May 27, 1942) because parachutists were found in the church of Saint Charles Borromeus.[71] The time of Reichsprotector Reinhard Heydrich (from September, 1941, until May 27, 1942) and of his successor, Kurt Daluege (May, 1942, until 1945) was the period of the worst terror, which increased as the Germans were pressed back by the Americans and Russians. In this period the Sokol Gymnastic Association was liquidated (October 12, 1941), and among those imprisoned or executed were many hundreds of high-school teachers, professors, and former army officers. The Prime Minister of the Protectorate government, General Eliáš, was executed in June, 1942. On June 10 of that year, all the inhabitants of the village of Lidice were massacred.[72] Many intellectuals were imprisoned. In 1942, in the period from May 28 to July 3 alone, 1,228 persons were tried and executed.[73] They were people from all professions and strata. The Germans were carrying out their revenge for Heydrich in a Teutonic manner. Because of his death, the Czech nation lost more than 10,000 lives. This was proof that the Nazis viewed all events as very dangerous for them. "Seventy thousand people were tortured in concentration camps and prisons; those who refused to divulge military and industrial secrets were killed by bestial methods."[74]

But the passive resistance of all Czech intellectuals was broad in its extent. The Nazis tried to seize theaters, centers of culture, education, and schools. The Czech people evaded all these snares by remaining at home. Farmers were struck in a brutal way by being expelled from all villages in the districts of Vyškov, Plumlov, and Blansko, a total of forty-two villages. North of Brno in Moravia and in Bohemia, they were expelled from twenty-nine villages between Pardubice and Žiželice, and from thirty-eight villages between Milovice and Nové Benatky. A total of 119 villages and towns were completely depopulated before September 1, 1941.[75] Others, such as Mirošov, Skořice, Mýto, Vichy, Přikonice, and Kolvin, followed.[76] Resistance of the farmers was increasing as they were forced to deliver all the prescribed amounts of their products to the Nazis, regardless of changing conditions.

In general, the workers in the beginning showed no resistance because the majority of them were working in ammunitions jobs, and were paid very well. Furthermore, from 1939 until 1942, they had no true concept of the alliance between Germany and Russia. The first sabotages in factories were discovered as the Nazis retreated from Russia in 1943. Four hundred thousand working people of all groups were sent to forced-labor camps in Germany.

To complete the picture of atrocities in the Protectorate of Bohemia and Moravia, the effect of the Nazi invasion on the Jews must be mentioned. Against the will of the government of General Eliáš, the so-called Nuremburg Laws were issued by Reichsprotector Von Neurath. The so-called "Magna Carta" of March 16 and the decree of June 21, 1939,[77] followed. Persecution of Jews was carried out not only for racial reasons, but for cultural, political, and economic reasons as well. The Nazis confiscated properties of Jews to support Germanization. Confiscation, arrests, deportations, and massacres of Jews were characteristic of the Nazi method. They were deported to Terezín in Czechoslovakia and Lublin in Poland, where Hitler set up a center for Jews. The Gestapo styled the Jews "enemies of humanity." Before the outbreak of the war, about 10,000 Jews succeeded in emigrating from the Protectorate of Bohemia and Moravia, so that at the beginning of the war the number remaining amounted to about 90,000.[78]

Obviously, there were excellent reasons for the Czech resistance against the Nazis and against the situation in the Protectorate from 1939 to 1945. Clashes, tension between Czechs and the occupying forces, caused trouble for the Germans from the cultural, military, and political point of view. This was the reason why the German Nazis were so cruel when detecting any resistance. They realized the importance of Bohemia and Moravia to their aims, and they wished to retain control under all conditions. They did not understand the mentality of the Czech and Moravian peoples, who had been humiliated and betrayed by Munich; but even in this condition, the Germans were unable to win them over. The Teutonic spirit was struck by blindness, and therefore they treated the population as slaves. This was the reason for the Nazi failure in the Protectorate of Bohemia and Moravia. A nation thus unified in resistance for its national heritage would work toward what it viewed as the reason for its existence and history.

In this nationalistic enthusiasm, people leagued themselves with the Church and the Catholic priests, suffering under the same force, fighting the same fight, expecting their liberation and peace. Progressivism was forced to retreat in its fight against the clergy and to work in unity for the liberation of the country.

In this fight there appeared a new factor, representing new strength, menacing all mankind: this was Communist Russia. The change came about in the 1941-1943 period, when it was necessary to use force to attain victory over nazism. It was a difficult choice. Considering the situation politically, one saw in Russia the disturbing element of communism, but the political combination was made desirable by the common enemy, Nazi Germany. This was the immediate reason for the Western Allies' decision to go into league with

Russia. For the democratic and Christian world it was anomalous, but the world needed a helper, and Russia was at hand. Shrewd Stalin stressed Russian nationalism, delivered speeches about democracy, dismissed the Comintern, and grew excited about the attack against Holy Russia and about the vandalistic Prussians, changing his former course which had been strictly anti-religious.[79] Thus he bridged the gap between East and West, being pressed by the quick German drive into Russia toward Moscow and Leningrad. Socialist aides of all nations in the West influenced and gave advice with the same intention. At once, all Communist atrocities, its revolutionary and demoniacal underground activity, its brutality and despotism were seemingly forgotten. Contact between West and East was established.

Inter arma silent musae is true also of political character. This change in Russian policy became apparent in its effect on the foreign policy of the United States and Great Britain, as well as on the Czechoslovak resistance movement at home and abroad. However, Czechoslovak Communists, at home and in exile, in the period of Russian neutrality toward Germany (from August 23, 1939 until June 22, 1941) were disorganized as they tried to uphold both patriotic and their own ideas. A group of Czechoslovak Communist exiles in Moscow including Klement Gottvald, Zdeněk Nejedlý, former ambassador Fierlinger, Šverma, and others cooperated with the group of Communist exiles in England, Václav Nosek, Dr. Vlád. Clementis, and others. They evoked discord, and, against official political representation, edited the pamphlet, *Guilty Men of Czechoslovakia*.[80] Of the same character were some events in the resistance movement in the country. The Communists separated themselves from other resisting factions,[81] and there were even instances of indiscretion and denouncements made by Communists. They did not perceive the national importance of the resistance. When Russia entered the war against Germany, Communists first began to take part in the resistance, but with the intention of serving their own interests. By every available means, they misused their influence and pressure.

In England, which was the sole powerful belligerent country at that time, Chamberlain's government determinedly changed its course when Winston Churchill took over the reins.[82] He announced in his speech of June 22, 1941, which he addressed to the world,[83] that Great Britain and the Soviet Union had become allies to defeat Hitler, Germany, and nazism. On July 13, 1941, the British-Soviet agreement was signed. This British-Soviet alliance included also the governments-in-exile of Czechoslovakia, Poland, Holland, Yugoslavia, and Greece.

The United States helped in this pact by securing ammunition, and President Franklin D. Roosevelt approved Churchill's policy by signing the Atlantic Charter.[84] There were also cultural and economic relations between the United States and the Soviet Union,[85] and Roosevelt himself was inclined toward them.[86] The United States entered World War II after the Japanese attack on Pearl Harbor on December 7, 1941. Germany and Italy, in their capacity as allies of Japan, proclaimed war on December 11, 1941, against the United States. Almost the entire world was involved in World War II. Russia, still undeclared, benefited from all supplies and military help from the West; the United States, fully appreciating the need for world cooperation, helped decisively.[87]

The development of a Czech policy by the government-in-exile in London, led by President Beneš and by Prime Minister Jan Šrámek, was influenced by the President's leanings, and by Socialists, Communists, and world policy. The trend was toward the Russian sphere, although this was contrary to the will of the conservatives, who did not trust Communists on principle. President Beneš had practiced this pro-Russian policy even before the war, when his political influence in Czechoslovakia was quite extensive. He continued to defend this policy in exile, and carried the point by the strength of his authority. Churchill said of this:

> The relations of Soviet Russia with Czechoslovakia as a state, and personally with President Beneš, were those of intimate and solid friendship. The roots of this lay in a certain racial affinity, and also in comparatively recent events which require a brief digression. When President Beneš visited me at Marrakesch in January, 1944, he told me this story: In 1935, he had received an offer from Hitler to respect in all circumstances the integrity of Czechoslovakia in return for a guarantee that she would remain neutral in the event of a Franco-German war. When Beneš

pointed to his treaty obliging him to act with France in such a case, the German ambassador replied that there was no need to denounce the treaty. It would be sufficient to break it, if and when the time came, by simply failing to mobilize or march. The small Republic was not in a position to indulge in indignation at such a suggestion. Their fear of Germany was already very grave, more especially as the question of the Sudeten Germans might at any time be raised and fomented by Germany, to their extreme embarrassment and growing peril. They therefore let the matter drop without comment or commitment, and it did not stir for more than a year. In the autumn of 1936, a message from a high military source in Germany was conveyed to President Beneš to the effect that if he wanted to take advantage of the Fuehrer's offer, he had better be quick, because events would shortly take place in Russia rendering insignificant any help he could give to Germany.

While Beneš was pondering over this disturbing hint, he became aware that communications were passing through the Soviet Embassy in Prague between important personages in Russia and the German government. This was a part of the so-called military and Old Guard Communist conspiracy to overthrow Stalin and introduce a new regime based on a pro-German policy. President Beneš lost no time in communicating all he could find out to Stalin. Thereafter there followed the merciless, but perhaps not needless, military and political purge in Russia, and the series of trials in January, 1937, in which Vishinsky, the Public Prosecutor, played so masterful a part.

Although it is highly improbable that the Old Guard Communists had made common cause with the military leaders, or vice versa, they were certainly filled with jealousy of Stalin, who had ousted them. It may, therefore, have been convenient to get rid of them at the same time, according to the standards maintained in a totalitarian state. Zinoviev, Bukharin, Radek, and others of the original leaders of the Revolution, Marshal Tuchačevský, who had represented the Soviet Union at the coronation of King George VI, and many other high officials of the Army were shot. In all not less than five thousand officers and officials above the rank of captain were 'liquidated.' The Russian Army was purged of its pro-German elements at a heavy cost to its military efficiency. The bias of the Soviet Government was turned in a marked manner against Germany. Stalin was conscious of a personal debt to President

> Beneš; and a very strong desire to help him and his threatened country against the Nazi peril animated the Soviet government. The situation was, of course, thoroughly understood by Hitler; but I am not aware that the British and French governments were equally enlightened. To Mr. Chamberlain and the British and French general staffs the purge of 1937 presented itself mainly as a tearing to pieces internally of the Russian Army, and a picture of the Soviet Union as driven asunder by ferocious hatreds and vengeance. This was perhaps an excessive view; for a system of government founded on terror may well be strengthened by a ruthless and successful assertion of its power. The salient fact for the purposes of this account is the close association of Russia and Czechoslovakia, and of Stalin and Beneš.[88]

Using all his opportunities diplomatically, Beneš successfully won cancellation of the Munich agreement, and established a directive for Czechoslovak policy in the future, with Russia as well as with the West. His pledge was the recognition of Russia *de iure,*[89] and in the same year, 1935, he signed the treaty of alliance with Russia. Evaluating world opportunities and fully trusting Russia, Beneš endeavored to pacify Russia by signing with her for the first time after World War II an agreement on December 12, 1943, in Moscow, against the will of Polish exiles,[90] and in spite of the great distrust of Great Britain engendered chiefly through Anthony Eden.[91]

World policy was swinging in the same direction, and in 1943, six meetings to achieve a settlement between East and West were held: in Casablanca, between President Roosevelt and Prime Minister Churchill, from January 14 to January 26; in Washington, from May 11 to May 14; in Quebec City, from August 11 to 24; in Moscow between the three great powers, from October 19 to November 1; in Cairo, from November 22 to 26; in Teheran, from November 28 to December 1.[92] The subject of these conferences was the formulation of reciprocal relations and preparations for the postwar period. Beneš, among others, was an influential adviser in Washington and London; he helped to accelerate negotiations between the great powers and Russia. At that time the veiled Communist sphinx was not recognized for what she was even by the great powers themselves. The world, having experienced nazism, was going in the wrong direction toward the sphere of communism. This influenced the mentality of the population in occupied Czechoslovakia. British broadcasts sent out by exiled Czechs and Slovaks were practicing this type of propaganda in a hegemonical, exclusive way. The broadcasting from Moscow inspired leftist factions and, by its exaggerated apologies for Russia and communism, influenced the mass of workers. Communists claimed to be a privileged class, and influenced nearly all groups in the underground movement.

In addition, the Czechoslovak government-in-exile in London officially described the future policy of Czechoslovakia. Hubert Ripka stated:

> The aid of Russia is necessary to help us attain our aim of securing our proper position in Europe.[93] We are proud that we have evaluated the development of world policy since World War I correctly, by taking an affirmative stand toward the Soviet Union. It should be generally recognized that we endeavored to prove that international cooperation with the Soviet Union is a fundamental prerequisite for securing peace and for opening peaceful competition of nations with equal rights.[94]
>
> The leading idea of this revolution (Russian revolution—November 7, 1917) should appeal to the conscience of the whole world. This is a supernatural idea of everlasting existence, an idea of cosmopolitan extent, an idea which since Plato and Christianity until the great revolution and from then on until today has inspired the minds of all generous men; the idea that all people are morally and legally equal, and that it is not permissible for someone's manpower to be exhausted and exploited by another man.[95]
>
> The people of the Soviet Union can be sure that the deep sympathy of the Czechoslovak nation is unchangeable and unshakeable.[96] We can be sure that this work (of alliance with Russia on December 12, 1943) would have had the blessings of Dobrovský, Kollar, Šafařik, Havlíček, Palacký, Rieger, Hurban Vajanský, Hvizdoslav, Stěfanik, and of all of them, especially of Masaryk.[97]
>
> I am surely not exaggerating when I declare the conclusion of the alliance pact between the Soviet Union and Czechoslovakia is an exceedingly important event for our foreign policy. I am happy to have been allowed to partici-

pate in this work.[98] The government in exile, as well as the state council, had taken an imposing unanimous stand, and thus proved to be worthy representatives of the will of our nation.[99]

On the occasion of a trip to Moscow, Beneš reported:

> My present trip to Moscow, and my trip to Moscow in 1935, are for me not only occasional acts of a beneficial character for the war policy, which could be changed by such events; this trip is for me a self-understood consequence, logical conclusion, and culmination of our policy in the last 100 years, which was made possible by the Russian revolution during World War I, by the strength of the Soviet Union, and by the constant future international policy.[100]

At another time, he said:

> If there are to be any changes in the constitution of Carpathian Ruthenia, or if these have to be made on account of considerable changes in neighboring countries, this will be done in agreement with the population . . . We will uphold the spirit of the first republic and its constitution.[101]

It should be mentioned in this connection that these quotations prove that the direction of the government-in-exile was not mere opportunism, but a deliberate policy of systematic endeavor and conviction, which was being practiced for many years. Carpatho-Ruthenia was detached from Czechoslovakia for the Soviet Union in 1945, but its population was not asked for its opinion. Also in 1945 was carried out the continuity as to the seat of the president, but not as to other constitutional organs.

Catholicism, through whose efforts all resistance factions were unified in the early days of Nazi occupation, was only tolerated after Czech Communists came into power. With the end of the war, concerted Catholic effort had become less important. Partisans were organized from new members chosen by Communists only. Parachutists of British and American origin assisted the underground movement very effectively.

Members and followers of rightist political parties were constantly changing the character of their propaganda. Fully disorganized, they lost sight of their former accurate appraisal of the substance of communism. A new antithesis, communism-democracy, was proclaimed. Communist leaders, masterful liars, cheated tirelessly. The communism which would come into liberated Czechoslovakia, so they said, was to be diametrically different from the communism practiced in Russia, and this type of Czech communism was to be true democracy. Socialists worked in the same direction, cooperating with Communists. Communists and radical Socialists displayed their real colors. Under cover of patriotism, they followed their own aims exclusively. Bloodshed continued when this group of usurpers of power in liberal Czechoslovakia calculated the division of their spheres. This state of affairs was supported by daily broadcasts from London, proclaiming vengeance for any form of collaboration with the Germans. People were frightened. Any who were conscious of some small collaboration were drawn toward the Communists, where they looked for and found protection. Many people, realizing what communism stood for, consoled themselves by saying, "We hope that it will perhaps not be wrong to the extent that people generally suspect."

Only the Catholic Church remained firm and unshaken at this period; her priests and her faithful were staunch. Their stand was based on religious, cultural, and social justice for all levels of citizens. They rejected the hegemony of socialistic-communistic ideals, which infiltrated everywhere, even indoctrinating many rightists. Some wise heads predicted an unhappy future for the nation under communism. During World War II, national interests had put aside any of the worries of those in the wise and conservative groups. Priests and the faithful hoped for the nation's deliverance, and were overjoyed when Nazi tyranny was ended. The sheer number of deported and suffering families from villages and towns moved all who were saved from these horrors by the help of God, to give help wherever it was needed. This faith and the horrors of the occupation unified all, despite the actions of Communists. The Catholic Church proved worthy of the trust of all, and was respected even by her enemies. Her traditional conservatism regulated all excesses, and she appeared as a protector of democracy. On May 9, 1945, at the end of the war, the Catholic Church in Bohemia and Moravia was busy with work for the nation and the people, having been appreciated for her efforts in the past, and thus becoming a hope the future of the nation.

However, the true face of the Communist sphinx was revealed after World War II in Czechoslovakia, when the enjoyment of liberation came quickly to an end and all inhabitants saw how very soon there had been established "partisans," "resistance movement leaders," "fighters on barricades," and the like. These seized power in a brutal way, without regard for justice and the opinions of wise and decent men. This was proof of the extent to which the national resistance movement was misused for political aims. They were carrying out the Stalin recipe: Seize power and rule brutally.

The quality of the ruling of national committees was an indication that the mob was the leading and ruling level of the state, in a true copy of the Russian Bolsheviks. The Red Army, occupying Slovakia, Moravia, Silesia, and the eastern part of Bohemia, protected these elements, and has been glorified since that time as the liberator of Prague, despite the fact that five days before this Russian Army arrived there, the American Army held a line at Plzeň, Rakovník, Rokycany, and Beroun, stopping near the capital of Prague. The American Army thus had an easy opportunity to occupy the capital and to save many lives which were lost in the fight with Nazis from May 4 to May 9, 1945. But the Communists needed an opportunity to glorify the Red Army as the liberator of Prague, and to turn this fact to their own political gain. Almost all the inhabitants of Prague and of the nation wished to be liberated by the Americans, and were disappointed when the Red Army came, since its bad reputation had preceded it in reports from eastern Slovakia. People, however, who had lived under the German yoke from 1939 through 1945 had to welcome any liberator who would help to end the horrors of Nazi occupation. Thus they welcomed the Red Army, suspecting that they were welcoming their future tyrants as well. Monsignor Jan Šrámek, Prime Minister of the government-in-exile, returned as minor member of the government because the Communists would not allow a Catholic priest to object to their actions. When the new Czechoslovak government was appointed, under the head of a corrupt politician, Social Democrat Zdeněk Fierlinger, with Communists and Socialists in the majority in its members, President Beneš's trip (to Moscow) was to be interpreted as Stalin's mockery of the West. This included Czechoslovakia, which found it difficult to believe any good of Stalin and communism.[102]

The tragic political error of compromising and cooperating with the communistic Soviet Union turned out to be the source of unlimited suffering for Czechoslovakia. Since 1945, when Czechoslovakia was liberated, the suffering has gone on. The tragedy of the Czechoslovak Republic was deliberately prepared and carried out by Communists, atheists, and followers of the slogan: "Religion is the opium of the people." This tragedy was shared by the Catholic Church, as we shall see in the following chapter.

PART THREE

THE CATHOLIC CHURCH AND THE COMMUNIST STATE

CHAPTER EIGHT

THE COMMUNIST INFILTRATION

IN THE PRECEDING CHAPTER, WE EXPOUNDED THE NEGATIVE attitude toward the Catholic Church, the development of this stand since Hussitism until certain periods in the first Republic (1918-1938), and its culmination in the cultural struggle against Rome. The developments during the German occupation (1939-1945) proved that Catholics were a trustworthy element in the life of the nation and that they could not be eliminated from historical participation in its fate. Catholics proved, by the stability of their ideals in the periods of left or right extremes, that they are a constant factor, insisting on their stand under all conditions. Even when a few of them altered their stand because of the pressure of special conditions, and made compromises, nevertheless Catholicism, on the whole, stood firm in the fight for the liberation of the nation.

The fights for democracy and Christianity are on parallel planes; therefore, they are both victims of Communist tactics. Christianity is being attacked as a spiritual base and democracy as a structure built upon it. This coherence is especially apparent in the case of Czechoslovakia because there, the Christian and democratic tradition proved to be on a very high level.

In this chapter we will treat of the struggle between communism and the Catholic Church since 1945, in which year the Czechoslovak Republic was re-established. The democracy of this republic had been destroyed by the Nazis; it perished in the period of Communist domination carried out in the name of the so-called people's democracy. But actually, as we will prove, the role of communism in Czechoslovakia was to make of this country a political satellite and bulwark for Russian imperialism and expansion.

It is a matter of historical fact that, according to the plan of President Beneš and of his chief adviser, Dr. Hubert Ripka, the orientation of the Czechoslovak government-in-exile in London was toward the Soviet Union. Of great historical importance was the signing of the Soviet-Czechoslovak agreement on December 12, 1943, in Moscow.[1] Minister Ripka viewed this act as a culmination of Czechoslovak foreign policy and he often expressed his opinion in this way.[2]

Another factor of historical importance was the co-operation of Czech and German Communists, which Minister Ripka encouraged. He expressed his opinion on the matter in his London speech which was broadcast on January 27, 1945, excepting German Social Democrats and Communists from the measures against the enemy prepared for the time after World War II.[3] This was an effective lesson for other collaborators who thereby learned where to look for protection. But under the Nazi regime, the suffering German Catholics were unprotected.

The memory of Munich strengthened this attitude. The weakening of French prestige, at Munich in 1938 and at Bordeaux in 1940, greatly increased the feeling of isolation in democratic areas east of Germany. This feeling increased in 1945 when it became apparent that France would not regain her former position as the most influential continental power. In Czechoslovakia the lesson of Munich would certainly always be remembered.[4] The disappointment evoked by Munich supported the trend of orientation toward Russia.

Red Army advances in 1944-1945 and Soviet or local Communist propaganda which pictured the Soviet Union as the only geographically close protection against any renewal of German aggression created the impression that the security of Germany's neighbors was in direct proportion to Soviet strength and interest in Central Europe.[5] The Soviets' entry into World War II, their impressive victories and advances, and later their propaganda condemning the absence of a Second Front, shifted Czech hopes and admiration from Great Britain to Russia. Furthermore, the symbols of the fighting spirit in the West, Churchill and De Gaulle, could hardly counterbalance the reality of Britain's insular position, its avoidance of all commitments in areas east of Germany, and the defeat and weakening of France. In any case,

Churchill and De Gaulle soon after the war were replaced in the hearts of the Czechs by other statesmen.[6]

Nearly all the Czechoslovak territory was occupied by the Red Army, and Prague was "liberated" by the army of Marshal Koněv. When the people saw that the American Army stopped before they arrived in Prague and Jáchymov, public opinion became wholly disorganized. The suspicions and fears of the people were confirmed by the fact that the Czechoslovak government-in-exile, returning from London, stopped first in Moscow for directions.[7] When the government was reorganized in Košice in Slovakia and then, when the Košice Program was proclaimed on April 5, 1945, the Czech and Slovak nations were thrown into the sphere of communism. This Košice Program became the principal and exclusive formulation of Czechoslovak internal and foreign policy.[8] Grave historical changes are indicated in it, as is apparent from its wording:

> Thanks to our great ally the USSR, it has been possible for the President to return to Czechoslovakia and a new government to be formed on home soil. The government should be of a wise National front of Czechs and Slovaks and composed of representatives of all social strata and political trends who at home and abroad led the struggle for national liberation for the overthrowing of German and Hungarian tyranny. The new government makes it its task, side by side with the Soviet Union and other allies, to lead the struggle to a complete liberation of the Republic, to contribute, with all the forces of the Czechoslovak nations, to the final defeat of Hitlerite Germany and to make the first steps for the building of a new and happier life of our nations in the liberated country.
>
> The government, in its present composition, considers its mission to have a time limit. After the liberation of the parts of the Republic, especially of the Czech lands, a provisional National Assembly, based on the National Committees, will be elected and called according to a constitutional President's decree which will confirm the President in his regular function until election. He will appoint a new government, having regard for the proportional representation of all the components of our national resistance, both at home and abroad. This government and the Provisional National

Assembly will prepare to carry out, as soon as possible, general secret direct elections for a new Constitutional Assembly which will work out a new Constitution and put her future on a firm and constitutional basis.

The war is yet unfinished and thus the main task of the government will be to strengthen in all possible ways Czechoslovakia's war effort till the complete liberation of the whole country and to complete the defeat of Hitlerite Germany. Therefore, the government will support the Red Army in every possible way, will carry out quick repairs of all communications and will support the transport of war supplies to the Red Army. All political, economic, social, and cultural measures in the liberated territory will also be governed by the needs of further war conduct. Expressing the great gratitude of the Czechoslovak nations to the USSR., the government will unwaveringly maintain as the leading line of Czechoslovak foreign policy the closest alliance with the victorious great Slav power in the East. The basis will remain the Treaty of December 12, 1943. The government will from the beginning safeguard practical collaboration with the Soviet Union, military, political, economic and cultural, and at the same time wishes a mutual exchange of representatives with the neighboring Ukrainian SSR. In the questions regarding the punishment of Germany, of setting new frontiers, of the organization of future peace, Czechoslovakia shall stand as near as possible at the side of the Soviet Union and in one line with other Slav and democratic countries. The government will endeavor to form a firm alliance and bond with democratic Poland so that, as soon as possible, the Treaty of December 12 will be widened into a three-power pact. The government will follow a Slav line in foreign policy also toward Yugoslavia and Bulgaria.

After retribution for all injustices and all crimes committed by the Hungarian occupants, the government will support endeavors for rapprochement of the new, really democratic Hungary and democratic Austria with the neighboring Slav nations and states. This main orientation of Czechoslovak foreign policy, carried on in the spirit of Slav friendship, will be established on a wide general basis of friendly relations with the Western democratic Powers and all the democratic states of the anti-Nazi front of the United Nations.

The government will strengthen friendly relations with England whose aid during the war we value highly and will seek particularly close friendship with the United States, the same as with France. It will be the government's endeavor that Czechoslovakia become an active component in the building of the new order in liberated, democratic Europe.

In its internal policy, the government starts from the basic paragraph of the Czechoslovak constitution that the people are the only source of state power.

A special charter program deals with the recognition of the Slovaks as a national independent nation. The government will, from the beginning, consistently endeavor that relations between the Czechs and Slovaks will be put into practice according to the maxim, 'equal among equal,' and thus assert the brotherhood between the two nations. The Slovak National Council is not only representative of the Slovak nation but also bearer of state power on Slovak territory.

The government, as a central government, will carry out the common state tasks in closest collaboration with the Slovak National Council and with the body of the Slovak National trustees as the executive governing organ of the Slovak National Council. In the United Czechoslovak Army, Slovak national units will be formed. The future division of competence between the central and Slovak organs will be directed by the legitimate representatives of the Czech and Slovak nations.

The government will take care that the Carpatho-Russian question, raised by the inhabitants of that country, will be settled as soon as possible. The government will wish this question solved according to the democratically expressed will of the Carpathian and Ukrainian people in complete friendship between Czechoslovakia and the Soviet Union.

The terrible experiences of the Czechs and Slovaks with the German and Hungarian minorities force restored Czechoslovakia to a deep and lasting action against the guilty. Loyal German and Hungarian citizens who proved their faithfulness to the Republic in the difficult times will not be affected. Czechoslovak citizenship for Germans and Hungarians will be confirmed only for anti-Nazis and anti-Fascists who fought for Czechoslovakia already before Munich and who, after March 15, were persecuted for their adherence to Czechoslovakia, or who fled abroad where they participated in the struggle for the restoration of Czechoslovakia. Czechoslovak citizenship of the other

Czechoslovak German and Hungarian citizens will be canceled. Although they may again express a choice for Czechoslovakia, public authorities will retain the right of individual decisions. Condemned transgressors, if not subject to capital punishment, will be expelled from the Republic. The government considers it its duty to punish all war criminals, traitors, and active helpers of the German and Hungarian oppressors.

The government will carry out its task without delay and will spare nobody. Persons guilty of high treason, like Hácha, all members of the Beran government who confirmed Hácha's so-called Berlin Pact, all members of the "Protectorate" government from March 16, 1939, Tiso and the members of the so-called Slovak government from March 14, and members of the so-called Slovak Parliament will be brought before the National Court. All of Hácha's political and official helpers, traitors, journalists and functionaries of all organizations who helped the Germans, and the people who handed Czechs and Slovaks to the Gestapo will be tried; in Slovakia, especially those who were active against the Slovak uprising. Bankers, industrialists, and big landowners who helped the Germans to plunder the land and wage war will also be punished. All Fascist organizations will be banned and a renewal of the Republican party, Agrarian party and its branches, and parties which in 1938 fused with the Slovak Hlinka party will not be tolerated.

To make reparation for the crimes committed by the occupants and their helpers against national and private property, a number of steps will be taken to place in custody the property of citizens of enemy States, especially of Germans, Hungarians, and of Czechoslovak citizens who betrayed the nation and actively helped the occupants.

Measures for a new land reform will be governed by the endeavor to free Czech and Slovak land once and for all from German and Hungarian aristocrats and traitors and give it into the hands of Czech and Slovak farmers and peasants. Confiscation of landed and other property connected with it will be done without compensation through the National Committees. Priority in land and property will be given to persons who helped the struggle for national liberation: partisans, soldiers, victims of foreign terror, etc.

Allotted land will pass into full ownership upon payment of a small compensation to be used for the improvement of agriculture. Compensation, which should not exceed

> the value of one or two years' harvest, will be paid in installments.
>
> The government will strive to restore economic life which was destroyed by the occupants and traitors, to restore quickly the production for war and for the civilian population, and to secure work and wages for all who will be able to work. It will also support private initiative or enterprise of artisans and other manufacturers by giving credits, allotting raw materials, etc. The whole money and credit system, industrial key enterprises, the insurance system, and natural and power resources will be turned over to the general state administration and put at the disposal of the reconstruction of national economy and of the renewal of trade and manufacture.[9]

This main text of the Košice Program comprises all the characteristics and outlines of the Communist and Socialist programs with its provisions for infiltration into the Czechoslovak Republic. The possibilities it opens were all used and abused by the Communists. The provisional government, in the time between April and September, 1945, and after some changes of personnel, until May, 1946, managed all affairs of internal and foreign policy in the spirit of communism.[10] The provisional National Assembly, composed of 300 deputies who were chosen on the basis of parity of parties (Communist, Social Democrat, National Socialist, and People's party), approved all decrees of the President of the Republic,[11] by which the whole social order was changed. The administrative instrument of the Communists was the policy of decentralization of government which was carried out by provincial national committees, ostensibly under the aegis of the policy of Abraham Lincoln: government of the people, by the people, and for the people.[12] The jurisdiction of these organs was really very extensive.[13] In Slovakia, the system of parity between only two political parties, Communist and Slovak Democrats, made the situation worse. Annihilation of all that was related to the past, coupled with the tactics of Communists aimed at the bolshevization of the country in a short time, formed the driving idea behind all these organs. Between 1945 and 1948 the Czechoslovak Republic stood politically to the left of British socialism and to the right of Russia's total state rule. The whole country became a laboratory for "socialism by decree."[14]

The prewar integrity of Czechoslovak territory was not respected. In virtue of the agreement between the President of the Supreme Soviet and the President of the Czechoslovak Republic concerning Carpatho-Ruthenia, made on June 29, 1945, and signed in Moscow,[15] the whole province of Carpatho-Ruthenia had to be given to the Soviet Union.

Economic life was regulated also by the decrees of the President of the Republic concerning nationalization from October 24, 1945 Coll.,[16] and land reforms effected under the idea of "revision of the first land reform."[17] The principles of private property were wholly ignored. The problem of land ownership was also regulated by the government, and the situation and conditions of life in the countryside were fully changed.[18] Within these reforms was also included the liquidation of ecclesiastical properties.

The Act of 1946, No. 128 Coll.,[19] concerning restitution, regulated economic matters from the time of occupation under the legal state in the spirit of the new development. The act, *in re* "The Two Year Plan" of October 25, 1946, No. 192 Coll.,[20] formulated its provisions fully in accordance with the principle of socialism.[21] It was amended and the date of its effectiveness was accelerated by the law concerning the Five Year Plan of October 27, 1948, No. 241 Coll.[22] When one considers that at the same time there was carried out the transfer of Germans and Hungarians from Czechoslovakia in accordance with the provisions approved by the Great Powers,[23] on the basis of Potsdam, the picture of the development in that time is complete. All affairs were drawn into the Communist sphere of thought, influence and action.

Into this revolutionary imbroglio were dragged also the Social Democratic and National Socialist political parties. Even the only non-Socialist group, the Christian People's party, could hardly resist this pressure and often just limped behind the rest.

Besides their operations in political spheres, the Communist party was willing to expend an almost limitless supply of "infiltrators," funds, and energy on nonpolitical organizations. Communist concentration in labor unions is well known.

The party was also applying the same effort to other nonpolitical organizations—peasant unions, youth clubs, student associations, intellectual groups, and purely professional associations.[24]

Communists have a tradition for organizing labor unions in all countries. The scheme of organizations set up in certain countries by the Nazis prepared the way to a unification later achieved by the Communists. Communists took over from the Nazis and first set up the central labor unions (ÚRO) under the despotic chairmanship of Antonín Zápotocký.[25] As the ÚRO increased the number of its members, so also its influence became very extensive. Under the pretext of being a nonpolitical organization ÚRO has made its influence and determinative procedure felt everywhere, acting as a reckless factor in the political life together with the supposedly national parties. A decisive part in the development of the ÚRO was played by the socialistic bloc, as a result of the compromise between the Social Democratic and National Socialist parties and the Communist party on June 17, 1945.[26] When the National Socialist party left the socialistic bloc in 1947, it was already too late. The nonsocialistic People's Christian party was left alone in its efforts.

When taking into consideration the whole situation of the year 1945, it is a matter of fact that all key positions were occupied by Communists. The Ministry of the Interior, Agriculture, National Defense, Education, economic centers of all kinds, and cultural and political life were controlled by them. Account must also be taken of the fact that what Communists were not commissioned to do by law, they carried into effect by an utter disregard for all trusts, and by circumvention of the law. They increased the chaos already caused by the activities of the national committees. For example, where the Communists had influence and control, they strengthened the idea of decentralization of administration; and where they were in a minority, they regularly took the opposite stand, thus always attaining their aims, either legally or illegally. And unfortunately the general elections of May 26, 1946, did not come up to the expectations and hopes of those who aspired to eliminate the extensive influence of Communists.

The following is a table of the results of the elections:[27]

Parties	Votes	Percentage	Deputies
Communists (Czech and Slovak)	2,695,915	38.00	114
National Socialists	1,298,917	18.50	55
Catholic People's party	1,110,920	15.65	47
Social Democrats	855,771	13.00	36
Slovak Democrats	988,275	13.05	43
Slovak party of Freedom (established after the Košice Program)	67,575	0.95	3
Slovak Labor party (established after the Košice Program)	49,983	0.85	2
Total	7,067,356	100.00	300

When taking into consideration the fact that the former Agrarian party, the middle-class Craftsmen party, and the National Democratic party had a political strength of 2,080,993 votes in the election of 1935, it is obvious that socialism and communism completely won in the general election of 1946. The three first-mentioned parties had already been disbanded by the Nazis. Their restoration had been forbidden by the Košice Program which instructed the persecution and elimination of the rightists. The position of Catholics became precarious due to the fact that the right-to-center political groups were entirely eliminated from the political scene. After this general election, the Communists strengthened their influence far beyond their due according to the results of the election, by creating so-called "experts." Thus they became the strongest and most influential power in the Republic.

Through the influence of the moderate elements, the situation was somewhat bettered in 1947 when the National Socialists started to support the policy of the Christian People's party under the leadership of Monsignor Jan Šrámek. Addresses by Minister Adolf Procházka of the People's party, by Dr. Prokop Drtina of the National Socialist party, and by Jan Masaryk were very critical, especially if one evaluates the situation at that time. These strongly worded speeches proved that communism was not fully accepted by the Czech and Slovak people. Even more courageous were the speeches of many other politicians, as for instance those by Dr. Bohdan Chudoba, Dr. Alois Rozehnal, Mr. Broj, M. P., Jindřich Nermuť, M. P., Dr. Helena Koželuhová, M. P., Vilém Pavlík, M. P., and of others from the People's party; and those of Dr. Kempný and Dr. Bugar from the Slovak Democratic party and others; and of Mr. Klátil, M. P., from the National Socialist party.

Very sharp criticism found a place in the periodicals of the People's Christian party, *Obzory*[28] and *Na výboj*. Very appropriate articles were known to echo even in the parliament. The newspapers *Lidová demokracie* and *Obroda* (Moravian) also began to publish articles containing very sharp criticism. Such magazines and newspapers were sold out very quickly, and gave proof of the interest of the readers and of the dissatisfaction of the people with the official policy of the government.

The relation of communism to the Catholic Church and to all religions is obvious from the nature of the Communist doctrine. It would have been absurd to hope that communism in Czechoslovakia would take on a form other than the one it had assumed in all other countries behind the Iron Curtain or in Russia.[29] Czechoslovak Communists proclaiming such developments or changes lied deliberately, especially when they promised Catholics that they would not be menaced. Actually they tried to diminish the merits of Catholic bishops, priests and the faithful who had done their duty during the Nazi occupation in a model way. Even when it became clear to thinking men that there would be no compromise between the Catholic Church and communism, there were those who believed that the Communists would take into consideration the fact that Catholicism was an important factor in the resistance during the war and for that reason would respect it. In view of this we can easily understand why even Archbishop Beran attended "people's meetings," invited there by the Communists themselves during the years 1946-47. Politicians of the People's Christian party actually hoped for such a development in an endeavor to avoid open conflict. They were willing to subscribe to almost any program in order to survive.

During the years 1945-1947, Communists used their influence to strengthen their hold on the government, economic life, national committees, and cultural institutions. In addition they exploited the feeling of relief and joy experienced by all who believed that peace had at long last arrived. In the territory left by the Germans and Hungarians, Communists divided the land and appointed national administrators in confiscated industrial and business enterprises from certain strata of the nation, so as to appear as Maecenases of state property. By this procedure they gained the support of masses of voters for the general election, putting them thus under their control.

It is an interesting fact that the Catholic Church in her opposition to communism stood alone at the beginning, while other non-Catholic Churches were collaborating with the Communists. This is astonishing because the hostile attitude of communism toward all religions was well known. For example, the Church of the Czech Brethren took a special stand. Bohdan Chudoba[30] critically analyzed the "stages in the Czech Protestant tragedy," in which the leading role was played by F. L. Hromádka (born 1889), Dean of the Hus Faculty in Prague. In his theological thesis *We Need a New Mission* he brought his Church ideologically into a positive stand toward communism, and induce people "to cooperate with the Communists toward social works."[31]

Even as early as World War II, while living in the United States, Hromádka had inclined toward this synthesis. In his work, *Masaryk as European* (Prague, 1936), he had already gone very far. In 1941, in his article, "The Modern Trends in European Protestant Theology," he proclaimed the aim of unifying not only all Christian Churches but also all political factors when he said, "We are living in a terrific crisis. However, this crisis is a great challenge for us. If we theologians are faithful to the divine truth, we might once be credited with having brought good news and a remedy to unhappy humanity."[32] In 1943 he explained the philosophy of Emmanual Rádl (1873-1942)[33] and in the year 1945, after analyzing Dostojewski, Masaryk, and Rádl, he said, "We cannot go back. We cannot save civilization by conservative caution or by reactionary devices. We cannot impose our abstract formulas and blueprints on the events of current history. Behind history, the Risen Lord is doing His work. What does it mean that the vast areas of Russia and the hundreds of millions of the Soviet people found themselves on the side of the Allies? What does it mean that the spiritual and moral motifs of Russian history have been released by revolution and war and are shaping the days to come? What does it mean that the liberal and democratic world has undergone a trial of blood and sweat?"[34]

Astonishing also are the opinions of the Czech Protestant philosopher J. B. Kozák, who in an unexpected way reversed his previous stand of vague Christian humanism and of T. G. Masaryk's realism to make a faulty evaluation of communism as a sociological symptom of a short period which was to be expected to occur according to Masaryk's theory of synergism. He thus betrayed Masaryk, who rejected materialism of all kinds for metaphysical reasons, as he did also Marxism, either of the Communist or of the Social Democrat variety. It was this same J. B. Kozák who, even before World War II, while connected with the philosophical faculty at Charles University in Prague, had taken a stand against the aim of Catholics who endeavored to open a university seat of Christian Thomistic philosophy, as idealized by the Catholic philosophers, Father Methodius Habáň, O.P., and Professor Jaroslav Beneš. J. B. Kozák did not want his leading position in the realm of philosophy to be surmounted by anybody from the Catholic bloc, in which there were philosophers of outstanding abilities like the Franciscan, Dr. Jan Urban, a pupil of Kozák, or Dr. Josef Kratochvíl of Brno.

The Czechoslovak Church followed the model of the Czech Brethren, although its membership was almost a traditional heritage of the national socialistic party. Only Bishop Tabach resisted. On the other hand, Bishop Novák even ordained "lady-priests," as a new specialty of this Church. Dr. Kovář, the patriarch of the Czechoslovak Church, in his comment on the new ecclesiastical laws of October 14, 1949, introduced by the Communist regime, openly declared: "It is possible to live in accordance with the spirit of Jesus only under the condition that we endeavor to nullify all class privileges and concentrate our efforts on attaining social justice. But there is only one way to attain social justice, and that is the way of socialism. Therefore our Church has decided, according to its best lights, to support this ideology."[35]

The Orthodox Church under Moscow's influence not only cooperated with the Communists, it even played the role of Trojan horse by dispersing the Greek Catholic Church in Slovakia, Ruthenia, Moravia and Bohemia. Unitarians in

Prague and other denominations were no exception in this collaboration but there were some individuals who understood the nature of the common danger.

In 1945, the Holy See sent to Prague its chargé d'affaires, Monsignor Raffaele Forni. President Beneš, appreciating the extensive services of Catholics in the resistance movement both at home and abroad, was anxious to make connections with the Holy See even as early as World War II. On January 7, 1941, President Beneš gave the Apostolic Delegate to Great Britain, Monsignor W. Godfrey, a letter in which he explained the stand he had taken:

> Immediately after the Armistice (1918) had been signed, acting in the capacity of foreign minister of the Republic, diplomatic negotiations with the Holy See were undertaken concerning the settlement of territorial extent of dioceses, of ecclesiastical properties, etc. There were many difficulties in the year 1924 and again in the year 1927, when new and serious misunderstandings appeared. But in the year 1927, it was possible to settle all problems definitely by establishing the legal basis for future relations. A *modus vivendi* between the Holy See and the Czechoslovakian Republic had been accepted; normal and even friendly relations were set up. Since that time mutual relations have been good and cooperation has developed without any difficulties. Especially one cannot forget the very sympathetic stand taken by His Holiness Pope Pius XI toward Czechoslovakia in the time of the September crisis of the year 1938, and the message which he sent in one of the most critical moments of the history of my nation.
>
> For this reason I hoped the time had come to establish unofficial relations between the new Czechoslovak government, with residence in London, and the Holy See. All agreements which had been made concerning ecclesiastical problems between the Vatican and the Republic were destroyed by the Nazi government. The situation in Slovakia is very sad and the existence of the present government of Tiso will doubtlessly deeply influence the position of the Catholic Church in Slovakia after this war. Persecution of Czech Catholics in the Czech Protectorate will influence the policy of the Czech nation in the time after the present war.
>
> Poles, Belgians, and others are maintaining similar relations and they are allowed to discuss with the Holy See all

their common interests and their policies concerning these problems that had arisen after World War II. Since March, 1939, such an opportunity was not granted to the Czechoslovaks. The Slovak delegate to the Holy See is the representative of the State, which is fully under the control of the Nazi government. I think that under such conditions it would be advisable to have suggestions for the future at the right time. Excuse me, please, if I give such an open explanation of my stand. But in this horrible war, by which the whole of Christian civilization is menaced, as is apparent from the Christmas Message of His Holiness Pope Pius XII, who has taken definite stand by demanding a just peace for all small nations, I think it is the duty of all responsible men to let no opportunity escape to do what they feel necessary for the interests of their suffering nations.[36]

Monsignor Godfrey gave President Beneš the answer of the Holy See on May 19, 1941, in which was stated:

His Eminence advises that he read with very great interest your participation in all negotiations, which, after serious difficulties, were concluded in the *modus vivendi* of the year 1928. His Eminence is especially delighted by your mention of the Church and the generous support given by Pope Pius XII who desires nothing more than to attain a righteous and constant peace, secured not by hate and vengeance, but by the generous reign of justice. His Holiness expressed this already in his good wishes of June 2, 1940, and recently in his Christmas message to the public of the world.

The Pope and the Holy See have sympathies for every suffering nation and by their concern are continually attempting to fulfill their pastoral mission, bestowed by God on the Church—that of helping in every manner all suffering people.

It is only natural that the Czechoslovak nation should have a special place in the maternal heart of the Church. As regards the suggestion that Your Excellency made, that of establishing unofficial relations between the Czechoslovak government in exile, which has been set up in London, and the Holy See, His Eminence is convinced that Your Excellency will understand to what extent this situation is delicate, and how difficult it would be at the present time, to grant the Czechoslovak people the privilege of such relations. His

Eminence is of the opinion that the favorable time for such a development has not as yet arrived.[37]

On July 15, 1943, through channels of the British government, there was sent to the Vatican a memorandum[38] of the Czechoslovak government in London, with an added explanation of its attitude and of the political situation. Therein it was urged that a regulation of relations and the preparation of diplomatic connections be made for the time after World War II. The Vatican, due to the complicated international situation, welcomed these efforts to prepare for conditions of the future. Unofficial negotiations were continued and by 1945, through the sending of Monsignor Raffaele Forni to Prague, prewar relations between the Vatican and Czechoslovakia were restored.

A preparatory status of diplomatic relations between the Czechoslovak Republic and the Vatican was accomplished through a compromise occasioned by the resistance of the Russian Ambassador in Prague because of the internationally recognized dignity of the rank of the papal nuncio as dean of the diplomatic corps. Pius XII appointed on May 13, 1946, the former nuncio to the Czechoslovak pre-war government, Monsignor Saverio Ritter, Bishop of Egius,[39] as Apostolic internuncio.[40] (While a nuncio is equivalent in diplomatic status to an ambassador, an internuncio is equal to a minister. Under the rules made by the Congress of Vienna in 1815, a nuncio is the dean of the diplomatic corps.) The interference of the Communists and the setting aside of the accustomed diplomatic etiquette was tolerated by the Vatican in a magnanimous way, thus proving again the Holy See's interest in regulating mutual relations. Nevertheless, the Communists made it clear that the relations with the Vatican were being viewed only as a necessity.

In the same year (1946), Dr. Francis Schwarzenberg was appointed by the Czechoslovak government as its chargé d'affaires at the Holy See, and Father Jaromír Machula was named ecclesiastical adviser. Later, Artur Meixner was appointed as Ambassador to the Holy See, on which occasion Pope Pius XII in a private audience of August 13, 1946, gave the following allocution:

The credential letters by which His Excellency the President of the Czechoslovak Republic communicates to us the nomination, in your person, of another Envoy Extraordinary and Minister Plenipotentiary to the Holy See, bring to an end a painfully troubled past and manifest the will to achieve a better and more serene future.

The words which Your Excellency has just pronounced on this solemn occasion attest your determination to cooperate efficaciously to guard the maintenance and development of normal and trusting relations between Church and state after the tragic circumstances of the most horrible of wars.

With the reëstablishment of this legation, the hope and conviction of having found a precious support and a solid prop for the safeguard of their rights and of their religious liberties, we are firmly convinced, shines for the Catholic faithful of your country. None would greet with more satisfaction than we, the realization of this hope. And none would desire more ardently than we, in order to fulfill this awaiting, to do all that is in our power and in conformity with the dictates of our conscience.

It is precisely from this point of view that we highly appreciate the noble expression with which Your Excellency so pleasingly recognized the courage that was manifested by the Catholics in the face of all the oppression which weighed on them during the years of foreign domination.

In the new Europe, that Europe which is now rising from the crisis and the upheavals of the war and its aftermath, the peoples of the Czechoslovak Republic have a special place, an assigned role, and, by that token, find themselves face to face with responsibilities and risks which, while they hazard their destiny, require wisdom and practical vigilance as well as moral conscientiousness on the part of their leaders, and a spirit of discipline and moderation on the part of all the citizens in their most vigorous and unceasing efforts.

All who sincerely have at heart the real interests of the peoples of Czechoslovakia wish that, in this decisive hour of their history, they may clearly understand how, over and above all the dissensions born of the war, the advent of a worthy, constructive and vital peace is indissolubly tied to the principles of the juridical and moral order which can never be replaced by all the abilities and the political energies of the world.

We request that you may transmit to the President of

> the Republic, with our thanks, the expression of our best wishes for his welfare. As for you, may you be assured that in the fulfillment of your high mission, you will always find in us understanding and cordial support.
>
> In token of the wishes which we formulate from the bottom of our heart for the prosperity and the peaceful progress of your people, we very readily grant, according to your request, to all the faithful Czechoslovak Catholics and particularly to Your Excellency and all his family, our Apostolic Blessing.[41]

The reaction of the Czech Catholics toward their government's action in appointing not a papal nuncio but only an internuncio had very strange repercussions in the press:

> This denial of the privilege belonging to the Pope's representative is a fresh insult to the feelings of many Catholic citizens. It is a fresh negation of the spirit and a submission to worldly force, the brutality of which we learned so well in the years past. We have few friends abroad, we are glad if someone shows us sympathy; we are glad if we are the winners in an international basketball tournament—but when our Hussite pride grabs hold of us, we do one silly thing after another.[42]

However, the internuncio, Monsignor Ritter, said in Prague on the occasion of his entering office on June 17, 1946:

> I have returned full of joyous hope, after more than seven years' absence, to the land of St. Wenceslaus, so rich in sacred Christian remembrances. My first thought goes to God in the spirit of gratitude for protection, help and strength given in every trial. This thought is naturally followed by warmest wishes for the happy future of your country and for those who direct its fate in various branches of social activity. My thoughts go as prayers for eternal atonement to your dead and ours who, for us, are always alive and who, today, are nearer to us than ever before in remembrance and love.[43]

The situation became very complicated because of state interference in ecclesiastical affairs, and was made even worse through the vacancy of episcopal sees in Prague, Brno,

Budějovice, and by complications in the diocese of Litoměřice. The same was true in Slovakia where, by persecution of some Slovak bishops, the situation became very precarious.

The first effort of the ecclesiastical authorities was to appoint new bishops. Thus, on March 10, 1946, Pope Pius XII appointed as Archbishop of Prague, Monsignor Josef Beran,[44] hitherto rector of the major seminary and professor in the theological faculty of Charles University. Dr. Beran had been imprisoned for many years by the Nazis in the concentration camp at Dachau, Germany, In June, 1947, Dr. Joseph Hlouch was appointed Bishop of Budějovice.[45] Up to that time he had been Professor of Pastoral Theology in the theological faculty of the Cyril-Methodius University in Olomouc, a zealous preacher and orator. On June 24, 1946, Monsignor Karel Skoupý was appointed as Bishop in Brno.[46] He had hitherto acted as rector of the episcopal major seminary and Professor of Biblical Studies in a theological college at Brno. His activities as an organizer of the movement for the revival of religious life in Moravia merited much praise.

The question of the German Bishop of Litoměřice (Leitmeritz), Monsignor Antonín Weber, who had always been loyal toward the Czechoslovak Republic, was solved in the following way: In March, 1947, in a secret consistory, Pope Pius XII appointed the Bishop of Litoměřice, Monsignor Weber, to the see of Samien.[47] The Czechoslovak government fixed an annual salary for him; thereby his episcopal see in Litoměřice became vacant and in his place the Czech Bishop, Dr. Štěpán Trochta, was appointed on September 27, 1947.[48] Up to that time he had been rector of the Silesian institute, *Cardinal Kašpar,* in Prague and a prominent member of the Silesian congregation. He, too, was a former prisoner in the Nazi concentration camp in Buchenwald, Germany.

In Slovakia, in February, 1946, Monsignor Eduard Necsey was appointed as Bishop in Nitra,[49] due to the fact that Archbishop Karol Kmet'ko, because of his advanced age, had been retired. The bishops of Slovakia had a really troublesome position because Communists held them responsible for Tiso's action in forming a free Slovak Republic (1939-1945).[50] Michael Buzalka, auxiliary bishop and military ordinariate of the Slovak Army in Bratislava, was severely persecuted. Bishop Vojtaššák of Spišská Nová Ves also suffered. Bishop

Josef Čarský, apostolic administrator in Košice, who during the occupation of South Slovakia by the Hungarians had his residence in Prešov, returned to Košice. No episcopal see in Slovakia was vacant until June 23, 1947, when Monsignor Pavol Jantausch, apostolic administrator in Trnava, died.[51]

In this way ecclesiastical matters were being organized for the first period after World War II. The Vatican recognized the situation in Czechoslovakia and gave it full attention. Catholics accepted the nominations of bishops with satisfaction and appreciation. All bishops began full-scale work. But by 1946, Communists had begun their encroachment on ecclesiastical affairs and, being in possession of all key positions in the state, they now claimed the right to decide on these affairs too. First in turn came the problems of education, and cultural and ecclesiastical properties.

Pope Pius XII himself carefully watched the development in Czechoslovakia, viewing analogically the cases of Archbishop Stepinac (in Yugoslavia) and Cardinal Mindszenty (in Hungary). In 1945, in a concise letter dated August 28, and addressed to all archbishops and bishops, he recalled the heroic stand taken by the Czechoslovak Catholic priests during World War II (1939-1945); he brought back to memory the courage and sufferings of Saint John Nepomucene and condemned all excesses against the Catholic Church and against her God-given rights. The text of this letter read:

> To the Most Reverend Archbishops, Bishops, and other local ordinaries in the Republic of Czechoslovakia: on the occasion of the completion of six hundred years since the birth of St. John Nepomucene.
>
> Venerable Brethren, health and apostolic benediction. We consider it a providential happening that you, Venerable Brethren and faithful of Christ in Czechoslovakia, are happily celebrating the completion of six hundred years since the birth of John Nepomucene, at a time when the light of a new age is dawning upon you who have emerged recently from war—an age which we hope will bring with it the gift of renewed peace and the growth of religion. Wherefore, we are unwilling to by-pass an event of such happy significance without extending to you salutary prayers and wishes, compelled as we are by our love for you and yours.

The awful war which has depopulated many parts of the earth, leaving them in deadening ruin and disaster, has brought you also many evils, the memory and recollection of which is not yet soothed and always intensifies our grief. In some of these regions, domination by foreign force is the affliction, and crowds of men, including many clerics and religious, are thrown into prison and are held in places of public detention, many of them liable to death. In other places are found deadly strifes, the destruction of homes, loss of goods, and exile. Everywhere there are groans, tears, and lamentations. But the Catholic Church in some parts of the republic of Czechoslovakia, besides finding itself molested by the power of the occupying nation, suffers from this source not a few injuries and exists in very severe traits. For the Archdiocese of Prague, the Diocese of Budějovice, and the Diocese of Brno have been bereaved of their most beloved Shepherds (bishops) and have remained for many years without legitimate successors, since we, although eager to appoint occupants to these sees, have decided that we must preserve unimpaired a good of supreme value, i.e., the liberty of the Church and your spiritual advantage. But the vicissitudes of time which take away many sorrows produce changes in things. Thus, the deeds and powerful image of Saint John Nepomucene, by being brought to the fore again, diffuse a shining light and bring back the prospect of good hope. Since the Saints, by reason of ties which an unconquerable love has fashioned, are never disjoined from those who inhabit the earth, they are as a most careful instruction for them in cultivating virtues and they map out the secure way of salvation, especially for those with whom they are closely bound by country, race, and speech. In the present circumstances, the star and guardian of your fatherland, who is to be honored by deserved emulation, offers austere admonitions which are a stimulation and an encouragement for all your assemblies, so that, with renewed efforts, they may conform themselves to the lofty precepts of the Gospel, whence flow eternal life, kindness, and culture worthy of the name, the strength of perpetual youth. This will be of great advantage: for if the extraordinary adornment of blossoms is lacking, i.e., generous and learned souls conspicuous for the charm of virtues, alas many go headlong into the cesspools of vice; having despised the law of God, they make the state of human society worse and liable to more severe castigations. Saint John Nepomucene rises up as an opportune teacher in whose life, strength and meekness, fortitude and gentleness, shone forth wonderfully. He teaches clerics the faith and care with which the duties of sacred ministers are to be fulfilled; that they ought to face death with scorn rather than to neglect their duty. He teaches the faithful that nothing is more precious than an undefiled conscience, and goods are to be weighed according to a just standard, so that the divine will always be preferred to the human, heavenly things to earthly, eternal to fleeting. There is now a pressing need for men attached to the service of the Church, i.e., clerics, or laymen endowed with great constancy, who will be outstanding in their desire to dedicate themselves to virtue and excellence, despising their own comfort and petty glory, and giving themselves energetically to the cause of the public welfare. For these, Saint John Nepomucene is not only a venerable name but an imitable exemplar. With his help and instruction, a perennial peace shall be established in your country. Not indeed a peace which by a falsification of the word contains pitfalls and insidious traps, but one which is based upon justice linked with charity. Without doubt, within the boundaries of your fatherland all the unfortunate things that have happened have led to dissension and hatred, which in turn stir up the passion for revenge. Lest these disturbances among souls pass beyond the limits of what is right and good, let the moderation of your own counsels and precepts not be lacking, Venerable Brethren. Is this not the true victory, to overcome through justice and charity? Do not allow the innocent to be punished along with the guilty; and if chastisement is inflicted upon the wicked, let this not be done beyond due measure and equity, lest in condemning violent men, the punishment be tainted with violence and be itself worthy of condemnation, or lest, having sown the seeds of hatred, the very unity of the people be injured. This same companion of justice, i.e., charity, moderate public and private morals—the noble insignia and undoubted mark of Christ's followers—when the sharp thorns of anger and revenge have been blunted, will incline hearts to moderation and agreement, and will bind the mutual needs of the citizens together. Such a mutually helpful union, when made strong through religion, righteousness, and peace, will provide a solid foundation for your state. Let that liberty worthy of the name flourish at the same time, always accompanied by virtue and reverence for the Supreme Being, lest that other liberty, which is in name only, lead to unbridled license or tyranny. "When a revolution will allay a war"—thus we spoke last year on the feast of Saint Wenceslaus to some of you who came to us in Rome—"it is lawful for you, under no constraint, by the full rights of liberty to establish your domestic society, to take care of the rearing of your children, to regulate your arrangements of a social nature and your institutes according to the directions which have been proposed to the whole world by our Predecessors and by ourselves, and which are rooted in the spirit and doctrine of Christ." With eyes fixed on the Heavenly Patron of your country, with one accord, Venerable Brethren, consecrate your powers and your works so that under the auspices and leadership of the Gospel, a new splendor may thereby be added to its ancient glory. Undertake the cause of God and your people. It is fitting that you, and under your initiative and inspiration, all who merit the name of Catholic, with all slothfulness put aside, should spare no labor and should earnestly make progress in the useful things that have been begun. We cannot now pass over in silence the Pontifical Nepomucene College in Rome, distinguished with the name of that heavenly Patron to whom you eagerly show reverence. Admire with us the harvest of learned priests with which it has enriched your land. It is greatly to be hoped that under your sponsorship this same college will receive, as soon as possible, a new and copious supply of students who will be imbued here in Rome, near the remains of the Princes of the Apostles, with knowledge of sacred sciences and zeal for Catholic activity. Finally, we pray God most earnestly, without Whom we can do nothing and in Whom we can do all things, that He may always assist you as a helpmate in your labors, so that hard duties may be met with evangelical kindness, that consolations may abound. All those things that are dear to your hearts and to ours, we commend to the patronage and intercession of Saint John Nepomucene. In pledge of heavenly gifts for you, Venerable Brethren, and for the clerics and multitudes of the faithful in the beloved Republic of Czechoslovakia, we lovingly impart the Apostolic Blessing.[52]

POPE PIUS XII

St. Peter's Rome, August 28, 1945

Even before the Communists spread through Europe, the

Pope rejected all totalitarian ideas and drew attention to the menace to democracy in his Christmas message of December 24, 1944,[53] declaring the Church to be a dependable protection for human dignity and freedom. He used every opportunity to encourage bishops by his letters. He sent a letter in 1946, on the occasion of the episcopal jubilee of Archbishop Karol Kmeťko and Bishop John Vojtaššák[54] in Slovakia, to strengthen the authority of the bishops who were in a fearful situation because of Communist terror.

On the occasion of the Saint Adalbert celebrations, in April, 1947, the Pope sent to Prague a letter dated March 21 and addressed to all ordinaries of Czechoslovakia, encouraging the faithful to embark on a religious revival. This was like encouragement from a father expecting his children to be involved in combat, as is apparent from the whole character of the letter:

> TO THE MOST EXCELLENT ARCHBISHOPS AND BISHOPS OF THE REPUBLIC OF CZECHOSLOVAKIA: ON THE FACT THAT IT IS NINE AND A HALF CENTURIES SINCE THE DEATH OF SAINT ADALBERT, BISHOP AND MARTYR OF PRAGUE.
>
> Greetings and Apostolic Blessings to you, Venerable Brethren. On this nine hundred fiftieth year since the death of Saint Adalbert, you have decreed the commemoration with solemn rites in all the dioceses of the Republic throughout this present year, for this truly outstanding man of your nation, who showed you an example of unwavering integrity in the Catholic faith and who, with unwearying toil in behalf of Christ's kingdom, even unto the martyrdom which he gloriously fulfilled during his missionary journey to Prussia, held the episcopal see of Prague. His distinguished memory, moreover, is fostered not only through Bohemia, Moravia, and Slovakia, but also among the Hungarians, the Poles, and the Germans. It is truly most opportune that these solemnities be carried out there, since the body of the holy martyr has been entombed from the year 1039 in the Cathedral Church of Prague, and the same Adalbert is numbered among the patrons of Bohemia. Accordingly, Venerable Brethren, you desire not only to recall to the mind of the faithful the life and outstanding accomplishments of this second Bishop of Prague, but you are also deeply anxious to promote among the flocks entrusted to

your care a profound renewal of morals through more frequent preaching of God's word, holy prayer, and pious pilgrimages to the tomb of the blessed man. In addition, the sacred head of the martyr, which is preserved most religiously in Prague, will be solemnly exposed for the veneration of the faithful in various cities of the Republic. These plans which you intend soon to carry out we fully endorse with the praise due them and encourage with sincere blessings and expectations. We are certain that such solemnities in honor of Adalbert will be a great inducement to your people so that, imitating the outstanding example of the Apostle and strengthened by his intercession before God, they may constantly and strenuously defend the Catholic faith handed down by their fathers and be able to foster zealously an intimate union of spirit and labor among themselves and with neighboring people to develop natural and Christian culture and prosperity. So, Venerable Brethren, upheld by such hopeful confidence, we lovingly impart in the Lord the Apostolic Blessing to each one of you and to the clergy and the faithful entrusted to you, as well as to all the strangers coming from other nations to share this sacred celebration with you, as a sign of heavenly gifts and a testimony of our special love.[55]

POPE PIUS XII

St. Peter's Rome, March 1, 1947

These celebrations of Saint Adalbert were arranged on the initiative of Archbishop Josef Beran, who opened the program of his episcopate with it. In these imposing celebrations, the relics of Saint Adalbert were carried from one town to another; everywhere an enormous attendance was recorded. Sermons were given by such prominent preachers as Dr. Silvester Braito, Dr. Hlouch, Monsignor Stříž, Monsignor Stašek, Abbot Jarolímek, Dr. Šingmayer, Dr. Jan Urban, O.F.M., and others. These celebrations were looked upon as a spiritual revival, and in a similar vein, missions were arranged in the cities and villages during which the relics of Saint Adalbert were brought and exposed for the veneration of all Catholic associations in the country. All the faithful attended in great numbers. In many towns, such as Mladá Boleslav, Liberec, Turnov, Litomyšl, Plzeň, and Budějovice, these celebrations especially gave the much needed encouragement against the fear of Communist oppression. In Moravia, enormous success followed these celebrations in Brno, Olomouc, Uh. Hradiště, Hodonín, and other places.

Slovakia did not take part in the solemnities because the first Slovakian President of the independent Slovak Republic (1939-1945), Monsignor Josef Tiso, was executed in Bratislava on April 18, 1947, after pardon had been denied him.[56] As a war criminal he was brought from exile, tried according to the regulations concerning war criminals and in accordance with the Košice Program, condemned. The harshness of the trial and all circumstances connected with it made it very difficult for Slovaks to condone.[57] Besides, since all this happened under instructions from Prague through Bratislava, Slovak bishops refused their participation in celebrations of Saint Adalbert which originated in Czech provinces. Otherwise it is impossible to explain the refusal of Catholic Slovakia, because Slovakia was included in the planning of these celebrations. But in Czech provinces these celebrations exceeded all expectation.

From the beginning of the celebrations, the government of Prague showed its true face. Although other state celebrations were sponsored by the government, it refused in the beginning to second these religious celebrations and did so later only by necessity. On official occasions, the government was represented exclusively by ministers of the Christian People's party. The attendance of people proved that Catholicism was capable of action, but this was not likely to be admitted by the Communists. It was an imposing act by which Catholics expressed their intention to defend their rights. It echoed in the country's press, and abroad, and proved that the Catholics of Czechoslovakia could be looked upon as a bulwark against communism.

After these celebrations, Archbishop Josef Beran became the central personality in the defense of Catholics until February, 1948, and in later times the prime figure in the whole Catholic resistance. He had fulfilled all prerequisites for this purpose. He excelled in all departments of Catholic Action, in the Catholic press, and in apostolic work. He lived a very modest and irreproachable life. Since 1933 he had educated young priests in modern pastoral work. He was a faithful cooperator with Cardinal Kašpar and eventually became his successor. The maxim of his life was, "All for the greater glory of God," and he consequently carried out all instructions of the Pope.[58] Born in Plzeň in 1888 of a family of teachers, he prepared himself for the profession of teaching. He studied theology in Rome, was graduated in 1912 as Doctor of Sacred Theology, and acted as chaplain in various institutions. Later he was appointed rector of the Teachers Institute of Saint Anne in Prague, and from 1934 he was rector of the major seminary. In 1942 he was arrested by the Gestapo and deported to the infamous concentration camp at Dachau. From there, after liberation by the American Army, he returned in 1945 to Prague. His membership card as a liberated prisoner also strengthened his position against Communists while they carried on their plan of infiltration.

All priests who had been arrested, imprisoned, or persecuted by the Nazis federated themselves into special associations, and these members became the mediators between ecclesiastical officials and the ruling socialistic and communistic elements. Thereby an immediate open fight was avoided in the year 1945. Some priests were even cited for distinguished service. On April 29, 1946, the Rev. Oldřich Bláha,[59] a priest of the Order of the Brethren of Charity in Brno, was decorated by President Beneš with the medal for outstanding courage. On July 15, 1946, Dr. Francis Cinek,[60] dean of the theological faculty of Saints Cyril and Methodius, in Olomouc, was decorated by President Beneš with the War Cross; Dr. Bohuslav Jarolímek, abbot of the Praemonstratenses of Strahov, was decorated on March, 1947, by the army general Boček.[61] Monsignor Eduard Oliva, manager of Catholic Charity, was distinguished with the medal of the government[62] for successful works of Catholic charity. On February 10, 1947, Monsignor Tylinek[63] was presented by the French government with the Cross for resistance. Monsignor Josef Beran was decorated on April 26, 1947, by the Minister of Interior, Václav Nosek,[64] with the memorial medal of the government for resistance. Thus did a whole line of Czech and Moravian priests gain distinction and honor from local and national authorities. Other priests became members and prominent functionaries in the association of political prisoners, *Svaz revoluce*. Some were distinguished by British and American military authorities. Even Communists themselves were compelled to honor Catholic priests, which is indisputable proof of the substantial contribution of Catholic priests to the cause of liberation and of the respect due them by even a Communist regime. Every distinction conferred on a priest was accepted by the faithful with feelings of satisfaction.

A general recognition was given Czech and Moravian priests officially on December 24, 1945, when President Beneš said to the delegation of Moravian priests, led by Monsignor Karel Skoupý of Brno:

> I well know the stand taken by the Catholic clergy in the last war. I know they were patriotic and that many had to suffer in concentration camps. You, on the other hand, know my political profile, so to speak, from the period before the war; you have known it during the war and you know it now. I have remained what I have been and I shall remain in the future what I have been. I have stood, I stand, and I shall stand for freedom of creed and religion and religious conviction uncompromisingly and clearly, just as I stand generally for tolerant objectivity and freedom in matters of conviction, both religious and political. In this spirit, I think, the Republic will go ahead, and every Catholic-minded citizen of the Republic, and the Catholic clergy may look forward with confidence to the development of conditions in our nation and state.[65]

Catholics believed these assurances given by the President and they even forgot that the Republic was actually under control of Communists who had no respect for official declarations of the President. His prestige gradually diminished because of the fact that he was kept subject to Communist dictates, to which he finally yielded.

In Slovakia there were not many political decorations. Only a few individuals were distinguished for their activities in the resistance movement, as, for instance, the Bishop of Košice, Monsignor Josef Čarský, Canon Andrej Cvinček of Nitra, Dean Pozdech of Bratislava, and some local resistance functionaries. Thus the ecclesiastical situation in Slovakia was more precarious than in the Czech provinces.

All power in Slovakia had been seized by the Protestant minority, who gave Catholics many lectures on morale, referring to Tiso's Slovak Republic. These depressing factors were surmounted by Slovak Catholics, however, and under courageous bishops they united with Czech and Moravian bishops, to defend the rights of their menaced Church.

Special attention must be given the tragic developments in the Greek Catholic Church in Slovakia.[66] Her fate in Carpatho-Ruthenia became evident as early as the year 1945. Two years later, the young Bishop Romža[67] was "liquidated" in a very mysterious way. From Poland and Carpatho-Ruthenia there came whole crowds of Greek Catholic refugees, some of whom took up temporary residence in Czechoslovakia, while others went farther, into Germany. In Slovakia, the Greek Catholic Church has her bishopric in Prešov where there is a major seminary. In the time of the strongest oppression, Greek Catholics were led by the very capable and irreproachable Bishop Pavol Gojdič. As aide in his missionary diocese there was appointed on March 10, 1947, as auxiliary bishop, Monsignor Basil Hopko.[68] Sufferings of the Greek Catholic Church in Czechoslovakia had begun in 1945 when Communists, under orders from Moscow, "liquidated" her according to a set plan. Orthodox priests endeavored to transfer all of her faithful adherents into the Orthodox Church, but they failed totally. Greek Catholics remained loyal to their faith. The aforesaid endeavors of Orthodox priests met the resistance of Bishop Gojdič and his faithful Basilians, under the leadership of the Reverend Sabol. The seizure of Greek Catholic Churches was a frequent event.

Because the jurisdiction of the Greek Catholic Bishop was extended also to Bohemia, where this Church had parishes in Prague and also in Liberec since 1947, and to Moravia, where there was a parish in Brno, Bishop Gojdič simplified regulations covering the holidays, and in August, 1946, issued a pastoral letter by which he canceled the use of the Julian calendar and introduced the Gregorian calendar.[69] This action proved to be very wise, owing to the practical needs of the Greek Catholic minority.[70]

Communists were aware of the heroic resistance of Greek Catholics in Poland and the Ukraine, and from 1945, through the harsh provisions of new laws and by persecution of priests, they set out to lessen the prestige of this Church in every possible way.

Bishop Gojdič had taken part in the conferences of all

the Czechoslovak bishops and joined them in issuing pastoral letters. Many Greek Catholic priests succeeded in escaping into exile, where they met the great majority of their fellow priests, thus proving their loyalty to Rome and the Faith by suffering for it as refugees. Communists arrested the heroic old Bishop Pavol Gojdič, and after a long imprisonment, in 1951 condemned him to life imprisonment.[71]

It was really a humiliating and unworthy role which was being played by the Orthodox Church, when, authorized by Communists, they undertook the task of digging the grave of the Greek Catholic Church. History proves that such state or national churches are directly or indirectly instruments of state policy, even of a bad policy.

But the calvary of the Catholic Church began in Slovakia. The Slovak National Council, in its capacity as a self-ruling legislative and executive body, on May 16, 1945, issued the decree about nationalization of private and ecclesiastical schools.[72] In this decree the Catholic Church was excoriated in a catastrophic manner with respect to her rights and aims in the education of Catholic children. In virtue of this law, there were seized from the Church in Slovakia, 1800 elementary schools, twenty-three high schools, and twenty vocational schools, or a total of 70 per cent of all the schools in Slovakia. At the same time regulations were issued governing procedure against religious and nonpolitical organizations, and against the Catholic press; according to the Košice Program, all prominent personalities of the former political parties were arrested in great numbers.

In the same week that saw issued the decree about nationalization of schools, Archbishop Karol Kmeťko, Bishop of Nitra and head of the Slovak hierarchy, issued a pastoral letter in which he attacked and opposed this decree as unjust and contrary to the will of the Slovak people, since, as early as 1924 some 770,000 people had signed a protest against such an attempt of the former Czechoslovak government; now the number of people who signed would be greater. The Archbishop pointed out the historical right of the Church to have her own schools, which had been established and maintained by her for many centuries. Slovak Catholics arranged manifestations and protests against this decree; but the Slovak police took these manifestations as a proof of disloyalty, and two bishops and many priests and faithful laymen were arrested. The bishops arrested were Jan Vojtaššak of Spišská Nová Ves, and Monsignor Michael Buzalka, auxiliary bishop of Trnava. A translation of Karol Kmeťko's protest follows.

NITRA, MAY 23, 1945.

ESTEEMED PRESIDENCY OF THE NATIONAL COUNCIL:

In the name of the Slovak R. C. Episcopate I present before the Esteemed Slovak National Council the following petition:

From the daily press I have found out that the Slovak National Council (SNR) by its decree of May 16 of this year has nationalized all schools: elementary, central, departmental and high.

Against this decree I am forced in the name of the Bishops' Committee of Slovakia to raise my voice and this from these motives:

With gratitude and appreciation responsible church authorities received the repeated announcement and assurance of the present governmental circles, that freedom of the Church will be spared and protected. I take the liberty to point out that the nationalization of schools conflicts with these announcements and encroaches upon the freedom of the Church in her *essential rights.*

According to Canon Law, the Constitution of the Catholic Church, the Church has the right and duty to found her schools, so that thus she may assure the religious and moral education of her faithful.

The Church can never renounce this right and violation or nonrecognition is felt by her as a very heavy and painful reaching into her life.

In all the States of the world where the freedom of the Church is assured, there is also recognized this her right and the Church not only in the Democratic States of America, the British Empire, but also in France, yes, even in the mission lands she has her schools, beginning with the elementary all the way up to universities. All these schools are recognized by the States as on an equal footing with the rest of the schools. It is worthy of mention that the French Republic after long years of bad experiences with the so-called neutral, lay school, in which leading French minds see one of the main reasons of the catastrophe of their country during this war, returned again to the religious school.

It would be odd if alone in the popular democratic Czechoslovak Republic this right of the Church were not recognized.

In Slovakia the Church has also *special historical right to schools.* The Church was the first one that founded schools and for many centuries it was she alone, who had the care of schools. Out of her own means the Church built and maintained many schools, and for this she should be thanked because thereby our nation became a cultured and civilized nation. Out of gratitude alone the school system of the Church should be spared and supported.

The esteemed SNR (Slovak National Council) by its decree reached deeply into our whole legislation on schools and voided a whole set of laws. The SNR (Slovak National Council) as a revolutionary organ should not have made so deep a reach, but could have left this to the elected representatives of the people. And even legal certainty itself and the legal order require that such important laws be enacted only after general and secret elections have been held which, according to the announcement of the responsible governmental functionaries, are to take place in Slovakia also while the people shall elect their representatives. Even if the SNR (Slovak National Council) faces the task that without asking the people it give out decrees about things which cannot suffer delay without jeopardy to the existence of the State or public order, such as military preparedness, supplies, transportation and the like, still *it cannot be claimed that the school question belongs among these, whose deference would endanger the existence of the renewed ČSR* (*Czechoslovak Republic*). For this reason it is fully reasonable to postpone the solution for such a time when the people at parliamentary elections assert themselves as to what direction they wish to have their State led, namely whether they accept the politics of this direction, which has in its program also the nationalization of schools, a State school monopoly or not.

The *popular democratic setup* of our State also requires that such an important question and one so directly affecting the education of the widest strata, should not be solved without asking the people. I take the liberty to mention *that this decree is not in agreement with the will of the Slovak people.* One of the proofs of this is also the signature action carried out in Slovakia in the year 1924. At that time in opposition to the designs of the then existing government of ČSR to nationalize all schooling, 775,040 adult and full-fledged citizens in Slovakia expressed themselves; they were followers (adherents) of various political parties and yet in this question they were of one mind. Their voting had the effect that the government of the then existing ČSR respected the will of the Slovak people and did not nationalize the Slovak Church schools.

The Slovak people have not changed their minds in this matter since then. If they have changed at all they have changed in this direction: that they adhere even more faithfully to their ideals of religious schools and religious education, for the sufferings and dangers of war noticeably strengthen the religious convictions of the people. A sign of this is already evident: open demonstrations of manifested impatience of parents, called forth by tactless assignment of teachers of denominations differing from the religion of the students, mixing of students of various religions in the grades, removing of religious symbols.

It is impossible not to wonder at these spontaneous manifestations, because after all *a parent has the natural, undeniable right to educate his child and to determine the direction in which such an education is to be given* when he entrusts to schools the further education of his children. Repeated and repeated announcements of responsible governmental functionaries assured the people that in the new popular democratic ČSR the will of the people would be decisive as to the kind of spirit, and the direction in which laws would be carried out and decrees given. If the former ČSR respected the will of the people in this question, it follows from the very essential ideas of the new ČSR that the will of the Slovak nation be even more taken into consideration, especially when there is a question of such a fundamental question of the internal structure of the State.

The nationalization of schools is entirely unjustifiable. It could be justified if religious schools harmed the interests of the State or citizenry. Any such thing of course cannot be claimed. For aside from the fact that even in the religious schools the teachers are citizens, these schools in every respect are under the supervision and management of the State. The teachers are appointed with its consent, they are State officials, the State has disciplinary power over them, the textbooks and textbook aids are approved by the State, and the study program is prescribed by the State.

State supervision over schools is so widespread that the

coexistence of State-recognized Church schools in no way can endanger the national culture and education of citizens, but will be definitely to their advantage; for the respective Church functionaries likewise caring for the national and religious-moral side of the school youth wish to contribute to the education of conscientious and responsible citizens, toward the strengthening and welfare of the State. When, however, I admit that a few consider the Church influence upon education to be undesirable or harmful, such thinking citizens among Slovaks are in so small a minority that their opinion beside that of the vast majority of citizens thinking otherwise cannot be directive.

Nor can this contra-argument stand, as though in the same district two different Church schools would divide the Slovak nation and thus harm the unity of the nation. If two or three churches of different religions can exist in the same district and do not harm the unity of the nation anywhere in the world, the same can be claimed about schools. But oppositely, where the State in regard to schools does not respect the difference in religious conviction of the people, there will ensue troubles—envy and unrest among the State citizens.

According to the daily press along with reference of the SNR to the order by which the Slovak schools are to be nationalized, there appeared also such words, that by this order the SNR does not intend to declare a cultural war, but oppositely, wishes the erection of a new Slovakia, the renewal of a new Czechoslovakia to be effected "by preserving the good relations toward the churches and incidentally also working with them."

Joyfully will the Bishops' Assembly of Slovakia welcome this proclamation and the Catholic Church willingly will take part in this important building program so that in the spirit of the principles of the gospel and national traditions and on the basis of her rich experiences she may actively help build a successful and firm country for all the citizens of the State. However it is impossible not to mention that so penetrating a reach into the internal life of the citizenry, carried out without previous agreement of the people, without discussion with the proper Church authorities, namely one-sidedly, already sets up at the very outset a cultural war, which the Catholic Church never wished for, and especially not now, when all energies are needed to concentrate on the removal of the terrible results of war.

Pleading that the SNR weigh the foregoing serious arguments and in consequence thereof make provisions so that the decree concerning nationalization of schools be not carried out, I am,

With expression of deep respect,

KAROL KMEŤKO

N. R. Archbishop, President of the Bishops' Conferences.[73]

On October 2, 1945, Archbishop Kmeťko issued a new pastoral letter[74] in which he reaffirmed his protest against this decree, reproving also the propaganda of those with anti-Catholic tendencies. As evidence of the hostility being enacted toward Catholics, the pastoral mentioned the removal of Catholic clerics from civil service positions and their replacement by non-Catholics, press campaigns against the clergy, and the arrest of Catholics on "disloyalty" charges, although similar measures were not taken against non-Catholic "collaborators." It protested against all restrictions of the Catholic press and the arrest of Monsignor Jan Pösteny, administrator of a nonpolitical organization known as Spolok Sv. Vojtěcha (Association of Saint Adalbert), for issuing Catholic books; against the nationalization of charitable institutions and the center of Catholic charities in Bratislava. It noted that, according to the last census (1938), 73.6 per cent of the total population was Catholic and stated that this Catholic majority should not be terrorized by a non-Catholic minority.

On January 10, 1946, a delegation of Slovak bishops[75] called on President Beneš and, having expressed their allegiance, asked in the form of a memorandum that—

1. Schools operated by religious orders should be returned to their communities;
2. Teachers, including nuns and brothers, who had been transferred by Slovak school authorities to remote places, should be reinstated in their former posts;
3. Permission should be given to place crucifixes in all classrooms of all those schools where the parents or the pupils asked for it;
4. All teachers should be instructed not to prevent pupils from praying before and after classes and from using the Catholic form of greeting;

5. All religious and nonpolitical organizations of Catholics, such as the Association of Catholic Young People, should be permitted to reorganize and their confiscated property should be returned;
6. Catholic "internats," particularly the dormitories for Catholic students in Bratislava, orphanages, and the charities buildings should be returned. These were built through Catholic contributions, many of which came from Catholic Slovaks in the United States;
7. More newsprint should be allotted for Catholic newspapers and magazines;
8. Catholics who had been unjustly interned should be released at once.[76]

Later, Slovak Catholics applied in March, 1946, to the National Front headquarters for permission to form a new political party to be known as the Christian Democratic party.[77] Some of the leaders of the proposed new party were Catholic deputies who had left the Democratic party in Slovakia because of its policy of not giving protection to the Catholics. Dr. Jan Kempný, Immrich Kruzlich, Stefan Harcar, Stephan Horvath, and Julius Spanik were the principal leaders of this movement. Featured in the program of the new party were these aims:

1. To work for reinstatement of Catholic control over schools which had been operated by the Church and by religious communities prior to the nationalization of all Slovak schools.
2. To work for full freedom of the press and to revive the Catholic periodicals which had not yet been permitted to resume publication.
3. To work for the freedom to reorganize Catholic associations.

The new party addressed its application to the "National Front," a body created by the government with the sole right to pass on the authorization of new political parties, the free formation of which was forbidden.

The fact that it was necessary to establish a new political organization for Catholics is proof that Catholics were not protected on any side to a satisfactory extent. Their organizing in a Democratic party under the leadership of Monsignor

Andrej Cvinček, Canon of Nitra, was enforced by a feeling of self-defense and necessity. Only thereby could the Democratic party which was mainly Catholic, under the chairmanship of the Protestant Dr. Josef Lettrich, gain sixty-one per cent of the votes in the general elections of 1946.

Despite all this, the position of Catholics in the Democratic party was only of secondary importance because very few Catholics were admitted as candidates owing to their past support of the Tiso Independent Slovak Republic. This state of affairs and its subsequent development was evidence of the good will of the Slovak Catholics. The Communist party of Slovakia, on the other hand, was very brutal toward Catholics. Its secretary issued all kinds of measures against Catholics, which the Democratic party was not in a position to moderate since it was forced to make compromises with the Communists.

As in Slovakia the People's party was forbidden, two groups were planned by the regime to replace it: the Slovak Democratic party and, later on, the Slovak party of Freedom. Both were organized in a spirit similar to that of the Czech People's party and under similar Communist supervision.[78]

In Bohemia, the most ardent interpreter among Communists was the Minister of Information, Václav Kopecký, who in his vituperations against Catholics surpassed even the former Nazi Minister, Dr. Goebbels. On every occasion he reiterated threats to Catholics. In his speech to the congress of the Communist party, April, 1946, he called the view of Catholics in fighting for their rights "the Vatican conspiracy stuff." He went on to say that "patriotic and democratic circles of the Catholic Church are expected to stand loyally by the Republic in spite of all intrigues emanating from the Vatican, which acts as defender of the defeated Germans, which even today helps fascism in Spain, and which is biased against our ally, the Soviet Union."[79]

The Communists were guided in their behavior toward Czech and Moravian Catholics by this estimate of what the Catholic situation should be. As Communists were not in a position to attack Czech and Moravian Catholics because of their meritorious work during World War II, they attacked the Vatican as the center of Christianity. The editor of the

Czech Catholic magazine, *Katolík,* the Reverend Adolf Kajpr, S. J., published in April an open letter, addressed to Minister Kopecký, in which he wrote:

> We all know, Minister, that your "Vatican conspiracy stuff" is an artificially provoked bugaboo, which will never undermine our confidence in the Holy Father. We shall not take lessons from you—either as regards our patriotism or our Catholicism. We are not engaged in politics; we do not strive for power or riches. What we want is a bit of real, manly, even if only modest freedom, because by our sufferings we have contributed to the preservation of that freedom which we fully deserve.[80]

That Czech Catholics were determined not to take "lying down" the baseless accusations hurled against the Holy See was manifested at a meeting of five thousand Prague Catholics held on the day of the final sessions of the Communist congress in Prague. There was a tremendous ovation when the Reverend Antonin Zgarbek, S.J., told a meeting of the Confraternity of St. Michael: "We love our country, but we shall not permit the Holy Father to be attacked and insulted."[81] A resolution pledging fidelity to the Pope was adopted at the meeting and cabled to Rome.

A further attack against Catholics was made by "Red" Professor Zdeněk Nejedlý, Minister of Education, when he announced officially in a cultural committee of the Provisional National Assembly, on March 4, 1946, his plan to nationalize private schools in Bohemia and Moravia.[82] "The main thing is that churches should not separate themselves from national unity and indulge in isolationism. From the viewpoint of a national and people's state, it is everybody's duty and right to participate in one way or another in the building up of the state. In this lies the question of ecclesiastical schools. It is not a question of religion, but a question of such isolation."[83] Under this plan, one thousand schools in Bohemia and in Moravia were included for liquidation. According to accurate published statistics, there were 699 kindergartens, 23 elementary schools, 19 higher-grade schools called "měštanky," 3 schools for retarded pupils, 2 institutes for the blind, 3 institutes for deaf mutes, 10 high schools, 8 industrial schools, 10 specialized artisan schools, 3 commercial schools, 21 farming schools, 1 orchard workers' school, 53 winter farmers' schools, 31 housewives' schools, 5 music schools, and 38 apprentices' schools.[84]

Another drastic measure against Catholics was the cancellation on October 10, 1946, of eight Catholic holydays, at the suggestion of the provisional National Assembly. The main supporter of this suggestion was Antonin Zápotocký, chairman of the ÚRO (labor unions). He maintained that "the economic reconstruction of Czechoslovakia is impaired by many legal holydays: Epiphany, Ascension, Corpus Christi, Assumption, Immaculate Conception, Saint Peter and Saint Paul, Saints Cyril and Methodius, and Saint Wenceslaus."[85] Catholics strongly opposed this measure. Eighteen Catholic organizations from Bohemia and Moravia submitted a protest. The Association of Moravian Catholic Women[86] arranged the collection of signatures for this protest and organized a delegation to call on the respective ministers. The Catholic press (*Našinec* in Olomouc, *Katolík* in Prague, *Katolické noviny* in Bratislava) wrote articles commenting on this protest, but all efforts were in vain.

The Communist plan was carried through, despite the fact that three hundred delegates of the Congress of Catholic Youth in Prague, November 11, 1946, joined the protest.[87] Even Catholic students were not left out of the persecution, mainly because of their contact with the world center, Pax Romana. Czechoslovak members of this organization were arrested in February, 1946. Also involved was Dr. Bohdan Chudoba[88] who, after his release from jail, had a private talk with President Beneš. Pardon was extended only to the Academic League of University Students, which was under the protection of the People's party headed by Monsignor Šrámek.

The Communist Minister of Interior, Václav Nosek, contributed greatly to the tragedy of Catholic persecution. He uncovered espionage everywhere and arrested thousands of people.

When on December 9, 1946, the National Assembly voted for the law of general censorship of all books and newspapers published in the country, Václav Kopecký was appointed minister of propaganda, controlling all publications in Czechoslovakia. Catholics especially were affected by this measure. Under various pretexts (e.g., lack of paper) Catholic magazines were suppressed, so that only political periodicals, protected by the People's party, could be issued.

The year 1947 proved to be for Catholics a period of general disappointment, as it also was for the President and ministers of other parties. They learned, as T. G. Masaryk had said, "Catholics will have only as many rights as they will be able to defend." That defense was very difficult, since Communists, supported in cultural affairs by Socialists, were recklessly carrying out their threats in accordance with the plan dictated by Moscow, even against the Catholic majority.

The determined defense of their rights by Catholics irritated the Communists, who broke every resistance by force. The political strength of the People's party was too weak, especially when National Socialists would not unite with the Catholics in cultural and ecclesiastical matters. Thus Communists were able to effect all that they proclaimed.

During March, 1947, Slovak school supervisors arranged conferences of teachers, in which the following resolution was accepted: "In the interests of the nation and state we most resolutely reject the attempts at denationalization and reorganization of the schools. The nationalization of the schools is the first precious prize of our glorious Slovak National uprising; it is a pillar of our future cultural development which the nation and the school workers will protect against any odds."[89]

The Czechoslovak government, by proclamation of Prime Minister Klement Gottwald, offered a solution to the problem of the whole educational system by calling the nationalizing action a "school reform." He referred to the existence of nationalized schools in England and America and declared it to be "incomprehensible" that there should be disputes in Czechoslovakia for and against the proposed "reform."

While acknowledging the basic right to freedom of opinion and freedom of religion, Beneš expressed the view in May, 1947, before the delegation of teachers, that "even if one had the most liberal concept in the world, one could not avoid the participation of the state in education."[90] By an earlier speech, given in May, 1947, before the delegations of teachers, Beneš betrayed the former stand he had expressed many times before. Thereby all hopes of Catholics were frustrated. Catholics were not resigned, however; on July 18, 1947, all Slovak bishops issued a pastoral letter[91] in which they rejected again the proposed school reform as unrighteous and anti-Christian, declaring that the Catholic Church would never resign her right to have her own schools and recalling this right, secured by the constitution of the first Czechoslovak Republic.

Influenced by this pastoral letter, the Central Council of Lutherans in Slovakia also declared on July 18, 1947, in Bratislava, their stand for freedom in education. At the same time, the Protestant students' association *Kuzmany,* in Bratislava, expressed its stand for nationalization of all schools, despite the fact that another association of Protestant students, the National Council of Students, had taken its stand for freedom in education. This is an indication that Protestants were not of one mind in this matter.[92]

The determined stand of Slovak bishops also later influenced the Slovak Democratic party, which strengthened its resistance against the Communists. The Minister of the Interior, Václav Nosek, discovered the "great fascist anti-government plot"[93] and on October 16, 1947, more than 237 persons were arrested. On November, 1947, Slovak bishops issued a new pastoral letter, emphasizing their stand and declaring that they would remain faithful guardians of the laws of God even though their voice should remain the voice of a Saint John the Baptist in the desert. They said, "Our hearts are also filled with sorrow over the antistate activity, which is now the object of investigation, but which we hope will be conducted in a correct and just manner. Hundreds of citizens, together with their families, must suffer because of this antistate activity, and the number of political trials, which was already diminishing, may again multiply. This greatly disturbs the peace of souls and the long-desired consolation of the nation and state."[94]

But the Minister of the Interior in Prague, Václav Nosek, on November 28, 1947, published a seventy-one-page pamphlet entitled *Conspiracy against the Republic.*[95] It contained a summary of the Ministry's investigation of the "extensive antistate conspiracy in Slovakia and photostat copies of documents." The list of arrested people was made up almost exclusively of Catholics: Pavel Čarnogurský, Dr. Miloš Bugar,

Dr. Jan Kempný, many priests, functionaries of the Catholic Charity office, Dr. Ludevít Obtulovič, and others. Careful perusal of this pamphlet, however, shows that there is only one suspect against whom there are what appear to be proofs: Otto Obuch, who came to Slovakia armed with recommendations from the exiled former Minister Durčanský and succeeded in getting an important confidential post as secretary to the recently resigned Vice President of the Slovak government, Jan Ursiny. Obuch was seeking to establish ties with the Slovak antistate movement abroad. While all the invectives in this pamphlet were not true, nonetheless it became apparent that Communists were devoting full attention toward strengthening their reprisals for past actions of the Slovaks. They thus frightened many people.

The Slovak Democratic party was falling into greater dependence upon the Communists, and, from that time on, Slovak bishops arranged conferences with bishops from Bohemia and Moravia. On December 4, 1947, the first conference of the Czechoslovak episcopate was held under the chairmanship of Archbishop Josef Beran. From this conference there was sent a memorandum to the Minister of Education, Dr. Jaroslav Stránský, a politician of the National Socialist party, asking freedom of religion and religious education in the schools. A delegation also was sent to President Beneš. Archbishop Beran, as their spokesman, expressed the hope that President Beneš would continue his interest "in preserving the religious peace and friendly relations between Church and state" and that in the framing of the constitution and the school law, as well as in the application of the land reform measures, "everything would be eliminated which might run counter to the best interests of the state." The Archbishop also voiced his displeasure at recent attacks on the Holy Father and the Vatican: "These attacks grieve us, since we ourselves cannot be accused of violating religious tolerance in a similar manner."[96]

President Beneš answered: "My standpoint today is the same. I understand your troubles, which are caused particularly by the great demoralization following the war. Yet, on the other hand, it must be seen by everybody that religious life and faith are gaining ground among the people here."[97]

A message was also sent to Prime Minister Klement

Gottwald. Present at this conference were all Czechoslovak archbishops and bishops, except Archbishop Karol Kmeťko who was absent because of illness. This conference compiled a pastoral letter which was very explicit and addressed to all officials of the government:

> It is a very sad fact that insincerity, dishonor, and false presentation of facts are spreading also in those circles of society dominant in the nation's culture with the consequence that public opinion is exposed to false influences. From the highest places it was repeatedly emphasized that cultural strife is quite undesirable in our country. We are grateful for this assurance but we would be bad guardians of religion if we silently tolerated a hidden, secret *Kulturkampf* which would block the way to a more effective application of the *Modus Vivendi* agreement between this country and the Holy See, a pact whose importance is recognized by every sensible and unprejudiced man.[98]

An appeal also was made to all Catholic laymen to cooperate, and because of the urgent lack of priests, to protect the cultural and ecclesiastical values in such a historical crisis. This pastoral letter of December 4 is really historical document, by which Czech and Slovak bishops warned government circles concerning the unfortunate consequences of their continued actions and advocated moderation in the interests of the nation. The voice of the bishops was not heeded. The close cooperation of Czech and Slovak bishops became a historical expression of Czechoslovak solidarity, following the extensive measures taken against Slovakia. This cooperation is also an indication of the extent to which the Catholic Church was being menaced.

The year 1947 was a landmark for the development of Czechoslovak democracy. When the Marshall Plan was made known, it was decided to accept it. But the strong intervention of Moscow forced the Czechoslovak government to cancel its previous affirmative decision. Prime Minister Gottwald, Minister of Foreign Affairs Jan Masaryk, Minister Prokop Drtina, and Secretary of the Ministry for Foreign Affairs Arnošt Heidrich were called to Moscow on July 9, 1947. There Stalin himself informed them that it was inadmissible for Czechoslovakia to participate in the Marshall

Plan.[99] This action proved to the whole world that there was no democracy in Czechoslovakia, since the government was forced to cancel its previous decision. Western tendencies were being driven from the land of Czechoslovakia. The trend of future development became manifest. This was the reason that the Christian People's party and the National Socialist party began to support each other in the face of Communist pressure.

In spite of everything, the Minister of Foreign Trade, Dr. Hubert Ripka, praised the Soviet-Czechoslovak economic agreement. By this agreement, Czechoslovakia was in reality being robbed.[100] Things developed very quickly after this. Communists occupied all key positions in the police corps and strengthened their position in the army; they established an armed civil militia corps in all factories. Speeches of Communist ministers and deputies were delivered in the open; now it took more courage for non-Communist ministers and deputies to make their speeches. It was apparent to all that the crisis had come. It culminated in the February 25, 1948, events, when the Communists took exclusive power into their own hands.

Democracy fully disappeared from Czechoslovakia. The sufferings of the Catholic Church increased. But the Church did not desist from defending her rights and mission under the leadership of the Archbishop of Prague, Dr. Josef Beran.[101] Before February, 1948, the Communists, having had no exclusive political power in legislative and executive procedure, held back their plan to subjugate all Christian churches. This hindrance vanished after the Communist *coup d'état* of February 25, 1948.

CHAPTER NINE

THE COMMUNIST CONSTITUTION AND ITS EFFECT ON ECCLESIASTICAL AFFAIRS

THE YEAR 1948 MEANT A COMPLETE CHANGE IN THE DEvelopment of the Czechoslovakian Republic. While it is true that events in that year were only a necessary consequence of the things that happened in 1945 when communism opened its drive on all satellite countries, which eventually fell under its sphere of influence, nevertheless the year 1948 meant the seizure of full power and exclusive control by the Communists. Infiltration of communism in the preparatory period since 1945 was carried out very skillfully and with the utmost caution. The ultimate purpose was the seizure of all key positions in the state. Concerning the relation of state, society and economic systems, communism and socialism had taken as their ideal the *Communist Manifesto,*[1] from which ten principles were taken to replace the Decalogue of God. This change, of course, became fatal to the Czechoslovak policy, because it caused the loss of democracy, which even the politicians who had previously cooperated in Communist plans and reforms were against.

The case of Czechoslovakia is very instructive from many points of view. "States are preserved by the ideas that give rise to their creation,"[2] and whenever Czechoslovakia failed to respect this principle it lost very much, especially after World War II. In the prewar period, Czechoslovakia was soundly based on democratic and Christian principles. Communists were able to seize power only because these principles were neglected at a time when their need was crucial.

The political situation in the year 1948 was proof of this. Already in the fall of 1947, the Communists had made their last preparations. In Slovakia, they arranged to pressure the Slovak Democratic party; they arranged so-called conspiracies against the state;[3] they arrested two courageous deputies of the parliament, the Catholics Dr. Kempný and Dr. Bugar.[4]

In Bohemia, the Communists arranged some incidents and through the Communist deputy, M. P. Losnar, in Krčman near Olomouc organized preparations for an assault on three Ministers; namely, Peter Zenkl, Prokop Drtina, and Jan Masaryk.[5] The plot was discovered by Dr. Krajina, Secretary General of the National Socialist party. In this way the public was made aware of the collusion between the Ministry of Interior, led by a Communist, Václav Nosek, and the Ministry of Justice, led by the National Socialist, Prokop Drtina. From the Christian People's party, Dr. Rostislav Sochorec, a great fighter for the rights of farmers, was arrested because he had opposed the drastic measures of the Communist Minister of Agriculture, Julius Ďuriš. Dr. Sochorec was tortured in jail and died. His burial was attended by great crowds from the whole district.[6] The crowds at the funeral in Staré Město-Velehrad in Moravia were an indication of the strong sentiment against communism and against the farmers' organization, which was being infiltrated by Communists. Non-Communist parties refused to continue with further nationalization, refraining from action until after the general elections which were prepared for the summer of 1948.

When the Communist Minister of Finance, Dr. Jar. Dolanský, suggested that the wages of civil service employees be 300 crowns monthly, the non-Communist ministers suggested a further raise of 500 to 800 crowns monthly. As a protest against this last suggestion, the chairman of labor unions (ÚRO), Antonín Zápotocký, convoked a congress of the labor unions in Prague for Sunday, February 22, 1948. Minister Ďuriš convoked the so-called farmers' committees for Sunday, February 29, 1948, also in Prague. In the meantime, the Communist Minister of the Interior, Václav Nosek, authorized Police Commander Dynybyl to appoint eight district commanders of the police in Prague to strengthen Communist positions. On February 13, 1948, the government decided by majority that these measures of Minister Nosek must be repealed. Nosek refused to do so and non-Communist ministers resigned: from the Christian People's party, Dr. John Šrámek, Rev. Francis Hála, Dr. Adolf Procházka, Ing. Václav Kopecký; from the National Socialist party, Dr. Peter Zenkl, Dr. Hubert Ripka, Dr. Jaroslav Stránský, and Dr. Prokop Drtina; from the Slovak Democratic party, Dr. Štefan Kočvara, Dr. John Pietor, Dr. Franěk and John Lichner. President Beneš did not accept these resignations and assured the Ministers that he would not accept them in the future either.[7] On Saturday, February 21, 1948, the Communists arranged a meeting in the Old Town Square in Prague; they demanded that the resignations of these Ministers be accepted and also that a new government be established without them.

On this occasion, Prime Minister Gottwald delivered the following speech, characteristic of the Communists:[8]

> Allow me please, first to show some causes and the whole background of the governmental crisis and after that to explain the manner in which we will solve it for the prosperity of the people, the nation and the Republic.
>
> You already know that yesterday, ministers representing the National Socialistic, People's, and Slovak Democratic parties resigned. The ministers of these parties established in the center of the Government a reactionary bloc, which was the reason why for over a month there was no possibility for the Government to do any positive work, especially the work of carrying out the program settled by all parties. On February 13, this reactionary bloc impelled, in the session of the Cabinet, the decision of the majority, according to which Minister Nosek was ordered, unlawfully and against the Constitution, to repeal the decision of the Provincial Commander of the Police in Prague. The matter was the transference of eight police officers. Please notice that this measure was carried out according to the law, that it was performed in full accordance with the central National Committee in Prague and with the Provincial National Committee for Bohemia. The Minister of the Interior was fully competent to make this decision in his own jurisdiction. I am mentioning in this connection a characteristic accusation, that this decision in the Cabinet was made in the absence of the constitutionally responsible Minister of Interior, that this question was discussed close to the end of the session, that the majority of ministers did not know the contents of the mentioned order and that under these circumstances the voting was carried out. Because of this, it happened that the Minister of Interior, who yesterday

returned to his office, having interrupted his convalescence, was not able to carry out this decision of the Cabinet, not only from the political and constitutional point of view, because it concerns and violates his jurisdiction, but also because the decision of a close majority was defective from the point of view of its form.

To explain all these and other things and to correct them, I convoked an extraordinary session of the Cabinet yesterday, to which the Minister of Interior was to report and to which the Minister of Interior, Václav Nosek, and the Minister of National Defense, General Ludvík Svoboda, were to make an important declaration in connection with invectives of the new paper *Svobodné Slovo*, printed yesterday in connection with the so-called espionage affair in Most. Attendance at this session had fallen off because the representatives of the National Socialist, People's and Slovak Democratic parties decided not to attend, pretending that the decision of the Cabinet from February 13 was not yet carried out. Representatives of these parties refused to listen quietly to reports of constitutionally responsible ministers and to make decisions only after that. They chose another way: they sent their resignations to the hands of the President and they caused this crisis in the Cabinet.

I am explaining these particulars to you so that you will understand the serious background of the whole matter. Everyone undoubtedly realizes that a crisis in the Cabinet is not usually caused by any eight appointed or removed police officers, so that the true reason must be of a deeper nature. The reason behind all this is that the reactionary forces are endeavoring to frustrate the constructive program of the Cabinet, especially in trying to ruin the efforts for the execution of the people's democratic constitution, laws concerning national security, new law reforms concerning taxes, relaxation for farmers and craftsmen, and the whole line of prepared measures in the favor of working people in towns as well as in the country.

The cause lies in the efforts of the reactionaries to annihilate the true national front, the fraternal bond of workers, farmers, craftsmen and intellectuals, according to the old slogan of exploiters: "Divide and conquer." The cause of it is that the reaction would bring our country into hostile relations with our Slavic allies, especially toward the most powerful of our allies, the Soviet Union. These reactionaries do not take into consideration that this new

Church would be the cause of a new national and state catastrophe in Czechoslovakia. The fault for all this really lies with the reactionaries of our nation, who, supported from abroad, are making an attempt to attain reactionary goals in our people's democratic order and the successive destruction of all that national revolution and liberation brought to our people. Our internal and foreign reactionaries are afraid of the results of free and democratic general election and they are making a desperate attempt, cost what it may, to seize power for themselves and to make possible the terrorizing of our peaceful nation.

But that is not all. Internal and foreign reactionaries want to make our republic the headquarters for spies and saboteurs sent to us from abroad, to arrange through them acts of all kinds against our republic and our allies, especially against the Soviet Union. This is proved especially by the treason committed yesterday by *Svobodné Slovo*, which is protecting spies and saboteurs. When they were caught and convicted, this newspaper called them "seduced people," and hurled invectives against our police organs who caught and convicted these spies. It is to be added that all lies and insults which are mentioned by Slavs against our police are based on the fabricated evidence of caught and convicted spies and saboteurs. In this connection we will conceive the true background of mongering by the reaction against the police and against all organs of the hierarchy of interior and of National Defense. It cries hysterically about a police regime, "terror," and even about Gestapoism.

Yesterday, in the Palace of the Prime Ministers, I welcomed many delegations. Among them was the delegation of the Armankt factory of Brno, whose members were followers of the mentioned parties. I asked them what they view as the difference between the police of today and the police corps in the time of the Republic before Munich. They replied determinedly, "We see the difference in the fact that the members of the Police SNB are greeting us, when we meet them, whereas under the former regime the police used their swords and sticks against us and were arresting us." Yes, my friends, there is a great difference between the police corps SNB under the leadership of Václav Nosek, and the former police under the leadership of the Agrarian, Dr. Josef Černý. This is the reason for the defiance and resistance of reactionaries against the police SNB. To get the police SNB in its hands, to transform the police into an instrument working for the reaction, against the working people, to return to the era of Černý when shots were being fired against people, this is the main aim of reactionary dissidents.

I am sure you all agree with me, when to the demands of this reaction we answer "Never!" We will never permit the Police Corps SNB to fall into their hands. This police corps will never act against the people, but it will always go with the people against reactionary saboteurs, black-marketeers, spies, and enemies of the Republic.

Citizens and dear friends! We have now a great task, which is to solve the cabinet crisis in a way helpful to the nation and Republic. We will solve it in a constitutional, democratic, and parliamentary manner, on the basis of a national front, representing all strata of working people in towns and in the country.

We suggest framing a cabinet, in lieu of the resigned ministers, with new men who have remained loyal to the original spirit of the national front, which was formulated in the common fight against invaders during the victorious revolution. We believe there are such men and women among Czechs and Slovaks in sufficient numbers, in all political parties and organizations. Ministers who really left the idea and program of the national front and thereby caused the cabinet crisis were acting without the consent of their parties and they did not secure the approval of their party members for their procedure. It is more necessary now that the members of their parties should express their true opinion and thus help to form a government of the national front with trustworthy men.

Having done this, the Government of the National Front, supported by trustworthy rulers of all progressive and democratic elements in all political parties and organizations can indeed take the task of carrying out the program of the government, especially as to the proclamation of a new constitution, National Security Act, and of the acts concerning new land reform, tax restriction for farmers and craftsmen, and to order new general elections in the term fixed by law. To achieve that, the new cabinet could lay its aims before the constitutional National Assembly, asking for the confidence and assistance necessary to fulfill the program already approved by the Constitutional National Assembly after the election in 1946.

We are sure that our people who have long and protestingly observed the invectives of internal and foreign reaction against our people's democratic regime, would not tolerate a return of the resigned ministers or its agents into the Cabinet of the Republic. We are sure, too, that the nation, in a determined stand, would frustrate any such attempt, and that it would decide to assure the peaceful development of the Republic.

We are taking the manifestations of today as a proof of the firm conviction and strength of our people, and this will be proved more by the historical Congress of Labor Unions tomorrow, and the Congress of Peasants' Committees next Saturday and Sunday. We do not doubt that our people through their determination and strength, will force through, in case of need, the more radical and determinative ways and means.

Citizens, dear friends! I am calling on all of you to be prepared. I am calling on all good Czechs and Slovaks, workers, peasants, craftsmen, and intellectuals, to be concordant, united. Establish local, district, and regional action committees of the national front from democratic, progressive representatives of all political parties and all national organizations and frustrate any provocations by reactionary agents. Be of one accord. Your truth will win!

This speech demonstrates the fraudulence of the official Communist policy in its endeavor to pretend that this *coup d'état* was legal.

President Eduard Beneš insisted on forming a democratic government.[9] In the meantime, Communists prepared through all local, district, and provincial committees, and also in all "action committees" which consisted of trustworthy and loyal Communist sympathizers, to seize power throughout the state. They armed civilian militia in the factories and exerted strong pressure on the President and dissidents of other parties. The Central Action Committee of the restored National Front was established in Prague.

In the first session of it, speeches were deliverd by Antonín Zápotocký, Klement Gottwald, General Ludwík Svoboda, Dr. Patková, Deputy Kobylka, Deputy Alois Petr, Zdeněk Fierlinger, Evžen Erban, and general representatives of the Czechoslovak Church.[10] The Communists prepared a list of men suggested by them for the Cabinet and threatened a revolution if the President refused to sign. Through the treason of such Social Democrats as Zdeněk Fierlinger and Bohumil Laušman, the opposition against the Communists collapsed, and by their endeavors they helped dissidents of the National Socialist and People's parties, especially when Jan Masaryk accepted the seat of Minister for Foreign Affairs and Ludwík Svoboda accepted the seat of the Minister of National Defense. The presence of Soviet Ambassador Valerian Alexandrovič Zorin in Prague strengthened the pressure and tension. It thus happened that the President, despite all his promises on February 25, approved by signature the establishment of the Gottwald government. and the Communists, in a great meeting on Wenceslaus Square, proclaimed seizure of power in the state. The main speech was delivered by Prime Minister Klement Gottwald, who condemned the reactionary Ministers who had resigned:

> First, I returned from the Hradčany, residence of our President. This morning I suggested that the resignation of ministers made on February 20, be accepted. At the same time I handed over to D. E. Beneš, President of the Republic, the list of men with whom the Cabinet should be reconstructed and who should be appointed as new Ministers. I can announce to you that the President accepted in full all my suggestions. Decrees, either of resignation or of nomination, have already been signed by the President and in a short time they will be signed by me, too.
>
> I consider it my duty to emphasize the fact that it was not easy for the President to make this decision but he recognized the necessity of such a measure. He realized that, especially when he saw that this was the true will of the people.
>
> We comrades are grateful to the President, because he respected the will of the people, even in a matter which was very difficult for him. Reaction, which prepared the strike against the people, was defeated and dispelled. Unity of our people, unity of working classes, unity of workers, peasants, craftsmen, and intellectuals supplied sufficient strength to annihilate any plots and riots of the reaction. Now that the attack of the reaction is repulsed, we will return to our work, to fulfill our two-year plan. Our work will be more encouraging because the influence of all

saboteurs has been almost eliminated by our meritorious acts.

It is necessary, my comrades, now that the will of our people has forced its way through in such a solemn manner, to increase our endeavor to surmount all obstacles which are ahead and to set up in our republic, deprived of all reactionaries, a happy home for all working people.[11]

In this way the *coup d'état* of the Communists was carried out, against the will of a great majority of the nation and against protests of the United States, Great Britain, and France.[12]

The nation was frightened and disorganized by all this. On February 24, university students arranged in Prague a protest procession on Hradčany Castle[13] to call on the President, but Communist police frustrated this. The nation was disappointed by the inconsistency of President Beneš, upon whom it relied. An impressive protest was the attempted suicide of Minister Drtina, a man who was always faithful and most loyal to the President. His confused state of mind over the decisions of the President caused him to jump out of a window. When awakened from the shock, he said: "If I could only understand him."[14]

Monsignor Šrámek, the first to resign as a member of the National Assembly,[15] and as chairman of the party, stopped all activities of the Christian People's party and despite his illness, tried to escape abroad with the Reverend Francis Hála, the former Minister of the Post. Their efforts were betrayed and they were caught in the forest near Rakovník just as they were preparing to enter an airplane.[16] At the end of February, 1948, the Minister of the People's party, Dr. Adolf Procházka, and his wife, Dr. Helena Koželuhová, succeeded in escaping. A short time thereafter the general secretaries of non-Communist parties, Dr. Adolf Klimek, Dr. Krajina, and Blažej Vilím succeeded in crossing the border.

At the first meeting of the National Assembly, after the aforementioned February events, on March 10, 1948, the program of the Gottwald government was proclaimed.[17] This meeting was attended by 230 deputies;[18] others either had been imprisoned or had succeeded in escaping into exile.

Dissidents of the People's party established an action

committee, with Alois Petr as chairman. His assistant, who became an infamous traitor, Reverend Josef Plojhar, Minister of Public Health, was a collaborator with the Communists. Dissidents of the National Socialist party were headed by Dr. A. Najman, J. B. Kozák, and Mrs. Pátkova. Dissidents of the Social Democratic party, under the leadership of Zdeněk Fierlinger and Bohumil Laušman, not only collaborated actively with the Communists, but even became very effective supporters of the Marxist program of the Gottwald government.

In this way the Communists pretended to the world that their February acts were legal, all the more so since President Beneš remained in office even after February 25, a fact of great historical importance. This fact was misused by Communists in manipulating foreign opinion. Behind this façade they sought to hide the death of Czechoslovak democracy. The suicide of Jan Masaryk on March 10 was certification of its burial.[19]

The relations of Czechoslovak Communists toward the Catholic Church became dependent on Communist tactics and her fate was regulated by a unification with Russia's policy:

> The Soviet hostility to the Church, resting primarily on hostility to the Church's claim that it is here to teach mankind, is increased by the universal character of Catholicism; it transcends boundaries and curtains and frontiers. And in this the Soviets are merely following and intensifying what many rulers, nominally Christian, have so often done in the past when they resented the idea of a spiritual authority outside their dominions not amenable to their control. But for Western Europeans today, the fact that there is this common religion each side of the great divide across Europe is a major asset; something which affords the best hope that, if only the submerged populations stand firm during what may be a long season of trial, the underlying unity of Europe, at present almost submerged, will become fully visible once more.[20]

Czechoslovak Communists and their fellow travelers faced this problem and wanted to solve it the Soviet way only, but they met strong resistance in the Catholic Church in Czechoslovakia; for this reason they decided to carry out their will in any way, legal or illegal—and finally succeeded.

In the critical days of February, 1948, many people wrote letters to Archbishop Beran, asking him to speak. He himself was not permitted to speak over the radio and so he wrote encouraging articles for the newspaper *Lidová demokracie,* which were taken by the people as an appeal, as is apparent from the contents:

> Awake! Do not destroy the bequest of the President-Liberator and the work of our President Establisher.
>
> It is understandable why in every period of tension, such as that in which we are living now, the number of anonymous advice-givers increases. Everybody is given advice as to what should not have been done. The conciseness of these writers is illustrated by one of these letters which says:
>
> Do not keep silent, Archbishop! You must not keep silent!
>
> I considered and meditated. "You must not keep silent." Will it really make any difference if I keep silent? . . . or I speak? A falling avalanche can be reclaimed, it is true, but an avalanche is material, whereas the movement of mind depends on people who are able to think and consider. You will speak in vain and, besides, it was said by Christ: "If I had not come and spoken to them, they would have no sin. But now they have no excuse for their sin." Perhaps it would have been better to keep silent and leave them unknowing. But Paul has written: "I charge thee, in the sight of God and Christ Jesus, who will judge the living and the dead by his coming and by his kingdom, preach the word, be urgent in season, out of season, reprove, entreat, rebuke with all patience and teaching." Therefore, I am not keeping silent. The good Czech nation knows us well. I have never betrayed my nation and I will never betray it. Therefore, I am speaking now.
>
> I am adjuring you all by the precious blood shed in concentration camps and in prisons by our brothers and sisters, and by the tears and pains of Czech women and mothers. Awake! I know you do not want to evoke any contentions among brothers, but this is not the way to evade them. Consider your responsibility. Maintain the legal order! You all approved the nationalization. Strive toward this aim. By legal means it is possible to achieve reform, even of the most radical nature. Read history!

> Convince yourselves! Do not destroy the bequest of the President-Liberator and the work of the President-Establisher! You called them by these names. Their work is being recognized by the whole nation. They worked and suffered for you and for your descendants. You had full trust in them and ingratitude causes pains; ingratitude is usually condemned by cursing!
>
> It is my sincere wish that everybody could look into my heart! I have compassion for all people, for all nations! Will my words be appreciated in a sincere way, too? I hope so.[21]

When the Communists seized power, they were quick to assure the Catholics that they had nothing to fear. The new Minister of Justice, Dr. Čepička, General Secretary of the Central Action Committee of the National Front, which was carrying on the revolution, and simultaneously chairman of the Commission on Religious Affairs, made in the last days of February a personal visit to Monsignor Josef Beran, the Archbishop of Prague and Primate of Bohemia, in order to give him this assurance. The bishops then met at Brno on March 4, and from this conference sent the following letter to Dr. Čepička:

> Referring to your call on the Archbishop of Prague, allow us to advise you that in the session of all ordinaries of Bohemia, Moravia, and Slovakia, held on March 4, 1948, in Brno, it was decided unanimously by them to send you the following letter:
>
> We did not consider and we do not consider now as necessary the issuance of a special declaration or special pastoral letter, relating to the contemporary political events, because the Catholic Church is not responsible to any political or state formulation, and, following her special mission, she will always serve the highest interests of the people. As Catholic bishops and ordinaries, we will fulfill in the future, diligently and faithfully, all duties toward God, church, nation, and state, and we are convinced that this loyalty will be believed by all priests and Catholic believers.
>
> As to any settlement of any ecclesiastical relations, we desire, as was stressed by us already, that an agreement should be negotiated between the Holy See and the state. Papal encyclicals and proclamations, either on the econom-

ic and social order or pertaining to matters of education and ideas, are clearly within this sphere. We hope with mutual good will to reach an agreement which will be in the best interests of the state and of the nation.

We accepted gratefully your assurance that nothing would be concluded whereby the good relations between Church and state would be menaced; but we point to serious excesses of the authorities with which we cannot agree; excesses by which the rights of our Church were dealt a blow, especially with respect to the forced seizure of church buildings and institutions and the deprivations of priests, monks, and nuns of their positions and rights. It is conspicuous, too, that the publishing of the majority of Catholic magazines was forbidden and that the activities of Catholic associations are meeting many difficulties and hindrances.

We wish to assure you that in all difficulties in all branches of Catholic activities we will maintain our passive attitude toward all political parties and their activities. We will devote all our efforts to religious matters; we will strengthen and defend Christian morality and the love of neighbor. We ask on the other hand that Catholics not be forced to enroll in political parties, and this under threat to their very existence, especially when at the time of signing the enrollment, a declaration about the ideology of the party is enclosed. Let the past be forgotten, but we hope these mistakes will be remedied in the future. For this reason we renew the decision, taken at our last session, forbidding any priest to accept any political positions.

We are sorry that the events of the last days evoked chaos among the people, which has hurt them morally and legally. This will never bring future blessings nor moral advancement to the nation and state. We pray that all who before God and the world are the responsible parties in this critical period, will make the decisions that will bring welfare, happiness, and peace to our nation. We pray for the good Czech and Slovak people, for only by their moral, decent, and diligent way of life can they continue to secure a happy future![22]

As a reaction to this letter of the bishops there followed the proclamation of the executive committee of the Central Action Committee, published in the official gazette on March 18, 1948: "The praesidium of the Central Action Committee

(CAC) of the National Front emphasizes that freedom of religion and of the performance of religious rites is one of the fundamental principles of our people's democratic regime. . . ."[23]

The Communists wanted to gain Archbishop Beran, and through regional committees, they sent a letter to all priests, asking them to enter the Communist party, mentioning at the same time that on the archiepiscopal chair there no longer sat an Austrian Duke, as was the case in previous times, but a son of the Czech nation.[24] The Archbishop of Prague replied by a letter to all priests on April 21, 1948, saying: "I learned that many of you received a letter from local authorities asking you to enter the Communist party. My name has been mentioned in this letter. I am proud to be a son of the Czech nation, but I am advising you to be on your guard."[25]

On April 26, 1948, Monsignor Beran, as chairman of the Czechoslovak hierarchy, sent a letter to Dr. Čepička, in which he wrote:

> Excuse me if I bother you by this, my letter. Until now I have not received any reply to my petition, in which I requested that Catholics be permitted in the case of working shifts, ordered and fixed by ÚRO (labor union) leaders, to be wholly exempt on all Sundays and holy days. Since we secured this right under the act concerning regulation of holy days, this regulation should be respected.
>
> The writing of this letter is occasioned also by the rebukes you made against the episcopate on the occasion of the first session of the newly established ecclesiastical section of the Central Action Committee held in Prague on April 15. I had hoped that the episcopate would get the memorandum you should have proclaimed in this session. Allow me, please, to declare that the establishment of an advisory commission for ecclesiastical affairs in the Central Action Committee would have been welcomed by the episcopate if they had been informed about it and if, on request, they could have sent to the session, priests enjoying their confidence. Priests who had been nominated to this commission without the knowledge of the episcopate do not enjoy the confidence of the bishops and hence they are not authorized to speak in the name of the Catholic Church. This was declared openly by the Archbishop of

Olomouc, as he told me; also by the Bishop of Litoměřice, and this on the occasion of his talk with you and the Prime Minister.

It would be necessary, too, to settle the competency of this Commission with the episcopate. You reproached the episcopate because it was said that the Catholic Church did not express her stand toward the program of the regime of today. The letter, which was handed over to you, Mr. Minister, dated March 4 of this year, as a result of the conference of all Czechoslovakian ordinaries in Brno, made clear the attitude of the Catholic Church. Not one of the Catholic bishops and Catholic priests would betray his state and nation, I can assure you, but none of us can accept a political program which injures in many points the rights of God and canon law. This cannot be accepted either by the Catholic Church or by any other church believing in our God.

We will never betray the state or the nation, but, on the other hand, neither will we betray God and the Church. By the new bill of education, the natural right of parents to decide freely about the education of their children is violated and because of this law an education regulated by one exclusive ideology is ordained. This nullifies the right of the Church to carry out any religious education of her faithful, in the spirit of a supernatural religion. Religious education regulated by an ideology which contests the existence of God and life after death is not a religious education at all. Therefore the two hours of education in religion are only a mask for a real annihilation of all religious freedom in education.

It is said you have declared that the episcopate is protracting any negotiation, making every possible delay, and that the negotiation concerning ecclesiastical goods and education would have been more favorably expedited had the episcopate been more willing to participate. This accusation, Minister, is unjust, because since 1946 the episcopate has expressed in two memorandums proposals for such a negotiation concerning ecclesiastical goods and in these memorandums drafted its aims. These documents expressed fully the will and demands of the majority of the Czechoslovak nation, which majority is formed by Catholics. We received our reply in the letter of January 29, 1948, No. 200895/48, sent by the Prime Minister's office, in which we were advised by order of the Prime Minister concerning certain remarks of the episcopate, especially about the Slovaks. There was no other negotiation with the episcopate. I myself spoke about all these things on the occasion of my official visits to the Minister of Information, or on the occasion of my earlier visits to the Prime Minister and Ministers of Education, namely, Dr. Nejedly and Dr. Stransky.

On April 13-17, 1949, the Archbishop of Olomouc spoke with the Prime Minister; with you, Mr. Minister; with the Minister of the Interior; and with others concerning land reform and reform of education; and Bishop Trochta in the name of the whole episcopate, in the same offices and in the office of the Minister of Education, in the presence of three clerks of highest rank, negotiated about the problem of education.

The episcopate never neglected anything within its jurisdiction. It was never invited to any official negotiations. Perhaps it will be objected that the Holy See was not interested in the negotiation. We are not authorized to defend the Holy See in this respect; we are not fully informed, but, as far as I know, the remarks made in this regard are not fully true. I myself, Mr. Minister, a half-year ago, in the Chamber of Deputies for the People's party, remarked to the ministers, and even to the Prime Minister in the office of the Ministry for Foreign Affairs, that the Holy See was expecting a reply. Hence its note concerning land reform and its willingness to negotiate. You remember when the answer was given to this note that I remarked during the aforementioned period authorities, that the government should follow the spirit of *modus vivendi;* the settlement concerning the relations between state and Church could have been decided between them, but the negotiation was made difficult because the law was already enacted, and especially because its regulations were unfavorable for the Church and her rights. There is not in this case any fault on the part of the Church or the episcopate.

It is said that you declared expressly that in case the priests were forbidden to participate in activities of the Central Action Committee, the Government would consider this a hostile act. Frankly and openly I told you, Mr. Minister, on the occasion of both my visits in your office, that no one of our ordinaries in Czechoslovakia can retreat from the principle based on canon law and proved by experience of priest-politicians in our country, that Catholic priests should not undertake any offices or functions annexed in any way to political affairs, or to administrative and financial activities. I cannot conceive that this attitude could be taken as hostile against the government, especially when Socialist parties fought against clericalism, which means against any misuse of religion for political aims and against any activities of priests in politics.

Besides that, due to the present lack of priests, when hardly one priest is able to fulfill all his clerical duties, there is no hope that he himself could devote any time to public affairs. Catholic priests will doubtless fulfill all their duties toward the state and government, but they cannot participate in political activities. Please take into consideration this respectful and sincere declaration of mine.

I think, Mr. Minister, so far as you came in contact with me, you could be assured of my sincerity and frankness. I am speaking openly, without any deceit. I love my people and my country; I will never break allegiance given to the government; I will never give any order which will not be advantageous to the happy development of the state and reinforcement of the welfare of the people; I will never permit priests to do anything inimical to the general welfare.

We recognize the discipline of members of your party; we are asking you to respect the discipline of believers in the Catholic Church. The episcopate is certainly willing to shoulder its responsibilities, but it requires that you act directly with it, and not with the priests without any knowledge of the episcopate, so that the episcopate can send a representative to the negotiations whom it can trust and whom it can properly authorize.

Please accept my sincere assertion that the Catholic bishops have really given earnest thought concerning all matters affecting the Czech nation, and that these bishops have decided, in case of need, to resign thereby all material privileges; but they can never betray the rights of God, because thereby they would not do well either for the people or for the country.

JOSEF BERAN,
Chairman of the Conferences of Czechoslovak Ordinaries.[26]

In this way and to this extent the Archbishop of Prague was forced to reprove the recriminations and false declarations of Minister Čepička, who in various meetings made fraudulent declarations about the state of ecclesiastical affairs as it appears from the pastoral letter of August 26, 1948.

The hierarchy of bishops was again filled when Monsignor Josef Matocha, Professor of Philosophy at Saint Cyril and Saint Methodius theological faculty in Olomouc, was appointed as Archbishop of Olomouc on March 23, 1948.[27] The installation of the Archbishop of Olomouc took place on May 3, 1948, in the presence of a very large attendance of the faithful.

On May 3 and 4 a conference of all ordinaries, archbishops and bishops, Czech and Slovak, was arranged in Olomouc. They formulated a resolution which was addressed to the government and to the Catholic priests. The government was informed that the conference had decided that no priest would be allowed to be a candidate in the general election on May 30, 1948, and that all priests must submit their resignations from all functions in action committees, national committees, and other political organizations; furthermore, that only priests individually nominated by the episcopate could be members of the Governmental Commission for Ecclesiastical Affairs, and this only for the purpose of negotiation.[28] This resolution, however, was not respected by the government which continued to issue further regulations concerning ecclesiastical affairs without any previous negotiations with the episcopate.

On May 9, 1948, in the session of the National Assembly held in famous Vladislav Hall in Hradčany Castle, the new constitution was proclaimed. In April, 1949, the Central Action Committee informed the public concerning substantial principles of the draft of the constitution which was approved on the third anniversary of Liberation Day. Before the declaration of the constitution, Dr. John Oldřich, chairman of the Constitutional Committee, Prime Minister Klement Gottwald, and the general reporter for the constitution, Dr. Vladimír Procházka, delivered their addresses. They asserted that to vote for the constitution meant "to give the country a new constitution of a people's democratic character; a constitution leading to socialism;[29] furthermore, that this constitution refers to the best tradition in the history of our nations, to the tradition of Hussitism."[30]

The constitution was promulgated as a constitutional act on June 9, 1948, in the official code, issue 42, no. 150.[31] This law is a compilation of the old constitution of Feb. 29,

1920, No. 121, Coll.,[32] but in the spirit of a "people's democratic institution."

This constitution introduced many new concepts.[33] In matters of an economic character, § 4, 146-164, the former order in favor of a socialistic thesis was reversed, and the cultural and educational systems were put under state control, whereas personal property rights were restricted (§ 9); personal freedom was bound by the conditions of the law (§ 2) and ecclesiastical matters were regulated as follows:

§ *13* *1*) Only state schools are recognized and admitted.
2) Elementary school education is uniform, obligatory, free.
3) Particulars and exceptions are to be fixed by the law.

§ *14* *1*) All education and teaching must be accommodated to and be in accordance with the result of scientific research, and not be in discord with the the people's democratic regime.
2) In the carrying out of all education and teaching, as also in the supervision of it, only the state is authorized to exert its influence.

§ *15* *1*) Freedom of conscience is guaranteed.
2) Faith and conviction may be a disadvantage for some but these cannot be taken as a reason for refusing to fulfill the duties of citizens as fixed by the law.

§ *16* *1*) Everybody is entitled to avow, in private as well as in public, any religious faith, or to be without confession at all.
2) All religions and atheists are equal before the law.

§ *17* *1*) Everybody is free to practice his religion, or to be without confession. The practicing of this must however not be in discord with public order or with good morals. It is not advisable to misuse this right for non-religious purposes.
2) Nobody can be forced, either directly or indirectly, to take part in religious acts.

§ *18* *1*) Freedom of speech is guaranteed.
2) Everybody can, within the limits fixed by the law, express his opinion by words, in writing, by picture, or by any other way. The exercise of this right must not be to the disadvantage of anyone.

§ *21* *1*) Freedom of press is guaranteed; preliminary censorship of the press is not admitted by principle.
2) The law will regulate who is authorized to edit and print newspapers, and periodicals, and conditions under which this may be done; especially regarding this last clause, profit alone should not be a motive.
3) The law will regulate regarding the freedom of sciences and arts and the protection of valuable works, the editing and publication of matters of a nonperiodical nature, especially of books, music, and reproductions of creative works.

§ 22 1) The right of production or publication of politically performed attractions is also of importance and export of films is preserved for the Slavs.
2) Transmission of broadcasting and of television is the exclusive right of the state.
3) Execution of these rights is regulated by the laws, which will also fix any exceptions.

§ *24* *1*) The right of holding meetings and of establishing associations is guaranteed so far as they are not a menace to the people's democratic institutions and to the public order. Execution of these rights is regulated by the law.[34]

Even though the Communists, wishing to safeguard their international reputation, tried to keep a semblance of religious freedom, nevertheless it soon became evident that it was very limited in comparison with the religious freedom expressed by the constitution of the Czechoslovak Republic of Feb. 29, 1920. The Communists did not keep and respect even this minimum guaranteed by their new constitution, as we shall see.

President Eduard Beneš, after a very spirited discussion

with Prime Minister Klement Gottwald, refused to sign this new constitution on May 4, and on June 7, 1948, submitted his resignation of which the following is a record:

> Having studied the proposed Constitution, the President decided on May 1 to resign. He informed the Prime Minister of his decision and requested him to call on the President.
>
> The differences between his view and those expressed in the Constitution are such, the President said, that full agreement cannot be reached. His main objection is to the formulation of the will of the people. The Constitution does not determine in what forms the will of the people should express itself. Eventually it might be the "street." In February he yielded; according to the Prime Minister, to the will of the people, but actually to the will of the "street."
>
> To Mr. Gottwald's objection that according to the Constitution the people are represented by the National Assembly, by the elected organs and National Committees and that the people's right to organize public meetings cannot be forbidden, the President replied: "I have already once been exposed to the pressure of the street—that is my argument. I do not wish to find myself in the same situation again." The Premier asked whether the street had forced the President to do something which was contrary to the law of the country. The Ministers resigned, the President accepted their resignation and nominated a new Government. The President reiterated that he had been forced to do so by the street. The Premier emphasized that what the President had done was not illegal. The President said: "I have been heavily burdened with this. I feel this as a humiliation of the President of the Republic and I cannot forget it. But I was pleased to hear from you that this was not directed against myself."
>
> The President then discussed other problems which he called less essential, among them civil rights. He admitted that, compared with the old Constitution, they had been considerably extended, but the pending Bill for the Defense of the People's Democratic Republic limited them to such an extent that their scope would practically be determined by the Ministry of the Interior. Nor did the new Constitu-

tion provide guarantees that these civil rights would be respected. There were many ambiguities and no provision had been made for the democratic control of civil rights.

The President then turned to the Electoral Law which he had signed, because its formulation appeared to him acceptable. But the elections which were being prepared were not at all democratic, because only one single, combined list of candidates was offered to the electors. The Premier defended the Electoral Law by pointing out that its formulation went back to the Laws of the First Republic. "It is true, the Government Parties have combined, but they have a right to do so. Whoever wishes can be in opposition, the combined list is not prescribed. And as to the secrecy of the elections, the word 'can' indicates that everybody who wishes has the right to vote secretly." The President retorted: "Why have they not inserted the word 'must'?"

The Premier acknowledged that they differed politically. If the President resigned at that moment, three weeks before the General Election, everybody would think so. The President replied that it was unbearable for him to remain in office. "Physically or politically?" asked Mr. Gottwald. Dr. Beneš replied that after February he had not wanted to remain long in office, but later had complied with Mr. Gottwald's wish that the President's flag should again be hoisted. Later he thought that he had made a mistake and he still regretted that he had not resigned at that time. His health was not improving, as he had expected, but he was convinced that he would recover in a few months' time.

The Premier asked whether the President had considered all aspects of his decision. After the February events, the people breathed freely once again—they understood. The President said that in February he had acted as he did, in order to ease the tension.

The President said that he did not wish to create a situation in which the Premier would not sign the Constitution: he realized how his refusal would affect the public both at home and abroad. He felt that it was his duty to make it possible for the Prime Minister and his Party to elect a President who could sign the Constitution without scruples. He wished to part in friendship, and remain in touch with the Premier. He expected that the situation might become difficult, even a war was possible, and therefore he wished to remain at Mr. Gottwald's disposal. He added: "While leaving, I am deeply concerned about the future. I see what they are preparing in the West. I do not look at these matters as some of our people. I am worried. When I go, my whole life goes. What will happen, I do not know, but I would like you to be convinced that I never had and never shall have designs against the State. I repeat this to you and to your Party." The President also said he would take part in no action against the State, the Communists, and the Soviet Union.

The Prime Minister pointed out that if the President resigned before the Constitution was approved, they would have to interpret his abdication politically and comment on it. It would cause excitement abroad. He urged the President that if he were determined to abdicate, not to do so before the General Election. Dr. Beneš admitted that people might misunderstand his resignation as Mr. Gottwald said. He was prepared to find together with Mr. Gottwald a formula in which his resignation could be announced to the public.[35]

The President then wrote to the Prime Minister Gottwald:

On May 4, I announced to you my decision to resign the presidential office. At that time we discussed my decision in connection with the general political situation. I also told you that the doctors recommended me to take into consideration my present state of health . . . . My wish for all my dear compatriots, their respective representatives and their Government, is that the Republic may be spared all disaster, that they may live and work together in tolerance, love and forgiveness, that they may grant freedom and enjoy freedom conscientiously. I believe in the good genius of our people, and I believe in a happy future for our dear Republic.[36]

This decision of Beneš, who had thus far allowed his name to be used by the Communists, to withdraw in the moment they most needed him,[37] is proof that the new constitution was not really democratic. In this melancholy at being deserted, and because of a feeling of depression occasioned by his political errors, Dr. Beneš died on September 3, 1948, in his residence in Sezimovo Ústí. His death made a deep impression.[38] The Communists denied any expression of gratitude to former President Beneš when, on the occasion of his burial, they failed to take official cognizance of it. Archbishop Beran, however, took part in the funeral procession to the grave, where he delivered a eulogy. Critics of Dr. Beneš vary. He is charged with drawing Czechoslovak life into the sphere of communism, and with having been the cause, in February, 1948, of the frustration of hopes which rested in him.

About two weeks before his death, Dr. Beneš sent to those in exile this pleading message:

> The Ministers are accusing me of failure, and I am accusing them of failing me in the critical moment. Without their intervention, which was promised me, I was helpless. When Gottwald gathered on the Old Town Square crowds of bloodthirsty militia, armed to the teeth, I expected others would gather on Wenceslaus Square. I could not imagine that organization and readiness were lacking to such an extent when any act was necessary. I believed the manifestation of unarmed students would make an appeal for a general revolt. But when nobody made a move, I could not permit the pugnacious hordes of Gottwald to carry out extensive massacres against the defenseless population of Prague. There were no limits to their threats.[39]

When Dr. Eduard Beneš died, Ferdinand Peroutka commented that his life resembled that of a playwright who wrote two excellent acts and added to them a weak final act.[40]

The hopelessness of the situation was evident to the people when, on the occasion of the general election, May 30, 1948, with a uniform candidates' list,[41] the new constitution was approved. Communists won this election completely. They gained 211 deputies; the Social Democrats got only 25, the National Socialists, 26, the People's party, 23, the Slovak Democratic party, 12, other parties, 3. In all, the Communists gained 89.2 per cent of the votes.[42] The fear of the voters was made evident by this result. The threat of the February events influenced the election, because people in general realized their position and no longer took any interest in anything.

The victory of the Communists was complete when the National Assembly on June 14, 1948, unanimously elected Klement Gottwald as President of the Republic "to personify the February victory."[43] It was an extreme expression of cynicism when, to mask their fraudulent stand toward the

Church, the newly elected President Klement Gottwald and the government, on their own impulse, attended the "Te Deum" celebration in St. Vitus Cathedral. This behavior was really a double-faced stand, which became apparent in all the actions performed by the Communists in ecclesiastical affairs.[44]

The greatest influence of the new constitution of May 9, 1948, centered on the point of religious and ecclesiastico-legal matters. In this regard the new constitution contained articles regarding freedom of conscience. Concerning its declaration on May 10, 1948, there were open negotiations of representatives of the episcopate in the Ecclesiastical Committee of the Central Action Committee in Prague.[45] Bishop Trochta was a delegate of the episcopate.[46] On May 13 the Archbishop of Prague sent to Minister Čepička, who was chairman of this committee,[47] a letter which read as follows:

> Reports about both sessions of the ecclesiastico-religious committee arranged on the tenth of this month were handed over to me. I thank you, Mr. Minister, for the patience you are demonstrating by presiding at these sessions.
>
> Allow me to make the following remarks: It is necessary to keep in mind, as was mentioned by Bishop Trochta at the beginning of the session, that the whole negotiation has only advisory importance. Delegates sent to the session are not authorized to settle anything which could be viewed as final. I am accentuating what I mentioned many times in the last half year, that in the spirit of *modus vivendi*, the government of the Republic should contact and negotiate both problems, land reform and educational reform, directly with the Vatican. Resolutions of the Advisory Committee for Ecclesiastical and Religious Affairs can only prepare the matter for negotiation between the government and the Holy See. Allow me, please, to request that secrecy be kept in the procedure of all negotiations before final settlement is reached, and to abstain from the publishing of any articles not fully conformable to the truth. May we hope that the ecclesiastical schools will be preserved, not only in the third grade, but even in the first and second grades, and including kindergartens.
>
> You yourself, Mr. Minister, have spoken twice already about preserving the present state of affairs, this after some modifications, especially as to the elimination of many reli-

gious schools. In the draft of the law which is being replaced, there are mentioned only ecclesiastical schools for young priests and religious persons and only the schools of the second and third grades.

It is the exclusive right of parents to make a choice of the manner of education of their children and should this be a republic of the people, in which the people will be respected or even have decisive importance, allow me to assert that the majority of people wish the continuation of the ecclesiastical schools with the teaching of religion. As I mentioned already, the two hours of religion in the schools, controlled by uniform teaching of religion, are not a satisfactory substitute for religious education. The possibility of the choice by parents who would decide to send their children to state religious schools should be permitted. This would correspond with the concept of freedom of religion, which is guaranteed by the constitution and which is being pointed out at public meetings arranged by governmental circles.

I have been informed that some said that, being against the agreement made with you, Mr. Minister, I have permitted to be published the resolution of the episcopal conference in Olomouc. I am not aware that I ever promised anything like that; in fact I could not have done so, because a resolution of such a character is willed by the public. I am surprised that the publication of the aforesaid resolution has been forbidden. On this occasion I am mentioning the pastoral letter of the Archbishop of Olomouc, to which some have raised objections. I read it through. The wording of it is general, words which concern all modern atheistic trends. But it is our duty to draw attention to the menace in religious affairs. Even if we devote our efforts to religious activities, nonetheless this activity is very important also for the general welfare, and we must stress the necessity of religious education which aims at the salvation of immortal souls.

This is our concept of freedom of religion, which is expressed by the new constitution. I assure you that I acknowledge the sincerity of negotiations by governmental organs, which I reaffirm. On our part we are acting with absolute sincerity; but our confidence is being shaken by the fact that a priest, unmindful of his ordination and position, was assigned by the Minister for Education to our ecclesiastical section, where those who left the Catholic Church are already working even in leading positions. Other cases also

> indicate that somewhere endeavors are being backed which are unfavorable to the Catholic Church. Attacks against the Holy See and Holy Father are published; but true informative articles and documents are officially suppressed. I hope that all these disturbances can be settled amicably, because they are ever disquieting Catholic believers.[48]

As has been said, it was decided at the bishops' conference at Olomouc on May 4, 1948, that the candidacy of priests for political positions was not permitted. The Communists did not publish this news because they were aware that their tactics of using priest candidates for public positions would be to their advantage in gaining votes of Catholics. The Communists were especially interested in Reverend Jos. Plojhar, Minister of Public Health, Reverend Lukačevič, and Reverend Straka as Commissioners of Slovakia.[49]

To make certain the carrying out of the resolution framed at Olomouc, on May 21, 1948, Archbishop Beran sent the following letter to the Reverend Josef Plojhar:

> Since it was said that I should by way of exception have granted you permission to be a candidate in the general elections on the thirtieth of this month, I hereby declare that I did not grant this permission and could not give it because in the conference in Olomouc the resolution was accepted to grant such permission to nobody, and this without any exception.
>
> I advise you of this resolution, because in case you do not repeal your decision to be a candidate, you would, as a Catholic priest, be *ipso facto* suspended and I would not be able to give you permission to celebrate Holy Mass in the Archdiocese of Prague, or to exert your priestly office.[50]

Apropos of this matter, the bishops, acting through Minister Čepička, sent the government the following letter, dated May 25, 1948:

> Referring to the action taken by the Ecclesiastical and Religious Committee in the matter of the candidacy of priests and in particular of Minister Plojhar, the Catholic bishops, gathered in a special session in Prague on May 24 of this year, advise: The bishops considered this matter

thoroughly and they repeat that they are unable to change their stand, based on the provisions of canon law as far as the appointment of priests as ministers and commissioners is concerned.

Regarding the candidacy for deputies, according to § 4 of the same canon, bishops cannot grant permission because Catholic priests could be, as deputies, in danger of approving laws which would be in discord not only with the ecclesiastical, but even with the natural law, and that means the divine law.

As to election, the Catholic people know their duties, regulated by principles of conscience as well as by ecclesiastical moral regulations concerning duties toward the state and its people. The bishops ask that this stand, taken on principle, which they must defend under whatever conditions, not be regarded as a negative attitude toward the government, but be judged as a sincere effort to serve the interests of the people, according to our best belief and knowledge.

Therefore, Catholic bishops expect in the future the successful cooperation which is necessary, especially at this time, for the moral and economical rehabilitation and consolidation of our dear country and for the prestige of the state before world opinion. Until now our bishops have not ceased to work and pray that our country attain flourishing conditions and promote the welfare of all.[51]

This letter was not respected and the Rev. Josef Plojhar, Rev. Lukačevič, and Rev. Straka remained as candidates. They were appointed as ministers and commissioners at the election of May 30, 1948. The Archbishop of Prague and the bishops of Slovakia were forced to take action. On June 15, 1948, Rev. Josef Plojhar, Minister of Public Health, was suspended and official notices were published in all churches, especially in the Church of Saint Aegidius in Prague.[52] To each notice was annexed an explanation of the Archbishop. Besides that, the Archbishop of Prague sent to all Catholic priests an instruction concerning the situation. It included the following six principles:

1) The Church is not an institution which should organize political consent or political resistance.

2) The Church cannot hinder anybody who wishes to bespeak God's help for his actions.

3) However, I remind with all seriousness that in doing so the Church does not accept the *Weltanschauung* (philosophy) of trends and movements that are at variance with the concepts of the Church.

4) The Church, even if she shows good will and readiness to meet peoples' wishes in a common effort toward the solution of temporal problems, can never betray her mission which commands her to discriminate between what is Christ's and what is not. In the name of this mission, the Church must chastize well, regardless of who may be the evildoer.

5) I call upon the faithful to stand firmly behind the Holy Father, behind their Archbishop and priests. On the other hand, I remind them that it is not always possible to give detailed and concrete precepts in each case; Christian knowledge and consciousness must live in Christians themselves; they themselves must carry personal responsibility which should go together with the spiritual maturity of the believing Christian.

6) Educate yourselves industriously, and more intensely than heretofore, in Catholic doctrine and in the principles of Christian social justice. Follow the pronouncements of the Holy Father.[53]

The procedure in Slovakia was similar. The measures of the Church against the priests who did not obey and did not abstain from candidacy were taken as an excuse by the government to proclaim all negotiations interrupted.[54]

Plojhar's case caused much controversy, since nearly all the Prague newspapers printed an endorsed statement on the subject by the runner-up in the People's party. This statement, printed in *Lidová demokracie,*[55] described the Reverend Plojhar's suspension as an example of the increased activity of the Church against the new government, and demanded her immediate withdrawal. It argued that there was no objection to the participation of priests in public affairs prior to last February; it was only now that the objections were being raised. The answer, of course, is that only then had the nature of the activities of the government made the bishops feel obliged to impose a ban which lies entirely within their discretion. The statement ended with an ominous sentence saying that the Church authorities were entering an ill-fated path of disloyalty toward the state.

Simultaneously an organization claiming to represent the farmers of Czechoslovakia, Jednotný Svaz zemědělců, sent a letter to the Pope protesting against the Reverend Plojhar's suspension, demanding that priests be permitted to work for the people "whenever and wherever they wish to." They asked the Pope to withdraw the suspension, and the official government news agency circulated an interview with Professor Josef Jureček of Charles University, an expert in canon law, claiming that the suspension was uncanonical. The *Osservatore Romano* replied to these interventions on behalf of Reverend Plojhar by saying that the Communists were using so-called Catholic Marxists to attack the faith of the Czechoslovak Catholics.[56]

The tension grew worse. The new Prime Minister of Czechoslovakia, Antonín Zápotocký, replied in a speech in his native village of Zakolany, near Kladno, to the ruling of the Church:

> Our constitution guarantees every citizen the right to vote unless he is disenfranchised because of dishonorable acts which he has committed. The constitution guarantees not only the right to vote but also the right to be elected to the government. No one, not even a church, has the right to make impossible what has been stipulated in the constitution. Therefore we are determined to defend the right to vote and to be elected against all efforts which may be made for the purpose of undermining this right of making its exercise impossible. People's democracy is for us the essence and basis of our movement. We allow everyone freedom for his convictions, even for his religious faith. Everyone may believe whatever he pleases. But religious beliefs give no one the right to harm others, especially when the nation and its republican institutions are at stake. Whatever religious convictions someone chooses to profess, and whatever faith he believes in, he owes obedience to the law. Every religious denomination has the right to instruct its members in its religious ceremonies, and every citizen has the right to attend such ceremonies. These rights must not be misused, however, for attacks against the people's democracy and the Republic, or for appeals to the citizens urging them not to fulfill their civic duties.[57]

Although the Central Action Committee of the National

Front, in a statement issued on March 19, 1948, declared: "We condemn arbitrary interference with the church schools . . ."[58] the fact of the matter is "there has been a gradual secularization of these schools."[59]

Reacting to this contradictory state of affairs, Monsignor Beran sent a letter to Minister Čepička, dated July 6, 1948, pointing out that, though negotiations on the future of the Catholic schools were still in progress, the Ministry of Education had drafted a decree which would render their continued existence impossible in practice. Besides this, copies of the encyclical of Pope Pius XI on the education of children, *Divini Illius Magistri* had been confiscated, and in these circumstances it seemed difficult to believe any promises or to continue the negotiations within the framework of the Ecclesiastical Commission of the Central Action Committee of the National Front.[60]

> Great bitterness has been caused among members of the Church by the fact that the question of maintaining the Church schools has not yet been settled. The same applies to the Church press, to religious and charitable organizations, and to various Catholic educational institutions. There has been great anxiety among the Catholic public because of recent measures tending toward the suppression of public church manifestations and addresses, the freedom of which was guaranteed by the constitution. Finally, many other points could be cited to show that a great and unacknowledged struggle against the Church is being carried on.[61]

The unfulfilled promises of the government and the case of the Rev. Plojhar caused the interruption of any negotiations between the episcopate and the government's Central Action Committee. The letter of Archbishop Beran stated as much. Double-faced practices of the government were stigmatized by the Catholic Church early in this period; and so the gap caused by distrust of the government was being increased.

Czechoslovak bishops informed the faithful of this situation in their pastoral letter of August 26, 1948, which was read in all the churches of Czechoslovakia on August 29.[62] In this statement from the hierarchy, the bishops accused the government of "a great and unacknowledged struggle against the Church" which "follows the pattern being pursued in other countries." The grievances of the Church were brought up anew: the state had prevented the expression of the mind of the Church, had suppressed the Catholic press of Bohemia and Moravia, and had carried on a propaganda against the bishops as though they were enemies of the people. Then the bishops spoke of the negotiations that had taken place since February for a settlement between Church and state and of the repeated assurances from the government that everything could and would be settled to the general satisfaction of all concerned:

> However promising these assurances were, only a start was made. The negotiations broke down and all the blame was put on the Church. We have been criticized on the ground that we did not endorse unconditionally all that was being done, as other churches did. We expressly announced that we would not betray our duties toward the state and its government, but we added that, in accordance with Christ's teaching, we would give to Caesar only that which is Caesar's, and that above all we must give God what belongs to God. We were unable to endorse everything unconditionally because, unfortunately, we had too much evidence of a hidden anti-Church and antireligious struggle that has begun in our country. This has been carried on according to a pattern used in other countries against the Church and religion. We would like to emphasize more particularly such breaches of religious law as the circumstance that leaders of the Church have been prevented from carrying out their functions for the sole reason that they had not participated in political demonstrations and public addresses.[63]

After a restatement of the reasons for the suspension by the Church of the Reverend Plojhar and other priests active in political life without the permission of their ordinaries, the bishops said:

> Full endorsement and full confidence on our part were not possible, because from the beginning of the negotiations the competent state representatives showed distrust toward the Church by banning almost all Catholic publications in Bohemia and Moravia, especially the widely circulated weekly, *Rozsevač*. The Catholic bishops have

> been described as enemies of the people, and our attitude has been characterized as unconstitutional on the basis of false interpretations of our public utterances. Pain has also been caused by unfounded attacks on the Holy See. An effort is being made to create an artificial gulf between ourselves and the people of the nation.[64]

It is evident from this letter that the bishops were fully aware of the tactics of the Communists. The struggle for eradication of the Catholic Church, mentioned by the bishops, was also led in a secret manner. Its characteristics are in evidence in the following documents, sent to all Communist secretaries.

Excerpts from the letter of Central Action Committee of the Communist Party in Prague, containing secret instructions for the party's secretaries:

1) Correspondence between archbishops and bishops and the Vatican will in future be carried out exclusively by the government.
2) The Czechoslovak Church and the Evangelical Church will be proclaimed as "national churches." The properties of the Catholic Church will be confiscated and assigned in case of need in the favor of the national churches.
3) Priests must be calumniated under whatever conditions, especially by hiring women for this purpose (especially women from Catholic families are wanted for the purpose).
4) Sermons and speeches of clerics and of all Catholic factions will be put under control.
5) Pastoral letters will be admitted only under permission of the government.
6) Catholic priests must be persuaded to apostatize and to enroll in the National Church. This campaign should be opened during October. Further instructions will follow.[65]

Concise extract from Instructions for Regional Action Committees of National Committees about their attitude toward the Catholic Church:

1) Undermine the authority of the Vatican by any means possible, especially by articles in the press.

2) Disrupt unity of clerics. Achieve separation of the hierarchy from the clerics of the lower degrees; especially separate bishops from priests and priests from the faithful. Persuade clerics; but for this purpose only specially authorized people should be used in the matter, e.g., in the form of discussions in the rectories, etc.
3) Do not come in contact with the hierarchy. Any negotiation with them is the exclusive matter of the Secretary General of the Central Action Committee of the National Front (Dr. Čepička); negotiations by regional centers, as has been proven by experience, would only cause retreats from the Action Committee, which must be avoided.
4) The task of the ecclesiastical committees in the Action Committee is not to come in contact and to cooperate with the Catholic Church, but to seize power without this Church and even against her. It is necessary to keep this in mind when members of these committees are being appointed and if they should be delegated by bishops.
5) Closest cooperation with the Czechoslovak Church is necessary. Encourage participation of their bishops on the occasion of any celebrations; welcome them with full honor.
6) Point out the religious chaos in the country and the necessity of unity. In the first phase use the Czechoslovak Church; in the next phases other means will be used. Cooperate with the Orthodox Church (Prague has been promoted as metropole).
7) In the fight against clerics, use a dependable weapon: celibacy, economic factors in the Church, capitalism, moral criminal cases, etc.[66]

Archbishop Beran did not give up the struggle despite the surrender of non-Catholic churches, and continued to oppose all similar actions by the government. Communists viewed him as a threat and opened a fight against him. On the occasion of Reverend Plojhar's suspension, the "Association of the Defenders of Freedom,"[67] of which Archbishop Beran, in consequence of his heroic stand under Nazi occupation, was vice-chairman, made a resolution to cancel his membership. This resolution was printed in the press,[68] and much publicity was given to the expulsion of Monsignor Beran from the "Association of the Defenders of Freedom" on account of his so-called "unfounded attacks"[69] on the Reverend Plojhar. This association protested on July 30 against the suspension of Reverend Plojhar and the Archbishop replied to the protest on August 3,[70] in terms which the association refused to publish but which they later cited as the reason for his expulsion.[71]

The Archbishop of Prague was forced to protest to the government against two bills newly introduced by Minister Čepička. The first provided for obligatory civil marriage[72] and constituted, as the ecclesiastical authorities later pointed out, a violation of the *modus vivendi* between Czechoslovakia and the Holy See, under which marriage contracted before a Catholic priest enjoyed the same recognition as that contracted before the civil authorities.[73] The second bill concerned the *protection of the democratic people's regime*[74] and contained a clause forbidding priests to read from the pulpit any pastoral letters or papal encyclicals which might contain what might be construed as references to that regime.[75] Since there was no longer any Catholic press, the pulpit was virtually the only means by which papal or episcopal messages could be brought to the notice of the faithful.

Archbishop Beran made his official *ad limina* trip to Rome[76] in October, 1948; so also did Bishop Trochta[77] and the Bishop of Hradec Králové, Mořic Picha;[78] likewise the Slovak Bishop Josef Čarský.[79] After their visits to Rome, appointments in the hierarchy of bishops were made. In the meantime Archbishop Karol Kmeťko,[80] Bishop of Nitra and head of the Slovak episcopate, had died in December, 1948. On July 25, 1949, Monsignor B. Pobožný was appointed as titular Bishop of Neilena; until then he had been vicar of the chapter in Rožnava, Slovakia.[81] On July 25, 1949, Monsignor Ambrož Lazik, Apostolic Administrator in Trnava,[82] was appointed as titular Bishop of Appia; on August 29, 1949, Reverend Kajetán Matoušek, from the archdiocese of Prague, was appointed Bishop of Sarigena and accredited as auxiliary Bishop to Archbishop Josef Beran;[83] on October 12, 1949, Monsignor Francis Tomášek, until that time Professor of Pedagogy in the theological faculty in Olomouc, was made titular Bishop of Butien and accredited as auxiliary Bishop to the Archbishop of Olomouc, Monsignor Josef Matocha.[84] This became a substantial reinforcement of the episcopate. The government did not recognize the appointment of Monsignor Matoušek to Prague, admitting, however, the others just mentioned.

The Pope had made use of his right to appoint bishops without previous consent of the Czechoslovak government. By this act he indicated that the Catholic Church was determined not to acknowledge any unlawful interferences by the government in religious affairs and indicated likewise that the Church was unwilling to resign her sovereign jurisdiction. The legal character and structure of the *modus vivendi* thereby was not affected.

This procedure taken by the Pope was very important because of the efforts of Communists to bring the Church under their control. Also the appointment of many priests loyal to the Church as monsignors was a reply to all who tried to arrange any kind of collaboration. The situation, however, became worse from day to day.

First, the Church was deprived of property which still belonged to her after the agrarian reforms[85]—property which allowed her means to provide for the most stringent needs of her clergy and for the most pressing wants of her churches and their maintenance.[86] According to statistics, expropriation of the Church land holdings in Czechoslovakia began with the seizure of 16,775 acres of farm lands and forests owned by the Prague monastery of the Premonstratensian Abbey and about 7,500 acres belonging to the bishopric of Nitra in Slovakia. In both cases, only 618 acres remained in the possession of the original owners, but there was no guarantee that they would retain these holdings indefinitely. The rate of compensation for the confiscated lands was not determined by any decree of the government.

Total land holdings of the Church in Czechoslovakia were estimated at 407,705 acres (165,000 hectares, with one hectare equaling 2,471 acres). Of this total, 61,115 acres are located in Bohemia, Moravia, and Silesia, and 345,940 acres in Slovakia. The holdings include 247,000 acres owned by the archdiocese of Olomouc (Moravia) and the archdioceses of Breslau (Germany) and Estergen (Hungary).[87]

The expropriation decisions, resulting from a "land reform" law passed by the Prague parliament, were undertaken by the so-called Revision Commission of the Ministry of Agriculture, under Julius Ďuriš, who was head of the commission. From the first decisions of this commission it was evident that land ownership by the Church in Czechoslovakia was practically doomed. The commission was composed of all parties.[88]

Priests were then asked to make a full inventory of all movable property belonging to their respective churches and parishes. This was done so that all ecclesiastical property, including valuable and artistic objects, would be under the control and provision of the state. Even the right of the priest to receive stipends for mass and spontaneous offerings of the faithful was abolished. Careful instructions were given to the district and local church commissioners "to keep watch over those members of the faithful who visit priests more often than others and who appear to support them financially."[89]

Another weapon of attack used by Communist leaders against the Catholic Church was the deprivation of the means for spreading and defending her doctrines.[90] In the field of the press all Catholic publications were gradually suppressed on the pretext that there was a shortage of paper.[91] Monthly publications, papers, pamphlets, and parochial bulletins were the first to be eliminated. Particular care was taken also to "purify" even the smallest libraries of publications having a religious character. Devotional works, particularly those concerned with the Eucharist and Our Blessed Mother, were classified as "immoral."[92] Textbooks, especially history books,[93] were revised and falsified by suppressing the least evidence of the benevolent influence of Catholicism.

Catechisms were compiled by school authorities in accordance with Communist mentality and aims.[94] The radio and other means of diffusing information were exclusively under government control. The purpose of all this was to enslave the Catholic Church and to place her in a position where she could no longer spread knowledge of her doctrines, nor defend herself against the calumnies of the Communist government.

As for the Catholic schools, the suppression had been practically universal.[95] Theoretically, a few schools were allowed to function, but their continued existence was becoming very difficult. A Communist commissioner was attached to each school as an informer whose task it was to watch the political conduct of teachers and students, both of whom were required to take special Marxist courses. Attempts were also made to compel nuns who were teachers to take the same courses.

School buildings belonging to religious congregations were confiscated, colleges directed by these congregations were occupied, and ecclesiastics who refused to submit themselves to practices adopted by communism were expelled from teaching posts. Nuns were prohibited from giving private lessons so that all possibility of support would be taken from them. In all government schools everything was being done to inculcate upon students the principles of communism, which was looked upon as the science of all sciences.[96]

Besides this, there were many calumniating attacks on the Holy Father[97] and the Vatican; the disbanding of all Catholic organizations, including Mojzes, the association of Catholic students in Slovakia;[98] the cancellation or restriction of holydays, especially of the Corpus Christi holyday.[99] Other indications made the picture completely Communist-controlled; for example, preference was given to the Russian Orthodox Church.[100]

All this indicated anything but good will on the part of the Czechoslovak government toward coming to terms. Under these circumstances it became evident that the speeches delivered by official representatives emphasizing the fact that religious freedom and protection of it was being upheld in Czechoslovakia were contrary to fact. The *modus vivendi* was continually being violated; new laws were being enacted, without previous negotiations with the Church. The Slovak National Council surpassed sometimes in this regard even the central government in Prague.

Even the constitution of May 9, 1948, was not respected. On the contrary, laws were later enforced counteracting this constitution. And the constitution itself seemed to exist only as a source of Communist propaganda for foreign countries.

CHAPTER TEN

THE CALVARY OF THE CATHOLIC CHURCH

THE EVENTS OF THE YEAR 1949 OPENED A NEW PERIOD IN the relationship between the Communist state and the Catholic Church.

While the time between 1945 and 1948 should be viewed as a period of tactical disturbances influenced by the past, the period after 1948 must be judged as a preparation for the total subjugation of the Church, which *de facto* was carried out in the year 1949.

Before the last step was taken, final negotiations were made. On January 17 and 18, 1949, all Catholic archbishops and bishops of Czechoslovakia met in Prague and made a resolution to send a delegation to the President of the Republic, Klement Gottwald. The delegation to the President was led by the Archbishop of Olomouc, Monsignor Matocha. Monsignor Beran did not take part in this delegation, most likely because a strong campaign had been carried on against him in the Czechoslovak press. The purpose of the visit to the President was to demonstrate that the Catholic Church was still willing to negotiate. The delegates gave a memorandum[1] to the President, Klement Gottwald, on the basis of which the new negotiations were opened.

Participating in the negotiations with the government were nine members of the delegation, authorized by the Church and headed by the Bishop of Litoměřice, Monsignor Stephan Trochta.[2] In the name of the Central Action Committee of the National Front seven members of the government took part. They demanded as a condition of further negotiations that all Catholic bishops and ordinaries, individually and as a body, give a declaration of their loyalty and fidelity to the state and the assurance for the future that the Church would not be misused as an instrument of any activities to overthrow the regime. They insisted on the delegates' making this declaration as part of their plans for the celebrations of the February anniversary of their reign of power, set for February 27, 1949. The negotiations themselves were very delicate and no records were published nor announcements made. However, it is known that the negotiations failed from the interview given a few days later by Archbishop Beran.[3]

At the end of February, the Archbishop of Olomouc, Monsignor Matocha, made an official visit to Rome,[4] returning on March 4. The Vatican legation had been vacant since the fall of 1948 when Monsignor Saverio Ritter had left;[5] but on March 12, 1949, Monsignor Gennaro Verolino arrived in Prague, having been appointed as chargé d'affaires.[6]

On March 17 Archbishop Beran gave an interview to the International News Service in which he said that negotiations between Church and state had failed. Recalling that up to that time some 120 priests had been arrested, he asserted that the negotiations had failed for three reasons. The government had asked the Church to declare its loyalty to the present regime; it had asked the Church to revoke the suspension of Father Josef Plojhar and the two other priests (from Slovakia) who held offices with the government; and finally it had asked for a further nationalization of Church property and had refused to allow the Vatican to take any part in the negotiations.[7]

On March 22 and 23 there was another conference of bishops in Dolní Smokovec in Slovakia[8] to take a stand against these demands of the government. The session was interrupted because in the hall a secret microphone, installed there by order of the government, was discovered. This event was announced by Archbishop Beran to the Prime Minister in a letter written March 26, and the Minister of the Interior was asked to investigate the matter. Since the reply of the Minister, Václav Nosek, was not considered satisfactory, the Catholic bishops met in Olomouc on April 29, 1949, and framed a resolution to send the following memorandum to President Gottwald:

> The Catholic bishops and ordinaries of Czechoslovakia, assembled at a conference held on April 29, 1949, have discussed the present status of negotiations between the government and the Czechoslovak episcopate, which were

opened after an audience given the Czechoslovak episcopate by you on January 19, 1949. They have decided to approach you again and to send you the following memorandum:

1) The body of Catholic bishops and ordinaries of Czechoslovakia, following their delegation's visit with you on January 19, 1949, and complying with your wishes, have handed you their proposals and demands. These were passed on for further action to competent authorities and in consequence thereof negotiations were opened on February 17, 1949, between representatives of the episcopate and the government on the premises of the Central Action Committee of the National Front in Prague. In the course of these negotiations, lasting for six hours, the demand was made by the government that the representatives of the Church make a new declaration of loyalty on the part of the Church toward the state as the main condition for any further negotiations.

On the anniversary of the February revolution such a declaration on our part could not be made because an important member of our house of bishops, the Metropolitan of Moravia and Archbishop of Olomouc, was then in Rome on an official visit. A conference of the bishops could not be convoked until March 22 and 23, 1949, at Dolní Smokovec in Slovakia, but their work was prematurely disrupted when a secret microphone was discovered fitted under the radiator in the conference room.

This fact was communicated to the Premier of the Government by a letter of the Archbishop of Prague dated March 26, 1949, No. 48/49. The Minister of the Interior was also asked to investigate that case in a letter dated March 25, 1949, No. 48/49. The reply of the Minister of the Interior, dated April 1, 1949, was, however, of such a nature that it cannot be regarded as satisfactory. This fact was communicated to the Minister of the Interior by a letter dated April 11, 1949.

2) As regards the required declaration of loyalty, we beg to remind you that the Catholic episcopate formulated their stand toward the February events immediately at their conference held on March 4, 1948, at Brno, which was conveyed by a letter of the Archbishop of Prague dated March 4, 1949, addressed to Dr. Alexei Čepička (Minister of Justice) in which it was clearly stated that the Catholic Church is not tied to any form of politics or government, and that she will continue to fulfill faithfully her duties both toward God and toward the state. The episcopate also promised that in all undertakings and branches of Catholic life they would carefully maintain aloofness from all partisan and political bias, and that they would devote themselves exclusively to religious activities. It was the episcopate's position that it was not their concern to express an opinion in political matters, maintaining that for this purpose there exist the people's political parties or representative bodies, formed under Article Four of the constitution, and that the right of privilege to express confidence in the government is reserved under paragraphs 82 and 83 of the constitution solely and only to the National Assembly.

For that reason the bishops refused to take any part in the election campaign of May, 1949, but they showed their loyalty toward the state by word and deed when you were elected President of the Republic. On June 15, 1948, you were visited by a delegation consisting of all the Roman Catholic archbishops and bishops, who in a manifestation of homage assured you that the Church and Catholics shall always fulfill faithfully their duties toward the state. They, however, asked at the same time that the duties of the Church and Catholics toward God be respected by the state. On Sunday, June 20, 1948, the order was given to hold solemn services in churches with a *Te Deum* and ringing of the bells.

In view of these clear facts we noted with surprise that at the start of the negotiations of February 17, 1949, a fresh declaration of loyalty was demanded. In spite of that, it was decided in principle at the above-mentioned conference in Smokovec that the Czechoslovak episcopate is willing to repeat its declaration of loyalty toward the state, as provided for in the *modus vivendi* agreement, but all this was marred by the incident (the secret microphone) which has not yet been satisfactorily explained.

3) In our afore-mentioned memorandum we asked, first, that systematic attacks and public utterances against the Church and her representatives be discontinued in press and radio, and especially that the campaign against the Holy Father be stopped. We regarded it as a matter of course that such attacks would be discontinued while the negotiations between the Church and the state were under way.

But we must state with sorrow that not even this most natural demand was met and that daily papers such as *Lidove Noviny* published further invectives against the Vatican: March 13, "Vatican, the Ally of Reaction," by Jar. Putik;

March 18, 1949, "Religion Is Not the Question," by S. Budin; March 25, 1949, "Philosophy of the Militant Vatican," by J. Putik; March 31, 1949, "Vatican and the Germans," by S. Budin; April 10, 1949, "In What Waters Do Vatican Fishermen Fish?"

Also in Slovakia, for instance, *Nové Slovo* published the article "Vatican's Policy in the Light of Documentation," by Frant. Chvojka, and the Ministry of Information and Culture in Bratislava published brochures in 1949 entitled "Vatican in the Service of American Reaction," by Segal. The Czechoslovak radio, for which the Minister of Information and Culture (Václav Kopecký) is responsible, broadcast news bulletins in which the Vatican was called the apostle of imperialism. That took place on March 15, 20, 23, and 30.

4) We asked for a just modification of the question of the Catholic press, which at the time the memorandum was issued was practically stopped, save for a few unimportant exceptions; for instance, official bulletins of the ordinates. Also in this field we must declare that anti-Church measures were adopted. In March, 1949, save for one exception, publication of the so-called "Pastoral Enclosures to Catholic Action" were stopped, and now in most of our dioceses also the official bulletins of Catholic action have been stopped by order of the Ministry of Information and Culture, although not even Nazi occupation authorities in their anti-Catholic press measures went so far as to interfere with the publication of these official bulletins. It is true that *Katolické Noviny* (Catholic weekly of Bratislava) is being published in Slovakia, but also in this case we must state that attempts have been made to make control of the paper by the Church hierarchy or its representatives impossible.

5) In our memorandum we asked for the right of free assembly and association for religious purposes, but instead we found that the Central Action Committee of the National Front gave quite unconstitutional orders prohibiting any training or assembly of Catholic youth outside the Church. This measure is strengthened by executive ordinances of the various authorities later issued by the Central Action Committee of the National Front and by the District National Committees. Let us cite, for example, the decision of KNV Gottwaldov, February 24, 1949, No.

263/00-2; the decision of ONV Uherské Hradiště, March 31, 1949, No. 370-29.349-III; the decision of ONV Valašské Klobouky, March 28, 1949, No. 267-28/III-B; the decision of ONV Kralupy, April 12, 1949, No. 457/49; the decision of OAV NF Rychnov, March 28, 1949, No. 645 49.

On the other hand, the manner of reorientation of government employees, with courses in which the faith and religion are mocked and treated with blasphemy, is contrary to all the principles of religious freedom and laws and prescriptions still in force regarding the protection of religions recognized by the state.

6) The Catholic Church was deprived of the remainder of her land property under the law No. 96/48 of the Collection of Laws and Decrees, a step against whose merit we did not protest; but we asked for compensation and for the regulation of all liabilities incumbent on that land property. We were given official promise that the matter would be taken care of. This fact was not explained to the public by the press. On the contrary, the press reports are worded so as to indicate that the Church is favored financially by the state.

Under the terms of paragraph 1, division 3, of the law No. 96/48 of the Collection of Laws and Decrees, and with the consent of the MRK (Ministerial Commission), the land holdings of an individual parish priest can not be taken if they are less than 30 hectares (about 75 acres). However, this explicit legal safeguard has been nullified as far as parish benefices are concerned in a manner that is quite contrary to the law of the ordinance of the Ministry of Agriculture dated November 16, 1948, No. 108435/48-A-11-1162/2. The result is that the Church has been left with only one source of income, namely collections among the faithful, but these too were a thorn in the side of the Central Action Committee of the National Front in Prague, which issued an order prohibiting all church collections. This order was applied, for instance, by a decision of ONV at Veseli n. Mor., ONV Kralupy, and OAV NF Rychnov, although collections are clearly internal church matters, fully respected by laws and decrees of the state administration now in effect.

7) We are citing these few instances which were obviously carried out according to a preconceived plan, carefully brought into effect, and which have as their aim

the gradual limitation of religious freedom. We pointed this out in our first memorandum, saying that what is being done constitutes a gradual limitation of the freedom of the Catholic Church, making it impossible for her to exercise her inalienable divine rights. In this connection we wish to emphasize that all these measures are at variance with the constitution in force. (See, for instance, paragraphs 18, 20, and 21, concerning the freedom of religious manifestations and professions of faith, and paragraph 24 regarding freedom of assembly). In fact, these measures constitute proof of insincerity on the part of the government representatives during the course of negotiations between the Church and the state.

Today, moreover, there is additional and irrefutable proof that the government has started an anti-Church campaign, using all means at its disposal, because orders with detailed instructions have been issued by county district commanders as by the state security force covering the campaign against the Church.

We are aware that these orders represent only a preparatory phase of the final decisive blow. We protest in our name and in the name of the Catholic people against these unconstitutional measures against the Church and her adherents—measures which mean a ban on Catholicism, the religion of the majority of the people of the state. We denounce all public reports which systematically insinuate that blame for the breakdown in negotiations falls on the Catholic hierarchy, and we hope that you, Mr. President, will recognize the merits of our complaints, supported by facts that do not contribute to the unification of the nation, but rather mar and destroy the peace and happiness in the nation which you wanted to unify.[9]

On May 17, 1949, the Catholic bishops held a conference in Prague and decided to send letters to Zdeněk Nejedlý, Minister of Education, to Minister Alois Petr, and to all priests. They determined also certain principles for their future procedure regarding the situation which had developed.

During the deadlock in the long-drawn-out negotiations between the Church and the government, Minister Alois Petr, chairman of the so-called People's Catholic party, informed the People's party that "the government has repeatedly shown its good will to fulfill all the justified claims of the representatives of the Catholic Church,"[10] but that there had nevertheless been no discussions on a National Front basis since the two meetings between representatives of the government and Catholic bishops in January and February. These delays, he concluded, were causing much disquiet in Catholic circles which sincerely wished to see the best relations between the Catholic Church and the state, fully aware that this would be in the interests of both the Church and the state.[11] Because Minister Petr, however, gave false information about the real state of conditions and because he misused the so-called Catholic People's party, Archbishop Beran sent him the following letter:

> On Wednesday, May 4, 1949, you received my letter, approved at the Episcopal Conferences on April 29, 1949, in which I asked for a reply. No reply has been received up to this day. On the contrary, according to newspaper reports, at a session of the presidium of the Czechoslovak People's Party held May 12, 1949, you again stressed that 'the National Front showed good will to fulfill all demands of the representatives of the Catholic Church, insofar as such demands should be justified'—this in face of the fact that you were present at the last meeting of the negotiations on February 17, 1949, where the demands submitted to the President in the form of a memorandum were not discussed at all, but, on the contrary, conditions of an ultimatum character were laid down which were known in advance to be unacceptable.
>
> It is possible to speak about 'the good will of the National Front' when by a one-sided process separation of the state and Church is being carried out? Or do you know nothing at all of what is being done against the Church? Are you aware—and all Catholics in your party and in other parties are aware—that they are accomplices in all anti-Church measures?
>
> Everything is directed by the Central Action Committee, so the blame falls on all participating parties of the National Front.
>
> Are you aware—in so far as you are still Catholics—that any form of direct or indirect collaboration and cooperation in laws and orders which restrict or abolish the rights of the Church cause automatic excommunication; i.e., that without any official declaration or promulgation (by the Church), every collaborator by mere participation

in such measures places himself outside the Church and thereby forfeits all rights which he or she has had as a member of the Catholic Church?

Do you not see what a sin you are committing when you mislead the faithful by inaccurate reports in your press while the Bishops are deprived of all means of informing the Catholic public?

We give you this final warning, and with all the more emphasis because, according to latest reports, the top assignment given the People's Party for the immediate future is the formation of a new Catholic Church, 'without the present Bishops and the supreme head in Rome.'

We therefore protest expressly against your speaking in the name of the Catholic faithful. We protest against the fact that the press material sent abroad calls the Czechoslovak People's Party 'Catholic,' because not even on the smallest scale do you safeguard the interests of the Church. You are participants and therefore acomplices in all the government's actions; also in those carried out in your name.[12]

Meanwhile the government, through the Ministry of Schools, Sciences, and Arts, launched on May 10 its own *Bulletin of the Catholic Clergy*, announcing it in the Prague press with an intimation that it intended "to inform Catholic priests and members of various orders about religious and Church matters. . . . It will give the clergy a proper basis for orientation and will provide all important means of repairing the harm done to the Church by some individuals in the Catholic hierarchy."[13]

This decision of the government affected all regulations and agreements determining ecclesiastical relationship between the Church and the state. Therefore, the Archbishop of Prague, in the name of the whole Czechoslovak episcopate, protested in a letter[14] sent to the Ministry of Education, Sciences, and Arts as follows:

We learn that your Ministry is sending to Roman Catholic clergymen the so-called *Bulletin of the Catholic Clergy*, which according to its preface should furnish 'correct information' especially to Roman Catholic clergy.

(1) We protest against the use of the term 'Bulletin

of the Catholic Clergy.' Such a name might mean either that the bulletin is published by the Catholic clergy or that it is published for Catholic clergy.

We protest the first meaning of the term. At the foot of the last page the publisher is stated to be the Ministry of Schools, Sciences, and Arts. That ministry surely cannot be described as 'the Catholic clergy' and, moreover, as we have found out, editorial work for the so-called *Bulletin of the Catholic Clergy* has been entrusted to apostate and suspended priests and to members of other denominations.

We protest also the latter meaning of the said term. The Roman Catholic clergy has been advised of all laws and ordinances of the Ministry of Schools, Sciences, and Arts and of other ministries and authorities so far as such laws pertained to the Church and religious life, through the intermediary of the Letters of the Ordinaries. It does not belong to the jurisdiction of state organs to issue instructions and impart information to the Catholic clergy, because such a right is reserved to authorities of the Church.

Because an unwarranted prohibition stopped publication of the Letters of the Ordinates, the Ordinaries have been deprived of the possibility of imparting to their clergy information about state laws and ordinances. The organs of the state could, of course, impart such information through the medium of an official bulletin insofar as they are the controlling or supervisory organs.

We must, however, point out the fact that while the Letters of the Ordinaries were discontinued for lack of paper, there seems to be enough paper for the publication of the so-called *Bulletin of the Catholic Clergy*, which is sent gratis to all the clergy, while the laws and directives of the Ministry of Schools and other ministries are promulgated in official bulletins of the respective ministries.

(2) We also protest the fact that all the clergy are ordered 'to acquaint all persons subordinate to them with the content of the Bulletin and to keep such copies for official reference.' The Bulletin, as published, is not signed by anyone and lacks official form. To be regarded as an official bulletin, it should have been marked as 'Official Bulletin of the Ministry of the Schools, Sciences, and Arts for the Catholic Clergy.'

(3) In the article entitled 'Congrua' on page 2 of the Bulletin, the clergy were not told how much the state profited by confiscating the property of the Church under

Law No. 142/47 and 46/48 whereby assets amounting to many millions have outbalanced the liabilities of the Religious Fund and the Náboženská matica (religious fund formerly formed). It was also promised by the Premier of the Government, who is now President of the Republic, that from the proceeds of confiscated church property at least three million crowns yearly would be used for purposes of the Roman Catholic Church.

Besides, a substantial portion of the Congrua is compensation to the clergy for tasks performed for the state, which is obliged to pay priests for the work performed. Therefore, these payments cannot be charged to the Religious Fund.

Among other things it should have been stated that the clergy refused the proposal for the new salary law; so did the non-Catholic clergy.

(4) We finally protest the interpretation of the ordinance of the Ministry of the Interior of May 9, No. 260/20-3-3/5-1949-VB-3a, published on page 3 under the heading 'Official reports.'

First, the law of November 15, 1868, No. 134 of the (Austrian) Reich Codex, about the right of association, states expressly in paragraph 3, division a): 'This law does not affect (a) religious orders and congregations, and other religious societies in general which should be regarded in the light of law and directives relating to them.' The law of the same date, No. 135, about the right to assemble, says in paragraph 5: 'Also exempt from this law are public festivals, nuptial processions, usual popular festivities and marches, funerals, processions, pilgrimages, and other assemblies or processions in the course of observance of a legally permitted cult if they are made according to ancient custom.'

Even if both these laws were repealed by paragraph 173 and paragraph 24 of the new constitution, the ban on associations cannot be construed as applying to religious associations and institutions of the Church. Therefore, quite incorrect is the inference printed in the *Bulletin* article (last paragraph) which reads: 'It is evident from the above circular that violations of these regulations will be prosecuted as infringements of the law. This applies to various free associatons in churches (such as Marian sodalities, associations of St. Adalbert, Eucharistic circles, Associations of Evangelical Youth, and Unions of Young People of the Czechoslovak Church).

We trust that this protest of ours will be considered,

> that further publication of the *Bulletin of the Catholic Clergy* will be discontinued and that we shall be given the opportunity to issue the Letters of the Ordinates (*Acta Curiae*) for official communication with our clergy.[15]

The first issue of *Věstník Katolického duchovenstva* (Bulletin of the Catholic Clergy) was sent free to all Catholic priests in the country and the principal article in it seemed in effect an attempt to "buy" them:

> The state is the source of a large part of each priest's income, since it pays 700,000,000 crowns a year in subsidies to the Church; rumors that these payments, the equivalent of some £3,320,000, are to be discontinued, is not to be believed. On the contrary, priests who show themselves amenable may expect their stipends increased. In this country, everybody is entitled to a reward for his work, and a priest must not be exempted from this principle. While fulfilling their religious duties they also fulfill the duties of good citizens of our People's Democratic party. Thus they do not have to fear that they will be deprived of a reward for their work. The People's Democratic Republic will improve the incomes of those who show by their deeds a positive attitude toward the efforts of our state. Therefore, all Catholic priests who march along with our people may, without fear for the future, concern themselves fully with the ecclesiastical tasks with which they are entrusted.[16]

On May 28, 1949, Archbishop Beran of Prague wrote, in the name of all bishops, a letter *ad clerium,* which was published on May 31.[17]

> 1) We once more call attention to the fact that any cooperation or collaboration with those who restrict the rights and the liberty of the Church means excommunication *ipso facto*. That applies to the contribution of articles or letters to journals which propagate the efforts of these people. This equally applies to the *Gazette of the Catholic Clergy*.
>
> The consequence of this excommunication for priests is that everything that they do along these lines becomes a sacrilege and has no validity before God and *pro foro ecclesiastico*.

2) The faithful are being asked by laymen to send to the Ordinary letters demanding that negotiations be opened with the Central Action Committee of the National Front.

But Minister Kopecký declared on Saturday, May 28, 1949, quite clearly, that scholastic education, as well as the youth movements, will be directed by the state according to Marxist ideology. After this declaration any attempt to renew conversations would be useless and hopeless. The Catholic Church cannot renounce her right to educate the young, nor indeed can any Christian confession renounce such a right.

Furthermore, these letters, which do not bear the signatures of priests and which are sent at the demand of the authorities, are valueless.

3) The journal *Christian Women*, which appears at Brno, and the journals *Lidová demokracie* and *Lidová Obroda* are not Catholic publications. It is forbidden to sell them inside or at the doors of churches.

Similarly, a Catholic Action movement is to be formed without the participation of the Bishops. It is forbidden under pain of ecclesiastical sanction to take part in this "Catholic Action" which is not Catholic. It appears that this Action is subsidized by the bureau of the Catholic People's Party. I remind you that this party has not the right to use the term Catholic.

4) Do not distribute, accept, or recommend journals, publications, or books that are not approved by the Bishop's office. In case of doubt ask for advice at the Bishop's office first.

The sale of objects of devotion and images of saints should also be authorized by the Church. For collections for the charitable society *Caritas* the measures previously laid down by the Bishop's office remain in force; only the Bishop's office has the right to modify them.

5) All the Church schools have been taken over by the state. The publication of all Catholic journals is forbidden. The journals which appear under the name of "Christian" or "Catholic" are not Catholic. Pilgrimages are being forbidden, as well as Catholic processions. Notes and protests remain unanswered.

A priest who cultivated forty hectares of land is a village and who was chosen by the Agricultural Commission as the best farmer of his village has by the higher Commission been classed as a "bad farmer," and his fields have been confiscated. The farmers who have refused to work the fields which belonged to this priest have been termed saboteurs.

The second issue of the *Gazette of the Catholic Clergy* praised the development of Catholic literature. You all know that Catholic books have been confiscated from all the bookshops and have been destroyed.

The *Gazette of the Catholic Clergy* states that the number of books published by the Catholic Church is constantly increasing. What do you say to that? Beware of this "Catholic" literature and this "Catholic" Church. There is only one Catholic Church.

The *Gazette of the Catholic Clergy* prints on page 3 a decree which has also been sent to the Archbishop's House. It is interesting to note that the phrases ("the measures . . . will be valid from the point of view of public administration") which appear in the letter addressed to the Archbishop's House have been suppressed in the *Gazette of the Catholic Clergy*, which claims to be well-informed.

The validity of all the decrees and laws published in the *Gazette is* from a juridical point of view contestable because this gazette is not official.

I hope that no priest will allow himself to be deceived by this *Gazette*. I hope, too, that all priests will have faith in their Archbishop to whom they have vowed their obedience and respect.

I am sure you will not sell your honor as priests for thirty pieces of silver, and that you will not betray Christ.[18]

The Communists knew of the harmony between the Catholic episcopate, the clergymen, and the faithful and they tried to penetrate the ranks of the faithful with the aid of prominent persons in the Communist-controlled People's party. They tried this by infiltration; they established the government-sponsored, so-called "Catholic Action" without any consultation with the bishops. This state organization became the instrument of the government, even in religious affairs. Unfortunately there were a few Judases even among the clergy, and in their articles in the magazine *Gazette of the Catholic Clergy* edited by the Ministry of Education, they supported the schismatic Catholic Action.

It was believed that this schismatic endeavor might work more easily in Czechoslovakia than in Poland or Hungary, because it was hoped that in the land of Hus there would be a more favorable ground for the establishment of a "Catholic National Church" directed by the Communist regime.[19]

The program for Catholic Action had been well prepared by the Cominform, which is an important organ[20] for accommodation, infiltration, regulation and intervening of the Moscow Politburo into foreign countries. On February 11 and 12, 1949, in the Grand Hotel Pupp in Karlovy Vary (Karlsbad) the "religious program" of the Cominform was elaborated.[21] According to this program the organization Catholic Action was established.[22] In the second secret meeting on October 4, 1949, at Karlovy Vary, which was presided over by a representative of the Kremlin, the Minister of Foreign Affairs of the Soviet Union, Andrei Vishinsky,[23] the establishing of the organization was approved. With the intention of liquidating the Catholic Church, an accurate but dangerous strategy in regard to the Catholic majority was adopted.

The following record of a secret document for the eventual elimination of the Catholic Church in Czechoslovakia was framed by the Cominform on October 10, 1949. It is known as the Protocol of Karlovy Vary. The meetings were arranged by Andrei Vishinsky, Minister of Foreign Affairs for Russia, and were attended by the following Czechoslovak representatives of the Cominform: Prime Minister Antonín Zápotocky; Zdeněk Nejedlý, Minister of Education; Václav Kopecký, Minister of Propaganda; Alexej Čepička, Minister of Justice; Ladislav Kopřiva, Minister of National Security; and Minister Zdeněk Fierlinger. The directions contained in this secret document became the basis for the attempted destruction of the activities of the Catholic Church in Czechoslovakia. The parenthetical explanatory notes are by the author. The document reads as follows:

> The Communist party must pretend that there is no intention to destroy the Catholic Church. Activities of the Church must be curtailed first of all in matters pertaining to education and to the press. The Catholic Church must especially be deprived of her position. It is necessary to restrict any activities of Archbishop Beran and of the other

bishops. Without paying attention to the protests by the Western nations, it is necessary to isolate the hierarchy from the clergy and to drive a wedge between the Vatican and the faithful. This drive must be successful, since it is undertaken under the auspices of Catholic Action and must become a national movement. According to the extent of its success in Czechoslovakia, it will be established in Poland, Hungary, and other countries, where there is as yet no Orthodox Church. The procedure must be carried out carefully. As soon as it is achieved, Prague will become a springboard against the Vatican. There is nothing to be changed in the liturgy or in the moral life of the people. For the time being, leave intact the hierarchical structure; but take care lest persons who are not acceptable to the party get control of the higher positions. It is necessary to make full use of salary regulations and to record all injustices concerning salaries among the clergymen. This action will inspire the clergy and separate them from the hierarchy, against whom a calumniating campaign must be arranged among the common people. Should the hierarchy conspire to raise a resistance, a "comrade" of high standing will be assigned to take care of matters. It is necessary to frighten the hierarchy and to break up any signs of resistance. Through salary regulations two aims will be achieved: the clergy will be isolated from the hierarchy and thereafter these same clergymen will be used for further activities. The government will order the formulation of an oath of allegiance. The law will be enforced in a cruel manner.

Moreover, it is necessary to observe the public opinion of the people, especially that of the farmers. Be firm with them in your conversations. They are the last remnants of the bourgeoisie and of the capitalistic system. If the clergymen stand by the farmers, we will charge them with anti-socialistic convictions; if the farmers adhere to the clergy—as we anticipate—we will make our stand clear when we we collectivize the farmlands. By reprisals against farmers, asserting that they supported the clergy, we will annihilate them and then will charge them with any upset in the flow of vital supplies. Against the hierarchy the fight must be carried out systematically, so that by the beginning of December, church affairs will be fully in our control. After our purge we will carry out the liquidation of the farmers.

The procedure against the Church will be carried out in the following steps. It is the duty of the Communist party to single out all weak, ambitious, avaricious and compromising priests in order to obtain, both in private and in public life, adherents for the ideology of Marx, Lenin and Stalin. Especially, however, we must approach priests who are in close contact with the people. Our comrades should call the attention of the clergymen to all that the Communist party has given, gives, and will give to them, and this according to the directions which will be issued by the party. In these instructions it will be pointed out how clergymen should be united according to the environment in which they live. The party must ask them to do propaganda work for the science of sciences, namely the doctrines of Marx, Lenin and Stalin. They should do this through their sermons, religious exercises, lectures, study-courses, etc., when they come in contact with the faithful. They too must be educated in the science of all sciences. These clergymen must be preferred everywhere and they must be supported. From these will be chosen the professors of religion, educators in the seminaries, leaders of camps and recreational centers, and rectors of the big city churches. To try to save money in this matter would be treason against the party. They must have a car and gasoline, and the radio and press must be at their disposal. The procedure must be directed cautiously. The priests who are loyal to the party will be made editors of the *Katolické Noviny* (*Catholic News*—a schismatic and Communist-sponsored, so-called Catholic press) and officials of Catholic Action, and they must be introduced to the public. They must be encouraged and protected against reactionary elements, against whom brutal retaliation must be taken. By the end of November more severe activities and methods must be taken by the press against the hierarchy. The latter must be accused of exploiting the lower clergy, for whom no regard can be taken, whether they will accept salaries or not. The hierarchy is a self-conscious enemy, to whom no mercy can be shown. Against them radio broadcasts and the press of the party will be put to work. A drive for the editing of appropriate books directed against the hierarchy and the Vatican must be undertaken. We will arrange contests and we will reward the clergy as well as laymen for their publications.

These are the tactics of our party. We know that religion will remain an opiate for the common people; but today we must exploit this theory as was done in the days of the great Lenin. We know for a certainty that in a classless Communist society there is no room for a hierarchy; neither is there a place for God or the farmer. This, therefore, is our immediate task—to liquidate the Church and the farmers. But also Zionists—i.e., national Jews—must be eliminated on account of the treason committed against the Union of Soviet Socialist Republics; for they are responsible for the state of Israel's not obtaining a Communist majority in the last general election.

The Communist party must work to the end that the people will condemn the clergy. The people who are faithful to them today are also the ones who side with the Vatican and with the hierarchy; therefore we must give preference to the people who hate the clergy. These emancipated ones we will assign to the rectories and to the schools. We know that this latter class of people will not send their children for their education to religious schools or to churches, because they condemn the clergy. The government will appoint the ones who are to supervise education and the police will be ordered to detect all children who go to religious schools and also their parents. It can be supposed that the majority of the clergy will refuse to draw salaries.

Where it is discovered that so large a number of people attend services that the churches are filled, the priest must be changed under the plea that he is not fulfilling his mission and cannot be relied upon to protect the interests of the party. These clergymen will be sent to an educational camp (for indoctrination) and another clergyman from another diocese will be appointed to his position—and as is understood, he will be a "comrade." We are preparing a special corps of reliable comrades to lead this agenda. After the arrival of the new comrade, who has been educated by us, the police will report that the number of faithful attending services in the churches and religious exercises in the schools has diminished. The government will then ask the faithful to go to church. Our propaganda will point out that now only a few are going to church and to religious instructions; even visitors from abroad will be invited. The people will then request that "booths with opiates" (meaning the churches and religious schools) be closed. The government will persuade the people, however, especially among the progressive population, to show resistance; these progressive people will thereupon request the government to eliminate the churches and in their places to establish clubs, theaters, and the like. It will be charged by the claimants that nobody wants to go to church and that for that reason these buildings should be converted to other uses. The government will resist these claims and seek through the radio and the press of the local Communist organizations to persuade the progressive majority of the population to repeal its original intention because the matter is a serious business, since the Church is being viewed as either a historical or an artistic monument; hence it will ask the local Communist organization to make it easier for the people to go to church and religious services (for easier indoctrination); also to secure proper clergymen (comrades, of course) who will have no connection with the Vatican and the hierarchy, which will be isolated and eventually disappear altogether. Through these efforts of the government, people will no longer want to go to church or to attend services, as will be certified by local clergymen, who will apply for another rectory, and even eventually for an assignment to another, more lucrative job. Under influence of this evidence and the attitude of the people, the government, after long hesitation, will accept the will of the people because it is a government of the people.[24]

It was proclaimed further that the Pontiff of Rome would be acknowledged as the head of the Church and supreme master only in matters of faith and morals, but that a practical solution to the question of the relations between the Church and the Communist regime would be better brought about by a Czechoslovak National Catholic Church.[25] This was of course intended only for the international forum. At home the attempt to lure the Catholics into schism through the spurious Catholic Action was embodied in the following measures:

1) The regime will make all clergymen entirely dependent on the state for their daily bread.
2) It will deprive the Church of every means of publicizing its view.
3) It will make a bold attempt to disseminate the Communist party line as Catholic news.
4) It will suppress practically all Catholic schools. The few that remain for window-dressing purposes will be subjected to the vigilance of the Communist Commissioner.

5) The regime will wage a ceaseless propaganda campaign to separate the priests from their bishops.[26]

According to a program arranged on June 10, 1949, a congress of so-called patriotic priests and faithful was held in the Prague National House. Speeches were delivered by the excommunicated priests, Rev. Josef Plojhar of Bohemia and Rev. Alexander Horák of Slovakia. As representatives of the laymen, prominent personalities in public life such as Minister Alois Petr, Dr. Dionysius Polanský, and Mr. Pujman addressed the assembly.[27]

At the first meeting of Catholic Action, on June 17 in Prague, the Central Committee of Catholic Action, of which Mr. Pujman became president, was established. In accordance with the principles of its regime, regional, district, and local committees of the same Catholic Action were established.[28]

Telegrams proclaiming allegiance were sent to the President of the Republic, to members of the government, and to all Catholic bishops. Since this Congress was convoked against the will of the bishops and with the aim of attacking them, Catholic bishops did not acknowledge the telegrams and, in accordance with ecclesiastical regulations, took corresponding measures.

President Klement Gottwald replied to the above-mentioned telegrams, "I welcome your address in which you express your loyalty to our People's Democratic Republic. I was especially delighted by your assurance that Catholic clergymen and faithful will cooperate in the setting up of our Republic. Your Catholic Action expresses an endeavor of Catholic clergymen and faithful to effect a sincere understanding between Church and state. This movement will be of very great importance for Catholicism in our country; it will fulfill all our aims."[29]

Likewise, Prime Minister Antonín Zápotocký and the Minister of Education, Nejedlý, in their letters to the Central Committee of Catholic Action, solemnly certified all the guarantees given to all the churches by the constitution of May 9, 1949.

What this state-sponsored Catholic Action really means is quite evident from the publications *Katolická Akce* (edited by the publication section of Catholic Action in July, 1949.[30]

This book contains very urgent invitations to Roman Catholics to cooperate with the people's regime) and *The Treason of the Vatican and the Bishops,* in which booklet the bishops are very strongly condemned.[31] These documents give very explicit testimony of the intentions of the government and its tactics against the Catholics.

By press, radio, and other means of propaganda, people were led to believe that a large number of priests had joined this bogus Catholic Action. Ecclesiastical personalities who had not even been approached in the matter, priests who were long since deceased, German priests who had emigrated to Germany, even nonexistent religious communities were made to appear as members. But despite the total suppression of the Catholic press, the truth became known. The answer given by the clergy and the faithful to the appeal of the fraudulent Catholic Action could not have been more significant, and of the six thousand or seven thousand priests living in Czechoslovakia, scarcely fifteen (not the one thousand and five hundred reported by Communist propaganda) actually became members of the schismatic movement.[32]

When the last Catholic publication still in existence, *Katolické Noviny,* in Slovakia, was confiscated on June 17, it was made the organ of the spurious Catholic Action. Neither the clergy nor the faithful were deceived by these tactics. The first government printing of this newspaper ran to 800,000 copies and its circulation was accompanied by all the means at the disposal of Communist organizations. After a few months, however, the number of copies was reduced to 24,000, and these were being sold without any great effort, mainly to members of the Communist party.[33]

Catholic bishops expressed their firm stand by sending on June 17, 1949, a letter[34] to all clergymen which read as follows:

> A government-sponsored preparatory committee of so-called Catholic Action is being formed. If you should be invited to join it, remember it is a schismatic movement, and will be prosecuted by Church penalties.
>
> The *Gazette of the Catholic Clergy*, published by the Ministry of Education in Prague, is not an official Gazette. Nor is it a Catholic magazine, as it is being published without the approval of the Church and is edited by non-

> Catholics. The reading and filing of this gazette is forbidden, and there is nothing to be done but return it.
>
> Preach in all churches on Sunday the 19th about the Papal power and the Papal primacy. If you should find it difficult to catch trains or buses, walk to this service as our fathers did.
>
> A national administration has been imposed on the *Caritas* organization. It has lost the right to use the name Catholic. Church collections for charity are forbidden except for local needs.[35]

On June 13, three days after the proclamation of Catholic Action, the secretary of the *authentic* Catholic Action in Prague, the Reverend Antonín Mandl, was arrested.[36] The bogus Catholic Action meanwhile constituted itself a representative of the Church and wrote to the President, Klement Gottwald, offering to resume the negotiations between Church and state.[37]

On June 14, the consistory office of the Archbishop of Prague received a letter from the Ministry of Education stating that to the archiepiscopal office a commissioner, Dr. Miroslav Houska, was being appointed. The Archbishop of Prague, Monsignor Josef Beran, protested strongly against this introduction of the state into purely ecclesiastical matters.[38]

On July 15, the Chancellor of the archdiocese, Rev. Doerner, was arrested, as was the consistory official clergyman, Rev. Karel Kučera. The Commissioner of the Ministry of Education, Dr. Houska, with the assistance of the police, occupied all premises of the archiepiscopal office of the Prague archbishopric.[39]

The keys of the consistory office were taken by a band of ten policemen who were stationed on the premises while government officials went through the Archbishop's palace, citing law No. 50 of May 7, 1874, as authority for their action.[40] In this way the administration of the Church by ecclesiastics was made practically impossible. In a similar manner the episcopal offices of all other bishoprics were occupied.[41]

Bishops experiencing this state of affairs canceled activities in their consistory offices and delegated by special jurisdiction their vicars in the rural areas (*vicarios foranneos*) to take care of matters referred to them. They thus prevented confusion and chaos and thereby clarified for the faithful priests and people alike the status of relations between the Church and the state.

On June 18, 1949, in the Strahov Church of the Abbey of the Premonstratensian Canons, Archbishop Beran preached and exposed the activities of the Czechoslovak Communist government in the following words:

> Perhaps you very soon will hear on the radio all sorts of things concerning me. You may hear that I have made a confession, or other statements. I hope you will trust me. If one day you learn of the conclusion of an agreement between the Church and the state, you should know that I would never conclude an agreement which would infringe on the rights of the Church and of the Bishops. It is possible that one day you will learn that I have concluded an agreement, or that I have given my consent. Maybe you will hear it from the wireless morning and night. But I declare before God and before the nation that nobody shall force me to do that. . . . No true Catholic can exist where the Bishops are not with the Church. . . . You know I would like to talk to you from here, but I will not. I do not want you to be persecuted. I do not know how often I shall be allowed to speak from the pulpit in the future. . . .[42]

The abbot of the historical abbey of Strahov, the Right Reverend Bohuslav Jarolímek,[43] a well-known figure in Czechoslovak Catholic and public life, was arrested after Archbishop Beran had left.

The following day, Sunday, June 19, 1949, a scandalous incident took place in the Cathedral of Saint Vitus in Hradčany-Prague. On this day a celebration of the Corpus Christi holyday was to take place. The faithful were hindered by all means possible from assisting at the celebration, but the services were attended by secret police and some hundreds of hired men sent there as members of the civilian militia corps. At the beginning of the sermon by Archbishop Beran, when he condemned the fraudulent Catholic Action, these men started to whistle and yell.[44] Since the secret police made no attempt to restore order, as was their duty, Archbishop

Beran, after making some effort to continue speaking, left the cathedral and thus the celebration of Corpus Christi was made impossible.

The tumult and scandal caused by the Communist party and its members of the civilian militia corps in the Cathedral of Saint Vitus had repercussions in the major seminaries of Bohemia and Moravia. As proof thereof we quote a circular letter issued by the Ministry of Education, Sciences, and Arts, No. 95.124/49-III 1, dated July 9, 1949:

> The Ministry of Education, Sciences, and Arts hereby declares that the deplorable incidents that took place during the services in the Cathedral of Saint Vitus in Prague on June 19, 1949, were participated in by clerics, students of the theological faculty of Charles University in Prague, and students from the seminaries of the dioceses and religious orders. The Ministry of Education, Sciences, and Arts, reserving its own jurisdiction and procedure against these students, nominates hereby an investigating commission consisting of the following members: Rev. Bohuslav Černocký, pastor in Slatina, Silesia, as chairman of the commission; Rev. Jan. Mára, Cooperator in Hloubětin; Rev. Kamil Filipec, curial counselor in Rychnov above Kněžna.
>
> I ask that all measures be provided to make possible for the members of the commission the execution of their duties, especially admittance to all school buildings and the investigation of students.[45]

In this manner the Communists sought to conceal the true nature of the scandal and to protect the real evildoers.

In spite of the afore-mentioned disturbance in the Cathedral of Saint Vitus, on June 19, 1949, there was read in almost all the churches in the Republic, as also in the Cathedral of Saint Vitus, a pastoral letter emanating from the conference of the episcopate held on June 15, 1949, in Prague and signed in the names of all the bishops by the Archbishop of Prague. Despite the efforts of the state commissioners who had sent from the episcopal offices an official statement forbidding the reading of any pastoral letters, the letter was read. The contents of this pastoral is of historical significance because its incisive analysis of the situation shows the almost hopeless position of the Church:

Recently, by all manner of propaganda, untrue statements have been spread that the discussions for solving relations between Church and state have failed through the fault of our Bishops. These accusations are untrue. We declare that we have been loyal, and are loyal, to this state. On taking office, we took oaths of loyalty to the Republic, and we declare that we have always been and are in favor of a just agreement with the state in all Church-political questions, as that is the basis for fruitful and successful cooperation between Church and state in their common tasks. This cooperation would, of course, only be possible on condition that the state did not interfere in Church and religious matters, just as the Church does not interfere in political matters.

In spite of all the assurances of the good will of government representatives, unfriendly actions have been taken against religious freedom and its rights. Some facts follow:

1. We have no means, by either press or radio, to inform you. You are yourselves witnesses of how, since February, 1948, all the Catholic press has been gradually stopped. Just remember the Catholic weeklies, *Neděle* and *Rozsevač*. In April, 1949, even the official gazette of the Archdiocese, *Acta Curiae*, was stopped. It had not been stopped even during the German occupation. In this connection, Chapter 18 of the new constitution guarantees us freedom of expression. But the fact is that the Ministry of Information, in its announcement of April 27, 1949, interfered even with the publication and distribution of information by means of a mimeographing machine. It has gone so far that there is interference in internal Church affairs, such as, for instance, the occupation of benefices.

2. With the participation of suspended priests and uninformed laymen, a hostile "Catholic Action" has been formed against the Bishops to cause confusion among the faithful and make it impossible for the Bishops to defend the freedom and rights of the Church. We have declared, and we declare again, that this false "Catholic Action" is schismatic, and that all participation in it and cooperation with it must be punished with ecclesiastical penalties. Those who inspired it and brought it into being fall under excommunication, *ipso facto*. That is to say, they are excluded from the Church under canons 2334, paragraph 2, and 2331, chapter 2. The telegrams of greetings sent to the Bishops do not

change the fact that the whole of this Action is directed against the unity of the Church and Church discipline. We expect that those who have associated themselves with so-called Catholic Action, either under compulsion or through ignorance, will renounce their declaration at the Ordinariate. Similarly, we hope that even those priests whose loyalty we do not doubt and whose signatures have been used without their knowledge on expressions of agreement with the so-called Catholic Action, and for agreement between Church and state, will act likewise.

3. From this fact, it is clear that it is a question no longer of agreement between Church and state, but of an undermining of Catholic ideology by a program which is anti-Christian and which proclaims the replacement of religion by Marxism and appropriates for the state all rights, even in matters of conscience, faith, and morals, something which no Christian can recognize.

For instance, at the Ninth Congress of the Czechoslovak Communist Party, the Minister of Information, Václav Kopecký, declared: "We must get rid of all that is old and outmoded, which has remained from the ideological structure of the capitalist order. We must awaken a new progressive attitude toward life, such as is given by dialectical materialism, Marxism, and Leninism, by the teachings of Marx, Engels, Lenin and Stalin." At the same Congress, the Minister of Education, Dr. Zdeněk Nejedlý, declared: "We still have with us much that is outmoded. We even have old feudal anachronism, old Church education. We must try to get rid of these anachronisms and create a new, truly Communist man."

We must, therefore, fight against the commissaries appointed by the state to all Church offiices under whatever pretenses, be it a national administrator in the Catholic organization *Caritas* or interference by Action Committees in our Catholic societies, or various plenipotentiaries nominated by the state to Bishop's consistories or clerical seminaries, or all those instructors in "social science" who have been appointed to the theological faculties of our Universities. We shall never give our consent to the Church being deprived of freedom and enslaved for money or subsidies. We declare that an agreement based on such principles is not acceptable to us, because it is aimed directly at extermination of the Creed and it violates all religious freedoms guaranteed by the new Constitution and violates all human rights as well.

Any further negotiations will be possible only if:

1. the Christian way of life and ideas is respected and recognized in public life and in education, not only in word but in deed;

2. the government is ready to recognize the spiritual jurisdiction of the Bishops, who are obedient to the Pope according to the current ecclesiastical law;

3. all measures which restrict and threaten the religious freedom of Catholics in Czechoslovakia are immediately revoked. In particular, the *Gazette of the Catholic Clergy*, which is published by the Ministry of Education and which calls us Bishops "isolated individuals inside the Church," must be stopped. All bills and decrees which limit freedom of assembly and association and hamper religious exercises and other tasks performed by the Church must be revoked. The state must be ready to stop its interference in Church administration.

We hope that real statesmanship as well as an interest for the well-being of the state—which is and must be before all political ideologies—will overcome the hostility toward the Church, whose freedoms and rights we are ready to defend by all means and with the help of all faithful clergy and laymen.

Every Czech and Slovak Catholic must realize that his time of test has come, in which (to tell the sheep from the wolves) there can be no compromise whatever; that in those issues a clear, strict proceeding is needed from the very start, as it is a question of the eternal salvation of every immortal soul.

We thank all the clergy and the faithful for their fidelity. We believe in their steadfastness, and to steel their Christian gallantry we bestow upon them our benediction. Be firm in your Holy Creed and pray fervently to the Sacred Heart of Christ. Pray for us all, as we pray for you.[46]

The establishment of the schismatic Catholic Action had, first of all, its repercussions in Rome. After the strong repudiation of this state-sponsored Catholic Action by the Czechoslovak Catholic episcopate, at a time when the Church was being attacked in a most severe manner, Rome issued a decree, enacted by the supreme Sacred Congregation of the Holy Office on June 20, 1949, which read as follows:

Schismatic "Catholic Action" in Czechoslovakia is condemned.

> Of late the enemies of the Catholic Church in Czechoslovakia put forward fraudulently the false name of "Catholic Action" by which they try to induce the Catholics of that Republic to abandon the Catholic Church and withdraw from the obedience due to the legitimate pastors of the Church.
>
> This "Action" is more wicked in that those who promote it have not hesitated to compel many, by violence or fraud, to lend their names to it; they have gone to such an extreme as to list and announce as supporters many priests and Catholic laymen who have never consented to it, but have rather manifested a will to the contrary.
>
> For this reason the Supreme Sacred Congregation of the Holy Office, discharging its duty of guarding the integrity of faith and morals, in the name and under the authority of our Most Holy Lord Pius XII, by divine providence Pope, rejects and condemns as schismatic the afore-mentioned "Action," deceitfully called "Catholic Action," and at the same time declares that all and every one, clerical and lay, who have already knowingly and willingly adhered to it or will do so in the future, and its authors and promoters by name, have incurred or are going to incur, by that very fact, as schismatics and apostates from the Catholic Church, excommunication reserved in a special manner to the Holy See, according to Canon 2314, other sanctions of Canon Law applying, by which they are to be punished if (which God forbid) they should rebelliously persevere in the censure.[47]

At the same time there was published in the *Osservatore Romano* by the papal theologian, Mariano Cordovani, O. P., an article, explaining this decree and designating the Czechoslovak regime as "a democracy surpassing the knavery of every tyrannical absolutism of the past."[48]

These strong words by the papal theologian stigmatize the interference by the state in ecclesiastical and religious affairs. The main issues concerning the jurisdiction of the Church as a perfect and public society and concerning jurisdiction of the Pope and hierarchy as expounded in the first chapter of this present work were directly violated or set aside.

On June 22, 1949, the government of Czechoslovakia held a session and passed a resolution against the bishops which was broadcast by Prime Minister Antonín Zápotocký as follows:

> Because the faithful do not follow them, they resort to direct provocation. They speak of the persecution of the believers, and, with the help of foreign radio, they diffuse calumnies on the situation of our Republic, the closing of churches, and the prohibition of religion, when they themselves violate the laws of the Republic and endeavor, by the use of lies, to heavily influence the free will of their fellow-countrymen.
>
> Our Constitution guarantees religious freedom to all citizens, to Catholics and others. This freedom has not been and is not limited. Services are freely held; all are free to attend. Religion is taught in the schools, and no influence is brought to bear on the parents as regards the religious instruction of their children. Our Constitution, however, determines that a religious belief must not serve as a pretext for a citizen to avoid his obligations, and the Constitution does not permit the misuse of religion for nonreligious purposes.
>
> The government notes with satisfaction that the believers have spontaneously expressed their attitude toward the government. The government will protect all who conduct themselves according to the principles of our popular democracy.
>
> The government of the Czechoslovak Republic will uphold the popular democratic Republic, its Constitution, approved by the population and parliament, and its laws now in force. The government will not tolerate the violation of the Constitution and the laws. Then it will guarantee religious liberty to the extent that the churches and religious services will not be used to give reactionary political speeches and to foment activities against the Republic. The government will not permit the Archbishop and bishops to violate the freedom of opinion of patriotic Catholic priests and to terrorize them. The government will protect the thousands of patriotic priests who remain faithful to the Republic and wish to labor for its welfare.[49]

There were two characteristics of the present situation that need in particular to be understood. The first was this cunning, but not at all successful, way in which the government tried to present all the trouble as being between two warring camps of Catholics, with the state concerned only as an arbiter, insuring proper freedom of religion for each side and favoring that which gave acceptable proofs of loyalty. Protestations such as those by the bishops in their pastoral letter on Sunday, June 19, were not regarded as acceptable. The second characteristic of the situation which needs to be emphasized is that, although there had in the past been a certain traditional readiness to prefer a national church in Czechoslovakia, such as the Communist government desired to have exclusively, nevertheless the Catholic Church, faithful to the Holy See and personified by Monsignor Beran, had the respect and allegiance of the people in a greater degree than ever before. One reason was her excellent patriotic record under the Nazi occupation, when, in 1942, Monsignor Beran himself was among the many Catholic priests sent to the concentration camp in Dachau.[50] The Communists themselves felt constrained to join in the general acclamation. Their newspaper after the war, in 1945, repeatedly praised Monsignor Beran as a good democrat and anti-Fascist, and even Mr. Gottwald, when he became President of the Republic, on June 14 attended a solemn *Te Deum* in Archbishop Beran's cathedral.

Meanwhile great pressure was being put on civil employees to sign declarations disassociating themselves from the Archbishop; the pressure became stronger on the clergy in proportion as the Archbishop urged them to resist.

On Saturday, June 25, 1949, a session of functionaries of the Action Committee of the National Front was held in Lucerna Hall in Prague. Minister Čepička on that occasion sharply attacked the Catholic Church in the following manner:

> The Vatican, which is serving the interests of international reactionary forces, is endeavoring in our country, just as was the case in Hungary, to transform the Church into a basis for organizing resistance against the establishment of socialism. In our country, there were found for the purpose of attaining this aim willing individuals among the hierarchy. . . . Catholic people remained loyal to their national traditions and by free and voluntary decision they established a movement which was called "Catholic Action." Our people and their government will not tolerate the persecution or injury of anyone for his voluntary activities. . . . The reactionary hierarchy will learn in the near future that in our country it is impossible to inspire priests and faithful in activities of an antistate nature. . . . Our people will never admit that the unity and freedom of the Church and the orthodoxy of Catholics can be injured and insulted by anyone.[51]

On the following day, Sunday, June 26, the second pastoral letter, issued also in the conference of bishops in Prague on June 15, 1949, was read in the majority of the Catholic churches of the Republic. This pastoral letter is proof of the unfortunate situation of the Church in Czechoslovakia. Every effort on the part of the bishops was being ironically calumniated by the government.

This pastoral letter, of an informative character for all the faithful, contains a statement to the effect that the bishops had taken all possible measures to reach an agreement, but unfortunately received no cooperation on the part of the government. In their letter, the bishops asked the faithful to remain loyal, consigning the Church to the protection of God. The letter reads:[52]

> In these overwhelmingly serious times of our religious and national life we turn to you with this letter of the Church, the guardian of truth.
>
> Love for the nation and for the people of Czechoslovakia leads us to speak in these decisive days, in which we have become witnesses of attacks on the unity and leadership of the Catholic Church in our own country. To know where truth and right and your place in the Church and nation lie, hear the voice of your pastors who, being conscious of their responsibility before God and the conscience of the whole world, after deliberate consideration cannot remain silent.
>
> Of late we have all been witnesses of a widely diffused action, the aim of which is to force the Czechoslovak Bishops to come to an agreement with the state. As the public knows, we too are aware of the fact that relations between Church and state are discordant and painful. This situation is surely unnatural, for both societies should complement each other and the present situation does not contribute to the general public peace nor to the internal peace of the faithful.
>
> The worst of it all is that many faithful Catholics suffer spiritually, as they sincerely love both their Church and their state and are filled with fears for their future.
>
> This causes no little pain to the Bishops, who are ordained by God as the guardians of the Commandments of Christ and are responsible before Him for the saving of your souls.
>
> It pains us all the more since people who are not suffi-

ciently informed put all responsibility for the failure in negotiations upon us to whom your eternal and temporal welfare is the greatest treasure, for which we are ready to sacrifice everything.

We understand your natural right—that you also wished to be informed truthfully about our side. Having no other possibility of presenting our case, we are endeavoring to do so, as our conscience bids us, by this pastoral letter, imploring God that the voice of the pastors reach your hearing and that it be heard with belief and rightly comprehended.

We also, the guardians of the truths and of the Lord, consider a sincere and just agreement with the state to be of no small importance. We cannot be indifferent as to whether our circumstances be favorable to the development of the Christian life or not. For, after all, the hindrances which today stand in the way of Christian thought in civilization and in everyday practical life are known.

We know well how many rights you have been deprived of, just as you are acquainted with the adversities which lately the Church has had to suffer.

We have always been aware of the burden of responsibility for the saving of your souls before God. We have always endeavored and we still endeavor today, even if only with small hope of success, to defend and insure the sacred rights of you Christians as free citizens of the state, as is naturally demanded by God's order.

To these humanitarian and commonly recognized rights of man belong not only the freedom of privately held religious convictions and the freedom to perform religious rites, but also the free realization of the principles of this faith as the norm of life of individuals and society—and this without fear of losing personal freedom and civic equality, and of endangering the right to existence.

For the realization and insuring of this religious freedom for Catholics it is the Church's understanding that by the ordinance of God, these further conditions are necessary prerequisites: the recognition of the authority of the Holy Father as the highest visible head of the Church and recognition and respect for the authority of his Bishops.

The nonrecognition of this fundamental principle means that the Catholic Church as Christ wanted it is not recognized and that every action taken apart from and against the will of the Bishops connected with the Pope of Rome disturbs the Church's basic structure, disrupts its unity, and necessarily leads to its destruction.

Further basic conditions for the recognition of the rights and freedom of the Church, stemming from natural law, are:

1) Respect for the sovereign right of parents over the education of their children. This includes education both in and outside the school.

2) Recognition of the family as a sacred tie, and the rights and duties stemming from this.

3) The right of the faithful to assembly in free congregations and organizations.

To these belong also the conditions of free religious life, which otherwise would be unattainable for the community or the individual. These conditions include the necessary number of church schools, educational, social and charitable institutions, cultural and philanthropic institutions, sufficient facilities for printing periodicals and books, and free and unlimited access to all possibilities of social and cultural life.

Finally, financial means and material security for these institutions and establishments is also necessary, as without them the Church cannot successfully develop this activity for the welfare of our people or save church buildings from deterioration and destruction.

All this we were once sufficiently provided with; of all this we have lately been deprived.

In difficult circumstances, with many hardships, the Church had built—with extreme sacrifices through your will and from your means for you and your children—social and educational institutions, schools, seminaries, presses, and an organization of societies. All these formed conditions for the spiritual life.

And what has become of all this in this short time? We need not put before you, dear Catholics, special proofs of this. Look around you. Follow what is happening and you will easily come to the conclusion that the Catholic Church in Czechoslovakia has received a very bitter reward for its hundreds of years of service to the nation, for its cultural and charitable activities, for its loyalty to the people, for its fearlessness and suffering during the (German) occupation.

It stands here today—robbed, deprived of the majority of its freedoms and rights, dishonored, soiled, persecuted secretly and openly.

Only observe how the Church is faring in Czechoslovakia at the present time. A concerted campaign is waged against it on the radio and in public proclamations, especially against the Holy Father and the Bishops, who are its God-ordained heads. The sacred character of the family and the sovereign rights of parents to the education of their children are willfully undermined.

All ecclesiastical publications, with a few completely insignificant exceptions, have been stopped. Even the official gazettes of the Bishops, which informed priests also of important state directives, have been discontinued. Instead, the Ministry of Education, Science and Arts has published the so-called *Gazette of the Catholic Clergy*, which is not Church-indorsed and is edited against the will of the hierarchy. Although this so-called gazette is intended for Catholic priests, it is a state-directed organ which interferes with affairs which are wholly ecclesiastical and thereby attempts to deter the Bishops from practicing their rights.

Every Catholic book which is to be published—even prayer books—is subjected to preliminary state censorship. State plenipotentiaries are planted in Catholic publishing houses. An interdict on assembly and schooling of Catholics outside churches has been issued at the threat of prosecution. Even the fate of church buildings, as was demonstrated by the forced inventory of ritual objects and sacred vessels, is, it seems, insecure.

The Church is deprived of the last remnants of its property: not even the minimum laid down by the law is respected. And in many cases the payment of the state stipend to priests has ceased.

Church schools practically no longer exist and the fate of the few remaining is painfully insecure, which causes sufferings to pupils and parents. Pressure has been brought to bear upon the parents to take their children out of church schools, and this under a direct threat of evil consequences.

Teachers of religion are tested ideologically and are given directives on how to teach religion in the materialistic spirit. All religious education of youth in societies, Eucharistic circles, and so on, is in many places forbidden under punitive threat, and is consistently made impossible by the fact that the state has formed a monopoly through materialist schools and extracurricular education, so that education in the Christian spirit is made impossible and considered practically illegal.

In this respect, we have come to the point that even in theological schools lectures in so-called social science were arranged, aimed at bringing it about that even theological students should be educated in the materialistic ideology.

An inventory of all church property, even church collections, was ordered, quite illegally. Such inventories were carried out in many cases under direct inspection; they were anti-constitutional searches.

Consistent attempts are made to deprive church buildings of their religious missions, especially by the taking over of monasteries and institutions for the education of clerical and monastic youth. Especially in Slovakia some monastic houses were forcibly cleared out and the priests taken away in trucks.

The Ministry of Interior gave instructions to the regional command of the state security (police) on how to deal with the Church and its members; in some places even the practice of religious rites has already been forbidden. Religious processions either were made impossible or were misused for irreligious purposes.

The conference of Bishops in Dolní Smokovec, which was to have taken a stand on the demands of the government, was broken up when listening devices were discovered in the conference room. The Ministry of Interior was asked to make an inquiry, but until now no satisfactory answer has been forthcoming.

The latest conference of Bishops in Prague was disturbed by the police. At the same time the Prague chancery was occupied by state officers and the Archbishop's residence put under secret police surveillance, so that the freedom of the chairman of the Bishops' conference was totally restricted. These restrictions represent extreme breaches of constitutional freedoms and many of the still existent laws. On the whole it can be said that outside the church any religious activity is impossible, and many fear to visit churches lest they be accused of reaction and deprived of their means of livelihood.

It is a certainty that by these measures conditions are created which are not only in defiance of the rights of God but are also opposed to the natural and commonly recognized rights of man.

Judge for yourselves, dear Catholics, after ascertaining these facts, whether the state was in any way harmed by the Church or whether just the opposite is true.

After all, the whole affair of an agreement between Church and state would actually have been a rather simple matter if it had not been for the fact that the state first harmed the Church and deprived it of the majority of its rights.

All this organized calling for an agreement would have been quite superfluous if government personages, on their own initiative, had not interfered before the start of negotiations in Church freedoms and rights and formed, by this one-sided action, a painful situation in which the Church was deprived beforehand of that which was supposed to have been the subject of the agreement.

So in reality the Church was deprived of all possibilities of successful negotiations and given this choice: submission to dictatorship or persecution.

In spite of all these painful realities the Czechoslovak Episcopate was always willing to negotiate and really did negotiate through its delegated representatives. It made extreme sacrifices to attain, at least in the most basic things, some regulation of affairs and to ensure its faithful at last the most necessary conditions of religious life.

It (the Episcopate) always found out, to its great sorrow, that in spite of all its good will this could not be done, except at the price of fundamental concessions and the price of misusing the Church against its divine mission.

At the same time, during negotiations the Church was frequently treated in a hostile way which consistently undermined the confidence of the Bishops in the success of the negotiations.

Ask yourselves these questions, dear Catholics:

Could we Bishops be satisfied with all this and accept every demand which is in defiance of the laws of God and humanity?

Could we approve, before our faithful people and before the whole world, any development not in accordance with the spirit of the teachings of Jesus Christ?

Indeed, with gladness we shall render unto Caesar the things which are Caesar's, but it would not be possible to sacrifice to him that which is God's because it behooves us rather than man to obey God.

Furthermore, this negative attitude of the state toward the Church cannot ever be justified by alleging that the Bishops refused a clear statement of loyalty to the Republic, because such reports are not in accordance with the truth. We declare again that we were always loyal to the Republic. We have stressed this many times and it can be deduced from the oath we undertook when we assumed office. A loyal attitude toward the Republic is, therefore, a matter of course for us and we are sure to remain faithful to our oath. Therefore, we have always demanded from our clergy that they refrain from any political activity, especially from any illegal and antistate activity.

But we cannot remain quiet when the rights of the Holy Church are violated and when political power is being misused against it.

If, therefore, we defend, as is our duty, the rights of the Holy Church, we in no way want to harm the interest of the state. On the contrary, we do it in the interest of the state itself and for the welfare of our dear nation.

It is a painful realization that we have no way of defending ourselves against these grossly untrue attacks. All manner of attempts are being made to force us out of our pastoral offices, and the management of the Church is being taken over by unbelieving people, people who have broken away from the Church and those who have no right, no competence, and no divine mission.

Nothing else remains for us but to waste our energy and time with unceasing protests and efforts against the confiscation of Church institutions, schools, and monasteries, against trampling on all Church rights and religious freedom—protests which nobody answers, which nobody takes any notice of, and which have no practical results.

In the present affair it is, therefore, not a matter, as we have stated before, of a lack of positive attitude of the Church toward the state. It is not a matter of reaction, because the form of government and regulation of social life are not the main subjects of our interest. The question is whether this state of affairs is favorable to the development of the religious life and whether it is possible to bring such a social reconstruction into harmony with the teachings of Jesus Christ.

Nor is it even a matter of inclination toward capitalism, for we know that not even a liberal-capitalistic society corresponds with all the ideals of Christianity, and capitalism has several times been condemned by the Church.

You, yourselves, know best that your present Bishops are not capitalists. They certainly would be better off today if they were willing to choose the path of Judas.

We desire for our working people every improvement in social standards and hope that their standard of life will improve so that, along with the growth of their material welfare, favorable conditions may be created for perfecting of moral and religious life. The seriousness of the times makes us act with absolute loyalty to principles and with consistency in negotiating. Indeed, this is a matter of a consistent, well-planned and steadily applied persecution of the Catholic Church in Czechoslovakia.

Not a whit of this can be changed by the resolution passed, on a plan prepared beforehand, at the meeting of the so-called (government-sponsored) Catholic Action in the Municipal Palace in Prague on June 10, 1949, even if it promised loyalty to the Holy Church, recognition of the Holy Father as its visible head, submission to him in matters of faith, morals, and Church discipline, and recognition of the authority of the Bishops in matters of faith and morals.

This meeting, secretly prepared, was convened without the knowledge and against the will of the Bishops. Its aim was clear: to hinder still further the authority and influence of the Bishops.

After all, the majority of delegates at this conference were paid delegates—appointed by action committees. They were delegates who often did not know what it was all about and who did not suspect that their signatures on the list of those present would be misused for the so-called Catholic Action.

Because of this, the Assembly of Bishops at its conference of June 15, 1949, was forced to declare that the so-called Catholic Action is not Catholic, but a separatist movement, and that participation and cooperation with it must be prosecuted with ecclesiastical penalties. The inspirers have, *ipso facto,* been excommunicated. That is, they were expelled from the Church according to Canon 2334, paragraph two, and Canon 2231, paragraph two, in accordance with the Ecclesiastical Judicial Code.

The whole action in fact is aimed against the unity of the Church and Church discipline.

By methods similar to that demonstrated above, many clergymen were misrepresented as voicing assent with the so-called Catholic Action. They knew nothing about its mission and they were enticed to sign under disguised slogans. They were asked if they favored a just agreement, if they were for the maintenance of Church rights, for the teaching of religion in schools, the recognition of the Holy Father as visible head of the Church. These priests did not want to undertake anything against the will of Church dignitaries. On the contrary, they wanted to support their efforts for the realization of such an agreement which would be in accord with the interests of the Church, in the spirit of Church directives.

These priests consequently gave their signatures under conditions of deceit and pressure. They did not act either consciously or of their own free will and therefore maintained, of course, their loyalty to the Holy Church and faithfulness to the Bishops, as many of them have already privately and publicly stated. Furthermore, the names of many priests were published without their knowledge, even against their will and protests.

The Catholic Bishops therefore call to everyone's attention that any attempt at the founding of diocesan, regional, district, or parochial so-called action committees is forbidden by the Church, and that clergymen and laymen who personally participate in the founding of such actions or center their committees or accept functions in them will thereby be excommunicated from the Catholic Church.

The so-called Catholic newspaper, published by the Committee of Catholic Action, of course, lacks the indorsement of the Bishops and cannot be considered as Catholic. Therefore, the reading and keeping and distribution of this newspaper is forbidden by the Church.

Moreover, the clergy must be aware not only that directives published by chanceries under government control are ecclesiastically not binding but also that the clergy is bound in conscience to observe only those directives and repeals which they are safely convinced were published by their respective authorities.

As the responsible representatives of the Catholic Church of the Czechoslovak Republic we, of course, feel heavy responsibility for the development of Church affairs in our country and we are not deluding ourselves about the fact that the decisive moment of great tests has come for our dear faithful and for our loyal clergy.

If it were true, as has been claimed, that the principal aim of all this which has now been organized against the Czechoslovak Catholic Church were to make the Bishops come to a just agreement between Church and state, then we declare that this whole campaign is superfluous.

Czechoslovak Catholic dignitaries had, and have, the greatest interest in reaching a sincere and just agreement between Church and state and will not cease to pray for this end. But they desire, too, that a real agreement be reached on the basis of which the Church can develop all its rich activity and put to use all its moral influence in favor of the state and its people. They want Catholics to be able to use their philosophy and to be able to direct their lives according to it, for religion should govern all acts of men. They do not want the Church to become a mere servant of the state —in other words, the bearer of a different philosophy under a cloak of Christian religion. Their wish is for an agreement, not dictation.

In this spirit the Czechoslovak dignitaries at the Bishops' conference of June 7, 1949, in Olomouc, laid down the basic conditions on which agreement would be possible and which should be accepted and guaranteed by the government beforehand. These conditions are:

(1) The Christian world viewpoint (philosophy) will be recognized and respected in public life and education, in word and deed.

(2) The government recognizes the spiritual authority of the Pope of Rome as the supreme head of the Church in matters religious and ecclesiastical, which, according to valid authority, does not touch the sovereignty of the state but is a natural consequence of recognized basic human rights. It especially recognizes the freedom of religion.

(3) Before the beginning of negotiations, all measures restricting and threatening religious freedom of Catholics in the Czechoslovak Republic, especially the religious freedom and education of youth, must be repealed.

In addition to this:

(a) The *Gazette of the Catholic Clergy*, published by the Ministry of Education, Arts, and Sciences, will be abolished immediately, and the publishing of all official Bishops' gazettes will be permitted.

(b) The decree of the Ministry of Education, Arts, and Sciences of May 23, 1949, about vacant Church offices and accompanying stipends, as well as the decree of the Ministry of Interior of May 5, 1949, restricting the freedom of assembly and congregation, and also the decree for regional and district command of state security police on the procedure against the Catholic Church must be revoked.

(c) All restrictions involving religious rights must be canceled.

To these conditions a further demand is added—that the government will not support the newly formed Catholic Action and will not grant it state sponsorship. To demand the fulfillment of these conditions we feel commanded by our archpastoral responsibility before God and before you and before the conscience of the nation, because without their fulfillment the Church would no longer be the Church of Christ and would not be able to fulfill its spiritual mission—that is, to teach, to sanctify, and to direct.

We are certain, dear brothers and sisters in Christ, that you approve of this, our standpoint and watchfulness. We would have to feel ashamed before you had we acted otherwise, had we acted not like pastors who are willing in the interest of your Savior to give even their lives for their sheep, but as hired pastors who forsake their flock treacherously in times of danger.

Help us and strengthen us with prayers, your truly Christian life, and your unconditional loyalty to the good Mother Church, so that with the help of the Holy Spirit, a negotiable path will be found for the regulation of Church-state relations.

But if such an agreement cannot be attained because it has been decided to begin a struggle of extermination by all means against the Church of Christ and misuse it in a cloaked way for ungodly purposes, then the hour of trial has come for the Catholics in Czechoslovakia.

The moment has come in which it is necessary to realize the words of the Apostle Peter: "Beloved, do not be startled at the trial by fire that is taking place among you to prove you, as if something strange were happening to you.

"But in as far as you are partakers of the sufferings of Christ, rejoice that you may also rejoice with exultation in the revelation of His glory."

Every test is of God's making and will surely contribute to the salvation of our souls. It is an opportunity to prove our faithfulness to Christ, to make amends for our trespasses, and to learn to be true and consistent Catholics. The nation looks upon you, anxious for your welfare in the historic moment of trial. The Catholics of the whole world are linked with you.

Remain loyal to your Bishops who suffer with you, and do not waver even if their voice does not reach you. The Church is indestructible, and to suffer for Christ is the greatest glory.

Do not let yourselves be misled by false prophets. Beware of ravenous wolves in sheep's clothing. Do not let yourselves be provoked to immediate actions. Be on your guard and pray: All ye saints of God who were imprisoned and tortured for Christ, plead for us; Sacred Heart, pierced for our sins on the grounds of a false sentence, be merciful to us.

We bless you all, especially those who suffer or will suffer adversities for the sake of justice. In the name of the Father, the Son, and the Holy Spirit. Amen.

(*Signed*)

JOSEF (BERAN), *Archbishop of Prague.*
JOSEF CHARLES, *Archbishop of Olomouc.*

JOHN, *Bishop of Spišská Nová Ves.*
JOSEF, *Titular Bishop of Thagora, Apostolic Administrator in Košice.*
PAUL, *Bishop of Prešov.*
MAURICE, *Bishop of Hradec Králové.*
ANDREW, *Bishop of Banká Bystrica.*
CHARLES, *Bishop of Brno.*
JOSEF, *Bishop of České Budějovice.*
STEFEN, *Bishop of Litoměřice.*
EDUARD, *Titular Bishop of Velicia, Apostolic Administrator of Nitra.*
FRANTISEK ONDEREK, *Apostolic Administrator of the Czech portion of Breslaw Archdiocese.*
AMBROSIUS LAZIK, *Apostolic Administrator of Trnava.*
ROBERT POBOŽNÝ, *Capitular Vicar of Rožnava.*
Prague, June 15, 1949.

This pastoral letter is to be read in all Church services on Sunday, June 26, 1949. Let the reverend priests not be intimidated from reading this letter by any threats in these so difficult and decisive times. They are bound in conscience to inform their faithful of the real state of affairs. Willful and intentional neglect of this duty will be prosecuted with ecclesiastical penalties.[53]

Under the same date, instructions for clergymen were added to this pastoral letter. The bishops explained the true state of affairs and asked all clergymen to fulfill the orders given by the bishops.[54] Priests were notified at the same time to listen to the true instructions given by Vatican broadcasts from Rome: "The distribution of this pastoral letter was a remarkable achievement, since the bishops' consistory offices remained in the occupation of government secret police and officials, who were using their seals and their stationery freely, so that, as one pastor explains, the very *imprimatur* on any new publications must be regarded with suspicion as possibly a forgery."[55]

In many places incidents occurred. Police watched the rectories, churches, and other places, to prevent the reading of the pastoral letter. For instance, in the old historical church of the Order of the Cross in Prague, the reading of this pastoral letter was interrupted by a group of youngsters who marched into the church crying: "Away with bishops!

. . . Hang them and their leader!" The faithful meanwhile sang a hymn as their answer to the invaders.[56]

There was severe rioting as a result of an attempt of the police in Slovakia to prevent the distribution and reading of the pastoral letter. The disturbances continued for a few days, during which an area of about a hundred square miles was cordoned off and placed under martial law. Carloads of police arrived early on Sunday morning and drew up outside the churches. The police entered the priests' houses not only to seize the pastoral letter but also to arrest the priests either for reading it or for having it in their possession.[57]

As an immediate sequel to the pastoral letter, the government, on June 26, decreed that any further pastorals and any meetings of the clergy would be illegal without the express permission of the Ministry of Education. A special issue of the now notorious *Gazette of the Catholic Clergy,* which was published by the Ministry of Education and circulated to all priests, contained three decrees to this effect.

The first law No. 50 of May 7, 1874, was cited to show that every bishop must submit to the approval of the Minister of Education all pastoral letters, circulars, instructions, orders, and other proclamations of this kind, intended either for priests or for the public. The second concerned "the invalidity of ecclesiastical penalties imposed for political reasons"; and the third ordained that no meetings of priests could take place, even in their presbyteries, without state permission.[58]

Besides, the Archbishop of Prague was notified that the Minister of the Interior had assigned police to safeguard him. The Archbishop protested, refused any escort, and declared that under such conditions he would rather not leave his palace. Similar was the case with the bishop in Hradec Králové, Monsignor Pícha, the oldest member of the hierarchy, who declared on the occasion of a confirmation in the town of Chrast:

> In my residence at Hradec Králové I am under police surveillance. I am not free to receive visits from my own functionaries. I am thus a semi-prisoner, cut off from the members of my own diocese. I solemnly protest against

> these exceptional police measures, in the name of the personal freedom guarantee in the second paragraph of our people's constitution, and in the name of the freedom of speech and freedom of press guaranteed in paragraphs 18 and 21 of that same constitution. According to the law that is valid all over the world, even a criminal has the right to be heard. Perhaps, therefore, the Bishops and the thousands of faithful priests and the millions of true believers will be given the right to defend themselves publicly, particularly when they are urgently demanding that right. This cannot be regarded as an act against the Republic. It is under protest that I relinquish my intention to preach, although not from fear of terrorism, punishment or persecution, for all this is already going on.[59]

By a decree of the Ministry of Schools, the bishops were ordered to submit the text of their sermons to the censorship of officials of the Ministry of Education. They preferred to discard them rather than deliver them with the changes made.

The Czechoslovak Communists struck at all ecclesiastical and religious affairs, having no regard for any religious regulations or traditional rights of freedom. Their procedure was not prevented even by those clergymen who had hoped that, by good will, cooperation with Communists would be possible. A typical case is that of Reverend Francis Fiala (b. 1911), a member of a religious order of Fathers Conventuals in Prague.[60] This priest participated in activities of the underground movement against the Nazis in the years 1940-1945. After the war he wrote in the Communist newspaper *Rudé Právo;* he was decorated by the government and even after the Communist *coup d'état* in 1948 he believed in cooperation and really cooperated with Communists. He attended public meetings and was an important personality among the patriotic priests; he helped in establishing the so-called Catholic Action, and he was authorized to perform many tasks. Among other things, he was appointed as manager of the national administration in Catholic Charities in Prague. His collaboration with Communists caused confusion among priests and the faithful. Father Fiala hoped that cooperation with the Communists, as in the case of the Protestant F. L. Hromádka, would be possible; but he soon learned his error and succeeded in escaping into exile in July, 1949, fleeing to Germany, Italy, and finally Argentina. This disillusioned priest awakened at the last moment to find that exile was his best chance to escape full apostasy from the Church, since he had caused many evils in ecclesiastical legal matters as early as 1945. The Communist press had chosen him as typical of a modern priest, but his case is important as an instance of the Communists' ill will toward the Church.

Reverend Fiala himself wrote some protests against the maddening policy of the Communists. To illustrate the character of Communist hatred, we are citing one of these letters. This is the letter of June 14, 1949, to Minister Čepička on the matter of charity, which reads as follows:

> The National Administration of Czech Catholic Charities takes the liberty of notifying you of the following facts. (We are giving here a summary of a few cases.) On June 4, 1949, the criminal police appeared in the home for children in Hluboká over the Moldau. They disbanded this home for children with the assistance of the local national committee and transferred the children to a local kindergarten. The chapel was also closed and the Sisters were removed by force. Similar cases occurred in the college for girls in Prague XIII, which is a branch institute of *Charities*. The district school supervisor, by order of the counselor for culture at the Central National Committee in the capital of Prague, accompanied by the counselor for security, came to the Sister Superior of the college and asked for the keys. They declared on this occasion that they were not interested in *Charities* and said that they would not even respect the decisions of the Action Committee.
>
> A typical case of violating the agreements between *Charities* and central organs of the government occurred when the National Administration in Social Institute was introduced in Hulín. The reason offered was that this Institute was not a branch of *Charities*, which is positively a lie.
>
> A further proof of how agreements between the chairman of the national administration of *Charities* and the authorities were maintained and practiced is the decision of the local National Committee in Lysá over the Elbe, nominating a branch commissioner in our institute! Also in the home for orphans and backward children in Záběhlice, a national administration was nominated, although it is not in accordance with the known decisions of the Minis-

try of Interior or of Social Security, and it is therefore unlawful.

In the Archiepiscopal Minor Seminary in Kroměříž, there was nominated as national administrator a man without any religious convictions who, according to the chairman of the local National Committee, was guilty of scandalous conduct, of impairing religious doctrine and causing trouble about reading during the dinner hour, etc. District national committees promised that this administrator would be removed, but this has not yet been done. And in Gottwaldov, Malenovice, the district school supervisor endeavored to close the house for children maintained by Sisters, it is said, on the pretext of the law about uniform regulation of the schools. However, these homes were not included under this particular law.

All these facts indicate that intentional obstacles were being placed in the way of the national administrator of Czech Catholic Charities lest he should fulfill his duties. Since the undersigned chairman assured the people that he guarantees the fulfillment of all laws and that they can fully rely upon his assurance, he is sorry to have to admit failure in his duties to the public. Thus is undermined the confidence due him as chairman and he is at a loss as to how to fulfill his tasks in the future.

The case in Hluboká is especially painful to me as a priest, and humiliating by the fact that among the Catholic public is being spread the opinion, which I tried always to disavow, that the National Administration of Catholic Charities will look only toward the liquidation of this organization having no other possibility. Since some are supporting this rumor, I am forced to consider this opinion in order to disprove it in some way. I cannot let it be thought that I was willing to stand by and passively watch the dissolution of some institutions of the Czech Catholic Charities.

Since I asked many times before that such actions stop, but all in vain, and amounting to some hundred during my activity, I am asking now that orders be given to all organs of the people's administration, bound by sanctions, so that such cases cannot be repeated in the future free of punishment, and that, as far as they have happened, they should be corrected. In the case of the forced removal of the Sisters in Hluboká, I am asking emphatically that to quiet the minds of the Catholic people and of Charities, these Sisters

> be reinstated, with the assistance of the Criminal Police and members of the local National Committee, into the Home for Children.
>
> I considered it necessary to give this intelligence to the Central National Committee of the National Front and to send a copy of this to the Ministry of Social Security.[61]

This is a real indictment against Czechoslovak Communists when even Father Fiala,[62] communizing monk, was compelled to protest against interferences of the regime which he had previously been supporting. Any promise, agreement, or law is not taken as binding on Communists; practice and theory are different matters. Theory serves only for propaganda; practice is good for revolution. This is what is done everywhere.

On June 27, 1949, the Executive Committee of the Czechoslovak People's party declared, "Everybody who desires to resist the movement of Catholic Action, as initiated by priests and believers, will not serve the interests of the Church and will take a stand hostile against the state and against its legal government. Therefore, our members will have no doubts as to where they stand . . . they will guard against marauders of public peace and order."[63]

The Executive Committee of the schismatic Catholic Action also took a stand in the situation and issued the following statement:

> We accepted with sorrow the news about the repudiation by ecclesiastical dignitaries of our "Action." . . . Religious freedom is guaranteed in our country and there is no reason to be afraid on that account. . . . The inimical stand of some ecclesiastical dignitaries cannot frighten us or shake us. Catholic Action in the future will flourish and grow strong. By all our efforts and with greater enthusiasm and courage we will endeavor that, as soon as possible, an agreement between the Church and the state will testify to our effort and desire to cooperate.[64]

Special attention must be paid to the relations of the Communist party to Catholic Action, it insisted.

On July 12, the Central Secretariat of the Communist

party sent to all regional Action Committees a circular bearing the signature of Rudolf Slanský, Secretary-general of the party.[65] It said:

> *1*) Selected comrades must constantly visit the priests who request dissolution of the Catholic Action, in order to prevent backsliding.
> *2*) Secret meetings of priests must be carefully watched in order to ensure that there be no pressure put on the clergy to recall their signatures.
> *3*) No obstruction of the activities of Catholic Action can be tolerated, and its organ, *Katolické noviny*, must be distributed.
> *4*) Members of the People's party, and even priests must watch and organize new recruits in order to bring the clergy closer to Catholic Action.
> *5*) Demonstration of loyalty to the government must be encouraged; organization of the clergy must be prevented; the clergy must be made members *en bloc* of the Regional Action Committees; and the attitude of all individual priests must be closely watched.[66]

Another circular of the Communist party, dated June 28, was issued and addressed to party members in the Gottwaldov (Zlín) district. The circular was concerned with urging mass participation in a government-organized pilgrimage to Velehrad in order to obtain a majority of progressive Catholics there. It called the Catholic Church "our most dangerous enemy" and insisted that "it is now necessary to cut all threads linking the Vatican and the Catholic hierarchy . . . to build a great dam around the bishops and Archbishop . . . to set honestly thinking Catholics against Archbishop Beran." It added that a final solution to the crisis between Church and state was not possible until a firm division between the good Catholics and the bishops had been achieved.

The circular further stated: "The first pastoral letter (June 19) was read by about 55 per cent of all priests; the second (June 26), on the other hand, by 90 per cent. Few priests, however, made any comment on the letter. We have divided the priests into three groups. To the first group belong those who read the pastoral letters without having been warned by the police or the Action Committee. The second group consists of those who read the pastoral letters after being visited by the police. They will have to pay a fine of 1,000 to 5,000 crowns. The third group comprises those who read the pastoral letters and added a commentary of their own. These will be persecuted, and will not receive their stipend. . . . We have the impression that the priests and the ecclesiastical hierarchy are courting punishment in order to become national martyrs. We shall handle them as we handled our own political reactionaries in 1948. We shall isolate them from the broad masses of the people, and then we shall accuse them of being in contact with traitors to the nation. Then we shall accuse them directly of high treason. . . ."[67]

In spite of all this propaganda, the papal document condemning the schismatic Catholic Action was generally accepted by the Czechoslovak people with satisfaction. This evoked a very strong reaction from the Czechoslovak government. Dr. Čepička, a member of the Executive Committee of the Central Action Committee of the National Front, declared on June 15, "Let no one doubt that anybody who tries to carry out the Vatican order (the decision of the Holy Office) commits treason against the principles of his own state and the people. . . . Anyone in our territory who tries to carry out the orders of the principal enemy of our state will be gambling with the right to call himself a Czech or a Slovak. If there is any fool who has confidence in the Vatican and its fellow-travelers, then the Vatican has taken care to make things clear. Even the remnants around Beran will now disperse very quickly."[68]

The Vatican took a very clear stand in its attitude toward those Communists who wished to crush Catholics, by issuing a decree of excommunication against Communists on July 1, 1949. The decree of excommunication read:[69]

It is asked of this Supreme Sacred Congregation:

1. Whether it is lawful to lend one's name to the Communist parties or to show them favor;
2. Whether it is lawful to publish, spread, or read books, dailies, or periodicals which support the actions or doctrines of the Communists, or to write for them;

3 Whether the Christian faithful who knowingly and freely do the acts mentioned in numbers 1 and 2 may be admitted to the Sacraments;

4. Whether the Christian faithful who profess the materialistic and anti-Christian doctrine of the Communists, and especially those who defend or propagate it, incur by that very fact, as apostates from the Catholic faith, excommunication reserved in a special manner to the Apostolic See.

The Eminent and Reverend Fathers, set up to watch over matters of faith and morals, having first received the vote of the Reverend Doctors Consultants in plenary session, on Tuesday, the 28th day of June, 1949, decreed that the answers should be:

To 1. *Negative*: for communism is materialistic and anti-Christian; for the Communist leaders, although sometimes in words professing not to oppose religion, do in fact show themselves to be hostile in doctrine and action to God, the true religion, and the Church of Jesus Christ.

To 2. *Negative*: they are forbidden by the law itself (Cf. Can. 1399 C.C.).

To 3. *Negative*: according to the ordinary rules about denying the Sacraments to those who are not disposed.

To 4. *Affirmative*.

And on the following Thursday, the 30th of the same month and year, Our Most Holy Lord Pius XII, by Divine Providence Pope, in regular audience granted to the Most Excellent and Most Reverend Lord Prefect of the Holy Office, approved, when it was presented to him, the resolution of the Eminent Fathers, and ordered it to be published in the Official Record of the Acts of the Apostolic See.

PETER VIGORITA,
Secretary of the Supreme Congregation of the Holy Office.[70]

The clear wording of this decree eliminated any doubts about the worth of any Communist assurances, which really were destroying the unity among Catholics and widening the gap between the nation and the Church. It gave a strong blow to that religious indifferentism which remained as an inheritance from the time of the first Republic. By this decree all Catholics were notified that they could make no compromise between theory and practice, which was the idea of progressives. In this and in similar cases, henceforth one could be either Catholic or Communist, never both at the same time!

The decree of excommunication demonstrated to the public that the Catholic faith is binding on the faithful and that it is not only the private matter of any individual. Besides this, the decree taught a lesson to politicians concerning the impossibility of differing in ideas and in public activities, or of making compromises that agree only with the opinions of politicians. Even they are bound, first of all, by faith and by conscience.

In order that the position of Communists and the Catholic Church be quite clear, the Holy Office also issued a declaration concerning the marriage of Communists in the following text:

SUPREME SACRED CONGREGATION OF THE
HOLY OFFICE
DECLARATION CONCERNING THE MARRIAGE OF COMMUNISTS

The question is whether the exclusion of Communists from the use of the sacraments in the decree of the Holy Office, issued July 1, 1949, also contains an exclusion from the celebration of matrimony; and if not, whether the marriages of Communists are regulated by the prescriptions of canons 1060, 1061. Concerning this matter, the Sacred Congregation of the Holy Office declared: in view of the special nature of the sacrament of matrimony, whose ministers are the contracting parties themselves, and in which the priest has only the role of official witness, the priest can assist at the marriage of Communists according to the regulation of canons 1065, 1066. In the marriages, however, of those about whom number 4 of the foregoing decree deals, the prescriptions of canons 1061, 1102, and 1109, paragraph 3, are to be observed.

Issued by the Congregation of the Holy Office, August 11, 1949.

MARINO MARANI
S. Officii Substitutus Notarius[71]

After this decree, the speeches of Czechoslovak ministers became still more pronounced in formulating their stand toward the Catholic Church. Henceforth they openly supported the schismatic Catholic Action, taking under their protection the so-called patriotic priests.[72] That such a decree would come was already apparent on July 5 and 6, 1949, when Prime Minister Antonín Zápotocký delivered the following address at Děvin in Slovakia:

> The Catholic Church is trying to sabotage the way to socialism, thus serving foreign Powers, but the people know their position and their enemies. The leaders and the patriotic priests are showing that they have nothing in common with those who want to betray the nation. Even today Czechoslovak priests feel that they are descendants of Cyril and Methodius and are on the side of the people. We hope they will remain with the people and will share all future victories with the people. The patriotic priests must not be persecuted by the Church Hierarchy. We shall resist subversive activity.[73]

In a similar vein and on the same day Minister Nejedlý spoke[74] in Sázava, the suspended priest Plojhar in Velhrad,[75] and Zdeněk Fierlinger in Husinec at Prachatice. On July 19, a few days before his departure for Moscow the latter declared, "The time has come when we have to settle the relation between Church and state forever . . . The Vatican is reckoning with our weakness and conflicts outside the nation, and is trying to feed them. We shall not allow ourselves to be threatened, because there is only one truth—the truth of the workingman."[76]

The press attacked the Czechoslovak episcopate systematically, and more especially the Vatican, so that on July 12, 1949, Monsignor Matocha, Archbishop of Olomouc, protested by open letter[77] against the attitude of *Rudé Právo,* in which on July 7, the article "People, State and Bishops" by Vilém Nový was published.[78] The letter reads as follows:

> The lead article by the editor-in-chief Vilém Nový in the *Rudé Právo* of July 7, 1949, Vol. 29, entitled "People, State and Bishops," is an insult to the Roman Catholic episcopate in Czechoslovakia. For this reason I am asking you hereby to publish within three days, in the same rank and place, and in the same type, under sanctions of the law, the following press statement. This request I make on the basis of the provisions in § 11 of the Act No. 126/33 Coll.

In the newspaper *Rudé Právo* of July 7, 1949, the lead article by the editor-in-chief, Vilém Nový, was "People, State and Bishops," in which was mentioned among other things that:

1) The attack against the people's democratic regime has been provoked by the bishops and ordinaries, and that, not for religious, but for political reasons. Furthermore, (so it was said) they announced themselves enemies of the people's democratic Republic; they took steps to change churches into places of political meetings, and pulpits into political rostrums for speeches against the state with the intention of provoking unrest and trouble.

2) Bishops and ordinaries, by suggestion of the Vatican and in full accord with the reaction abroad, rejected any proposed agreement. They rejected any agreement, because they are planning the fight against the regime.

3) They cannot expect anything but to remain alone, along with other (secret) enemies of our people and our state. Our progress will continue without them and in spite of them. But nonetheless there will be a Catholic Church . . . a Church which will not be subversive and an anti-state organization, as bad shepherds are now trying to make her.

(To these accusations the Archbishop answered:)

1) This charge of yours is completely false. In proof thereof I ask: who is responsible in Czechoslovakia for the closing of ecclesiastical schools; who has forbidden the operation of every religious and ecclesiastical press; who is introducing dialectic materialism into educational matters and into examinations, even into theological schools; who is forcibly making appointments in ecclesiastical offices; and who has put their own administrators in these places; who has established the schismatic Catholic Action if not the people's democratic regime?

All these measures menace the freedom of the Church. It is the absolute duty of bishops to defend this freedom of the Church. Evident infringements by state totalitarianism, such as attacking the religious freedom which is guaranteed by the constitution, are occurring continually. For this reason it is wrong to reproach the bishops, because they make a just defense, or to denounce them as guilty of anti-state activities or of any other subversive intentions.

Every unprejudiced observer must realize the fact that all clergymen and believers must remain faithful to their bishops. Suspended and excommunicated priests are cut off from the Church, even though they call themselves patriotic. The faithful themselves have realized the deceitful maneuvering, and they are of the opinion that this is not a struggle involving loyalty to the state, but that the cause of all the trouble has been the evident and undeniable interference of the state in religious freedom and in the self-government of the Church. The Catholic Church in Czechoslovakia under no condition will be a church in which puppets, chosen by the so-called Catholic Action and by government commissioners, will represent the ruling authority. We repudiate all the unjust and untrue accusations that we are serving the reactionaries, when the truth is that we are defending the legacy of Jesus Christ and the freedom of His Church.

It is not the bishops who are violating the quiet and public order of religion, but the guilty persons are rather those who are endeavoring to repeat in Czechoslovakia the case of Henry VIII, when believers and clergymen alike became heretics and schismatics because they resisted and repudiated the Pope and the bishops. The whole situation has already been clarified and it has been shown that the culprits have failed. It is advisable that the authors of this destructive idea cease their unsuccessful activities in the future because clergymen and believers are well acquainted with the real issues in this struggle. In our circular letter of June 15, 1949, it was pointed out that we are ready to enter into negotiations with the state under what conditions are necessary.

2) The second accusation is slanderous, as is quite evident from the statement by the episcopacy on the occasion of Klement Gottwald's election as President of Czechoslovakia. Negotiations between the Church and the state have been stopped not through the fault of the episcopacy, but because of the government. The government took as its pretended reason the disciplinary steps against those priests who did not obey the prohibition to refrain from accepting any candidacy. This negotiation was renewed at the invitation of the bishops, in January, 1949, when we called on the President of the Republic, Klement Gottwald, and submitted to him the

memorandum containing our demands. When even then our bishops were harassed in their meetings, all my bishops and ordinaries stated clearly in their memorandum of April 19, 1949, sent to the President of the Republic, that they were ready to repeat an oath of loyalty to the state. It will be sufficient only to publish this memorandum which has remained entirely unanswered. The public will then be able to make their own judgment.

3) If some think it possible to eliminate bishops from the Catholic Church, let them remember that the bishops are the successors of the apostles. These people are promoting schisms, even though they constantly proclaim their loyalty to the Pope, and to the bishops. Just as in the state there can be only one government, so also in the Church there can be only one spiritual power, which lies in the hands of the episcopate. The establishing of any new organization against the bishops is schismatic, such as the organization that unjustly styles itself "Catholic Action." This is not really "catholic action" but schismatic action. They are responsible for this who establish "spontaneous" secular movements against the bishops.

In case this statement is not published, I am reserving to myself the power to take steps according to § 14 of the act.[79]

The publication of the decree of the Holy Office on July 1, 1949, excommunicating all those who either joined or assisted the Communist party was received with great interest and its timing was thought to have been chosen with an eye to local events.

On July 15, the Archbishop of Olomouc (Primate of Moravia), Monsignor Matocha, in the following statement announced the Holy Office's decree of June 20, whereby the schismatic Catholic Action in Czechoslovakia was repudiated:

According to this decree those were excommunicated who knowingly and voluntarily joined the Catholic Action. If any signed the register without knowing that this association was of a schismatic character, and that it resisted ecclesiastical authority, and did not know that assistance given to this action is punishable by ecclesiastical regulations—

they are not excommunicated. Much less are they who signed a declaration that they are for an agreement between the state and the Church. For the future, however, all who join Catholic Action, or sign a declaration or sign the enrollment, or accept any function in the organization, will incur the penalty of this decree, because the character of that Catholic Action is now publicly known. The excuse of force or threat to one's life is not recognized because it is a betrayal of the faith, which is not permitted even when life, liberty or property is menaced. The ecclesiastical penalty of excommunication cuts off such a person from all union with the other faithful. It means that the excommunicated person does not partake in indulgences, prayers and sacraments of the Church. He cannot receive the sacraments, he cannot be a godfather at baptism or at confirmation. If the excommunicated person does not receive absolution and if he dies without giving signs of penance, he may not receive Catholic burial. An excommunicated priest is forbidden to celebrate Holy Mass and to administer the sacraments. If a priest has been proclaimed excommunicated by the decision of his superiors, the faithful must not accept the sacraments administered by him, except in the case of danger of death. Confession to this priest is invalid. Invalid is the marriage contracted before such priests. If any priest is excommunicated, the faithful will be advised by their pastors.

Those priests who were excommunicated for their participation in activities of Catholic Action and who will not repudiate their participation, nor correct their lapses—those priests must be deprived of ecclesiastical offices, dignities and pensions, if they are drawing any. They will be proclaimed as dishonorable, and after repeated warning, they will be discharged from their positions. Also laics, if they are excommunicated and if they do not express their sorrow in an effective way, will be unable to accept any ecclesiastical function.

Absolution from this excommunication is reserved in a special way for the authority of the Holy See. It is permissible, however, to request either directly or through a priest the services of a competent archbishop, who can give absolution to any penitent after that penitent takes an oath repudiating his error. The archbishop can also authorize another priest to give absolution. In such a case the declaration of the repudiation of error and of the profession of the faith must be made before such an authorized priest and two witnesses. It is always necessary to correct wrong or false ideas in people's minds, so that those who gave their signa-

> ture or consent to the activities of the schismatic Catholic Action without understanding the full nature of their act must now repudiate this—penitents should always be given a heavy penance.[80]

Attacks were concentrated against the chargé d'affaires of the papal internunciature in Prague, Monsignor Gennaro Verolino. In June the papal representative was stopped at Košice in Slovakia, while making his official trip. Despite all protests, his diplomatic immunity was not respected. On July 10, 1949, Rev. Ludvík Zmrzlík, a Czech priest of the Silesian Congregation, who was the interpreter of the internunciature in Prague, was arrested. Protests of the chargé d'affaires were not respected.[81] On June 25, the Minister of Justice, Čepička, had already attacked Monsignor Verolino directly in his radio speech,[82] accusing him of a plot with Cardinal Mindszenty to help the reactionary clergy to carry out activities aimed at disrupting the peace of the people and the peaceful development of socialism. Since an agreement between Church and state in Czechoslovakia was likely to frustrate his actions (so said Čepička), the Archbishop of Prague, by order of the Vatican, was acting disloyally when he intervened to prevent the agreement.[83] On July 19, Monsignor Gennaro Verolino returned to Rome.

As a consequence of all this, diplomatic relations with the Vatican practically ceased, and Monsignor Verolino's successor, Monsignor Paulo Bartoli, could not even get an entry visa into Czechoslovakia.[84] The Communists had achieved their aim: the elimination of any influence of the Vatican upon Czechoslovak Catholics, and the reinforcement of the state-sponsored "Catholic Church." Prime Minister Zápotocký in his speech in Trutnov expressed his view on this situation:

> We shall not allow any reactionary power, even the Vatican, to interfere in our internal affairs. If the Pope today excommunicates all Communists, and with them all the cooperating and believing Christians, then we are aware of the fact that he is excommunicating nearly the entire Czechoslovak working people. Our people have found a real friend and ally in the East. We never posed for ourselves the question, Rome or Moscow. But if that question is posed for us

> by the other side, then we shall leave nobody in doubt that the answer of our nation will be that there is no alternative for us but Moscow, Stalin, and Socialism.[85]

By such a stand, the government's determined attitude against the Catholic Church was made evident. The decree of excommunication by the Pope clarified the situation from the ecclesiastical and canonical point of view. There remained now only the one or the other alternative: the Catholic Church or communism. Czechoslovak Communists took the stand that the carrying out of papal decrees was to be judged as an act hostile to the state.[86]

Coalition between the Vatican and Czechoslovak communism was from then on a sheer impossibility. On the basis of a strange verdict of the court, every bishop and priest, just for exercising his office and profession, could be condemned.

The time of the enslavement of the Catholic Church had arrived. The Catholic Church was from then on viewed as inimical to the state, and since her representatives—the bishops and priests—were systematically being put under severe censorship, the Church was continually hindered in her activities. Czechoslovak Communists did not neglect any opportunity to impede Catholic priests in the exercise of their duties of an official nature. Typical of this is the following letter sent by Dr. Houska, the state commissioner of the archiepiscopal consistory office in Prague, pertaining to all priests. It bore the date of July 26, No. 10721.

> According to the instruction of the Ministry of Education, Sciences, and Arts of June 20, 1949, No. P-13096/49-P 16, concerning the invalidity of ecclesiastical penalties, proclaimed for political reasons, and according to the statement of June 21, 1949, by the government, any punishments proclaimed by ecclesiastical authorities are not recognized as effective by the government of the country, if those punishments are aimed against clergymen who did not commit any crime against the dogmas or ethics of the Church and who did not refuse obedience to their ecclesiastical superiors in matters of faith and morals.
>
> Penalties proclaimed by ecclesiastical authorities contrary to this instruction and this statement are against the sovereign interests of the Czechoslovak government. They contradict the legal order, especially the constitution of the Czecho-

slovak Republic, and such a procedure is punishable under valid regulations. Clergymen, struck by such ecclesiastical penalties, do not lose their capacity for appointment and continuance in their offices, and nothing will be changed in their official position. The state administration will grant them all assistance and will protect anyone who insists on the principles of the people's democratic regime. According to these regulations:

1) Every clergyman is obliged to report to the archiepiscopal consistory office in Prague if he himself or another clergyman, subordinate to him, or a parishioner in his care is struck by ecclesiastical penalties. He is obliged to send to the Minister of Education a copy of his report.

2) Clergymen are further obliged to send the decree, by which the penalty was proclaimed, directly to the archiepiscopal curial office in Prague.

3) Clergymen must report without delay any events which refer to persecution by ecclesiastical authorities of clergymen, laity, professors of religious studies, or parishioners for their affirmative stand toward the people's democratic institution of the state. Those who were included in the penalty are directed to remain in their positions and to exert fully all functions they were hitherto exercising.
Clergymen are directed to proceed in full accordance with this instruction and for this they are held responsible.[87]

A similar circular letter, which was shorter and contained a milder threat, was sent also by Jan Dolek, commissioner of the episcopal consistory office in Hradec Králové, on July 6, 1949, to all priests of that diocese. Jan Dolek encroached on the internal affairs of ecclesiastical administration, as is proved by the following documents. On July 18, 1949, he again sent a circular letter, No. 6858/49, to all Catholic rectories concerning an agreement before contracting marriage, which read as follows:

We notify you that the statements which are required to be made by Catholic and non-Catholic parties, by which prospective husbands and wives are obliged to fulfill their ecclesiastical duties and to influence the non-Catholic party to accept the Catholic faith, and held liable for the baptism of their children, are not in accord with the law No. 96/25 Coll. of April 23, 1925, and therefore equal to force, and contradict the constitution of May 9, 1948, which guarantees to all citizens, without distinction, freedom of religion and confession.[88]

By another letter of July 18, 1949, No. 6857/49, all clergymen of this diocese were instructed:

You are hereby notified that the *Gazette of the Catholic Clergy* is the official newspaper of all Catholic clergymen and that every rectory is obliged to subscribe to it. Notices which are published in its official sections have an official character and are binding on clergymen. Any instructions published in any other way are not legally valid. Therefore all rectories must, after reading the *Gazette*, file it in their archives, and, on the occasion of a supervisory visit, they must present it for inspection.[89]

These documents prove the extent of pressure against Catholic clergymen and show how the state commissioners enforced their influence in ecclesiastical affairs. That this course of action was directed by the government is apparent from the following document, No. 25-26.7.1949, Litoměřice, July 26, 1949, signed by Dr. Janota, Commissioner of the Ministry of Education, Sciences, and Arts.[90]

In re: INSTRUCTION OF THE MINISTRY OF EDUCATION, SCIENCES, AND ARTS OF JULY 20, 1949
No. 13096/49

Obligations to Report: TO ALL VICARS AND RECTORIES:

The episcopal consistory office of the diocese of Litoměřice gives notice that, according to instruction of the Ministry of Education, Sciences, and Arts, of July 20, 1949, No. 13096/49, every activity tending to circulate the decision concerning excommunication of clergymen or the faithful as far as these excommunications or other ecclesiastical penalties are proclaimed not for religious, but for political reasons, is liable to punishment. To the same extent any other activity against such convicted clergymen or faithful is also punishable.

Against those ecclesiastical functionaries who do not respect this instruction, legal measures will be taken on the ground of the cited instruction by the Ministry of Education, Sciences, and Arts, and also on the basis of other valid laws.

We ask all administrators, in case they should receive any declaration concerning excommunication, to keep this declaration and to send it to the episcopal consistory office and to report the matter to the consistory office by telephone.

Every clergyman active as a priest or leader of religion, as also every lay teacher of religion who was placed under excommunication or any other ecclesiastical penalty proclaimed for political and not for religious reasons, is directed, according to the decision of the Ministry of Education, Sciences, and Arts, not to respect such a penalty and to remain in his position.

We ask you to notify all clergymen and lay teachers of religion appointed in your area of this instruction and to let them sign this circular letter as a proof that they have read it. Thus signed, this circular letter is to be returned to the Ministry of Education, Sciences, and Arts' episcopal curial office within eight days.[91]

What the replies were to these circular letters and similar letters by commissioners of episcopal consistory offices is evident from the following:

No. 25-26, VII 1949 Zh
In re: INSTRUCTION OF THE MINISTRY OF EDUCATION, SCIENCES, AND ARTS OF JULY 20, 1949

To: THE EPISCOPAL CONSISTORY OFFICE IN LITOMERICE

Referring to your letter of July 26, 1949, we wish to advise you of our position in the name of all rectories in our vicariate. Neither our episcopal vicariate nor the rectories in our vicariate were officially notified that the administration of the episcopal consistory office in Litoměřice had been taken over by some commissioner of the government and that his name is Janota. We really do not know the reason why this measure has been issued. Hitherto, such a measure, during the history of ecclesiastico-political relations in our country, has never been in use. Therefore official notice of any letters of this commissioner cannot be heeded, all the more so since the signature is illegible and covered by the seal of the episcopal consistory office. From practice we have learned that important official acts must have legible signatures of the responsible and assigned person, and that it must be officially proved that the person signing the document is authorized to send such letters.

The letter of July 26, 1949, cannot be accepted, not only for the reasons already mentioned, but also because the commissioner is attempting to encroach on all internal affairs of the Church, and this in affairs of absolutely religious character, which means he is acting outside his jurisdiction.

Furthermore, this letter is unacceptable because the ordinaries are the executors of papal decrees concerning excommunication of clergymen or of the faithful and they alone are competent to make decisions in such matters.[92]

In the state's further attempts to gain control in this matter, a meeting of episcopal vicars by the regional National Committee was called at Hradec Králové on July 30, 1949. This regional National Committee convoked on July 30, 1949, all episcopal vicars from the Hradec Králové diocese, although the sphere of jurisdiction of this diocese is not the same as that of this regional National Committee.

Some vicars did not appear; those who came met in the bishop's residence at ten o'clock and, despite the disapproval of Commissioner Jan Dolek, called on Bishop Pícha. At eleven o'clock the conference was opened. Cooperation with communism was asked. Finally, threats of punishment for high treason were made should the decree concerning excommunication be exercised against clergymen who were participating willfully and effectively in the schismatic Catholic Action.

But as a protest in the name of all vicars who appeared, one of them read the following statement:

According to the letter of the regional National Committee in Hradec Králové on July 27, 1949, episcopal vicars of the Hradec Králové diocese were called under penal sanctions to the regional National Committee in Hradec Králové to attend these unusual official proceedings.

1) We protest, first of all, against the unlawful convocation, since it is contradictory to Act 24, No. 8, of January 13, 1928, Coll. According to this act, the summons to the party should contain the subject matter and a mention of the capacity in which the summoned party should appear. This provision was not respected, probably purposely, because the invitation was addressed not to episcopal vicars but to religious administrators, rectors, deans, archdeans, etc. We feel, therefore, that we are misrepresented, since for the first time we here experience that we are to be known as vicars.

2) We protest against this convocation because the Hradec Králové diocese comprises, besides the region of Hradec, also parts of the regions of Pardubice, Jihlava, Liberec, and Prague; the regional National Committee encroached thereby on the jurisdiction of the Hradec ordinariate, for nobody is authorized to convoke episcopal vicars except the bishop of the diocese exclusively.

3) We protest against the threats for not appearing, that we would be punished by a fine of 2000 crowns and five days in jail, and that we would be interned by the police. These threats are contrary to § 35 of the constitution of May 9, 1948; these threats are unreasonable because the session is unlawful and therefore invalid.

4) We protest against appointments by the commissioner in the consistory episcopal office, for this commissioner forbids admittance to the diocesan bishop and the free official proceedings, which is contrary to §§ 2, 3, 5, 6, 9 of the constitution of May 9, 1948.

5) We episcopal vicars declare that with our subordinate clergymen, we will remain unanimously and firmly loyal to the bishop of our diocese, of whom, in our vicariates, we are the competent representatives.[93]

The relation of the government to the Catholic Church became even more hostile as appears from the following document—a letter by which the spiritual retreat of priests in Turnov was disbanded.

From: District National Committee in Turnov
No. 2119/1949, July 21, 1949

To: Vicariate of the Roman Catholic Church in Turnov

This office learned that, without permission of the district National Committee in Turnov, a meeting of clergymen of your church from the whole region is being arranged to take place in the building of the Roman Catholic church on Kozak Street.

According to the instructions by the Ministry of Interior, of May 9, 1949, No. 260/5-5/4 1949 12a, the law of Nov. 15, 1867, No. 134, the law No. 135 of the same date, and the constitution of May 9, 1948, §§ 173 and 24, the afore-mentioned meeting is not to be held as arranged and it should be immediately dismissed. The holding of and the reason for this meeting were not announced to this National Committee, either by writing or by oral announcement in the prescribed terms; this made it impossible to send to this meeting an official permit of the National Committee, as is prescribed by law and by official instructions.

The instructions of the Ministry of Interior, as well as the cited law, refer to the activities of all associations and public gatherings and therefore to your meeting. In case this meeting is not being arranged by your vicariate, this memorandum is to be handed over to the responsible association. The signed National Committee asks for a report regarding the form of the meeting and any questions discussed therein.

The signed National Committee expects clergymen also to respect the afore-mentioned instructions as well as the law, and as good citizens of the state, not to act contrary to the law.

J. Novák,
Security Officer of National Committee.[94]

It is interesting that even the Commander of the National Security Corps was afraid lest the people should hear of their actions against the priests. To illustrate this point, we are reproducing here a circular letter of the regional command of the National Security Corps:

No. 3371/1949-III-7

In re: Unpermitted Publishing of Verdicts

To: All administrators of Roman Catholic Rectories in the Gottwaldov (Zlín) District

On a previous occasion some priests of the Roman Catholic Church, in accordance with legal regulations, were punished for administrative misdemeanors which they committed in their official capacities.

> It was learned that some of these priests made these verdicts known to their faithful through sermons and in their ecclesiastical functions, in order to evoke in the faithful an unreasonable compassion, or to evoke a hostile trend against these measures of the administrative offices.
>
> This publishing of verdicts by private persons is not permitted. Their contents can be made known to the public only by the office which proclaimed them, as is mentioned in the proclaimed verdict itself. I am notifying you hereby that any announcement to the public of the content of verdicts which was not ordered by this office is inadmissible and will be prosecuted severely as an act threatening public order and security.
>
> I am asking you to notify all subordinate ecclesiastical servants concerning this circular letter.
>
> V. Červinka
> *Security Officer.*[95]

In spite of these events, priests remained loyal to their bishops, and whenever the bishop appeared, sympathies were expressed. Thus in Prague, on July 18, a great meeting of priests, who had promised firm fidelity to the bishops, was held.[96] On August 12, 1949, the clergy of the diocese of České Budějovice, in southern Bohemia, met in the Cathedral of Saint Nicholas, to pay homage to their Bishop, Monsignor Hlouch, and to renew publicly in the face of the governmental campaign seeking to separate the clergy from the hierarchy, their vow of loyalty and absolute obedience to him.[97] This also happened in other places, such as Litoměřice and Olomouc, and in Slovakia. On these occasions, in Catholic churches and before the faithful, the following declaration was solemnly proclaimed:[98]

> It was announced recently to the public that a great part of the Catholic clergy had decided to give its help to the activities of the so-called Catholic Action. As that allegation does not correspond to the truth and since for the most part our signatures were obtained by trickery, pressure and fraud, we hoped that competent authorities, whose task it is to protect the citizens' honor, would contradict that false rumor. Since this hope has been disappointed, we consider it expedient to make the following declaration:
>
> We Catholic priests declare that we will remain loyal and faithful to our beloved Archbishop, Dr. Beran, and to

all Czechoslovak bishops, that we are ready to suffer with them if need be, and that we condemn the so-called Catholic Action as non-Catholic and schismatic. We are, like our bishops, favorable to a fair agreement between the state and the Church, but we reject the mistaken way in which the so-called Catholic Action would like to realize that agreement. We are certain of the support of the faithful population, if it could express itself freely. We make this declaration in virtue of the article of the constitution that guarantees liberty of religion and of opinion. We make it spontaneously and free from pressure, so that our names cannot be misused in falsely proclaiming that thousands of priests and faithful give their allegiance to Catholic Action and that our good bishops persecute us by threatening us with ecclesiastical penalties. We make this declaration because we know our responsibility toward the whole nation, and in order to obey the dictates of conscience that command us to put the interests of God above those of the state.[99]

The occupation of episcopal consistory offices by state commissioners like the Ministry of Education was unlawful. Therefore Archbishop Beran wrote to the Czechoslovak State Prosecutor the following letter, dated August 5:

Since neither the Ministry of Education, Science, and Arts nor the Ministry of Interior nor the Czechoslovak government has answered my letters, I am forced to turn to the State Prosecutor.

And perhaps even the State Prosecutor will not consider it worthwhile to answer. However, I turn to the State Prosecutor with the question:

Is the Roman Catholic Church in Czechoslovakia still recognized by the state? If so, by what law was the Roman Catholic Church deprived of its legal independence in internal matters?

By note No. P-12, 388 49-P6 of June 13, 1949, from the Praesidium of the Ministry of Education, Science, and Arts, in accordance with paragraph 60 of May 7, 1874, No. 50, Dr. Miroslav Houska, plenipotentiary of the Ministry of Education, Science, and Arts, was named as the supervisor in the chancery of the Archbishop of Prague.

The note mentioned was sent to the chancery of the Archbishop in Prague. In protest against this measure, the

Archbishop announced that on June 15 his chancery would not be opened. The representative of the Ministry of Education was informed that he would have to await the reply to the protest. But neither this protest nor the Archbishop's letter was acknowledged, and on the afternoon of June 15, 1949, Doctor Houska, assisted by the security police, occupied the chancery offices.

Doctor Houska who, according to the note already mentioned, was to act as supervisor, immediately took upon himself the task of administering the chancery of the Archbishop and completely carries out everything that is connected with the office of the chancery, even though the mentioned law speaks only of supervisory work.

I take the liberty of asking whether Doctor Houska, according to paragraph 60 of law No. 50, dated May 7, 1874, has authority—

1. to carry on completely the work of the chancery, for which work he did not receive the permission of the Archbishop?

2. to use the official seal and official stationery, when the chancery of the Archbishop functions in the name of the Archbishop and the plenipotentiary does not have his approval?

3. to confiscate the treasury of the chancery and in his name, without knowledge of the owner of the postal (checking) account, announce that he is authorized to dispose of the account as he sees fit?

4. to confiscate even the central treasury of the Diocese of Prague, which legally is not a part of the chancery? Is he authorized to terminate and hinder the paying of salaries to employees of the palace of the Archbishop from this central treasury?

5. to restrict the regular functions of the diocese, which is shown by the fact that the Archbishop does not receive even official correspondence?

Here are examples of what happened as a result of this unlawful seizure of ecclesiastical authority:

1. The Archbishop's palace in Dol. Břežany was placed under the national administration. The Archbishop was never informed of this measure.

2. When the remaining 50 hectares (123.5 acres) of the Archbishop's property in Červená Řečice (District Pelhrimov, Province Jihlava) was nationalized, the Archbishop was never officially informed and his representatives were

not permitted to intervene; the diocese was represented by a delegate sent by the government's plenipotentiary in the chancery of the Archbishop.

3. Liquidation of the property of the diocese is being conducted without the knowledge of the Archbishop, who is still owner of the property.

Are all these actions legal? Do they stem from the mentioned decree of 1874?

Since June 19 I have been interned in the palace of the Archbishop. I am not permitted visitors, and it is said that the Archbishop forbade such visits.

All correspondence of the Archbishop, both personal and official, and correspondence of the employees in the palace is being withheld. Only postal cards and publications are delivered.

I am deprived of all personal freedom and all rights as the Archbishop, and all this without any investigation and without any decision of any court or any other official authority. The plenipotentiary of the chancery acts in the name of the Archbishop and the diocese.

On June 19 of this year services in the Church of St. Vitus were interrupted by whistling and shouting. And on Saturday, June 18, I was warned that, in Prague, factory employees were told to come to Mass at the Church and create a disturbance.

The faithful were detained and kept from attending the services. All around the church and in the streets of Hradčany, police and security measures were undertaken.

Why was all this done? Of those creating the disturbance no one was apprehended, even though there were many members of the security police present.

Is the law dealing with the prohibition of interruption of religious services still in effect? Why was not the Archbishop informed prior to this? Why were all the police measures taken?

I have requested the Ministry of Interior to investigate the incident. To date I have received no reply.

The above are some of the questions I should like the State Prosecutor to answer.[100]

On Sunday, August 14, the Apostolic Administrator of Trnava, Monsignor Ambrož Lazík, and the Vicar-Capitular of Rožnava, Monsignor Robert Pobožný, appointed by Pope

Pius XII to be titular Bishops of Appia and of Neila, were consecrated at Trnava, Slovakia. The Archbishop of Olomouc, Monsignor Matocha, was the consecrating prelate, and the Bishop of Spiš, Monsignor Jan Vojtaššák, and the Greek Catholic Bishop of Prešov, Monsignor Paul Gojdič, were the co-consecrators. It should be remarked that under the *modus vivendi* of 1928, which still governed relations between Czechoslovakia and the Holy See, the approval of the government had to be sought for diocesan bishops only, and that in these particular cases it was not required, since the new bishops were appointed to titular sees. Both, however, were among the signatories of the last pastoral letter, circulated in behalf of the hierarchy on June 15, and described by the government as a "subversive and antistate document."[101] It is interesting to note that both men came from working-class families.

All the members of the hierarchy were present for the consecration except the Archbishop of Prague, Josef Beran, and the eighty-two-year-old Bishop of Hradec Králové, Mořic Pícha.

Outside the cathedral a great crowd heard mass at an open-air altar and sang hymns, even though the Communists tried to drown them out by relaying popular music through loudspeakers. There was much enthusiasm when the procession of clergy passed through the crowd which afterward tore up or trampled into the mud the leaflets handed out by the Communists. Similarly, the reaction was great when the newly nominated Bishop Monsignor Stefan Barnas,[102] hitherto rector of the seminary in Spišská Nová Ves, was consecrated auxiliary bishop of Spiš, under Bishop Jan Vojtaššák in Spiš.

This was, in fact, the most important assembly of the hierarchy since March, when they adjourned a meeting in Dolní Smokovec because secret microphones had been found hidden in the room and they had felt that they could not, under the circumstances, continue the deliberations on the relations between Church and state.

The Catholic bishops in the Czechoslovak Republic who met on the occasion of the episcopal consecration on August 14, 1949, in Trnava, sensing the disquiet felt by the faithful and led by the endeavor to secure the fundamental requisites of religious life for their people, submitted to the government of the Czechoslovak Republic the following memorandum:[103]

> We were publicly accused that the bad state of the relationship between state and Church has been caused by the episcopate, and we were reproached that we even deny to take an oath of allegiance to the state. After the frustration of our last episcopal conference in Dolní Smokovec, which has not been investigated even until now, we sent to the president Klement Gottwald a memorandum as of April 29, 1949, and we declared our willingness to repeat the oath of allegiance to the Republic according to the text advocated in the *modus vivendi;* our memorandum remained unanswered, but nonetheless we were accused of refusing to take an oath of allegiance to the state, and even those of the bishops who were appointed after the year 1945 were attacked.
>
> We declared that we were willing at any time to repeat the oath of allegiance to the Republic, and this in the words agreed upon in the *modus vivendi.*
>
> That we desire to achieve agreement between state and Church, we proved by our statements proclaimed on the occasion of the serious encroachments on religious freedom and self-rule. Minister Dr. Alexej Čepička, in his speech of July 15, 1949, admitted a whole line of these measures of anti-ecclesiastical character, as, for instance, the appointment of commissioners to consistory offices, discontinuation of the *Acta Curiae*, encroachments in seminaries, ecclesiastical schools, Catholic charity, and limitation of the freedom of assembly. Besides, the so-called Catholic Action was established under the pretext that chaos and disturbances among Czech and Slovak believers would arise; and this was proclaimed with all our authority not only by us, but also even by the supreme head of the Church as schismatic. It is our idea that the right moment has come to bring this inimical stand against the Church under supervision. For this reason we approach the government with these remarks and demands, being convinced that our good will and proffered right hand seeking to achieve an agreement will not remain without favorable reply:
>
> 1) We sorrowfully discover that our episcopal conferences could not be attended by the chairman of the episcopate, Archbishop of Prague and Czech Primate Monsignor Josef Beran. We ask therefore that all measures limiting his personal and domestic freedom be canceled.

2) We protest against assignment of commissioners by the Ministry of Education in the episcopal consistory offices (resp. in Slovakia in episcopal offices). The assignment of these commissioners makes impossible the free practice of religious confessions because to every decision made by the occupied office, without any regard to its character, is attached the signature of the assigned commissioner. The state adopted for itself the jurisdiction to make decisions even in the matter of sacraments, of religious rites and the practice of worship and in matters of ethics and conscience.

This measure was introduced as a penal sanction according to §60 of the law concerning external affairs of the Roman Catholic Church in historical provinces although there are no objections against the activities of consistory offices. In Slovakia this measure has not even a presumably lawful basis.

The short period of the activities of these commissioners makes the essence of their unlawful jurisdiction apparent; in some dioceses they adopt the right to decide exclusively to the full extent of jurisdiction of the respective ecclesiastical office, and they use for their orders, even without permission, the legal seal, marks of ecclesiastical jurisdiction, and forms with these marks, and they issue their own decisions without any knowledge of the bishops. These commissioners also take to themselves the right to make decisions concerning ecclesiastical properties, and in some cases our freedom to dispose of ecclesiastical properties was limited.

3) We ask abstention from any encroachments on the education of candidates for the priesthood and novices. We protest against any hindrance and limitation of contact of bishops with the faithful and against resisting our right of defense against unjust accusation and persecution. We protest against the persecution of the Catholic priests for reading pastoral letters and for the faithful execution of their priestly duties. We protest against further issues of the so-called *Gazette of the Catholic Clergy*, and we ask full freedom of the press for all forbidden Catholic magazines, periodicals and press.

We ask the full renewal of constitutionally guaranteed freedom of assembly, and we protest against all hindrances to arrangements for retreats for clergymen and other meetings for religious education, which is the substance of such meetings; they are usual in our country (exercises, religious courses, etc.).

We protest against the closing of all church schools, the seizing of ecclesiastical buildings, monasteries and convents, and against all measures which are a menace to religious freedom. We ask the cancellation of all measures concerning limitations of Catholic Associations and Institutions; especially do we ask that the national administration of Catholic Charities and of Church associations in Pelhřimov, Unitas in Olomouc be canceled.

4) We protest against so-called Catholic Action, which unlawfully adopted the name of Catholic Action, because this name has become a symbol for a certain sort of cooperation by laymen headed by the bishops, and therefore it is inadmissible to call this movement by the same name, when the schismatic so-called Catholic Action is aimed against episcopal authority.

We ask that this "action" be not allowed to organize, supported and backed by state organs, and that it abstain from any threats by terror to enforce consent to this action on the faithful.

5) As to the drafted law concerning reimbursement of personal and material needs for the Church, in full accord with our priests we declare that the preparation of this draft was made from only one point of view, so that we cannot accept the suggested solution, especially as a substitution for the seized ecclesiastical properties. We insist on the right to reimbursement for these properties and we declare hereby that there is need of an agreement about appointments in ecclesiastical offices when these have a relation to the congrual salary for us; also for our priests, all regulations of Canon Law have a binding character. From this point of view, our consent cannot be replaced by inviting to the session the representatives of the schismatic so-called Catholic Action, and we warn not to make such suggestions a valid law, because such regulations would not be acceptable to our priests in conscience. We reserve the submission of further specified remarks if some proceedings with us should be opened.

6) We protest determinedly against brazen libels and slanders of the Czechoslovakian episcopate and of the Holy Father, as are especially contained in the speech of Minister Čepička of July 15, 1949.

We protest against accusations that we are in the services of capitalism and that we oppose any social improvements. It was the great social Pope, Leo XIII, who by his encyclical *Rerum Novarum* condemned capitalism and its excesses, which Pope Pius XI in his encyclical *Quadragesimo Anno* also condemned. The Church supports and will support any improvement of standards of living for all people. The dignity and freedom of man has been and will always be protected by the Catholic Church.

Capitalism must not be identified with private ownership, which the Church has always defended as a natural basis of human society. Private ownership is guaranteed also by our constitution of May 9, 1948.

We protest against any attacks insulting the Holy Father (Vatican) who is described as an enemy of our people and state, although the evidence of the late president, Mr. E. Beneš, proves all these charges to be totally untrue.

7) We protest against all cases in which our priests are humiliated, accused, and condemned for high treason for the exercise of their ecclesiastical and religious duties, acting thus in accordance with the regulations of the Catholic Church, which is a recognized church in our country, and the believers in which form the majority of all the population. The faithful of our Church are all on a voluntary basis, and it is the right of the Church to excommunicate every believer who does not respect and who violates ecclesiastical discipline. The Church abstains from forcing her doctrines on anybody, but she cannot permit that her priests be forced to sacrilegious administration of the sacraments to the excommunicated members of the Church. It is unheard of in the cultural world that somebody could be accused of high treason because he is an obedient son of the Catholic Church.

All these complaints and pledges, only roughly outlined, are supplemented by our love for our people and for our native country, in spite of all the bad experiences of these latter times, nor do we lose our hope of achieving agreement about all ecclesiastical-political problems. We repeat our willingness to negotiate about the right settlement of mutual relations between Church and state, if endeavors will be made to respect the freedom of the Church and if there will be previously fulfilled the already mentioned conditions and prerequisites, to wit:

1) The Christian ideal will be respected and recognized in public life and education, in words and in deed.

2) The government will recognize the jurisdiction of the Pope of Rome as the Supreme Head of the Church, as also the jurisdiction of bishops, loyal to the Pope, and this according to valid ecclesiastical regulations.

3) All measures limiting and menacing religious freedom of Catholic in Czechoslovakia, as has been specified by this memorandum and by our previous declarations, will be repealed.

TRNAVA, August 14, 1949

JOSEF KAREL, *Archbishop in Olomouc and Metropolitan of Moravia (chairman of the episcopal conference)*
JAN, *Bishop in Spiš*
PAVEL, *Bishop in Prešov*
JOSEF, *Tit. Bishop of Taregoram, Apostolic Administrator in Košice*
ANDREJ, *Bishop in Banská Bystrica*
KAREL, *Bishop in Brno*
JOSEF, *Bishop in Budějovice*
STEPÁN, *Bishop in Litoměřice*
EDUARD, *Tit. Bishop of Beliae, Apost. Adminis. in Nitra.*
AMBROŽ, *Tit. Bishop of Appia, Apost. Adminis. in Trnava*
ROBERT, *Tit. Bishop of Neilla, Capitular Vicar in Rožnava*
FRANK ONDEREK, *Apost. Administrator of the Czechoslovak part of the Archdiocese of Breslau*[104]

By this memorandum the Catholic bishops expressed their view of the situation at that time, declaring again their willingness to negotiate. This document is of historic significance in a time of tragic and menacing omens for the future.

Because of the strong tension at that time, state officials were not willing to modify their excesses; nevertheless they felt some sort of a conciliatory gesture had to be made. In the session of the Executive Committee of the Central Action Committee of the National Front in Prague on July 15, 1949, a draft of a bill concerning payment for personal and material needs of the churches and denominations recognized by the state was unanimously accepted.[105]

The draft of the bill contained nineteen paragraphs. In the first eight paragraphs all the advantages were described. The rest of the bill was devoted to an enumeration of all the demands and conditions under which the state was willing to improve the position of the clergy; for instance, clergymen were promised substantial raises in their salaries. In reality, however, these ten paragraphs meant ten fetters by which the freedom of the Church and independence of priestly jurisdiction were further limited. For instance, § 10 required the previous approval by the state administration for any assignment or promotion; § 12 required the making of a strict inventory of properties of all kinds of an ecclesiastical nature; §13 claimed that the supervision of all ecclesiastical properties was the province of state administration, without whose approval nothing could be changed, sold or mortgaged.

Maintenance of all institutions and the education of candidates for the priesthood also belong to the state. In virtue of § 15 all private and public rights of patronage over churches and prebends were transferred to the state and all donations in favor of clergymen, for instance in the form of exemption from taxes, were proclaimed canceled. The threat that all acts or omissions contradicting this law would be punished by a fine of 100,000 crowns was listed under §17. It was thus apparent that the state had adopted for itself rights which it never had and which could not be resigned by the Church. By these provisions the Church would become fully state-controlled.[106]

It was for this reason that voices of dissatisfaction were raised against this draft of the bill. The bishops and ordinaries, in their memorandum to the government of August 14, 1949, expressed their protest, stipulated their stand and issued their instructions for lay teachers of religion.

During August and September hundreds of letters signed by priests from all the vicariates in the Republic arrived at the Central Action Committee of the National Front in Prague. In these the clergy admitted that the prepared bill would indeed improve their salaries, but this at the price of their freedom and of bringing the spiritual mission of the Church under subjugation to and dependence upon political interests and powers. Moreover, since the raise of salary for priests could be blamed for the reduction in wages of other working people, the priests voluntarily resigned all privileges which were offered to them by the law as then drafted, and declared themselves satisfied if in agreement with the ordinaries the basis for serious laws would be accepted and if all national ecclesiastical monuments and sites of the churches would be secured.[107]

As a general protest to the bill, the following memorandum, signed by a great majority of the priests, was presented to the government prior to the passage of the proposed bill on October 14, 1949:

MEMORANDUM OF THE CLERGY CONCERNING THE PROPOSED LAW ON FINANCIAL GUARANTEES

Having attained the consent of all the bishops, the clergy declares that it does not intend to accept the new law relative to the reimbursement of expenses pertaining to the personal material needs of the Church and the religious organizations, and that the representatives of the parochial clergy have unanimously determined to publish the following declaration and to submit it to the government of the Czechoslovak Republic.

1) The clergy gratefully recognizes that the government of the Czechoslovak Republic realizes, as is actually the case, that the social position of the clergy does not correspond with the educational work and other duties which it performs for the common welfare and the supreme interests of the nation.

2) However, the projected law will ameliorate the social position of the clergy at the price of an independence which was guaranteed by church lands; it places the spiritual duties of the clergy under the total dependence of political agents and interests, as can be seen from Article 10 of the proposed law. Because of this, the clergy publicly declares that it will accept ecclesiastical assignments only from the hands of an authorized Church dignitary.

3) The proposed bill to ameliorate the position of the clergy and to increase the material contribution to Church activity gives the unfavorable impression that the Church is satisfied to accept a compensation for properties and lands which it has lost against its will as a result of the unilateral intervention of the state and without previous agreement with the Holy See.

4) An increased salary is proposed for the clergy at a time when, for various economic reasons, it is possible to reduce the salaries of workingmen and the pensions of the retired workers. Under such conditions, the clergy willingly renounces the benefits of the increase proposed in the new law, and respectfully requests that the social condition of the workers and pensioners be maintained at its actual level, or better yet, be improved.

5) The seventeenth article threatens even light infractions with very grave sanctions which, in extreme cases, would be antisocial and unjust; at all events, it is imperative that we reject it.

6) The clergy will be satisfied if, after an agreement with the higher dignitaries of the Church, the fundamental law on the *congrua* is maintained, with the possibility of adjustments in special cases, if the repair of religious monuments of historical value is financed and if the needs of the Church are fulfilled.

7) It is requested in particular that the religious liberty of the people and the liberty of the clergy to fulfill its sacerdotal duties and to pursue its religious objectives which are aimed at both the eternal and the temporal welfare of the people, be completely respected and maintained.[108]

This was the reply of the bishops and priests to the draft of the proposed law; they declared they would refuse any raise in salary rather than injure the freedom of the Church. This naturally did not please the body politic, and the government tried by terror to enforce a contrary action. Within a few days more than ten vicars and deans in Bohemia and Moravia were arrested. Commissioners attended meetings of priests, trying to persuade them to take an affirmative stand for the bill. In other cases threats were used. Finally, the Apostolic Administrator in Těšín, Monsignor Francis Onderek, after a police hearing lasting some hours, sent a circular letter to his priests counseling them to refrain from sending any more letters protesting against the bill.[109]

To gain further control of the Church the Czechoslovak government on October 14, 1949, decreed the establishment of a special state office for Church affairs.[110] On October 14, the following resolution on new laws was accepted by the National Assembly.[111] It bore the title: "New Church Laws."[112]

A

The Law of October 14, 1949, Establishing the Government Bureau for Church Affairs

(Law No. 217 of 1949, Coll. promulgated on October 17, 1949)[113]

The National Assembly of the Czechoslovak Republic has passed the following law:

Section 1

A governmental Bureau for Church Affairs shall be established as a central governmental body; a minister assigned by the President of the Republic shall direct it.

Section 2

The purpose of the Bureau for Church Affairs shall be to see to it that church life and religious life develop in accordance with the constitution and the principles of the people's democratic order and thus secure for everyone the right of freedom of religion based upon the principle of religious tolerance and equal rights for all denominations as guaranteed by the constitution.

Section 3

The jurisdiction in all matters of church and religion which until now were exercised by other central departments shall pass to the governmental Bureau for Church Affairs.

Section 4

The Minister directing the governmental Bureau for Church Affairs shall exercise his jurisdiction in Slovakia, usually through the Slovak Bureau for Church Affairs, which shall be directed by a commissioner assigned by the Cabinet.

Section 5

Detailed provisions on the jurisdiction and organization of the governmetal Bureau for Church Affairs and the Slovak Bureau for Church Affairs, and on the procedure, shall be established by a decree of the Cabinet.

B

CABINET DECREE OF OCTOBER 14, 1949, ON THE JURISDICTION AND ORGANIZATION OF THE GOVERNMENT BUREAU FOR CHURCH AFFAIRS

(*Cabinet Decree No. 228, Coll. promulgated on November 4, 1949*)

Section 1

The Bureau for Church Affairs shall exercise, as the central governmental body for ecclesiastical matters, all jurisdiction in the matter of church and religion, in particular also the jurisdiction exercised, until now, by other central government departments.

Section 2

The jurisdiction of the Bureau for Church Affairs shall cover the following matters:

a) Issuance of general rules, direction and supervision in all matters of church and religion.

b) Administrative matters of the churches, religious associations, and their branches, communities, institutions, foundations, temples, prebends, funds, monastic orders and monasteries, as well as their economic and financial affairs (legal transactions relating to property, matters involving building constructions, administration of church funds and foundations, and the like).

c) Protection of religious monuments.

d) Matters involving the budget, credit, and planning, in the ecclesiastical and religious fields, without prejudice to the jurisdiction of the Central Planning Office.

e) Personnel and payment matters relating to clergymen, teachers and employees of the theological schools of the universities, theological schools and seminaries, as well as teachers of religion.

f) Regulation of the teaching of religion, approval of the syllabus, textbooks, equipment and services, and supreme supervision, in agreement with the Ministry of Education, Science, and Arts, over the teaching of religion and over denominational educational institutions of any kind.

g) Expert revision of the ecclesiastical press and publications.

h) Issuance of an official gazette for clergymen, and issuance of information bulletins and publications.

i) Matters involving religious associations and organizations without prejudice to the jurisdiction of the Ministry of the Interior.

j) Matters involving charitable activities of churches and religious associations.

k) Taking care of the development of religious life in harmony with the constitution.

l) Keeping informed on the development of the international relations of churches and religions.

Section 3

1) The work of the Bureau for Church Affairs shall be performed in a section for religious affairs, a personal section, an information section, and an economic and administrative section.

2) For the performance of accounting, clerical, typewriting, messenger and similar work the Bureau for Church Affairs shall be provided with its own accounting office, disbursing office, and clerical and economic service.

Section 4

The Slovak Bureau for Church Affairs shall be organized in accordance with the provisions of Section 3.

Section 5

In provinces and counties the jurisdiction in religious and church matters shall be exercised by competent provincial and county people's committees which, in this respect, will act as subordinates of the Bureau for Church Affairs.

Section 6

The present decree shall take effect on the day of its promulgation; it shall be carried out by the Minister charged with the direction of the Bureau for Church Affairs in agreement with the interested members of the Cabinet.

C

Law of October 14, 1949, to Provide Economic Security to Churches and Religious Associations through the Government

(Law No. 218 of 1949, promulgated on October 17, 1949)

Section 1

According to the provisions of the present law, stated below, the government shall grant emoluments to the clergymen of churches and religious associations who perform, with the consent of the government, strictly religious functions, or are employed in church administration or in establishments for the training of clergymen. The Bureau for Church Affairs may, in agreement with the Ministry of Finance, grant, as an exception, emoluments also to the clergymen who are engaged in other activities.

Section 2

The consent may be granted by the government only to ministers of religion who are Czechoslovak citizens, are politically reliable, irreproachable, and otherwise meet the general requirements for employment with the government.

The Bureau for Church Affairs may waive the requirement of citizenship in cases worthy of special consideration.

Section 3

1) The emoluments of clergymen shall consist of:

a) a basic salary

b) additional pay according to rank

c) efficiency bonuses

2) The Cabinet shall fix, by decree, the amount of the

basic salary, the method and rates of its increase, requirements for granting of additional pay according to rank, and its amount, and efficiency bonuses and details concerning them.

Section 4

Concerning the compensation for travel, removal, and other expenses, clergymen entitled to emoluments shall also be entitled to compensation for travel, removal, and other expenses according to the general provisions.

Section 5

The clergymen performing strictly religious functions are under the obligation to teach religion in schools without remuneration, unless there is another arrangement for the teaching of religion. The extent of this obligation and its further regulation shall be fixed by the Minister directing the Bureau for Church Affairs in agreement with the Minister of Education, Science, and Arts.

Section 6

Social benefits, in particular the allocations for dependent children and pension benefits for clergymen and members of their family, shall be granted in accordance with provisions for governmental employees. The details shall be determined by the Cabinet.

Section 7

Activities and Appointment of Clergymen

1) Only those persons may exercise the activities of a minister of religion (preacher and the like) in a church or religious association, who have obtained the consent of the government and have taken an oath.

2) Every employment (by election or appointment) of such persons shall require the consent of the government, given in advance.

3) The vacant posts must be filled within thirty days. If this is not done, the government may take the necessary measures to secure the regular performance of the religious functions, church administration, or education of clergymen.

Section 8

Expenses of Upkeep

1) The government shall reimburse churches and religious associations for regular expenses of upkeep relating to the divine service and other religious functions and the church administration in accordance with their budgets, approved by the Bureau for Church Affairs.

2) The government may grant a special subsidy for extraordinary expenses of upkeep which are justified.

Section 9

Budgets

1) The representatives of churches and religious associations and administrators of church property must prepare budgets and final accounts and submit them to the Bureau for Church Affairs for approval.

2) The budgets of current expenses of upkeep shall be set up in conformity with actual needs in accordance with the rules for the drafting of the governmental budget; the particulars shall be determined by the Bureau for Church Affairs in agreement with the Ministry of Finance.

Section 10

The Property

1) The government shall supervise the property of the churches and religious associations.

2) The representatives of churches and religious associations and administrators of church property shall take an inventory of all personal property, real property, and property rights of the churches and religious associations, their branches, communities, institutions, foundations, churches, prebends and funds, and submit them to the Bureau for Church Affairs within three months after the date on which the present law takes effect. The details shall be determined by the Bureau for Church Affairs.

3) Any disposal or encumbrance of the property of churches and religious associations requires the consent of the governmental administration in advance.

Section 11

The Termination of Obligations

1) All private and public patronage of churches, prebends, and other church institutions shall pass over to the government.

2) All obligations to contribute to the purposes of churches, religious associations, their branches, communities, institutions, foundations, churches, prebends, and funds based on patronage or other legal reasons, or on long-standing custom, shall cease to exist with the exception of the obligations of members of the churches and religious associations resulting from establishments approved by the government.

Section 12

Schools for the Education of Clergymen

The government shall maintain schools and institutions for the education of clergymen.

Section 13
Penal Provisions

Acts or omissions contrary to this law or other provisions based on it shall be punishable—if not by courts, then by the country's people's committees—as administrative offenses with a fine of up to 100,000 Czechoslovak crowns. A substitute penalty of imprisonment up to six months, according to the gravity of the offense, shall simultaneously be determined for the case where the fine is uncollectable.

Section 14
Repeal of Previous Provisions

All provisions of law which govern the legal relations of churches and religious associations are hereby repealed.

Section 15
Implementation of this Law

The present law shall take effect on November 1, 1949; it shall be carried out by all members of the Cabinet.[114]

By these laws the Church was subjugated to the state. Freedom of religion as granted by the Communist constitution of May 9, 1948, was entirely eliminated. In spite of all the protests, memorandums, and pastoral letters of the bishops, whose voices were not respected, the Catholic Church came under the yoke of the state. The "patriotic" priests conformed without further ado. In its anti-Catholic attitude, the government surpassed all former regimes. State absolutism of the People's Democratic Republic celebrated its triumph. The main creator of this campaign against the Catholic Church was Dr. Alexej Čepička.[115]

On October 11, 1949 (the Feast of the Maternity of the Virgin Mary), representatives of the majority of Czech and Slovak dioceses met at Prague to discuss the situation created by the new government laws on Church affairs. The delegates were informed of the opinions of their ordinaries who enjoyed the complete confidence of the majority of the clergy. They were also informed in detail on the attitude of the clergy on all matters pertaining to their respective dioceses. After a detailed discussion of the general situation from the ecclesiastical, legal, personal and material points of view, the delegates resolved unanimously to make the following declaration:

1. Both the bills drawn up on clerical pay and the estab-

lishment of a State Office for Church Affairs are, by the nature of their content and their spirit, in sharp conflict with the inalienable divine rights of the Church, and signify her complete subjugation and misuse for political ends.

2. Though it is true that the bill for the adjustment of the pay of the clergy and material expenses of the Church was discussed at the religious committee of the Central Action Committee of the National Front, it was not accepted or approved by the Czechoslovak Ordinaries, nor were their comments and amendments heeded. By the establishment of the State Office for Church Affairs, of which there was no talk at the religious committee of the Central Action Committee of the National Front, the whole problem has been placed on an entirely different and unexpected basis, and neither bill can in any way be connected with the negotiations at the Central Action Committee of the National Front.

3. The establishment of the State Office for Church Affairs is an unheard-of usurpation of the internationally recognized constitution of the Catholic Church, and an attempt to liquidate it; for here, in place of the divine spiritual authority, which had its origin in the Sacrament of Holy Orders, comes lay authority, which takes over the right of decision not only in purely material matters but also in mixed matters, and, indeed, even in matters which are purely spiritual or jurisdictional.

4. The bill, as proposed, cannot be accepted by any faithful priest in his own heart, and even less can it be approved inwardly or publicly without sinning against his faith, his loyalty to the Church and his vow of obedience to his bishops.

5. It has been ascertained that the absolutely predominant majority of the Czech and Slovak clergy do not agree with the proposed bills, and realize with the greatest personal bitterness that they have no means of defending themselves against them. If, however, in spite of the resistance of the Catholic clergy, these two bills should be enacted and become law, the clergy would be obliged to look upon such a law as forced upon them, and all its consequences must be judged from this point of view.

6. It has been learned that in some localities priests were put under pressure by local authorities to come out in favor of both bills. While these recurring compulsory methods of the government are condemned as being a contradiction of personal civil liberties, an appeal is made to those priests

who have expressed their approval of the Church bills to put their conscience in order. Whether they have done so knowingly and of their own free will, or whether they did so involuntarily, or whether their approval was obtained by fraud, they owe an apology and an explanation to the faithful.

7. We leave a definite decision in the matter of increased pay and the demanded oath to the Republic to the Very Reverend Ordinaries themselves. However, it is clear to us from the way they were proposed together—i.e., the forced acceptance of pay and the taking of the oath at the same time—that it is not merely a question of salaries or of taking the oath, but it is a question of approval of the Church bills, and therefore no priest can make any decision in his conscience, without exact directives from his Ordinaries, without betraying the Holy Church.

8. We and His Excellency the Archbishop of Prague, Mgr. Josef Beran, wish to remind our brethren that they did not become priests to enrich themselves or to assure their worldly existence, but to administer to souls and to ensure their eternal salvation. It is in this way that the faithful regard you, and it is thus that Almighty God will judge you. To give preference to temporal interests before spiritual at such a critical hour means soiling your priestly honor and admitting before your faithful that you have not the true priestly calling, that you are not shepherds but hired laborers.

9. Do not forget that hundreds of our brethren are in prison or labor camps. To accept material advantages at a time when many of our brothers are suffering would be a gross violation of brotherly love. Do not forget that every day many poor people knock at your doors who, in spite of all the progress of socialism, are suffering immeasurably and can barely maintain existence. By accepting advantages at a time when so many people given into your care are suffering and in want spiritually and materially, you would call upon yourselves the contempt and hatred of those who look for you to be their shining example, moral support and encouragement.

10. It must also be clear to you that to accept material advantages at a time when tens of thousands of the faithful and our fellow citizens are forcibly separated from their families, and hundreds of thousands are groaning in prisons and labor camps, is not honorable and manly for shepherds of souls, for by such actions they estrange them-

selves from their people for the sake of material interests, and show themselves unwilling to suffer with the sufferers and mourn with the mourners.

Rather, let material advantages be granted to all those who need them even more; especially to the hard-working class, the aged, the sick and the brethren who are finding themselves in need now. Do not forget that if you seek first for the Kingdom of Heaven and its justice, Almighty God will not desert you, and will see that you do not perish of hunger. And our Czech and Slovak people will regard you with respect, admiration and sincere gratitude, because you have not forsaken them at the most difficult times, and because you knew how to suffer with the suffering nation.[116]

The bishops also took a stand against this situation created by the new ecclesiastical laws, in a conference held at Prague on October 21, 1949. On that same day they sent to the government their petition asking revision of the new laws. It read as follows:

The new juridical order established by the ecclesiastical laws that were recently approved (by the National Assembly) with regard to the economic status of the Church and the creation of a State Office for Church Affairs, leads the bishops and the Roman Catholic ordinaries to define their attitude toward these laws. Consequently, in conformity with Article 23 of the constitution of the Czechoslovak Republic of May 9, 1948, we present to the government of the Czechoslovak Republic the following petition. The new laws and their decrees of execution constitute an infraction of the religious rights and liberty of the Czechoslovak people guaranteed by the constitution because these regulations are destined to serve as the basis and framework for justifying and strengthening the measures used prejudically against the rights of the Church and to restrain her liberty.

1) We observe that this situation leaves the organization and the mission of the Roman Catholic Church without any guarantee, not even a guarantee of norms for public worship; on the contrary, the juridical order in force up to the present, even though it was not in full agreement with the needs of the Church, has been so radically changed that the Roman Catholic Church has in fact been outlawed in our country. The new regulations of the right of worship constitute a flagrant violation of international law on ecclesiastical affairs, represented until the present time in our country by agreements between the Church and the state, the basis for good reciprocal relations.

2) The Church's autonomy, including freedom of constitution and organization, has been taken away because the state henceforth claims the right to meddle with the internal organization of the Church and to withhold for ideological and political reasons its consent to the nominations of clerics to ecclesiastical positions. This ruling is contrary to the fundamental provision of the constitution of the Czechoslovak Republic concerning religious freedom, because that freedom includes the freedom of the Church to provide for itself its own internal organization.

3) Although (according to the new legislation) priests do not cease to be ministers of the Church, the public power arrogates to itself the right to regulate their working conditions unilaterally according to principles in force for servants of the state, thus violating the Church's fundamental and exclusive right of nomination of ecclesiastical servants.

4) The law from the State Office for Ecclesiastical Affairs no longer respects the power of the Church to regulate, in conformity with existing laws, questions concerning faith, morals, ritual, discipline, religious teaching and membership in the Church. On the contrary, it gives this government office unlimited rights to interfere in ecclesiastical and religious affairs. Thus not only is freedom of religious practice insecure, but professing one's faith, the corollary of Church membership, runs the risk of being hampered or made impossible by public authority.

5) One of the purposes of these laws is ostensibly to eliminate worship characteristic of a past age, especially of feudalism. It is therefore with great astonishment that we see these same laws introduce a new feudal institution: state patronage. Ecclesiastical law rejects absolutely the establishment of new patronages, survivals of the Middle Ages. On the other hand, patronage rights that were tolerated and still in force were based on bilateral agreements between the patron and the Church, and their application was subordinate to membership in the Roman Catholic Church on the part of the patron.

6) The exposition of the motives of the law for the creation of a State Office for Church Affairs indicates in the latter the faculty to exercise every legislative and executive power in ecclesiastical and religious questions. On the other hand, there is no guarantee for the liberty of the Church to direct in an autonomous manner spiritual affairs that are certainly of the internal order: questions of conscience, questions related to the sacraments, membership in the Church and ecclesiastical discipline. Hence there is a justifiable fear that in the future the Church will be vilified precisely with regard to the exercise of those powers of the internal order, her spiritual activity judged from the purely political angle and declared illegal and contrary to national interests. Under these conditions both laws are directly contrary to the constitution of the Roman Catholic Church as well as the constitution of the Czechoslovak Republic of May 9, 1948, because they are in flagrant contradiction to the rights and liberties guaranteed by Articles 15, 16, 17 of the said constitution. Besides, the decree for the execution of these laws, which was not discussed with representatives of the Church, only reënforces the prejudice of the new laws toward the Church. Certain requirements seem to be practically impossible to apply even with the best of intentions.

This is why we have serious reasons to fear consequences like those foreseen by Article 172 of the constitution of the Czechoslovak Republic. The Catholic bishops and ordinaries of the Czechoslovak Republic ask, by virtue of the right of petition provided for in Article 23 of the constitution, that the government take account of our present request and put an end to the difficulties which now disturb relations between Church and state, by an agreement between the two, and by a revision of the laws in question as well as their decrees for execution, thus assuring to the Roman Catholic Church, in conformity with the norms of public worship, a position founded on juridical guarantees and a real autonomy in its internal affairs.[117]

The bishops maintained, in the statement sent to the government, that the new law was incompatible with the assurances of religious freedom given in the constitution of the Republic of May 9, 1948. By it the Catholic Church was put beyond the pale of the law, and the organization of the Church was no longer guaranteed by any common standards. The state, they declared again, was interfering by political means in the internal affairs of the Church, especially in regard to the appointment of priests to their posts, making priests in effect civil servants. The State Office for Religious Affairs would be usurping the functions that should be reserved to the Church. The state had declared that it would remove from public life all vestiges of feudalism, but the laws for the control of the Church brought into existence a new feudal institution of state patronage. However, according to canon law no new patronage can be established.[118] Therefore the new state patronage could not be accepted by the Catholic Church. Moreover, not only were the new laws unconstitutional, but some of their provisions were impossible to carry out. The Catholic bishops and ordinaries demanded that the Czechoslovak Republic remove the present difficulties between the Church and the state through the revision of the recently approved laws for the control of the Church and orders concerning their application. "We demand from the government a guarantee of worship. We demand a firm legal status for the Church. We demand that the government guarantee the autonomy of the organization concerning itself with the internal affairs of the Church."[119]

An instructive pastoral letter to the clergymen dated October 21, 1949, proves that the Catholic bishops always took a conciliatory stand, even under such critical conditions:

> Peace be unto you, beloved brethren in Christ. You are waiting for words of guidance in these weighty days. We, the bishops and ordinaries, have met for discussion and send you our heartiest greetings and the most essential instructions in the situation in which you have been placed as a result of the enactment of the laws which interfere with the vital affairs of the Church, and thereby also interfere with our bishops' and your priestly activity.
>
> You have rejected unanimously the schismatic so-called Catholic Action. God knows the people are proud of you, and we thank you. You deserve no less respect and gratitude because you did not let yourselves be tempted into expressing your approval of the announced salary regulations, which were needed by many of you, if this meant surrender of your freedom and the subjugation of the Church. Loyalty to the Church and its religious freedom is, in our opinion, preferable to a salary regulation. You know that we have fatherly feelings for you and wish you a just social improvement. It is a salary regulation that has been agreed on without regard to our common wishes or to the recommendations we clearly expressed; and if you, without knowledge, accept the raised salaries, this is the result of pressure of external circumstances. You are changing nothing in your

magnanimous attitude, your material unselfishness, your unshakable loyalty to the Church, as you proved them long before the said law was enacted.

Our common fears for the freedom of the Church have been made stronger by the enactment of the law for the establishment of a State Office for Church Affairs.

In the knowledge of the sacrifices of the highest order which the Catholic people and their priests have laid on the altar of the fatherland by their suffering, work, and moral standards, and in view of the undeniable fact that the Holy Church has been the mother of the most beautiful things the nation possesses, we regret that laws were enacted which conflict with the constitution of the Republic because they are against the freedom of the Church. Without negotiations with the Church, the legal order of the Church has been altered and violated. As a result of all this, and by reason of a unified practice, we give you these directions:

1. According to Clause 20 of the government Ordinance, an oath of loyalty to the Czechoslovak Republic of the following wording will be laid before you.

I (name) promise before God that I will be loyal to the Czechoslovak Republic and its People's Democratic Order, and that I will not undertake anything that would be against her interests, security and integrity. As a citizen of the People's Democratic Republic, I shall conscientiously fulfill my duties, which arise from my position, and I will try according to my strength to support the constructive efforts directed toward the prosperity of the Czech and Slovak people.

The promise is to be made before God, and the consequence of this is that what you promise and what the state demands from you must be compatible with the inalienable rights which originate directly from God, on whose standards, as expressed by the Ten Commandments, every valid law must depend. Therefore, our conscience dictates us to add to the formula of the promise this oral or written reservation: Provided that this is not in conflict with the natural rights of man.

2. As far as the new salaries are concerned, we proclaim:

The bishops and ordinaries will not accept the newly regulated salaries, which are prepared also for them. For these salaries and the question connected with them, as well as the establishment of the new State Office of Church Affairs—without doubt a matter of far-reaching significance today—were not negotiated with them, as should have been an obvious preliminary necessity. We rely on the assistance of the providence of God, into whose service we have given ourselves completely.

You, however, will not be acting against your conscience and priestly honor, which you have unmistakably proved in this matter, if you accept the newly regulated salaries. On the one hand, it is necessary to protect you from the possible unpleasant consequences and to preserve you for the spiritual care of the faithful. On the other, it is necessary to take into account that your salary is a well-earned reward for your devoted work for the welfare of the people.

The state intends to remunerate you for from eight to ten hours of teaching at school, and as compensation for payments in kind which have been abolished. And finally it must be remembered that the pay, especially in the case of bachelors, increases taxes.

However, make this declaration to your ordinaries:

I declare that I have accepted the newly regulated salary because it is an ordinance which has gained legal validity. By accepting this salary, however, I am not taking upon myself any obligation which would be in conflict with my priestly conscience and with Church laws. I declare again that the spiritual interests of the Church and the undisturbed freedom of my priestly work are preferable to the material security of my existence.

3. If we are invited to do so, we are prepared to send our representatives to the Church Commission established with County National Committees, as we formerly sent members to the Land School Council in Bohemia and Moravia. Should anyone accept membership in this Commission without our approval, he will be reprimanded. It would be necessary to proceed according to Canon Law against those who disobey.

In conclusion, we wish to thank you for your unwavering loyalty to the Church, as shown up to now, and we charge you to be mindful of the fact that it is necessary also in the future to keep absolute unity and to believe firmly in the assistance of God. In recent times, in defending the rights of the Church, you have suffered much. Scores of your best brethren are languishing in prison. We have fatherly sympathy with their sufferings, and we pray for them and we ask you to remember them in your priestly prayers, as well as by *orationes pro incarceratis* (prayers for those in prison). Your courage, your sterling character, and

> Your incorruptibility are a guarantee to God, to the people, and to us, that, with the help of God, you will remain loyal also in the future to your priestly mission and the happiness of the people and our fatherland.
>
> We are constantly linked with you in our prayers, and we bless you and our work in the name of the Father, the Son, and the Holy Ghost. Amen.[120]

It is apparent from this letter that the Catholic bishops were not satisfied with the situation as formulated by the aforementioned laws but wanted to try to make the best of it.

President Gottwald in a broadcast in connection with the Czechoslovak Independence Day, October 28, declared that he regarded the dispute between the Church and the state now settled:

> A most important domestic political problem was the relationship between Church and state, which was solved when the National Assembly passed the Church Bills. Those bills swept away all the fears of the people who thought that the people's democratic regime had a hostile attitude toward the Church and religion. But we shall not allow anyone, either at home or abroad, to misuse religion to cloak hostile activities against our republic.[121]

To demonstrate before the people, especially the international public, that Catholicism still had great freedom, a proclamation was made on the occasion of the national holy day of October 28, 1949, to the effect that 127 convicted or suspected priests were to be either released from jail or relieved of being investigated. The announcement was broadcast by radio and by the Czechoslovak press. An amnesty was offered to the priests in the Pankrác Penitentiary of Prague. They were called at midnight into a room where they were advised that they could obtain amnesty if they showed repentance and if they promised full collaboration. Some of the foreign newspapers called the procedure a mockery.[122] The procedure in other cities was similar. Officers for so-called higher culture called on rectories and monasteries, persuading priests to repent. A real amnesty was granted to some priests; others preferred to remain in jail.[123]

To eradicate any resistance of Catholic priests, the government prescribed in the official *Věstník Katolického duchovenstva* of November 4, 1949, that all clergymen must take an oath of allegiance to the people's democratic regime. It read as follows:

> I promise on my honor and conscience to be faithful to the Czechoslovak Republic and to its People's Democratic order, and I will not undertake anything contrary to its interests, security, and integrity. As a citizen of the popular democratic state, I shall perform conscientiously the duties inherent in my office and I will do all according to my ability to support the constructive efforts directed toward the welfare of the people. (Decree No. 219, sec. 19)
>
> The pledge is given to the chairman of the competent people's committee. But the higher dignitaries give the pledge to the minister in charge of the governmental Bureau, bishops and all ordinaries to the Prime Minister.[124]

On November 12, the Minister of the Interior, Václav Nosek, announced in a conference of the chairman and the secretaries of the regional National Committees in Prague that Catholic bishops had agreed that the priests might accept the state regulation of their salaries and take the oath as prescribed. He did not take notice of any amendments or subjoined declarations since the oath is valid only as fixed by law. He repudiated any reservation which had been asked by the bishops in case of an orally taken oath or any written clause "as far as it is not contradictory to divine or ecclesiastical regulations and natural human rights."

In the same meeting the "agreement" was announced by the Minister of the Interior, even though the necessary bill had yet to be approved by the National Assembly. The bill, which was notable for relieving the clergy of many of those public duties and ceremonies for which they had long received from the state the small stipends known as the *congrua*,[125] had a very important bearing on marriages. It ordained that:

> 1) A civil marriage in the office of a National Committee will be the only marriage legally recognized by the government. If, however, couples desire a church wedding after the civil ceremony, this will be permitted.
>
> 2) The posting of the banns of marriage will be dis-

continued. A declaration by the contracting parties that they know of no circumstance which would invalidate their marriage will be considered sufficient.

3) The property of one partner will become the property of both after marriage.

4) A divorce will only be granted when the marriage cannot fulfill its social function, although it will be made difficult to obtain a decree if a minor is involved.

5) Separation will no longer be legally recognized.

6) A Registry of births, deaths, and marriages will be established by the National Committees, thus taking over a duty formerly executed by the Church.

7) Both man and wife will be able either to keep their own names or to adopt the name of either partner, as they may choose.

8) The legal age limit for marriage will be reduced from 21 to 18.[126]

On November 16 and 17, 1949, a conference of all Catholic bishops and ordinaries from the whole Czechoslovak Republic was held in Prague. Archbishop Beran did not attend but his signature was affixed to the pastoral letter issued on that occasion. Delegates of the conference appeared before his palace, but they were not permitted to enter. From this conference the bishops sent again a memorandum to the government and a circular to all clergymen. These documents[127] were of great significance, especially from the theological point of view, because in these papers the bishops explained their stand on fundamental principles concerning ecclesiastical jurisdiction.

Besides that, these documents were solemn declarations before God and the world that the rights of the Church concerning the episcopate, priests, and the faithful would remain and would always be viewed by them as inalienable and sacred, and this under all conditions. The documents were impressive in their wording and true in their contents, and they characterized the severe persecution of the Catholic Church in Czechoslovakia. The bishops' wise leadership in this most critical situation was well illustrated in these declarations, in which nothing remained unobserved concerning the possibility of the Church's bearing her hard task. The text is as follows:

The Catholic bishops took the liberty of sending a petition, addressed to the Czechoslovak Republic, from their conference held in Prague on October 21, 1949. In this petition they asked for the revision of the new laws involving and concerning the Church. These bishops sent their priests a conciliatory instruction concerning the matter of salaries and the oath of loyalty to the Republic. This petition was answered by letters of the President of the Republic under date of November 11, 1949, sent to all the bishops who had signed, treating them as individuals, and not as signers of a petition permitted by the constitution (§ 23 of the consitution) in the interest of public peace, but it was answered as if it had been a criminal act. Ordinances were changed, as though they had ceased their loyalty as citizens; had made (fictitious) remarks about an assumed religious freedom; as though they had disturbed public order; and as though their religious activities had been in disharmony with public order and the principles of good morals, etc. Therefore the letter does not contain threats.

Meanwhile, by the very way these instructions are being issued and carried out, they are even attacking the organic structure, order, and life of the Church, menacing thus any and all religious life in our country. About the extent of these new laws, so far as they concern the Church the bishops are still competent and obliged to express their viewpoint first of all.

We recognize the secular power and its jurisdiction and we are willing to support it in a just administration, but we also demand freedom for the Church. Therefore, being conscious of our responsibility before God, the Church, the whole Catholic world, and all the people of our Republic, we ask the government to reconsider all these laws and to regulate them in harmony with the constitution of the Church. The hitherto provided stipulations are not practicable, and they contradict the divine law, which even the Church cannot change. The new laws, furthermore, eliminate any freedom of the Church. They oppose the spiritual interest of a majority of the population. Even in states where the Church has not as yet been recognized, the freedom of the Church was not touched in such a way and to such an extent.

The Church was established by Christ, who has given her constitution to her. All jurisdiction in this Church has been given by Christ. The Church, in its activities and missions, is free and independent of any human power. By the grace of God, the Pope is head and the bishops are the connecting members in the Apostolic Church; they teach, consecrate, and manage their dioceses, as is fixed by Canon Law. Legal instructions protect the interests of this work of Christ. To reduce the jurisdiction of bishops means to menace the organic life and structure of the Church.

Should the Church resign her rights and preaching, which are to the same extent her duties, she would cease to be the Catholic Church; religious life would be the victim of tempers and delusions.

The new state laws and restrictions make the Church an outlaw. They endow the state authorities with spiritual jurisdiction. Bishops should be either eliminated, or become instruments of secular power. Paragraph 2, art. *a* of instruction No. 228 entitles the administration and Bureau for Church Affairs especially to formulate norms, manage and supervise activities in all ecclesiastical matters. Thereby the Bureau for Church Affairs has become the supreme authority in religious matters. The Church cannot fall back and bow before a law which contradicts the divine law. It is better to obey God than man (Acts 5:2). The constitution guarantees religious freedom to us, and this means the right to fulfill the divine law; but by the afore-mentioned Order enacted by the Council this freedom is substantially restricted.

1) In the record of the Ministry of the Interior of Oct. 20, 1949, No. 142/19 1/2 of the draft of the Order of 220, 1949, it is said *ad* No. 9 that the supervision of the teaching of religion will be carried out in harmony and cooperation with the section for schools, education, and gymnastic education, and will be limited in the inspection of the educational scheme. The state preserves for itself the determination of what can be taught. There is danger that the teaching of Catholic truth could be forbidden, and the teaching of error could be ordered. Such interference in religious education can never be binding and admissible.

2) Paragraph 16 of the Order says: All spiritual activities can be executed by secular and religious clergymen but by state consent. Christ authorized the Church to work for the salvation of the souls. If the state demands worse conditions for the activities of clergymen than it asks for assignment in the civilian services, it is unjust. State consent could be denied even for activities which have been ordered by divine law. We are asking therefore maintenance of § 17 of

the constitution. Everybody is free to practice activities, demanded by any religious confession . . . . It is therefore the inalienable right of clergymen to perform activities for which they have been ordained and authorized by the Holy Father or by their Bishop. If somebody should be found guilty, the state has the possibility of investigating and punishing.

3) On the ground of § 18, art. 3 of the same Order, the state will take measures to secure the proper performance of spiritual administration. But nobody can celebrate Holy Mass who was not ordained by the Bishop; so also nobody can exercise any spiritual jurisdiction if he is not authorized by the granting of the canonical mission. No loyal priest can accept or practice any spiritual office if he has been assigned thereto only by the state. Such activities as preaching would be sinful and void (Can. 2394, 2395). So also no clergyman, without consent of his bishop, may leave the office to which he was appointed (Can. 2399). The discharge and removal of priests by state power is evidently terror against the Church.

4) The establishment of ecclesiastical offices as outlined by Paragraph 5 should be repudiated. "As instituted by the consent of the state" means any of the offices which have been declared such by the Bureau for Church Affairs.

If such an office should be instituted by state consent, the Church must have the decisive right over this, which cannot be questioned. Only the Ordinariate is the organ of ecclesiastical jurisdiction (cf. Can. 1414-18).

5) a) The vast interference in the organization and order of the Church is the manner of assignment on the basis of § 30 of the state's ruling. Accentuating their inalienable jurisdiction, the undersigned ordinaries hereby declare:

All vacant places will be made known by the ordinariate, not by the consistory office. Not even the state can force a bishop to give any jurisdiction to any office (curial office) especially after the state has proclaimed that all laws hitherto enacted are being canceled.

b) On the basis of the same order, all vacant places should be noted in the *Gazette for Catholic Clergymen.* In this *Gazette* the ordinary can note all vacancies. Priests refused and will refuse the *Gazette* in which attacks were made against the Holy Father, and bishops, and by which the schismatic Catholic Action was backed.

Ordinaries would be willing to accept this *Gazette*, if

it would remain exclusively the official organ to the Bureau for the confessions and if they would be allowed to issue a *Gazette* of ordinariates, where vacant places will be noted. To achieve such a general review, they are willing to note all vacancies and personnel changes in the *Gazette*.

c) Impracticable is the demand of the paragraph which asks that the curial office submit applications of all applicants (and state reasonable objections). Often there might be matters of internal extent and of a moral nature, sometimes secrets of higher grade than an official nature (and these cannot be made public).

The ordinary cannot surrender his duty, after interviewing the examiner, by eliminating all applicants found incapable for the proposed office. If the Church should view and judge ability, she would be liable to assign all applicants offered her by the state. A civilian servant cannot know, even to the best of his knowledge, all prerequisites of one assigned to the spiritual office of preaching. It could happen that he might choose an incapable person, the same as an ecclesiastical superior would do if he were inexperienced in the knowledge of the conditions regarding the prerequisites for a military office.

d) According to § 18, for every assignment of clergymen to a position instituted by state consent, the preceding consent of the state is required. It is necessary to fix a time limit in which the state should proclaim its stand, the same as the state assumes for the Czechoslovak Church (by the Order 220, § 17)—within 30 days. Confessions should be equal before the law. Besides, from the obligation of preceding consent, it is necessary to eliminate the positions of cooperators and administrators, because in these cases it is necessary to take measures without any delay.

6) According to the record of the Ministry of the Interior to the Order . . . No. 20, the Bureau for Church Affairs should give approval and grant vacations for clergymen.

But in this way the interests of souls can be menaced. The divine law directs under certain conditions, even under sin, that pastors do not desert their faithful. The ecclesiastical superior can and should know if, and for how long a time, a clergyman is to leave his position. His dependence from the state will be proved by the needed certification of the official doctor of medicine. Besides, according to § 1 of the Order, 219 clergymen are employed by the Church. The Church usually grants a vacation to its employees.

7. We are asking cancellation and repeal of commissioners assigned to the episcopal offices because this measure contradicts the divine law and also the secular law. A layman is unable to exercise spiritual jurisdiction. Even the state did not authorize commissioners to use their jurisdiction independently, but only to supervise. Commissioners themselves are sending letters, even assigning priests, and granting them canonical mission, which is fully unlawful, void, and unreasonable. Therefore, clergymen will not and cannot respect any such measures. Even by the new laws, the assignment of Commissioners is not reasonable. We are asking that offices seized by these be returned.

All this we declare and ask, convinced that we asked this many times before, warned, and exhausted all possibilities for settling an agreement between the Church and state. If the state will cancel these new laws and repeal them, since they injure the structure of the Church to a very damaging extent, it would be possible to restore rather quiet times, development, and cooperation. We assure you that the matters in which we are interested are not our personal rights but the inalienable rights of God. We ask, therefore, freedom for the Church, freedom in administration, organization, teaching, and spiritual administration.

Our demands are backed by the faith of millions of the faithful who know that we are of their blood; they know we are living to foster their highest interests and that already we are suffering much. They are backed by all the clergymen. Some individuals, forgetful of their ordination and mission, left the unity of their brothers. Even if the people despise them, we pray for them and are waiting their return in a fatherly way.

We ask the representatives of the people to realize that we cannot act against the divine law. What belongs to God we cannot give to the Emperor. This is our clear stand. Should a cultural fight be opened, which may God avert, the whole world will know we did not cause it, because we are defending only divine things. We are defending the rights of those who were attacked. We did not attack anybody. In love of peace and quiet, for which we are willing to make all efforts, together with priests and faithful, we ask the government of the Czechoslovak Republic to abstain from any violation of the divine law and not try to enforce by threats a fulfillment of an impracticable law.

Persecution of the Church has always belonged to the

saddest chapters of the respective country. Our country has suffered enough already, enough lives are already lost.

The solemn history of the Church, the Mystical Body of Christ—the history of our Saints, the religious life of the Church through our priests, bind us and give guarantee to the state that in the country of the Saints, of martyrs, of Duke Wenceslaus, of Bishop Adalbert, of the priest John Nepomucene, and of the three martyrs of Košice, there are priests and people enough who are willing, including their bishops, to fight for the divine law, for the rights of the Church and for real freedom of religious life and for them to sacrifice all.[128]

From the same conference of bishops a touching letter was sent to the clergy, which reads as follows:

From our conference we send you a greeting and we assure you of our admiration for the brave stand you have taken thus far; also for your fearlessness in defending the rights of the Church, a thing which God Himself will appreciate and for which the Czech people will be grateful to you.

Troubled by the lot of the Holy Church and the religious life of our country, we, by apostolic right and before God and the Holy Church, hereby give warning:

If the latest government provisions are fully and consistently carried out, the very organization of the Church, its liberty, and its spiritual power will be threatened, and the Church founded upon Peter will become some sort of religious association directed almost entirely by the laity and by some timorous priests who have voluntarily separated themselves from her.

Aside from the grace of God, all will depend upon you, upon how completely you recognize the Church as the Mystical Body of Christ, on your bravery, on your unselfishness and on your sincere supernatural love for the faithful.

Be priests! Not only ordination but also jurisdiction is necessary to exercise your office. One as well as the other is given by the Bishop. The priest is a helper of the Bishop, carries on his work by his authority and is dependent on him. Only in union with the Bishop is he also united with the visible Vicar of Christ, the Holy Father, Bishop of Rome. Only thus united does he validly and licitly exercise his spiritual mission and its inherent office.

If, on the contrary, the civil authorities were to decide about you on this point, you together with the Bishop would become a tool of the secular power, and this is repugnant to the order willed by God. In such a way often not the most worthy individuals would be put into the most important offices, as the law of God and the interest of souls demand, but others who would be harmful to the faith and religious life. And if the Church were to renounce her authority she would cease to be the Church of Christ. We defend, therefore, not our own authority but the rights of God.

We give you the following directives for the coming days.

Conscious of our responsibility and apostolic power we proclaim that all provisions which are contrary to the rights of God are invalid:

(1) We ask the competent authorities not to require the consent of the National Regional Committees for the exercise of spiritual activity, for that is contrary to religious liberty.

There can be no competing for offices (*concursus*) advertised only by the *Gazette of the Catholic Clergy*, which we have justly rejected.

Our unfavorable attitude remains unchanged towards the so-called *Catholic News* and toward the *Gazette of the Catholic Clergy* in its present form.

(2) Possession of any ecclesiastical office cannot be taken without previous canonical order. Just as no one can validly celebrate Mass if he has not been ordained a priest, so no one can exercise spiritual jurisdiction if it has not been given to him by him who possesses it. Consequently, he who even provisionally accepts some spiritual office without the consent of his Ordinary is *ipso iure inhabilis* (by very law incapable) of exercising the same and, moreover, will incur suspension (Canon 2394).

(3) Applications for vacations must be made, as before, to the Ordinary and a substitute must be sought. The permission of the state office does not, in the eyes of the Church and in conscience, give a priest the right to abandon the parish. It is sinful to disregard ecclesiastical prescriptions. The Bishop knows best when and for how long the priest can be absent.

In the case of a permission to absent oneself for reasons of health the priest must present the certificate of the attending physician.

Even the new law declares you employees of the Church. It is obvious that it pertains to the superior, that is to the Church, to grant permissions to its employees.

(4) By ordination and canonical jurisdiction you have been authorized to exercise your spiritual functions. He who would wish to impede you would be acting contrary to the law of God. It is necessary to obey God rather than man. Preaching forms part of the sacred ministry. No civil power has the right to dictate what must be preached. Likewise, only the spiritual authority can determine what must be taught. We will request from the state authority approval of the texts for the religious instruction in schools, as has been the practice.

(5) You have accepted the increased salary in order to avoid a greater evil. But be disposed to deprive yourselves of it at once if anyone should demand for it the service of a Judas. You will not be traitors! Think of the poor, especially of your brother priests; be full of consideration in asking stipends for religious services.

We serve notice that even after the reform, the state payments to priests on pension have up to now remained unchanged. Show them fraternal charity!

(6) Since as Christians and much more as priests, you can promise and fulfill only what is not repugnant to the laws of God and of the Church and to the natural rights of man, it is necessary to add to the oath prescribed by law, either vocally or in writing: ". . . on condition that it is not contrary to divine and ecclesiastical laws and the natural rights of man."

(7) In making an inventory of property "to determine the source and amount of the income of the Church" (Section 26, no. 4 of government decree 219), it is necessary to keep in mind the following prescriptions: Goods which yield no return are subject to inventory. However, in no case are the following articles, those purely for worship, to be set down: vestments, sacred vessels, furnishings, pictures, statues. These cannot be sold and their price cannot be determined in any way. Moreover, it is difficult to find persons who can form a just estimate of them.

(8) The balance sheet should be made out according to directions which will be given later (government decree 219, section 25, no. 2).

(9) There is no need to make mention of the schismatic Catholic Action which has been condemned by the supreme

ecclesiastical authority and by the judgment of the entire nation.

(10) According to newspaper reports, civil marriage will be introduced as obligatory from January 1. This will impose upon you a very serious duty to instruct the faithful concerning the obligation of contracting the sacrament of Matrimony. All ecclesiastical prescriptions which are in force concerning marriage (publications, records, receiving the Sacraments) remain unchanged. Be always at the disposal of those to be married so they may not be deprived of receiving the Sacrament.

In case the state wishes to introduce its own registers, you will still be obliged to keep ecclesiastical registers and you will not be able to assume the obligation of keeping also the state registers. Your attention is also called to the fact that the ecclesiastical registers remain also for the future the property of the Church. Priests charged with their custody are therefore obliged to produce certificates upon requests of public or private offices. The oldest registers are considered as "precious" and are to be kept with other books of value in the safe.

(11) Prepare yourselves for the Holy Year 1950. Organize tridua, spiritual retreats, processions of penance. This must be a year of sanctification for souls by means of prayer and penance. It will be by strengthening your fidelity to Christ and the Church, by exerting yourselves to convert those who have strayed, by effecting social justice in helping the miserable and suffering, by labor for peace and the defense of the Holy Places.

Do not allow yourselves to deviate from the path upon which you have entered, but remain faithful to the Church, to the Holy Father and to us who wish in all circumstances, even at the cost of the heaviest sacrifices, to remain loving, spiritual fathers.

You know that we have not provoked the struggle, for the Church is here now for a thousand years. We defend ourselves with the right of him who is attacked. If it shall be necessary for us to suffer for these directives and for the defense of the faith, you know that even in suffering we remain united with you. Stay with your people for whose salvation we are jointly responsible before God.

If you have often exhorted the faithful to bear sacrifices for the holy faith, know now that the hour has come in which you must give the example. The whole nation looks to you. May neither threats nor promises separate you from love for the Holy Church. The most humiliating thing for you would be to become, for reasons of money, faithless to the Church which ordained you and to which you have promised an irrevocable obedience.

If then anyone of you—which God forbid—has forgotten his holy Priesthood, we wish to address a paternal word also to him. If he has denied obedience to his Bishop and the laws of the Church, he has betrayed Christ in one of the most important epochs. He has betrayed his brother-priests who in an absolute majority, as a block, remain faithful. He has betrayed the nation, falls under the judgment of God, and becomes the scandal to the whole country.

Such a one has no longer the right to be a Catholic priest and is deprived of jurisdiction even for confessions. Even the simple people know today that such a priest exercises his spiritual functions sacrilegiously and hears confessions invalidly.

You who are faithful, then, if you had much to suffer for fidelity to your vocation; you know that sufferings borne for Christ constitute the greatest glory on this earth and are always the seed of an even stronger faith. A life shortened through sufferings has more value and is more fruitful for souls than a long and comfortable life in which the work of Christ is wrecked, the faith stained by errors, the order of God upset, while the enfeebled life of faith gives way to paganism.

Be faithful; we have faith in you! Proceed unanimously and faithfully according to these directives. Preserve unity with your Bishops and among yourselves. In uncertainties and hesitations take counsel with your brother-priests and encourage each other.

We exhort you, all of you who will remain united with your people, with the words of the Holy Apostle: "If we suffer with Christ we will be glorified with him."

We bless you in our prayers, cares, and sufferings, united always with the Holy Father, with you, and with the faithful.[129]

As a reply to this articulate declaration of good will by the Catholic bishops, the Czechoslovak government published a book on December 6, 1949, entitled *The Conspiracy Against the Republic.*[130] It accused the hierarchy of high treason and claimed that Monsignor Beran was the most guilty; furthermore, that the criminal policy of the Vatican was driving the bishops into treason against their government and that the ecclesiastical aristocracy, headed by Archbishop Beran, was willing to perform this high treason. They stated that Beran was the most guilty, because his sufferings in a German concentration camp had engendered the government's faith in him. They said further that the bishops had organized a treacherous counter-revolution which started a campaign against the Republic and that they had begun to dictate to ordinary priests orders to commit treason. Monsignor Gennaro Verolino, the former chargé d'affaires in the internunciature in Prague, was described as the Vatican's most able diplomat and spy, who organized the antistate plot. It was said also that Monsignor Beran tried to stir up unrest through a devilish plan and that on June 19, 1949, when he was knocked down in his own cathedral, he planned to get himself arrested because the Church needed a martyr. Instead, it was claimed, the police protected him from the faithful who had refused to let him speak against the state.[131]

The newspapers, radio, and other propaganda media which reviewed the book urged people to obtain copies of this document of the treason of the ecclesiastical aristocracy against the Czech and Slovak people, adding that the danger point in the conspiracy was passed after June and that all was now quiet. The conspiracy against Czechoslovakia had been unveiled. To the organizers—the treacherous bishops—nobody had done anything, they said piously, and concluded: "We are marching toward a socialistic society."[132]

The year 1949 meant a breakdown in ecclesiastical affairs. Every act of the bishops calling for the preservation of the freedom of the Church was viewed as an act inimical toward the state and as a reaction against the people's democratic institution. The state ceased to recognize the Church as an independent and perfect society, and a society of the public order. It eliminated the jurisdiction of the Pope, under the plea of its being that of a foreign power, and of the hierarchy, which it sought to subordinate to the state. But the Church would not accept the concepts; the tragedy of the situation increased consequently.

During 1950 and 1951 the Catholic Church became a victim of a still greater persecution, being exposed to juridical humiliation, and in spite of protests by the Vatican and the hierarchy, was severely hampered in her freedom.

In closing this chapter, it is necessary to summarize developments in Church-state affairs in 1952-1953, in order to stress the persistence of the Communists in their enmity toward the Church. A small distinction should be drawn: the Catholic Church is not being clubbed over the head so much as it is being fed doses of slow poison. In other words, to quote Father Heidler, it can be compared to "an unfaithful wife who is plotting to get rid of her husband. To avoid suspicion she tells everyone how wonderful her husband is and poses as an affectionate spouse, yet adding, as she does so, small doses of poison to his food that will cause his slow but sure death."[133]

In like manner, the Communist regime loudly proclaims religious freedom, mainly in regard to the international forum, and evens feigns some benevolence toward the Church, but at the same time it is slyly injecting a whole series of poisons into the body of the Church. These poisons do not make headlines, but they eat away at the Church's very structure. The cruel face of the policy is veiled in nice phrases. Pretending to patronize the Church, bishops and a majority of the clergy are jailed or isolated, and a watch is put upon all Church activities, which are drastically restricted. Secret "trials" are held, and both the clergy and the faithful are sentenced; state-supervised "seminaries" are organized to replace the old ones; religious instruction in the schools is curtailed; insidious efforts are made to keep the people from attending church; priests are inducted into the army:[134] such are the regular, day-to-day phenomena of Communist policy.

In 1953, two more bishops, Monsignor Pobožný, Bishop of Rožnava, and Monsignor Karel Skoupý, Bishop of Brno, were put in jail, the latter because he organized a Marian Year.[135] Officials appointed by the Communist regime completely took over active direction of all dioceses, thus facilitating the aims of the atheistic state in Church affairs, and silencing real Church officials.

In the year 1954, the situation of Church-state affairs reached another milestone of antagonism: the moderator and promoter of negotiations with the government, Bishop Štěpán Trochta, after being silenced for two years in his residence, was put on shameful trial in May and received a sentence of twenty-five years in jail at hard labor on the grounds of espionage on behalf of the Vatican. His Vicar General, Monsignor Francis Vlček, and Reverend Francis Rabas also received twenty years in jail. In July, the Archbishop of Olomouc, Joseph Matocha, was reported to be jailed, as well as one hundred fifty priests and over three thousand Catholic laymen. These recent incidents indicate very clearly that communism cannot coexist peacefully with any religion. The "Church of Silence" will continue to be heard in every country outside the Iron Curtain, despite the alluring tactics of the Czechoslovak Communists.

CHAPTER ELEVEN

THE ATTACK ON THE VATICAN

WHEN THE CZECHOSLOVAK GOVERNMENT BEGAN ITS DIRECT persecution of the Catholic Church it centered its attacks on the hierarchy, sought to curb and control Catholic education and press, and endeavored to nullify canon law, especially those sections of the code dealing with ecclesiastical offices. Archbishop Beran was charged with non-coöperation with the government and of being "a tool of the Vatican and of imperialist agents."[1] A government directive desired to see "the Church and religious life develop in accordance with the constitution and the principle of the people's democratic regime."[2] The directive further stipulated that the press, radio and theater must systematically propagate the new church policy; that private gifts and other independent sources of income of the churches must be eliminated; that subsidies will be provided to maintain the charitable work of the churches —this to prove "the generous attitude of the regime toward religion"; and that every encouragement must be given priests to show their loyal attitude by positive acts.[3]

On January 8, 1950, Monsignor Andrej Škrabík, Bishop of Baňská Bystrica in Slovakia, died.[4] In accordance with ecclesiastical law[5] the canons of the episcopal chapter elected Monsignor Daniel Briedon as the vicar capitular.[6] The Czechoslovak government insisted that the vicar capitular must request the permission and the consent of the government in order to exercise his office. The vicar capitular, however, abiding by the decision of the canons, refused to seek ecclesiastical authority from secular government sources. Thereupon the government prevented him from exercising any powers and named Father John Dechet as "ecclesiastical administrator."[7] By accepting the appointment, Dechet became guilty of "a most grave infraction of ecclesiastical discipline and a no less grave usurpation of the rights of the Holy See, falling therefore under ecclesiastical censure."[8] Against such interference in ecclesiastical affairs, the Vatican took a determined stand and issued the following decree of excommunication against Father Dechet:

SACRED CONGREGATION OF CONSISTORY
First Decree

Since the priest John Dechet presumed to accept the office of "Administrator" of the vacant church of Baňská Bystrica, and after accepting it, also presumed to fulfill this office, the Sacred Consistorial Congregation inflicts upon the aforesaid priest the penalty of excommunication, specially reserved to the Apostolic See, and commands that he must be avoided.

Therefore, it warns clerics and faithful that they conduct themselves with the aforesaid priest according to the rules of Canon 2261, n. 3, of the code of canon law.

Given at Rome, from the Sacred Consistorial Congregation, on the eighteenth day of February, 1950.[9]

The decree was commented on in *L'Osservatore Romano,*[10] which analyzed this interference by secular power as: *Teocrazia dello Stato ateo nello Cecoslovacchia*[11] (theocracy of the atheistic state in Czechoslovakia).

During 1949 several new laws were passed to allow the government to intervene further in the appointments of other ecclesiastics, so that they might send the appointee to any parish they wished; thus the law of October 14, 1949, No. 218, Coll., and the decrees issued in its implementation on October 18, 1949, Nos. 219-223, Coll. The laws themselves bear a rather harmless title: "Decrees to Provide the Economic Security of Churches and Religious Associations by the Government." The decree No. 219, Coll., deals specifically with the Roman Catholic Church.

Although this law and the consequent decrees deal with "economic security" only insofar as they provide for emoluments of the clergy, supervision over the management of church properties and current expenses connected with the upkeep of the churches, matters are regulated in such a manner as to give the government complete control over the material conditions necessary for the existence of churches.

It is true that clergymen are declared to be the employees

of the Church and not of the state. However, they must satisfy "all general requirements for employees of the government" (Law No. 218, Sec. 2; Decree No. 219, Sec. 7). Furthermore, no clergyman may perform his duties without the consent of the government (Law No. 218, Sec. 7, Par. 1; Decree No. 219, Sec. 16), and for every appointment a governmental consent must be given in advance (Law No. 218, Sec. 6, Par. 2; Decree No. 219, Sec. 17).

Consequently, for any activity of a clergyman the consent of the government is required. Section 7 of Law No. 218 stipulates expressly that only those persons may exercise the activities of a minister of religion in a church or religious association who have obtained the consent of the government, given in advance. Similar provisions are to be found in Section 16 of Decree No. 219. The consent for the clergy is required from the provincial people's committee of the priest's permanent residence, or from the governmental Bureau for Church Affairs if he is of higher rank, or from the Cabinet if he is an archbishop, a diocesan bishop, or an apostolic administrator (Sec. 17, Paragraph 2, Decree No. 219).

Furthermore, the government emolument is paid only to those clergymen who are appointed, with the consent of the government, to posts and offices established with the consent of the government (Law No. 218, Sec. 1). To eliminate any doubt, Decree No. 219 states that this applies to clergymen with or without monastic vows, performing strictly religious functions (Sec. 2); to clergymen active in Church administration, e.g., in episcopal consistories or as members of chapters (Sec. 30); or as teachers in theological schools (Sec. 4).

The governmental Bureau for Church Affairs is authorized to indicate the posts which are considered as being established with the consent of the government. In so doing, it must hear the opinion of the competent church authorities, but it is not bound to follow them.

The express consent of the government is needed for the establishment of new posts. If the post is filled without the consent of the government given in advance, it is considered vacant and the clergyman appointed will receive no emolument from the government (Decree No. 219, Sec. 18). The vacant posts must be filled within thirty days; otherwise, the government is authorized to take steps "to ensure the carrying on of the wholly religious functions, church administration, or theological teaching involved in the post."

In other words, the government proceeds, in such cases, as an ecclesiastical administrative authority. In this connection a significant stipulation concerning the exercise of the right of patronage, contained in Section 30 of Decree No. 219, may be noted. According to it the government shall exercise patronage in nominating suitable candidates to the competent ordinary. The applications for a vacant prebend shall be sent to the episcopal consistory which shall submit all of them to the government with a designation of those applicants whom the consistory does not consider as suitable for nomination. It is from applicants who were not eliminated that the government shall nominate its candidate. The ordinary is, however, bound to appoint the nominee. This stipulation means that appointments to ecclesiastical offices are under the control of the government.

Finally, the government is to give consent only to ministers of religion who are Czechoslovak citizens, politically reliable, irreproachable, and who otherwise meet the general requirements for employment with the government. In exceptional cases, however, the requirement of citizenship may be waived (Section 2 of Law No. 218 and Section 7 of Decree No. 219).[12]

These laws formed the basis for the nomination of the administrator, the Rev. John Dechet, who was sponsored by the state. His installation was set for January 9, 1951, by the authorities and was to be carried out in a very solemn manner. Governmental personalities, excommunicated priests, and members among the "patriotic" clergymen participated in the celebration.[13] Understandably, Church dignitaries did not attend the installation of one who was looked upon as an illegal usurper.[14]

To attain an even stronger influence over the Church, Czechoslovak Communists assigned district commissioners for church affairs to every district. From January 19 until February 4, 1951, in the building of the State Office for Church Affairs in Prague, a special course was given for training these commissioners,[15] representing all the regions and districts. Attendance at these meetings was obligatory. To indicate the trend of the course, it will be sufficient to single out one lecture entitled "Aims of Vatican Policy and Means of Frustrating Them."[16] It reads:

> To destroy religion directly is not suitable, especially in Central Europe, where we are continually observed. This could damage the development of revolutionary activities in Western countries. We need, above all, believers who can help us carry out the plan of our reconstruction and reform. From this viewpoint, priests who can help us by encouraging people to work more can be useful. We will succeed in taking from the people their faith by more natural means, by sciences, progress and better-organized education. If we can succeed through science to free the people of the fear of supernatural forces, religion will shortly be destroyed. Therefore it is our immediate task not to destroy religion directly, but only to achieve reconstruction of the Church, to make of her an available instrument in our behalf, in accordance with our intentions. It is necessary to give Western countries the impression that communism is not an adversary of religion, but of capitalism and of the hierarchy.
>
> Our revolution concerns the whole world and it should be viewed under this broad aspect. Thus our fight here is not different from the fight of Italian workers against the Vatican. The Vatican forms the greatest danger to all people's democracies which are being sponsored by the U.S.S.R. To eliminate this menace, every possible means should be used. The main problem will be to destroy the strength of the hierarchy—to frustrate its influence. Because of the single-mindedness and determination of our adversary we must proceed in a ruthless way. The State Bureau for Church Affairs will take care to respect all state laws concerning religion. We must penetrate into the organizational structure of the Church. By regulating salaries we destroyed the social independence of the clergymen; by ordering them to take the oath we secured their obedience and loyalty. Bishops, seeing that they are losing the confidence of the secular clergymen, are beginning to transfer their activities to clergymen of religious orders. The faithful who go to church should be put under control, and full evidence concerning them must be secured. Catholic Action fulfilled its mission, but not to the expected extent. It has not attracted the masses through its activities and the leaders of it are not equal to their mission. It is necessary to give it a new program, and new moral content; it is necessary to change officers and to gain the unrest of the masses

> for its ideas. We will give to it the necessary financial assistance. It is necessary, too, to use Catholic Charities. Instructors for priests should be trained. Even Catholic confession must not evade our control and attention. The designation of rectories must be made strictly in accord with our political aims, because the preliminary consent of the state authorities is of primary importance. The number of rectories will be regulated and the number of parishes will be reduced. Where there are few Catholics, the Church will be disposed of and given to another religion. The preferred churches will be the Orthodox Church, because it is amenable to socialism, and the Czechoslovak Church, because it is flexible in any direction.[17]

The mentioning of the Orthodox and Czechoslovak National Churches as instruments of Communist aims is really a poor tribute to both these Churches. The remark about the Czechoslovak National Church is readily understood in the light of a statement of February 1, 1950, made by a high representative of the latter Church:

> For us and our Church these laws mean an end of the discrimination from which our Church suffered during the first Republic and under the occupation. The people's government found a just solution to the problem of the standing of the various Churches, so that no Church can complain that its present position in the Republic is worse than it was before, when the Church did not enjoy equality.[18]

The Catholic bishops, however, took a different stand. They expressed their view by a circular letter to the clergymen, dated February 17, 1950, to explain why the government-appointed "ecclesiastical administrator" of Baňská Bystrica, Father John Dechet, had been excommunicated, and why a similar fate was in store for other priests who accepted ecclesiastical appointments at the hands of the state. It described the government's present appointment as "an attempt to violate Church rights," and demanded that it should be withdrawn. It also forbade priests to attend the special evening classes in Marxist theories which were being organized all over Czechoslovakia, and concluded by saying: "Be aware of your dignity and your duties towards the Church and the nation, and pray for all who are wavering."[19]

The sequel to this was that Minister Čepička sent to

Monsignor Beran and all the bishops of Czechoslovakia a letter dated March 3, in which, after repeating his arguments concerning the diocese of Baňská, he said:

> You are, of course, not concerned with truth, nor with the welfare of the Church and the state, nor yet with the calm and peaceful life of the priests and the faithful. You have for a long time now been working for subversion and sowing disquiet. You therefore do not consider it beneath your civic and episcopal dignity openly and in an unheard-of manner to attack the new Church Laws, which the nation has given itself in the interests of the Republic and of the Church, and which must unconditionally be kept. On the contrary, the Bishops have obediently carried out the Vatican's orders, and have even approved its medieval punishment of a fellow-churchman. They have also forbidden priests to make contact with public officials entrusted with Church affairs, showing that the taking of oaths of loyalty to the state by priests had become a mote in your eye (sic). Your circular is a further act proving your deep hatred of and enmity to the People's Democratic Order. It is not the first time that your attention has been drawn to this state of affairs. It is unthinkable that we should in the future tolerate any form of incitement of priests or faithful, or any disturbance of the calm development of our state. In the interest of calm and order the working people will find means to prevent the future disturbance of its efforts to build a just social order.[20]

The text of the letter was released at a press conference in Prague which M. Čepička called for the purpose.[21]

Similarly a letter was sent to the clergy of Slovakia by the Slovak Bureau for Church Affairs in Bratislava:

> We draw the attention of those who would become the instruments of reaction and spread the illegal circular of February 17th that they do so at their own risk. We hope this letter will help you to devote yourselves to peaceful religious work. We are sure that in the future you will remain firm against any attacks and intrigues of the enemies of our Republic. The bishops' circulars are a service to the capitalists. This is proved from enemy broadcasts. The British and Americans apparently have only a political interest in the Catholic Church.[22]

The unified stand of Catholic bishops was unfortunately broken on January 31, 1950, when the auxiliary bishop of Prague, Monsignor Antonin Eltschkner, took an oath of allegiance, as did Monsignor Theofil Opatrný, Vicar-General of the archdiocese of Prague, and Monsignor Francis Kutal, Dean in Kroměříž in Moravia. These were the first cases among clergymen of the upper echelons of the hierarchy.[23] The contrast of this with the firm stand which until that time had generally been taken by the clergymen of higher rank and by the episcopate evoked feelings of displeasure among the people.[24]

On February 28, 1950, President Klement Gottwald delivered a speech in which he attacked the "nonconformist" clergymen, by saying:

"The higher clergy of the Catholic Church in Czechoslovakia is an enemy of our regime. They are against the spirit of our government and act as a center of internal reactionary forces. All Czechoslovak reactionaries, at home and abroad, are in contact with high Catholic clergy and they are preparing a *coup d'état* against the Republic."[25]

The Minister of Justice, Alexej Čepička, leveled a new blast at the Archbishop of Prague, Josef Beran, whom he charged with working a long time to spread disruption and to incite the masses.[26] In December, 1949, a pamphlet had been published, entitled *Conspiracy Against the Republic,*[27] in which Archbishop Beran was attacked. In a pamphlet entitled *Vatican between Two World Wars,*[28] the Vatican was derided as though it had collaborated with nazism and fascism. By means of these frequently published pamphlets the Communists endeavored to eliminate the Vatican as the supreme center of jurisdiction for Catholics and to nullify Catholic universalism from the religious sphere.

This was the main reason for their hostile stand against the Vatican. This was also the reason why the contact with the Vatican was disrupted. The Czechoslovak government expelled on March 18, 1950, the papal diplomat, Monsignor Ottavio de Liva, who was secretary to the papal internunciature in Prague. He was accused of conspiring in the miracle at Čihost. Because these occurrences at Čihost were commented on by the Czechoslovak government as events "inspired by the papal representative Monsignor de Liva"[29] it is necessary to show what actually happened in Čihost.[30]

On the eleventh of December, 1949, the third Sunday in Advent, the parish priest, Father Joseph Toufar, said at the end of his sermon, "Among you stands one whom we know not. In the sanctuary here is your Saviour," and he made a movement toward the altar. And at this moment all who looked in this direction saw the crucifix moving at an angle of 45 to 50 degrees, first to the epistle side, then to the gospel side. This was repeated twice. Then the crucifix came back into the middle—not in its original position, but turned to the pulpit; in the place where it is fixed to its stand, it bent forward so that its center of gravity was very far above the base of the stand. Under normal circumstances, according to the investigation made by Rt. Rev. Abbot of Želiv and the head of the District Hospital, the crucifix would have turned over and fallen down. This phenomenon was seen by nineteen people, most of them adults, men and women. Some students and some religiously indifferent people were among them. They could see it from all points in the church, from the front pews, from under the gallery, behind the benches and even from places where they could not see the preacher in the pulpit but only the altar. They all wrote an official report under oath of what they had seen. They repeated it at the police investigation. The witnesses are all normal and healthy persons.

The crucifix is about 19 inches high. The base of the stand is round, and made of wood, with a diameter of about 8½ inches. Magnetic activity is out of the question. Soon after this phenomenon occurred, thirteen priests arrived; many people came day after day. On Sundays there were rows of cars and tractors in front of the church. Some of them came from as far away as Prague. The same movement of the crucifix occurred also at Christmas time. The police came from Kolín to investigate, but nobody wanted to touch the crucifix. People began making pilgrimages to Čihost.

On the eve of Saturday, January 28, 1950, two cars arrived at the priest's house. A group of men stepped out and introduced themselves to Father Toufar as journalists and representatives of the foreign press and asked for a short explanation of the recent events. The priest, dressed only in his ordinary clothes, wanted to take them into the church, but outside his house the men forced him into the car and departed. (Since that time he has been in prison. Similarly, Monsignor Burýšek, rector of the major seminary of Hradec Králové, the Abbot of Želiv, Rt. Rev. Vít Tajovský, Father Slavíček of Ledeč-upon-Sazava, one theologian, and the sacristan of Čihost have been imprisoned.)

The state police then began to be interested and made a thorough search. They tried to explain the movement of the crucifix as being effected with the help of a string, controlled by someone behind the altar. Because many Christians came to Čihost, the police ordered that no nonresident people be allowed to enter the church. Finally the church was closed entirely during the week by order of the police and only on Sundays, the priest Morish, who arrived by car from Pardubice, celebrated the Mass.

The first one who officially mentioned the events at Čihost was the President of the Republic himself in his speech to the Central Committee of the Czech Communist party on February 24, 1951. He denounced all that had happened at Čihost as a great fraud and deception and said, "Faithful Christians will take due note of how their sacred symbol is handled by these fairground magicians; how disgracefully, disgustingly, and cheaply the feelings of these simple people have been misused."[31]

Minister Čepička also took action. He arranged a press conference on Friday, March 3, when he denounced as yet another crime of Vatican diplomacy, this attempt to produce a miracle in order to distract the believers' attention from their work. Not only was the miracle at Čihost manufactured, he continued, but news about other miracles was spread with the intention of preparing other actions to harm the people's democratic republic.[32] Several other speakers took part and without giving any proof, described the events at Čihost as a mere fraud.

There was another press conference on Monday, March 6, at the office of the Minister of the Interior, Václav Nosek, where a detailed report on the investigation of the miracle at Čihost was given to Czechoslovak and foreign journalists.[33] It was stated that the recorded events were a fraud; that the priest had constructed a mechanism of thin wire, steel and elastic springs and made the crucifix move by pulling the wires from behind the pulpit. However, in all the statements that had been made, not a single proof had been given to show that the miracle with the crucifix was a fraud, organized, as it was claimed, by the bishops and the Vatican.[34]

There are differences in the details concerning the supposed fabrication of the miracle even in the reports of the government representatives. According to one statement, it was dark in the church and a thin steel wire would have been practically invisible. According to the President a spring was used which the priest put up from the altar extending to the pulpit. According to another version the priest confessed that on the eleventh of December, at his sermon at 9:30 A.M., he had made three movements of the crucifix with the help of the described mechanism. Then he supposedly put away his contrivances after two on the same afternoon so that nobody could ever ascertain what had been done. But according to a unanimous statement of the whole Czech press, the same movements of the crucifix occurred again on December 25, 1949. Yet it is not stated anywhere that the priest set up his mechanism again.[35] A detailed analysis would show other differences. So far the Church has not expressed its opinion.[36]

A very interesting side effect of this case was that although the Czechoslovak government drew so much attention to the miracle in its endeavor to prove the event a fraud, the psychological effect was quite different. The faithful were greatly reinforced by this event. A critical analysis of the explanations of the police investigations was published in the central bulletin of the Saint Cyril and Saint Methodius League, *Nový Život* (New Life).[37] They tended to show that the strange event in Čihost was true.

After leaving his office as chargé d'affaires Monsignor Verolini became the last member of the papal legation.[38] *De facto* it was now closed, because the Czechoslovak government refused to give an entry visa to Monsignor Bertoli and two other diplomats appointed by the Vatican, who were to become the successors of Monsignor Verolini in the legation at Prague.[39]

This situation was severely criticized by the Vatican press.[40] However, if we recall that as early as July 1, 1949, the Central Action Committee of the National Front had issued a pamphlet, entitled *Treason of Vatican and Bishops,*[41] the expulsion of the papal diplomat is not surprising.[42] The

Czechoslovak Ambassador to the Holy See, Artur Meixner, was recalled to Prague on December 23, 1949. His successor, the Slovak Dr. Ilja Rath, was to function as secretary of the Czechoslovak legation, but he too was recalled at the end of April, 1950. The last member of the Czechoslovak Embassy, Josef Minařík, left Rome without notifying the Vatican of his departure.[43]

The rupture of diplomatic relations with the Vatican was followed by the seizure of religious houses in Czechoslovakia. This action of the government was taken under the pretext that "monasteries are centers for espionage and subversive activities for the Vatican."[44] A psychological preparation for this adverse policy against monasteries and convents was made in the important trial held from March 30 to April 5, 1950, in Prague, involving well-known superiors and members of religious orders and congregations.[45]

The accused were Rt. Rev. Augustin Machalka and Rt. Rev. Bohumil Tajovský, Abbots of the Premonstratensian Abbey of Nová Říše and Želiv; Father Frant. Šilhan, S.J., Provincial of the Jesuits; Father Sylvester Braito, O.P., Professor of Theology at Olomouc; Father Mastilák, C.SS.R., professor at the seminary at Obořiště in Bohemia; Father Adolf Kajpr, S.J., and Father Frant. Mikulášek, S.J., both of Prague; Father Jan Blesík, C.SS.R., of Prague; Father Jan Urban, O.F.M., of Prague; and Rev. Stanislav Barták, a Premonstratensian monk of Nová Říše. Most of them had been arrested only a few days before.[46]

The Prague radio, announcing that the trial had begun, reported that it was open to the public, and that many foreign and Czech reporters were present; but according to a dispatch from Prague to the British United Press, two Western correspondents who tried to get into the court were told there were no more seats available.[47] In fact the only journalists present were those from the Communist press of Eastern Europe; and with them in the public benches were a few of the apostate priests who had given their services to the regime.[48]

The five-day trial of these ten religious ended on Wednesday, in Holy Week. Dr. Jan Mastilák, C.SS.R., was given a life sentence. Rt. Rev. Augustin Machalka and Dr. Frant. Šilhan, S.J., were given twenty-five-year sentences. Rt. Rev. Bohumil Vít Tajovský was given twenty years; Dr.

Sylvester Braito, O.P., fifteen years; Dr. Jan Urban, O.F.M., of Prague, fourteen years; Father Adolf Kajpr, S.J., of Prague, twelve years; Father Jan Blesík, C.SS.R., ten years; Father Frant. Mikulášek, S.J., nine years; Rev. Stanislav Barták, of Nová Říše, two years. There were no acquittals. The last named was the only one who was found not guilty of high treason and espionage, and was sentenced because "he knew about the high treason and espionage and did not denounce the group to the authorities."[49] The first four defendants named were also fined 50,000 crowns each; the two following 30,000 crowns each; Father Kajpr and Father Blesik, 20,000 crowns each; and Father Mikulášek 10,000 crowns. Since the property of all except Father Barták was to be confiscated, the fines would appear to be something of a formality. All defendants lost their civil rights for ten years, except Father Barták, who lost his for three years only.[50]

It is interesting to note that many of the accused priests were men well known for their literary activities. Dr. Kajpr was the former editor of the suppressed weekly *Katolík*. Incidentally, he spent four years in the concentration camp Dachau in Germany. Father Mikulášek had been a leader of the suppressed Catholic youth movement, and the editor of the youth magazine *Dorost*. Father Braito was head of the publication *Krystal,* which was confiscated in February, 1950, and supplanted by the organ of the government's bogus Catholic Action, and up to the time of his arrest was editor of the religious review *Na Hlubinu.*[51] Father Urban was a founder of the special women's lay organization of the Third Order of Saint Francis, for the exclusive purposes of the Catholic Action; he was also head of Studium Catholicum in Prague, a private university.[52] Father Mastilák spent six and a half years studying in Rome at the papal institute, Russicum, which the Communists called the "Vatican's school for spies."[53]

The juridical basis for the arrest of monks for being engaged in "espionage and subversive activities" was explained by Professor Hobza in his speech at the trial:

> The existence of a religious order with the demand of complete and strictest obedience is in vociferous conflict with the established law in the Czechoslovak Republic. As long as there is a question of a concrete situation, effected

by the presentation of the complaint against the ten ecclesiastical functionaries, I formulate my criticism thus: the complaint of the "delicti" class, which the known functionaries committed, I place in two categories: 1) the delicti, falling under the concept of the crime of arch-treachery; 2) the delicti, falling under the concept of espionage—both within the sense of the laws of Czechoslovakia. If the court acknowledges that by judicial proceedings the committing of these crimes was proven, we must deal with such criminals even against international law.[54]

On April 13 and 14, monasteries in Bratislava, Trnava, and Nitra in Slovakia[55] were forcibly seized and the monks deported[56] and insulted in the Czechoslovak press.[57] To emphasize the guilt of monasteries against the regime and seemingly to justify its action in the eyes of the international forum, as a final step the government on April 18, 1950, announced:

It has recently been established that Catholic Religious Orders have become the instruments of the foreign enemies of the Republic. In the court trials for subversive activities it has been proved that many monasteries have sheltered hostile agents, spies and even assassins. Weapons and secret broadcasting stations have been discovered in monasteries, and many monasteries have served as centers for espionage and subversive activities. Particularly since the publication of the new Church laws, which put an end to the hope that the secular clergy would continue their subversive activities, the reactionary Catholic Church hierarchy, on orders from the Vatican, have used monks as their chief helpers for the realization of their disruptive plans.

In order to discontinue the hostile activities of the Catholic Orders, measures have been taken which bring back those Orders to their original and truly religious missions. It has been noted that the large monasteries were inhabited by only a few people, who did no work and were mostly engaged in inciting the people. For this reason the Religious Orders have been concentrated in several monasteries, where they will be able to devote themselves to their purely religious missions according to the rules of their Orders. The vacated monastery buildings will continue to serve mainly the needs of the Catholic

Caritas, and also social and health purposes. Some will be converted into flats which are badly needed by the people living nearby.[58]

In accordance with the final phases in this edict, abbots and other superiors of religious houses were interned in a monastery,[59] Pezinok, near Bratislava, while monks and friars were similarly interned at Jasov, near Košice in Slovakia. Both these "concentration camps" were surrounded by triple police cordons.[60]

Similar "concentration camps" were established in various other places in the country[61] and it was asserted that the purpose of them was "to return sisters and monks to their original mission."[62] In reality, however, these places have become like the Nazi concentration camps, having the same purpose as they had under Adolf Hitler in Germany and as they have now in Soviet Russia.[63] They have become centers of manpower for slavery and forced labor.[64]

The destruction of monasteries struck a tragic blow at Czechoslovak culture. Each monastery was equipped with a library which was open, not only to the members of Orders or congregations, but also to the public. The strongly worded documents which followed these events, such as the one below, are proof of the severity of Communist methods:

"The State Officer for Church Affairs has authorized local National Committees to conduct the liquidation of monastery libraries. We have received reports that delegates of the State Office for Church Affairs have transferred such books from liquidated monastery libraries directly to provincial purchasers. Among the sold material we have discovered a great percentage of books which could still be profitably sold on foreign markets.

"You are therefore requested to inform local purchasers not to accept such books from monastery libraries and to inform us of any instances where such books have been offered for sale. We alone take these books over for the purpose of classifying them more expertly.

"We draw your attention to the fact that this action has been requested from us by the competent official for the exploitation of old books at the Ministry of Information and Culture in Prague.

"In your report please indicate the location of the occurrence, the amount of books, and the name of the person authorized to handle the liquidation.

"We thank you and remain with

Cheer to the Five-Year Plan
'Raw Material Collection'
National Enterprise
Enterprise # 21—Paper
Action 'K'
Prague, I., Revoluční tř. I"[65]

That suppression of any religious opposition against Communist atheism was the official aim of the Czechoslovak government is indicated in an official government memorandum[66] concerning the handling of religious matters:

Instructions for the political activities of the Bureau for Church Affairs are shaped by the general trend of the Communist party, as expressed in the resolution of the tenth congress and speeches delivered at this congress, especially in the speech of Minister Kopecký. The main purpose of the aforementioned bureau is to see that religious and ecclesiastical life follows the provisions of the constitution and the principles of the people's democratic institutions. All regulations aim to attain this goal. This bureau must therefore see that churches have a loyal attitude toward the people's democratic regime and express this stand by affirmative acts, thus morally supporting the endeavor to solidify the country. The bureau must systematically win the sympathy of clergymen for the people's democratic order. It must strengthen and improve our people's democratic administration, making purges and disposing of members of the staff.

Plan of Tasks:

Staff office:

1) to deepen and improve planning services; to prepare the plan for the year 1951;

2) to compile drafts of the laws and regulations for its activities and to cooperate by the issuing of regulations, sent out by subordinate offices of the Bureau;

3) to establish a staff office and coordinate activities;

4) to limit personal responsibility of staff officers;

5) to give instructions on the occasion of suspicion in the central office, as also in the subordinated offices.

Section I (ritual)

1) making notes about vacancies in church administration, religious administration in seminaries for education of priests, all of which are fixed with the consent of the state;

2) giving permission to the activities by clergymen of all religions and religious associations;

3) taking an oath of allegiance to the Republic;

4) regulation of salaries and services of teachers of religion of all degrees;

5) regulation of legal positions of theological faculties, seminaries and educational institutes;

6) carrying out the equalization of all churches and religious associations which in previous times were not recognized by the state;

7) carrying out liquidation of former German Evangelical churches;

8) setting up evidence of all properties about all churches and religious associations (monasteries and convents).

Section II (membership)

1) Political training of employees of the Bureau for Church Affairs and of subordinated offices (to adopt the doctrine of Marx-Lenin) and continue in deepening and improving political level of all employees;

2) political training of clergymen;

3) constant political work among clergymen, gaining them for the people's democratic regime and their active assistance for reconstruction of the working ability;

4) screening all staff officers as to political security and working ability;

5) regulating legal position of employees of the Bureau, church-commissioners of regional and district national committees;

6) regulation of legal position of employees in church sections of regional and district national committees and regulation of their salaries;

7) transfer all employees of the Bureau and of subordinated offices into the scheme that is valid for other civilian servants, and formulate and draft all respective regulations.

Section III (information)

1) by press, radio, film and theater systematically to make propaganda for new church policy;

2) to endeavor to inform the public about church affairs;

3) to make tests of public opinion concerning church policy;

4) to collect documents and material for our new church policy;

5) to promote church life through the press and radio at home and abroad.

Section IV (economical-administrative)

1) in budget and financial agenda to draft and submit to the Ministry of Finance and to the control office all prescribed statements;

2) prepare the draft of budget for the year 1951;

3) supervise means for economy and budget in bureaus and departments, subordinated to the Central Bureau, and in all churches;

4) make statement for the year 1950;

5) regulate the competence of economical sections in the church departments of regional and district national committees;

6) establish organization of production and distribution of enterprises dealing with articles of worship;

7) examine all church monuments and care concerning them;

8) take inventory of all church properties;

9) investigate all investments as to churches and other church buildings;

10) pay subsidies to all social institutions of the churches;

11) liquidate the rights of patronage, religious funds and church committees;

12) pay subsidies for extraordinary expenses of churches.[67]

It seems evident from all this that the Czechoslovak government was bent on gaining sovereign control over the Catholic Church.[68]

Besides monasteries, the main source of the strength of the Catholic Church are seminaries and theological faculties in universities, where recruits for the priesthood are educated. Czechoslovak Communists focused their attention next on these institutions. The first step in this regard was the taking over of the regulation of education and the maintenance of these institutes, in order to obtain full and exclusive control over the education of young priests.

Based on some previous laws, Law No. 218 of 1949,

Sec. 12, was passed, and the government gained control of theological schools and seminaries. The teaching of religion in public schools was first authorized by the law on schools of April 21, 1948, No. 95, Coll. Section 19 of this law reads:

> 1) The school must take care of the religious instruction of children in accordance with their religious denomination with the exception of cases where the parents (persons authorized by law to represent the child) renounce such instruction.
>
> 2) Religious instruction shall be given and its control shall be exercised by church authorities (religious communities) without prejudice to the right of the supreme control and direction which shall be reserved to the Ministry of Education (Sec. 7).
>
> 3) The syllabus of religious instruction shall be established by the Ministry of Education, on the proposal of the church authorities (religious communities); this Ministry shall examine the syllabus from the point of view of civil and religious tolerance.
>
> 4) Teachers of religion (church authorities and religious communities) shall observe the regulations issued by the school authorities according to the statute.
>
> 5) Religious instruction must be in accordance with the educational activity of the school . . .[69]

It must be noted that Paragraphs 2 and 3 of Section 19 were superseded by Cabinet Decree No. 228 of Coll., which considerably tightened the governmental control of religious teaching and transferred it to the governmental Bureau for Church Affairs. Its Section 2, Clause 1, stipulates that the jurisdiction of the governmental Bureau for Church Affairs will cover: regulation for the teaching of religion, approval of the syllabus, textbooks, equipment and devices, and supreme supervision, in agreement with the Ministry of Education, Science and Arts, over the teaching of religion and over denominational educational institutions of any kind.[70]

A recent Cabinet decree of July 14, 1950, No. 112, Coll., goes even further in governmental effort to influence the teaching of religion.[71]

Its Section 3, Paragraph 1, reads: "Teachers of religion shall be appointed within the framework of the approved plan of employment after the church authority of the respective denominations has been heard."

Thus the appointment of teachers of religion is completely in the hands of the governmental Bureau for Church Affairs, which may or may not take into consideration the suggestions of the church authorities.

The qualifications required for a teacher of religion are explicitly stated in Section 4, Paragraph 2: "Only a teacher who proves *his higher political ability,* higher special knowledge, and who has had good results in his work shall be eligible for the higher grade of the basic salary."[72]

There is no doubt that this provision is another efficient tool in the efforts of the government to restrain the influence of churches and, in particular, of the Roman Catholic Church.

The Cabinet Decree No. 112 of July 14, 1950, Coll., regulates all theological schools. All Roman Catholic theological schools must be abolished with the exception of the Roman Catholic divinity school of Cyril and Methodius in Prague and Bratislava. Likewise, Evangelical theological teaching shall be conducted in three divinity schools, two in Prague and the third in Bratislava. An Orthodox theological school is established in Prague. The dean and his deputy are appointed by the Minister charged with the direction of the governmental Bureau for Church Affairs (Sec. 5, Par. 2). The dean is responsible to the Minister for the activity of the faculty (Sec. 51, Par. 3).

Other provisions of Cabinet Decree No. 112 should be noted. Section 4, Par. 2, reads:

> The government, in conjunction with the churches, will see to it that the instruction of students of theology is carried out in the people's democratic spirit and in accordance with the principles of the Church.

Section 9 reads as follows:

> 1) Students shall be received by theological faculties according to the abilities of the applicants and with regard to the planned needs of churches and religious communities.
>
> 2) Plans of studies and examinations, statutes, syllabi and rules for admission of students shall be decreed by the governmental Bureau for Church Affairs which shall take into consideration propositions of the Council of the Faculty and of representatives of the respective churches.[73]

The provisions concerning the theological schools and the teaching of religion, quoted above, clearly show tendencies to restrain the influence of churches and religious communities in theological schools and in the teaching of religion; to tighten the control of the government, which gradually takes over the rights reserved to the churches in order to infiltrate the theological schools and the teaching of religion with Communist political doctrine.[74]

All former seminaries were abolished; instead, the faculties of Saint Cyril and Saint Methodius in Prague and Bratislava, sponsored by the government, were established. Nearly the same thing had happened under the reign of Emperor Joseph II, but the Communists surpassed his Caesaro-Papism by dictating the education of theology in the Marx-Lenin spirit.[75]

Exclusive control over the theological faculties created for the bishops an urgent problem concerning ordination. To ordain or not to ordain? It was a very difficult problem to solve in this crisis. Every solution was dangerous. An affirmative reply to the question meant resignation of the sovereignty of the Church over the education of the priests. A refusal to ordain could mean a new tension and total official persecution. To meet the situation as best they could, well-meaning professors accepted their assignments in theological faculties to achieve some control over the education of priests.[76] When one recalls the urgent lack of priests, it can be realized how difficult the situation of bishops was. The stand taken by the bishops in this problem resulted in the present-day conditions. Some bishops like Monsignor Ambrose Lazik[77] in Slovakia, and the auxiliary bishop of Prague, Eltschkner,[78] ordained new priests, while other bishops took a defiant stand: they refused to confer ordinations.

After so many seminaries for the education of new priests had been closed by an order of the government, by law No. 112/50, Coll., issued on July 15, 1950,[79] students of theology realized the new situation and only a few took up theological studies in the universities. Students of theology who refused to go on with their studies were forced to ask for work from the Office of Labor, which, however, would not assign them any jobs. Instead, as early as September, 1949, all these students of theology were conscripted for compulsory military service and were assigned to infantry regiments in Olomouc in Moravia, and in Bratislava and Komarno in Slovakia.[80] Thus the theological faculties, despite all appeals by the official press and radio, remained almost empty.

The ruthlessness of the State Bureau for Church Affairs increased when Minister Zdeněk Fierlinger was appointed head of this bureau to succeed Minister Čepička.[81] Dr. Čepička was bad enough, but according to Vatican sources, Minister Fierlinger proved to be much worse. Immediately after entering office he assigned new vicars-general and more commissioners to the episcopal consistory offices of all dioceses. These were chosen from among the so-called "patriotic" priests; thus the influence of the bishops was destroyed. Rev. Josef Buchta[82] was appointed vicar-general in Budějovice; Monsignor Eduard Oliva,[83] former manager of Catholic Charities in Prague, vicar-general in Litoměřice; Rev. Ladislaus Hronek,[84] vicar-general in Hradec Králové (this greatly against the wishes of Bishop Pícha); the infamous Rev. Andreas Schafer, vicar-general in Spiš in Slovakia;[85] Rev. Žoltan Belák in Rožnava; Rev. Michal Beňo in Nitra; Rev. John Tuleja in Košice; Rev. Josef Minařík in Trnava; and Rev. Kristek in Brno.[86]

The commissioners (laymen) assigned to the episcopal consistory offices expedited all the agenda, and newly appointed vicars-general replaced the former ordinaries in bestowing the prescribed consent in religious affairs, thereby giving the semblance of a new hierarchy of patriotic priests.[87]

The sequel to this development was pitiful. The number of "patriotic" priests continued to increase. Among these were Monsignor John Sobota, papal prelate and provost of Poděbrady;[88] Monsignor Macháček, dean of Bratislava; and Monsignor Eduard Oliva. The oath of allegiance was taken by Monsignor R. Pobožný, capitular vicar of Rožnava,[89] and by all university professors of theology in Prague and Bratislava.[90] Surprise was registered when among the "patriotic" priests appeared also the names of such men as Rev. Kasan, Premonstratensian; Rev. Kubáň, Franciscan; Rev. Polak, Dominican of Košice; and others. These collaborators arranged congresses and meetings of patriotic priests in Hořice, where ninety-two patriotic priests were already present.[91] The reasons for their defections were numerous and varied. Their creed was expressed by the words of Rev. Plojhar, leader of the "patriotic" priests, who declared in the conference in Litoměřice on June 22, 1950: "As patriotic priests, we are and we will remain members of the Catholic Church."[92] "We must distinguish between the authority of the Pope as head of the Church and the Vatican state policy."[93] This distinction was many times officially proclaimed in many different ways, as, for instance: "We recognize the Pope only in matters of faith and morals; we do not recognize his jurisdiction." At the conference of July 2, 1950, in Luhačovice, and on June 3 in Prague,[94] these "patriotic" priests made the following declaration: "We must differentiate between the Vatican's authority in matters of faith and morals and its capacity as a sovereign state with its own political activity. It is clear that in the matter of faith and morals, the Vatican is the authority for us, but nobody will convince us that there is a necessity to follow and obey Vatican policy."[95]

Further reforms following the secularization of priestly life were almost the same as that of the union of Catholic clergymen known as *Jednota Katolického duchovenstva* from the year 1920,[96] which was adopted as a program by the patriotic priests. This, however, proved to be another unavailing attempt to reconcile Catholic theology with communism.[97] This spurious "Catholic Action" turned out to be the right hand of the state in Church Affairs.

The Communists' main purpose in organizing this group of priests was to mask the true character of Communist policy, not only in Church affairs, but also to whitewash it before an international forum. "The Stockholm Resolution for Peace"[98] and similar conferences for peace were abused by Czechoslovak Communists, and the patriotic priests played an important role by trying to show that the policy of the Communists is right and peaceful. The Czechoslovak people's democratic regime showed ingratitude by giving them its confidence and by bestowing on them material rewards.[99] In 1949 they helped to subdue the Church to such an extent that the Communist regime, having been encouraged by their servile stand, arrested all the faithful bishops, and in this way expressed its sovereignty over the Catholic Church.

The systematic assignment by the Bureau for Church Affairs of vicars-general and commissioners brought on a still greater persecution of bishops, as the Communists tried to eliminate them entirely from the government of the Church.

Each day brought greater limitations to their freedom. At first the bishops were guarded in their resistance; later, they found it necessary to be constantly vigilant. After June, 1950, they were forbidden to celebrate Holy Mass in their cathedrals;[100] finally they were arrested.

To make the trials of clergymen and members of the hierarchy easier, the Czechoslovak Communists issued on July 12, 1950, a new administrative penal code,[101] the regulations of which, especially those concerning "crimes" relating to activities of priests, seemed very cruel.[102] Extracts from the new penal code, which came into effect in Czechoslovakia on August 1, 1950, are as follows:

Penal Code of 1950

Section 123

Misuse of Religious Functions

Anyone who misuses his position in the Church for the purpose of influencing political affairs in a manner injurious to the People's democracy shall be deprived of his personal freedom for a period varying from three months to three years.

The perpetrator shall be deprived of his freedom for a period varying from one year to five years:

a) if he refuses to perform a religious function to which he is called as a pastor, or in a similar capacity; or

b) if there are any other aggravating circumstances.[103]

Section 173

Interfering with the Supervision of Churches and Religious Societies

1) Whoever performs pastoral functions in a church or religious association without governmental consent shall be punished by confinement not to exceed three years.

2) Whoever performs pastoral functions in a church or religious association at a post for which he was not appointed with governmental consent shall be punished in like manner.

3) Whoever, without governmental consent, appoints

another for performance of pastoral functions in a church or religious association, shall be punished by confinement for from one year to five years.

Section 174

1) Whoever intentionally frustrates or obstructs the governmental supervision over a church or religious association shall be punished by confinement for from one year to five years.

2) Whoever intentionally violates in any other manner the provisions of laws protecting the churches and religious associations by the government shall be punished in like manner.

Administrative Penal Code of 1950

Section 101

Protection of Order in Church Affairs

Whoever does not discharge his duties in provisions pertinent to the legal relations of churches or religious associations; in particular, whoever endangers or interferes with the execution of supervision over the property of churches or religious associations shall be punished by a fine not to exceed 100,000 crowns or by confinement not to exceed three months.[104]

Since every exercise of religious duties by priests, in accordance with instructions given by their bishops, was proclaimed a crime, the jails and penitentiaries were full of priests.[105] At first priests who were popular among the people and who were beloved by them were arrested. Before arresting the bishops, the Communists arrested vicars, aides and monsignors[106] of the completely isolated Catholic bishops. This practice is also known to have been used in Bulgaria,[107] Roumania,[108] Hungary,[109] Poland,[110] and Yugoslavia.[111] The same procedure was followed in Czechoslovakia.

Later, bishops were arrested. In August of 1950, Monsignor Michal Buzalka, auxiliary bishop of Trnava, was taken;[112] somewhat earlier, on July 14, the Greek Catholic Bishop Pavol Gojdič was arrested; taken also at the same time were Josef Čarský, Apostolic Administrator of Košice,[113] and Bishop Ambrose Lazík, Apostolic Administrator of

Trnava. On September 22, Bishop John Vojtaššák was arrested and placed in a concentration camp in Mučedníky, near Nitra, but was later transferred for trial to Bratislava;[114] arrested at the same time were the auxiliary bishop of Olomouc, Monsignor Stanislav Zela,[115] the auxiliary bishop, Monsignor Štefan Barnas of Spiš, and the Greek Catholic auxiliary bishop of Prešov, Monsignor Hopko; Monsignor Štěpán Trochta, Bishop of Litoměřice, and Monsignor Josef Hlouch, Bishop of Budějovice, were put under police guard in their residences.[116] Finally, Bishop Monsignor Pícha of Hradec Králové, who had been put under police guard in his residence, was arrested and placed in the cellar of the monastery in Broumov.[117]

Those who remained free because they took the oath of allegiance were one auxiliary bishop of Prague, Monsignor A. Eltschkner; Monsignor R. Pobožný, Apostolic Administrator of Rožnava; and Monsignor F. Onderek, capitular vicar in Č. Těšín.[118] The second auxiliary bishop of Prague, Monsignor Kajetan Matoušek, was admitted only as cooperator at the Church of Saint Adalbert in Prague, but was not recognized by the government as a bishop.[119]

By these same measures all loyal vicars-general were removed. All other episcopal offices fell into the hands of the commissioners of the new vicars-general chosen from among the so-called "patriotic" priests.[120]

Since all these nominations and appointments by the Bureau for Church Affairs in Prague and in Bratislava were proclaimed as invalid by a decree of the Sacred Congregation of the Council on June 29, 1950,[121] the stand of the Church became juridically clearer, even in such a complicated situation as existed in Czechoslovakia.

The Czechoslovak government carried on the same policy. The trial conducted in the state court from November 21 to December 1950, was a monstrous travesty of justice.[122] Similar trials were given to the auxiliary bishop of Olomouc, Monsignor Stanislav Zela; the Abbot of the Benedictine Abbey in Břevnov, Rt. Rev. John Opasek; the Abbot of the Premonstratensian Abbey in Prague, Rt. Rev. Bohuslav Jarolímek; canons of Saint Vitus Cathedral in Prague, Monsignor Josef Čihák, Monsignor Otakar Švec, and Monsignor Jaroslav Kulač; secretary of Catholic Action in Prague, Rev.

Antonin Mandl; aide to Archbishop Beran, Monsignor John Boukal; and the monk, Rev. Wenceslaus Mrtvý.

According to the official indictment[123] they were charged: (*a*) with an attempt to overthrow the people's democratic regime and the economic and social order in the Republic, the attainment of which necessitated coming into direct contact with foreign powers; and (*b*) with exploring state secrets with the intention of betraying them to foreign powers. Bishop Zela, Monsignor Kulač of Olomouc, and Monsignor Boukal of Prague were accused of having been active as confidants of the Gestapo during the German occupation, and through willful collaboration with the Gestapo, of having caused danger to the lives, health and security of the people; Bishop Zela and Monsignor Švec were accused of misrepresentation in 1947, by fraudulent handling of the relief funds of the Priest Insurance Associations, in consequence of which the Central National Insurance lost four million crowns; furthermore Bishop Zela was accused of having given false testimony before the court in 1946 in Olomouc, and of inspiring others to do the same as a result of his activities.

L'Osservatore Romano[124] characterizes the whole indictment as a mockery of truth. According to the Vatican press, confessions were forced[125] from the accused.[126] The verdicts were as follows: Bishop Stanislav Zela was sentenced to twenty-five years in jail and fined 150,000 crowns; Abbot John Opasek, condemned to life-time imprisonment and fined 100,000 crowns; Abbot Bohuslav Jarolímek, jailed for twenty years and fined 50,000 crowns. Regarding the canons: Monsignor Otakar Švec was sentenced to twenty years and fined 50,000 crowns; Monsignor Josef Čihák was sentenced to ten years in jail and fined 150,000 crowns; Monsignor Jaroslav Kulač was sentenced to seventeen years in jail and fined 40,000 crowns; Rev. Antonin Mandl was given twenty-five years in jail and fined 20,000 crowns; Monsignor John Boukal was given eighteen years in jail and fined 100,000 crowns; Rev. Wenceslas Mrtvý was given fifteen years in jail and fined 10,000 crowns.[127]

The penal sanctions were fixed according to the new penal code of 1950.[128] Espionage, with which all accused were charged, was under the jurisdiction of Dr. Antonin Hobza, professor of International Law at the Charles University in Prague.[129] Professor Hobza, considered by the court to be an expert, explained that "canon law and ecclesiastical regulations have no validity in Czechoslovakia; every dignitary or religious functionary who places canonical obedience before state loyalty is to be viewed as a traitor,[130] and is in discord with the state laws. Direct contact of a Czechoslovak citizen with the papal legation or with the Pope himself is not allowed."[131] By this exposition, Professor Hobza tried to prove why all accused were condemned as traitors. According to Dr. Hobza apparently every faithful Catholic, loyal to the Pope, is a traitor.[132]

To achieve this purpose the Ministry of Justice in Prague published, in 1950, a book entitled *Proces proti vatikánským agentům v Československu* (Process Against Vatican Agents in Czechoslovakia).[133]

Of course, the purpose of this trial was to dishonor the excellent reputation of famous Catholic dignitaries. It should be mentioned in this connection that all of those accused had proven their courage under German occupation, especially Bishop Zela and Monsignor Švec, who suffered in Nazi concentration camps and never faltered. The Western press condemned this travesty of truth and justice.

On July 12, 1950, a new penal code was enacted, and promulgated under No. 86 of the Collection of Laws. It provides in Section 36 (1) that a person who by his criminal deed has proved hostile toward the people's democratic order and has not, while serving his sentence, changed his attitude, may after the expiration of the punishment be assigned to a forced labor camp for a period of three months to two years. The procedure is regulated by Section 27 (9) of the new Code of Criminal Procedure, also enacted on July 12, 1950, No. 87 of the Collection of Laws.

The Forced Labor Camp Act of 1948 has been embodied into the new Administrative Criminal Code of July 12, 1950, No. 88 of the Collection of Laws. The normal rates of imprisonment liable under the code never exceeded six months. However, Section 12 (3) stipulates that if it appears from the manner in which the offense was committed that a hostile attitude toward the people's democratic order of the Republic or toward its socialist framework was demonstrated or intended to be demonstrated, the period of imprisonment determined by the verdicts of the criminal commissioner or commission of the respective national committee may be extended from three months to two years. In such cases the punishment is not carried out by detention at a court or administrative prison but in a forced labor camp.[134]

Under Section 85 (2) of the Code of Administrative Criminal Procedure, dated likewise July 12, 1950, No. 89 of the Collection of Laws, the Minister of National Security, acting in concord with the Minister of Interior, can issue detailed regulations on the detention in forced labor camps.[135]

During 1949 and 1950 more than seventy forced labor camps were established in Czechoslovakia and their number is still increasing.[136] They were either attached to mines (especially uranium and black coal mines), to large factories or constructions, or to independent institutions. The number of detainees in each of these camps varied from a few hundred to ten thousand and a very conservative estimate puts the total figure of persons deported and interned in such camps at 200,000 but most probably by 1951, it was nearer to 300,000 people.[137] Delinquents with higher rates of imprisonment were being deported into Russia.

After the aforementioned trial in Prague, another was held in Bratislava from January 10 to 15, 1951, to try the Slovak bishop, Monsignor John Vojtaššák, Bishop of Spiš; Monsignor Michal Buzalka, auxiliary bishop of Trnava; and Monsignor Pavol Gojdič, Greek Catholic Bishop of Prešov.[138]

The official indictment against them accuses them of collaboration with nazism, with mishandling of finances, and with espionage. The same "travesty of justice," to quote *L'Osservatore Romano,* that had happened in Prague[139] in December, 1950, was repeated in Bratislava with the intention of destroying every resistance of the bishops.[140]

The court delivered very severe verdicts.[141] Bishop John Vojtaššák was condemned to twenty-four years in jail; Bishops Pavol Gojdič and Michal Buzalka were condemned to life imprisonment.[142]

It is interesting to note that these bishops were tried for crimes which they were supposed to have committed at the time of the old Slovak Republic (1939-45), but even from this point of view, these verdicts were unjust because Bishop

Pavol Gojdič was generally known as an adherent of Czechoslovak state unity. Ostensibly his crime was that he had been a Greek Catholic bishop, working intensively for union with Rome. All of them were accused and condemned for the sole reason of being Catholic bishops.[143] The trial was condemned by the Western press: "The verdict of the Bratislava tribunal expresses nothing more than a disregard for truth and for the most elementary moral sense; this verdict will render our martyrs even more dear to us."[144]

Other bishops were completely isolated. They did not even have the opportunity to go to confession. Permission to do so was given once to the Bishop of Litoměřice, Monsignor Štěpán Trochta, but he had to speak aloud, in the presence of two agents of the secret police, who never left him. But he outsmarted them by making his confession in Latin.[145]

At the same time, more trials were held for ecclesiastics: Rev. Vladimir Pícha of the parish of Our Lady of Victory, Church of the Infant of Prague, was condemned to twenty years imprisonment; Rev. Antonín Dvořák of Olomouc was condemned to thirteen years;[146] Rt. Rev. Heřman Tyl, provost of the Abbey Teplá, was condemned to twelve years. Rev. Alfons Kovač was condemned to eleven years; Rev. Wenceslaus Pácha, aide to Archbishop Beran, Rev. Jos Ryška, aide to the Archbishop of Olomouc, and Rev. Rudolf Rykýr, aide to the Bishop in Hradec Králové, were all condemned to thirteen years imprisonment. Rev. Josef Hynek, superior of the Redemptorist Order of Svatá Hora, and Monsignor Thomas Beránek, dean of Vodňany,[147] were condemned to from four to thirteen years and also fined.[148] Many other priests also were sentenced.[149]

In addition to all this, there were trials against Catholic priests before district and regional courts, so that rectories were abandoned, monasteries were emptied, and parishes were left without priests.[150] The rest of the priests endeavored to serve the faithful with the administration of the sacraments and by worship, but there were very few remaining. The "patriotic" priests were busy attending the many congresses or meetings of the Stockholm Resolution for Peace and various activities arranged by the Communist party.[151] They were not very much interested in their faithful.

After putting on trial the hierarchy and leading churchmen in Prague and the Slovak bishops in Bratislava, another persecution was begun after January, 1951. The Communists completed the occupation of all episcopal offices and other positions, and exercised enormous pressure on the clergy.[152] In an attempt to destroy completely the spirit of the clergy, the state police enforced a strict screening of all priests based upon a detailed questionnaire,[153] the text of which follows:

I. Personal information concerning the cleric:

1. What are his relations with people? Does he readily mingle with people, or does he live a retired life? Has he any influence on public opinion? With what type of persons does he associate—reactionaries or progressives?
2. Does he seek material security and the quiet life?
3. What are his personal interests?
4. Does he regularly contact certain persons? Whom? Does he receive many people at his home? Does he often visit the same places?
5. Does he actively work among the faithful? Do they visit the parish house? Does he work with young people?
6. How does he fulfill his priestly functions? With zeal? With suitable interest? Or is he indifferent and negligent?
7. Who lives with him? What is the conduct of his personnel?
8. Is he loyal and open or is he a hypocrite?

II. Political information concerning the cleric:

1. Was he formerly interested in political questions?
2. Was he or is he a member of a party or of some popular organization and does he actually belong to it? Is he interested in political literature? Does he collaborate in some way with the Communist party or with other organizations of the National Front? Does he fulfill official duties?
3. How does he conduct himself with the working class and with the wealthy?
4. What is his environmental background?
5. What is his attitude toward the Soviet Union and the West?
6. What is his attitude toward the episcopate? Is he faithful to ecclesiastical authority in a fanatical way or does he adopt a critical attitude toward it? Has he difficulties with his superiors?
7. What is his attitude and position in regard to the Vatican and its policies?

III. EVALUATION OF THE POLITICAL LEANINGS OF THE CLERIC:

1. What was his political stand during the years of the First Republic, 1918-1938?
2. What was his behavior during the occupation? Did he have altercations with the Gestapo?
3. What was his political activity between May, 1945, and February, 1948?
4. What position did he take toward the events of February, 1948? What did he say on this subject? Did he accept a function and show that he was ready to collaborate with the National Front?
5. What did he have to say of the elections of May, 1948? Did he take part in the campaign in favor of the single list? How did he vote?
6. Did he give an opinion on the activities of the priests against the state and what was it? What was his conduct during the fall and winter of 1948?
7. Did he give his opinion on the proposed law of the incorporation of the clergy to the state, during the summer and fall of 1949?
8. How did he express himself in February, 1949, on the renewed relations between the government and the bishops? What was his conduct in 1949 during the campaign of the episcopate against the state?
9. What was his reaction to the emergence of the new Catholic Action? Did he sign the declaration of the Catholic Action or voice his loyalty? When and how did he revoke his loyalty to Catholic Action?
10. Did he take part in the episcopate's campaign against Catholic Action; if he did, in what way did he act against Catholic Action?
11. Did he read the pastoral letter on Corpus Christi, 1949? or during the following week? With or without comment? Or did he read it at all?
12. What is his judgment on the *Katolické Noviny* (a publication of the state Catholic Action to inform the Catholic population)? Does he recommend this newspaper or does he forbid it?
13. What is his attitude concerning the *Bulletin for the Catholic Clergy* edited by the Ministry of Education?
14. What was his position on the circular of the Catholic bishops which appeared in early June, 1949? What was his position on the emergence of Catholic Action? What was his opinion on the conduct of the episcopate and of Archbishop Beran?

15. How did he greet the decree of excommunication?
16. Was he ever imprisoned or fined? When and why? In what measure was the penalty carried out?
17. Did he take part in the campaign for signatures launched in the fall of 1949 by the vicars-general?
18. What did he say concerning the regulation of salaries before and after the discussion of this question in the parliament? Did he give an oral or written consent? Did he take part in the relative sessions of the parliament?
19. If he was ever punished with imprisonment or fine, did he seek amnesty later in October, 1949?
20. What was his reaction, November 1, upon first receipt of payment of his salary?
21. Did he sign the congratulatory address to Marshal Stalin and what was his conduct on this occasion?
22. What did he say relative to the budget prepared for the Church?[154]

From this text it is evident that this detailed classification of the mind of every priest would serve as a basis for respective measures in every given circumstance. This questionnaire determined the fate of every priest.

On January 19, 1951, the first congress of the "Defenders of Peace" was held in Prague, in which Zdeněk Fierlinger, Minister of the Bureau for Church Affairs, and Rev. Jos. Plojhar, Minister of Public Health, both made addresses strongly attacking the Catholic Church.[155] A delegation of the "patriotic" priests was present.

In 1951, all measures prepared by the government against clergymen were used to a greater extent. The more the persecution increased, the stronger and more severe and vigorous were the purges carried out among the Communist functionaries themselves,[156] men who until that time were in leading positions.[157] The trend of this development, directed by the Moscow Kremlin, is indicated in the arrests of Dr. Vládŏ Clementis,[158] Minister of Foreign Affairs; Mr. Šling,[159] deputy; Mrs. M. Šwerma,[160] deputy; Rudolf Slánsky,[161] secretary-general of the Communist party; Ladislav Kopřiva,[162] Minister of the State Police, and other powerful figures.[163] Other arrests or screenings occurred during 1952.[164]

An important trial in Prague on November 20, 1952, was held for some formerly very powerful figures in the Communist party in Czechoslovakia.[165] This is the consequence of political dictatorship, which eliminates by purges any personal opposition in its bid for power. This factor does not minimize the basic problem of Communists versus the Catholic Church, because "purged" or "deviating" or "governing" Communists remain the same in their opposition to the Church.[166]

The position of the Catholic Church became even more precarious as it became more apparent that Prague was only a branch of the Kremlin in Moscow, from which it received its orders. The best proof of the real situation during 1951 can be seen in the fact that over three thousand priests were arrested, two thousand of whom were placed in the "concentration camp monasteries," while many other priests were discharged from their positions, and over 70 per cent of the parish rectories were abandoned.[167] Secret police watched and intervened in all activities of faithful priests and laymen. The Communists sought to exercise control over every person[168] who favored some religious life or showed interest in the fate of the Catholic Church, or who in some way or other helped Catholic priests and bishops.

Through these experiences the Czechoslovak people were learning that democracy has a strong ally in the Catholic Church.[169] The Communists, however, did not respect the opinion of the citizens of Czechoslovakia and since 1951 have been openly boasting of having buried the Catholic Church.[170]

But the persecution of religion in Eastern and Central Europe and especially in Czechoslovakia[171] has been loyally and courageously resisted by the laity, priests, and bishops, and by the noble reaction of the Vatican. A struggle exists between the spiritual and the secular powers, a struggle that is just one part of that great, world-wide struggle.

CHAPTER TWELVE

THE REACTION OF THE VATICAN (ACCORDING TO THE DOCUMENTS ISSUED IN: ACTA APOSTOLICAE SEDIS)

THE STRUGGLE BETWEEN THE SPIRITUAL AND THE SECULAR powers in the Czechoslovak Republic had its beginning in the attacks on, and interference with, ecclesiastical affairs by the government. This evoked and even necessitated reaction by the Vatican. From the previous chapters it is apparent that the struggle for the sovereignty over the Catholic Church led in two directions. The Czechoslovak government had taken a view that the spiritual power is exclusively subordinated to the secular power of the state, and its acts were directed by this attitude. The Catholic Church, on the other hand, could not resign the sovereignty of her spiritual power, endeavoring only to adjust the life of the Church in Czechoslovakia in accordance with the *modus vivendi,*[1] already settled under the first Czechoslovak Republic (1928), and to achieve full respect for the jurisdiction exerted by the spiritual power of the Church.

The endless negotiations between the episcopate and the Czechoslovak government, as also pastoral letters of Czechoslovak bishops, are eloquent proof of this. On its part, the Czechoslovak Communist regime made all negotiations for the achievement of any agreement impossible. It wanted to enforce only that state of affairs in which the Church would be fully subjugated by the state. To achieve this, the state carried out its program in the following stages:

(a) From April, 1945, until the year 1948, a *modus vivendi* was tolerated, due to the influence of the coalition of noncommunistic parties of the government.

(b) Between February 25, 1948, and October 14, 1949,

the *modus vivendi* was repeatedly violated, and only regard for foreign public opinion and foreign policy kept it still alive.

(c) By the establishment of the State Bureau for Church Affairs (October 14, 1949) and by the issuance of corresponding laws, all sovereignty of Church power in Czechoslovakia was annihilated and subdued by a state power of force.

(d) Since 1950 theocracy by the state has been practically exercised, and the systematic persecution of the Catholic Church has accompanied the program.

Although some of the documents referred to in this chapter were mentioned on previous occasions they will bear a brief repetition for the sake of a unified treatment.

The Church defended herself by "the right of those who are attacked," as expressly stated by the Czechoslovak bishops in their pastoral letter of November 17, 1949.[2] She made her stand clear by every possible means until forced to keep silent. The voice of Czechoslovak Catholic bishops exerted its influence over the faithful, but since this voice was unbearable for the Communists, almost all of the bishops were eliminated.[3] Through the events of 1950 and 1951 the Iron Curtain had also fallen over the Catholic Church in Czechoslovakia. Behind the Iron Curtain, through the officials of the people's democratic regime, bishops as well as priests and the faithful fell victims.[4] The last diplomatic representative of the Vatican was expelled[5] so that Communists would not be disturbed in their work by his protests.

The Vatican devoted extraordinary attention to the struggle of Czechoslovak Catholics and showed its reaction in a very ready and strong answer. The semi-official press of the Vatican and the Vatican radio commented on this in the Bohemian language three times a week and in Slovak with the same regularity. *L'Osservatore Romano* and the Sacred Congregations intervened at opportune times, so that nobody could have any doubt that the sovereignty of ecclesiastical power was binding even on Czechoslovak Communists.

The first proof that the Vatican was not willing to discuss the principal matter, not even with Communists, was the *declaration* that the so-called "Catholic Action"[6] sponsored by the state was schismatic.[7] The decree of "excommunication"[8] distinguished a clear stand between Catholicism and communism and exposed to the public the great danger and evil of communism. It is interesting to note that this decree was issued immediately before Archbishop Beran of Prague excommunicated priests who were collaborating with communism. Through the *declaration*[9] concerning marriage with Communists, Catholics were directed to be careful not to endanger the Catholic family by Communist infection. This is an important proof of the antithetical nature of Catholicism toward communism in the official eyes of the Church. Even more: the Holy See paid great attention to youth, especially its education and spiritual progress. Therefore the Supreme Congregation of the Holy Office gave a special warning with regard to the bad conditions in which youth finds itself. The document bears the date of July 28, 1950, and reads as follows:

SUPREME CONGREGATION OF THE HOLY OFFICE

A Warning

It is widely known that associations have been organized under the impulse and the direction of the Communist party, for the purpose of inculcating on boys and girls principles and a doctrine which are drawn from materialism and attacking the Christian religion.

The faithful are hereby warned that such organizations, whatever the name they bear to hide their true identity, are the object of the penalties put in force by the decree of the Holy Office on July 1, 1948 (*AAS*, 41: 334):

1. As a result, parents or their substitutes, who, contrary to the prescription of canon 1372, paragraph 2 of Canon Law, and the above-mentioned decree of the Holy Office, entrust the education of their children to these organizations, may not be admitted to the reception of the Sacraments.

2. Those who will have taught boys and girls doctrines contrary to the faith or to Christian morality, incur the excommunication *speciali modo* reserved to the Holy See.

3. The children, boys as well as girls, may not be admitted to the sacraments during the entire period of their association with such organizations.

Given at Rome, Palace of the Holy Office, July 28, 1950.

MARINUS MARANI,
Notary of the Supreme Congregation of the Holy Office.[10]

Objection to the usurpation of the jurisdiction of the Church by the state was manifested in the case of Rev. John Dechet, through a decree of the Consistorial Congregation,[11] asking the faithful to abstain from any of his activities, thus demonstrating that such interferences of the secular power are entirely illegal and inadmissible. This stand was further emphasized by the decree of the Congregation of the Council of June 29, 1950, intended to impede more effectively any atheistic theocracy of the state. The text follows:

THE SACRED CONGREGATION OF THE COUNCIL

Decree: Concerning the canonical institution and the provision of ecclesiastical offices and benefices

The Catholic Church, by the institution of Christ Himself, is a perfect society founded on the hierarchy whose supreme rule and jurisdiction are in the possession of the Roman Pontiff successor to Saint Peter in the primacy. Wherefore no one can presume to take possession or give possession to others of ecclesiastical offices and benefices without legitimate canonical institution or provision.

The first rule of Canon Law in *VI°* already recalled the natural norm on this matter—'An ecclesiastical benefice cannot licitly be obtained without canonical institution.' And the Council of Trent decreed: 'They who are called and instituted only by the people or the secular power and office to exercise this office and who through their own temerity take it upon themselves, all these are to be considered not as ministers of the church but as ones who have not entered through the door but as thieves and robbers (Cap. IV, sess. XXIII, de reform.). Moreover the same Holy Synod defined: If anyone says that they who have been neither rightly ordained nor commissioned by the ecclesiastical and canonical power, but come from another source, are the legitimate ministers of the word and the Sacraments, let him be anathema (*Ibid.*, can. VII; cf. Syllab. Pii Pp. IX, n. 50).

Besides the Code of Canon Law sanctions these same principles by statutes and by penalties against the transgressors. (Cf. cc. 2331, § 2; 2334, 1°-2°; 147, §§ 1-2; 332, § 1; 2394.)

In order to restore, protect, and preserve the more these same sacrosanct principles and at the same time to be careful of abuses in a matter of such great importance, our Holy Father is obliged to decide:

They automatically incur the excommunication reserved in a special manner to the Apostolic See:

(1) who scheme against the legitimate ecclesiastical authorities or who try in any way to subvert their power;

(2) who occupy or allow themselves to be placed illegitimately in possession of an ecclesiastical office or benefice or dignity without canonical institution or provision according to the norm of the sacred canons;

(3) who take part in any manner, either directly or indirectly, in the crime mentioned in numbers 1 and 2.

Notwithstanding anything else, even that deserving of special mention.

Given at Rome, the twenty-ninth day of June, 1950.

I. CAROL. BRUNO, *Praefectus.*
F. ROBERTI, *a Secretis.*[12]

Such interferences by state power into the properly ecclesiastical affairs demonstrate the situation of the Catholic Church in Czechoslovakia. Only increasing persecution during the year 1951 effected the forced prevalence[13] of state power in this struggle.

On February 15, 1951, the state office's newly assigned so-called vicars-general and capitular vicars from all the dioceses of the Republic met in the National Club in Prague. The conference was attended by Zdeněk Fierlinger, Rev. J. Plojhar, the Slovak commissioners, Rev. Horák and Rev. Lukačovič, and representatives of the State Bureau for Church Affairs of Prague and Bratislava. At the speaker's desk were seated also the Auxiliary Bishop of Prague, Monsignor Antonín Eltschkner; the dean of the theological faculty in Prague, Rev. Adalbert Šanda; the dean of the theological faculty in Bratislava, Dr. Nicolas Višnovský; and Monsignor John Sobota of Poděbrady. The object of this consultation was the same as the former episcopal conferences.[14] But this was the first of its kind that indicated that episcopal conferences would be in the future replaced by conferences of "patriotic priests." Thereby it became evident that in the future no regard would be taken for the objections of Catholic bishops.

On February 13 four new residential canons were installed in the Cathedral of St. Wenceslaus in Olomouc: Rev. J. Glogar, Rev. Otakar Drtílek, Rev. Frank Kubíček, and Rev. Rud Havelka, and this in the presence of a representative of the State Bureau for Church Affairs, Mr. J. Dolek. The installation was accompanied by an oath of allegiance to the state regime.[15]

On February 28, 1951, the schismatic "Catholic Action" in Prague, sponsored by the state, held its annual meeting which was attended by "patriotic priests" from the Czech provinces, as also from Slovakia.[16] In all the addresses a close co-operation with the regime was accentuated; this same spirit characterized all the resolutions passed. These in turn were sent to the president and to all governmental officials.[17]

On February 28, in the Cathedral of Sts. Peter and Paul in Brno, in a solemn ceremony the vicar-general and canon Rev. Jos. Kristek and the canons Monsignor Jos. Toman, Rev. Dr. Frank Falkenauer, and Rev. Peter Franta were installed. According to the Czechoslovak press, this installation[18] was made with the approval of the Bishop Karel Skoupý of Brno.

On February 28 seven new canons were installed in the cathedral of Košice; in Spiš, the infamous Rev. Andreas Schafer became Capitular Vicar.[19]

In this way assignments to all ecclesiastical positions were made by the State Bureau for Church Affairs. The infiltration and influence of the Communist regime in Church affairs was accordingly still more strengthened and augmented.[20]

In the meantime some of the faithful bishops,[21] in their isolated and guarded residences,[22] as also in the jail,[23] were forcibly trained and prepared[24] to make addresses in favor of allegiance to the regime.[25]

Since the very courageous anti-Communist Prelate, Archbishop Joseph Beran, was considered by representatives of the regime an obstacle to their plans, the Communists forced through the following measures: on March 10, 1951, Archbishop Beran was banished from the Archdiocese of Prague.[26] According to the press, he was deported to the Castle Rožmital,[27] and later to Nová Říše,[28] having been even fined 50,000 crowns for his "negative stand toward new Church laws in Czechoslovakia."[29]

Since Archbishop Beran, according to the reports of the State Bureau for Church Affairs, "for his negative stand to the new church laws was condemned to pay a fine in virtue of an assessment by respective administrative officials on the ground of §§ 101 and 23 of the administrative criminal code, the office of the ordinariate in Prague has become vacant."[30] So the state declared.

Already on March 3 four new canons were assigned in Prague: Rev. Joseph Kubík, Rev. Antonín Stehlík, Rev. Oswald Novák and Rev. Francis Kotalík. The installation took place in the Cathedral of St. Vitus in Prague and was attended by the Auxiliary Bishop, Monsignor Antonín Eltschkner, by Monsignor Francis Onderek of Český Těšín, Monsignor Eduard Oliva; by Plíhal, substitute of the Minister of the State Office for Church Affairs, and by many deputies of the National Assembly.[31]

On March 8, 1951, a session of the metropolitan chapter of Saint Vitus was held. Having accepted the forced[32] resignation of the vicar-general, Monsignor Dr. Theofil Opatrný, the Rev. Antonín Stehlík was nominated from among the new canons capitular vicar in the Archdiocese of Prague.

In this way a *coup d'état*[33] in the affairs of the Catholic Church was carried out by the state power. All these measures, from the viewpoint of the Church, are void and invalid.[34]

The development and resolutions made in the case of Archbishop Beran are contrary to ecclesiastical regulations:

a. No secular power is entitled to punish members of the hierarchy. Canon 2214, §1: The Church has the innate and proper right, independent of all human authority, to punish her guilty subjects with both spiritual and temporal penalties.

b. The State Bureau of Church Affairs is not entitled to make any disposition of the rights of patronage. This right is illegally usurped. Canon 1453, §1: The personal right of patronage cannot validly be transferred to infidels, public apostates, heretics, and schismatics, who are enrolled in secret societies condemned by the Church, or to any person excommunicated by a declaratory or condemnatory sentence.

§2: The written consent of the Ordinary is required to transmit validly the personal right of patronage to others, due regard having been taken for the laws of foundation and the prescription of canon 1470, §1, n. 4.

§3: If anything, to which a real right of patronage is attached, is transferred to any of those persons mentioned in section one, the right of patronage remains suspended.

The right of patronage exerted by the state has no title for its existence, being in contradiction with canon 1450, § 1: No right to patronage can in future be validly constituted under any title. For this reason the Czechoslovak Catholic bishops protested already in their *Memorandum to the Government of the Czechoslovak Republic.*[35]

A declaration[36] by the State Bureau for Church Affairs in Prague that the ordinariate of Prague had become vacant was contrary to law:

(a) Archbishop Beran was deported by force, and by this fact alone every act lost its validity because, as provided for in the following canons, the see of Prague is not vacant. Neither is the Auxiliary, Bishop Eltschkner, his Vicar.

(b) An episcopal see becomes vacant by the death of the bishop, by his resignation accepted by the Roman Pontiff, by his transfer, and by the privation of his office after he is notified thereof. (Canon 430, § 1.)

(c) When the see is so embarrassed by the captivity, relegation, exile or incapacity of the bishop that he cannot communicate with his diocesans even by letter, the government of the diocese, unless the Holy See shall provide otherwise, shall be in the hands of the vicar-general or of some other ecclesiastic delegated by the Bishop. (Canon 429, § 1.)

Archbishop Beran, during the time in which he had been forcibly held a captive under house arrest, had as his legal substitute the vicar-general, Monsignor Theofil Opatrný, and no one else was delegated by him for the administration of the archdiocese.

The assignment therefore of the Rev. Ant. Stehlík as capitular vicar is unlawful, because:

(a) the archiepiscopal see in Prague has by no means become vacant;

(b) the functioning of a capitular vicar presupposes a canonical vacancy of the seat;

(c) whoever assumes the government of the diocese as above provided shall as soon as possible inform the Holy See of the fact that the see is embarrassed and that he has taken charge (Canon 429, § 4);

(d) there was no reason to assign a capitular vicar, since there was a vicar-general, Monsignor Theofil Opatrný;

(e) the capitular vicar should be a doctor or licentiate in theology or in canon law, or at least well versed in these sciences; his character must be blameless, and he must possess piety and soundness of doctrine combined with prudence. (Canon 434, § 2.)

The resignation of the vicar-general, Monsignor Theofil Opatrný, was in this case contrary to canon law, since only Archbishop Beran was authorized to accept it; and this was not the case. If Monsignor Opatrný resigned and his resignation was accepted by the new chapter, this serves only to indicate the great pressure which was used to carry out the whole *coup d'état* against the Catholic Church in Czechoslovakia. The new canons were assigned by secular power because the true canons, Monsignor Josef Čihák, Dr. Otakar Švec, and Dr. Jaroslav Kulač, had been imprisoned. Since the provisions of canon law were not respected in this case, there is no doubt that these assignments are totally void, unlawful, and null.[37] Even if, according to the notions of the State Office for Church Affairs, the archiepiscopal see were vacant, the appointment of the new canons by the state is contrary to canon law (canon 436): "During the vacancy no innovations shall be made."

Likewise, against the will of Bishop Hlouch, the State Bureau for Church Affairs assigned new canons to the cathedral in Budějovice, and installed on March 15, Rev. Frank Čech, Rev. Francis Gabriel, and Rev. Al. Titman.[38]

The question of assignment of new canons in Slovakia was solved in virtue of a compromise by Bishop Ambroze Lazík of Trnava who installed, on March 23, Rev. Leopold Adamček, Rev. Josef Greguška, Rev. Nicolas Višnovský, Rev. Ladislav Mogyprossy, Rev. Cyril Dudas, Monsignor Pavol Macháček, Rev. Stěfan Zarecký, and Rev. Karol Czokaš.[39]

A very special case occurred in Litoměřice. On July 12, Monsignor Stěpán Trochta, Bishop of the Litoměřice diocese, carried out the solemn installation of Monsignor Edward Oliva, vicar-general of the diocese, as Provost Capitular in St. Stephen's Cathedral of Litoměřice, of which the installed was the first canon.[40] Monsignor Oliva, a "patriotic priest," was earlier appointed by the state as vicar-general while Bishop Trochta was under arrest. Later the same bishop promoted him to become his own "commissar."[41]

Against these and previous infringements on ecclesiastical affairs, the Vatican reacted by the following declaration of the Sacred Congregation of the Consistory:[42]

Sacred Consistorial Congregation

Declaration

For many months past and in many unheard-of ways, the Church's rights in the Republic of Czechoslovakia have been attacked unjustly: namely, local ordinaries have been impeded in the performances of their functions; their pastoral rights have been usurped; even the office of the curia, as well as the ecclesiastical benefices, have been bestowed upon intruding persons at the decision of laymen who presumed to mingle in the government of the dioceses.

Moreover, freedom has been taken away from many of the clergy and religious; some bishops, with impious boldness, were dragged before a lay judge and imprisoned; recently, His Excellency, Josef Beran of Prague, after having been held captive under house arrest for a long time and entirely hindered in the exercise of jurisdiction, has been most wickedly banished from his See and Archdiocese.

Against those who carried out such crimes there are many sacred canons, by which they automatically incur excommunication, reserved simply or in a special manner to the Apostolic See according to the differences of circumstances:

a. those who dare to cite a bishop before a lay judge (Can. 2341);
b. those who lay violent hands on the person of an archbishop or bishop (Can. 2343, § 3);
c. those who either directly or indirectly impede the exercise of ecclesiastical jurisdiction, having recourse for that purpose to any lay authority (Can. 2334, § 2);
d. those who contrive against lawful ecclesiastical authorities, or in any way strive to overthrow their power (Dec. S.C. Concilii Diei 29 Junii 1950; *AAS*, Vol. XXXXII, anno 1950, p. 601);
e. those who occupy ecclesiastical office or benefice or dignity, without institution or canonical provision, made according to the norm of the sacred canons; or permit someone to obtain them unlawfully or hold them.

Therefore, the Sacred Consistorial Congregation declares that all those who have concurred either physically or morally to carry out the forementioned crimes, or have cooperated in them, according to Can. 2208, §§ 1-3, have incurred the enumerated excommunications and they will remain subjected to them until they obtain acquittal from the Holy See.

Given at Rome, from the Sacred Consistorial Congregation, on March 17, 1951.

Fr. A. I. Card. Piazza, Ep Sabinen et Mandelen. a Secretis, L. S.

I. FERRETTO, *Assessor*.[43]

This declaration makes it clear that the Catholic Church never resigned the rights which belong to her by divine authority. It exposes her basic stand and principles, proving[44] that the *coup d'état* in Church affairs which had been carried out by the State Bureau for Church Affairs was unlawful from the viewpoint of canon law.

This document of the Holy See evoked a very strong and favorable echo in Czechoslovak public opinion. *L'Osservatore Romano*[45] commented on it.

In the face of this declaration of the Holy See, strange indeed must have appeared the announcement of March 12, 1951, to the effect that the highest representatives of the Catholic Church in Czechoslovakia, Monsignor Mořic Pícha, Bishop of Hradec Králové; Monsignor Josef Čarský, Bishop and apostolic administrator of Košice; Monsignor Stěpán Trochta, Bishop of Litoměřice; Monsignor Ambroze Lazík, Bishop and apostolic administrator of Trnava; Monsignor Francis Onderek, Apostolic administrator in Česky Těšin, and Reverend Antonín Stehlík, the new "capitular vicar" in Prague had made an oath of allegiance to the people's democratic Republic. The Slovak bishop, Most Reverend Josef Čarský, in the name of the dignitaries just mentioned is reported to have declared among other things:

> We know our responsibility which we have as ecclesiastical dignitaries, before God and the nation. Allow us to declare in a solemn way that all of us recognize the validity of state laws. . . . We do not recognize ecclesiastical penalties and we will not punish our clergymen and the faithful, if these penalties are imposed for political reasons. We will endeavor to establish forever a good relationship between Church and state. We will support the efforts of our working people and of our people's democratic order, because we all see that this endeavor serves the general welfare

and that it is in full harmony with the moral principles of our Holy Church. We sincerely welcome every endeavor of our people to preserve peace in the world.[46]

The text itself of this declaration seems to suggest, as the Vatican later indicated, that it was not made freely, because evidently a Catholic bishop could not declare, when speaking freely, that "ecclesiastical penalties will not be recognized" and the "efforts of the Czechoslovak people and of our people's democratic order are in full harmony with the moral principles of our Holy Church." The fact that this declaration seems to have been gained by force and terror should be accentuated all the more, due to the fact that Bishop Čarský and the aforesaid bishops were the most courageous in their previous stand.[47] This declaration contradicts all the provisions of ecclesiastical law as well as the dogmatic principles of the Catholic Church, which just and upright bishops worked strenuously to teach and to enforce.[48] It parallels the similar alleged admissions of Cardinal Mindszenty in the Budapest trial.[49]

To understand this surprising stand of the aforesaid bishops, it is advisable to add an explanation. Communists, as it is clear from their practice, as illustrated in previous chapters, always try to cover up their most undemocratic methods, and by propaganda methods seek to create a seemingly lawful basis for their supposedly democratic liberty. To this aim they use all possible means such as trials, the whole structure[50] of which has a tendency to justify their revolutionary and violent putsches, purges, and actions. Especially self-accusations[51] on the part of those who are on trial always favoring the Communists and disfavoring themselves, is a proof that the trials are intended only as a guise for Communistic justice and democracy.[52] This phenomenon itself is psychologically unnatural and seems to indicate an unfree procedure in Communistic trials.[53] This policy is systematically practiced not only in politics but above all in ecclesiastical matters affecting the international form. It is sad to hear of forced self-accusations and statements of some bishops or priests by which Communists pretend to display justice, although nobody believes them.

Since the Communists themselves know that only the

bishops govern in the Catholic Church,[54] and that by Divine Institution,[55] they concentrated all their attacks against the bishops, and that by a double method: (1) they endeavored by every means to coerce the bishops to collaborate with the people's democratic regime, thereby making them tools of the regime; (2) in case they were unsuccessful in eliminating them entirely, they used every means at their disposal to compel the bishops during the year 1950 both psychologically and tactically to make every conceivable concession.[56] But this was conceivably not enough for the Communists. Their aim was to coerce bishops to take a positive stand in favor of the people's democratic regime; and for this purpose they resorted to even violent provisions and methods.[57] In this regard it is necessary to accentuate to the honor of the Czechoslovak bishops that not one of them except Auxiliary Bishop Eltschkner of Prague[58] and Bishop Pobožný of Rožnava[59] lent themselves to the collaboration with the Communists. The official and firm stand of all the other bishops expressed in their many memoranda in pastoral letters[60] issued individually or jointly from their meetings is a great testimony to their fidelity as careful and courageous guardians of the rights of the Catholic Church, such as will redound to their favor for all times.

From the direct written protocols of the refugee Czech and Slovak priests[61] collected in the CML Archives in London and by *Veritas* of Mariazell in Austria and of Rome, and partly published in many newspapers and periodicals, as e.g., by *Nový Život, Katolík, Národ, Vinculum, Hlas z Československa, Zpravodaj, Dobrý Pastier,* and in NCWC news release, Washington, D. C., and in *Kipa* (Switzerland), in reports over the Vatican radio and especially in Free Europe in Munich (Germany) in *la Documentation catholique and Civiltà Cattolica* it seems evident that violent methods were used against the Czechoslovak Bishops.

The cruel fate of the Greek Catholic bishops Theodor Romža of Mukačevo,[62] Pavol Gojdič[63] of Prešov, and his Auxiliary Bishop Basil Hopko[64] became the overture of the persecution of Roman Catholic bishops, against which the Communists used tactics to obviate their great popularity with the people. They isolated them in residences which they completely controlled, forbidding any kind of contact with clergy and people. After this isolation, all bishops except Archbishop Joseph Beran of Prague, Archbishop Joseph Matocha of Olomouc, Bishop Skoupý of Brno, and Bishop Joseph Hlouch of Budějovice were put in jails where they were prepared by violent means and even by drugs[65] to make the declaration of March 12, 1951. This refers especially to the following bishops: Stěpán Trochta, Bishop of Litoměřice, Mořic Pícha, Bishop of Hradec Králové, Bishop Ambrose Lazík of Trnava, and Bishop Joseph Čarský, Apostolic Administrator of Košice. Later also, Bishop Necsey of Nitra made an oath of allegiance to the regime[66] due to pressure brought to bear against him on the ground of past public activities.

If we consider further that Auxiliary Bishop Stanislav Zela of Olomouc, Bishop Vojtaššak of Spiš, and Auxiliary Bishop Buzalka of Trnava were eliminated by the famous trials in Prague and in Bratislava as early as at the beginning of 1951, the situation of Czechoslovak bishops after this declaration became tragic. Great pressure was brought to bear also upon other bishops, e.g., Bishop Skoupý of Brno.[67] In the meantime, Bishop Hlouch of Budějovice, who like Archbishop Beran of Prague was later banished from his diocese, and Archbishop Matocha of Olomouc resisted heroically without any compromises.

The Communists made profit of this desolate situation of the bishops and tried to force them more and more to make proclamations[68] in favor of the people's democratic regime. They hoped thereby to make an impress of a legal nature in ecclesiastical matters, although already by 1952 it was evident that they no longer needed the bishops since "figure heads" in the form of the so-called capitular and general vicars from the ranks of patriotic priests governed the various dioceses—always, of course, under the supervision of state commissioners. The Vatican radio itself gave instructions to the priests and people in Czechoslovakia to be careful of the proclamations of bishops because of the confused situation.[69] Even signatures of bishops were falsified.[70] All new proclamations of bishops thereafter had to be accepted with caution because we know from previous chapters that the signatures of many hundreds of priests in connection with the so-called Catholic Action and the Church Laws of October 14, 1949, were not authentic. Loyal priests protested against these abuses, but the bishops could not take even this course because of their complete isolation.

Substantially nothing was changed in the latter's resistance to the Communist regime, and if they endeavored to make some agreement with the people's democratic regime they did so in accordance with the Vatican's intentions and regulations as already expressed by Pius XI in his well-known encyclical *Ubi Arcano Dei* of 1922.[71] It was once necessary for the Catholic Church to live in catacombs. And thus even today the bishops must strive to govern their churches, even though living—to use a biblical expression—in a "den of lions"[72] as in Czechoslovakia.

The report declaring that on March 19, 1951, the ordinaries of Prague had granted to Rev. Jos. Plojhar "permission to celebrate Mass" created a consternation.[73]

It was said that his *celebret* was issued on the ground of a declaration made by bishops and ordinaries involving repeal of his religious suspension imposed by Archbishop Beran on June 15, 1949.[74] The Communist Czechoslovak press looked upon this (false) rumor as a justification of Plojhar's actions.[75]

The Vatican radio countered very strongly on March 29 when it declared among other things:

> The Catholic Church is determined to continue in her resistance against totalitarian pressure and terror by the Communist regime. Only a few priests betrayed the Church of Christ either from human weakness or from vanity and secular ambitions.
>
> Regarding the report that permission has been granted to Plojhar to celebrate Holy Mass, it is necessary to mention that such a repeal of ecclesiastical censure is nonsense and that a decision of this kind is invalid, since it concerns a priest who has been excommunicated and who, in virtue of his excommunication, is excluded from exercising all spiritual religious functions. As to the pledge of allegiance made by some ordinaries, judgment for the time being must be reserved until the bishops concerned can come freely in contact with their head. The true faithful will not attend any acts performed by excommunicated priests who do not serve God but atheistic communism.
>
> The faithful will remain true to their real ecclesiastical leaders, personified by Archbishop Beran, who, having been

banished from his archdiocese for his loyalty to the Church, must suffer in jail. Beran belongs to the greatest men in the history of the Church and good priests will follow his heroic example.[76]

Because of the critical situation arising from the fact that several bishops took the oath of allegiance to the existing Communist government, there arose serious danger for the authority of the Church. Realizing also the danger of a new schism that might arise, the Sacred Congregation of the Holy Office on April 9, 1951, issued the following decree:

THE SACRED CONGREGATION OF THE HOLY OFFICE

Decree:

Concerning the Consecration of a Bishop without Canonical Provision.

The Sacred Congregation of the Holy Office, by the special faculty given it by the Sovereign Pontiff, publishes this decree:

The Bishop, of whatever rite or dignity, who consecrates to the episcopacy some one neither nominated by the Apostolic See nor expressly confirmed by it, and he who receives the consecration, even though they are coerced by grave fear (c. 2229, § 3, 3°), incur automatically the excommunication reserved in a very special manner to the Apostolic See.

This decree takes effect on the very day of its promulgation.

Given at the Holy Office, the ninth day of April, 1951.

MARINUS MARANI,
Notary of the Supreme Congregation of the Holy Office.[77]

This decree is a very important memorandum to every bishop and a strong reminder to them to be firm in all circumstances that might arise.

Compromising acts made by some Catholic bishops, as for instance by Monsignor Ambroze Lazík, Monsignor R. Pobožný, and Monsignor Stěpán Trochta, can be explained by reasons of utmost emergency, in order that Catholic priests might not be pitted against them through the tactics of Communists and that complete influence of so-called patriotic priests sponsored by the state be prevented. In this way can be explained and conceived also why, for instance, the Bishop of Brno, Monsignor Karel Skoupý, rather approved some new canons for the Cathedral of Brno or why Monsignor Lazík installed canons himself in Bratislava, namely, to prevent full infiltration by "patriotic priests."

The Vatican even endeavored to maintain diplomatic relations with Czechoslovakia, despite all unwarranted intrusions into the activities of Monsignor Verolino by the state police, and of Monsignor Bertoli who was assigned as his successor but was refused an entry visa. Monsignor de Liva remained in Prague until he was expelled by the police at the airport Prague-Rome. Thereby diplomatic relations with the Holy See were definitely broken off. The Vatican had done its level best to co-operate with the Czechoslovak government, but in vain. Even if in accordance with St. Paul[78] the Church is not bound by any form of government, she cannot, for that reason, resign her sovereignty in ecclesiastical matters. The sovereignty of secular power is not and cannot be unlimited; on the contrary, it must be restricted so that the sovereignty of the Church in ecclesiastical matters remain untrammeled as defined by Christ. To attain this aim and to defend her rights—these were the reasons for the just and rightful struggle of the Church in Czechoslovakia.

Co-operation between state and Church is, of course, an ideal envisioned and desired by the Church. In past years the Church's viewpoint has been set forth frequently, stressing the peculiar urgency of the problem in our times. Pope Pius XII, considering the aims and policies of states the world over and making special reference to those states now veiled by the Iron Curtain, reiterated this position of the Church in his allocution of Christmas Eve, 1951.[79] Therein he presented a clear analysis of this important question which is, in point of fact, the underlying reason for the present chaotic relations between Church and state in so many regions. The Holy Father said in part:

> Statesmen, and at times even churchmen, who want to make the Spouse of Christ their ally or the instrument of their political alliances, either national or international, would do injury to the very essence of the Church and would inflict

damage on the life which is proper to her; in a word, they would bring her down to the same level on which conflicting temporal interests are locked in struggle. And this is and remains true, even where there is question of ends and interests legitimate in themselves.

Whoever, then, would wish to detach the Church from her supposed neutrality, or bring pressure to bear on her in the question of peace, or diminish her right freely to determine whether, when, or how she may wish to come to a decision in the various conflicts, such a one would not make the Church's co-operation in the work of peace easier. For any decision on the Church's part, even in political questions, can never be purely political, but must always be *sub specie aeternitatis*, in the light of the divine law, of its order, its values, its standards.

It is not rare to see purely temporal powers and institutions abandon their neutrality and align themselves today in one camp, tomorrow perhaps in another. It is a game of alliances which can be explained by the constant shifting of temporal interests. But the Church keeps herself aloof from such unstable alliances. If she passes judgment, that does not mean that she is thereby abandoning a neutrality hitherto observed; for God is never neutral toward human events in the course of history, and so neither can His Church be. If she speaks and judges on the problems of the day, it is with the clear consciousness of anticipating in the power of the Holy Spirit the sentence which at the end of time her Lord and Head, judge of the universe, will confirm and sanction.

Such is the proper and superhuman function of the Church regarding political questions. What, then, is the meaning of that empty phrase about a neutrality which the Church should abandon?

The Church does not judge according to purely political norms.

Others, on the contrary, in the interests of peace, demand the neutrality of the Church. But neither have these a correct idea of the place of the Church in the midst of the world's great events. She cannot come down from the lofty supernatural sphere where political neutrality has no meaning, in the sense in which this concept is applied to earthly powers. This does not exclude, but rather increases, her share in the toils and sufferings of her divided members in either camp, and intensifies her grief at the clash of opinions and desires in her own ranks.

The Church cannot consent to judge according to exclusively political norms; she cannot tie the interests of religion to particular policies of a purely earthly scope; she cannot run the risk of giving any reason for doubt about her religious character; she cannot forget for an instant that her role of representative of God on earth does not permit her to remain indifferent, even for a single moment, between "good" and "evil" in human affairs. If that were asked of her, she would have to refuse, and the faithful on both sides would, in virtue of their supernatural faith and hope, have to understand and respect her stand.

The Church is not a political, but a religious society. That, however, does not prevent her from assuming not merely external, but internal and vital relations with states. The Church has in fact been founded by Christ as a society that is visible, and, as such, meets states in the same territory, embraces in her solicitude the same people, and in many ways, and under different aspects, makes use of the same means and the same institutions.

And since the Church and the states live together, there are, besides these external and what might be called natural relations, others, too; interior and vital relations, which have their principle and origin in the person of Jesus Christ as Head of the Church. For the Son of God, by becoming man, and truly man, has by that very fact entered into a new relationship, a truly vital relationship, with human society, with human nature. And this is true whether we consider human nature a single unit implying equal personal dignity in all men, or human nature as found in multiple particular societies, especially those societies which, within the fundamental unity of human nature, are necessary to effect, or at least to perfect, external order and sound organization.

And here we have in mind primarily the family and the state, as well as the society of states, since the common good, the essential purpose of every state, cannot be attained or even imagined without the intrinsic relation of the states to the human race as a whole. Under this aspect the indissoluble union of states is demanded by nature. It is a fact which is imposed upon them. And in consent to it, although sometimes hesitantly, they answer the voice of nature. This natural union they strive to embody in an external stable framework, an organization.

As human experience teaches them, the state and the society of states, with its external organization, in spite of all their defects, are naturally, given the social nature of man, forms of union and order among men; they are necessary for human life; they contribute to its perfection. Their very concept involves the tranquillity of order, that *tranquillitas ordinis* which St. Augustine gives as a definition of peace. These societies of their very essence exist for peace.

With them, as societies which exist for maintaining peace, Jesus Christ, the Prince of Peace—and with Him the Church in whom He continues to live—has entered into a new and intimate relationship which elevates and strengthens society. This is the basis for the singular contribution which the Church, by her very nature, makes to the cause of peace—that is, when her life and her action among men occupy the place that is their due.

And how will all this come about, except through the continuous enlightening and strengthening action of the Grace of Christ on the minds and hearts of citizens and statesmen, so that in all human relationships they recognize and pursue the purposes of the Creator, that they strive to enlist the collaboration of individuals and nations for effecting these purposes, that within as well as among nations they practice social justice and charity.

If men, obeying the Divine Will, will use that sure way of salvation, a perfect Christian order in the world, they will soon see the possibility of even a just war practically disappear. For there will be no reason for such a war, once the activity of the society of states, as a genuine organization for peace, is made secure.[80]

With this appeal for genuine co-operation between Church and state, the Pope not only solves the question of peace for the world, but also shows how that peace may be attained. It is an indirect answer to the Communist interpretations of the "Stockholm resolution for peace" and various propaganda actions of their so-called defenders of peace.

To stress this contrast between the real stand of communism and the Church, the decree of excommunication demonstrates that the struggle which we are expounding was not a fight only between the state and hierarchy; it was also the struggle between the Communistic regime and the Catholic faithful as such.[81] When we consider that in Czechoslovakia seventy-five per cent of the population is Catholic, we can easily realize that the Communist rulers were frightened by the resistance of Catholics, as appeared from the occasional speeches of the state ministers. They were not sure about their influence over their own fellow travelers and, therefore, they accentuated nationalism as the substance of Czechoslovak Communist activities, accusing the Church of reactionary activities and of high treason.

The Pope strengthened the Czechoslovak Catholics in their struggle by consoling them in their suffering. He let them realize that he understood their endeavors, and that he was very much concerned about their sad fate. In this sense all Czechoslovaks in exile or at home were overjoyed by the Pope's friendly address to the archbishops, bishops, faithful and all Czechoslovak people, dated October 28, 1951, in commemoration of the memorable day of Czechoslovak independence. This apostolic letter, with its beautiful contents, excited the attention of foreign newspapers.[82] It reads as follows:

> To Our Venerable Brothers the Archbishops and Bishops, and to Our beloved sons of the clergy and laity of the Republic of Czechoslovakia having peace and communion with the Apostolic See.
>
> With greater intensity does Our affection embrace those who are living in hardships and in difficult conditions, particularly when such sufferings derive from their unwavering fidelity and their ardent love for the Divine Redeemer and for the Church which He founded. It deeply grieves Our heart to know that you are numbered amongst those sufferers.
>
> There is nothing more glorious in your history than the Catholic religion, nothing more suited to bring about concord or to consolidate peace, to promote justice and charity, to safeguard human dignity or to advance civilization. Yet We know that unfortunately the Catholic religion is at present either denied its rightful liberty, or it is obstructed by difficulties and obstacles of all kinds, to such an extent that it is almost impossible for it to fulfill its mission properly, to promulgate laws in public or in private, to exert openly its beneficent influence on the minds of individuals, on the family, on the school, and on all classes of society—that beneficent influence which contributes so much to the common good. We know that amongst you there are Bishops who have been imprisoned or thrown into concentration

camps, confined to their residences or subjected to an unceasing surveillance and control even in the discharge of the duties of their office.

In the same lamentable conditions are to be found hundreds of priest, religious and nuns; and a great number of lay people who, because they tenaciously uphold, strongly defend and strive to put into practice the precepts and teachings of the Catholic Church, are regarded as destructive and subversive enemies of the state. But this redounds to their honor and not to their shame: for Christian teaching, when it is uncontaminated by error, is not opposed to the good of citizens, of peoples or of nations, but rather does it consolidate, reinforce and confirm the foundations of human society; it equitably regulates rights and duties and, while safeguarding the liberty of everybody, it calls and leads all to peaceful and undisturbed prosperity, under the protection of true justice.

Catholics, without any doubt whatsoever, yield to no one in their love of the fatherland, in their observance of public laws and in their respect for public authority, provided that nothing is commanded to them which violates their Christian conscience or the rights of the Church. Wherefore they—if the true good of the nation is being promoted—should not be hampered, nor should they be unjustly punished for their tenacious fidelity to their ancestral religion, but they should have the possibility of freely and openly professing their faith and their way of thought, teaching and life. And in striving to do this, despite the very great dangers which threaten them, they win the admiration not only of the whole Catholic world but of all men of good will.

But that which causes Us the greatest anxiety of heart is that every guile is being used to induce youths and young children to abandon the Christian faith and Christian morals, in order that they may be deprived of those principles and norms which guide their formative years and which constitute the safeguard of innocence, the food of virtue, and make them citizens worthy of the name of Catholic. You see, Venerable Brethren and beloved children, what an important matter We are treating: if youth does not walk the straight path, but, deprived of the light that comes from on high, succumbs to the gratification of the passions, then, without doubt, they will do harm not only to themselves but also to your future generations.

For this reason, every effort should be made to avoid

such a lamentable calamity, and to see that young children grow healthy and upright in their habits, and that they are carefully educated in accordance with the norms of Christian teaching which alone can preserve them immune from so many evils and incite them to virtue. Above all, We earnestly exhort fathers and mothers of families not to spare any efforts or attention in this matter, as to them above all, in these conditions, falls the duty of making good with all diligence the work which priests and teachers are prevented from doing.

Another matter also afflicts Our heart. We are well aware of the efforts that are being made, through accusations falsely represented as true or by means of open calumny, to drag the faithful away from the unity of the Catholic Church, and, if it were possible, from its very center, that is, from this Apostolic See. The Roman Pontiff is represented as an enemy of your people, when on the contrary he is their most loving father; the point is reached where he is accused of preparing a new and more terrible war, when in reality, after having made every effort to alleviate the wretchedness and sufferings of the last conflict, he now lets no opportunity pass to promote brotherhood and peace among all peoples.

Nevertheless, Venerable Brethren and beloved children, let no one lose heart on account of extreme difficulties of this kind; above all, let not the sacred pastors lose heart, whose duty it is, as a special office accredited to them by God, to nourish the faith of their flock, to uphold their courage and to strengthen the bond of union between them and this Apostolic See. Already, during the course of centuries, your people have overcome other and most extreme difficulties. More than once in times past your ancestors have been obliged to choose between martyrdom sustained with strength and treachery to the faith of their forefathers; but with invincible spirits they clung to their Catholic religion, and sometimes confessed it by shedding their very blood.

The ancient glories of your people are well known to you; emulate them with soul undefiled, relying on the firm hope that, when error has been overthrown and the due liberty of the Church restored, then at last the example of such fidelity and fortitude will be set forward for the admiration of all.

Remember this above all else: men can rob you of your liberty, they can afflict you with torments, they can subject you to public derision, they can cast you into prison, they can even put you to death; but they can never pluck the Catholic faith from your breasts nor sully your conscience. They will be able to make martyrs if they wish; but they will not—thus We trust, so do We ask of God with suppliant prayers—be able to make traitors to the Christian religion, provided that all with resolute will persevere in their obedience to the laws of God and the Church.

May those Saints in whom your people glory assist you from Heaven in this present struggle: SS. Cyril and Methodius, who, so it is related, succeeded by enduring tremendous labors and by travelling enormous distances, in bringing the light of the Gospel to you and to the other Slavic peoples; St. Adalbert, who made your lands fertile by his apostolic toil and who constitutes for all ages a most striking example of fidelity to the Apostolic See; St. John Nepomucene, who in defense of the rights of the Church and the protection of the sacramental seal underwent martyrdom with heroic strength; the martyrs of Košice, who were solemnly beatified as courageous champions of Christ by Our Predecessor Blessed Pius X; St. Wenceslaus, who confirmed his faith with his blood, and his grandmother, St. Ludmilla, who, in this grave moment, constitutes for the mothers of families an example of strength of soul in the Christian education of children, and finally, innumerable others who shone in your midst with the splendor of their sanctity.

But, above all, may the Virgin Mother of God who, as she has been in the past and is in the present, will, without doubt, be also in the future the most sure defense of all your people, assist you benignly with her powerful protection. She, who with burning devotion is honored among you in so many sanctuaries, most loving Mother that she is, will not fail to obtain for you from her only-begotten Son the necessary help of which you have so great need in these times. Already on other occasions, she has done this; We implore her that, invoked by so many prayers, she may deign to do so again in this our age, when evil and the assaults of the impious against religion, which keep Our soul in such anxiety, are no less terrible.

May there be everywhere restored to the Church that due liberty which she uses in order to promote the progress of civil society itself and to consolidate its foundations. May those who, in order to defend their faith, have been thrown into prison, and those who live in concentration camps, be able finally to return to their homes and there lead a tranquil life in the free exercise of their religion. May there return that peace and concord of citizens and of all peoples, wherein the proper rights and dignity of the Church, of nations and of individuals will be recognized. May this true peace, founded on truth, on justice and on charity, that peace which Jesus Christ came to bring to men of good will (Luke 2:14) soon gladden you and all men.

We have, during the past month of September, exhorted the Catholic world, by means of the Encyclical Letter, *Ingruentium Malorum*, to gain those goals in union of prayer. Now, in this letter, We turn in a particular way to you, most Venerable Brethren and beloved children, paternally inviting you to implore the protection of the Virgin Mother Mary to grant you divine consolations and most copious aid. May the Divine Redeemer, without Whom We can do nothing and with Whom all is possible, in answer to His mother's supplications, and in His infinite mercy, graciously and speedily hear Our prayers and Our wishes, to which are joined your petitions and those of the whole Catholic world.

Know that Our fervent love and Our paternal affections are ever with you, and that your sufferings are also Ours; nor ever forget that your anguish and your sorrows are benevolently received by God, Who transforms them into a rain of heavenly graces.

Meanwhile, in token of divine favor, and as a pledge of Our most particular benevolence, We impart, from the fullness of Our Heart, to all of you Venerable Brethren and beloved children, and especially to those "who suffer persecution for justice's sake" (Matt. 5:10) the Apostolic Benediction.

Given at Rome from St. Peter's, this twenty-eighth day of October, 1951, the Feast of Christ the King, and in the thirteenth year of Our Pontificate.

PIUS PP. XII[83]

The encyclical letter *Orientales Ecclesias* and the above apostolic letter to the Bishops of Czechoslovakia are important documents, not only because of their paternal tone showing the Holy Father's anxiety about the sorrowful fate of the Catholic faithful in Czechoslovakia, but also because they are historical documents evidencing the urgency of the times—the Iron Curtain must be lifted not only for enslaved Czechoslovakia, but for all the satellite countries as well. The freedom so desired for all should be given to all, for to be free once more is the unanimous wish of all of these nations.[84] The Holy Father paid especial attention to the persecution of the oriental churches, including those of the Greek Catholic Church in Czechoslovakia, and rewarded them for their fidelity to Rome by the special encyclical letter *Orientales Ecclesias* under date of December 15, 1952.[85] Therein their tragic fate under Communist domination is documented. The text reads as follows:

> The Oriental Churches, rendered illustrious by the doctrine of the Holy Fathers, and bathed by the blood of martyrs in ancient times, in more recent ages, and also in our own day, have always formed in a special manner the object of Our solicitude, a fact which is known to all.
>
> Indeed, as soon as We, without any merit of Our own, but through the inscrutable design of God, were raised to the Chair of the Prince of the Apostles, We turned Our mind and heart to you, and to those also who "find themselves outside the Catholic Church" (Cf. Radio message, March 3, 1939; *AAS*, XXXI [Ser. II, Vol. IV], p. 86), and who We ardently desire may return as soon as possible to the fold of the Common Father, the abode of their ancestors (Cf. Encyclical *Summi Pontificatus; AAS*, XXXI [Ser. II, Vol. VI], pp. 418-419; and Encyclical *Mystici Corporis; AAS*, XXXV [Ser. II, Vol. X], pp. 242-243).
>
> We have given you other proofs of Our paternal benevolence during the course of Our Pontificate. As is known to you, We have conferred the dignity of the Roman purple on another of your Bishops, the Patriarch of the Armenians of Cilicia, and We are providing for the codification of the canonical laws which affect you: a work of the greatest importance, and one which is already in part completed.
>
> But it is not necessary to speak at length of matters without doubt already well known to you; as for the rest, We have followed in the footsteps of Our predecessors (Cf. Encyclical *Rerum Orientalium; AAS*, XX, pp. 277 ff.), who from the very first days of Christianity not only surrounded your ancestors with a particular affection, but were accustomed besides to grant them all possible aid on every occasion when they were besieged by heresy or groaned under the terror and persecutions of enemies.
>
> Thus it was that through the Apostolic Authority entrusted to the Prince of the Apostles and to His Successors by the Divine Redeemer, the Roman Pontiffs defended the

integrity of Catholic doctrine in the First and Second Councils of Nicea, in the First, Second and Third of Constantinople, and in those of Ephesus and Chalcedon; and when a lamentable dissension separated a great part of the Oriental Churches from Rome, they not only reproved it through their Legates in the Fourth Council of Constantinople, but they exerted themselves in every manner possible in order that, in the common interest, the situation might happily be resolved. After numerous praiseworthy and difficult efforts, they were able to do this in the Council of Florence, although against the hopes of all good men the deliberations taken were not afterward put into practice.

Again when the Eastern regions were invaded by new peoples who devastated even the sacred places of Palestine, consecrated by the Divine Blood of Jesus Christ, the Roman Pontiffs then urged the Christian Princes to the great undertaking of the defense of religion. Nor has this eager solicitude and this benevolence of Our Predecessors toward your fellow-countrymen become less in intensity or diminished in Our day, but rather appears to be ever increasing.

As you in fact know, many were sent among you to expose Catholic doctrine and to convince all to return to the highly desired unity of faith and of rule. Here, too, at the See of Peter, there was founded a Sacred Congregation with the express purpose of regulating the interests and rites of the Oriental Church. Thus also there was founded an Institute for Oriental Studies with the object of cultivating and promoting with every care a suitable knowledge of all matters concerning you.

At the present time, unfortunately, other motives require Our care and solicitude. In many regions where the Oriental Rite particularly flourishes, there has been unleashed a new tempest, which seeks to overthrow, devastate and destroy in misery flourishing Christian communities.

If in past centuries some particular dogma of Catholic doctrine was impugned, today, as you well see, our enemies rashly go even further. They seek to banish from public life and the domestic scene, from the universities, from the schools, and from the life of whole populations, sacred rights, institutions and laws, indeed, all that is divine or that has relations to divinity, almost as if they were dealing with matters of mythology and evil omen.

Therefore, however greater the accumulation of evils which oppresses a most elect part of Christianity, in that degree, Venerable Brothers, is Our benevolence toward you increased, that much more ardent is the paternal love which We cherish for you all.

And in the first place We wish that it be most clearly manifested to you that We consider your sorrow and your grief as Our own, and that there is nothing We desire more ardently than to bring some relief to your sufferings, above all by means of Our prayers, and those of every Christian for all those who are being persecuted for having defended, as was necessary, the Catholic religion and its sacred rights.

We know that today there are multitudes of the faithful in Oriental regions who weep bitterly as they see their Bishops put to death or dispersed, or so impeded that they are unable freely to address their flocks and, as they rightfully should, exercise over them their authority; as they behold so many of their churches destined to profane uses or left in squalid abandon; as they realize that no longer in these churches can they now raise up to heaven in prayerful union their voices harmonized in the wonderful modulations that are prescribed in your Liturgy, to call down the dew of heavenly graces that minds be elevated, hearts consoled and remedy found for such great evils.

We know that many from among you have been sent to prisons and concentration camps, or if they are living in their homes, are unable to exercise those sacrosanct rights which are theirs; that is, not only the right to profess their faith in the intimate sanctuary of their own consciences, but also to be able to teach it openly, to defend and propagate it in the family circle for the proper education of the children, and in the school, for the proper training of the pupils.

On the other hand We also are aware that the faithful of the Oriental Churches, in fraternal union with their brethren of the Latin Rite, are together bearing with fortitude the sorrowful burdens of these persecutions, and in like manner are together sharing in the martyrdom, the triumph and the glory that are resulting therefrom. Indeed, they are persevering with heroic courage in their faith. They are resisting the enemies of Christianity with the same unconquerable fortitude with which your forebears did in times past. They are raising their supplications to Heaven—if not publicly, at least in private. They are remaining faithfully attached in closest union to the Roman Pontiff and to their pastors. So also are they continuing to revere, beseech and love in a very special way the Blessed Virgin Mary, most loving and powerful Queen of Heaven and of earth to whose Immaculate Heart they have all been consecrated by Us.

All this is unquestionably the augury of most certain victory in the future; of that victory, however, which flows not from the blood of men in conflict among themselves, nor is nourished by unbridled desire for earthly power, but which is founded on just and legitimate liberty: on justice, practiced not only with words but also with deeds, justice to citizens, peoples and nations; on peace and fraternal charity, which unites all in the bonds of friendship; on religion, above all, which rightly orders customs, moderates private aspirations by placing them at the service of the public welfare, raises up minds to heaven, and, in fine, protects civil society and peace of all.

This is the object of Our most ardent hopes. But in the meanwhile, however, the information that reaches Us is such as to render more bitter Our sorrow.

By day and by night We turn with paternal solicitude Our mind and Our heart to those who have been confided to Us by divine mandate (Cf. John 21:15-17), and who We know are treated in so unworthy a manner as to be the object of calumnies for their firm attachment to the Catholic faith, and to be deprived of their legitimate rights, not excluding at times even those so innate to human nature that whenever they are curtailed by violence, fear or other means, the very dignity of man is lessened and subjected to injury as a result.

Among those saddening communications brought to Our notice, there is one which in these latest days has afflicted more than any other not only Us, not only all Christians, but also all those who hold in honor the dignity and liberty of citizens.

We would refer to Bulgaria, where there existed a small but flourishing community of Catholics, and where a terrible catastrophe has caused profound mourning in the Church. With the usual method of accusations, public crimes were imputed to the ministers of God. Among these, Our Venerable Brother, Eugene Bossilkoff, Bishop of Nikopol, was condemned to death, together with three other of his priest collaborators in the pastoral ministry. Furthermore, many others already are imprisoned or impeded by the restraint of public authority, and to these are added a not inconsiderable number of Catholics punished in various ways, and thus invested with the same distinction and honor.

As a duty of conscience, We raise Our protest against all of this, while to the whole of Christendom We denounce the injury inflicted upon the Church.

These victims, in fact, have been condemned as enemies of the state not only because of having professed, but also for having striven openly and strenuously to defend the Catholic religion, when in truth they are second to none in their observance of the law, provided these be not contrary to the natural, divine or ecclesiastical law.

What indeed has happened, especially in more recent times, in Bulgaria, unfortunately has been happening already for some time among other peoples where the Church of the Oriental Rite flourishes—for instance, among the peoples of Rumania and the Ukraine.

As far as the first nation is concerned, by an Apostolic Letter of last March (Cf. *AAS*, XLIV, Ser. II, Vol. XIX, pp. 249 ff.), We have already protested vehemently against the many afflictions by which the faithful of your own and the Latin Rite are oppressed, and with fatherly sympathy We have exhorted them all to persevere, with that indomitable steadfastness by which they are distinguished, in the religion of their forefathers.

For the present, however, We sadly turn Our thoughts and affection to another people, truly dear to Us, namely, to the people of the Ukraine, among whom are not a few of the faithful who look toward Rome with immense desire and earnest love, and venerate this Apostolic See as the center of the Christian religion and as the infallible teacher of Christian truth by reason of the mandate of Jesus Christ (Cf. Matt. 16:18-19; John 11:15-17; Luke 22:32).

These people, nevertheless, as We have learned with overwhelming grief, are oppressed in no smaller degree with persecution and find themselves already for some time in a situation no less grave than the other peoples of whom We have spoken to you, Venerable Brothers, in this letter.

In a special way We would recall the memory of those Bishops of the Oriental Rite, who were among the first in the defense of their religion to endure hardship, affliction and outrage; who, transported to the city of Kiev, were there tried and condemned to various punishments—in the city of Kiev, We say, whence once shone forth throughout all those regions the light of Christian doctrine, and whence Christian worship was propagated.

Some of these have already met a glorious death, and so, as one may hope, from the abode of heavenly blessedness which they enjoy, lovingly look down upon their sons and their companions in their unarmed struggle, and implore for them the all-powerful protection of God.

Besides, We cannot pass over in silence those faithful of the Latin and Oriental Rites, who, after being driven from homeland and hearth, and deported into unknown and distant lands, are now there deprived of their rightful priests, who could console, help and direct them, and extend to them the heavenly comforts of religion.

All this is for Us a cause of grief so heart-rending that We cannot restrain Our tears. Meanwhile We beseech the all-compassionate God and Father of Mercy that He would deign graciously to enlighten those who are responsible for such a sad state of affairs, and that He would deign likewise to put an end as soon as possible to the accumulation of so many evils.

Nevertheless, Venerable Brothers, in the midst of so many and such great calamities, on account of which Our soul and yours are overwhelmed with grief, We have reason to derive some consolation from news We have received. For it is made known to Us that those who are reduced to such a lamentable and critical situation remain steadfast in their faith with such intrepid constancy as to excite Our admiration and the admiration of every honest person.

Let all these receive from Us this merited recognition of Our paternal praise, and may it serve to increase and strengthen more and more their fortitude. And let them know for certain that We, as the Common Father Whom "the care for all the churches" (II Cor. 11:28) urges and the "love of Christ" (*ibid.*, 5:14) impels, raise up each day ardent supplication that the reign of Jesus Christ, bearer of peace to souls, to peoples and to nations, may everywhere triumph.

Before the sad spectacle of these afflictions—which have stricken not only Our sons among the laity, but more especially those who, raised to the priestly dignity, are for that very reason afflicted, that the words of Sacred Scripture may be verified: "I will smite the shepherd and the sheep of the flock will be scattered" (Matt. 26:31; Cf. Mark 14:27; Zach. 13:7)—We feel obliged to recall to the mind of all that throughout the course of the centuries, not only among civilized but also among barbaric peoples, the ministers of religion have always been treated, in so far as they are intermediaries between God and men, with due honor and veneration.

When, moreover, the Divine Redeemer, after the dispelling of the darkness of error, taught to us heavenly truth and through His profound condescension wished to make us partakers in His eternal priesthood, this showing of honor and veneration was then greatly increased, so much so that Bishops and priests were regarded as most loving Fathers, desirous of nothing else than the common good of the people entrusted to their care.

Yet the Divine Redeemer has said Himself: "No disciple is above his teacher" (Matt. 10:24); "if they have persecuted me, they will persecute you also" (John 15:20); "blessed are you when men reproach you, and persecute you, and, speaking falsely, say all manner of evil against you, for my sake. Rejoice and exult, because your reward is great in heaven" (Matt. 5:11-12).

We should not wonder, therefore, if in Our days, and perhaps more than in past centuries, the Church of Christ, and in a particular way its ministers, is made to suffer from persecutions, falsehoods, calumnies and afflictions of every kind; but rather place Our secure trust in Him, Who if He has already foretold these future calamities, wished also to forewarn us with these words: "in the world you will have affliction. But take courage, I have overcome the world" (John 16:33).

Do not be downhearted, therefore, Venerable Brothers. Just as your forebears overcame so many difficulties, wiles and dangers by fighting with heroic fortitude even unto martyrdom, so also you who belong to the Oriental Church, together with the faithful of Latin Rite, trust in the aid of heavenly grace and be not afraid. Supplicate together the Lord and His Most Loving Mother, praying especially for those who are today in greatest danger, that they may be endowed with Christian fortitude.

Pray too that all may finally understand certain truths, which are, in fact, clearer than the light of the sun, namely: that "the weapons of our warfare are not carnal but powerful before God" (II Cor. 10:4), that the Church does not seek temporal power but the eternal salvation of souls, that she does not intrigue against governing authorities, but, by means of the Gospel teachings which are capable of forming first-class citizens, she strengthens the very foundation of human society.

If, therefore, she is allowed to enjoy the liberty given her by God, if she is allowed to display her strength publicly and carry on her activities openly in the midst of the people, she can undoubtedly contribute much toward promoting the common good, toward bringing the various classes of citizens closer together in justice and in concord, and toward leading all nations to that true peace and tranquillity which, just as it is desired by all, must also be willed by all.

In order to obtain these things, We desire, Venerable Brothers, that you have public prayers said and that you exhort the faithful entrusted to you to perform also works of penance, so that the Divine Majesty, outraged by so many and so grave offenses, may be appeased.

Let all remember the words of Sacred Scripture: "Pray for those who persecute and calumniate you" (Matt. 5:44); "let the members have care for one another. And if one member suffers anything all the members suffer with it" (I Cor. 12:25-26). It is necessary, furthermore, to imitate the example of the Divine Redeemer Who, in the midst of terrible pain, cried out from the Cross: "Father, forgive them for they do not know what they are doing" (Luke 23:34). It is necessary likewise to fill up in our flesh what is lacking of the sufferings of Christ for His Body, which is the Church (Cf. Col. 1:24). Wherefore, not only must we pray to God for our distressed sons and brothers, but we must willingly offer up to Him our sufferings, our voluntary penances and afflictions.

If, toward the numberless persons in those regions who are suffering infirmity, sorrows and anxieties, or who are in prison, We cannot put into practice the words of Jesus, "I was sick and you visited me; I was in prison and you came to me" (Matt. 25:36), there is, nevertheless, some way in which we can accomplish the same thing: namely, by our prayers and works of penance we can beseech the Most Merciful God to send His comforting angels to these our suffering brothers and sons, and to grant them most copious gifts from on high which will console and fortify their minds and elevate them to heavenly things.

In a particular manner, however, We desire that all priests who are able to offer the Eucharistic Sacrifice every day should make a remembrance of those Bishops and priests, who, far from their churches and their faithful, have not the possibility of ascending the altar to offer the Divine Sacrifice and nourish themselves and their faithful with that divine food, from which our souls attain a sweetness surpassing all desire and receive that strength which leads to victory. And, united together in fraternal union, let the faithful who approach the same holy table and partake of the same sacrifice do likewise, in such wise that in every part of the world and in all the rites which constitute the ornament of the Church, there shall be raised to God and His Heavenly

Mother unanimous voices imploring the divine mercy on behalf of those afflicted communities of Christians.

Since, next January, there will be celebrated as usual in many places the octave of prayers for the unity of the Church, it seems to Us particularly opportune that, especially on that occasion, earnest supplications should be made to God, not only that there be verified as soon as possible the desire of the Redeemer: "Holy Father, keep in thy name those whom thou hast given me, that they may be one even as we are" (John 17:11); but also that the prisons may be opened and the chains unlocked which today pitifully afflict so many for heroically having tried to defend the rights and institutions of religion; and also that Christian truth, justice, concord and peace, which are the greatest gifts of all, may triumph everywhere.

As an earnest of that and as a pledge of Our paternal benevolence, We impart from Our heart to you, Venerable Brothers, to the flocks entrusted to your care, and in a particular manner to those living in these difficult conditions, the Apostolic Benediction.

Given at Rome, from St. Peter's, on the fifteenth day of December, 1952, in the fourteenth year of Our Pontificate.

PIUS PP. XII[86]

Moreover, the Pope seems to want to awaken the whole world and to rouse it to a common concern for the untold sufferings of the people behind the Iron Curtain; he wishes to stimulate all to a keener understanding of the matter so that they may be more lavish in their help and prayers. This was the sense of the encyclical *Ingruentium Malorum* of September 15, 1951,[87] which in part reads as follows:

You know well, Venerable Brethren, the sad conditions of our times. Fraternal union among nations, broken for such a long time, has not yet been re-established everywhere. Yet, everywhere we see souls upset by hatred and rivalry, while threats of new bloody conflicts still hover over the peoples. To this, one must add the violent form of persecution, which, for a long time, has been unleashed against the Church, saddening it very cruelly with calumnies and miseries of all kinds, making the blood of martyrs flow again.

To what and to how many snares are the souls of so many of Our sons submitted in those areas to make them reject the Faith of their fathers, and to make them break, with the utmost disgrace, the tie of union which links them to this Apostolic See. Nor can We pass over in silence a new crime to which, with utmost sorrow, we want earnestly to draw not only your attention, but the attention of the clergy, of parents, and even of public authorities. We refer to the iniquitous campaign that the impious lead everywhere to harm the shining souls of the children. Not even the innocent age has been spared. On the contrary, audacious efforts are unfortunately made to snatch, with a gesture, from the mystical garden of the Church even the most beautiful flowers, which constitute the hope of religion and society. Considering this, one cannot be surprised if peoples groan under the weight of the Divine punishment, and live under the nightmare of even greater calamities.

However, consideration of a situation so pregnant with dangers must not depress your souls, O Venerable Brethren. Instead, that Divine teaching: "Ask and it shall be given to you; seek, and you shall find; knock, and it shall be opened to you" (Luke 11:9), spontaneously raises your hearts with greater hope toward the Mother of God. There, the Christian people have always sought refuge in the hour of danger, because "she has been constituted the cause of salvation for the whole human race."[88]

From these documents it is evident that the reaction of the Vatican to the suffering Catholic Church in Czechoslovakia was not only noble and measured to meet each new situation as it arose, but also in accord with the fundamental human rights as expressed in the *Universal Declaration of Human Rights,*[89] in which human rights are guaranteed in the international forum. Thereby it became evident to the whole world that the impassioned pleas of the Holy See represent a recognition of human dignity, a realization of human worth and of the inviolability of human rights that is embedded in the international consciousness of mankind. To prove this point we reproduce here a few of the articles in this Declaration:

Article 3

Everyone has the right to life, liberty and security of person.

Article 4

No one shall be held in slavery or servitude; slavery and the slave trade shall be prohibited in all their forms.

Article 5

No one shall be subjected to torture or to cruel, inhuman, or degrading treatment or punishment.

Article 6

Everyone has the right to recognition everywhere as a person before the law.

Article 7

All are equal before the law and are entitled without any discrimination to equal protection of the law. All are entitled to equal protection against any discrimination in violation of this Declaration and against any incitement to such discrimination.

Article 8

Everyone has the right to an effective remedy by the competent national tribunals for acts violating the fundamental rights granted him by the constitution or by law.

Article 9

No one shall be subjected to arbitrary arrest, detention, or exile.[90]

Article 17

(1) Everyone has the right to own property alone as well as in association with others.

(2) No one shall be arbitrarily deprived of his property.

Article 18

Everyone has the right to freedom of thought, conscience and religion; this right includes freedom to change his religion or belief, and freedom, either alone or in community with others and in public or private, to manifest his religion or belief in teaching, practice, worship and observance.

Article 19

Everyone has the right to freedom of opinion and expression; this right includes freedom to hold opinions without interference and to seek, receive and impart information and ideas through any media and regardless of frontiers.

Article 20

(1) Everyone has the right to freedom of peaceful assembly and association.

(2) No one may be compelled to belong to an association.[91]

Thus the reactions of the Vatican were enhanced and became more important in the eyes of the world.

CHAPTER THIRTEEN

CZECHOSLOVAKIA IN EXILE

EVERY REVOLUTION IS ACCOMPANIED BY A POLITICAL EMIgration. This forms the crowning testimony of the suppression of freedom before an international public. A Communist *coup d'état*[1] is inevitably accompanied by emigration because the Communists cannot tolerate any political opposition.

After the events of February, 1948, in Czechoslovakia, emigration began by the escape of political leaders and ministers and by resignation of ambassadors, consuls and clerks in diplomatic legations.[2] Among the first refugees were Catholic priests, journalists, members of the parliament and many political rightists.

The Czechoslovak refugees increased in number very rapidly. In May, 1948, *L'Osservatore Romano*[3] published an article revealing the number to be about ten thousand. According to statistics, at the beginning of 1950 there were about 45,000 Czechoslovak refugees,[4] and this figure increased during the year 1950 and later to 55,000.[5] If one recalls the difficult conditions under which Czechoslovak refugees crossed the frontier, there is no doubt that under such forbidding circumstances this extraordinary number of refugees is dramatic testimony to the impossibility of the situation in Czechoslovakia. It can be estimated that about the same number were caught crossing the frontier or were betrayed when preparing their escape; unknown also is the large number fugitives who were shot. Enormously greater is the number of those who would have escaped from Communist prisons, concentration camps and captive monasteries in Czechoslovakia if the opportunity had presented itself. This is a very important factor because it demonstrates first of all that the majority of people in Czechoslovakia are resisting and fighting against the Communist regime. There is little doubt that nobody leaves his native country unless he has a very good reason. The emigration of refugees from Czechoslovakia strongly indicts the Communist regime in that country.

It is quickly agreed that a great number of the *émigrés* exiled themselves because of political differences with the party in power. However, what is noteworthy about the emigrations from Czechoslovakia is this: among the refugees are found not only those opposed on principle to communism, followers of the Christian bloc and non-socialist parties, but even Socialists and Marxists.

The hard life of refugees in D.P. camps is a matter of public knowledge. Under difficult conditions Czechoslovak refugees spent some years in D.P. camps in Austria, Germany and Italy, and then emigrated into various countries: the United States, England, Canada, France, Norway, Sweden, Chile, Brazil, New Zealand. A substantial number of them went to Australia. The International Refugee Organization (IRO), the National Catholic Welfare Conference, the Young Men's Christian Association, Protestant and Jewish organizations, and others, helped in charitable cooperation to facilitate emigration. To all these organizations the refugees are profoundly grateful for the assistance rendered.

Furthermore, exiles before an international forum have the status of representatives of their subjugated nations. It is not only their privilege but rather their solemn duty to inform the world of the necessity of helping Czechoslovak people and other nations behind the Iron Curtain in their struggle to regain their liberty and freedom. Although every refugee is, so to speak, an ambassador of his nation, nevertheless the establishment of official Czechoslovak representation in exile has been troublesome because the Czechoslovak problem is so complicated. (*See Appendix*)

In Paris in 1948, Ferdinand Peroutka established the Masaryk Democratic Federation, which was a nonpolitical body. In February, 1949, after negotiations of leading Czechoslovak political personalities, the Council of Free Czechoslovakia was established in Washington, D. C., as the central representative body of Czechoslovaks in exile. Dr. Peter Zenkl, former deputy of the Prime Minister and chairman of the National Socialist party, became chairman of this council.

Socialists re-enforced their own majority in all the branches of this council by appointing certain sympathetic people who were entitled to vote as equal members of the committee, so that the Socialists, in addition to the representation of their own parties, had the votes of these fellow travelers.

Likewise, branches of the Council of Free Czechoslovakia, regional committees, were established in Paris, where the chairman was Dr. Hubert Ripka, former Minister for Foreign Trade and a politician of the National Socialist party. Another regional committee was established in London. Václav Majer, former Minister for Food and member of the Social Democratic party, became the chairman. A few members of the Christian People's party (Dr. Adolf Procházka, Dr. Ivo Ducháček and Dr. Adolf Klimek) were taken into these groups. Dr. Josef Černý was admitted as the representative of the former Agrarian Peasants' party. Other non-Socialist parties such as the National Democratic party and the Craftsmen Middle Class party, which had been disbanded by the Communists, had to fight for admission. There were no representatives of the Carpatho-Ruthenians, the province of Czechoslovakia that was detached by the National Front government in 1945 for the Soviet Union. Socialists, under the leadership of Dr. Peter Zenkl, occupied a disproportionate number of positions under their tactics of hegemony.

Czechoslovak refugees in D.P. camps expressed their dissatisfaction with such procedures when they learned the policies of the council, especially of its regional body in Paris. In 1950, another regional committee of the council was established in Canada (Ottawa) where the former Ambassador Francis Němec, a member of the Social Democratic party, was elected chairman.

From January 6 to 19, 1951, meetings were held of all the thirty members of the committee of the Council of Free Czechoslovakia in Washington, D. C. There was an exhausting debate between leftists and rightists, as well as a clash of personalities in matters of negotiation. The crisis, which was evoked by the question how the election period should be fixed finished in a surprising way.[6] The defeated minority of thirteen members of the committee left the Council of Free Czechoslovakia, proclaimed the council dissolved, and established a new body: the National Committee (Národní výbor). The other seventeen members of the committee of the Council of Free Czechoslovakia remained in the original organization so that Czechoslovakia in exile had now been split into two representative groups. The fact that the minority refused to accept a decision of the majority is typical and instructive. It proves that the Socialists are not willing to give to others what they demand for themselves. This is contradictory to the mission of those in exile, all the more so since official representation should be antithetical to the practices of communism. It is surprising that in establishing Czechoslovak representation abroad, very little consideration and regard was taken for the proportion of non-Socialists in Czechoslovakia.

Representation in the groups in exile did not take into account the fact that 75 per cent of the Czechoslovak population is Catholic. It would have been of more benefit to Slovakia to admit a greater representation of Slovak Catholics. When it is recalled that the Catholic Church is the principal factor in the fight against communism, as is apparent from the foregoing exposition, it is to be regretted that a proper representation was not permitted.

Although the Council of Free Czechoslovakia claimed, according to its statutes, to be representative of the interests of the whole Czechoslovak Republic in the free world, this council did not take any stand on the events, laws, injustices and oppressions that took place in Czechoslovakia before February, 1948, under the regime of the National Front. This council did not repudiate the treaty of alliance and close cooperation between the Soviet Union and Czechoslovakia. They did not repudiate the Košice Program of April, 1945, in accordance with which non-Socialist parties were forcibly disbanded, and property was nationalized. They did not repudiate the unconstitutional detachment of Carpatho-Ruthenia to the U.S.S.R. in 1945, and did not repudiate many laws which now form the basis for Communist practices in Czechoslovakia.

It was therefore apparent that it was necessary to strengthen the effectiveness of representation in exile, and to use representatives of the different ideologies which had been persecuted for their meritorious work. This was all the more necessary because, while political exiles cannot directly correct the persecution and evil in the fatherland, they should nevertheless be able to take an eloquent stand against the tyranny of communism.

Since Catholics, despite their prevailing majority among the refugees, were not officially represented in fair proportion, they established a nonpolitical association, the Saints Cyril and Methodius League,[7] with headquarters in London, for the purpose of promoting Catholic action among Czechoslovak Catholic refugees dispersed throughout the world. Besides this, Christian refugees in exile established under the sponsorship and leadership of the Rt. Rev. Ambrose Ondrák, Abbot of St. Procopius in Lisle, Illinois, aided by Dr. Vilém Stranecký, editor-in-chief of *Katolík* and *Národ,* the Bohemian newspapers in Chicago, the Conference for the Restoration of Christian Tradition in Czechoslovakia.[8]

On the occasion of the convention of the National Federation of Czech Catholics on October 16 and 17, 1951, in Chicago, Rt. Rev. Ondrák addressed a message to the exiles and to those still suffering in their subjugated homeland:

> We American Czechs cannot be uninterested in the fate of the homeland of our fathers once it is liberated from communism. Nor can we be uninterested in the way in which Czechoslovak exiles, through radio and other media, are preparing conditions for future activities once the country is liberated. Some things, however, are developing to the disadvantage of Catholics, and this despite our sincere desire that in liberated Czechoslovakia there should be a democratic Christian state, which all Czech countrymen in America are willing to support. It is not directly necessary to enter political life in exile, but it is necessary to draw attention to the Catholic and cultural interests of refugees and to help restore Catholic traditions in Czechoslovakia, which will someday be liberated. As chairman of the Conference for the Restoration of Christian Traditions in Czechoslovakia I have the opportunity of knowing more fully many problems which should be considered by all Catholics as their own. These are really serious problems, which will meet the Catholic Church in Czechoslovakia when Bohemia, Slovakia and Carpatho-Ruthenia will be free.
>
> The education of priests in Nepomucenum will be pro-

vided through contributions of money, so that Czechoslovakia will have after its liberation at least some young priests to serve in the immediate future. But many difficulties will meet these priests and the whole Catholic Church in Czechoslovakia, when they face conditions brought on by communism, even after their restoration to freedom. Keeping silence in the face of anti-Christian propaganda now flooding Czechoslovakia will only aggravate the condition of the Catholic Church in Czechoslovakia.

The Czechoslovak exiles established Catholic Action called the Saints Cyril and Methodius League. The weakened Catholic Church in Czechoslovakia, which has been robbed of her properties and deprived of her leaders, will need extensive activities of the apostolate by laymen. All Catholics of Czech origin should be pleased to know that there is now in exile this true Catholic Action for Czechoslovakia, which for the time being is working for Czechoslovak exiles and is spreading the lay apostolate among refugees. Because of the misunderstanding and willful steps of a noted individual, it happened that this apostolate here in America was not always correctly understood, namely that the Czech exiles should do more for God, the Church and the nation.[9]

Dissatisfaction with the Council of Free Czechoslovakia as a representative of Czechoslovakia became almost general. As a protest to the Socialist majority of this council, a *Sdružení demokratických úprchliků* (alliance of democratic refugees) was originated in Chicago. This organization protested very often against the council's representation and its construction.[10] Strong criticism of some members of the Council of Free Czechoslovakia was systematically publicized by Jiří Hálek in *Katolík* and *Národ*. Similar articles of other authors appeared in many newspapers. Under the pressure of this opposition and criticism, and on the advice of American officials of the National Committee for a Free Europe, Czechoslovak representatives of both organizations (the Council of Free Czechoslovakia and the National Council) advised the groups to make some personnel changes and then re-establish one national representative organization under the name, Council of Free Czechoslovakia.

The split among the Czechoslovak exiles was thus seemingly abolished,[11] and the necessary conditions for membership were stabilized by agreement of both groups. On May 4, 1952, a first meeting of the so-called Reunited Council of Free Czechoslovakia[12] met in Washington, D. C. At this meeting general regulations and a program were announced.[13]

To understand a confusing situation it is suitable to say this: during these negotiations only two parties, the National Socialistic party and the Slovak Democratic party, made an agreement unknown in content and extent but known concerning only statutes, structure and competence of the organs of the Council, and the choice and appointment of functionaries. Such a state of affairs was created by only two parties and recommended to other parties. It is evident that this was an undemocratic procedure and it seems that this desperate situation of the National Council of Free Czechoslovakia as a central representative organ of Czechoslovak exiles came also to the careful attention of the National Committee for a Free Europe in New York, and subsequently a reorganization of the Council of Free Czechoslovakia was recommended.[14] Currently, a reconstruction of this council is going on—we hope with more satisfactory results, especially for Catholics.

Of course this reorganization was not satisfactory to some politicians, especially those from the former Agrarian party, and therefore, under the leadership of Dr. Francis Král, professor at the University of Pennsylvania, a new and independent organization was established in 1953 under the name *Alliance for Liberation and Freedom in Czechoslovakia.* It had an entirely anti-Socialist program.[15] Besides this, many of the Slovaks in exile who were fighting for a free, independent Slovak state[16] gathered in separate Slovak organizations under the leadership of Karol Sidor and of Dr. Ferdinand Durčanský. Meanwhile, Czech separatism was represented by General Prchala. These separatists did not, of course, participate in political representation in the Council of Free Czechoslovakia.

Disregarding these political trends, Catholics in exile sought to infiltrate Catholic ideas into the public life of the exiles and edify their hosts by concertedly conforming to the Catholic majority at home. The Rt. Rev. Abbot Ambrose Ondrák, O.S.B., in an encouraging address to a political conference of Czechoslovak politicians in New York, on April 19, 1953, clarified the situation in the following words:

My original intention was to convoke a plenary session of the Conference for Renewal of Christian Tradition in Czechoslovakia. I wanted all Catholic laymen who are interested in political ideas and who are now residing in the United States to participate. I am sorry to say there were some individuals who worked against our intentions. This is a very sad state of affairs. I have decided, therefore, to postpone the meeting.

I was very interested to know the opinion of those Catholic laymen who are not living under political pressure as is the case with the majority of refugees, most of whom live in the eastern part of the United States. In view of this, I decided to invite only a restricted number of Catholic laymen from the area in and around New York, especially those who have taken part in establishing this conference.

This address, however, is meant for all Catholic exiles. I welcome you sincerely to this meeting which is being held in the presence of the relics of our dear national saints. Their presence should remind us of the glory and greatness of these patrons of our nation. We should also remember their lives, and how they suffered for Christ.

I am sorry to say that among you there are some who want to force the Church and her activities into catacombs. They want to remove Christian activities from public life. They do not respect God or his commandments, and they do not work to achieve the liberation of their country, but rather, are trying to gain political power. These exiles have forgotten Christ's words: ". . . . and who will deny me before people, I will deny him before my Father in heaven."

The Devil never sleeps; he does not work only among Communists, but prompts others also to hate all that is from God: his divine rights, his justice, and his believers.

I was surprised and disappointed by the defects in the principles for a program set forth by the Council of Free Czechoslovakia. I could not find one reference to God's truths. Neither did I find anything expressing honor to our Creator. One politician in exile tried to prove to me that the Christian tradition is mentioned in the program of the Council of Free Czechoslovakia. However, upon further investigation, it turned out that this "mention" of Christian tradition was so understated that it wasn't even there! For example, for many months, Czechs in America have been preparing celebrations in honor of Saint Procopius who left our country such a valuable heritage. Yet the Council of Free Czechoslovakia, although busy honoring Slansky and

> Gottwald, have completely ignored Saint Procopius. And this in spite of the fact that the Pope has asked the Christian world, in a special apostolic letter, to honor this saint, giving his apostolic blessing to those who did this.
>
> The courageous bishops on whose behalf I feel bound to speak since they are not allowed to do so, would be very sad if they knew that there are some Catholics who are not attempting to fight at all. They refuse to help, and close their eyes to the slander and vilification of God and the Church. However, I have confidence and faith that the situation will improve and that those who are now persecuting Catholic exiles for their convictions will see the light.[17]

Representatives of the former People's Party under the leadership of the exile, Dr. Adolf Procházka, made remarkable progress. Besides an official representation in the Council of Free Czechoslovakia, they formed a Christian union with six other nations.[18] The first meeting was held on March 15, 1953, in New York and evoked great attention. Very gratifying is the fact that a magazine *Nové Obzory* (New Horizons) appeared in 1953, in which Christian Democrats tried to continue along the moderate lines of the People's Party for the conservative policy of Rt. Rev. Jan Šrámek.

This moderate tendency of the Czechoslovak Christian Democrats with their constructive intentions was a peaceful element in the restless political situation of the Czechoslovak exiles despite the fact, to use James Burnham's expression,[19] that politics in exile is usually dreary and stultifying.[20] Furthermore, to solemnly represent the Catholic viewpoint to the world, a Catholic gymnastic organization called Orel (Eagle) was established under the leadership of Dr. Frank Hradil and held its first meeting in Chicago, on July 4-5, 1953.

In the field of religion, Catholic Czech and Slovak priests in exile, through their Catholic organizations such as the Saints Cyril and Methodius League, worked for the restoration of Christian and democratic traditions at home. They tried to let the world know what the real situation of the Church was in Czechoslovakia by separating the truth from the propaganda. To this end many protests or memorandums were sent to internationally important political or diplomatic organizations, especially to the United Nations Assembly in New York. An example of this is a document issued at a meeting of Czech priests in Camp Morton, Manitoba, Canada, on August 29, 1953:

> Mr. Dag Hammarskjold
> Secretary General of UN
> New York, N. Y.
>
> Catholic priests, refugees from Czechoslovakia, living now in Canada and in the United States, assembled at a meeting held at Camp Morton, Manitoba, Canada, on August 25-27, 1953, discussed the religious situation in their enslaved country and resolved unanimously to send a protest against the religious persecution in Czechoslovakia to the United Nations.
>
> All Catholic bishops and ordinaries, with Archbishop Joseph Beran of Prague as head, were deprived of liberty. Many of them were unjustly sentenced to many years in prison, others were held in their residences, but without the possibility of contact with the faithful.
>
> Many priests were executed for ostensibly illegal activity; many hundreds of Catholic clergy are suffering in prisons and civil or military forced labor camps. The education of priests is impossible due to the closing of all episcopal seminaries.
>
> All religious societies have been dissolved. Nuns were forced to leave their schools and charitable institutions and were sent to factories under degrading conditions.
>
> The religious education of young people has been made almost impossible. Children, against the conviction of their parents, are educated by the public schools in atheistic thinking. The religious life has been totally suppressed. All church property was confiscated by the state.
>
> The above-mentioned facts are evidence of the cruel persecution of the Catholic Church in Czechoslovakia. The priests who were present at the meeting request that the suppression of religious freedom in Czechoslovakia be discussed by the Division of Human Rights at the United Nations.[21]

A restoration of Czechoslovak democracy depends first of all on religious freedom. The natural conflict between communism and Catholicism makes it imperative for Catholic representatives in exile to work for the defeat of communism and to restore again a democracy based on the freedom of the children of God.[22] Their hope is strengthened by the idea of a future united or federated free Europe,[23] in which the Christian spirit of Europe[24] will be a foundation for the restoration of the democratic ideal of freedom, fraternity and equality.[25]

EPILOGUE

TO MAKE THE SUFFERINGS OF THE CATHOLIC CHURCH IN Czechoslovakia more understandable, we quote the following from the Bible: "Now there was a certain man among the Pharisees, Nicodemus by name, who was a ruler of the Jews. This man came to Jesus one night, and said to him, 'Rabbi, we know that thou art a teacher from God, for no one can work these signs which thou workest, unless God be with him.' Jesus answered, and said to him, 'Amen, amen I say to thee: Unless a man be born again, he cannot see the kingdom of God.' Nicodemus said to him, 'How can a man be born when he is old? Can he enter a second time into his mother's womb, and be born again?' Jesus answered, 'Amen, amen I say to thee: Unless a man be born again of water and the spirit, he cannot enter into the kingdom of God. That which is born of the flesh, is flesh; and that which is born of the spirit, is spirit. Do not wonder that I said to thee, those must be born again. The wind blows where it will; thou hearest its sound, but thou dost not know where it comes from or where it goes; thus is every one who is born of the spirit,' Nicodemus answered, and said to him, 'How can these things be?' Answering him, said Jesus, 'Thou art a teacher in Israel, and dost not know these things? Amen, amen I say to thee: We speak what we know, and we bear witness to what we have seen, but you do not understand. If I have spoken of earthly things to you, and you do not believe, how will you believe, if I speak to you of heavenly things? And no one has ascended into heaven, except he who has descended from heaven.[1]

" 'And as Moses lifted up the serpent in the desert, even so must the Son of man be lifted up: That those who believe in him, may not perish; but may have life everlasting.[2]

" 'For God so loved the world, that he gave his only begotten Son; that those who believe in him, may not perish, but may have life everlasting. For God did not send his Son into the world, in order to judge the world, but that the world might be saved through him. He who believes in him is not judged. But he who does not believe, is already judged; because he does not believe in the name of the only begotten Son of God. Now this is the judgment: the light has come into the world, yet men have loved the darkness rather than the light, for their works were evil. For every one who does evil hates the light, and does not come to the light, that his deeds may not be exposed. But he who does the truth, comes to the light, that his deeds may be made manifest, for they have been performed in God.' "[3]

The conversation between Christ and Nicodemus is very instructive for an analytical understanding of the historical mission of Christ's Church among those of mankind who do not understand it. Despite all the good deeds that the Church performs by the mandate of Christ, she is constantly being persecuted; yet at the same time she is loved in proportion to the graces granted.

Even those unwilling to accept the principles and commandments are able to see and appreciate the meritorious activities of the Church, but for lack of grace and of faith, they are unable to understand. There are those who are willing to admire a beautiful cathedral: they walk around it, but they will not enter, nor are they interested in its history. The demand of Christ: "Unless a man be born again, he cannot see the kingdom of God" is a condition of the Church about which a modern Nicodemus should be concerned.

Concerning the Pharisees who were unable to understand him, Christ once said: "Woe to ye Pharisees."[4] Thus he reproached their lack of understanding and their "hardened hearts."[5] There are those who will not look upon facts about the works and aims of the Catholic Church as satisfactory proof of her divine mission and insist on persecuting the Church.

Latter-day Nicodemuses who are too busy with earthly things do not take the time to understand the Church. They ignore her or even persecute her. This is analogous to the fate of the Church in Communist Czechoslovakia. The faithful believers are the sufferers; the Nicodemuses are the silent ones; and the Pharisees, having a free hand, are the persecutors of the Church.

The Catholic Church is fighting a good fight in Czechoslovakia. She is convinced of her divine mission, and in working for the benefit of all Czech and Slovak people, she is at the same time working for the betterment of the whole world. Furthermore, she is convinced that even in Czechoslovakia "the gates of Hell shall not prevail."[6]

APPENDIX

AIMS AND PRINCIPLES OF LIBERATION

(This statement was adopted by exiles from ten Communist-dominated countries at ceremonies outside Independence Hall, Philadelphia, Pa., February 11, 1951.)

I

Whereas

The peace ardently desired by the people of the whole world requires conditions of order and justice;

These times of great trouble will persist in the world so long as peoples aspiring to liberty are kept in isolation from the free world and in slavery;

This trouble prevails particularly in Europe, where people, brutally separated from each other by an arbitrary will, see the ancient ties, both spiritual and material, ties formed by history and a common civilization, severed between them;

This division in Europe keeps the West in a continual state of insecurity and weakness, depriving the countries that are still free of conditions indispensable to well-being and to the re-establishment of strength;

This division isolates the countries of Eastern Europe and, despite their aspirations and natural tendencies, confines them against their will in the sphere subjected to Soviet communism;

Whereas

The isolation of an entire part of Europe can be maintained only by constraint and terror exercised equally against nations and individuals;

The nations held prisoners in an enemy camp are arrayed against the West as the advance guard of the new aggression which is being prepared;

Individuals tortured in mind and in body must suffer an unnatural warping of their spirit by a despotic rule or perish;

In the domain of fact, the Communist experiment is doomed to failure; the economy of a country subjected to incessant levies, deprived of its markets and its natural outlets, moves toward catastrophe; the social order succumbs under a dictatorship which abolishes liberty of thought, creativeness, research and enterprise, deprives the peasant of his land, the worker of the product of his labor, separates the child from the customs, faith, education and patriotic inspiration of his parents, and denies to an entire category of citizens the right of life;

In the domain of the spirit, the pitiless struggle of communism against man leads to the debasement of the human being; in spite of the heroic resistance of our martyrs, to whom we render a tribute of deep emotion, our most precious heritage and our highest values, the very groundwork of our civilization, must suffer outrage and violence from a hostile mentality; in the systematic spreading of moral confusion, with no distinction between good and evil, the only law is an immense and brazen falsehood;

Under cover of a treacherous system of thought, designed to gain command of the mass mind but incapable of fulfilling its promises, obscure forces are at work hostile to the entire world whose only aim is to exercise absolute and limitless power; the exercise of this power becomes an end in itself, with the world as its victim; and the unlawful occupation of the Eastern European countries is the starting point for new conquests.

II

Whereas Moreover

The dangerous process of disintegration which threatens to extend over all Europe cannot be checked without restoring a rule of liberty to the countries in the East; and these countries are worthy of such a rule, having fought through centuries on the front lines of Europe to win freedom for themselves and for the Continent;

The word "liberty" has gained heightened meaning and new value through the sufferings endured by these countries, sustaining their peoples in hope of the deliverance for which they long with all their hearts;

And Whereas

Such a deliverance calls for a great effort of constructive organization fired by a creative urge;

This effort must aim at the liberation of man as well as nations;

The liberation of man must restore his natural rights—fundamental, inalienable, not to be proscribed, but protected in their very finality against the abuses of power and the interference of public authority;

This liberation, consecrated by legal guarantees of a national and international order, must deliver man from the fear that has permeated his being and give back his indispensable sense of physical and spiritual security; the freedom thus assured must be the essential element in the formation of states, and of those ties which are destined to draw more and more closely together the commonwealth of man;

The freeing of the nations must put an end to unlawful dominion by any alien power acting through the intermediary of servile government imposed and maintained by violence;

It must restore to the people their right of adopting freely the laws and institutions of their choice, so that the just power of governments shall derive from the consent of the governed;

Further, it must provide means for remedying as promptly as possible the social ills produced by Communist rule, which has created a much sharper social division than existed before between ruled and rulers: between the mass of half-starving and downtrodden people and a small upper ruling group, politically and economically privileged and self-perpetuating, which wields power of life and death unrestrained by any civil or moral law; this deadly distinction must be abolished;

And Whereas

The reconstruction of Eastern Europe involves problems of a political, economic and social order beyond the capabilities and powers of nations to resolve separately; the dangers to which they remain exposed have prepared them to seek salvation through union; this tendency toward close international collaboration is in harmony with the present order of events; the federal principle, signifying union in liberty and implying the creation of organic ties, is the most appropriate and sure means of uniting the states; the people of the East are resolved to apply this principle to the regional organization which they envisage; these same people proclaim their right and their desire to take part in a United Europe on a federal basis, which they regard as the realization of all their prayers; and in spirit these continental and regional unions signify further steps along the road to this indispensable organization of the free world as a whole;

The great movement which carries the people of the East toward union springs likewise from a desire for security, from their need of opposing unitedly the menace of any totalitarian dictatorships whatsoever and of preventing any imperialist power from subordinating their countries to its will—as happened with Nazi Germany and Soviet Russia.

Consequently the peoples of the East feel themselves brothers not only to all the free nations of the West but also to the Russian people and all the other people of the Soviet Union aspiring to a common deliverance;

III

And Whereas Finally

Continents, like men, are related to each other, and in the sense of the words spoken by the great American, Abraham Lincoln, whose memory we honor at this time, the world cannot live half free and half slave;

The principles written into the Atlantic Charter could assure peace to the world under conditions of order and freedom; the present crisis results from the fact that certain of these principles have been abandoned; to cope with this crisis, and the grave disorder provoked by the division of the world, there is no better way than to return to these principles and to restore to the Charter its original authority; in order to bring about this restoration it is necessary to possess a definite program and real strength;

The people of the United States of America, conscious of the mission before them, have resolutely given leadership to the free world in order to create, through new efforts and sacrifices, the preponderant strength able to assure a just and durable peace.

The free world is the bearer of a political idea which it must share with all people eager to rally in a great and just cause; it is now for the United States of America, the nation which marches at the head of the line, to speak the word; here where the representatives of the people, in a time of revolution against autocracy and in touch with the most enlightened minds of the Western world, once gathered to inspire the Constitution of a free people, and where the wisdom of a free people with authority gained from glorious experience can restore to the world, in a time infinitely troubled, the belief in liberty.

IV

Now Therefore We

Exiles from Albania, Bulgaria, Czechoslovakia, Esthonia, Hungary, Latvia, Lithuania, Poland, Rumania, Yugoslavia, loyally united and single in thought, dedicated by the profound suffering and the high aspirations of our native lands;

Faithful to the example of predecessors who, in the course of centuries, have forged in exile, but in contact with the free world, the framework of the institutions, the laws, the liberties of their countries;

Wish to send from the great Republic of the United States of America, where we have the good fortune to see the forces of freedom assembling, a message of confidence to our faraway peoples;

And to proclaim solemnly together the Principles and Aims of Liberation:

1. All men and all nations are endowed by their Creator with an inalienable right to liberty. The cause of freedom is, like the cause of peace, one and indivisible. The suppression of freedom in one part of the world endangers the freedom of all nations and of all men.

2. The principles of law and liberty embodied in the Atlantic Charter offer solid foundations for just peace in our time. Therefore, as an earnest of the determination in the free world to replace lawlessness and tyranny now rampant, with liberty under law, there must be a return to the principles of the Charter.

3. The world can have no peace so long as no real peace reigns in Europe. This cannot be achieved so long as that Continent is sundered in two. The Iron Curtain divides Europe into halves which are vitally necessary to each other. In the Eastern half a ruling group irresponsible to the will of its own people is forging powerful arms for an aggressive war. Liberation of Central and Eastern Europe is therefore a condition essential to the establishment of international democratic order, justice and lasting peace.

Having been violated by the same Soviet Communist aggressor, the freedom and independence of our peoples deserve to be defended with the same determination as that with which the United Nations are defending the freedom of the Korean people.

4. The great powers cannot achieve their purpose of safeguarding Western Europe if they base their endeavors upon a recognition, even implied, of the present enslavement of Central and Eastern Europe. Let the free world give to the oppressed peoples of Eastern and Central Europe at every possible opportunity assurance that its purpose is to bring the principles of the Atlantic Charter into effect in their unhappy lands. It is for the free world to demand that all further deportations from our countries cease, that prisoners of war and persons deported from their homes be repatriated immediately, that all Soviet troops and foreign police units be withdrawn, and that all political prisoners wherever they are held be set free. The deliberate destruction of the best in our nations, steadily pursued, must be stopped. The first goal is the establishment of

democratic governments and the holding of free elections under effective international supervision.

5. All our peoples, from the Baltic to the Black and Adriatic Seas, from the Iron Curtain into the heart of the Russian lands, anxiously await action that would herald their approaching liberation. They are confident that the spiritual and material forces gathering under the leadership of the United States of America are capable of establishing a peace based on freedom and justice. Despite its impressive military might, the ruthless power confronting the free world is undermined by hatred and latent revolt among the people it oppresses. Their contribution to the fight for freedom can lead to decisive results only if it is related to positive and determined action by the free world.

Pledge of Democracy

6. The peoples of Central and Eastern Europe are firmly resolved, upon their liberation, to join the community of free nations and to establish government of the people, by the people and for the people. The right of *habeas corpus*, as well as freedom of religion, freedom of research and artistic creation, freedom of opinion and of information, freedom of assembly, among other essential freedoms and fundamental political and social rights, shall be assured. No one shall be barred from education because of national origin, religious or political belief, or social and economic circumstances. Parents shall have the right to send children to such schools as they may establish or choose. There shall be special care for the oncoming generation of the young, who have a right to the widest opportunities to use their enthusiasm and capacity in building a better new order of society. The machine of mutual extermination shall no longer roll through our countries. Crimes against humanity shall be dealt with through the regular process of justice and on grounds of personal responsibility for the definite acts. Eastern European democracy cannot be revived through vengeance. "Thou shalt not kill" is the basic commandment for us.

7. The movement of ideas and persons, goods and services shall be free. Individual initiative shall be stimulated. Choice between private and public enterprise should be determined on the basis of merit; those methods which can produce better results both for consumers and workers should have preference.

There shall be no more Iron Curtains. Our countries shall again be integrated into the world economy and be able to

raise their standard of living and add their contribution to H
general welfare.

8. The land shall be owned by the peasant as his private property in accordance with the desire of the whole peasantry, which forms a major part of our populations and the backbone of our nations. Cooperatives and other forms of association voluntarily entered into by the peasants for economic ends shall be free from government interference. Advanced scientific methods and modern implements will help to raise the standard of living of the rural and urban populations.

9. The workers, manual and intellectual, shall be protected against exploitation whether by private or by public enterprise and shall be free from the fetters of arbitrary and competitive forced standards in work and from repressive labor laws. They shall be free to choose their employment and the places where they wish to live and work. Free and independent trade unions and organizations shall be the guardians of workers' rights and interests. There shall be responsibility on the part of the public authorities and private administrators that technological and scientific resources be employed to increase output and improve levels of living. The workers shall be entitled to a just share in the profits earned by their industries. Before the interest of the machine comes the interest of man.

10. The peoples of Central and Eastern Europe are eager to take their natural place in the great movement of free peoples toward better relationship and closer union. They are desirous of establishing among themselves strong ties of a federal character and of joining in the formation of a United Europe. Such a fraternal federation must prize and respect the distinctive values of each nation, for the common good of our European civilization and for the cultural heritage of mankind throughout the world.

Our belief in the need of close and loyal cooperation has prompted us to come forward with this joint declaration. We pledge ourselves to remain faithful to this belief after liberation.

In this great country, where the idea of liberty is so closely bound to that of union, we pray God to give us the strength we need to bring to a successful outcome the fight for the freedom and the union of our nations.

ABBREVIATIONS

AAS—Acta Apostolicae Sedis.
ASS—Acta Sanctae Sedis.
BKV—Bibliothek der Kirchenväter.
CIC—Codex juris canonici.
ČČH—Bohemian historian periodical—*Český časopis historický* (Prague).
CML—Archiv of the SS. Cyril and Methodius League, Fitzjohn Avenue, London, N.W. 3.
Coll.—Collection of the laws and regulations of the Czechoslovak Republic.
DTC—Dictionnaire de la théologie catholique.
ES—Denzinger-Bannwart-Umberg: *Enchiridion Symbolorum* (Friburgi Brisgoviae: Herder and Co., 1931).
LA—Leonis XIII acta. Romae: Ex Tipographia Vaticana, 1881-1905, 23 vols.
La DC—La Documentation catholique.
KA—Katolická Akce (Catholic Action).
NCFE—National Committee for a Free Europe, New York.
NCWC—NCWC News Service, Archives in Washington, D. C. (News service issued by the Press Department of the National Catholic Welfare Conference.)
PA—Pii IX Acta, Rome 1854-78.
Veritas—Institution of the Czechoslovak Catholic Documentation (Christian Academy, Rome, Via Concordia 1).
NŽ—Nový Život (New Life). Organ of the SS. Cyril and Methodius League, London, 1949-53; Rome, 1954—
SST ser. 2—The Catholic University of American Studies in Sacred Theology.
RBi—Revue biblique.

FOOTNOTES

FOOTNOTES TO CHAPTER I

1. Alaphridus Ottaviani, *Institutiones juris publici eccliastici*, I, 176-77.

2. The complete text of this letter is given in Chapter X. Cf. *La Documentation Catholique*, 46 (1949), 1055, col. 1453-64. Cf. *The Red and the Black: the Church in the Communist State*, 23.

3. The complete text of this memorandum is given in Chapter X.

4. Ottaviani, *op. cit.*, I, 184-5.

5. CIC, can. 218, par. 1-2.

6. Gerald A. Ryan, *Principles of Episcopal Jurisdiction*, 19-29.

7. Amleto Giovanni Cicognani, *Canon Law*, 44. Consequently public law is the law of the Church as a perfect society.

8. *AAS*, XLII, 601.

9. Antonius Straub, *De Ecclesia Christi*, abundantly quotes from Holy Scripture concerning these truths, with corresponding theological analyses and proofs.

10. *ES*, 1821, 1822, 1824, 1826, 1842.

11. Professor Hobza, having been accepted by the court as an expert, contended that canon law and ecclesiastical regulations have no validity in Czechoslovakia; that every dignitary or religious functionary who prefers canonical obedience to state loyalty is to be viewed as a traitor. See "Report on Czechoslovakia," in *NCFE,* April 1-15, 1950, 7. Cf. *The Jurist*, January, 1951, 157-58; and *Nový Život* (The New Life), December, 1950, 18.

12. Ottaviani, *op. cit.*, I, 176-77.

13. Hobza's speech against superiors of orders and congregations. See "Svobodné Slovo" (April 4, 1950). Cf. Joseph A. Mikuš (trans.), *The Three Slovak Bishops*, 38-41.

14. Taken from the official Bohemian text in *Proces proti vatiskánským agentům v Československu* (Process against Vatican agents in Czechoslovakia), Biskup Zela a společníci, 135-38. English translation by the author.

15. Reginald M. Schultes, O.P., *Die Autorität der Kirche in Weltlichen Dingen*. Cf. Ottaviani, *op. cit.* II, 130.

16. Jacques Maritain, *The Things That Are Not Caesar's*, 6.

17. *Katholische Sociallehre*, 198-204.

18. Jacques Maritain, *The Man and the State*. I cannot agree with the opinion expressed by Father Sherrin in his article, "Catholic Position on Church-State Separation Clear," in *The Catholic Observer*, LII, No. 31 (Aug. 2, 1953), 9, because of the position of the Catholic Church in the United States. Cf. Heinrich A. Rommen, *The State in Catholic Thought*, 586-605.

19. Theodor Schnitzler, *Im Kampfe um Chalcedon*, 104-8.

20. Francis Dvorník, "Church and State in Central Europe," in *The Soviet Union: a Symposium*, 203. Cf. Francis Dvorník, *The Making of Central and Eastern Europe*, 44-47.

21. Francis Dvorník, *op. cit.*, 212.

22. ES, 627, 629, 631, 632. Cf. Josef Kratochvíl, *Otázky a problemy* (Questions and Problems), 90.

23. *ES*, 633, 635, 636, 637, 638, 639, 646, 648, 649, 650.

24. *Ibid.*, 656.

25. Herbert B. Workman, *John Wyclif: A study of the English Medieval Church*, II, 8-10; 83-118.

26. Hartmann Grisar, *Martin Luther: His Life and Work*, 245-48.

27. Johannes Gottschick, "Hus's, Luther's und Zwingli's Lehre von der Kirche," 3, 3, 346-97, 577-616.

28. R. A. Knox: *Enthusianism: A Chapter in the History of Religion*, 109-113.

29. Dvorník, *op. cit.*, 207.

30. "Josef II," in *Catholic Encyclopedia*, VIII, 509.

31. Emmet John Hughes, *The Church and the Liberal Society*, 203-31.

32. *ES*, 2093.

33. *Pii IX Acta, pars prima*, 2, 465-87. Cf. Mercati, *Raccolta di concordati fra la Santa Sede e le autorite civili*, 821-84.

34. *ASS*, IV, 10-13, *Papae Pii IX Allocutio habita in consistorio secreto die* 22 *Junii* 1868. The Pope calls these laws "*leges abominabiles, vehementer reprobandae et damnandae*."

35. Franz Stauracz, *Los von Rom*. Cf. T. G. Masaryk, *Los von Rom*.

36. Cf. *NCWC*, Mar. 2, 1922, Cf. Hanuš, *Viktor Dyk*, 25.

37. *AAS*, XX, 65-55.

38. Felix J. Vondráček, *The Foreign Policy of Czechoslovakia* 1918-1935, 92; Cf. Kamil Krofta, *A Short History of Czechoslovakia*, 161-67. Cf. Ottaviani, *op. cit.*, II, 342,345.

39. *I celostátni katolický sjezd v Praze* (I. Catholic Congress in Prague). Cf. Dvorník, *op. cit.*, 212.

40. *Four Fighting Years*.

41. Otto Friedman, *The Break-up of Czech Democracy*, 147.

42. N. S. Timasheff, "Religion in Russia, 1941-1950," in *The*

Soviet Union, A Symposium, 193-94; Cf. *La DC*, 45 (1948), 1013, col. 395-419.

43. *La DC*, 46 (1949), 1048, col. 995.
44. Timasheff, *op. cit.*, 159.
45. *The Clergy Review*, May, 1951, xiii.
46. The complete text of this pastoral letter is in *La DC*, 46 (1949), 1055, col. 1454-64.
47. *Ibid.*
48. Otto Friedman, *op. cit.*, 145.
49. *Ibid.*
50. *The Clergy Review*, May 1951.
51. *AAS*, XIV, 698. The English translation is from *The Pope and the People: Selected Letters and Addresses on Social Questions*, 251.
52. The complete text of this letter will be found in Chapter X.
53. Thomas McDermott, *Keeper of the Keys*, 252.
54. *AAS*, XIII, 521-524. For the English translation see *Principles for Peace*. Selections from papal documents, Leo XIII to Pius XII, 316-17.
55. See *AAS*, XIV, 674-700, for English Text. *Ibid.*, 353.
56. Ludvík Němec, *Episcopal and Vatican Reaction to the Persecution of the Catholic Church in Czechoslovakia*, 16-60.
57. Samuel A., Cardinal Stritch, *The Papal Peace Program*, 9.
58. John Courtney Murray, S. J., "The Problem of the Religion of State," in *American Ecclesiastical Review*, May, 1951, 330.

FOOTNOTES TO CHAPTER II

1. Joseph Gredt, O.S.B., *Elementa Philosophiae Aristotelico-thomisticae*, II, 121.
2. Gredt, *op. cit.*, II, 154.
3. Gen. 1:26.
4. Gen. 1:27.
5. Gen. 1:31.
6. Henry Kalloch Rowe, *Society, Its Origin and Development*, 1-2.
7. Elmer Pendell, *Society Under Analysis*, 146-147.
8. Jacques Maritain, *The Things That Are Not Caesar's*, 139.
9. Leo XIII, Enc. *Immortale Dei*, Nov. 1, 1885.
10. Gredt, *op. cit.*, I, 253. Ordo sumitur: pro speciali relatione secundum prius et posterius.
11. Garrigou-Lagrange, *De Revelatione*, II, 192: Societas est adunatio hominum ad aliquid unum perficiendum.
12. Felix Cavagnis, *Institutiones Juris Publici*, I, lib. I, 23.

13. Ottaviani, *Institutiones*, I, 11.
14. Ottaviani, *op. cit.*, I, 14.
15. St. Thomas Aquinas, II a II ae q 188 a. 7 ad 1.
16. Gredt, *op. cit.*, II, 411.
17. *The Catholic Encyclopedia*, III, 760.
18. Ottaviani, *op. cit.*, I, 31; see *The Catholic Encyclopedia*, III, 760; see Gredt. *op. cit.*, II, 422.
19. Herman Dieckmann, *De Ecclesia*, I, 256. . . . et necessariam, fundatam in voluntate legitimi superioris.
20. Wernz-Vidal, *Ius Canonicum*, II, 29.
21. Capello, *Institutiones*, I, 13.
22. Gredt, *op. cit.*, II, 421, . . . illa societas est perfecta, quae per se immediate ordinatur ad finem supremum in aliquo genere bonorum supremo.
23. Gredt, *op. cit.*, II, 422.
24. St. Augustine, *Confessiones*, I, 1, 1; PL 32, 661; Cf. Vernon Y. Bourke, *Augustine's Quest of Wisdom*, 145.
25. Ant. Straub, *De Ecclesia Christi*, I, 5. See Aemil Dorsch, *Institutiones Theologiae Fundamentalis;* II *De Ecclesia Christi*, 3. See Carolus Passaglia, *De Ecclesia Christi*, I, 70.
26. Capello, *op. cit.*, I, 27; Cf. Gredt, *op. cit.*, II, 205.
27. Dieckmann, *De Ecclesia*, II, 247.
28. "The Idea of the Church in St. Thomas Aquinas," in *The Thomist*, I, 331-359.
29. Dieckmann, *op. cit.*, II, 247. This definition is from St. Robert Bellarmine.
30. Ottaviani, *op. cit.*, I, 157; Cf. Braito, *Základy*, 110.
31. Dieckmann, *op. cit.*, II, 247. Triplex denique vinculum, quo eius membra ligantur, eiusdem auctoritatis, fidei, caritatis.
32. Ottaviani, *op. cit.*, I, 158.
33. Friedrich Heiler, *Urkirche und Ostkirche*, I, 61-67. Cf. Garrigou-Lagrange, *De Revelatione*, II, 188.
34. Dieckmann, *op. cit.*, I, 280-283: Nomen Ecclesiae ad Jesum Christum ut auctorem reducitur, p. 183; consentimus igitur verbis M. J. Lagrange; non erit facile determinare, quam vocem Jesus adhibuerit in lingua Aramaica . . . eo sensu, ut salvo meliore juditio, praeferamus gehala. . . .
35. Garrigou-Lagrange, *op. cit.*, II, 189.
36. Ottaviani, *op. cit.*, I, 159. Cf. Emmet John Hughes, *The Church and the Liberal Society*, 207.
37. Ottaviani, *op. cit.*, I, 169-170; Cf. Lenin, "*Discours aux jeunes Communistes, Oeuvres*, XVIII, 320. Cf. *The Red and the Black: The Church in the Communist State*, 1953, 3.
38. Ant. Straub, *De Ecclesia Christi*, I, 19.
39. Conc. Vat. S. IV, D1667.
40. Ant. Straub, *op. cit.*, 20.

41. John 20:21; Matt. 7:29; Matt. 23:10; Luke 4:43; John 17:1-4; John 17:19; Heb. 5:5-10; Matt. 28:18; John 5:26-27; Phil. 2:9-10; John 10:11-16; Acts 20:28; Eph. 5:23.
42. Luke 24:33; John 20:19; Matt. 28:16; Luke 6:13; Matt. 10:18; Mark 3:14; Acts 1:2-8; 1:21-26; 10:40-42.
43. Matt. 28:16-20; Luke 22:19; John 20:22-23; Matt. 18:16-18; Matt. 28:19-20.
44. Matt. 16:18-19.
45. Matt. 16:18.
46. I Cor. 4:1.
47. Tit. 1:5; Acts 20:28-31; I Pet. 5:1-5; I Tim. 4:11; 6:13-14; II Tim. 1:6-14.
48. Schultes, *De Ecclesia Catholica*, 260.
49. Matt. 28:18-20.
50. Luke 21:12; Mark 13:9.
51. Acts 4:19.
52. Acts 5:29; Acts 5:42: "And they did not for a single day cease teaching and preaching in the temple and from house to house the good news of Jesus as the Christ."
53. Schultes, *op. cit.*, 261.
54. *ES*, 469.
55. Matt. 18:18.
56. Schultes, *op. cit.*, 262; see *The Catholic Encyclopedia*, III, 761.
57. Billot, *De Ecclesia Christi*, 133.
58. *ES*, 714, 1646, 1677, 1716.
59. Jacques Maritain, *The Things That Are Not Caesar's*, 123-132. See M. Gosselin, *The Power of the Pope*, II, 360 ff.
60. *ES*, 714; cf. Bulla Bonifatii VIII: *Unam Sanctam* Con Flor.; decretum pro Jacobitis (*ES*, 714). Formulam: Extra Ecclesiam nulla salus . . . iam dixit Origines; cf. Schultes, *op. cit.*, 269; cf. Billot, *op. cit.*, 727.
61. J. V. de Groot, *Summa Apologetica de Ecclesia Catholica*, 736.
62. Schultes, *op. cit.*, 265.
63. Billot, *op. cit.*, I, 123.
64. *Ibid.*, 123.
65. Dieckman, *op. cit.*, 272.
66. Caroli Passaglia, *De Ecclesia Christi*, I, 123. Cf. Schultes, *op. cit.*, 144.
67. Billot, *op. cit.*, 67.
68. *Ibid.*, 68.
69. Garrigou-Lagrange, *op. cit.*, II, 197.
70. Matthias Joseph Scheeben, *The Mysteries of Christianity*, 540.
71. De Groot, *op. cit.*, 67.

72. Ottaviani, *op. cit.*, I, 166.
73. Dieckmann, *op. cit.*, I, 272.
74. Mark 16:15; cf. St. Thomas Aquinas, I-II, q. 90, a. 4.
75. Garrigou-Lagrange, *op. cit.*, II, 201.
76. Francis C. Kelly, "Society," in *The Catholic Encyclopedia*, XIV, 76.
77. Ottaviani, *op. cit.*, I, 164.
78. Cavagnis, *op. cit.*, 116.
79. Leo XIII, Enc. *Immortale Dei*, Section 45. Ecclesiam vero.
80. Billot, *op. cit.*, 122.
81. Dieckmann, *op. cit.*, 257. Jurisdictio definire potest auctoritas in societate perfecta.
82. Raymond Corrigan, *The Church and the Nineteenth Century*, 296.

FOOTNOTES TO CHAPTER III

1. Dieckmann, *De Ecclesia*, I, 526.
2. Gredt, *Elementa Philosophiae*, II, 411.
3. Felix Cavagnis, *Institutiones*, I, no. 80, 47.
4. Ottaviani, *Institutiones Juris Publici Ecclesiastici*, I, 81.
5. Dieckmann, *op cit.*, I, 257. Cf. Billot, *De Ecclesia Christi*, I, 440. "Et si societas sit perfecta, perfectam quoque in ea oportet esse auctoritatem regiminis, id est, in suo saltem ordine independentem, et ad omnia imperii iura sese extendentem. Et si insuper, non modo perfecta societas sit, verum etiam suprema inter humanas societates, eo ipso necesse est ut eius jurisdictio nulli omnino humanae potestati, quacumque tandem ratione et modo, etiam mero indirecto, subiaceat."
6. *CJC*, can. 107.
7. St. Thomas Aquinas, *Summa Theologiae*, Suppl. q. 17, a. 2. ad. 2.
8. Matthias Joseph Scheeben, *The Mysteries of Christianity*, 546.
9. Ottaviani: *Compendium Juris Publici Ecclesiastici*, 140.
10. *Ibid.*, 208.
11. F. X. Wernz and P. Petrus Vidal, *Ius Canonicum*, II, 62.
12. *CJC*, can. 118.
13. St. Thomas Aquinas, *op. cit.*, II, II, q. 39, a. 3.
14. Wernz-Vidal, *op. cit.*, II, 66.
15. *ES*, 960.
16. *ES*, no. 1822; cf. Ottaviani, *op. cit.*, 243-4.
17. Matt. 16:19.
18. Matt. 18:17-18.
19. Billot, *op. cit.* 128.
20. *Ibid.*, 129. Cf. Ad Tanquerey-F. Cimetier, *Synopsis Theologiae Moralis et Pastoralis*, 15. Cf. Dieckmann, *op. cit.*, 263.

21. Billot, *op. cit.*, 139.
22. Aemil. Dorsch, *Institutiones Theologiae Fundamentalis*, II, 79.
23. Matt. 16:13; cf. Ant. Straub, *De Ecclesia Christi*, I, 39.
24. Matt. 3:1; 4:5; Eccl. 48:1.
25. II Macc. 15:14.
26. Matt. 16:15; cf. Dorsh, *op. cit.*, 86.
27. John 21:15-17.
28. Matt. 16:13.
29. John 10:11.
30. Dieckmann, *op. cit.*, 315.
31. Matt. 5:14.
32. Matt. 28:18-20.
33. St. Thomas, III, 8, 6.
34. Dorsch, *op. cit.*, 111.
35. Straub, *op. cit.*, 136.
36. Wernz-Vidal, *op. cit.*, 463.
37. *ES*, 1823.
38. John 21:15-17.
39. De Groot, *Summa Apologetica de Ecclesia Catholica ad mentem S. Thomae Aquinatis*, 501.
40. John 1:42; Mark 3:16.
41. I Cor. 10:4.
42. Luke 5:3-4.
43. John 13:6.
44. Mark 16:7; I Cor. 15:5.
45. Acts 2:14-41.
46. Acts 15:7-12. Cf. Straub, *op. cit.*, I, 116 ff.
47. De Groot, *op. cit.*, 512.
48. *Ibid.*, 527.
49. St. Thomas Aquinas, *Contra Gentiles*, IV, 76.
50. Dorsch, *op. cit.*, 100.
51. De Groot, *op. cit.*, 529-555.
52. *AAS*, XLIII, 51. In Nuntius rudiophonicus universi orbis episcopis et Christi fidelibus latus, pridie pervigilium nativitatis D. N. Jesu Christo, anno 1950. Cf. *America*, 34, no. 74, 394. Ritravomento della Tomba del Principe degli Apostoli, p. 57: Le perodurante l'anno Santo la Confessione de S. Pietro in Vaticano e stata testimone e centro di cosi imponenti manifestazioni della unita dei cattolici di tutto il mondo nella fede e nell'amore, la gloria di questo luogo sacro ha avuto auche in an altro aspetto il suo compimento: gli scavi sotto la confessione medesima, almeno in quanto concernono la tomba dell' Apostolo (ricerche alle quali Noi volgemmo l'animo fin dai primi mesi del Nostro Pontificato), e il loro ezame scientifico, sono stati, nel corso di questo anno giubilare, condotti felicemente a termine. Nel piu

breve tempo uno documentata publicazione portera a conoscenza del publico il risultato delle diligentissime esplorazioni.

Questo risultato e stato di somma riccherra e importanza. Ma la questione essenziale e la seguente. E stata veramente ritrovata la tomba di S. Pietro? A tale domanda la conclusione finale dei lavori e degli studi risponde con un chiarissimo St. La Tomba del Principe degli Apostoli e stato retrovata.

Una seconda questione, subordinata alla prima, riguarda le reliquie del Santo. Sono state esse rinvenute? Al margine del sepolcro furono trovati resti di ossa umane, dei quali pero non e possibile di provare con certezza che appartenessero alla spoglia mortale dell' Apostolo. Cio lascia tuttavia intatta la realta storica della tomba. La gigantesca cupola s'inarca esattamente sul sepolcro del primo Vescovo di Roma, del primo Papa; sepolcro in origine umilissimo, ma sul quale la venenarione dei secoli posteriori con meravigliosa successione di opere cresse il massimo tempio della Cristianita.

53. Francis Dvorník, *The Photian Schism: History and Legend.*

54. II Thes. 2:4.

55. De Groot, *op. cit.*, 557.

56. Schultes, *De Ecclesia Catholica*, 409.

57. Edm. Richers, *De Ecclesiastica et Politica Potestate.*

58. *ES*, 1322-24.

59. St. Thomas Aquinas, *op. cit.*, IV, 76.

60. Scheeben, *op. cit.* 552-3.

61. Matt. 26:31.

62. Jacques Maritain, *The Things That Are Not Caesar's*, 116-118.

63. *Ibid.*, 57.

FOOTNOTES TO CHAPTER IV

1. Garrigou-Lagrange, *De Revelatione*, II, 192. Cf. Straub, *De Ecclesia Christi*, 336.

2. Timotheus Zapelena, S. J., *De Ecclesia Christi*, 171.

3. Schultes, *De Ecclesia Catholica*, 99.

4. Zapelena, *op. cit.*, 172.

5. Schultes, *op. cit.*, 100; cf. Billot, *De Ecclesia Christi*, 5.

6. Garrigou-Lagrange, *op. cit.*, 192.

7. *ES*, 2104.

8. Matt. 10:5-8; Mark 6:7-13; Luke 9:1-6.

9. J. V. De Groot, *Summa Apologetica de Ecclesia Catholica ad Mentem S. Thomae Aquinatis*, 86.

10. Kleros; by divine institution or the Lord is a part.

11. I Peter 2:10; cf. Straub, *op. cit.*, 336.

12. Conc. Trid., Sess. XXIII, cap. IV; Conc. Vat. Const.

Pastor Aeternus; ES, 1821; cf. Dieckmann, *De Ecclesia* 258; cf. Zapelena, *op. cit.*, 173.

13. Hebr. 7:24.
14. S. Thomas Aquinas, III, q. 64, a. 3.
15. *Ibid.*, III, q. 64, a. 1.
16. Col. 1:18.
17. I Cor. 4:1.
18. Billot, *op. cit.*, 33.
19. Tit. 2:14.
20. Eph. 5:25-28.
21. Eph. 1:22.
22. Schultes, *op. cit.*, 100.
23. *Ibid.*, 132-139.
24. De Groot, *op. cit.*, 104-109.
25. St. Thomas Aquinas, *Contra Gentiles*, IV, 74. Matt. 18:18. Matt. 18:1-35; Matt. 18-17; John 17:18; John 20:21-23; Matt. 26:20; 28:18; Mark 14:17; Luke 22:14-30. John 20:21-23.
26. John 17:18-19.
27. Matt. 28:18.
28. Mark 16:16.
29. Zapelena, *op. cit.*, 181.
30. Schultes, *op. cit.*, 101.
31. John 15:16.
32. Luke 6:13.
33. Luke 10:16.
34. Matt. 28:18-20.
35. Schultes, *op. cit.*, 107.
36. Aemile Dorsch, *Institutiones Theologiae Fundamentalis*, 55.
37. Gerald Aloysius Ryan, *Principles of Episcopal Jurisdiction*, 19-29.
38. Dorsch, *op. cit.*, 61.
39. I Tim. 5:19.
40. Billot, *op. cit.*, 222; cf. Dieckmann, *op. cit.*, 394.
41. I Thess. 2:7.
42. Catech. Rom., II, cap. VII, 9.
43. Conc. Trid. Sess. XXIII, can. 6; *ES*, 960, 966.
44. Luke 10:1.
45. II Tim. 1:6.
46. De Groot, *op. cit.*, 114.
47. St. Thomas Aquinas, *Contra Gentiles*, IV, 76; *Summa Theologica Supl.* q. 37, a. 1.
48. Acts 20:28; cf. Billot, *op. cit.*, III, 5.
49. Pius XI, Ep. ad Enc. Card. A. Bertram, 13 Nov. 1928. In *AAS.*, XX, 384 ff.
50. Schultes, *op. cit.*, 139.

51. Francis J. Connell, *Morals in Politics and Professions.*
52. Schultes, *op. cit.*, 122.
53. Zapelena, *op. cit.*, 173.
54. Schultes, *op. cit.*, 127; cf. Dieckmann, *op. cit.*, 487.
55. Giuseppe Ricciotti, *Paulo Apostolo: Biografia con introduzione critica e illustration*, 201 ff., and 195-207.
56. I Cor. 13:1-13; cf. Adolph Tanquerey-Herman Branderis, *The Spiritual Life*, 710-711.
57. Eph. 4:12.
58. Eph. 4:11.
59. Dieckmann, *op. cit.*, 323-324.
60. Billot, *op. cit.*, III, 35.
61. *ES*, 1821.
62. *Ibid.*, 495-500.
63. *Ibid.*, 1502, 1504, 1505.
64. *Ibid.*, 960, 966.
65. *Leonis XIII, Pontificis Maximi Acta*, XVI, 182-183.
66. Matt. 28:18-20; John 14:16-17; Eph. 4:11-16; I Cor. 11:23-26; Matt. 4:23; 9:35; 13:19-35; 21:31; 43; 24:14; Luke 1:35; I Cor. 14:34, 35; I Tim. 2:11-12.
67. Straub, *op. cit.*, 341 ff.
68. Acts 20:28; I Tim. 5:19-20; Acts 11; 30; Acts 12:17-18; I Tim. 4:6; II Cor. 3:6; Eph. 3:7; Rom. 15:8.
69. Straub, *op cit.*, 362.
70. *ES*, 960.
71. *Ibid.*, 967.
72. *Ibid.*, 968.
73. St. Thomas Aquinas, *op. cit.*, IV, 76.

FOOTNOTES TO CHAPTER V

1. Matt. 13:24.
2. Francis Dvorník, *Les Légendes de Constantin et de Méthode vues de Byzance*. Cf. F. Dvorník, *Sv. Vojtěch, II Biskup Pražský*.
3. Dvorník, *The Making of Central and Eastern Europe*, 95-196.
4. Ludvík Němec, "*Catholicism in Exile*," in *Katolík*, April, 1950, LVII, no. 5948.
5. Mikuláš Šprinc, *Sv. Andrej-Svorad.*
6. Dvorník, *The first Wave of the Drang Nach Osten*. Reprinted from the *Cambridge Historical Journal*, VII, no. 3, 134.
7. Bohdan Chudoba, *Czekoslovakia*: *A Study in Disintegration*. Reprinted from *Thought*, XXV, no. 96, 83.
8. August Naegle, *Einfuehrung des Christentums in Boehmen*, I.

9. Kamil Krofta, *A Short History of Czechoslovakia*, 4.

10. Francis Dvorník, *Saint Wenceslas, Duke of Bohemia.*

11. B. Ráček, *Československé dějiny* (*Czechoslovak History*), 693. Cf. *Slovakia*, 3, no. 2 (July, 1953), 57.

12. Joseph Pekař, *Československé dějiny* (*Czechoslovak History*), 48.

13. Joseph Loserth, *Hus und Wiclif* (Zur Genesis der Husitischen Lehre), 13-24; *ibid.*, 302-303; *ibid.*, *Document No. 12*, "Missa Wiklefistarum," 299-303. Loserth is very eloquent in showing how great was Wyclif's influence in Bohemia, and that the strongest invective against Wyclifism in Bohemia originated just at the time of the Council of Constance.

14. S. Harrison Thomson, *Czechoslovakia in European History*, 99.

15. Ludwig Pastor, *Geschichte der Paepste*, 166.

16. Joseph Hergenroether, *Handbuch der Allgemeinen Kirchengeschichte*, II, 878.

17. *ES*, 581-82.

18. Gotthard Victor Lechler, *John Wiclif and his English Precursors*, 123-154; cf. John Lingard and Hilaire Belloc, *The History of England*, III, 268. Cf. David Wilkins, *Concilia Magnae Britanniae*, III, 344 ff.

19. Pastor, *op. cit.*, 168. Cf. Loserth, *op. cit.*, 281. According to Loserth, Hus was a mere *plagiarist* of Wyclif, who, in all probability, "with the exception of the Bible and some few of the fathers consulted in his theological studies no other sources than those of Wyclif only." Cf. Jan Sedlák, *Studie a Texty*, II, 526. "This certainly is not copied from one or two of Wyclif's treatises, but he did take from the literary production of Wyclif everything that was relevant to his purpose, and he put it together into a whole which was relatively independent." Cf. Herbert B. Workman, *John Wyclif: A Study of the English Medieval Church*, II, 7.

20. Mansi, *Sacrorum Conciliorum nova et amplissima Collectio*, XXVII, 1207 ff.

21. Kamil Krofta, *Malé Dějiny Československé*, 30.

22. Karl Joseph von Hefele, *Conciliengeschichte*, VI, 684, 704, 719.

23. Ráček, *op. cit.*, 167-170. The description of John of Jenštejn, in the novel *Mezi Proudy* (*Between the Streams*), by Jirásek, is wrong. Historian Pekař, in his *Tři Kapitoly o Sv. Janu Nepomuckém* (*Three Chapters about St. John Nepomucene*), 17, described John of Jenštejn in his true light.

24. E. Winter, *Tausend Jahre Geisteskampf im Sudetenraum*, 87.

25. Count von Luetzow, *Bohemia, An Historical Sketch,* 92.
26. Winter, *op. cit.,* 85.
27. Frantisek Palacký, *Dějiny husitské,* I, 40. Ed.
28. Joseph Pekař, ČČH, 460.
29. Winter, *op. cit.,* 96.
30. V. Flajshanš, *M. Jan Hus,* 68, 74.
31. Ráček, *op. cit.,* 187.
32. Joseph Kratochvil, *Otázky a Problemy* (*Questions and Problems*), 86.
33. *Ibid.,* 86.
34. Palacký, *op. cit.,* 39.
35. Winter, *op. cit.,* 102.
36. Ráček, *op. cit.,* 188.
37. This event was disclosed by the historian Flajshanš. Cf. Ráček, *op. cit.,* 189.
38. Jan Sedlák, *Mister Jan Hus,* 173.
39. K. Hoefler, *Geschichtschreiber der Husitischen Bewegung in Boehmen,* I, 52. Cf. Höfler, *op. cit.,* II, 156-169.
40. Palacký, *op. cit.,* 32; cf. Von Hefele, *op. cit.,* VI, 928.
41. Josef Pekař, *Československé dějiny,* 49.
42. Thomson, *op. cit.,* 100.
43. Von Lutzow, *op. cit.,* 100.
44. Gustave Schnuerer, *Kirche und Kulture im Mittelalter,* 275.
45. Von Lutzow, *op. cit.,* 102.
46. Ráček, *op. cit.,* 209.
47. Reuben Parsons, *Studies in Church History,* III, 6; cf. A. Neuman, *Hus dle nejnovéjší literatury* (*Hus According to the Newest Literature*), 38.
48. Palacký, *op. cit.,* 190.
49. Ráček, *op. cit.,* 217.
50. Pekař, *op. cit.,* 50.
51. Mansi, *op. cit.,* XXVII (1409-1418), 530 ff.; XXVIII (1419-1431), 4 ff.; cf. Schnuerer, *op. cit.,* III, 274.
52. Palacký, *Documenta,* 69; cf. M. Greighton, *A History of the Papacy during the Period of the Reformation,* I, 324-325.
53. Mansi, *op. cit.,* Vol. XXVIII (1414-1421), 4 ff.; cf. Palacký, *Dějiny Husitské,* II, 183-186.
54. T. G. Masaryk, *Jan Hus,* 118.
55. Palacký, *op. cit.,* 598-599.
56. Palacký, *Dějiny Husitské,* 196; cf. Paul Roubiczek and J. Kalmer, *Warrior of God: The Life and Death of John Hus,* 192.
57. Palacký, *Dějiny České,* III, 197; cf. Philip Schaff, *History of the Christian Church,* V, Part II, 379-384. Cf. K. Hoe-

fler, *Geschichtschreiber der Husitischen Bewegung in Boehmen*, II, 306-308 (ordo et processus qualiter sententiatus examinatus et crematus fuit Johannes Hus).

58. T. G. Masaryk, *Česká Otázka* (*The Czech Question*).
59. Pekař, *Der Sinn der Tschechischen Geschichte*, 57.
60. *ES*, 627; cf. Johannes Gottschick, *Hus', Luther's und Zwingle's Lehre von der Kirche.* In *Zeitschrift fuer Kirchengeschichte*, III, no. 3, 357-394.
61. *ES*, 632.
62. *Ibid.*, 629.
63. *Ibid.*, 631.
64. Palacký, *Dějiny Husitské*, 189.
65. *ES*, 633.
66. *Ibid.*, 635.
67. *Ibid.*, 637.
68. *Ibid.*, 636.
69. Paul Roubiczek and Joseph Kalmer, *op. cit.*, 188-189.
70. Gottschick, *op. cit.*, 374.
71. Reuben Parsons, *op. cit.*, III, 6.
72. *ES*, 638.
73. *Ibid.*, 639.
74. *Ibid.*, 648.
75. *Ibid.*, 646.
76. *Ibid.*, 645.
77. *Ibid.*, 641.
78. *Ibid.*, 656. Cf. Bohdan Chudoba, *The Meaning of Civilization*, 175.
79. *ES*, 651; cf. Von Hefele, *op. cit.*, VI, 955.
80. Pekař, *op. cit.*, 50.
81. Palacký, *op. cit.*, 41.
82. Ráček, *Dějiny Československé*, 230; cf. Pekař, *op. cit.*, 49.
83. Pekař, *Der Sinn der Tschechischen Geschichte*, 57. Cf. Chudoba, *op. cit.*, 175.
84. *Ibid.*
85. Pekař, *Kniha o kosti*, II, 124.
86. Pekař, *Dějiny Československé*, 50.
87. *Ibid.*, 50.
88. Palacký, *op. cit.*, 535.
89. Pekař, *Jan Žižka*, II, 176.
90. Pekař, *Dějiny*, 52.
91. Kamil Krofta, *op. cit.*, 42.
92. *Ibid.*, 43.
93. Palacký, *op. cit.*, 416.
94. Pekař, *Jan Žižka*, I, 174.
95. Pekař, *Dějiny Československé*, 52.

96. *ES*, 641.
97. Pekař, *op. cit.*, 52.
98. Ludwig Pastor, *op. cit.*, V-VII, 170.
99. *Ibid.*, 170; cf. Gustav Schnuerer, *op. cit.*, 283.
100. Hoefler, *op. cit.*, III, 214. Quae vos vocatis compactata oratores insignes, apostolica sedes neque novit unquam neque accepit.
101. Gustav Schnuerer, *op. cit.*, III, 283.
102. Pastor, *op. cit.*, 355 ff.; cf. Hoefler, *op. cit.*, III, 213. Georgius ad omnia simulanda dissimulandaque paratus. . . .
103. Krofta, *Malé déjiny Československé*, 40.
104. Pekař, *op. cit.*, 73.
105. *Ibid.*, 72.
106. Dvorník, *op. cit.*, 265.
107. Pekař, *Dějiny*, 73.
108. Ludwig Pastor, *The History of the Popes*, XXVII, 279-281.
109. Pekař, *op. cit.*, 88.
110. Pekař, *Smysl českých dějin* (*The Sense of Czech History*), 15.
111. Krofta, *op. cit.*, 78.
112. *Ibid.*, 83.
113. *Ibid.*, 94.
114. Winter, *Tausend Jahre Geisteskampf im Sudetenraum*, 376-377.
115. K. Hilgereiner, "Husiten," in *The Catholic Encyclopedia*, V, 211. Cf. Vlastimil Kybal, *Czechoslovak Independence.*
116. Ráček, *op. cit.*, 196.
117. Kamil Krofta, "University Speeches"; Ráček, *op. cit.*, 318.

FOOTNOTES TO CHAPTER VI

1. Kirsch-Veit, *Kirchengeschichte*, IV, 245.
2. Kirsch-Veit, *op. cit.*, 246.
3. T. G. Masaryk, *Česká Otázka*, 192. Cf. T. G. Masaryk, *Jan Hus*, 35; cf. J. A. Quigley, *Condemned Societies*, 51-68.
4. Kirsch-Veit, *op. cit.*, 320-322. Cf. T. Vonásek, *Po stopách Českého Zednářství* (Chicago, 1913).
5. Winter, *Tausend Jahre Geisteskampf im Sudetenraum*, 333.
6. Winter, *op. cit.*, 334.
7. Winter, *Bolzano und Sein Kreis* (Sebastian Merkle gewidmet). Cf. Winter, *Leben und geistige Entwicklung des Sozialethikers und Mathematikers Bernard Bolzano* (1781-1848).
8. T. G. Masaryk, *Karel Havlíček*, 282.
9. Winter, *Tausend Jahre*, 342.

10. Kirsch-Veit, *op. cit.* 61.
11. *Ibid.*, 63.
12. Pii IX, *Acta*, pars prima, Vol. II, 465-484. Cf. Mercati, Raccolta di concordati su materie ecclesiastiche fra la Santa Sede et le Autorita Civili, 821-844.
13. Felix John Vondráček, *The Foreign Policy of Czechoslovakia* 1918-1935, 91. It was decreed that the state should preserve the Roman Catholic religion "with all its rights and prerogatives according to God's order and the Church's laws." Thereby the Church had been granted control over all matters pertaining to marriage, morals, and education.
14. Kamil Krofta, *Stará ústava Česká*, 72.
15. Franz. Lud. Rieger, "*Ein Charakterbild aus Boehmens Neuester Geschichte.*" 633-651; 734-752.
16. Kirsch-Veit, *op. cit.*, II, 301.
17. *ASS*, IV (1868), 10-13: Papae Pii IX. Allocutio habita in consistorio secreto die 22 Junii 1868. The English translation by Father John Gallagher, of Duquesne University, Pittsburgh.
18. Winter, *op. cit.*, 356.
19. T. G. Masaryk, *Moderní člověk a náboženství* (Modern Man and Religion), 187-224.
20. Joseph Cardinal Hergenroether, *Handbuch der Allgemeinen Kirchengeschichte*, III, 976-977.
21. Hergenroether, *op. cit.*, 978.
22. Joseph Schmidlin, *Papstgeschichte der Neuesten Zeit. (Papsttum und Paepste gegenüber den modernen Strönungen. Pius IX und Leo XIII*, 1846-1903). Vol. II, 255-283.
23. *Ibid.*, 271.
24. *Ibid.*, 275-283.
25. *Ibid.*, 271-272.
26. Beiser J. Ryan, *The Vatican Council and the American Secular Newspapers*, 1869-70, 10. Most of the adversaries accepted papal infallibility as a dogma but were opposed to its definition on various grounds.
27. Winter, *op. cit.*, 380.
28. Hergenroether, *op. cit.*, 980.
29. Winter, *Die geistige Entwicklung Anton Guenthers und seiner Schule*, 381.
30. Schmidlin, *op. cit.*, 291.
31. Hergenroether, *op. cit.*, 980.
32. Raymond Corrigan, *The Church and the Nineteenth Century*, 207-214.
33. Lillian Parker Wallace, *The Papacy and European Diplomacy*, 1869-1878, 222.
34. Corrigan, *op. cit.*, 213.

35. Emil Ludwig, *Bismarck*, 417.

36. *Ibid.*

37. Corrigan, *op. cit.*, 212. Cf. Julien De Narfan, *Pope Leo XIII*, 186. Cf. Thomas P. Neill, *They Lived the Faith*, 71-93.

38. Kirsch-Veit, *Kirchengeschichte*, IV, part 2, 302. Cf. James McCaffrey, *History of the Catholic Church in the Nineteenth Century*, I, 333.

39. Hergenroether, *op. cit.*, 984.

40. Winter, *op. cit.*, 382.

41. Count von Luetzow, *Bohemia, An Historical Sketch*, 351.

42. *Lexikon fuer Theologie und Kirche*, 2d. ed., VI, 652.

43. *Loc. cit.*

44. Franz Stauracz, *Los von Rom*, 16-17.

45. *Der Grosse Brockhaus*, XVI. Cf. Adolf Hitler, *Mein Kampf*, 10. Schoenerer's movement was strongly anti-Semitic.

46. Elizabeth Wiskemann, *Czechs and Germans: A Study of the Struggle in the Provinces of Bohemia and Moravia*, 42-44.

47. T. G. Masaryk, *Los von Rom*, 100.

48. *Der Grosse Brockhaus*, XVI, 99.

49. *Lexikon fuer Theologie und Kirche*, VI, 652.

50. Adolf Hitler, *Mein Kampf*, 97-108.

51. *Der Grosse Herder*, VII, 1207. Cf. Blažej Ráček, *Československé Dějiny*, 624.

52. R. W. Seton-Watson, *Masaryk in England*, 9.

53. Kirsch-Veit, *op. cit.*, 306.

54. Winter, *op. cit.*, 386.

55. Kamil Krofta, *Malé Dějiny Československé*, 95.

56. Schmidlin, *op. cit.*, II, 479.

57. Leonis XIII, Pontificis Maximi *Acta*, V, 1-7. De collegio clericorum bohemorum in urbe condendo.

58. Theodor Grentrup, *Volk und Volkstum im Lichte der Religion*, 151.

59. Grentrup, *op. cit.*, 150; cf. Schmidlin, *op. cit.*, 479.

60. Leonis XIII, *Acta*, XXI, 137-144; 164-165; XXII, 239-240 Congratulations for the successful absolving of the episcopal conference in Olomouc.

61. Winter, *op. cit.*, 383.

62. Leonis XIII, *Acta*, XI, 91-144.

63. Wiard Klapp, *Leben und Wirken des Sozialpolitikers Karl Freiherr von Vogelsang* (Nach den Quellen bearbeitet).

64. Franz Stauracz, *Dr. Karl Lueger*. Cf. Adolf Hitler, *Mein Kampf*, 99, 55. Hitler writes about him with great admiration, commenting especially on his political works.

65. Winter, *op. cit.*, 384.

66. Masaryk, *Jan Hus*, 27.
67. Winter, *op. cit.*, 387.
68. Masaryk, *Los von Rom*, 15.
69. Count von Luetzow, *op. cit.*, 354.
70. Hitler, *op. cit.*, 108, 113.
71. Masaryk, *op. cit.*, 12; Cf. Alfred Rosenberg, *Der Mythus des XX. Jahrhunderts*, 456-458; Cf. *Der Grosse Herder*, 555; Cf. *Der Grosse Brockhaus*, XI.
72. Franz Stauracz, *Los von Rom.*
73. "Die Los-von-Rom Bewegung in Oesterreich," in *Hist. Pol. Bl.* CXXVI, CXXVII (1900-1901), in many articles.
74. *Lexikon fuer Theologie und Kirche*, VI, 653. Cf. Kirsch-Veit, *op. cit.*, 464.
75. Winter, *op. cit.*, 387.
76. Goyau, "L'Allemagne en Autriche: un épisode d'histoire religieuse," in *Revue des Deux Mondes*, (1903), 276.
77. Winter, *op. cit.*, 388.
78. Kirsch-Veit, *op. cit.*, IV, part 2, 306.
79. Winter, *op. cit.*, 387.
80. Sarda-Pallen, *What is Liberalism?*, 19.
81. Stauracz,. *op. cit.*, 89-90. Die Maurer waren in der Arbeit . . . especially Italian masone Mazzini: "Oesterreich muss zu Grunde gerichtet werden . . ."; see *ibid.*, 7.
82. Masaryk, *op. cit.*, 16.
83. Masaryk, *Česká Otázka*, 241.
84. Zdeněk Nejedlý, *T. G. Masaryk*, 310.
85. *Ibid.*, 313.
86. *Ibid.*, 284.
87. Otto Krause, *Franz Brentano.*
88. Karel Čapek, *Hovory s Masarykem*, 97.
89. Nejedlý, *op. cit.*, 459.
90. Harald Hoeffding and Josef Král, *Přehledné Dějiny Filosofie* (History of Philosophy), 330.
91. Otakar Machotka, *T. G. Masaryk*, 15.
92. Hoeffding and Král, *op. cit.*, 330.
93. Masaryk, *Jan Hus*, 10. Cf. R. W. Seton-Watson, *Masaryk in England*, 10.
94. Masaryk, *Česká Otázka*, 13.
95. Jaroslav Werstadt, *Ve jménu Husově pro svobodu Národa* (In the name of Hus for freedom of the nation), 7.
96. Masaryk, *Jan Hus*, 157.
97. Masaryk, *op. cit.*, 158-59.
98. Werstadt, *op. cit.*, 13.
99. Masaryk, *Česká Otázka*, 184.

100. John Herben, *T. G. Masaryk*, 380.
101. Masaryk, *Ein Katechetenspiegel.*
102. Machotka, *op. cit.*, 9.
103. Nejedlý, *op. cit.*, 48.
104. Masaryk, *Jan Hus*, 45.
105. Machotka, *op. cit.*, 21. For information see Arthur Robert Pennington, *The Counter-Reformation in Europe*, 50-68.
106. Jan Papánek, *Czechoslovakia*, 17.
107. Papánek, *op. cit.*, 21.
108. Winter, *op. cit.*, 386.
109. Krofta, *op. cit.*, 91.
110. Nejedlý, *op. cit.*, 273.
111. Adolf Srb, *Politické Dějiny Národa Českého* (1861-1918), II, 168.
112. *Ibid.*, 168.
113. *Ibid.*, 349.
114. Seton-Watson, *op. cit.*, 8.
115. The Reverend Francis Sušil was a great scientist, theologian, and patriot. He was a professor at the theological seminary in Brno. He was active in promoting Catholic organizations.
116. Monsignor Stojan was a generous benefactor and worked arduously for social reforms that would benefit the people. The success of the Catholic center in Velehrad is one result of his work. Cf. *Nový Život* (The new life), III, No. 7, July 1951. "*Můz modlitby a práce*" (Radio broadcast by Cardinal Clement Micara on the 100th anniversary of Archbishop Antonín Cyril Stojan, on May 22, 1951). See a detailed study in articles, appearing weekly in *Katolik*, LXI (1954), by Monsignor Dr. Josef Bezdíček: "Antonín Cyril Stojan, God's faithful servant."
117. Masaryk, *Jan Hus*, 10.
118. Masaryk, *Česká Otázka*, 200.
119. Masaryk, *op. cit.*, 228.
120. Masaryk, *Jan Hus*, 89.
121. Masaryk, *Česká Otázka*, 210-11.
122. Masaryk, *op cit.*, 224.
123. Polivka, "O Kontroversich Cyrilomethodějských," in the *Athenaeum*, Oct. 15, 1885.
124. Winter, *op. cit.*, 389.
125. Oldřich Zlámal, "Povídka mého života" (The Story of My Life), in *Katolik*, 60 (1953). Many articles from May-December, 1953, and April, 1954.
126. Winter, *Russland und die slawischen Völker in der Diplomatie des Vatikans* 1878-1903, 108-10.
127. Pius X, Encyclical, *Pascendi Domini Gregis*, Sept. 7, 1907, in *ASS*, 40, 38 ff.

128. Pius X, *Motu Proprio*, Sept. 1, 1910; in *AAS*, II, 655-680.

129. Viktor Dyk declared that atheists and Socialists are anti-Catholic to the point of insanity. His statement is well-known. NCWC., May 4, 1925. Cf. Hanuš Jelínek, *Viktor Dyk*.

130. J. Godrycz, *The Doctrine of Modernism and Its Refutation*, 121.

131. *Slovenská Čitanka* (1925), 358; cf. V. Chaloupecký, *Zápas o Slovensko*.

132. Konstantin Čulen, *Po Svätoplukovi druhá naše hlava*, I, 32.

133. Von Luetzow, *op. cit.*, 355; cf. Seton-Watson, *op. cit.*, 168.

134. Zdenka and John Munzer, *We Were and We Shall Be*, 81-86. Cf. Beneš, *Le Problème Autrichien et la Question Tchèque*. Beneš and Masaryk realized the necessity for the Hapsburg monarchy before the war, but were against it after the war.

135. Masaryk, *Světová revoluce*, 13.

136. Milada Poulová, *Dějiny Maffie*.

137. Rudolf Gajda, *Moje Paměti*, 9.

138. Krofta, *A Short History of Czechoslovakia*.

139. Augustin Neumann, *Katolici a naše národní osvobození*. Cf. Zlámal, *op. cit.*

140. Sindelař, Z *boje za svobodu*, 73.

141. This letter was deposited in the museum of the Czechoslovak legions in Prague.

142. Masaryk, *op. cit.*, 261.

143. Felix John Vondraček, *The Foreign Policy of Czechoslovakia* 1918-1935, 92.

144. Neumann, *op. cit.*, 23; cf. Masaryk, *op. cit.*, 74.

145. Schmidlin, *op. cit.*, III, 287.

146. Orazio U. Premoli, *Contemporary Church History*, 239.

147. Antonín Šorm, *Ve jménu demokracie* (The Name of Democracy), 26.

148. Premoli, *op. cit.*, 239.

149. Alaphridus Ottaviani, *Institutiones*, I, 394; cf. *Civiltà Cattolica*, I, 376.

150. Frant. Cinek, *K náboženské Otázce v prvních letech Samostatnosti*.

151. Premoli, *op. cit.*, 239.

152. Schmidlin, *op. cit.*, III, 287.

153. *AAS*, XI, 382, 489.

154. *AAS*, XII, 33, 57.

155. *Ibid.*, 34.

156. Ráček, *op. cit.*, 693.

157. Vondráček, *op. cit.*, 93.

158. *AAS*, XII, 37.
159. Schmidlin, *op. cit.*, III, 288.
160. Premoli, *op. cit.*, 240.
161. *AAS*, XII, 583-588.
162. Dr. Jos. Hanuš, *The First Council of the Czechoslovak Church*, in *NCWC*, April 5, 1921, 1-4.
163. Premoli, *op. cit.*, 242.
164. *NCWC*, April 5, 1951, 3.
165. *AAS*, XIV, 379, 380, 593.
166. Liscová Míla, *The Religious Situation in Czechoslovakia*, 36-60. The census of 1921 listed 10,384,833 Catholics and 990, 319 Protestants.
167. Ráček, *op. cit.*, 694; cf. Krofta, *op. cit.*, 114.
168. *NCWC*, March 12, 1921, 1.
169. *NCWC*, Feb. 21, 1921—for. p. 2.
170. *NCWC*, 4/5/21—for. p. 2; Dr. Hanuš, *Religious Chronicle of Czechoslovakia*, *NCWC*, April 5, 1921, 2.
171. *AAS*, XII, 291.
172. Schmidlin, *op. cit.*, III, 289.
173. *AAS*, XIII, 554-559.
174. The constitution was compiled by Alfred Meisner, Social Democrat. See: "The Constitution of the Czechoslovak Republic," a reprint of the English version published in Prague in 1920 by the Société de l'effort de la Tchécoslovaquie, with an introduction by Jiří Hoelzel and V. Joachim (New York: Czechoslovak Government Information Office Service, 1947).
175. The Pittsburgh Agreement was dated May 30, 1918. A photocopy of the text may be seen in Gottfried Żarnow, *Masaryk-Benesch, Philosophen, Abenteurer Staatsgründer* (Berlin, 1939), 182.
176. The English texts of these laws are in "*Czechoslovakia: Church and Religion*," compiled by Stephen Kočvara and Henry Nosek, and edited by Vladimir Gsovski. Cf. *Digest-Index of Eastern European Law* (Washington, D. C.: Library of Congress, National Committee for Free Europe, 1951), 5-8.
177. Schmidlin, *op. cit.*, IV, 132.
178. Schmidlin, *op. cit.*, IV, 288.
179. *Osservatore Romano*, Aug. 28, 1925.
180. Premoli, *op. cit.*, 242.
181. S. Harrison Thomson, *Czechoslovakia in European History*, 324.
182. Schmidlin, *op. cit.*, IV, 133.
183. *Ibid.*, 133.
184. *AAS*, XIX, 93-96.

185. *AAS.*, XX, 277-288.
186. Eduard Beneš, *Paměti*, 494.
187. Schmidlin, *op. cit.*, 133; cf. Beneš, "Exposé Ministra Dra Beneše o modu vivendi mezi Československem a Vatikánem," in *Zahraniční politika*, VII, 200-203. Text of speech of February 1, 1928.
188. *AAS*, XX, 65-66; cf. Thompson, *op. cit.*, 323-324.
189. *AAS*, XX, 307. Sabato, 10 Giugno, Sua Santita ha ricevuto in solemne udienza Sua Ecc. il Sig. Vladimiro Radimsky, Inviato-Straordinario e Ministro Plenipotenziario Czechoslovacchia per la presentatione delle Lettere Credenziali.
190. *AAS*, XIX, 134-36.
191. *AAS*, XXI, 129-37.
192. *Ibid.*, 598.
193. *AAS*, XXIII, 442.
194. *Ibid.*, 518.
195. *AAS*, XXII, 340.
196. *Nový Život* (The New Life), II, no. 5. (Organ of the SS. Cyril and Methodius League. Cf. *AAS.*, XLIII, 443. 21 Aprilis 1951 mortuus est Mons. Saverio Ritter, Arcivescovo di Egina, nunzio apostolico.
197. *AAS*, XXIX, 366-69. English translation by the author.
198. Bohdan Chudoba, "Czech Protestants and Communism," in *America*, Nov. 12, 1949, 149.
199. Brackett Levis, *Democracy in Czechoslovakia*, 93.
200. Masaryk, *Moderni člověk a naboženství* (*Modern man and religion*), 32.
201. *De Civitate Dei*, IV, 4; I, 153A; cf. Bourke Y. Vernon, *Augustine's Quest of Wisdom*, 254.
202. *Czechoslovakia Fights Back*, 71.

FOOTNOTES TO CHAPTER VII

1. Adolf Hitler, *Mein Kampf*, 109.
2. *Czechoslovakia Fights Back*, 30.
3. Josef Pekař, *Jan Hus;* cf. T. G. Masaryk, *Jan Hus*, 108.
4. Cf. Franz Stauracz, *Los von Rom*, 94.
5. Hitler, *op. cit.*, 31.
6. Eduard Beneš, *Paměti*, 104. Cf. Shepard Stone, *Shadow Over Europe*.
7. Eduard Beneš, *Boj o mír a bezbečnost státu*, 710-788.
8. Karl Marx, *Communist Manifesto;* cf. Karl Marx-F. Engels, *Das Kommunistische Manifest*.
9. Fulton J. Sheen, *Communism and the Conscience of the West*, 58.

10. John F. Cronin, *Catholic Social Principles*, 173.

11. Sheen, *op. cit.*, 62. Cf. Henri De Lubac, *The Un-Marxian Socialist. A Study of Proudhon.*

12. *Der Grosse Herder*, VI, 1384-85; cf. Sheen, op. cit., 70.

13. Zdeněk Nejedlý, *T. G. Masaryk*, 44.

14. T. G. Masaryk, *Marx Studien*, VII, 693-700.

15. T. G. Masaryk, *Česká Otázka*, 195.

16. *ES*, 1694, 1718, 1849; cf. John F. Cronin, *op. cit.*, 158-61. See Benjamin L. Masse, "Socialism in Name Only," in *America*, 89, no. 17 (July 25, 1953), 419-20. "Socialists who do not profess atheistic materialism and do not fight against religion, freedom and private and public morality, as for example the English Socialist party of Laborites, are not condemned by the Church." Cf. *Osservatore della Dominica*, May 24, 1953.

17. Hitler, *op. cit.*, 37-65. A very precise description of Nazi policy during World War II (1938-45) based on documents is in *Nazi Conspiracy and Aggression*, I-VIII and Suppl. A-B. Office of United States Chief of Counsel for Prosecution of Axis Criminality, Washington, D.C.: United States Government Printing Office, 1946.

18. Brackett Lewis, *Democracy in Czechoslovakia*, 61-63.

19. Winston S. Churchill, *The Gathering Storm*, 280.

20. Kamil Krofta, *Malé Dějiny Československé*, 136.

21. Churchill, *op. cit.*, 285.

22. *Ibid.*, 287.

23. Krofta, *op. cit.*, 137.

24. *Crisis: A Report from the Columbia Broadcasting System*, 9.

25. Frank P. Chambers, Christina Phelps Grant, Charles C. Bayley, *This Age of Conflict*, 794-99: The Sudeten crisis.

26. *Ibid.*, 104.

27. Churchill, *op. cit.*, 298-321. Cf. Fritz Berber, *Tvář pod Maskou Europské Politiky* 1933-1938, 168. Cf. *Nazi Conspiracy and Aggression: Opinion and Judgment.* Office of United States Chief of Council for Prosecution of Axis Criminality. Washington, D.C.: United States Government Printing Office, 1947, 9.

28. Krofta, *op. cit.*, 141.

29. Beneš, *op. cit.*, 73-75.

30. Joseph Hanč, "Czechoslovakia," in *A Handbook of Slavic Studies*, 594.

31. Čulen, *Po Svätoplukovi druhá naše hlava* (After Svatopluk Our Second Head), I, 210-214; cf. *Four Fighting Years*, 14. Cf. Peter P. Yurchak, *The Slovaks: Their History and Tradition*, 211.

32. Krofta, *op. cit.*, 143. Cf. Jozef Paučo, *Dr. Jozef Tiso o*

sebe (Dr. Jozef Tiso About Himself), 328-329.

33. *Czechoslovakia Fights Back*, 32; cf. Count von Luetzow, *Bohemia*, 370; cf. *Nazi Conspiracy and Aggression*, 27. The proposal was made to Hácha that if he would sign an agreement consenting to the incorporation of the Czech people in the German Reich at once, Bohemia and Moravia would be saved from destruction. He was informed that German troops had already received orders to march and that any resistance would be broken with physical force. The defendant Goering added the threat that he would destroy Prague completely from the air. Faced by this dreadful alternative, Hácha and his foreign minister, Dr. Chvalkovský, put their signatures to the necessary agreement at 4:30 in the morning and Hitler and Ribbentrop signed on behalf of Germany.

34. Churchill, *op. cit.*, 343.

35. Čulen, *op. cit.*, 234-248.

36. *Two Years of German Oppression in Czechoslovakia*, 30-32.

37. *Czechoslovakia Fights Back*, 33.

38. Vojta Beneš, *The Vanguard of the Drang nach Osten*, 144; cf. *Speeches of John Masaryk in America*, 15.

39. Churchill, *op. cit.*, 354.

40. Krofta, *op. cit.*, 149.

41. Churchill, *op. cit.*, 394; cf. Beneš *op. cit.*, 202.

42. Churchill, *op. cit.*, 364; cf. Beneš, *op. cit.*, 194. *Nazi-Soviet Relations*, 1939-41. (Documents from the Archives of the German Foreign Office, Washington, D. C., Department of State, 1948. Publication 3023.)

43. Churchill, *op. cit.*, 367-368.

44. Mario Bendiscioli-Gerald Griffin, *Nazism versus Christianity*, 110.

45. Hitler, *op. cit.*, 563-565.

46. Alfred Rosenberg, *Der Mythus des XX Jahrhunderts*. Cf. Bendiscioli-Griffin, *op. cit.*, 44-45, 47-51. Cf. Andrew J. Krzesinski, *Religion of Nazi Germany*.

47. According to the Nazi philosophy, the State is a centrum of all actions of the people, and also for the education of children.

48. Friedrich Nietzsche, *Der Antichrist*, 20-1. Cf. Roger Lloyd, *Revolutionary Religion: Christianity, Fascism, and Communism, 53*.

49. *AAS*, XXV, 177-194.

50. *AAS*, XXV, 389-413.

51. Michele Maccarrone, *Il Nazional socialismo e la Santa Sede*, 117-140.

52. Bendiscioli-Griffin, *op. cit.*, 217.

53. *AAS*, XXIX, 145-167; cf. Maccarrone, *op. cit.*, 140-194. Cf. Anonymous, *Czechoslovak Catholics*, 20.
54. *AAS*, XXIII, 285-312; cf. William Teeling, *Pope Pius XI and World Affairs*, 135; cf. Chambers, Grant, Bayley, *op. cit.*, 278.
55. *AAS*, XXIX, 65-106.
56. Igino Giordani, *Le Encicliche Sociali dei Papi* (Da Pio IX a Pio XII, 1864-1946.).
57. *AAS*, XXIX, 189-199.
58. *AAS*, XXVII, 460.
59. *Two Years of German Oppression*, 68.
60. *Ibid.*, 68.
61. *Ibid.*, 69.
62. *Ibid.*, 69.
63. Eduard Beneš, *Paměti*, 164.
64. *Two Years of German Oppression*, 78.
65. "Svatovaclavský Choral of the 12th century," in *Český Kancional svatovaclavský*, 11.
66. From the Choral of the Hussites of the 15th century.
67. Otakar Odložilik, *The Way of Light* (The Glory and Martyrdom of Czechoslovak Schools). Cf. *Two Years of German Oppression in Czechoslovakia*, 111-117.
68. *Czechoslovakia Fights Back*, 80.
69. *Two Years of German Oppression*, 74.
70. *NCWC*, Mar. 18, 1946, 5.
71. *Four Fighting Years*, 129-130.
72. *Lidice* (A document of the Ministry of Interior).
73. *Czechoslovakia Fights Back*, 137.
74. Brackett Lewis, *op. cit.*, 86.
75. *Ibid.*, 88.
76. *Two Years of German Oppression*, 65-66.
77. *Ibid.*, 84.
78. *Ibid.*, 86; cf. *Speeches of Jan Masaryk in America*, 75-76; cf. *Nazi Conspiracy and Aggression: Opinion and Judgment*, *op. cit.*, 77.
79. N. S. Timasheff, *Religion in Soviet Russia* (1917-1942), 137, 159, 161. Cf. Paul B. Anderson, *People, Church and State in Modern Russia*, 208.
80. Beneš, *op. cit.*, 212.
81. Beneš, *op. cit.*, 217.
82. Churchill, *op. cit.*, 666.
83. Beneš, *op. cit.*, 233.
84. Beneš, *op. cit.*, 252.
85. *Cultural Relations between the United States and the Soviet Union;* cf. Pitirim A. Sorokin, *Russia and the United States*, 163-177.

86. John T. Flynn, *The Roosevelt Myth*, 207.
87. Frances Perkins, *The Roosevelt I Knew*, 347-387.
88. Churchill, *op. cit.*, 288-289.
89. E. Beneš, *op. cit.*, 11.
90. E. Beneš, *op. cit.*, 359, 363.
91. "Retreat from Moscow," in *America*, LXX (December 25, 1943), 322. Cf. Hanč, *op. cit.*, 595. Cf. Eduard Beneš, *Czechoslovak Policy for Victory and Peace*, 38: "That guarantee against a German *Drang nach Osten*, which is contemplated by the Soviet-Czechoslovak pact."
92. E. Beneš, *op. cit.*, 366-7.
93. Hubert Ripka, *S východem a Západem*, 39.
94. *Ibid.*, 62.
95. *Ibid.*, 96.
96. *Ibid.*, 99.
97. *Ibid.*, 104.
98. *Ibid.*, 108.
99. *Ibid.*, 109.
100. Dr. Beneš by radio from Moscow on Dec. 21, 1943.
101. Beneš, *op. cit.*, 47-48.
102. *Speeches of Jan Masaryk in America*, 30, 37-38; cf. Štefan Osuský, *The Way of the Free*, 130: ". . . Dr. Beneš' information and his views exerted considerable influence on those who were in touch with him. . . ."

FOOTNOTES TO CHAPTER VIII

1. E. Beneš, *Paměti*, 363-65, 379-91. Includes the text of this treaty. Cf. E. Beneš, *Czechoslovak Policy for Victory and Peace.* The fourth message of the President of the Republic to the State Council of February 3, 1944. Jiří Hálek, "Neblahé výročí," (The Sad Anniversary), in *Katolík*, 59, no. 6221 (Dec. 16, 1952). There is a critical and historical explanation of the Czechoslovak agreement with Russia from Dec. 12, 1943.
2. H. Ripka, *The Soviet-Czechoslovak Treaty* (Speech delivered before the State Council on the 15th of December, 1943, in London), 23. This treaty is a historic landmark in the relations between the two countries.
3. H. Ripka, "Address to the German Social Democrats and Communists from Czechoslovakia (London, January 27, 1945)," in Louise W. Holborn, *War and Peace Aims of the United Nations*, 1037.
4. Ivo Duchaček, "The Strategy of Communist Infiltration in Czechoslovakia, 1944-1948," in *World Politics*, II, no. 3 (April, 1950), 346-347.
5. *Ibid.*

6. *Ibid.*

7. F. Cavalli, S. J., *Governo Communista e Chiesa Catholica in Cecoslovacchia*, 7.

8. Alliance for Liberation and Freedom in Czechoslovakia, *Declaration.* In this declaration the Košice Program is called the main source of all the troubles in national policy.

9. Louise W. Holborn, *War and Peace Aims of the United Nations,* 1038-1042. There is an English text of the Košice Program.

10. Josef Hanč, "Czechoslovakia," in *A Handbook of Slavic Studies*, 595-597.

11. The President signed various decrees which were later approved by the National Assembly.

12. Ivo Duchaček, *op. cit.*, 355.

13. J. Fusek, *Organisace a činnost okresnich výborů.* Cf. Jindřich Veselý, *Bezpečnostní agenda národních, výborů.* Cf. Pavel Levit, *Jednací řád mistních národních, výborů*, XV.

14. Martin Ebon, *World Communism Today*, 58.

15. Holborn, *op. cit.*, 1043. The Presidium of the Supreme Soviet and the President of the Czechoslovak Republic, *Treaty on the Transcarpathian Ukraine*, signed at Moscow, June 29, 1945. Text of treaty, 792-794. Cf. *Cecoslovacchia* (Squardo alla Storia politica e religiosa d'un popolo schiavo del communism), 4. Cf. Michael Zibrin, "Edward Beneš—Stalin's Stooge," in *Slovakia*, 2, no. 3 (Dec., 1952), 52-57.

16. *La Nationalisation en Tchécoslovaquie*. Cf. Ebon, *op. cit.*, 65-67; cf. Cavalli, *op. cit.*, 42-47.

17. Jaroslav Michl-Josef Nový a František Petruv, *Revise první pozemkové reformy*.

18. Alois Rozehnal, *Land Reforms in Czechoslovakia.*

19. Victor Knapp-Tomaš Berman, *Vracení majetku pozbytého za okupace.*

20. Václav Vlk, *Zákon o dvouletém hospodářském plánu ze dne 25. října 1946 č. 192 Sb.* Cf. *The First Czechoslovak Economic Plan.*

21. *Czechoslovakia on the Road to Socialism.*

22. *The First Czechoslovak Economic Five Year Plan, Act. No. 241.*

23. Robert A. Graham, "Orderly and Humane Inhumanity," in *America* (Jan. 24, 1948), 457-459. See Chapter XIII, on the Potsdam Conference decisions of August 2, 1945. Under the heading, "Orderly Transfers of German Population," it states that the transfer to Germany of German populations or elements thereof remaining in Poland, Czechoslovakia, and Hungary will have to

be undertaken. It states further that these transfers are to be effected in an "orderly and humane manner."

24. Duchaček, *op. cit.*, 359.

25. Alois Rozehnal, *Odborové hnutí v Československé republice* (Trade Unions in the Czechoslovak Republic).

26. This Socialist block was formed by Communists, Social Democrats, and National Socialists. See *Katolík*, 60, no. 6273 (June 16, 1953), 3, for a text of this agreement between Social Democrats, National Socialists and Communists.

27. Hanč, *op. cit.*, 598.

28. The Christian Democratic party in exile has published a magazine under the same name, *Nové Obzory* (New Horizons), in New York, since 1953, which reflects the moderate political trends of the People's party in Czechoslovakia.

29. *Communism in action.* A documented study and analysis of Communism in operation in the Soviet Union (prepared at the instance and under the direction of Representative Everett M. Dirkson, of Illinois, by the Legislative Reference Service of the Library of Congress, under direction of Ernest S. Griffith), Washington. D. C.: U. S. Government Printing Office, 1946, 126-139. Cf. Alaphridus Ottaviani, *Institutiones Juris Publici Ecclesiastici*, II, Jus publicum externum, 134-140.

30. Bohdan Chudoba, "Czech Protestants and Communism" in *America* (Nov. 12, 1949), 149-151.

31. Joseph L. Hromádka, *Between East and West*, cited in Chudoba, *op. cit.*, 151. Cf. R. H. Markham, *Communists Crush Churches in Eastern Europe*, 16. Cf. *Time*, 60, no. 13 (Sept. 29, 1952), 52.

32. Joseph L. Hromádka, "The Modern Trends in European Protestant Theology," in *The Univ. of Pennsylvania Bicentennial Conference, Religion and the Modern World*, 21-25.

33. Joseph L. Hromádka, *Don Quijote české filosofie, Emanuel Rádl 1873-1942.*

34. Joseph L. Hromádka, *Doom and Resurrection*, 121. Cf. *The Red and the Black*, 28: "Hromádka's Protestants." Hromádka's point of view regarding the Communists is here well expressed.

35. *Nové církevní zákony*, 39. Cf. J. B. Kozák, *The Future of Czechoslovakia*, 46, 49, 62. Cf. J. B. Kozák, *Democratic Ideas in Postwar Education in Central and Eastern Europe*. See *The Red and the Black*, 28: Patriarch Kovář, head of the Czechoslovak Church, declared on many occasions that the Communists were fighting the Catholic hierarchy only to protect the people from clerical oppression.

36. E. Beneš, *Paměti*, 494-495. There is a Czech text of this document.

37. Beneš, *op. cit.*, 495-496. There is a Czech text of this document.

38. Beneš, *op. cit.*, 496-504. There is a Czech text of this memorandum.

39. *NCWC*, May 13, 1946, 9.

40. *CIC*, Can. 267, par. 1-3; cf. Ottaviani, *Institutiones juris publici ecclesiastici*, 405-412.

41. *AAS*, XXXVIII, 323-324. Ad Exec. Virum Arthurum Meixner, novum Reipublicae Cecoslovachiae Legatum extra ordinem liberis cum mandatis, die 13 mensis augusti a. 1946, Summo Pontifici litteras publicas porrigentem.

42. *NCWC*, May 27, 1946, 23.

43. *NCWC*, June 24, 1946, 12.

44. *AAS*, XXXVIII, 400.

45. *AAS*, XXXIX, 315.

46. *AAS*., XXXVIII, 209, 240.

47. *AAS*, XXXIX, 112.

48. *AAS*, XXXIX, 420.

49. *AAS*, XXXVIII, 118.

50. Jozef Paučo, *Dr. Jozef Tíso o sebe* (Dr. Joseph Tiso About Himself). Cf. *Slovenská Republika, 1939-1949.*

51. *AAS*, XXXIX, 318.

52. *AAS*, XXXVII, 252-254. There is a complete Latin text of this papal letter.

53. *AAS*, XXXVII, 10-23. A complete Italian text of this message.

54. *NCWC*, Mar. 15, 1946, 15.

55. *AAS*, XXXIX, 223-224. There is a complete Latin text of this.

56. Konstantin Čulen, *Po Svätoplukovi druha naše hlava*, 588-590.

57. Josef Cieger, "Prvý Prezident Slovenskej Republiky" (First President of the Slovak Republic), 90-101.

58. *Nový Život* (*The New Life*), February, 1951, 18.

59. *NCWC*, Apr. 29, 1946, 19.

60. *NCWC*, July 15, 1946, 17.

61. *NCWC*, Mar. 10, 1947, 2-3.

62. *NCWC*, Jan. 13, 1947, 2.

63. *NCWC*, Feb. 10, 1947, 9.

64. *NCWC*, May 26, 1947, 28.

65. *NCWC*, Dec. 31, 1945, 1.

66. *Primi incatenati*, 49-60.

67. *AAS*, XXXVI, 308. Ssmus D. N. Pius, div. Prov. Pp. xii; decreto S. Congregationis pro Ecclesia Orientali, die mensis Septembris anno 1944 dato, titulari episcopali Ecclesiae Appianae, praefecit Rev. mum Dominus *Theodorum Georgium Romza*, directorem in Seminario Munkacsiensi, quem deputavit auxiliarem Exc. P. D. Nicolai Dudas, Administratoris Apostolici dioecesis Munkacsiensis. Cf. *AAS*, XXXIX, 648. Monsig. Romza Teodoro Giorgio Vescovo tit. de Appia died Oct. 25, 1947. Cf. *Katolík*, 60, no. 6235 (Feb. 3, 1953), 3, 4.

68. *AAS*, XXXIX, 110.

69. *NCWC*, Sept. 23, 1945, 3.

70. *Statistique annual Praha*, 1931, gives the number of Greek Catholics as 585,041, or 4½ per cent.

71. *The Trial of the Treasonable Slovak Bishops Jan Vojtaššák, Michel Buzalka, Pavol Gojdič*, (30 102-84-III/1 66), 120-146; 214-222; 225-226.

72. *NCWC*, Mar. 11, 1946, 22-24.

73. *Ibid.*, 3. This document was never published. The original is in the *NCWC* archives in Washington. The translation into English is by the Rev. Florian C. Billey, O.F.M., Conv. Secretary of the Slovak Catholic Federation of America.

74. *NCWC*, Feb. 4, 1946, 3.

75. *NCWC*, Mar. 11, 1946, 24.

76. *NCWC*, Mar. 25, 1946, 1, 2.

77. *NCWC*, Apr. 22, 1946, 1-2.

78. Bohdan Chudoba, *Czechoslovakia, a Study in Disintegration*, in *Thought*, XXV, no. 96 (March 1950), 93.

79. *NCWC*, Apr. 22, 1946, 1-2.

80. *Katolík* (Apr. 16, 1946), 1.

81. *Ibid.*

82. *NCWC*, Mar. 11, 1946, 8-9.

83. *Ibid.*

84. *NCWC*, Apr. 14, 1947, 14.

85. *Ibid.*

86. *NCWC*, May 27, 1947, 7.

87. *NCWC*, Nov. 18, 1946, 10.

88. Chudoba, *op. cit.*, 93.

89. *NCWC*, Mar. 24, 1947, 3.

90. *NCWC*, June 30, 1947, 30.

91. *NCWC*, July 21, 1947, 11-12.

92. *NCWC*, Aug. 4, 1947, 5; Oct. 20, 1947, 405.

93. *NCWC*, Nov. 17, 1947, 16-17.

94. The original of this pastoral letter is in the *NCWC* archives, in Washington.

95. *NCWC*, Dec. 8, 1947, 11-12. Cf. *Conspiracy Against the Republic*.
96. *NCWC*, Dec. 8, 1947, 8.
97. *NCWC*, Dec. 8, 1947, 9.
98. *NCWC*, Dec. 15, 1947, 17.
99. Stewart Alsop, "Stalin's Plans for the U.S.A." in *The Saturday Evening Post* (July 14, 1951), 17. This article is very interesting because it is based on information from Arnošt Heidrich, who was a member of this delegation in Moscow, and heard Stalin talk about his private intentions regarding America. Cf. *Zpravodaj*, no. 10 (August, 1950), 6-8. "Československo nesmí býti pro Západ ztraceno." Cf. Stefan Osuský, *The way of the Free*, 130-131. Cf. Andrew Gyorgy, *Governments of Danubian Europe*, 103. Cf. "*Which Plan for Czechoslovakia.*" In *America*, January 10, 1948, 420.
100. This economic Russian-Czechoslovak agreement replaced the Marshall Plan, including political orientation.
101. Edward Duff, S. J., "Beran of Prague." In *America*, July 2, 1949, 397-398.

FOOTNOTES TO CHAPTER IX

1. Karl Marx and F. Engels, *Das Kommunistische Manifest*, 19-20.
2. Francis J. Connell, *Morals in Politics and Professions*, 1-9.
3. *America*, Mar. 6, 1948, 622.
4. *Ibid.*
5. F. Cavalli, *Governo Communista e Chiesa Cattolica in Cecoslovacchia*, 10.
6. *Katolík*, 62, no. 5948, 5. *See Nové Obzory*, May-June, 1950, 6.
7. *L'Osservatore Romano*, Feb. 24, 1948, 1, 4; and Feb. 25, 1948, 1.
8. Klement Gottwald, *Ku předu, Zpátky ni krok*, Documents and speeches of the prime minister, Feb. 17-29, 1948. (Translation by the author.)
9. *L'Osservatore Romano, loc. cit.*
10. A. J. Jandáček, *Život za železnou oponou* (Life Behind the Iron Curtain), 61. Documents concerning the Communist coup in Czechoslovakia in February, 1948.
11. Gottwald, *op. cit.*, 40-1. (Translation by the author.)
12. *L'Osservatore Romano*, Feb. 28, 1948, 1.
13. *America*, Mar. 13, 1948, 632.
14. Ferdinand Peroutka, *Byl Eduard Beneš vinen?* (Was Eduard Beneš Guilty?), 24.

15. *Lidová demokracie*, Feb. 27, 1948, 1. Cf. *L'Osservatore Romano*, June 25, 1948, 1.

16. *L'Osservatore Romano, loc. cit.* See *Lidová demokracie*, Mar. 23, 1948, 1.

17. *Akční program nové Gottwaldovy vlády.* (Speech by Prime Minister Gottwald in the Constitutional National Assembly on Mar. 10, 1948.)

18. Cavalli, *op. cit.*, 16.

19. Robert B. Lockhart, "The Czechoslovak Revolution," in *Foreign Affairs* (July, 1948), 641. Cf. *Lidová demokracie*, Mar. 11, 1948, 1, and Mar. 14, 1948, 1. Cf. *L'Osservatore Romano* (Mar. 12, 1948), 2: *Le impressioni internacionale sulla morte di Masaryk.* "... Minister Nosek ha detto, altressi, che sul tavolo di lavoro del defunto sono stati rinvenuti anche parecchi telegrammi di amici britannici e americani i quali esprimevano il loro disappunto perche Masaryk si era unito ai communisti del nuovo governo; questo, a detto del Ministro degli Interni, deve aver contributo a creare in Masaryk una grave depressione nervosa..."

20. *The Tablet*, June 12, 1948, 363-4.

21. *Lidová demokracie*, Feb. 25, 1948, 1, in which the entire Bohemian text may be found. (Translation by the author.)

22. Transcribed from the original letter in the *CML* archives.

23. *The Tablet*, May 22, 1948, 324.

24. *The Tablet*, June 12, 1948, 312: in which the full text may be found. See *La DC*, 46 (1949), 1048 col. 996-7. Cf. *L'Osservatore Romano*, June 28-29, 1948, 3: in which an Italian translation of this document is given under the title of "La mano tesa in Cecoslovacchia."

25. *The Tablet*, June 12, 1948, 372.

26. The original, in Bohemian, is in the *CML* archives in London.

27. *AAS*, 40 (1948), 272, 358. Cf. *Lidová demokracie*, Mar. 24, 1948, 1.

28. *The Tablet*, *loc. cit.*

29. *Ústava ze dne 9 května 1948* (Constitution of May 9, 1948). Cf. *Lidová demokracie*, Apr. 15, 1948, 1-2.

30. *La DC*, 46 (1949), 1051 col. 1178. Cf. *Lidová demokracie*, May 11, 1948, 1.

31. Albert Flory, "La constitution tchécoslovaque," in *La DC*, 46 (1949), 1051 col. 1178-9.

32. This Constitution was compiled by Alfred Meisner, Social Democrat. See *The Constitution of the Czechoslovak Republic*, a reprint of the English version published in Prague in 1920 by the Société de l'effort de la Tchécoslovaquie.

33. *Constitution of May 9, 1948*, 81.

34. This English translation is from the *Digest-Index of Eastern European Law*, "Czechoslovakia: Church and Religion." Edited by Vladimir Gsovski. Washington: U. S. Law Library of Congress, 1951.

35. The record of Beneš' conversation with Gottwald on May 4, to which the President refers in his letter of abdication, is fortunately available. It is in Otto Friedman's *The Break-up of Czech Democracy*.

36. Friedman, *op. cit.*, 121.

37. Peroutka, *op. cit.*, 24; cf. *Lidová demokracie*, June 8, 1948, in which Beneš' abdication letter is printed. Cf. Michael Zibrin, "Edward Beneš—Stalin's Stooge," in *Slovakia*, Dec. 1952, 52, 57.

38. *L'Osservatore Romano*, Sept. 5, 1948, 1: La morte dell' ex-Presidento Beneš ha provocata viva impressione in tuta l'Europa.

39. Peroutka, *op. cit.*, 28.

40. Peroutka, *op. cit.*, 7.

41. *L'Osservatore Romano*, May 27, 1948, 1: "Le elezioni in Cecoslovacchia." Cf. Ivo Duchaček, "Czechoslovakia Under the Communists (The Eve of the Bogus Elections)," in *The Tablet*, May 29, 1948, 334. Cf. P. Korbel, *Parliamentary Elections in Czechoslovakia*, 13-16.

42. Cavalli, *op. cit.*, 19: "La lista unica ipotecheca per i communisti 211 seggi, dividendo le briciole del bottino parlamentare tra gli oltri partiti 25 ai socialdemocratici, 26 ai socialisti nazionali, 23 ai populari, 12 e 3 rispettivamente ai due partiti slovacchi della rinascita e della liberta. In teoria era possibile presentare altre listi, ma per questo si rendeva necessario una richiesta firmata di mille elettori una enorme trappola tesa ai 'traditori.' Esclusi dal voto i 'nemici delle istituzione democratiche populari' e costretti tutti gli altri alle urne con gravi pene (fino a 6 mesi di carcere), il 30 maggio i Cechi e gli Slovacchi si recarono ai seggi elettorali, dove gli ultimi accorgimenti erano predisposti per asicurare ai communisti, nasco sti dietro la maschera del Fronte Nazionale, la schiacciante vittoria dell' 89.2 per cento, nel cui calcalo bisogna far entrare le manipolazioni notturne compiute negli scrutini tra fidi compagni." Cf. Bohdan Chudoba, "Czechoslovakia: A Study in Disintegration," in *Thought*, March, 1950, 98.

43. Cavalli, *op. cit.*, 20; cf. "Gottwald Presidente della Republica Cecoslovacchia," in *L'Osservatore Romano*, June 14-15, 1948, 1.

44. *NCWC*, July 19, 1948, 6.

45. *NCWC*, May 24, 1948, 3.

46. *Lidová demokracie*, May 11, 1948, 1.
47. *Ibid.*
48. The original of this letter is in the *CML* archives. Cf. *L'Osservatore Romano*, July 12-13, 1948, 3. An Italian translation of the letter may be found in "La questione scholastica in Cecoslovacchia."
49. *The Tablet*, June 12, 1948, 372.
50. The original of this letter, in Bohemian, is in the *CML* archives.
51. The original of this letter, in Bohemian, is in the *CML* archives.
52. *The Tablet*, June 26, 1948, 404.
53. *NCWC*, June 28, 1948, 10-11. See *L'Osservatore Romano*, July 5-6, 1948, 3: "La Chiesa Cattolica in Cecoslovacchia," in which an Italian translation of this document may be found.
54. *NCWC, loc. cit.*
55. *Lidová demokracie*, June 19, 1949, 1-2.
56. *L'Osservatore Romano*, Sept. 8, 1948, 3: "Una notaficazione dell' Arcivesco di Praga."
57. *The Tablet*, Aug. 14, 1948, 108.
58. *Ibid.*
59. F. Cavalli, "La nazionalizazione delle scuole cattoliche."
60. The entire text of this letter is from the *CML* archives. See *The Tablet*, Aug. 11, 1948, 108, for the English text.
61. *The Tablet, loc. cit.*
62. The text of this letter in Bohemian is in the *CML* archives.
63. Partial English translation of above.
64. Partial English translation of above.
65. This document is in the *CML* archives. It was also published in the Bohemian newspapers *Katolík* and *Národ*.
66. The complete document is in the *CML* archives.
67. The Association of the Defenders of Freedom was organized in 1945, just after the end of World War II. Its members were former prisoners from Nazi camps and any others who actively participated in the resistance against the Nazi occupation. The members were given preference in filling important government and political posts, especially the latter. Communists occupied key positions in the organization, although a large majority were non-Communists. Through their leadership, however, the Communists used the opportunity to obtain political power in the state.
68. *Lidová demokracie*, July 30, 1948, 1, *České Slovo, Rudé Právo*, and others.
69. Coming from the Communists, the expression "unfounded

attacks" means that Archbishop Beran had publicly attacked Father Plojhar because of his German origin. He also asserted that Plojhar had been in the German block in the Dachau concentration camp, not in the Czech block.

70. The Archbishop's reply was known only through a letter that the Association refused to publish as its contents disclosed details of Plojhar's priestly life.

71. *The Tablet*, Oct. 2, 1948, 220.

72. This bill was later approved by the National Assembly. On Nov. 12, 1949, the Minister of the Interior, Václav Nosek, announced the legal provisions of obligatory civil marriage.

73. Alaphridus Ottaviani, *Institutiones Juris Publici Ecclesiastici*, II, 346: "Viget ex lege 22 Maii 1919, matrimonium civile facultativum; hinc parochi habentur ut officiales status in re matrimoniali, sicut etiam pro nonnullis *aliis* actibus (nativitatum, funerum, etc.) Eadem lege sancitum est divortium."

74. *The Tablet*, Oct. 16, 1948, 252.

75. The "pulpit act" was put into effect during the first Czechoslovak Republic (see Ottaviani, *loc. cit.:* Lege 20 februarii 1919 sanctiones poenales statutae sunt contra sacerdotem, qui abutitur sacro ministerio verbi ad fines politicos.), but it was abused by the government. Using the slogan: "Protect the people's democratic regime!" the interpretation of the law was widened so that it forbade the reading of pastoral letters and papal encyclicals. Thus, in Czechoslovakia, the ordinary, universal jurisdiction of the Pope was tacitly denied and the jurisdiction of the bishops suspended. The "ratio status" and the old "placetum regium," as they were known in times past, were again put into operation.

76. *L'Osservatore Romano*, Oct. 30, 1948, 1.

77. *Ibid.*, Nov. 25, 1948, 1.

78. *Ibid.*, Nov. 24, 1948, 1.

79. *Ibid.*, Nov. 25, 1948, 1.

80. *AAS*, 41 (1949), 88. Archbishop Kmet'ko, before his death, was honored by Rome. See *L'Osservatore Romano*, June 19, 1948, 1: "Nelle Pontificie Opere Missionarie della Cecoslovacchia su proposta dei consigli Superiori delle Pontificie Opere della Propagazione delle Fede e di S. Pietro Apostolo, la Sacra Congregazione 'de Propaganda dello Fede' ha riconosciuto come Presidente Onorario delle Pontificie Missioni in Cecoslovacchia S. E. Rev. ma Mons. Carlo Kmet'ko, archivescovo vescovo di Nitra."

81. *AAS*, XLI (1949), 372, 584.

82. *Ibid.*

83. *AAS*, XLI (1949), 563, 585.

84. *Ibid.*

85. In the spring of 1948 the churches began to fear their

right to conduct their own schools (Law no. 95 Coll.) would be abrogated, and shortly after land owned and possessed by them was taken over by the state (Law no. 96 Coll.). It was left to the local people's and farmers' committees to contribute to the upkeep of the parish clergy (but not the higher clergy), not to exceed 30 ha (about ten acres) for each parish. Also, as a result of the laws effecting the nationalization of industry (Presidential decrees nos. 100 and 101 of 1945, and laws nos. 114 and 115 of 1948), the Church lost practically all its profit-producing enterprises. See *Digest-Index of Eastern European Law*, *op. cit.*, 10. Cf. P. Korbel, *Some Basic Information on the Czechoslovak School System* (*NCFE*, September, 1952), 2-6. Cf. *La Nationalisation en Tchécoslovaquie.*

86. Jaroslav Michl, Josef Nový, František Petrů, *Revise první pozemkové reformy*. Cf. Ottaviani, *op. cit.*, II, 364. The "first land reform" refers to the law of Apr. 8, 1920 Coll.

87. *NCWC*, Feb. 9, 1948, 19-20.

88. *Loc. cit.*

89. *Loc. cit.*

90. On Dec. 9, 1946, when the National Assembly voted a general censorship of all books and newspapers published in the country, Václav Kopecký had already been appointed Minister of Propaganda, controlling all publications in Czechoslovakia. (See *NCWC*, Mar. 24, 1947, 3.) This Ministry of Propaganda, little by little, restricted all civil freedom. The Christian People's party and leading magazines like *Na výboj* and *Obzory* fought strongly but vainly against these restrictions. (See *NCWC*, Feb. 2, 1948, 2.)

91. The Czechoslovak bishops protested against the suppression of the Catholic press on many occasion; for instance, in pastoral letters dated July 6, 1948, Aug. 26, 1948, and again in 1949.

92. Under the pretext of a shortage of paper, purges of the libraries took place. The classification of devotionals as "immoral" originated with Minister Nejedlý.

93. Especially eliminated from the schools were histories by the great Czech historian Josef Pekař and his pupil Zdeněk Kalista. In a special letter of instruction issued by the Ministry of Schools, teachers and professors were directed to teach history only in the spirit of Hus and of the Revolution.

94. Old catechisms, long officially sanctioned, such as Podlaha's and Kubíček's, were abolished and a special commission of so-called patriotic priests was formed to compile a new catechism. These priests were under the control of the Ministry of Schools. The new catechism was issued in 1948, and its chief compilers

were the Fathers Mára and Černocký. It was, of course, not approved by the ecclesiastical authorities.

95. Practically speaking, Catholics in Slovakia lost their schools under the decree of May 16, 1945, issued by the Slovak National Council, and in Bohemia and Moravia by Law no. 95 Coll., passed on Apr. 21, 1948. Czechoslovak bishops frequently protested against the nationalization of Catholic schools, as is evidenced in their pastoral letters in which the whole controversy is extensively treated.

96. *NCWC*, Dec. 15, 1948, 31.

97. *Ibid.*, Nov. 15, 1948, 17.

98. *Ibid.*, May 17, 1948, 11.

99. *Ibid.*, Apr. 12, 1948, 5.

100. *Ibid.*, Nov. 22, 1948. 2.

FOOTNOTES TO CHAPTER X

1. *America*, Jan. 29, 1949, 450.

2. *Lidová demokracie*, May 11, 1948, 1.

3. *La DC*, 46 (1949), 1048, col. 999.

4. *L'Osservatore Romano*, Feb. 25, 1949, 1.

5. Internuncio Monsignor Saverio Ritter left Czechoslovakia in the fall of 1948 because of illness. He died Apr. 22, 1950, in Italy. He loved Czechoslovakia very much. See *Veritas*, May 22, 1951, 1.

6. *Vinculum*, Sept., 1951, 5. Monsignor Gennaro Verolino was in Prague until July 13, 1949, when he returned to Rome (see *L'Osservatore Romano*, July 27, 1949, 1), where he helped Czechoslovak exiles. On Sept. 6, 1951, he was named nuncio to the republics of Guatemala and San Salvador.

7. *The Tablet*, Apr. 2, 1949, 220.

8. *La DC*, 46 (1949), 1048, col. 999.

9. *The Tablet*, June 25, 1949, 418-20. Cf. *NCWC*, June 10, 1948, 1-4, in which the entire English text is given, Cf. *La DC*, 46 (1949), 1048, col. 1006-1009.

10. *The Tablet*, May 21, 1949, 340.

11. *La DC*, 46 (1949), 1048, col. 1000.

12. The English text of this letter is from *NCWC*, June 10, 1949, 5. Cf. *La DC*, 46 (1949), 1048, col. 1011-1012.

13. *The Tablet*, *ibid.*, 340.

14. The original of this letter, in Bohemian, is in the *CML* archives in London.

15. The English translation of this letter is from *The Tablet*, June 25, 1949, 420-21. Cf. *NCWC*, June 10, 1949, 6-7; Cf. *La DC*, 46 (1949), 1042, col. 1010-1011.

16. *Věstník Katolického duchovenstva*, May 10, 1949, 2; cf. *NCWC*, May 23, 1949, 3.

17. The original of this letter, in Bohemian, is in the *CML* archives in London.

18. This English translation is from *The Tablet*, June 25, 1949, 421-22; cf. *NCWC*, June 13, 1949, 6-7; cf. *La DC*, 46 (1949), 1048, col. 1013-1014.

19. The scheme whereby the Church was to be subjugated and brought under Communist domination was generally given in the *Communist International Program of the Comintern in 1928*. It declared: "One of the most important tasks of the cultural revolution affecting the wide masses is the task of systematically and unswervingly combating religion—the opium of the people. The proletarian government must withdraw all state support from the Church, which is the agency of the former ruling class; it must prevent all church interference in state-organized educational affairs . . . it carries on antireligious propaganda with all the means at its command." The foregoing text is from Edgar Snow, *The Pattern of Soviet Power*, 184. This general declaration regarding religion was only part of the program which centered on world revolution as formulated by the Comintern . . . Cf. Sumner Welles, *The Time for Decision*, 313. See Christopher Dawson, *Understanding Europe*, 119-122. See *The Red and the Black*, 3-8.

20. "Autour du Cominform," in *La DC*, 46 (1951), 1090, col. 297-99.

21. *L'Osservatore Romano*, July 2, 1949, 1: "L'azione Cattolica vittima designata del Cominform." Cf. *NCWC*, Apr. 24, 1950, 1-3; cf. F. Cavalli, *Governo Communista e Chiesa Cattolica in Cecoslovacchia*, 112: "Il nuovo assalto alla chiesa in Cecoslovacchia entro come un capitolo del grande 'programma religioso' del Cominform, elaborato l'11 e il 12 Febraio 1949 el grand-hotel 'Pupp' di Karlovy Vary (Karlsbad). Si sa che il cominform ha qui definito meglio le forme della lotta contro il cattolicismo, specie per neutralizzare gli effetti religiosi dell' Anno Santo. La tattica convenuta si proponeva di non urtare le tendenze e le tradizioni religiose cui i popoli dei paesi satelliti si erano mostrati devoti; per coprire, quindi, la manovra con cui si voleva imporre un ateismo esecrato, il *Cominform* escogito per i paesi europei soggetti alla Russia l'idea di una 'chiesa cattolica orientale,' il cui centro sarebbe stato Praga."

22. Cavalli, *ibid.*, 112.

23. *The Clergy Review*, June, 1951, 5: "The liquidation of the Catholic Church in Czechoslovakia was decided at Karlsbad

(Karlovy Vary) in October, 1949. It is known as the Protocol of Karlsbad. This document declared that the first steps must be to restrict the activity of the Church in the field of education and the press, and to curtail the freedom of action of Archbishop Beran and the other bishops, without paying too much attention to what might be said in the West—in other words, without worrying about the worldwide effects which had followed the imprisonment of Cardinal Mindszenty in Hungary. Our 'Catholic Action'—that is, the bogus organization then recently created—had already, it was said, successfully directed a blow at the Vatican and the faithful. The next thing was to exploit such questions as that of the salary of the lower clergy." This document was taken from *Veritas*, the valuable bulletin of the Accademia Christiana dell'Azione Cattolica Cecoslovacca in Rome. The first issue of *Veritas* is dated Apr. 1, 1951. It appears twice a month.

24. The English translation is by the author from a Bohemian text that appeared in *Veritas*, Apr. 31, 1951, 23. Cf. *Katolík*, Jan. 27, 1953, 3.

25. *NCWC*, July 24, 1950, 1-3.

26. *Ibid.*, Apr. 27, 1950, 1-2. The author of this measure was Minister Čepička, who was also present at the meeting at Karlovy Vary.

27. *Lidová demokracie*, June 18, 1949, 1-2.

28. *La DC* 46 (1949), 1048, col. 1001.

29. *Lidová demokracie*, June 17, 1949, 1.

30. *Katolická Akce.*

31. *Zrada Vatikánu a biskupů*, 5. This is a 48-page booklet that repeats the arguments contained in the addresses of government spokesmen. The Czechoslovak Embassy to the Holy See in Rome also published a 41-page booklet entitled *Documenti cecoslovacchi.* This one is in Italian and defends the policy of the Czechoslovak government. It says that in Czechoslovakia everything possible was done to avoid a Kulturkampf. A criticism of this booklet will be found in *L'Osservatore Romano*, Oct. 29, 1950, 1-2, in an article signed by F. A., entitled "Documenti cecoslovacchi." Cf. *La DC* 48 (1951), 1088, col. 165-68; cf. *NCWC*, Aug. 1, 1949, 5.

32. *The Tablet*, June 25, 1949, 413. Cf. the *declaration* of the Catholic clergy of July 18, 1949.

33. *NCWC*, Apr. 24, 1950, 3. The Vatican radio announced that Father Ladislav Škoda, editor of the Communist-controlled *Katolické Noviny*, organ of the bogus "Catholic Action," is the only one among two hundred parish priests of the Bratislava region who has been excommunicated under the Decree of the

Holy Office. Dr. Škoda was removed by his bishop from his parish of Prievoz, a suburb of Bratislava. The Vatican radio added that his successor was arrested and maltreated.

34. A copy of this letter in Bohemian is in the *CML* archives in London.

35. *The Tablet*, June 25, 1949, 404; cf. *La DC* 46 (1949), 1048, col. 1014.

36. *NCWC*, June 13, 1949, 6; cf. *The Tablet*, June 18, 1949, 404.

37. *Loc. cit.*

38. *NCWC*, June 20, 1949, 4.

39. *NCWC*, June 20, 1949, 1-2.

40. Francis Dvorník, "Church and State in Central Europe," in *The Soviet Union: A Symposium*, 208: "The Czechoslovak Communist regime, when ordering the police to enter the palace of the Archbishop of Prague, Joseph Beran, and to survey his activities, invoked law No. 50 of May 7, 1874. This law contains prescriptions regulating the juridical status of the Catholic Church. According to paragraph 60 of the law, state authorities are empowered to use forceful methods to insure the execution of the law." Cf. Boh. Bunž, "Poměr Cirkve a státu v Československu," (The Relations between Church and State in Czechoslovakia), in *Record of the Cult. Commission*, No. 3 (London: Council of Free Czechoslovakia, 1950), 5.

41. *Record on Czechoslovakia* (New York: *NCFE*), March, 1951, 71-73.

42. *The Tablet*, June 25, 1949, 412; cf. *La DC* 46 (1949), 1048, col. 1002. Cf. Vilém Stránecký, "Vyroči požehnaného dne," (Anniversary of the Blessed Day), in *Katolík*, Dec. 9, 1952, 3. Cf. Jiří Hálek, "Kristův bojovnik" (Christ's Warrior), in *Katolík*, Dec. 9, 1952, 3-4.

43. Dr. Stanislav Koutnik, "Velký vlastenec opat Jarolímek komunistickou obětí," (The great patriot, Abbot Jarolímek, as a Communist victim), in *Nový Život*, June, 1951, 13.

44. *NCWC*, June 20, 1949, 3-4.

45. This document is in the *CML* archives in London.

46. The original Bohemian text of this pastoral letter is in the *CML* archives in London. The English translation appeared in *The Tablet*, June 25, 1949, and also in *La DC*, 46 (1949), 1048, col. 1014-1017.

47. This decree is in *AAS*, 41 (1949), 333. See the English text in *NCWC*, June 20, 1949, 1.

48. *L'Osservatore Romano*, June 30, 1949, 1.

49. This entire text is from *La DC*, 46 (1949), 1048, col. 1003; cf. *The Tablet* (June 25, 1949). 412.

50. "Msgr. Josef Beran," in *La DC* 46 (1949), 1048 col. 995-96.

51. *Katolická Akce* (Catholic Action), 36-40.

52. The Bohemian version of this letter was edited by *CML* in London as a separate document, and printed in the periodical *Nový Život*, April, 1950. The English translation is partly from *The Tablet*, July 2, 1949, 4-5.

53. The English text is from *NCWC*, June 27, 1949, 5-13; cf. *La DC* 46 (1949), 1055 col. 1453-64.

54. *The Tablet*, July 2, 1949, 13.

55. *Ibid.*

56. *Nový Život*, April, 1951, 10.

57. *The Tablet*, July 9, 1949, 29-30.

58. *Věstnik Katolického duchovenstva*, 1-2.

59. *The Tablet*, July 16, 1949, 44. Cf. *L'Osservatore Romano*, July 10, 1949, 1: "Una protesta di Mons. Picha."

60. Cavalli, *op. cit.*, 77, 78, 121, 122.

61. The Bohemian text of this letter is in the *CML* archives in London.

62. Max Jordan, "Fr. Fiala, Long Aide of Czech Red Flees Country," in *NCWC*, July 25, 1949, 1-3. Father Fiala was also accredited by the government to participate in the negotiations between Church and state. See *Lidová demokracie*, May 11, 1948, 1.

63. *The Tablet*, Aug. 6, 1949, 92.

64. *Katolická Akce*, 42.

65. *The Tablet*, July 30, 1949, 76. The Bohemian original is in the *CML* archives.

66. *La DC* 46 (1949), 1055, col. 1468-69.

67. This document is from *The Tablet*, July 23, 1949, 52-53. "The tactics of confusion." Cf. *L'Osservatore Romano*, July 13, 1949, 1. "Direttive del partito communista cecoslovaccho."

68. *The Tablet*, July 23, 1949, 53.

69. *AAS*, 41 (1949), 334.

70. The English translation of this decree appeared in *The Tablet*, July 23, 1949, 53; cf. *La DC*, 46 (1949), 1048 col. 961-62.

71. *AAS*, 41 (1945), 427-8, gives the Latin text. Cf. *L'Osservatore Romano*, August 16-17, 1949, 1.

72. *L'Osservatore Romano*, July 13, 1949, 1.

73. *The Tablet*, July 9, 1949, 29.

74. *L'Osservatore Romano*, July 6, 1949, 1: "La giornata religiosa in Cecoslovacchia."

75. *Ibid.*, July 7, 1949, 1: "Nuovi echi delle celebrazioni pseudo-catholiche cecoslovacche."

76. *The Tablet*, July 16, 1949, 44.
77. The original letter, in Bohemian, is in the *CML* archives in London.
78. Vilém Nový, "Lid, stát a biskupové," (People, State and Bishops), in *Rudé Právo*, July 7, 1949, 1. A strong attack upon the bishops and the Vatican.
79. This letter was never published in the Czechoslovak press.
80. This pastoral letter of the Archbishop of Olomouc is in the *CML* archives in London. See *AAS*, 41 (1949), 333.
81. *L'Osservatore Romano*, July 11-12, 1949, 1.
82. *The Tablet*, July 9, 1949, 30.
83. *Ibid*., Aug. 20, 1949, 124.
84. *L'Osservatore Romano*, July 27, 1949, 1.
85. *Ibid*., July 18, 1949, 1: "Dopo il decreto del Sant'Officio contro il communismo."
86. *L'Osservatore Romano*, July 17, 1949, 1: "Nuove minacce e antichi minacciati in Cecoslovacchia."
87. This document is in the *CML* archives in London.
88. This circular is in the *CML* archives in London.
89. This document, in Bohemian, is in the *CML* archives in London.
90. This document, in Bohemian, is in the author's possession.
91. *Ibid*. The English translation is by the author.
92. For reasons of security, neither the place nor the person of this representative of the vicariate is given. The Bohemian original of the document is in the *CML* archives in London and was never published.
93. This document is in the *CML* archives in London.
94. This document, in Bohemian, is in the *CML* archives in London.
95. This document is in Bohemian and is from the *Veritas* archives in Rome. The English translation is by the author.
96. "La fedeltá del clero cecoslovaccho," in *L'Osservatore Romano*, July 18-19, 1949, 1.
97. *The Tablet*, Oct. 15, 1949, 252. Recently this same bishop, Joseph Hlouch of Budějovice, has been ordered banished from his diocese because of his "negative attitude" toward the Communist regime, the Prague radio announced. The broadcast said he was being replaced by Joseph Buchta, a "patriotic priest" who was appointed Vicar General of the Diocese by the Communist authorities last year. No mention was made of the whereabouts of Bishop Hlouch, *The Register*, April 13, 1952, 2.
98. The complete text affirming the clergy's loyalty to the

hierarchy was read on July 18, 1949, in the churches of Czechoslovakia. Its purpose was to cut short the attempt of Communists to dissociate the "lower clergy" from the hierarchy.

99. The text is from *La DC*, 46 (1949), 1055 col. 1463-64.

100. The post of a Czechoslovak State Prosecutor is similar to that of the Attorney General of the United States. The complete text of this letter appeared in *NCWC*, Aug. 22, 1949, 4, 5, 6. Cf. *L'Osservatore Romano*, Aug. 19, 1949, 1: "Una lettera di Mons. Beran al Procuratore di Stato." Part of this letter reads: "L'Arcivescovo, infine, domanda; Lo Stato cecoslovacco riconosce tuttora la chiesa Cattolica Romana in Cecoslovacchia? Nel caso che la chiesa Cattolica sia tuttora riconosciuta, in base a quale legge essa è stata illegalmente privata della sua indipendenza in affari strettamente interní?" Cf. *La DC* 46 (1949), 1055 col. 1465-66.

101. This statement was made by Dr. Čepička on June 25, 1949, at a session of the officials of the Action Committee of the National Front in Prague. See *Lidová demokracie*, June 26, 1946, 1.

102. *AAS*, 41 (1949), 615.

103. This document, in Bohemian, is in the *CML* archives in London.

104. For the English text see *The Tablet*, Oct. 1, 1949, 220. Cf. *L'Osservatore Romano*, Sept. 14, 1949, 1: "Uno memorandum dell' Episcopato cecoslovacco."

105. *Digest-Index of Eastern European Law*, 29.

106. *Ibid.*

107. Special record from the *CML* archives in London. A unanimous protest against these bills was expressed by many vicariates. Many copies are in the archives.

108. The complete text is from *La DC* 46 (1949), 1055 col. 1467.

109. *The Tablet*, Oct. 29, 1949, 285. The Vatican radio severely criticized the Apostolic Administrator of Teschen, Dr. F. Onderek, for issuing a statement in support of the bill. "This," said the Vatican radio, "has caused dismay, and has compromised the spirit of unity with which the clergy rejected the bill." Cf. "Nationalizing the Church in Czechoslovakia," in *The Tablet*, Oct. 15, 1949, 244-45.

110. *Ibid.*

111. Rev. Stanley Evans, *Church and State in Eastern Europe*, 13.

112. *Nové Cirkevní Zákony*. This is an official propaganda book for foreign countries, with sermons of the deputies, ministers, and representatives of the churches.

113. "Czechoslovakia; Church and Religion," in *Digest-Index of Eastern European Law*. This contains a translation of the principal laws. Cf. F. Cavalli, *Op. cit.*, 159-68.

114. *Digest-Index, op. cit.*, 29-39.

115. *The Tablet*, Oct. 29, 1949, 218.

116. This English text is from *The Tablet*, Nov. 5, 1949, 300.

117. This text is from *La DC* 47 (1950), 1064 col. 371-73; "Une petition de l'épiscopat tchécoslovaque."

118. *Codex Iuris Canonici*, can. 1450, § 1: Nullum patronatus ius ullo titulo constitui in posterum valide potest. (No right of patronage can be validly established in the future under whatsoever title.)

119. From a document in Bohemian received from the *CML* archives in London. Cf. "Una petizione dell' Episcopato cecoslovacco," in *L'Osservatore Romano*, Nov. 19, 1949, in which the complete Italian text is given.

120. The English text appeared in *The Tablet*, Oct. 29, 1949, 278-79.

121. *Lidová demokracie*, Dec. 28, 1949, 1.

122. *NCWC*, Dec. 12, 1949, 11: "The Czech government's claims of widespread amnesties for priests are false."

123. *Loc. cit.*

124. *The Tablet*, Nov. 12, 1948, 322, gives the English text.

125. Boh. Bunža, *Poměr Cirkve a Státu v Československu.* (The Relation Between Church and State in Czechoslovakia), 6. Cf. Felix J. Vondraček, *The Foreign Policy of Czechoslovakia*, 1918-1935, 91. Cf. Ottaviani, *op. cit.*, 376.

126. *The Tablet*, Nov. 26, 1949, 360. This provision became effective on January 1, 1950.

127. These documents are from the *CML* archives in London. Translations appeared in *The Tablet*, Dec. 3, 1949, 395-96, and Dec. 10, 1949, 412-13. Cf. *NCWC*, Dec. 5, 1949, 1-8.

128. This complete English translation is by the author. Cf. *La DC* 47 (1950), 1064 col. 376-81.

129. The English translation of this letter is from *NCWC*, Dec. 16, 1946, 1-3. Cf. *La DC*, 47 (1950), 1064 col. 373-76. Cf. *L'Osservatore Romano*, Dec. 7, 1949, 3-4. Slovenský Národ, Nov. 15, 1949, contains a letter from the bishops dated Oct. 21, 1949.

130. *Spiknutí proti republice* (The Conspiracy Against the Republic).

131. *NCWC*, Dec. 12, 1949, 11-12.

132. *The Tablet*, Dec. 10, 1949, 416.

133. *NCWC*, Jan. 25, 1954, 1-2.

134. *Katolík*, Jan. 15, 1954, 3; F. E. Křištan: "Náboženský

útlak v Československu za r. 1953" (Religious Persecution in Czechoslovakia in 1953). Cf. *NCWC*, Jan. 18, 1954, 1-3.

135. *Národ* (Czech-American Calendar, 1954), 225. Bishop Skoupý prepared a special pastoral letter about a Marian Year in 1954 and distributed it to the people. Police searched him and took him to an undisclosed place of detention. This was the second time he had been put in jail.

FOOTNOTES TO CHAPTER XI

1. *NCWC*, Feb. 6, 1950, 6.
2. *Ibid.*, 7.
3. *Ibid.*, 7.
4. *AAS*, 42 (1950), 216.
5. *CIC*, can. 432, § 1: Capitulum ecclesiae cathedralis, sede vacante, intra octo dies ab accepta notitia vacationis, debet Vicarium Capitularem qui loco sui dioecesim regat et, in fructuum percipiendorum ei munus incumbat, economum unum vel plures fideles ac diligentes constituere. (In case of a vacancy in the episcopal see, the cathedral chapter, within eight days from the date of notice received, must appoint a vicar-capitular, who shall govern the diocese in the place of said chapter. If the chapter also administers the revenues, it must appoint one or more trustworthy and industrious persons as administrators thereof). English translation by Charles Augustine, O.S.B., *A Commentary on the New Code of Canon Law*, II, 481.
6. F. Cavalli, *Governo Communista*, 185.
7. Cavelli, *op. cit.*, 186.
8. *NCWC*, Feb. 20, 1950, 12.
9. *AAS*, 42 (1950), 195. Cf. *La DC* 47 (1950), 1064 col. 369-70.
10. *L'Osservatore Romano*, Feb. 19, 1950, 1: A norma dei Sacri canoni il capitolo della cathedrale provvedera al governo della vacante diocesi mediante l'elezione, del Vicario Capitolare. Senonche il governo avanzava la pretesa che il Vicario Capitolare, per potere exercitare le sue funzioni, dovesse chiedere il consenso governativo. Non avendo il Vicario Capitolare ritenuto di potere aderire a tale pretesa, perche glielo vietava il Diritto della Chiesa, l'autorita civile gli impediva l'esercizio della giurisdizione ecclesiastica.
11. *Ibid*, 4: Una volta di piu il governo cecoslovacco ha preferito il colpo di forza alla regionevolezza, mostrando nuovamenta l'assurdo di uno Stato, che interpreta ad applica in tal modo la separazione fra chiesa e Stato, da esse voluta e proclamata.

Ognuno deve riconoscere in questo suo atto un autentico abuso di potere, senza precedenti nella storia contemporanea, che pure ha veduto arbitri e prepotenze d'ogni genere: infatti, neppure i nazional-socialisti di Hitler sono giunti a tal regno con le loro ingerenze nelle cose ecclesiastiche. L'arbitrio del governo di Praga raggiunge poi il colmo nel designare ad 'Amministratore Ecclesiastico' il sacerdote Jan Dechet, definito da un portavoce governativo, 'leale servitore' della Republica.

Sappiano auche troppo che significhino queste parole nel lessico progresista: voglione dire, cioe, che il Dechet e uno sleale ribelle a quell autorita ecclesiastica, che sola gli ha conferito la dignita ed i poteri ecclesiastici, affinche li usasse a salvare le anime e non a scandalizzarle col degradarsi al servizio degli atei:

Cosi un indegno ecclesiastico, colpito ora giustamente dalla scosmunica, e messo da un'authorita illegittima, a capo, sia pure provisoriamente, di una diocesi; naturalmente egli non sara diconesciuto da nessun cattolico, ecclesiastico e laico che sia.

Ne nasceranno, percio, difficolta, attriti, inconvenienti d'ogni generi: ma di tutto questo non si preoccupera il governo di Praga, il quale, anzi, trovera il modo di rallegrarsene.

Si, perche esso spera, forse, di giungere per questa via a sopprimere la chiesa cattolica in quella Nazione; ma la solida Fede ed il tradizionale attacczamento di quei cattolici alla Sede di Pietro, ci fanno certi che essi, nomori dei loro glorisosi antenati, usciti vittoriosi dalle lotte, sapranno mostrarsi degni eredi dalla loro fortezza e della loro costanza nel difenders il piu prezioso patrimonio che un popolo possa avere.

12. Gsovski-Kočvara-Nosek, "Czechoslovakia: Church and Religion," in *Digest-Index of Eastern European Law*, 13-16.

13. *NCWC*, Apr. 17, 1950, 1-2.

14. *Report on Czechoslovakia. NCFE*, Jan. 1951, 54.

15. *NCWC*, May 8, 1950, 1-2.

16. This document, in Bohemian, is in the *CML* archives in London.

17. The English translation of this document is by the author. The original document was never published.

18. *The Tablet*, Feb. 11, 1950, 116.

19. This document is in *Nový Život*, Mar., 1950, 17-18; cf. *L'Osservatore Romano*, Mar. 3, 1950, 1: "Un monito dell' Episcopato cecoslovacco."

20. *The Tablet*, March 11, 1950, 196.

21. *NCWC*, Mar. 6, 1950.

22. *The Tablet*, Mar. 18, 1950, 216.

23. *Nový Život*, Feb., 1950, 27; cf. *NCWC*, Feb. 27, 1950, 8-9.

24. *Loc. cit.*

25. Cavalli, *op. cit.*, 189.

26. *NCWC*, Mar. 6, 1950, 9.

27. *Spiknutí proti republice* (Conspiracy Against the Republic). Cf. *NCWC*, Mar. 6, 1950, 8 This booklet marks the opening phase of a campaign to charge the Archbishop with antidemocratic activity.

28. *Vatikán mezi dvěma světovými válkami* (The Vatican Between Two World Wars).

29. Cavalli, *op. cit.*, 193-194.

30. This document is in the *CML* archives in London.

31. *Rudé pravo*, March 8, 1949, 1.

32. Cavalli, *op. cit.*, 190.

33. *Nový Život*, April, 1950, 19.

34. Cavalli, *op. cit.*, 194-195.

35. *Nový Život*, *loc. cit.*

36. Cavalli, *op. cit.*, 194.

37. *Nový Život*, 2, nos. 4, 5, 6 (1950). Against this apparent miracle the booklet *Excommunications, Miracles and Sabotages* was published in Prague, May, 1950; cf. *Nový Život*, June, 1950, where a complete critique of the booklet is given.

38. *Universe* (British Catholic newspaper), March 24, 1950, 1: "Czechoslovakians expel last Vatican Official." The government ordered Msgr. de Liva to leave the country within three days. Msgr. de Liva was escorted to the Prague airfield by three police cars.

39. Cavalli, *op. cit.*, 192.

40. *L'Osservatore Romano*, March 29, 1950, 1: Il Ministero degli Esteri per parecchio tempo non ebbe, come era naturale, nulla da osservare. Ad un certo punto peró cominció a muovere difficoltá, affermando che a Mons. De Liva non spettava la qualifica di Incaricato d'affari ad interim, e vane riuscirono le delucidazioni date dallo stesso Mons. De Liva al Ministerio degli Esteri e dalla Segretaria di Stato all 'Incaricato d'affari di Cecoslovacchia per far comprendere l'insostenibilitá della tesi e del modo di agire del Governo. Il quale, da una parte, si rifiutava di ammettere che Mons. De Liva—L'unico diplomatico pontificio, rimasto a Praga—reggesse quella Internunziatura ad interim, cioe fino all'arrivo del nuovo Incaricato d'Affari, e, dall'altra, impediva—per ben nove mesi!—l'ingresso in Cecoslovacchia agli ecclesiastici che la Santa Sede destinava a quell'Ufficio. Prosequendo nell'attuazione dei suoi piani, il governo cercó in piu modi di ostacolare il funzionamento della Rappresentanza Pontificia. Incominició ad opporre difficolta a che l'incaricato d'Affari trattasse con funzionari del Ministero degli Esteri, indi gli rese difficile, e talvolta gli impedí, l'ingresso allo stesso Ministero . . . Un communicato del 16 corrente annunziava che il Governo aveva invitato Mons. De Liva a lasciare entro tre giorni il territorio della Republica.

41. *Zrada Vatikánu a biskupů* (The Treason of the Vatican and the Bishops). This is a highly defamatory pamphlet.

42. *NCWC*, Mar. 27, 1950, 1-4; cf. *NCWC*, Apr. 10, 1950, 3.

43. *The Tablet*, May 6, 1950, 368. M. Josef Minařík left Rome without notifying the Vatican. This signified the final rupture of diplomatic relations between Czechoslovakia and the Holy See.

44. Vojtěch Dolejší, "Rozvratná činnost řádových kněží ve službách imperialistů." (The Subversive Activities of Religious Priests in the Service of Imperialists.) In *Rudé Právo*, Apr. 16, 1950, 1. Cf. *Report on Czechoslovakia*, Apr. 1950, 14. Cf. *L'Osservatore Romano*, Apr. 2, 1950, 1: "Recrudescenza della persecutione anti-religiosa in Cecoslovacchia."

45. "Processo dei sacerdoti cattolici in Cecoslovacchia," in *L'Osservatore Romano*, Apr. 1, 1950, 1. Cf. *ibid.*, Apr. 5, 1950, 1; Apr. 10, 1950, 1; Apr. 6, 1950, 1.

46. *La DC*, 48 (1951), 1088 col. 157-62.

47. *Ibid.*, col. 157.

48. *NCWC*, April 10, 1950, A.

49. *Ibid.*, D.

50. *L'Osservatore Romano*, April 7, 1950, 1: "Il significato anticattolico e politico del processo di Praga."

51. *La DC*, 46 (1949), 1048 col. 994.

52. *Ibid.*, col. 993.

53. *La DC*, 48 (1951), 1088 col. 158; The Papal College Russicum, Roma, Piazza Santa Maria Maggiore, educates priests for two rites, Roman and Oriental, and practically follows the trends of unionism.

54. The complete text of this address may be found in *Svobodné Slovo*, Apr. 4, 1950, 1. For the English text see *Dobrý Pastier*, Nov. 1951, 15-17.

55. *Nový Život*, May, 1950, 32-3. Cf. *NCWC*, May 29, 1950, 4-6; cf. *L'Osservatore Romano*, Apr. 22, 1950, 1: "Dopo l'arresto di religiosi a Bratislava." Cf. *ibid.*, Apr. 19, 1950, 1: "Violente attivita politiche contra religiosi."

56. *L'Osservatore Romano*, Apr. 19, 1950, 1.

57. *Rudé Právo*, Apr. 20, 1950, 1: "Monasteries for better purposes." *Ibid.*, Apr. 25, 1950, 1: "Vestiges of monastery mysteries." See especially *Tvorba*, Apr. 12, 1950, for charges against monasteries and the Vatican under the title "The Father of Darkness and His Environs." Cf. *Report on Czechoslovakia*, Apr. 1950, 15. Cf. *Nový Život*, May, 1950, 32.

58. *The Tablet*, May 13, 1950, 389.

59. *L'Osservatore Romano*, May 3, 1950, 1: "Conventi di concentramento in Cecoslovacchia." Cf. *Zpravodaj*, November, 1950, 15-18.

60. *The Tablet,* May 13, 1950, 389.
61. *L'Osservatore Romano,* Oct. 29, 1950, 1-2.
62. *Report on Czechoslovakia,* Apr. 16, 1950, 15.
63. *Denni Hlasatel,* nos. 138-147, September, 1951. In various articles Dr. Francis Polák explains the terrible conditions in concentration camps in Russia. According to statistics, 12-15 million persons are living in these camps. The Vatican radio and the Voice of America gave many broadcasts during September, 1951, concerning this problem. See also *Národ,* the only Czech Catholic daily in the United States, Sept. 23, 1951, 3. Cf. Edward Crankshaw, "Cracks in the Kremlin" (Ten Million Soviet Slaves), in *The Washington Post,* Oct. 29, 1951, 9. Cf. Elinor Lipper, *Eleven Years in Soviet Prison Camps.* A very interesting article about life in the Soviet prison camps, taken from this book, is in *Reader's Digest,* June, 1951, 141-162. Cf. James M. Gillis, *This Our Day,* 2.
64. P. Korbel and V. Vagasský, "Forced Labor, Population Transfers, and Deportation in Czechoslovakia," in *NCFE,* Sept., 1952, 2-11.
65. *Veritas* (English Edition), September 15, 1951, 1-2. This letter was sent by Dr. Suchánek, official of the national "Raw Material Collection," to all provincial committees. This national enterprise trades in waste material. Action "K" covered all actions contemplated by the political section of the Ministry of Interior against monasteries and religious orders.
66. *Nový Život,* Feb., 1950, 27-28.
67. This document appeared in Bohemian in *Nový Život,* Feb., 1950, 24-25.
68. The jurisdiction of the state, from the Communist point of view, not only controls "mixed matters" (*res mixtas*), a limitation contained in the *Modus Vivendi* of 1928 and in some laws dating from the first Czechoslovak Republic, but also extends directly into ecclesiastical affairs, sufficient proof of which may be seen in the laws of 1949 and thereafter.
69. Gsovski-Kočvara-Nosek, "Czechoslovakia: Church and Religion," in *Digest-Index of Eastern European Law,* 21. Cf. *The Jurist,* October, 1950, 491: Catholic and Protestant seminaries in Czechoslovakia have been abolished as independent institutions and replaced by state-controlled theological schools.
70. By this provision of the state, the *magisterium ecclesiae* is endangered, since it is practically replaced by the State Ministry of Education and the government bureau for church affairs.
71. *The Clergy Review,* February, 1951, vi.
72. Gsovski-Kočvara-Nosek, *op. cit.,* 21.
73. *Ibid.,* 22.

74. *Ibid.*, 23. Cf. "Theology in Chains," in *The Clergy Review,* February, 1951, xiii-xiv.

75. *NCWC*, July 31, 1950, 1-2.

76. Several other professors refused to accept the assignment of the government. An impressive instance was that of the Reverend Dr. John Koutný, of Brno, who refused an appointment to the theological faculty of Prague in these words: "Death rather than treason!" Cf. *Nový Život*, May, 1951, 16. Cf. *Report on Czechoslovakia,* June, 1951, 67. Some professors escaped into exile. Among them were Dr. Felix Mikula, Dr. Alexander Heidler, and Dr. Vojtech Bucko of Bratislava. The well-known historian Dr. Francis Dvorník clearly foresaw political developments in Czechoslovakia and did not return to Prague in 1945. He remained in exile in France and England. At present he is in the United States, a professor at Harvard University. He is doing research work at Dumbarton Oaks, Washington, D. C.

77. *Report on Czechoslovakia*, June, 1951, 66. Eight seminarians from the theological faculty in Bratislava were ordained by Bishop Ambroze Lazik (Czech broadcast, June 19, 1951).

78. *Ibid.*, 65. Bishop Eltschkner ordained two priests in February, 1951, in Prague.

79. *Report on Czechoslovakia,* November, 1950, 49. Cf. *Veritas*, no. 7, 1951.

80. *Ibid.*, 50. Some seminarians, of course, escaped into exile and finished their theological studies in Austria, Germany and especially at the Nepomucenum, in Rome.

81. *NCWC,* June 12, 1950, 12.

82. *L'Osservatore Romano,* May 26, 1950, 1: "Cose di Praga." Rev. Josef Buchta is from Silesia and was a member of the Communist party for a long time.

83. Msgr. Edward Oliva was made a monsignor in February, 1948, for his successful work in establishing Catholic Charities in Prague. In 1949 he was deposed by the Communists as director of charity organizations and in 1951 was elevated by the same Communists to vicar-general in Litoměřice.

84. *Report on Czechoslovakia,* November, 1950, 20-21.

85. *Op. cit.*, December, 1950, 60.

86. *Ibid.*, 61.

87. By this provision of the State, Catholic bishops were practically denied all control of their dioceses, for they were faced with the dilemma of either collaborating with the state, which gave the orders, or being ousted. The large number of them that resisted this virtual enslavement and pressure shows the firm stand they took, even under duress, against the state's encroachments in matters ecclesiastical. The apparent weakness

displayed by some of the bishops in attempting to collaborate can be excused, perhaps, by their sincere desire to salvage what they could in so great a crisis. It does not necessarily invalidate the official stand of the resisting bishops, as recorded at their meetings. (See footnote 88.)

88. *Report on Czechoslovakia*, May 16-31, 1950, 14. Msgr. Sobota was removed from the list of monsignors by the Vatican.

89. *Op. cit.*, April 16-30, 1950, 15-16.

90. *The Clergy Review*, February, 1951, xviii.

91. *Ibid.*, May 16-31, 1950, 14.

92. *Lidová demokracie*, June 24, 1950, 3.

93. *Ibid.*, June 17, 1950, 3.

94. *Ibid.*, June 2, 1950, 12. This speech was made by Plojhar on the occasion of a meeting of "patriotic priests" on June 1, 1950, in the Archbishop's palace in Prague.

95. *Report on Czechoslovakia*, June 15, 1950, 9.

96. *AAS*, 12 (1920), 34, 37, 583-588; cf. *AAS*, 14 (1922), 379-380, 593. Cf. Ottaviani, *Institutiones*, I, 394; cf. *Civiltà Cattolica* (1920), 376.

97. *The Clergy Review*, February, 1951, xviii.

98. *La DC*, 47 (1950), 1083 col. 929-939; 37 (1950), 1074, col. 991-1000; 47 (1950), 1078 col. 1133-1254; 47 (1950), 1079, col. 1318-1339; 47 (1950), 1081 col. 1441-1443. These contain reports on the entire controversy. Cf. *Report on Czechoslovakia*, June 1-15, 1950, 7-8.

99. The patriotic priests received more pay than other state employees. Cf. Cary MacEoin, *The Communist War on Religion*, 46. The Communists announced that these "patriotic priests" would receive salaries as high as 15,000 crowns (about $300 at the official rate of exchange). The average civil-service salary was about 5,000 crowns, and high police officials got 12,000.

100. *The Tablet*, May 13, 1950, 389. Cf. *ibid.*, June 10, 1951, 469; cf. *Report on Czechoslovakia*, May 16-31, 1950, 15.

101. *Nové trestné právo správni* (The new penal administrative law); cf. *Zpravodaj*, December, 1950, 21.

102. *L'Osservatore Romano*, July 29, 1950, 1: "Il nuovo codice penale cecoslovacco."

103. The English translation is from *The Clergy Review*, February, 1951, xviii.

104. The English translation of these laws is from the *Digest-Index of Eastern European Law*, 24-5.

105. *L'Osservatore Romano*, Oct. 29, 1950, 1-2: Due mila circa sono in prigione o internati nei campi di lavoro.

106. *NCWC*, July 24, 1950, 2; cf. *The Tablet*, August 12, 1950, 186.

107. *La DC*, 46 (1949), 1051 col. 1205-09.
108. *Ibid.*, 47 (1950), col. 1201-06.
109. *Ibid.*, 48 (1951), 1100 col. 907-23.
110. *Ibid.*, 48 (1951), 1104 col. 1195-1202; 47 (1950), 107 col. 807-29.
111. *Ibid.*, 48 (1951), 1104 col. 1187-94.
112. *L'Osservatore Romano*, August 25, 1950, 1: "Si annunzia l'arresto di Mons. Buzalka."
113. *NCWC*, July 17, 1950, 1.
114. *Ibid.*, June 19, 1950, 8.
115. *The Tablet*, Dec. 9, 1950, 196.
116. *Ibid.*
117. *NCWC*, October 13, 1950, 1.
118. *Report on Czechoslovakia*, April, 1950, 15-6. Cf. *Ibid.*, November, 1950, 51. According to this explanation, Bishop Eltschkner and General Vicar Opatrný had always shown a tendency toward compromise, and this was now exploited by the Communists. Bishop Pobožný of Rožnava was put under pressure because of his former public activities as far back as World War II. Later this bishop was arrested.
119. Msgr. Matoušek was secretly ordained in Prague.
120. *Report on Czechoslovakia*, November, 1950, 51.
121. *AAS*, 42 (1950), 601, 602, Cf. *The Jurist*, January, 1951, 134-35. The decree of the Sacred Congregation of the Council of June 29, 1950, also inflicts specially reserved automatic excommunication on those who unlawfully usurp or permit themselves to be intruded into ecclesiastical offices. *AAS*, 42 (1950), 601 ff.
122. Cary MacEoin, *op. cit.*, 49.
123. *Report on Czechoslovakia*, December, 1950, 47-48.
124. *L'Osservatore Romano*, November 30, 1950, 1: "Il processo nelle carceri di Praga . . . E' necessario infamare, et necessario calumniare . . . ."
125. *Ibid.*, December 1, 1950, 1: "Continuano gli interrogatori al processo di Praga: alcune confessioni tipiche-Processo alle intenzioni."
126. *Ibid.*, December 2, 1950, 1: "Al processo di Praga si esagera."
127. *Report on Czechoslovakia*, November, 1950, 48; cf. *L'Osservatore Romano*, December 3, 1950, 1: "Mons. Zela e i suoi compagni condannati a gravi pene di carcere (concluso il dramma di Pankrac)."
128. See Chapter III.
129. *Nový Život*, December, 1950, 16-20: "Rub pražskéko soudu." This periodical published a complete analysis and critique of this trial. Cf. Dr. Adolf Procházka, "Na okraj pražského

procesu proti čs. katolické Hierarchii," in *Zpravodaj*, January, 1951, 6-7. Cf. *Dokumentarní brožura*. This booklet was published to give information concerning the trials of the hierarchy. Cf. *Report on Czechoslovakia*, December, 1950, 60.

130. *Report on Czechoslovakia*, April 1-15, 1950, 7: Dr. Hobza said that the trial of members of religious orders began on April 5, 1950, in Prague. Cf. *The Jurist*, January, 1951, 157-58: "Attrition in Czechoslovakia." The article refers to the testimony of the so-called expert in international law, Dr. Antonin Hobza, professor at the University of Prague, who denied the validity of the norms of canon law in relation to the state, and asserted that bishops automatically became traitors by telling priests how to act in regard to the law of Czechoslovakia.

131. *NCWC*, December 4, 1950, 5.

132. We wonder how Dr. Hobza can come to such a conclusion. It is sufficient to recall that the validity of the ecclesiastical right is based on the ontological fact that "through baptism a person becomes a member of the Church of Christ with all the rights and duties of Catholics. The Catholic Church and the Apostolic See have the nature of a moral person by divine institution itself." The "*stabilité de l'Église*" is a "*stabilité de son droit*," to quote Cardinal Villeneuve ("Pages d'introduction à l'étude du droit canonique," in *Les Cahiers Canoniques de Laval*, (Cahier No. 2 Quebec: Université Laval, 1944, 94). Cf. *Proces proti vatikánským agentům v Československu.*

133. *NCWC*, December 4, 1950, B.

134. *L'Osservatore Romano*, April 8, 1951, 1: "Una nuova documentazione: Il lavoro forzato in Cecoslovacchia."

135. Korbel and Vagasský, *op. cit.*, 9-10.

136. *Orel*, a monthly review published in New York, and the well-known Catholic gymnastic organization in exile, recently reproduced a map which, according to official, unofficial, and top-secret sources shows the forced labor camps and jails in Czechoslovakia, with special statistics on the persons incarcerated. According to the map, there are 152 principal jails and 97 investigation stations, which include forced-labor camps and special camps for the clergy. The data on the map are in Bohemian. The map was further elaborated by members of the Presidium of the organization, especially by Vladimír Richter, See *Orel*, January, 1953, 8-9.

137. *Ibid.*, 5. Cf. *Zpravodaj*, November, 1950, 15-18.

138. *The Trial of the Treasonable Slovak Bishops, Jan Vojtaššak, Michal Buzalka, Pavol Gojdič.*

139. *L'Osservatore Romano*, January 13, 1951, 1: "La turpe commedia di Bratislava: . . . In conclusione—sempre la stessa—a

Bratislava si rinnova la turpe commedia che ormai e nelle consuetudini della considetta, giustizia democratica e populare."

140. *Ibid.*, January 12, 1951, 1: "Processo a Bratislava: Nel caso presente questo interesse comanda la distruzione nel cattolicismo; e la calumnia la versazione legalistica . . ." Cf. *ibid.*, January 14, 1951, 1: "Il processo di Bratislava."

141. *The Trial of the Treasonable Slovak Bishops, op. cit.*, 43-91 (Msgr. Jan Vojtaššak); 92-119 (Msgr. Michal Buzalka); 225 (Msgr. Pavol Gojdič).

142. *L'Osservatore Romano*, January 15-16, 1951, 1: "Chiesa con una condanna iniqua l'infame 'processo di Bratislava.' L'ergastolo del Vescovo di Prešov e all'auxiliare di Tirnava—24 anni al Vescovo di Spis."

143. *Report on Czechoslovakia*, January, 1951, 53-54.

144. *NCWC*, Jan. 15, 1951, 7; cf. *ibid.*, Jan. 29, 1951.

145. *The Tablet*, Jan. 27, 1951, 76.

146. *Ibid.*, Feb. 3, 1951, 96.

147. *Report on Czechoslovakia*, Feb. 1951, 57.

148. *The Tablet*, Feb. 10, 1951, 117.

149. See *La DC*, 48 (1951), 1088 col. 155-58: "Les procés contre le clergé."

150. *The Jurist*, April, 1951, 346.

151. The well-known Stockholm resolution was used by the Communists for their own political advantage and as a seeming pretext for peace.

152. *NCWC*, Feb. 27, 1950, 8. The first phase of this fight was led by the District Action committees, to which priests were invited for so-called "talks with clergymen," and where meetings were arranged, attended by the officials of the people's administration or by "stachanors" (best workers) from the factories. These meetings were used to promote animosity against ecclesiastical authorities. Following the meetings dinner parties were arranged, photos and films were taken and these were shown in theaters. It was pointed out that these dinner parties were arranged by the working people. It is clear that shameful tactics were used to discredit priests before the public, and to induce the faithful to desert their bishops. The same aim was followed through the training of priests where systematic attacks against the hierarchy and the Holy Father were brought into play.

Besides this stand toward the clergy, another form of attack was used. The faithful and courageous priests were becoming discouraged and the resistance of arrested priests was being broken by torture. The number of priests arrested constantly increased as more demands were made on them by the government. Czechoslovak Communists had many opportunities to arrest priests, for all they had to ask were questions against church-directed regulations, against religious doctrine, or against the principles of conscience. Some priests were arrested and released twice or more, which is proof that they were not frightened by the measures of the government in fulfilling the directives given by their bishops, for in the face of the threatening menace, every loyal act of a Catholic priest to his bishop was construed as grounds for an accusation of subversive activity.

153. The Swiss agency *Kipa* published this questionnaire of the Czechoslovak secret police on February 17, 1950, but it was put into general use only since January, 1951, although in some districts before that time. This form of questionnaire was given in connection with the so-called "religious problem" of the Cominform in Karlovy Vary, in 1949, as a method of ascertaining the true stand of the Catholic clergy. Through it the government intended to eliminate the bishops and priests faithful to the Holy See. The results of these tactics were relayed to the secret meetings of the Cominform in Racisdorf, near Bratislava, 1950. Cf. Cavalli, *Governo Communista*, 208.

154. This document is in the *CML* archives in London. All details regarding every Catholic priest are specified in it. A complete text is also in *La DC*, 48 (1951), 1088 col. 153-55.

155. *Report on Czechoslovakia*, March, 1951, 55.

156. P. Korbel and V. Vagasský, *Purges in the Communist Party of Czechoslovakia*, in *NCFE*, October, 1952, 1-50. This account sets forth the political background which gave rise to the screenings and the purges, mass and individual, in Czechoslovakia during these years.

157. *News from Behind the Iron Curtain*, in *NCFE*, January, 1952, 5-6.

158. *L'Osservatore Romano*, March 3, 1951, 1: "La nuovo epurazzione in Cecoslovacchia." Cf. *ibid*, March 16, 1950, 1: "Dopo le dimissioni di Clementis . . ."

159. *Report on Czechoslovakia*, September, 1951, 6-7; cf. *ibid.*, August, 1951, 6.

160. *Ibid.*, May, 1951, 5.

161. *Ibid.*, August, 1951, 6; cf. *ibid.*, November, 1951, 6-12, in which authentic documents concerning the case of Slansky will be found. Cf. *ibid.*, November, 1951, 6.

162. *The New York Times*, Feb. 28, 1952, 1, 5: Col. Gen. Jaroslav Procházka.

163. In 1951 and 1952 general purges took place in the district and central committees of the Communist party under the pretexts of deviation and sabotage. See, for example, the news story in the New York *Daily News*, December 8, 1952, "Czechs Seize Six Reds in Purge Move."

164. The issues of *Veritas* for this period carry reports on all the purges.

165. See "Fourteen Ex-Red Leaders Brought to Trial in Czechoslovakia," in the New York *Daily News*, Nov. 20, 1952, 1, 8; cf. Pittsburg *Post-Gazette*, Nov. 28, 1952, 1, 5; cf. the *Daily News*, Dec. 2, 1952, 8: "Prague Trials Embarrassing to U. S. Reds." The free press all over the world commented on this trial with surprise, because the victims were mostly Jews. The press termed the trial anti-Semitic and anti-Zionist. Cf. "Open Anti-Semitism Marks New Attacks," in *News from Behind the Iron Curtain*, February, 1952, 8-9. Cf. *Time*, December 8, 1952, 31: "Spiders, Bugs, Rats." Cf. *ibid.*, December 15, 1952, 31, in which economic sabotage is given as one reason for the trial. Cf. *Report on Czechoslovakia*, January, 1952, 8-10.

166. The best example is that of Tito's government in Yugoslavia, where the Catholic Church was persecuted under the same pretexts as those employed in Russia. It should be noted that the Czechoslovak government "purged" Communists like Slanský who were the main enemies of the Catholic Church. Many secretly issued instructions and circulars were originated or signed by Slanský, who was particularly responsible for information from so-called main Catholic sources. These "deviationists" were such only to the extent of preparing to seize power for themselves. Their "deviationism" bears the stamp of personal opposition to other cliques in the struggle for power in the Communist government. The policy remained the same, with the same aims, theories, and practices. In purges, it is a question of an exchange of persons, not programs. So under a deviationist government like Tito's, the Catholic Church is persecuted by the same tactics. See the *Memorandum* of Yugoslav bishops to Marshal Tito in *NCWC*, Jan. 26, 1953, 1-6. Cf. *The Catholic Digest*, April, 1953, 33-8: "Stepinac Speaks." The situation of the Church in Yugoslavia is no better than in Russia or the satellite countries. Cf. Anthony Henry, Count O'Brien of Thomond, *Archbishop Stepinac*, 94-95. Cf. "Letter to Marshal Tito," in *The Catholic Mind*, May, 1953, 314-20.

167. *NCWC*, Jan. 22, 1951, 2. Cf. *The Jurist*, April, 1951, 346: Czechoslovakia still has a few clerical victims left—70 per cent of all parishes are without pastors. Cf. *The Evangelist*, November 23, 1951, 1.

168. *NCWC*, Dec. 15, 1948, 31. This practice was stressed in many circulars after the Ninth Congress of the Communist party in Prague, in 1949. After the influence of the priests had been eliminated, important Catholic laymen were persecuted and brought to trial, as, for instance, in June, 1951, in Prague, the leading figures in the real Catholic Action. See *Veritas*, nos.

7 and 8, 1951; cf. *Nový Život*, March, 1952, 9. A great trial that took place in Brno, June 11-13, 1952, was also directed against Catholic laymen. See *Report on Czechoslovakia*, June, 1952, 65-6. The main purpose of these trials was to frighten and terrify the faithful in order to prevent them from giving any aid to Catholic priests.

169. "La Chiesa e la democrazia," in *L'Osservatore Romano*, July 6, 1950, 1. Cf. Fulton J. Sheen, *Liberty, Equality and Fraternity*, 10: The liberty which the Church defends starts with the spiritual nature of man . . ." Cf. *Enciclica di Leone XIII*, "Graves de Communis," *re sulla Democrazia Cristiana*, January 18, 1901, 13.

170. *Report on Czechoslovakia*, March, 1951, 10.

171. Cary MacEoin, *op. cit.*, 190-1. See also "The New Religion," in *The Tablet*, June 19, 1948, 381-382.

FOOTNOTES TO CHAPTER XII

1. Giannini Amedeo, *Il modus vivendi fra la S. Sede e la Cecoslovacchia*. Anonima romana editoriale (1928).

2. Pastoral letter of all the Czechoslovak Archbishops and Bishops of November 17, 1949; quoted above in Chapter X.

3. Exceptions were Bishop Eltschkner, the Auxiliary of Prague and Bishop Pobožný of Rožnava.

4. It is necessary to stress that not only bishops and clergy were victims of this persecution, but also many active Catholic laymen, especially the Catholic intelligentsia, against whom many trials were held from the end of 1951 and during 1952. They were thus liquidated from public influence on the ordinary people. They were expelled from important state jobs. Especially well-known Catholic professors of universities were suspended from teaching or forced to conform to the new situation. Many of them unwaveringly proved their fidelity to the Church. Pope Pius XII, himself, glorified the laymen of Czechoslovakia for their great valor in times of persecution. See *AAS* 43 (1951), 768-78.

5. Monsignor de Liva, Secretary of the Internunciature in Prague.

6. La *DC* 46 (1949), 1055 col. 1460-61.

7. The decree of the Sacred Supreme Congregation of the Holy Office, June 20, 1949; *AAS*, 41 (1949), 333. Cf. *L'Osservatore Romano*, June 20, 1949, 1; *Clergy Review*, 32 (1949), 273-75. The English text is found in Chapter II, C.

8. The decree of the Sacred Supreme Congregation of the Holy Office, July 1, 1949; *AAS*, 41 (1949), 334; the whole English text is in Chapter II, C; cf. *La DC* 46 (1949) 1050, col. 1099-

1110; cf. Josephus Sirna, "Adnotationes ad decretum S. Officii de Communismo," in *Apolinaris*, An. 26, Nos. 1-2 (1949), 56-70.

9. *De Communistarum matrimonio declaratio*. The declaration of the Supreme Congregation of the Holy Office, given on August 11, 1949; *AAS*, 41 (1949), 427; cf. *L'Osservatore Romano*, August 16-17, 1949, 1; cf. *La DC*, 46 (1949), 1050, col. 1095-96.

10. *AAS*, 42 (1950), 553; cf. *La DC*, 47 (1950), 1076, col. 1095-96.

11. The Decree of the Sacred Consistorial Congregation, February 18, 1950, in *AAS*, 42 (1950), 195. By virtue of this decree the Rev. John Dechet became an *excommunicatus vitandus* (an excommunicated person to be avoided); cf. *La DC*, 47 (1950), 1064, col. 370.

12. Decree of the Congregation of the Council concerning the canonical institution and provision of ecclesiastical offices and benefices, June 29, 1950; in *AAS*, 42 (1950), 601-02.

13. Theoretically, new laws were enacted; practically violent methods were used.

14. *Report on Czechoslovakia*, 2, No. 2 (February, 1951), 56.

15. *Ibid.*, 56-57.

16. *Report on Czechoslovakia*, 2, No. 2 (February, 1951), 56.

17. *Ibid.*, 56; cf. *Lidová demokracie*, 7, No. 60 (March 1, 1951), 1.

18. *Lidová demokracie*, 7, No. 60 (March 1, 1951), 1.

19. *Report on Czechoslovakia*, 2, No. 3 (March, 1951), 74.

20. See Vilém Stránecký, "Kapitulni a generalni vikári-nástroj rozvratu cirkevní organisace v ČSR" (Capitular and general vicars—tool of the split of the ecclesiastical organization in the Czechoslovak Republic), *Katolík*, No. 6056 (May 18, 1951), 2; cf. *ibid.*, No. 6057 (May 22, 1951), 2, and *ibid.*, No. 6058 (May 25, 1951), 2; cf. J. Fatran, "Obsadenie biskupskych uradov 'vlasteneckymi' kňazmi" (Occupation of bishops' offices by patriotic priests) in *Dobrý Pastier*, 26, No. 11 (November, 1951), 7-11.

21. All bishops except Auxiliary Bishop Eltschkner of Prague and Auxiliary Bishop Matoušek of Prague, who was not recognized as a bishop by the Czechoslovak government, and Capitular Vicar Monsignor Onderek of Český Těšín, who had earlier been coerced (December, 1949) to make a declaration favoring the state policy of new Church laws, refused cooperation with the state. Monsignor Onderek was subjected to "third degree" torture. See *The Tablet*, 194, No. 5710 (October 29, 1949), 284: He was questioned continuously for eight hours under glaring lights and held out until the police threatened the safety of all the priests in his charge.

22. Archbishop Beran of Prague, Archbishop Matocha of Olomouc, Bishop Hlouch of Budějovice, Bishop Pícha of Hradec Králové, Bishop Skoupý of Brno were thus under house arrest.

23. Bishop Trochta of Litoměřice, Auxiliary Bishop Zela of Olomouc, Auxiliary Bishop Tomášek of Olomouc, and all Slovak bishops except Bishop Pobožný of Rožnava were jailed.

24. Bishop Trochta of Litoměřice, Bishop Mořic Pícha of Hradec Králové, Bishop Ambroze Lazik of Trnava, Bishop Joseph Čárský, Apostolic Administrator of Košice, were among those thus "indoctrinated." See *RNS*, March 26, 1951 (Vienna); cf. *The Sun-Herald*, New York (March 28, 1951), 4: Four Czechoslovak bishops took an oath of loyalty to the Communist government and did so after weeks of torture at the hands of the security police; Bishop Pícha and Trochta were subjected to injections which induced a state of fever and finally led to brain paralysis. Bishop Pícha also underwent special treatment in a "revolving chair," used by the Communist police to soften up "stubborn cases." Other methods of physical violence were used on Bishop Joseph Čarský and Bishop Ambroze Lazik. Cf. *The Ensign* (Canada's National News Weekly), 3, No. 23 (March 24, 1951), 2, "Drug Treatments." Cf. *The Tablet*, 196 (March 17, 1951), 205. Bishops Michael Buzalka, Pavol Gojdič and Vojtaššák were prepared by drugs for the trial in Bratislava. See *Nový Život*, 3, No. 1-2 (February 1951), 14. Cf. quotation No. 65. Besides these direct proofs we can get the same impression indirectly from the analysis of "surprising declarations" or still more "surprising self-accusations" of those bishops, who up to now always took a firm stand. This becomes evident also by analysis with cases in other countries. An indirect proof of the pressure that must have been brought to bear on our bishops in their "surprising declarations," and still more "surprising self-accusations" can be deduced from the fact that before that period these bishops had always taken a firm stand. No one outside of the Iron Curtain today believes that Cardinal Mindszenty *voluntarily* changed his former stand toward communism in Hungary. The same would logically seem to apply to the so-called "confessions" of the Czechoslovak bishops. See document No. 1 in *Veritas* (Czech edition) of April 1, 1951: "Regarding the Ecclesiastical Situation in Czechoslovakia."

25. *The New York Times* (March 13, 1951), 15, under the caption "Six Churchmen Take Czech Regime Oath" says: "The Czech Government through intimidation and pressure had succeeded in insuring at least formal collaboration of some members of the episcopate."

26. Cf. *The Ensign*, 3, No. 23 (March 31, 1951), 2, 16; cf. "Beran Banished by Prague" in *The New York Times*, 61 (Sunday, March 11, 1951), 1, 12.

27. *Christian Democratic News Service* (The organ of the Christian Democratic Union of Central Europe, 2020 P. St. N.W.; Washington, D. C.), 1, No. 8 (September 29, 1951), 4. Cf. *Czechoslovak newsletter* (New York: NCFE No. 15, October 10, 1951, 14): It was reported from Vienna on September 24, 1951, that Monsignor Beran was removed from the Nová Říše monastery to a monastery near Šternberk in Northern Moravia during the night of September 14-15. In view of growing resistance activities in the Czechoslovak-Austrian border region Nová Říše was no longer considered as safe place of internment.

28. P.K.V.V., *Population transfers, deportations and forced labor camps* (New York: NCFE, 1951), 6.

29. "L'Arcivescovo di Praga cacciato dalla sua sede," in *L'Osservatore Romano*, An. XCI, No. 61 (March 15, 1951), 1: "Le autorità amministrative hanno inflitto una ammenda a Mons. Beran, arcivescovo di Praga, per il suo attegiamento negativo nei riguardi delle leggi sulla Chiesa, e gli hanno impasto di soggiornare fuori della diocesi di Praga." Cf. *The New York Times*, 61 (March 11, 1951), 1.

30. *Report on Czechoslovakia*, March, 1951, 71.

31. *Ibid.*, 71.

32. *Catholic Digest*, November, 1952, 29: "The Forced 'Resignation' of Vicar General Opatrný of St. Vitus Cathedral announced."

33. Cirkevní puč (Ecclesiastical coup d'état) in *Record on Czechoslovakia* 2, No. 3 (March, 1951), 70-76.

34. See Chapter E, 242: Declaration of the Sacred Consistorial Congregation under date of March 17, 1951. Cf. *Katolik*, 58, No. 6037 (March 13, 1951), 1, 10.

35. *Memorandum to the Government of the Czechoslovak Republic*, November 17, 1949, *cit. supra*, Chapter II, C. But the right of patronage in Czechoslovakia was regulated to read: All private or public patronage of churches and prebends has passed over to the government (Law No. 218, sec. 11, 1949 Coll.) whereas all obligations to contribute to the Church have ceased. The law concerning patronage is evidently contrary to Canon Law.

36. This declaration was given by the State Bureau for Church Affairs in Prague immediately after the banishment of Archbishop Beran and was published in the Czechoslovak Press. See *Rudé Právo*, March 11, 1951, 1.

37. *C.J.C.*, see canons, caput VII de personis: De sede impedita

aut vacante ac de Vicario Capitulari. Cf. *Dobrý Pastier*, 27, No. 8 (August, 1952), 13-16; *ibid.*, No. 9 (September, 1952), 10-11.

38. *Rudé Právo*, 31 (March 16, 1951), 1.

39. *Report on Czechoslovakia*, 2, No. 3 (March, 1951), 13.

40. *Research and Information Center, N.C.F.E.* (Czechoslovak Section), 2, No. 4 (July 25, 1951), 12: A Bishop promotes his own commissar.

41. *Record on Czechoslovakia*, 2, No. 7 (June, 1951). Cf. *The Ensign*, 3, No. 22 (March 24, 1951), 2: Well-informed sources told the *Ensign* there is no doubt that Monsignor Oliva had been subjected to drug treatments by the Communists. See footnote No. 24.

42. *AAS*, 43 (1951), 173-74 where the Latin text will be found. Cf. *L'Osservatore Romano*, March 18, 1951, 1: cf. *La DC*, 48 (1951), 1092, col. 421-422.

43. The English text is by the author; see also *The Tablet*, March 24, 1951, 236; the Italian text of this declaration is in *L'Osservatore Romano*, (March 21, 1951), 1.

44. N.C.W.C. March 19, 1951. A-B. Cf. *The Washington Post*, March 18, 1951, 3 M: "Pope Bans Czechs for Church Crimes." Cf. *Times-Herald*, 13, Sunday, March 18, 1951, 1: "Czech Reds Expelled by Vatican Edict."

45. "Rispetto in Cecoslovacchia," in *L'Osservatore Romano*, March 24, 1951, 1: "Una longa notizia da Praga, apparsa su l'Unità, riferisce alcune affermazioni del Vice-presidente del consiglio Zdenek Fierlinger e di un altro 'autorevole portavoce' sulla sistematica oppressione della chiesa cattolica in Cecoslovacchia e sulla, 'Dichirazione della Sacra Congregatione Consistoriale.' Vi si parla, tra l'altro, di-'fidelta'-ai principi della chiesa cattolica e di 'pieno rispetto delle norme del diritto canonico.' Come e quanto, principi della Chiesa e i Sacri Canoni siano rispettati dai governanti di Praga non e necessario dire: basta rileggere i punti della Dichiarazione suddetta."

46. *Report on Czechoslovakia*, 2, No. 3 (March, 1951), 70-71.

47. Bishop Stěpán Trochta of Litoměřice, in particular, showed a special diplomatic ability as an intermediator between the government and bishops. For that reason these bishops could hardly be styled "four puppet bishops." See *Catholic Digest*, 17, No. 1 (November, 1952), 29. Bishop Trochta was forcibly deported from his see by the Czechoslovak Communists on Deceember 30, 1952, Cf. *NCWC*, January 5, 1953, 3-4.

48. E. M. Lynskey, *The Government of the Catholic Church* (New York: Kenedy and Sons, 1952), 19-24.

49. Bela Fabian, *Cardinal Mindszenty*, 169-198. The declaration of the Czechoslovak bishops under date of March 12, 1951 regarding an agreement with the state church is very similar to the written statement given by Cardinal Mindszenty at his trial. See *ibid.*, 180-81.

50. See *Bulletin* (of the International Peasant Union, Washington, D. C.), 2, No. 6 (June, 1951), 21: "Organization of the Judiciary": To conform with the Communist thesis that the law is the totality of the rules of conduct "expressing the will of the dominant class and of customs and rules of community life sanctioned by state authority the application of which is being guaranteed by compulsive force in order to guard, secure and develop social relationships and social orders advantageous and agreeable to the dominant class," the Communist regime in Czechoslovakia has made of the judiciary an instrument for complete annihilation of all the last traces of democracy.

51. *Katolík*, January 2, 1953, 3: Krištan, F. E. "Posudek katolického theologa o Kommunistickém soudnictví" (A judgment of Catholic Theology concerning the Communist Judiciary).

52. See *Time*, December 29, 1952, 24: "Stronger than truth itself." Cf. Dr. Joseph Mikuš, "The Truth about Three Slovak Bishops" in *Dobrý Pastier*, November, 1951, 13-18.

53. A strong reaction to the trials of bishops and priests and the procedure of these trials was voiced by the Vatican radio and press. See, e.g., the reaction of *L'Osservatore Romano* to the trials, of Prague and Bratislava, already quoted. Many protocols of Czech and Slovak refugee priests give sufficient testimony collected by the Research Centre of Free Europe testifying to the lack of freedom and justice of these trials. The many protests of a free world against the trials are so many manifestations that justice was corrupted, e.g., "Protest of the Executive Committee of the Slovak Catholic Federation of America against the persecution of the Slovak bishops," in *Slovakia*. It calls the Bratislava trial "the kangaroo court." See *Dobrý Pastier*, June 1951, 5. See footnote No. 69.

54. Gerald A. Ryan, *Principles of Episcopal Jurisdiction*, 19-29.

55. *CIC*, canon 329, 335.

56. It is known that Czechoslovak bishops gave a conciliatory advice to the clergy after October 14, 1949 in the pastoral letter of November 17—see Chapter X. After the new Church's laws had been enacted there was no longer any basis for a relation between Church and state according to a theological point of view, for the Communists began to exercise complete subordina-

tion of the Church to the state. This new situation also evoked new tactics on the part of the bishops. Active resistance was followed by passive resistance. See *L'Eglise persécutée en Tchécoslovaquie* (Paris: Centre d'études et de diffusion catholiques, 1951) (brochure No. 7), 13; cf. Cardinal Tisserant, *La Persécution Religieuse derrière le Rideau de fer* (Paris: Centre d'etudes et de diffusion catholiques, 1951), (No. 5), 18.

57. The first violent provision was against Monsignor Francis Onderek, apostolic administrator of Český Těsin, 1949; then from May, 1950, on against all bishops. See previous pages.

58. It now seems evident from the previous exposé that Auxiliary Bishop Eltschkner of Prague collaborated fully with the regime and took part in public manifestations arranged by the State Office for Church Affairs in Prague, in charge of patriotic priests.

59. See *Report on Czechoslovakia*, 1, No. 8 (April, 1950), 15-16. This favorable stand taken by Bishop Pobožný can be explained only as a result of his former public activities, namely "political revisionism" in favor of Hungary. This situation was pressed by Communists from a national point of view against Bishop Pobožný and forced him to take, it seems, a compromising stand to save himself from being accused of political treason. In 1953 the Bishop was arrested anyway.

60. See Chapter X and XI. In these memoranda and pastoral letters will be found the answers and opposition to every step of state policy from a theological, canonical, political point of view. De facto the whole development of ecclesiastical affairs in Czechoslovakia is contained in these official actions of the bishops, collectively taken. Every government action was followed by a reaction on the part of the bishops until they were silenced by force.

61. Over one hundred Slovak and Czech priests are in exile. Rev. Dr. Alexander Heidler, National Delegate for Czech refugees in Germany and director of religious broadcast "Free Europe" in Munich, uses their testimonies for radio services.

62. See *Katolík,* January 2, 1953, 2: "Karpatorusini vzponinali biskupa Romži (Karpato-Ruthenians remember Bishop Romža). He was killed in 1947.

63. Bishop Pavol Gojdič was given a life sentence in the trial of Bratislava, January, 1951.

64. Auxiliary Bishop Hopko was put in jail August, 1950, without a trial and according to latest news has been deported to Russia. For the elimination of these three bishops as a part of the brutal liquidation of the Czech Catholic Church in Czechoslovakia, see J. Fatran, "Zlikvidovanie Greckokatolickey Cirkvi

na Slovensku (A Liquidation of the Greek Catholic Church in Slovakia), in *Dobrý Pastier* (Good Shepherd), December, 1951, 12-16.

65. *Veritas*, April 30, 1951, No. 13: "A Persuasive Document of Forced Declaration of Six Bishops": According to reliable sources Monsignor Trochta, Bishop of Litoměřice, and Monsignor Picha, Bishop of Hradec Králové, were given a twenty-four-hour period to decide whether they wanted to take the oath to the government. Added to this message was the urgent remark that refusal would mean internment for the majority of the clergy of their respective dioceses; consent would bring restoration of their standing in their diocese under the watchful eyes of the police. The bishops, of course, did not know what text Bishop Čarský would subscribe over their names.

It has been proven beyond a doubt that there was a systematic use of drugs, served with meals to the bishops. *Veritas* has a direct document which at present cannot be quoted. . . . It will be released when there is no fear of danger to the author; it will be made public so that judgment can be made about the methods of communism as well as the fortitude of the Czechoslovakian Episcopate. At present, this document rests in the *Veritas* archives in Rome.

(English translation by the author.) See also *Veritas*, April 1, 1951, No. 12: "A Declaration of Bishops was forced by the Communists."

Cf. *Dobrý Pastier*, November 1951, 10; *Nový Život*, December, 1951, 3, Methods Used by Communists; Cary MacEoin, *The Communist War on Religion*, 54.

66. *Report on Czechoslovakia*, 2, No. 4 (April, 1951), 79; Bishop Neczey stressed on the occasion of taking an oath to the regime, that he identifies himself with the declaration of Bishop Josef Čarský of March 12, 1951. His action can be explained the same as that of Bishop Pobožný.

67. *Report on Czechoslovakia*, 2, No. 8 (August, 1951), 59-60. Great pressure was also brought to bear on Archbishop Matocha of Olomouc. See *Národ*, June 1, 1952, 3 (The Communist Fraud in the Case of Archbishop Matocha).

68. See *Katolické Noviny*, 2 (August 24, 1951), 1, wherein an exhortation by Bishop Josef Čarský to the peasants to comply with the demands of the government is given. *Rudé Právo*, 31 (April 19, 1951), 1, contains a letter sent on April 17 by the bishops to the French Government concerning the activities of the secratariat of the World Council for Peace (supported by Moscow). Cf. *Rudé Právo*, 31 (March 28, 1951), 1: Pastoral

letter on peace according to the aims of World Council for Peace (under the influence of Moscow), signed by the aforesaid bishops. Besides this every bishop had to compile a similar copy for his diocese.

69. *Report on Czechoslovakia*, 2, No. 5 (May, 1951), 67. The Vatican radio on May 3, 1951, gave six instructions to the clergy in Czechoslovakia, the third instruction of which reads thus: "Priests are warned lest they accept as true declarations of bishops who are now submitted to the Communist censure. Bishops are not able to manifest their own free opinions. It is necessary to hold those declarations as true, which were made before they were submitted to the Communists' violent methods."

70. This practice of misusing the signatures of bishops was often made use of by the State Commissioner in episcopal curias and chancery offices. The purpose was to stimulate the consent of the bishop and thus confuse priests and the faithful to get similar signatures. Documents of this nature can be found in *Veritas* and in the *CML* archives in London.

71. *AAS*, 14 (1922), 673 ff.

72. Dan. 6:16.

73. *Report on Czechoslovakia*, 2, No. 3 (March, 1951), 73.

74. *Ibid.*

75. *Rudé Právo*, 31 (March 20, 1951), 1.

76. *Veritas* (A Catholic Documentation of the Christian Academy, Rome), 1 (April, 1951); cf. *Report on Czechoslovakia*, 2, No. 3 (March, 1951), 74.

77. *AAS*, 43 (1951), 217-18. Cf. "Unlawful Consecration of Bishops," in *The Tablet*, May 12, 1951, 385; *Zpravodaj*, No. 19 (May, 1951), 16.

78. I Tim. 2:2; Tit. 3:1; Rom. 13:1-7; cf. Matt. 22:15-21; Mark 12:13-17; Luke 20:20-26.

79. *AAS*, 44 (1952), 5-6. Cf. *L'Osservatore Romano*, December 24-25, 1951, 1-2. "La chiesa e la pace" (Il radio messaggio natalizio del Sommo Pontifice Pio XII." Cf. *AAS*, 43 (1951), 57-58 in "Nuntius radio-pnonicus 1950."

80. The English translation is from *The Tablet*, January 5, 1952, 16-17.

81. *La DC*, 46 (1949), 1050, col. 1099-1110.

82. *The New York Times*, October 28, 1951, 9: "Pontiff Condemns Czech Persecution."

83. *AAS*, 43 (1951), 768-78. The authorized English translation of this apostolic letter is from the editorial information *NCWC*, October 30, 1951, 1-4. The text of the apostolic letter was cited also in the broadcasts of the Vatican and "Free Europe"

in Munich and in the "Voice of America," New York. The whole Bohemian text is in *Katolík,* Bohemian Catholic newspaper, Chicago, November 9, 1951, 3: "Poselství sv. Otce Pia XII do Československa" (The message of the Holy Father Pius XII to Czechoslovakia).

84. *Declaration of the Aims and Principles of Liberation of the Central and Eastern European Peoples* (Philadelphia: Independence Hall, February 11, 1951). This document is a solemn official expression of the deliberations of the delegates, in exile, of all nations behind the Iron Curtain in their important meeting held in Independence Hall, Philadelphia, February 11, 1951.

85. See *AAS*, 45 (January 16, 1953), 5-14 for the original Latin text. Our English translation is taken from the files of the *NCWC* press release of January 6, 1953. The Latin text of this encyclical letter was also published in *Primi incatenati.* Libro bianco sulla persecutione religiosa in Ucraina (Rome 1953. Published by the Ukrainian priests in Rome), 70-79.

The English translation appeared also in *The Catholic Mind*, April, 1953, 244 ff.

86. Our English translation of the encyclical letter *Orientales Ecclesias* of December 15, 1952, is from *NCWC*, January 6, 1953, 1-6.

87. *AAS*, 43 (1951), 577-82. Cf. *L'Osservatore Romano*, September 17, 1951, 1: "Il Somno Pontifice Pio XII con una epistola Enciclica: *Ingruentium malorum* all 'Episcopato esorta a rinnovato fervore nella pia practica del S. Rozario durante il mese di Ottobre in vista delle presenti necessità della Chiesa a conforto dei perseguitati e di tutti i sofferenti."

88. The English translation of this encyclical *Ingruentium Malorum* is from *NCWC*, September 17, 1951, 1-4.

89. *Universal Declaration of Human Rights* (Complete text adopted on December 10, 1948, by the General Assembly of the United Nations at the Palais de Chaillot, Paris). The text of this declaration will be found in *Human Rights* Comments and Interpretations (A Symposium edited by UNESCO with an Introduction by Jacques Maritain. New York: Columbia University Press, 1949, 273-80).

90. *Ibid.*, 275.

91. *Ibid.*, 277; cf. *A Declaration of Human Rights* (Statement drafted by a Committee appointed by the National Catholic Welfare Conference and Submitted to the Human Rights Commission of the United Nations; Washington, D. C.: National Catholic Welfare Conference, 1948), Part I, The Rights of the Human Person, arts. 1-18.

FOOTNOTES TO CHAPTER XIII

1. Ferdinand A. Hermens, *Europe Between Democracy and Anarchy*, 88-93.

2. *L'Osservatore Romano*, March 5, 1948, 1: "Dimissioni di diplomatici cecoslovacchi." (Dr. Juraj Slavik, ambassador in U. S. A.). *Ibid.*, March 6, 1948, 1: (General Sergei Ingr). Dr. Francis Schwarzenberg, counsel of the delegation to the Holy See, resigned in March, 1948. *Ibid.*, June 19, 1948, 1: (Dr. Bedrich Veliz, commercial counsel in Cairo). *Ibid.*, February 25, 1949, 1: Le diminizion del capo della missions militare cecoslovacchia a Berlino (General Dastich). *Ibid.*, January 1, 20, 1950, 1: Nuovi orientamenti di diplomatici ceco (Vladislav Matějček, Arnost Fried in New York). *Ibid.*, March 26, 1948, 1: Le dimissioni dell Ambasciatore cecoslovacco in Francia (Mr. Nosek) etc.

3. *L'Osservatore Romano*, May 5, 1948, 1: 10,000 personne sono fuggite della Cecoslovacchia . . ."

4. "In Search of Haven: The Story of Czechoslovak Refugees," 7: "The figures are based on official IRO statistics which included the DP's born or residing in Czechoslovakia before the war. They are adjusted to include only political refugees who escaped after February, 1948. Persons without an IRO mandate and those who did not apply for IRO assistance are not included."

5. *Hlas Československa*, June-July, 1953, 27.

6. *Zpravodaj*, May, 1951, 20. *Ibid.*, February, 1951, 2-3; "From the meeting of the Council of Free Czechoslovakia."

7. The world center of the Saints Cyril and Methodius League is 39 Fitzjohn Ave., London. There are district committees in Germany, France, Italy, Australia, and the United States. The magazine of this organization is *Nový Život* (New Life). Especially important is the documentary institution of the Christian academy in Rome, *Veritas*.

8. These conferences are arranged periodically in various cities, for instance, in February, 1951, a conference was held in New York; May, 1951, in Washington; September, 1951, in Cleveland; again in Washington in 1952; and in 1953 in Chicago. Attendance is entirely voluntary and the resolutions agreed upon serve as a program for real work in various parties.

9. The message of Abbot Ambrose Ondrák, of Lisle, Illinois, to Catholic people of Bohemian origin in America, was sent on October 12, 1951. It was printed in many newspapers in America. This text is from *Katolík*, October 16, 1951, 3.

10. See the protest of May 8, 1952, to the National Committee

for Free Europe, New York. Almost every activity of the Council of Free Czechoslovakia was criticized by this organization.

11. Communication of the Council of Free Czechoslovakia, Jan. 18, 1952. The text is as follows: In the two days of January 26-27, 1952, a four-member commission composed of an equal number of representatives of the Council for Free Czechoslovakia and the National Committee for Free Czechoslovakia was held in Washington, D. C. This Commission was established by the agreement of January 15, 1952, which was settled and signed by the representatives of the Council and of the National Committee, being aware of the extraordinary importance which a united political leadership among Czechoslovak democratic exiles has for the Czechoslovak cause.

The Commission has to prepare a political program on organization for the United Czechoslovak democratic exiles. The serious intentions of the representatives of both organizations in creating a union of exiles is clear from the fact that, according to the agreement of January 15, the statute organs of the Council and of the National Committee for Free Czechoslovakia stopped all their activities. A provisory two-member leadership was established to carry out the current agency.

A negotiations Commission held its first open meeting to consider the principles of the political program and authorized a four-member committee to prepare for the coming meeting a version of these principles. The Commission will hold its next meeting February 2 and 3, at which time the Commission will approve a plan of the program and discuss organization for the final leadership of Czechoslovak Democrats in exile. Washington, D. C., Jan. 18, 1952.

12. This document of the Council of Free Czechoslovakia, dated May 5, 1952, was published in *Zpravodaj*, and also separately.

13. This program was formed before the time of the first Council of Free Czechoslovakia, and was criticized in the speeches of Abbot Ondrák for its lack of Christian spirit.

14. *Katolík*, Nov. 17, 1953, 3.

15. The Alliance for Liberation and Freedom in Czechoslovakia published this declaration in February, 1953, in New York City. It is written in an impressive tone and strongly criticizes the political situation from 1945 to 1948. It also takes a definite stand on the conditions of political exile.

16. *Slovenska Republika* (*Slovak Republic*), 1939-49 (Scranton, Pa.: the Obrana Press, Inc.).

17. This document is from *Katolík*, April 28, 1953, 1-2. The English translation is the author's.

18. Christian Democratic Union of Central Europe. Its headquarters are in New York. Its semimonthly bulletin is the Christian Democratic News Service.

19. *Nové Obzory*, May-June, 1953, 8.

20. James Burnham, *The Coming Defeat of Communism*, 212.

21. This document is in the *CML* archives. It was published in *Katolík*, September, 1953.

22. The liberty of human beings is rightly based upon a religious concept, as is generally known.

23. Robert A. Graham, "The Unification of Europe," in *The Role of the Christian in the World for Peace*, 98-103.

24. See the speech of Pope Pius XII to the group of professors and students from the College of Europe, Bruges, Belgium, in *NCWC*, April 16, 1953, 1-3. Cf. Ludvik Němec, "Papežova péče o sjednocenou Evropu" (The Pope's concern over a united Europe), in *Katolík*, Apr. 14, 1953, 3.

25. Fulton J. Sheen, *Liberty, Equality and Fraternity*.

FOOTNOTES TO EPILOGUE

1. John 3:1-13.
2. John 3:14-15.
3. John 3:16-21.
4. Matt. 23:13-33; Luke 11:42-44.
5. Matt. 11:20-24; Luke 10:13-15; I Rom. 2:4-5.
6. Matt. 16:18.

BIBLIOGRAPHY

SOURCES

Acta Apostolicae Sedis (AAS), Commentarium Officiale, Romae, 1909-
Acta Sanctae Sedis (ASS), 41 vols., Romae, 1865-1908.
Acta et Decreta Sacrorum Conciliorum Recentiorum, Collectio Lacensis, 7 vols., Friburgi Brisgoviae, 1870-1890.
Acta Ss. D.M. Pii Pp. IX. ex quibus excerptus est *Syllabus* editus die VIII Decembris 1864, Romae: typis rev. Camorae Apostolicae, 1865.
Akční program, Nové Gottwaldovy vlády (Programme of Action of the New Gottwald Government), Předneseno předsedou vlády Klementem Gottwaldem v ústavodárném Národním shromaždění dne 10 března 1948.
Alliance of Czechoslovak Exiles in Chicago, Protesting Memorandum of May 8, 1952. Chicago, 1952.
Alliance for Liberation and Freedom in Czechoslovakia, Declaration, New York, 1953.
Better Men for Better Times, Washington, D.C.: The Catholic University of America Press, 1943.
Bible. New Catholic Edition of the Holy Bible. Translated from the Latin Vulgate. The Old Testament Douay Version and the New Testament Confraternity Edition. New York: Catholic Book Publishing Co., 1949-50.
Československo a norimberský proces; hlavní dokumenty norimberského processu o zločinech nazistů proti Československu (Czechoslovakia and the Nürmberg trial; the main documents of the Nürmberg process about the crimes of Nazis against Czechoslovakia), Praha: Ministerstvo informací, 1946.
Český kancional svatováclavský, Praha: Vyšehrad, 1947.
Codex Juris Canonici (CJC), Pii X, Pontificis Maximi iussu digestus, Benedicti Papae XV auctoritate promulgatus, Romae: Typis Polyglottis Vaticanis, 1917.
Conspiracy Against the Republic, Ministry of the Interior, Prague: Orbis, November, 1949.
The Constitution of the Czecho-Slovak Republic, with introduction by Jiří Holtzel and V. Joachim, October, 1922, No.

179. New York: American Association for International Conciliation, 1922.

The Constitution of the Czechoslovak Republic, a reprint of the English version published in Prague in 1920 by the Société de l'effort de la Tchécoslovaquie, with an introduction by Jiří Holtzel and V. Joachim. New York: Czecho-Slovak Government Information Service, 1944.

Concilia Magnae Britanniae et Hiberniae, 4 vols., Londini: Sumptibus R. Gosling, F. Gyles, T. Woodward, C. Davis, 1737.

The Constitution of the Czechoslovak Republic, translated from the Czech by F. O. Stein, 2. ed., Prague: Czechoslovak Ministry of Information and Public Culture, 1948.

Conventiones, de rebus ecclesiasticis inter S. Sedem et civilem potestatem initae, sub Pontificatu Ssmi D. N. Leonis PP. XIII, usque ad diem 7. Nov. 1893, Romae: ex Typographi a Vaticana, 1893.

Cultural Relations Between the United States and the Soviet Union, Washington, D. C.: Department of State Publication, No. 3480, 1949.

Czechoslovak National Insurance, a Contribution to the Pattern of Social Security. The Czechoslovak National Insurance Act with an Introduction by Evžen Erban, Czechoslovak Minister of Social Welfare, Prague: Orbis, June, 1948.

Czechoslovak Policy for Victory and Peace; the Fourth Message of the President of the Republic to the State Council, February 3, 1943, London: Czechoslovak Ministry of Foreign Affairs, Information Service, 1944.

Czechoslovakia Fights Back. A document of the Czechoslovak Ministry of Foreign Affairs, American Council on Public Affairs, Washington, D. C., 1943.

Czechoslovakia on the Road to Socialism. Presented by the editorial team of *Rudé právo* to the IXth Congress of the Communist Party of Czechoslovakia. Prague: Orbis, 1949.

Declaration of Human Rights. (Statement drafted by a committee appointed by the National Catholic Welfare Conference and submitted to the Human Rights Commission of the United Nations.) Washington, D. C.: National Catholic Welfare Conference, 1949.

Declaration of Independence of the Czechoslovak Nation by its Provincial Government, New York: Printed for the Czechoslovak Arts Club by the Marchbanks Press, 1948.

Declaration of the Aims and Principles of Liberation of the Central and Eastern European Peoples, Independence Hall, February 11, 1951. (This document is a solemn expression of the delegates in exile of all the respective nations to be free again. Meeting was held in Philadelphia, February 11, 1951.)

Dictionnaire de la Théologie Catholique, 13 vols., Paris: Vacant-Mangenot, 1903-1907.

Digest-Index of Eastern European Law. Czechoslovakia: Church and Religion compiled by Stephen Kočvara and Henry Nosek; edited by Vladimir Gsovski, Washington, D. C.: Library of Congress, Law Library (National Committee for Free Europe), 1951.

Documenta mag. Joannis Hus, vitam doctrinam, causam in Constansiensi concilio actam et contraversias de religione in Bohemia, annis 1403-1418 *notas illustrantia quae partim adhuc inedicta, partim mendose vulgata, nunc ex ipsis fontibus hausta* . . . Ed. František Palacký, Prague, 1869.

Documentation Catholique, 48 vols. Paris, 1918-

Documents Relating to the German-Czechoslovak Crisis, September, 1938 (Published by authority of the Secretary of State for External Affairs, Canada), Ottawa: Printer to the King's Most Excellent Majesty, 1938.

Dokumentární brožura (Documentary booklet), Prague: Ministry of Justice, December, 1950.

Dokumenty o ústavnom postaveni Slovenska (Documents concerning the constitutional position of Slovakia), ed. Josef Kovačik and Karel Král, Praha: Ministerstvo informací, 1947.

Draft Declaration of the International Rights and Duties of Man and Accompanying Report. Formulated by the Inter-American Juridical Conference on Problems of War and Peace, held in Mexico City, Feb. 21-Mar. 8, 1945. Washington, D.C.: Pan American Union, March, 1946.

Enchiridion Symbolorum definitionum et declarationum de rebus fidei et morum, ed. Henri Denzinger and Clem Bannwart, 10. ed., Friburgi Brisgoviae: Herder, 1908.

Encyclopedia Americana, 30 vols., New York and Chicago: Americana Corporation, 1949.

Encyclopaedia Britannica, 9th ed., 24 vols., Boston: Little, Brown and Co., 1889.

First Czechoslovak Economic Plan (Explanatory memorandum on the Bill and the text of the two-year economic plan act, with a preface by Edward Outrata, Jr., chairman of the Central Planning Commission), 1st. ed., Prague: Orbis, April, 1947.

First Czechoslovak Economic Five-Year Plan, Act. No. 241,

dated October 27, 1948, and government memorandum. Trans. from the Czech by F. O. Stein, 1st ed., Prague: Czechoslovak Ministry of Information and Public Culture, 1948.

First Czechoslovak Economic Five-Year Plan, Act. No. 241, dated October 27, 1948, with introduction by Antonin Zápatocký. Translated by F. O. Stein, 2d ed., Prague: Czechoslovak Ministry of Information and Public Culture, 1949.

Fontes Rerum Austriacarum: Oesterreichische Geschichts-Quellen. Herausgegeben von der Historischen Kommission der Kaiserlichen Akademie der Wissenschaften in Wien. Erste Abtheilung, Scriptores II Band, Geschichtsschreiber der Husitischen Bewegung in Boehmen, Wien, 1856, 2 vols., 1856, 3 vols., Aus der Kaiserlich Königlichen Hof- und Staatsdruckerei.

Four Fighting Years. Published on behalf of the Czechoslovak Ministry of Foreign Affairs (Department of Information), London-New York-Melbourne: Hutchinson and Co., Ltd., 1943.

German Cultural Oppression in Czechoslovakia. Memorandum of the Czechoslovak National Committee, London: G. Allen and Unwin, Ltd., 1940.

German Massacre in Occupied Czechoslovakia Following the Attack on Reinhard Heydrich, London: Czechoslovak Ministry of Foreign Affairs, Department of Information, 1942.

Handbuch des Wissens (Der Grosse Brockhaus), 20 vols., Leipzig: F. A. Brockhaus, 1930.

Harvard Slavic Studies, Volume II, Cambridge, Mass.: Harvard University Press, 1954.

Heroes and Victims (preface by Jan Masaryk), London: Czechoslovak Ministry of Foreign Affairs, Information Service, 1945.

Human Rights, Comments and Interpretations. (A Symposium conducted by UNESCO with an Introduction by Jacques Maritain), New York: Columbia University Press, 1949.

Index Librorum Prohibitorum, Ss. mi D. M. Pii PP. XII iussu editus. Typis polyglottis Vaticanis, Roma, 1948.

In Search of Heaven, the story of Czechoslovak refugees, Washington, D. C.: Council of Free Czechoslovakia, 1950.

Katholische Soziallehre (Lexikon paepstlicher Weisungen: Pius IX (1846)—Pius XII (1948), Eichstädt-Rom-Muenchen: Roma Verlag, 1948.

Katolická Akce (Catholic Action), edited by the Publication

Section of the Catholic Action, Prague, July, 1949.

Leonis XIII, Pontificis Maximi Acta, 23 vols., Romae: ex typographia Vaticana, 1881-1905.

Leonis XIII, enc. Graves de communi re, Jan. 18, 1901, ed. A. B. W. S., Bologna: Enciclica de SS. Leone XIII, sulla Democrazia Christiana.

Lexikon fuer Theologie und Kirche, 10 vols., Freiburg im Breisgau: Herder and Co., G.M.B.H., Verlagsbuchhandlung, 1930.

Lidice (Document of the Ministry of Interior), Prague, 1945.

Lista Katyňská (Jency Obozow Kozielsk-Starobielsk-Ostaszkow zaginieni w Rosji sowieckiej) ed. Adam Moszynski, London, 1949.

Long Term Planning in Czechoslovakia, a speech . . . given at the extraordinary meeting of the Central Planning Commission of Czechoslovakia on October 10, 1947 (translated and edited by Bedřich Rothbaum), Prague: Czechoslovak Ministry of Information, 1947.

Memorandum of the Czechoslovak Government: On the Reign of Terror in Bohemia and Moravia under the Regime of Reinhard Heydrich, Czechoslovak Ministry of Foreign Affairs, Department of Information, London: Williams, Lea and Co., Ltd.

Miscellaneous No. 8 (1938), Further documents respecting Czechoslovakia, including the agreement concluded at Munich on September 29, 1938 (presented by the Secretary of State for Foreign Affairs to Parliament by command of His Majesty), London: Printed and published by His Majesty's Stationery Office, 1938.

Nachschlagewerk fuer Wissen und Leben (Der Grosse Herder), 4th ed., 12 vols., Freiburg im Breisgau, 1931.

Nationalisation en Tchécoslovaquie: les décrets du président de la République Tchécoslovaque du 24 Octobre 1945, concernant la nationalisation des mines et des enterprises industrielles, de quelques banques par action et des sociétés d'assurance privées, Prague: Orbis, 1946.

Nazi Conspiracy and Aggression, Vols. 1-VIII and Suppl. A-B. Office of United States Chief of Counsel for Prosecution of Axis Criminality, Washington, D. C.: U. S. Government Printing Office, 1946.

Nazi Conspiracy and Aggression, Opinion and Judgment, Office of United States Chief of Counsel for Prosecution of Axis Criminality, Washington, D. C.: U. S. Government Printing Office, 1947.

Nazi-Soviet Relations 1939-1941 (Documents from the Archives of the German Foreign Office), edited by Raymond James Sontag and James Stuart Beddie. Department of State, Publication 3223, Washington, D. C.: 1948.

New Family Legislation in Czechoslovakia, translated from the Czech by F. O. Stein and W. Beardmore, Prague: Ministry of Information and Public Culture, 1950.

New Testament, The, The Confraternity of Christian Doctrine edition. Paterson, N. J.: St. Anthony Guild Press, 1951.

Nové cirkevni Zákony (The New Church Laws), Statní úřad pro věci cirkevní, Praha, 1949.

Nové trestní právo spravni (The New Criminal Administrative Law), 3 vyd., Praha: Ministerstvo Vnitra, 1950.

Novum Testamentum graece et latine, 6th ed. Ed. Augustinus Merk. Romae: Sumptibus Pontificii Instituti Biblici, 1948.

Occupation of Germany, Policy and Progress 1945-1946. Department of State, Publication 2783, European Series 23, Washington, D. C.: U. S. Government Printing Office.

Ochrana lidově domokratické republiky (The protection of the people's democratic republic, commentary to sections 78-129 of the criminal law, No. 86/50 Coll.), ed. Juraj Vieska. Praha: Orbis, 1950.

Pages d'introduction à l'étude du Droit canonique par Son Eminence le Cardinal Villeneuve (Cahier, No. 2), Québec: Université Laval, 1944.

Pastoral Letters of Czechoslovak Archbishops and Bishops from March, 1948 *until* 1951 (From the *CML* Sts. Cyril and Methodius archives in London and the *NCWC* archives in Washington).

Persecution of the Catholic Church in the Third Reich (Facts and documents translated from the German), New York: Longmans, Green and Co., 1940.

Persekuce českého studenstva za okupace (The persecution of Czech students during the time of occupation), Praha: Ministerstvo Vnitra, 1945.

Pii IX, Pontificis Maximi Acta, 9 vols., 1846-1857, Roma: tipografia delle Belle Arti. 1857.

Primi incatenati. Libro bianco sulla persecutione religiosa in Ucraina, Rome: "Ars-graf," 1953.

Principles for peace. Selections from papal documents Leo XIII to Pius XII. Washington, D. C.: National Catholic Welfare Conference, 1943.

Proces proti vatikanským agentům v Československu (Process against the Vatican's Agents in Czechoslovakia), Biskup Zela a společníci, Praha: Orbis, 1950.

Protocol of the Locarno Conference. Final protocol of the Locarno conference, 1925, and annexes together with treaties between France and Poland and Czechoslovakia, Washington, D. C.: U. S. Government Printing Office, 1925.

Raccolta di Concordati su materie ecclesiastiche fra la Santa Sede et le Autoritè Civili (Mercati), Roma: Tipografia poliglotta Vaticana, 1919.

Red and the Black, The: The Church in the Communist State, New York: The National Committee for a Free Europe, 1953.

Role of the Christian in the World for Peace, Washington, D. C.: The Catholic Association for International Peace, 1953.

Sacrorum Conciliorum Nova et Amplissima Collectio, 53 vols., ed. Joannes Mansi, Parisiis, 1901-1907.

Sbírka zákonů a nařizení statu československého (Collection of laws and Proclamations of the Czechoslovak State), Praha: Statní tiskarna annual.

School Reform in Czechoslovakia (Translated from the Czech by Stephen Jolly and F. G. Stein), 1. ed., published with the public relations Department of the Ministry of Education, Science and Arts. Prague: Orbis, 1948.

Selected letters and addresses of Pius XII. London: The Catholic Truth Society, 1949.

Six Social Documents of Pope Pius XII, Huntington, Ind.: Our Sunday Visitor Press, 1953.

Slovenska Republika (The Slovak Republic) 1939-1949, published by Nicholas Šprinc. Scranton, Pa.: The Obrana Press, Inc., 1949.

Smlouva mezi Československem a sovětským Svazem, Praha-Orbis: Ministerstvo Informace, 1945 (Publikace č. 5/45).

Soviet Union, The: A Symposium. Ed. Waldermar Gurian. Notre Dame, Ind.: University of Notre Dame Press, 1951.

Spiknutí proti republice (The conspiracy against the Republic), Ministerstvo Vnitra, Praha, prosinec 1949 (pamphlet).

Trial of the Treasonable Slovak Bishops: Jan Vojtaššák, Michal Buzalka, Pavol Gojdič. Published by Orbis in Prague for the Ministry of Information and Public Culture in February, 1951.

Universal Declaration of Human Rights (Complete text adopted on December 10, 1948, by General Assembly of United Nations at the Palais de Chaillot, Paris).

Ústava ze dne 9, května 1948, 8. ed. v. květnu 1950. Praha-Orbis (The Constitution of May 9, 1948, 8. ed. in May, 1950, Prague-Orbis).

Ustavní zákony Československé republiky, Pro potřebu Národniho Shromaždění, Státní tiskarna, Praha, 1920.

Vatikan mezi dvěma světovými válkami (Vatican between Two World Wars), Praha: Ministerstvo Vnitra, prosinec, 1949.

What Happened in Czechoslovakia, An Account of the Government Crisis in February, 1948, Prague: Orbis, April, 1948.

White Book on Aggressive Activities by the governments of the USSR, Poland, Czechoslovakia, Hungary, Rumania, Bulgaria and Albania toward Yugoslavia, Ministry of Foreign Affairs of the Federal People's Republic of Yugoslavia, Belgrad, 1951.

Zrada Vatikanu a biskupů (The treason of the Vatican and the Bishops), Edited by the Central Action of the National Front in Prague, July, 1949 (pamphlet).

AUTHORS

Acton, Lord, *Essays on Church and State*, New York: The Viking Press, 1953.

Adler, Georg, *Geschichte des Sozialismus und Komunismus von Plato bis zur Gegenwart*, 2 vols., Leipzig: Verlag von O. L. Hirschfeld, 1899.

Anderson, Paul B., *People, Church and State in Modern Russia*, New York: The Macmillan Company, 1944.

Anonymous, *Cecoslovacchia*, sguardo alla storia politica e religiosa d'un popolo schiavo del communismo. Edizioni La Civiltà Cattolica, Roma, 1950.

Anonymous, *Czechoslovak Jewry: Past and Future*, New York: Spett Printing Co., 1943.

Anonymous, *Czechoslovakia, Its Sacrifice and Future*, Chicago: Czechoslovak National Council of America, 1939.

Anonymous, "Europe's Christian Democrats," in *Time*, CX I, No. 21 (May 25, 1953), 32.

Anonymous, *Human Relations and Efficient Production*, New York: National Association of Manufacturers of the United States of America, 1946.

Anonymous, *The Slovaks and the Pittsburgh Pact*, Chicago: The Slovak Catholic Federation of America, 1934.

Anonymous, *Slovakia's Plea for Autonomy by an Autonomist*, Middletown, Pa.: Slovak Literary Society, 1935.

Anonymous, *Základy první československé pětiletky*, 1. ed. (Fundamentals of the Czechoslovak Five Year Plan). Praha: Ministerstvo informací a osvěty, 1948.

Antonelli, *De regimine ecclesiae episcopalis*, Venetiis, 1705.

Aquinas, St. Thomas, *Opera Omnia*, 32 vols., Parisiis: Vives, 1871-1879.

———, *Summa Contra Gentiles.*

———, *Summa Theologiae* (ed. Marietti), Romae, 1948.

Armstrong, Hamilton Fish, *Tito and Goliath*, New York: The Macmillan Co., 1951.

Augustinus, Aurelius St., *Sancti Aurelii Augustini episcopi de civitate Dei*, libri XXII, recensuit et commentario critico instruxit Emanuel Hoffman . . . Vindobonae, Pragae, F. Tempsky, Lipsiae, G. Freytag, 1899-1900.

———, *Sancti Aurelii Augustini Confessionum libri tredecim.* Recensuit et commentario critico instruxit Pius Knoell, Vindobonae, Pragae, F. Tempsky, Lipsiae, G. Freytag, 1896. For an English translation see F. J. Sheed, *Confession of St. Augustine* (New York: Sheed and Ward, 1943).

Barron, J. B., and Waddams, H. M., *Communism and the Churches.* New York: Morehouse-Gorham Co., 1950.

Barth, Karl, *The Church and the Political Problem of Our Day*, New York: Charles Scribner's Sons, 1939.

Bartlett, Vernon, *East of the Iron Curtain*, London: Latimer House, Ltd., 1949.

Beaumont, A., *Heroic Story of the Czecho-Slovak Legions*, Prague: Czechoslovakian Foreign Office, 1919.

Bednař, F., *Sbirka zákonů a nařizení ve věcech nabožensých a cirkevních v Republice československé*; *normy platné v celém území republiky*, *zvláštni předpisy týkajici se cirkví zemich českých*, Praha: Náklad Husovy čs. ev. fakulty bohoslovecké, 1929.

Beisner, Y. Ryan, *The Vatican Council and the American Secular Newspapers, 1869-1870*, Washington, D. C.: The Catholic University of America Press, 1941.

Bela, Fabian, *Cardinal Mindszenty*, New York: Charles Scribner's Sons, 1949.

Bellarmine, Robert Francis H., *Power of the Pope in Temporal Affairs against William Barclay*, Cologne, 1610. Translated and edited by George Albert Moore, Chevy Chase, Md.: Country Dollar Press, 1949.

Bendiscioli, Mario, *Marxism versus Christianity* (translated from the Italian by Gerald Griffin), London: Skeffington and Son, 1939.

Beneš, Eduard, "Expose Ministra Dra Beneše o modu vivendi mezi Československem a Vatikánem," *Zahranični Politika*, Vol. VII (Text of speech of February 1, 1928), 1928.

———, *Czechoslovak Policy for Victory and Peace*, London: Czechoslovak Ministry of Foreign Affairs, Information Service, 1944.

———, *The Future of the Small Nations and the Idea of Federation*, New York: Czechoslovak Information Service, 1942.

———, *Boj o mir a bezpečnost státu* (The Struggle for Peace and Security of the State), Praha: Orbis, 1934.

———, *Paměti* (Memoirs), Od Mnichova k nové válce a k novému vitězstvi, Praha: Orbis, 1947.

———, *The Way to Victory*, London: Czechoslovak Ministry of Foreign Affairs, Information Service, 1942.

———, *Le problème autrichien et la question tchèque* (Thèse pour le doctorat) Etude sur les luttes politiques des nationalités slaves en Autriche, Paris: V. Girard et E. Brière, 1908.

———, *Nazi barbarism in Czechoslovakia*, Chicago: Czech National Council of America, 1940.

Beneš, Vojta, *The Vanguard of the Drang nach Osten*, Chicago: Czechoslovak National Council of America, 1943.

Beneš, Václav; Drucker, Alfred; Táborský, Edward, *Czechoslovak Yearbook of International Law* (London: Published under the auspices of the Czechoslovak Branch of the International Law Association), Domington House, March, 1942.

Berber, Fritz, *Tvář pod maskou* (The Face Under the Mask), Praha, Evropská Politika, 1933-38, Praha, 1942.

Bernhart Joseph, *The Vatican as a World Power*, New York: Longmans, Green and Co., 1939.

Bernus, P., "L'Autriche tchèque et le Vatican," in *Le Journal des débats*, Vol. XXIII, pt. 2, July 18-25, 1925.

Berry, E. Sylvester, *The Church of Christ*, 2. ed., St. Louis and London: B. Herder Book Co., 1927.

Bezdíček, Josef, "Thomáš G. Masaryk—Katolická Církev. Historie učitekelkou i v životě českeho národa (Thomas G. Masaryk—Catholic Church. History as a Teacher in the Life of the Czech Nation)." In *Katolík*, Vol. 60, 1953-4.

Bidlo, Jaroslav, *Jednota bratrská v prvnim vyhnanstvu*, Praha, 1900.

Billot, Ludovicus, S.J., *Tractatus de Ecclesia Christi*, 3. ed., 2 vols., Prati, 1909.

Birley, R., *Czechoslovakia* (Oxford Pamphlets on World Affairs, No. 15), Oxford: at the Clarendon Press, 1939.

Blanshard, Paul, *Communism, Democracy and Catholic Power*. Boston: The Beacon Press, 1951.

Boffa, Rev. Conrad Humbert, *The Historico-Canonical Devel-*

opment of Legislation on Catholic Schools, Washington, D. C.: Catholic University Library, 1938.

Bourke, Vernon Y., *Augustine's Quest for Wisdom* (Life and Philosophy of the Bishop of Hippo), Milwaukee: The Bruce Publishing Co., 1945.

Brackett, Lewis, *Democracy in Czechoslovakia*, New York: Czechoslovak Information Service, 1943.

Braden, Charles Samuel, *War, Communism and World Religions.* New York: Harper and Brothers, 1953.

Braito, P. Silvester, O.P., *Základy* (Elements), 3. ed., Rozsévač, Velehrad, Olomouc, 1947.

Brierly, J. J., *The Law of Nations*, An Introduction to the International Law of Peace, Oxford: at the Clarendon Press, 1928.

Browder, Earl, *What Is Communism?* New York: The Vanguard Press, 1936.

Brown, Francis Joseph, *Social Justice in the Modern World*, on Reconstructing the Social Order (*Quadragesimo Anno*), Outline Encyclical Series, Vol. I, Chicago: Outline Press, Inc., 1947.

Budenz, Louis F., *The Cry Is Peace*, Chicago: Henry Regnery Company, 1952.

———, *The Techniques of Communism*, Chicago: Henry Regnery Company, 1954.

Bruechmueller, Gerhard, *Der politische Katolicismus*, Mannheimer Grossbrückern G.M.B.H., Mannheim, 1941.

Burnham, James, *The Coming Defeat of Communism*, New York, The John Day Co., Inc., 1949.

Bušek, Vratislav; Hendrych, Jaroslav; Laštovka, Karel; Muller, Václav, *Československé cirkevni zákony* (Czechoslovak Church Laws), Praha: Československý Kompas, 1931.

Cairns, Huntington, *Legal Philosophy from Plato to Hegel*, Baltimore: The Johns Hopkins Press, 1949.

Campbell, Thomas Y., *The Jesuits*, 1537-1931, 2 vols., New York: The Encyclopedia Press, 1927.

Capello, Felix, *Institutiones juris publici Ecclesiastici*, 2 vols., Augustae Taurinorum Typographia Pontificia, Eg. Petri Marietti, 1907-1908.

Cavagnis, Felix, *Institutiones iuris publici Ecclesiastici*, 2. ed., 2 vols., Romae, 1888.

Cavalli, F., *Governo Communista e Chiesa cattolica in Cecoslovacchia*, Edizioni "La Civiltà Cattolica," Roma, 1950.

Chaloupecký, Václav, *Zápas o Slovensko* (The Struggle for Slovakia), Praha: Cin. Pub. Co., 1930.

Chambers, Frank P.; Phelps, Christina; Bayley, Charles C., *This*

Age of Conflict: a contemporary world history, 1914-1943, New York: Harcourt, Brace and Co., 1943.

Chmelař, Josef, *Political Parties in Czechoslovakia,* Prague: Orbis, 1926.

Chlup, Otakar; Kahuda, Frant; Král, Karel, *Školský zákon ze dne 21 dubna 1948* č. 95 Sb. (School law of April 21, 1948, No. 95 of Coll.), Výklad zákona a prov. předpisů, Praha, Orbis, 1949.

Chudoba, Bohdan, *A Study of Disintegration,* reprinted from *Thought,* Fordham University Quarterly (Vol. 25, No. 96, March), 1950.

———, *The Meaning of Civilization,* New York, P. J. Kenedy and Sons, 1951.

Churchill, Winston S., *The Gathering Storm: The Second World War,* Boston: Houghton Mifflin Company, 1948.

———, *The Hinge of Fate,* Boston: Houghton Mifflin Co., 1950.

Cianfarra, Camile M., *The Vatican and the Kremlin,* New York: E. P. Dutton and Company, 1945.

Cicognani, Amleto Giovanni, *Canon Law* (authorized English version by the Rev. Joseph M. O'Hara and Msgr. Francis Y. Brennan), second rev. edition, Westminster, Maryland: The Newman Bookshop, 1934.

Cinek, F., *K. náboženské otázce v prvnich letech samostatnosti* (Concerning the Religious Question in the First Years of Independence), Olomouc, 1926.

Cockburn, J. Hutchison, *Religious Freedom in Eastern Europe.* Richmond, Va.: John Knox Press, 1953.

Coleman, Christopher B., *The Treatise of Lorenzo Valla on the Donation of Constantine.* Text and translation into English. New Haven: Yale University Press, 1922.

Commager, Henry Steele, *Documents of American History,* 5th ed., New York: Appleton-Century-Crofts, Inc., 1948.

Connell, Francis J., *Morals in Politics and Professions,* Westminster, Md.: The Newman Bookshop, 1946.

Conran, Rev. Edward James, *The Interdict* (a dissertation on canon law), Washington, D. C.: Library of the Catholic University, 1929.

Cook, Arthur H., *Readings in Modern and Contemporary History,* New York and London: D. Appleton-Century Co. 1950.

Corrigan, Raymond, *The Church and the Nineteenth Century,* Milwaukee: The Bruce Publishing Company, 1938.

Crankshaw, Edward, *Cracks in the Kremlin Wall,* New York: The Viking Press, 1951.

Creighton, M., *A History of the Papacy During the Period of Reformation*, 2 vols., London: Longmans, Green and Co., 1892.

Cronin, Rev. John F., *Catholic Principles*, Milwaukee: The Bruce Publishing Co., 1950.

Čulen, Konstantin, *Po Svätoplukovi druhá naše hlava* (After Swatopluk, our second head), 2 vols., Cleveland, Ohio, The First Catholic Slovak Union, 1948.

David, C., *Werdegang der Los von Rom Bewegung bis 1899*, Wien, 1906.

Dawson, Christopher Henry, *Religion and the Modern State*, London: Sheed and Ward, 1935.

———, *Understanding Europe*, New York: Sheed and Ward, 1952.

Day, Donald, *Woodrow Wilson's Own Story*, Boston: Little, Brown and Co., 1952.

De Lubac, Henri, *The Drama of Atheist Humanism* (translated by Edith M. Riley), New York: Sheed and Ward, 1950.

———, *The Un-Marxian Socialist: A Study of Proudhon* (translated by R. E. Scantlebury), New York: Sheed and Ward, 1948.

Demeruan, Y. Louis, *L'Eglise: Constitution-droit public*, Paris: Gabriel Beauchesne, Editeur, 1914.

Diamond William, *Czechoslovakia Between East and West*, Published under the auspices of the London Institute of World Affairs, London: Stevens and Sons, Ltd., 1947.

Dieckmann, Hermanus, S.J., *De Ecclesia* (tractatus historico-dogmatici), 2 vols., Friburgi-Brisgoviae: Herder and Co., Typographi editoris Pontificii, 1925.

Doležal, Jaromir, *Masarykova cesta životem* (Masaryk's Way Through Life), Brno: Náklad Polygrafie, 1920-1921.

Dorsch, Aemilianus, *Institutiones theologiae fundamentalis*, 2 vols., Oeniponte, Typis et sumptibus Felicani Rauch, L. Pustet, 1914.

Douglass, Paul Franklin, *God Among the Germans*, Philadelphia: University of Pennsylvania Press, 1935.

Druce, Gerald, *Czechoslovakia: Past and Present*, Prague-Orbis, May, 1948.

Duchaček, Ivo, *The Strategy of Communist Infiltration in Czechoslovakia, 1944-1948*, reprinted from *World Politics*, 2, No. 3, April, 1950.

———, *The February Coup in Czechoslovakia, Ibid.*, 2, No. 4, July, 1950.

Dvornik, Francis, *The First Wave of the Drang nach Osten* (Reprinted from *The Cambridge Historic Journal*, Vol. VII, No. 3, 1943), Cambridge: at the University Press, 1943.

———, *Les Légendes de Constantin et de Méthode vues de Byzance*, (Byzantino-Slavica, Supplementa, Vol. I), Prague, 1943.

———, *The Making of Central and Eastern Europe*, London: The Polish Research Centre, Ltd., 1949.

———, *National Churches and the Church Universal*, London, 1944.

———, *The Photian Schism (History and Legend)*, Cambridge: at the University Press, 1948.

———, *The Study of Church History and Christian Reunion*, reprinted from *The Eastern Churches Quarterly*, Vol. VI, No. 1, 1945, Exeter: The Catholic Records Press.

———, *The Life of Saint Wenceslas, Duke of Bohemia*, Prague, 1929.

———, *Les Slaves, Byzance et Rome au IXe siècle*, Paris: Librairie Ancienne Honoré Champion, 1926.

———, *Sv. Vojtěch, II. biskup pražský*, Chicago: Bohemian Benedictine Press, 1950.

Eberdt, Mary Lois, and Schnepp, Gerald J., *Industrialism and the Popes*, New York, P. J. Kenedy and Sons, 1953.

Ebon, Martin, *World Communism Today*, New York: Whittlesey House, McGraw-Hill Book Company, Inc., 1948.

Eichmann, Eduard, *Kirche und Staat*, 3 vols., Paderborn (Press and ed. von Ferdinand Schoningh), 1925.

Eisenhower, Dwight D., *Crusade in Europe*, Garden City, N. Y.: Doubleday and Co., Inc., 1949.

Evans, Rev. Stanley, *Church and State in Western Europe*, New Central European Observer Pamphlet, No. 3., London, 1950.

Eyre, Rev. W. H., *The Pope and the People* (Select Letters and Addresses on Social Questions), London and Leamington Art and Book Company, 1895.

Fainsod, Merle, *How Russia Is Ruled*, Cambridge: Harvard University Press, 1953.

Fasnacht, G. E., *Acton's Political Philosophy*, New York: The Viking Press, 1953.

Feketekuty, Laszlo, *Christentum und Staatsgedanken zu einer christlichen Verfassungslehre*, Koeln am Rhein, 1953.

Father George, as told to Gretta Palmer, *God's Underground*, New York: Appleton-Century-Crofts, Inc., 1949.

Flynn, John T., *The Roosevelt Myth*, New York: The Devin-Adair Co., 1948.

Frank, Karl Herman, *Boehmen and Maehren im Reich*, Prag: Volk und Reich Verlag, 1943.

Franzelin, Joannes Bapt., *Theses de Ecclesia Christi* (opus posthumum), Rome: ex typographia polyglotta, 1887.

Friedman, Otto, *The Break-up of Czech Democracy*. London: Victor Gollancz, Ltd., 1950.

Fusek, J., *Organisàce a činnost okresnich národnîch výborů* (Organization and Action of the District Nation Committees), Praha: Ministerstvo Vnitra, 1946.

Garrigou-Lagrange, Reginald, *De Deo Uno* (Commentarium in primam partem S. Thomae), Paris: Bibliothèque de la Revue Thomiste, Desclée de Brouwer et Cie., 1938.

———, *De Revelatione* (per Ecclesiam Catholicam proposita), 2 vols., 4. ed., emendata, Roma: Libraria Editrice Religiosa F. Ferrari, 1945.

Giannini, Amedeo, II "Modus vivendi," fra la S. Sede e la Cecoslovacchia, Roma: Anonima romana editoriale, 1928.

Gilby, Thomas, *Between Community and Society: A Philosophy and Theology of the State*, New York and London: Longmans, Green Co., 1953.

Gillis, James F., *This Our Day*, volume two, New York: The Paulist Press, 1949.

Giordani, Igino, *Le Eciccliche sociali dei Papi* (da Pio IX a Pio XII—1864-1946), 3. ed., Roma: Editrice Studium, 1946.

Glaser, Kurt, "The 'Russia first' Boys in Radio Free Europe," in *Slovakia*, April, 1953, 31-37.

Godryck, Y., *The Doctrine of Modernism and Its Refutation*, Philadelphia, 1908.

Gordello, Mauricius, *Compendium Theologiae Orientalis*. Ed. altera. Romae: Pont. instit. Orientalium Studiorum, 1939.

Gordon, George Stuart, *Anglo-American Literary Relations*, Oxford University Press, 1942.

Gosselin, Md., *The Power of the Pope*, 2 vols. Translated by Rev. Matthew Kelly. Baltimore: J. Murphy and Co., 1853.

Gottschick, Johannes, *Hus', Luther's und Zwingli's Lehre von der Kirche mit Rücksicht auf das zwischen denselben bestehende Verhältnis oder Verwandschaft oder Abhaengigkeit* from *Zeitschrift fuer Kirchengeschichte*, Vol. III, No. 3, pp. 345-394; 543-618.

Gottwald, Klement, *Long-term Planning in Czechoslovakia*, a speech . . . given at the extraordinary meeting of the Central Planning Commission of Czechoslovakia on October 10, 1947. Tr. and ed. by Bedřich Rothbaum. Prague: Czechoslovak Ministry of Information, 1947.

———, *Programme of Action of the New Czechoslovak Government*. Statement made in the Constituent National Assembly on March 10, 1948 (translated from the Czech by

D. Kleinova, R. Shepherd and Stephen July), Prague: Czechoslovak Ministry of Information, 1948.

———, *Statement of Policy of Mr. Gottwald's Government*, Prague: Czechoslovak Ministry of Information, 1946.

Gredt, Josephus, O.S.B., *Elementa philosophiae Aristotelico-Thomisticae* (editio octava recognita), 2 vols., Barcelona: Herder, 1946.

Grentrup, Dr. Theodor, *Volk und Volkstum im Lichte der Religion*, Eine grundsätzliche Studie zur Gegenwartslage, Freiburg im Breisgau: Herder and Co., 1937; Verlagsbuchhandlung: 1937.

Grisar, Hartman, *Martin Luther:* His Life and Work, trans. from 2nd German ed. by Frank Y. Eble, Westminster, Md.: The Newman Press, 1950.

Groot, Y. V. de, O.P., *Summa Apologetica de Ecclesia Catholica ad mentem S. Thomae Aquinatis*, Ratisbonae, 1906.

Gurian, Waldemar, *Bolshevism: An Introduction to Soviet Communism*, Notre Dame, Ind.: University of Notre Dame Press, 1952.

———, *Der Kampf um die Kirche im 3. Reich*, Luzerne: Vita Nova, 1936.

———, *Hitler and the Christians* (translated by E. F. Peeler), London: Sheed and Ward, 1936.

Gurian, Waldemar and Fitzimons, M.A., *The Catholic Church in World Affairs*. Notre Dame, Indiana: University of Notre Dame Press, 1954.

Gyorgy, Andrew, *Governments of Danubian Europe*, New York: Reinhart and Company, 1949.

Hadsel, Winifred M., *Czechoslovakia's Road to Socialism*, New York: Foreign Policy Association, 1947.

Haffert, John M., *Russia Will Be Converted*, Washington, New York and London: AMI International Press, 1951.

Hagedorn, Rev. Francis Edward, *General Legislation on Indulgences* (A dissertation in canon law), Washington, D. C.: Library of the Catholic University, 1923.

Halaga, Ondrej R., *Slovanské osídlenie Potisia a východoslovenskí gréckokatolici* (Slavic Population of Potisia and East Slovakia Greek Catholics), Košice: Svojina, 1947.

Hall, Jerome, *Living Law of Democratic Society*, Indianapolis: Bobbs-Merrill Co., Inc., 1946.

Hanuš, Franciscus, *Church and State in Silesia Under Frederick II (1740-1786)*, Washington, D.C.: The Catholic University of America Press, 1944.

Hayes, Carleton J. H., *The United States and Spain*, New York: Sheed and Ward, 1951.

Hearley, John, *Pope or Mussolini?*, New York: The Macaulay Co., 1929.

Hefele, Carl Joseph, *Conciliengeschichte*, 6 vols., Freiburg im Breisgau: Herder, 1890.

Heiler, Friedrich, *Urkirche und Ostkirche*, 2 vols., München: Verlag Von Ernst Reinhardt, 1937.

Herben, Jan., *T. G. Masaryk* (Life and Work of the President Liberator), Praha: Ed. Sphinx and B. Janda, 1938.

Hergenroether, Joseph, *Handbuch der allgemeinen Kirchengeschichte*, 2 vols. 2. ed., Freiburg im Breisgau: Herder, 1870-1880.

———, *Anti Janus.* An historico-theological criticism of the work entitled: "The Pope and the Council" by Janus. Translated from the German by J. B. Robertson, Dublin: Kelly, 1870.

———, *Catholic Church and Christian State;* a series of essays on the relation of the Church to Civil Power, London: Burns and Oates, 1876.

Herman, Stewart Winfield, *Report from Christian Europe.* New York: Friendship Press, 1953.

Hermen, Ferdinand A., *Europe Between Democracy and Anarchy*, Notre Dame, Ind.: University of Notre Dame Press, 1951.

Herron, Matthew, *The Binding Force of Civil Laws*, North Miami, Fla.: Brower Press, 1952.

Heston, Edward L., *The Holy See at Work*, Milwaukee: The Bruce Publishing Company, 1950.

Hillquit, Morris and Ryan, John A., *Socialism: Promise or Menace?* New York: The Macmillan Co., 1941.

Hitler, Adolf, *Mein Kampf* (translated by Ralph Manheim), Boston: Houghton Mifflin Co., 1943.

Hodde, William G., *The Concept of Nation, State and Sovereignty in the Philosophy of Saint Thomas*, Washington, D. C.: The Catholic University of America, 1948.

Höffding, Harald, and Král, Josef, *Přehledné dějiny filosofie* (Concise History of Philosophy), 2d rev. ed., Praha: Česká Grafická Unie A. S., 1946.

Holborn, Louise W., *War and Peace Aims of the United Nations* (from Casablanca to Tokio Bay), January 1, 1943—September 1, 1945, Boston: World Peace Foundation, 1948.

Hrobák, Philip A., *"Czechoslovakism" versus Americanism.* (An Exposé of the pro-Soviet "Czechoslovak National Fronters" in the Council of Free Czechoslovakia). Middletown, Pa.: Jednota Press, 1953.

Hromadka, Joseph L., *Doom and Resurrection*, with an introduction by John A. Mackay. (Dedicated to Henry A. Wallace, a man of deep social and spiritual vision). Richmond, Va.: 1945.

———, *Don Quijote české filosofie, Emmanuel Rádl 1873-1942*, New York, 1943.

———, "The Modern Trends in European Protestant Theology," in *University of Pennsylvania Bicentennial Conference: Religion and the Modern World*, Philadelphia: University of Pennsylvania Press, 1941.

Huber, Raphael M., O.F.M., *Our Bishops Speak: 1919-1951*, Milwaukee: The Bruce Publishing Company, 1952.

Hughes, Emmet John, *The Church and the Liberal Society*, Princeton, N. J.: Princeton University Press, 1944.

Hughes, Philip, *History of the Church*, 3 vols., New York: Sheed and Ward, 1942.

Hurter, H., *Theologia Generalis Complectens tractatus quattuor*, ed. XIX. recognita. Oeniponte: Libraria Academia Wagneriana, 1903.

Husslein, Joseph, S.J., *The Christian Social Manifesto* (An Interpretative Study of the Encyclicals *Rerum Novarum* and *Quadragesimo Anno* of Pope Leo XIII and Pope Pius XI), Milwaukee: The Bruce Publishing Co., 1931.

———, *The Reign of Christ* (The Immortal King of Ages), New York: P. J. Kenedy and Sons, 1928.

Jandaček, A. J., *Život za železnou oponou* (Life Behind the Iron Curtain), Dokumenty o únorovém puči v Československu v únoru 1948. Vyd česká tiskarna benediktinů v Chicago, 1948.

Jansen, Rev. Raymond Josef, *An Historical Conspectus of Canonical Legislation on Catechetical Instruction to the Code of Canon Law* (A dissertation in canon law), Washington, D. C.: Catholic University Press, 1936.

Jaynor, Eamonn, "Is Communism the Enemy of Religion?" In *The Catholic Mind*, March, 1953, 162-70.

Jedin, Hubert, *Katholische Reformation oder Gegenreformation?* (Ein Versuch zur Klärung der Begriffe nebst einer Jubiläumsbetrachtung über das Trienter Konzil), Luzern in Switzerland: Verlag Josef Stocher, 1916.

Jelinek, Hanuš, *Viktor Dyk, Náklad.* České akademie věd a umění, Praha, 1932.

Journet, Charles, *La Jurisdiction de l'Église sur le cité*, Paris: Desclée, de Brouwer, et Cie, 1931.

Joyce, G. H., "The Church a Perfect Society," in *Catholic Encyclopedia*, Vol. III.

Jung, Nicholas, *Le droit public de l'Église dans ses relations avec les états;* préf. de M. l'Abbé Andrien-Ouitramcourt, Paris: Procure Générale du Clergé, 1898.

Kars, Hans, *Kanzler und Kirche*, Bismarck's grundsätzliche Einstellung zu den Kirchen während des Kulturkampfes, Giessen: A. Toepelmann, 1934.

Keller, Emile, *Les syllabus de Pie IX et Pie X et les principles de 1789, en l'église, l'état, et la liberté*, 3. ed., Paris: P. Lethielleux, 1909.

Kettler, Wilhelm Emmanuel, *Die Katholiken im Deutschen Reich.* Entwurf zu einem politischen Programm, Mainz: F. Kirchheim, 1873.

Kirch, Johann P. and Veit, Ludwig Andreas, *Kirchengeschichte*, 4 vols., Freiburg im Breisgau: Herder, Verlagsbuchhandlung, 1930.

Kirsch, Johann P., *Kirchengeschichte*, 4 vols., Freiburg im Breisgau: Herder, 1930.

Klopp, Wiard, *Leben und Wirken des Sozialpolitikers Karl Freiherr von Vogelsang* (nach den Quellen bearbeitet), Wien, 1930.

Knap, Victor and Berman, Tomáš, *Vráceni majetku pozbytéo za okupace*, Restitučni zakon; výklad Zákona č 128/1946 Sb. o neplatnosti některých majetkovych právnich jednani z doby nesvobody a o nárocich této neplatnosti, l. ed., Praha: V. Linhart, 1946.

Knox, R.A., *Enthusianism.* A Chapter in the History of Religion. New York: Oxford University Press, 1950.

Kohn, Hans, *Pan-Slavism: Its History and Ideology*, Notre Dame, Indiana: University of Notre Dame Press, 1953.

Korbel, Josef, *Tito's Communism*, Denver: The University of Denver Press, 1951.

Korbel, P., *Sovietization of the Czechoslovak Judiciary*, New York: NCFE Research and Publication Service, 1953.

———, and Vagasský, *Purges in the Communist Party of Czechoslovakia*, New York: National Committee for a Free Europe, October, 1952.

Kotátko, J., *Land Reform in Czechoslovakia* (translated from the Czech by B. Bohan and F. Stein), Prague: Orbis, April, 1948.

Kozák, Jan Blahoslav, *Democratic Ideas in Postwar Education in Central and Eastern Europe* (a sociological survey), New York: "New Europe," 1943.

———, Vboji a duchovni hodnoty, Praha-Čin., 1930.

———, *The Future of Czechoslovakia*, Washington, 1944. Reprinted from the *Slavonic and East European Review*, Vol. XXII, 1944.

Kramer, K., *Die russische Krisis: Geschichte und Kritik des Bolschewismus*, München and Leipzig: Duncker and Humbolt (autorisierte Uebertragung aus dem tschechischen von A. Schebek), 1925.

Kratochvil, Josef, *Otázky a problemy*, Olomouc: Matice Cyrilo-Methodějská, 1916.

Kraus, Karl, *Franz Brentano*, München, 1919.

Krofta, Kamil, *Malé dějiny československé*, Praha: Orbis, 1947.

———, *A Short History of Czechoslovakia* (translated from the Bohemian by William Beardmore), London: Williams and Norgate, Ltd., 1935.

———, *Stará U'stava Česká a Uherská, Praha*, 1931.

Kybal, Vlastimil, *Czechoslovak Independence*, Los Angeles, Calif.: The College Press, 1940.

Langer, William L., *The Diplomacy of Imperialism, 1890-1902*, 2. ed., with supplementary bibliographies, New York: Alfred A. Knopf, 1951.

La Pira, Giorgio, *et al.*, *The Philosophy of Communism*, New York: Fordham University Press, 1952.

Lechler, Rev. Gotthard Victor, *John Wiclif and His English Precursors* (translated from the German by the Rev. Peter Lorimer), 2 vols., London: C. Kegan Paul and Co., 1878.

———, *Johann von Wiclif und die Vorgeschichte der Reformation*, 2 vols., Leipzig, 1873.

Lecler, Joseph, *L'église et la souveraineté de l'état*, Paris: Flammarion, 1946.

Leen, Edward, C.S.Sp., *The Church Before Pilate*, Silver Spring, Maryland: The Preservation Press, 1939.

Leites, Nathan, *The Operational Code of the Politburo*, New York: McGraw-Hill Book Company, 1951.

Levit, Pavel, *Jednací řád místních národnich výborů* (The order of business of local national committees), Praha: Ministerstvo Vnitra, 1947.

Lingard, John, and Belloc, Hilaire, *The History of England* (with an introduction by James Cardinal Gibbons), 11 vols., New York: The Catholic Publication Society of America, 1912.

Lipper, Elinor, *Eleven Years in Soviet Prison Camps*, Chicago: Henry Regnery Co., 1950.

Liscová, Mila, *The Religious Situation in Czechoslovakia*, Prague: Orbis, 1925.

Lloyd, Roger, *Revolutionary Religion: Christianity, Fascism and Communism*, New York and London: Harper and Brothers, 1938.

Lockhart, Robert B., "The Czechoslovak Revolution," in *Foreign Affairs*, July, 1948.

Lord, Daniel A., *His Passion Forever*, Milwaukee: The Bruce Publishing Co., 1951.

Lorwin, Lewis L., *The International Labor Movement*, New York: Harper & Brothers, Publishers, 1953.

Loserth, Johann, *Hus und Wiclif* (Zur Genesis der husitischen Lehre), Prag: F. Tempsky; and Leipzig: J. Freytag, 1884.

Lowry, Charles W., *Communism and Christ*, New York: Morehouse-Gorham Co., 1953.

Ludwig, Emil, *Bismarck* (The Story of a Fighter), (Translated from the German by Eden and Cedar Paul), New York: Blue Ribbon Books, 1926.

Lunt, W. E. *History of England*, New York and London: Harper and Brothers, 1945.

Luetzow, Count von, *Bohemia, an Historical Sketch*, London, 1939.

Lynskey, E. T., *The Government of the Catholic Church*, New York: P. J. Kenedy and Sons, 1952.

MacCaffrey, James, *History of the Catholic Church in the Nineteenth Century*, 2 vols., St. Louis: B. Herder, 1910.

Maccarrone, Michele, *Il Nazional Socialismo e La Santa Sede*, Roma: Editrice Studium, 1947.

Machotka, Otakar, *T. G. Masaryk* (Published on the occasion of T. G. Masaryk's Centenary by the Council of Free Czechoslovakia), Washington, D. C., 1950.

MacEoin, Cary, *The Communist War on Religion*, New York: The Devin-Adair Company, 1951.

MacShane, Eduardus, S.J., *A Critical Appraisal of the Antimendicantism of John Wyclif* (Excerpta ex dissertatione ad Lauream in facultate Historiae Ecclesiasticae Pontificiae Universitatis Gregorianae), Romae: Officium libri Catholici, 1950.

Manhattan, Avro, *The Catholic Church Against the Twentieth Century*, London: Watts and Co., 1947.

Mansi, Joannes, *Sacrorum Conciliorum Nova et Amplissima Collectio*, 53 vols., Parisiis, 1901-1927.

Maritain, Jacques, *Man and the State*, Chicago: The University of Chicago Press, 1951.

———, *The Things That Are Not Caesar's* (a translation of *Primauté du Spirituel* by J. F. Scanlan, London: Sheed and Ward, 1939.

Markham, R. H., *Communists Crush Churches in Eastern Europe*, Boston: Meader Publishing Co., 1951.

Maroto, Philippo, *Institutiones iuris canonici ad normam novi Codicis*, 2 vols., Matriti, 1918.

Marshall, Charles C., *The Roman Catholic Church in the Modern State*, New York: Dodd, Mead and Company, 1931.

Marx, Karl, *Capital*, 3 vols., Chicago: Charles H. Kerr and Co., 1906-09.

Marx, Karl, and Engels, F., *Das kommunistische Manifest*, I Aufl. Lingen, Hohentwiel, Oberbadische Druckerei und Verlagsanstalt, 1946.

Masaryk, Jan, *Speeches of Jan Masaryk in America*, New York: The Czechoslovak Information Service, Czechoslovak Sources and Documents, No. 1, 1942.

Massaryk, Thomas G., *Česká Otázka* (*The Czech Question*), 2 vyd. Praha: Nakl. Pokrok, 1908.

———, *Jan Hus* (Naše obrozeni a naše reformace), Praha, 1923.

———, *Ein Katechetenspiegel* (Autorisierte Uebersetzung aus dem Tschechischen), Frankfurt am Main, Neuer Frankfurter Verlag, 1906.

———, *Idealy humanitní* (Ideals of Humanity), Autor vyd. Praha: Nakl. Domov, 1919.

———, *Die philosophischen und sociologischen Grundlagen des Marxismus*, Studien zur socialen Frage, Wien: C. Konegen, 1899.

———, *Karel Havlíček* (Snahy a tužby politického probuzeni), 2 vyd, oprav. a dopl. Praha: Nakl. Jana Laichtera, 1904.

———, *Los von Rom* (an address by Thomas Garrigue Masaryk), Boston: Unitarian Historical Society, 1902.

———, *Les Slaves après la guerre*, Prague: Orbis, 1923.

———, "Marx Studien" (Sonderabdruck aus der *Zeitschrift für Sozialwissenschaft* von Julius Wolf), II. Band, ii Heft, Verlag von Georg Reiner in Berlin, 1904.

———, *Moderni Človék a náboženstvi*, Praha: Jan Laichter, 1934.

———, *Modern Man and Religion*, London: C. Allen and Unwin, 1938.

———, *The Spirit of Russia*, 2 vols., London: Allen and Unwin, 1919.

———, *Světová revoluce za války a ve válce 1914-1918* (The World Revolution During the War, 1914-1918), Praha: Orbis, 1933.

———, *Sur le Bolchevisme*, Geneva: Sonor, 1921.

———, *Die Weltrevolution, Erinnerungen und Betrachtungen, 1914-1918*, Berlin: E. Reiss, 1925.

McDermott, Thomas, *Keeper of the Keys*, a life of Pope Pius XII, Milwaukee: The Bruce Publishing Co.

McIlwain, Charles Howard, *Constitutionalism: Ancient and Modern*, rev. ed., Ithaca, N. Y.: Cornell University Press, 1947.

McFadden, Charles J., O.S.A., *The Philosophy of Communism* (with preface by Fulton J. Sheen), New York: Benziger Brothers, Inc., 1939.

McGovern, William Montgomery, *From Luther to Hitler* (The History of Fascism as a Political Philosophy), Boston: Houghton Mifflin Co., 1941.

Meyer, Peter; Weinryb, Bernard D.; Duschinsky, Eugene; Sylvain, Nicolas, *The Jews in the Soviet Satellites*, Syracuse: Syracuse University Press, 1953.

McKnight, John P., *The Papacy: A New Appraisal*, New York: Rinehart and Co., 1952.

Michl, Jaroslav; Nový, Josef; Perů, František, *Revise první pozemkové reformy* (Revision of the First Land Reform), Praha: Orbis, 1948.

Micklem, Nathaniel, *National Socialism and the Roman Catholic Church*, New York: Oxford University Press, 1939.

Mikolajczyk, Stanislav, *The Rape of Poland*, New York: Whittlesey House, 1948.

Mikula, Felix, "Ze života arcibiskupa Msgra Josefa Berana (k jeho 65. narozeninám)." (From the Life of Archbishop Beran.) In *Katolik*, (Dec. 29, 1953), 1, and (Jan. 1, 5, 8, 1954), 2, 2, 2.

Mikuš, Joseph A., *The Three Slovak Bishops: Their Struggle for God and Slovakia*, Passaic, N. J.: Slovak Catholic Federation of America, 1953.

———, *La Slovaquie*. Individualité politique de l'Europe Centrale, Paris: Centre de Documentation Internationale, 1952.

Moody, Joseph N., *Church and Society: Catholic Social and Political Thought and Movements, 1789-1950*, New York: Arts, Inc., 1953.

Mudrý, Michal, *Milan Hodža v Amerike*, Chicago: Geringer Press, Inc., 1949.

Murray, John Courtney, "The Problem of 'The Religion of the State,'" in *The American Ecclesiastical Review*, May, 1951, 327-352.

Naegle, August, *Kirchengeschichte Boehmens* (Quellenmässig und kritisch dargestellt), 2 vols., Wien and Leipzig: Wilhelm Braumueller, 1915.

Nejedlý, Zdeněk, *T. G. Masaryk* (Kniha první: Masarykovo mládí 1850-1876), Praha: Orbis, 1949.
Neill, Thomas P., *They Lived the Faith.* Milwaukee: The Bruce Publishing Company, 1950.
———, *The Rise and Decline of Liberalism*, Milwaukee: Bruce Publishing Co., 1953.
Němec, Ludvík, *Episcopal and Vatican Reaction to the Persecution of the Catholic Church in Czechoslovakia*, Washington, D. C.: The Catholic University of America Press, 1953.
Nešpor, Zdeněk, *Vráceni majetku persekvovaným*, Prague: Orbis, 1946.
Neuman, Aug., *Hus dle nejnovější literatury*, Olomouc, 1931.
———, *Katolictví a naše osvobozeni*, Olomouc, 1922.
———, *Katoličtí mučednici doby husitské* (Catholic Martyrs of Hus's time), Olomouc, 1927.
———, *Z dějin bohoslužeb doby husitské* (From the history of the divine services of Hus's time), Olomouc, 1927.
Nietzsche, Friedrich, *Der Antichrist* (Versuch einer Kritik des Christentums), Herausgegeben von Dr. Wilhelm Matthiessen, Wordland Verlag-Berlin, 1941.
———, *Thus Spake Zarathustra* (translated by Thomas Common), The Modern Library, New York.
———, *Jenseits von Gut und Boese*, Zur Genealogie der Moral (Aus dem Durchlass 1885/1886), Leipzig: E. C. Naumann Verlag, 1906.
Nussi, Vincenzo, *Conventiones de rebus ecclesiasticis inter S. Sedem et civilem potestatem variis formis initae ex collectione romana a Vincentio Nussi . . . excerptae*, sumptibus Francisci Kirchheim, 1870.
O'Brien, Anthony Henry, Count of Thomonnd, *Archbishop Stepinac: The Man and His Case*, Westminster, Md.: The Newman Bookshop, 1947.
O'Brien, Sister Mary Consilia, *Catholic Sociology*, New York: P. J. Kenedy and Sons, 1939.
Odložilík, Otakar, *The Way of Light* (The glory and martyrdom of Czechoslovak schools), Chicago: Czechoslovak National Council of America, 1942.
O'Neill, James M., *Catholicism and American Freedom*, New York: Harper and Brothers, 1952.
Osuský, Stěfan, *The Way of the Free*, New York: E. P. Dutton and Co., Inc., 1951.
———, *Pravda vitězí* (Pohled do zrkadla druhého obboje), 1 vol. ed. London, "Pravda," 1942.

Ottaviani, Alaphridus, "Church and State: Some Present Problems in the Light of the Teaching of Pope Pius XII," in *The American Ecclesiastical Review*, May, 1953, 321-34.

———, *Institutiones Juris Publici Ecclesiastici*, 2 vols., ed. tertia, Typis Polyglottis Vaticanis, 1947.

Palacký, František, *Geschichte von Boehmen, groesstentheils nach Urkunden und Handschriften*, 5 vols., in 10. Prague: In Commission bei Kronberger und Neber, 1846-67.

———, *Dějiny husitské*, 2 vols., Praha, 1850-1851.

———, *Die Geschichte des Hussitenthums und Prof. Constantin Hoefler; Kritische Studien*, 2. ed., Prag: F. Tempsky, 1868.

———, *Dějiny narodu českého* (History of the Czech Nation), Praha, 1848.

———, *Dějiny národu českého w Čechách a w Moravě dle puvodnich pramenů*, Praha: B. Tempsky, 1850-76.

———, *Oesterreichs Staatsidee*, Prag: J. L. Kober, 1866.

Papánek, Jan. *Czechoslovakia*, New York: International Universities Press, Inc., 1945.

Parsons, Reuben, *Studies in Church History*, 6 vols., 3. ed., Philadelphia: John Joseph McVey, 1886-1900.

Passaglia, Carolus, *De Ecclesia Christi*, 2 vols., (ed. C. Joseph Manz), *Ratisbonae*, 1851.

Pastor, Ludwig, Freiherr von, *Geschichte der Paepste seit dem Ausgang des Mittelalters. Mit Benutzung des paepstlichen Geheimarchives und vieler anderer Archive*, 16 vols., Freiburg im Breisgau: Herder, 1899-1933.

———, *Geschichte der Päpste* (im Zeitalter der Renaissance bis zur Wahl Pius II, Freiburg im Breisgau: Herder, 1886.

———, *The History of the Popes* (translated by Don Ernest Graf, O.S.B., and others). 37 vols. have been edited to date (1952). St. Louis: B. Herder Book Co., 1923 ff.

Pattee, Richard, *The Case of Cardinal Stepinac*, Milwaukee: The Bruce Publishing Co., 1953.

Paučo, Jozef, *Dr. Jozef Tíso o sebe* (Dr. Josef Tiso About Himself), Passaic, N. J.: Slovenský Katolícky Sokol, 1952.

Paulová, Milada, *Déjiny Maffie* (odboj Čechů a jihoslovanu za světové války 1914-1918), Praha: C. G. Unie A. S., 1937.

Pekař, Josef, *Smysl českých dějin* (The Sense of Czech History), Praha, 1929.

———, *Masarykova česká filosofie* (Masaryk's Czech Philosophy), Praha, 1912.

———, *Tři kapitoly o sv. Janu Nepomuckém* (Three Chapters About Saint John Nepomucene), Praha, 1921.

———, *Der Sinn der tschechischen Geschichte, Eingeleitet von Josef Pfitzner*, Brünn: Verlag Rudolf M. Rohere, 1937.

———, *Dějiny československé* (Czechoslovak History), Praha, 1921.

———, *Jan Hus* (Address delivered on the occasion of Hus's anniversary in Old Town Square), Prague, 1902.

———, *Bílá Hora*, Praha, 1922.

———, *Die Wenzels und Ludmila Legenden und die Echtheit Christians*, Prague, 1906.

———, *K sporu o zakládací listiny biskupství pražského* (A contribution to the controversy on the foundation charter of the bishopric of Prague), in *Czech Hist. Rev.*, vol. X, 1904.

Pendell, Elmer, *Society Under Analysis* (An introduction to sociology), Lancaster, Pa.: The Jogues Cattell Press, 1942.

Pennington, Arthur Robert, *The Counter-Reformation in Europe*, London: Elliott Stock, 1899.

Perkins, Frances, *The Roosevelt I Knew*, New York: The Viking Press, 1946.

Peroutka, Ferdinand, *Byl Eduard Beneš vinen?* (Was Eduard Beneš Guilty?), Paříž: Masarykuv demokratický svaz, 1950.

———, *Budování státu*, I-IV, (The Making of a State), Prague: Fr. Borový, 1934-6.

Pošvar, Jaroslav, *Nástin spravného práva trestního* (Outline of the administrative criminal right), studie o některých pojmech, zejmena o vině, 2 vols. Praha: Orbis, 1936-46.

Premoli, Orazio M., *Contemporary Church History, 1900-1925* (authorized English translation), London: Burns, Oates and Washbourne, Ltd., Publishers to the Holy See, 1932.

Quigley, Rev. J. Anthony, *Condemned Societies* (a historico-canonical dissertation in canon law), Washington, D. C.: Catholic University Press, 1926.

Ráček, Blažej, T. J., *Československé dějiny* (Czechoslovak History), II. dopl. vydání, Lad. Kuncíř v Praze, 1933.

Rádl, E., *La Question religieuse en Tchécoslovaquie*, Prague: The Gazette de Prague, 1922.

Rašín, Dr. Miroslav, *Svoboda si žádá obvahy* (Freedom Needs Courage), New York: C. S. Publishing Co., Inc., 1952.

Riccioti, Giuseppe, *Paulo Apostolo* (Biografia con introduzione critiche e illustrazioni), 2. ed., Roma: Coletti Editore, 1946.

Rieger, Franz Ladislaus, "Ein Charakterbild aus Boehmens neuester Geschichte," in *Histor-pol. Bl.* CXXXII, 1903).

Ripka, Hubert, *Czechoslovakia Enslaved: The Story of the Communist Coup d'État*, London: Gollancz, 1950.

———, *East and West*, London: Lincolns-Prayer Ltd., 1944
———, *The Repudiation of Munich*, London: Czechoslovak Ministry of Foreign Affairs, Information Service, 1943.
———, *The Soviet-Czechoslovak Treaty* (Speech delivered before the State Council on December 15, 1943, London), London: Czechoslovak Ministry of Foreign Affairs, Information Service, 1943.
———, *Speech on Relations Between Czechoslovakia, Poland and the Soviet Union as Part of Their Policy to the State Council*, London, May 17, 1943, London: Department of Information, Czechoslovak Ministry of Foreign Affairs, 1943.
———, *S východem a západem*, Londyn: "Cechoslovák," 1944.
Rommen, Heinrich Albert, *The State in Catholic Thought:* a Treatise in Political Philosophy, St. Louis and London: B. Herder Book Co., 1950.
Rosenberg, Alfred, *Der Mythus des 20. Jahrhunderts* (Eine Wertung der seelischgeistigen Gestaltenkaempfe unserer Zeit), ed. 176, Muenchen: Hoheneichen-Verlag, 1941.
Roubiczek, Paul and Kalmer, Joseph, *Warrior of God* (The Life and Death of John Hus), London: Nicholson and Watson, 1947.
Rowe, Henry Kalloch, *Society, Its Origin and Development*, New York: Charles Scribner's Sons, 1916.
Rozehnal, Alois, *Land Reforms*, New York: NCFE Research and Publications Service, 1953.
———, *Odborové hnutí v Československé Republice* (Trade Unions in the Czecho-Slovak Republic), NCFE Research and Publications Service, 1953.
Růžek, Ant., *Ochrana lidové demokratické republiky* (Protection of the People's Democratic Republic) (Zákon č. 231/1948, Sb.), Praha: Linhart, 1949.
Ryan, Rev. Gerald A., *Principles of Episcopal Jurisdiction* (a dissertation in public ecclestiastical law), Washington, D. C.: The Catholic University of America Press, 1939.
Ryan, John A., *The State and the Church* (written and edited for the Department of Social Action of the *NCWC*), New York: The Macmillan Co., 1936.
———, *Catholic Principles of Politics*, Rev. ed. of *The State and the Church*, New York: The Macmillan Co., 1940.
———, *Distributive Justice: The Right and Wrong of Our Present Distribution of Wealth*, 3. ed., completely revised, New York: The Macmillan Co., 1942.
Salin, Edgar, *Civitas Dei*, Tübingen: Mohr, 1926.

Salvany, Don Felix Sarda Y and Pallen, Conote B., *What is Liberalism?* St. Louis, Mo.: B. Herder, 1899.

Satolli, Francesco, *Loyalty to Church and State*, Baltimore: J. Murphy and Co., 1895.

———, *Prima Principia Juris Publici Ecclesiastici de Concordatis*, Roma: Typis A. Befani, 1888.

Schaff, Philip, *History of the Christian Church*, 5 vols., New York: Charles Scribner's Sons, 1910.

Scheeben, Matthias Joseph, *The Mysteries of Christianity* (translated by Cyril Vollert, S.J.), London: B. Herder Book Co., 1947.

Schmidlin, Josef, *Päpstgeschichte der neuesten Zeit*, 3 vols., Muenchen: Verlag Josef Koesel and Friedrich Pustet, 1933-1939.

———, *Päpstgeschichte der Neuesten Zeit*, Vol. II, Papsttum und Päpste gegenüber den modernen Strömungen, Pius IX und Leo XIII, 1846-1903, München: Josef Koesel und Friedrich Pustet, 1934.

Schmidt, Dana Adams, *Anatomy of a Satellite*, Boston: Little, Brown and Co., 1952.

Schmidt, Hermann Josef, *Der Kulturkampf*, Paderborn: F. Schöningh, 1926.

Schnitzler, Theodor, *Im Kampfe um Chalcedon* (Geschichte und Inhalt des Codex Encyclius von 458), Rome: Gregorian University, 1938.

Schroeder, Rev. H. J., *Disciplinary Decrees of the General Councils* (text, translation and commentary), London and St. Louis: B. Herder, 1937.

Schubert, v. H., *Der Kampf des Geistlichen und Weltlichen Rechts*, Akademie Heidelberg, Hist. Phil. Bl., 1927.

Schultes, Reginaldus Maria and Prantner, Edmund M., *De Ecclesia Catholica* (Praelectiones apologeticae), 2 vols., Paris: Symptibus F. Lethielleux editions, 1931.

Schuman, Frederick L., *The Nazi Dictatorship* (A Study in Social Pathology and the Politics of Fascism), 2. ed., New York: Alfred A. Knopf, 1936.

———, *The Nazi Dictatorship*, 2 ed., New York, 1936.

Schwarze, W. N., *John Hus, The Martyr of Bohemia*, London and Edinburgh: Fleming H. Revell Co., 1915.

Šebestík, Josef and Lukeš, Zdeněk, *Přehled předpisů o Němcich a osobách považovaných za němce*, Praha: Ministerstvo vnitra, 1946.

Sedlák, Jan. M., *Jan Hus*, Brno, 1915.

Seton-Watson, H. W., *Masaryk in England*, New York: The Macmillan Co., 1943.

Shea, F., *Man and the State*, Chicago: University of Chicago Press, 1951.

Sheen, Fulton J., *Communism and the Conscience of the West*, Indianapolis: The Bobbs Merrill Co., 1948, 1. ed.

———, *Communism: the Opium of the People* (pamphlet), Paterson, New Jersey, 1937.

———, *Liberty, Equality and Fraternity*, New York: The Macmillan Co., 1938.

———, *Freedom under God*, Milwaukee: The Bruce Publishing Co., 1940.

———, *Love One Another*, New York: P. J. Kenedy and Sons, 1944.

———, *Religion Without God*, New York-London-Toronto: Longmans, Green and Co., 1928.

———, *The Cross and the Crisis*, Milwaukee: The Bruce Publishing Co., 1937.

———, *The World's First Love*, New York: McGraw-Hill Book Co., 1952.

Shotwell, James T. and Loomis, Louise, *The See of Peter*, New York: Columbia University Press, 1927.

Shub, David, *Lenin* (A Biography), Garden City, New York: Doubleday and Co., Inc., 1948.

Shuster, George N., *Religion behind the Iron Curtain*, New York: The Macmillan Company, 1954.

Siegfried, André, *Nations Have Souls* (tr. by Edward Fitzgerald), New York: G. P. Putnam's Sons, 1952.

Snow, Edgar, *The Pattern of Soviet Power*, New York: Random House, 1945.

Šorm, Antonín, *Ve jménu demokracie*, Praha, 1922.

Sorokin, Pitirim A., *Russia and the United States*, New York: E. P. Dutton and Co., Inc., 1944.

Spinka, Matthew, *Christianity Confronts Communism*, New York and London: Harper and Brothers, 1936.

Šprinc, Mikuláš, *Sv. Andrej—Svorad*, Cleveland, Ohio: Opátstvo sv. Andreja-Svorado, 1952.

Srb, A., *Politické dějiny národa českého od počatku doby konstituční* (Political History of the Czech Nation from the beginning of the Constitution), 1861-1918, 2 vols., Praha, 1926.

Stalin, Joseph, *Leninism*, 2 vols. London: G. Allen and Unwin, 1933.

Stauracz, Franz, *Los von Rom* (Wahrheitsgetreue Schilderung der Osterreichischen Verhaeltnisse), 2. ed. Hamm i. Westf. Druck and Verlag von Breer and Thiemann, 1901.

———, *Dr. Karl Lueger, Zehn Jahre Buergermeister*, Wien and Leipzig: Wilhelm Braumuller, 1907.

Stone, Shepard, *Shadow Over Europe* (The Challenge of Nazi Germany), New York: The Foreign Policy Association, 1939.

Strakhovský, Leonid I., *A Handbook of Slavic Studies*, Cambridge, Mass.: Harvard University Press, 1949.

Stranský, Jan, *East Wind Over Prague*, London: Hollis and Carter, 1950.

Straub, Antonius, *De Ecclesia Christi*, 2 vols., Oeniponte: Sumptibus Felizian Rauch, 1912.

Stritch, Cardinal Samuel A., *The Papal Peace Program*, an address to the College and University Section of the National Catholic Youth Council, Washington, D. C.: National Catholic Welfare Conference, 1948.

Sturzo, Luigi, *Church and State*, New York: Longmans, Green and Co., 1939.

———, *Inner Laws of Society: A New Sociology*, New York: P. J. Kenedy and Sons, 1944.

Šusta, Josef, *Dvě knihy českých dějin*, Praha, 1917. (Two books of Czech history.)

Táborsky, Eduard, *Czechoslovak Democracy at Work*, Preface by Sir Ernest Barker, London: G. Allen and Unwin, Ltd., 1945.

Tanquerey, Adolf, *The Spiritual Life*, A Treatise on Ascetical Mystical Theology, translated by Herman Branderis, 2. ed., Tournai (Belgium), 1930.

———, *Synopsis theologiae moralis et pastoralis*, ed. 12, Typis Societatis Sancti Joannis Evangelistae, Desclée et Socii, Paris-Tornaci-Romae, 1936.

Taracouzio, T. A., *The Soviet Union and International Law* (A study based on the legislation, treaties and foreign relations of the Union of Socialist Soviet Republics), New York: The Macmillan Company, 1935.

Teeling, William, *Pope Pius XI and World Affairs*, New York: Frederick A. Stokes Co., 1937.

Telepun, Rev. L. M., *The Bloody Footprints*, New York: Vantage Press, Inc., 1954.

Thomson, S. Harrison, *Czechoslovakia in European History*, Princeton, N. J.: Princeton University Press, 1943.

Timasheff, N. S., *Religion in Soviet Russia, 1917-42*, New York:

Sheed and Ward, 1942.
Ulan, Adam B., *Titoism and the Cominform*, Cambridge: Harvard University Press, 1952.
Vajs, Josef, and Vašica, J., *Literárni památky o sv. Václavu a sv. Ludmile* (collection of old Slavonic literary records on St. Wenceslas and St. Ludmila), Praha: Sbornik Star Pamiatek, 1929.
Veit, Andreas Ludwig, *Die Kirche im Zeitalter des Individualismus 1648 bis zur Gegenwart*, 2 vols., Freiburg im Breisgau: Herder and Co., 1931.
Veselý, Jindřich, *Bezpečnostní agenda národních výborů* (Agency for Security of National Committees), Praha: Ministerstvo Vnitra, 1946.
Vlk, Václav, *Zákon o dvouletém hospodařském plánu* (Law concerning the two-year economic plan of October 25, 1946, No. 192 of Col.), 1. ed. Praha: Orbis, 1948.
Vogeler, Robert A., *I Was Stalin's Prisoner*, New York: Harcourt, Brace and Company, 1952.
Voigt, H. G., *Adalbert von Prag*, Berlin, 1898.
Vojíř V., *Slováci a koncepce Československá* (Slovaks and an idea of Czechoslovakia), Chicago: Color Printing Co. (Louis Malý), 1954.
Vondraček, Felix John, *The Foreign Policy of Czechoslovakia*, 1918-1935, New York: Columbia University Press, 1937.
Voste, M. Jacobus, O.P., *Studia Paulina*, ed. altera, Roma: Libreria del Collegio Angelico, Salita del Grillo 1, 1941.
Vrchovecký, Josef, *T. G. Masaryk a náboženství* (Masaryk and Religion), Prague, 1937.
Vyshinsky, Andrei, *The Law of the Soviet State*, New York: The Macmillan Company, 1948.
Wallace, Lillian Parker, *The Papacy and European Diplomacy, 1869-1878*, Chapel Hill: The University of North Carolina Press, 1948.
Welles, Sumner, *The Time for Decision*, New York and London: Harper and Brothers, 1949.
Wernz, Franciscus, S.J., and Vidal, P. Petrus, S.J., *Ius Canonicum*, 7 vols., 3. ed., Romae, 1938.
Werstadt, Jaroslav, *Ve jménu Husově pro svobodu národa* (In Hus's name for the Freedom of the Nation), Praha, 1935.
Wiemer, Peter F., *Martin Luther, Hitler's Spiritual Ancestor*, Hutchinson and Co., Ltd., 1939.
Wilmot, E. M.-Buxton, *A Catholic History of Great Britain* (with an introduction by C. C. Martindale, S.J.), London: Burns, Oates and Washbourne, Ltd., 1921.

Winter, Edward, *Bernard Bolzano und sein Kreis* (Sebastian Merkle gewidmet), Leipzig: Verlag von Jacob Hegner, 1933.

———, *Die geistige Entwicklung Anton Günthers und seiner Schule*. Paderborn: Verlag Ferdinand Schöningh, 1931.

———, *Der Josefinismus und seine Geschichte. Beiträge zur Geistesgeschichte Oesterreichs, 1740-1848*, Brünn-München-Wien: Rudolf M. Rohre, Verlag, 1943.

———, *Leben und geistige Entwicklung des Sozialethikers und Mathematikers Bernard Bolzano* (1781-1848), Hallische Monographien herausgegeben von Otto Eissfeldt Naz Niemeyer Verlag, Halle (Saale), 1949.

———, *Russland und die slawischen Völker in der Diplomatie des Vatikans 1878-1903*, Akademie-Verlag Berlin, 1950.

———, *Tausend Jahre Geisteskampf im Sudetenraum* (*das religiöse Ringen zweier Völker*), II. Auflage, Salzburg, Lepzig: Otto Müller, 1938.

Wiskemann, Elizabeth, *Czechs and Germans* (A Study of the Struggle in the Historic Provinces of Bohemia and Moravia), Issued under the auspices of the Royal Institute of International Affairs, London: 1938.

Workman, B. Herbert, *John Wyclif: A Study of the English Medieval Church*, 2 vols., Oxford: at the Clarendon Press, 1926.

Yurchak, Peter P., *The Slovaks: Their History and Traditions*, rev. ed., Whiting, Ind.: Obrana Press, Inc., 1947.

Žampach, A., *Katolici v zahraničnich bojich za československou samostatnost* (Catholics in foreign struggles for Czechoslovak independence), Praha, 1928.

Zapelena, Timothy, S.J., *De Ecclesia Christi*, 2 vols., Editio quarta recognita et aucta, Romae: apud Aedes Universitatis Gregorianae, 1946.

Zarnow, Gottfried, *Masaryk-Benesch, Philosophen* (*Abenteurer*) *Staatsgruender*, Dortmund Berlin: Volkschaft-Verlag, 1939.

Zlámal, Msgr. Oldřich, "Povídka mého života" (The Story of My Life), in *Katolik* (a series of articles), vol. LX, 1953-54.

Zrkesinski, Andrew J., *Religion of Nazi Germany*, Boston: Bruce Humphries, Inc., 1945.

COMMENTARIES ON CANON LAW

Abbo, John A. and Hannan, Jerome D., *Sacred Canons*, A concise presentation of the current disciplinary norms of the

Church, 2 vols., St. Louis-London: B. Herder Book Co., 1952.
Augustine, Chas.: *A Commentary on the New Code of Canon Law*. 10 books in 8 vols., St. Louis and London: B. Herder Book Co., 1919.
Woywood, Stanislav and Smith Callistus: *A Practical Commentary of the Code of Canon Law*. 2 vols. New York: Joseph F. Wagner, Inc.; London: B. Herder Book Co., 1919.

Periodicals

America (A Catholic review of the week, edited and published by the Jesuit Fathers of the United States), New York: The America Press, 1909-
American Ecclesiastical Review, The, published by the Catholic University of America Press, 127 vols.
Apolinaris (Commentarium juris canonici) Roma: Pontificium institutum utriusque juris, 24 vols.
Ark, The (A Catholic monthly concerning the Eastern rites), published by the Ukrainian Catholic Diocese, under the patronage of His Excellency Bishop Constantine Bohachevsky, D.D., Apostolic Exarch. 11 vols.
Bulletin of the International Peasant Union, Washington, D. C., 1950-
Catholic Digest, New York, 17 vols.
Catholic Mind, The, a publication of the America Press, 1902-
Československý přehled (Czechoslovak review), published by Free Europe Committee, Inc., New York, 1954.
Český časopis historický (Bohemian Historical Periodical), Praha.
Christian Democratic News Service, bi-monthly, published by Christian Union of Central Europe, Washington, D. C., 1951-
Civiltà cattolica, Società grafica Romana, Roma, Italy, 1850-
Clergy Review, The, London, 35 vols.
Congressional Record (Proceedings and debates of the 82nd Congress, first session), Washington: U. S. Government Printing Office, 1951.
Czechoslovak Newsletter (NCFE, Research and Information Center—Czechoslovak Section), New York, 1951.
Dobrý Pastier (The Good Shepherd), published by the Slovak Catholic Federation of America, Passaic, N. J., 1925-
Goloc Spasitelja (*The Redeemer's Voice*). Yorkton, Sask: Kalendar, 1952.

Hlas Československa, published by Rada Svobodného Československa, Washington, D. C., 1951-

Jurist, The, Review of the School of Canon Law, The Catholic University of America, Washington, D. C., 1941-

Keryx, The, published semi-annually by St. Basil's College, Stamford, Conn., 1945-

News from behind the Iron Curtain, published monthly by the Research and Publications Service. New York: NCFE, 1952-

New York Times Magazine, New York, 1896-

Nové Obzory (New Horizons), List čs. křestanské democracie, New York, 1953-

Nový Život (The New Life), published by the SS. Cyril and Methodius League, London, 1949-53, Rome, 1954-

Pope Speaks, The (Addresses and Publications of the Holy Father), The American Quarterly of Papal Documents, Chevy Chase 15, Maryland, 1954-

Review of Politics, The, Notre Dame, Ind.: The University Press, 1938-

Saturday Evening Post, The, Philadelphia, 1728-

Sign, The (National Catholic Magazine), published by the Passionist Fathers, Union City, N. J., 1921-

Slovakia, published by the Slovak League of America, 1950-

Tablet, The, a weekly newspaper and review pro-Ecclesia Dei, pro Rege et patria (Printed in Great Britain at Pettys Press by C. Nicholls and Co., Ltd., Reading, London and Manchester, and published by the proprietors, The Tablet Publishing Company, Ltd.), London, 1840-

Thomist, The, a speculative quarterly review of theology and philosophy (Dominican Fathers, Province of St. Joseph), Washington, D. C., 1939-

Thought, Fordham University Quarterly, New York: Fordham University Press, 1926-

Time, New York City.

Veritas, Czechoslovak Catholic documentation, published by the Christian Academy, Rome, 1951-

Věstník katolického duchovenstva, Ministerstvo školstvi, Prague, 1949-

Vinculum, Rome, 1951-

World Politics, a quarterly journal of international relations, Yale Institute of International Studies, Yale University, New Haven, 1948-

Zpráva o Československu (Report on Czechoslovakia), National Committee for a Free Europe, Research and Information Center, New York, 1950-

Zpravodaj, bulletin published by the Council of Free Czechoslovakia, Washington, D. C., 1949-

NEWSPAPERS

Denní hlasatel, the leading Czechoslovak daily in Chicago and suburbs, 1891-
Katolík, chief Catholic Bohemian newspaper in the United States, Chicago: The Bohemian Benedictine Press, 1895-
Lidová demokracie, list československé strany lidové, Praha, 1945-
Lidové noviny, list svazu československých spisovatelů, Praha, 1892-
L'Osservatore Romano, giornale quotidiano politico religioso, Città del Vaticano, 1861-
Národ (The Nation), the only Czech Catholic daily in the United States. Chicago: The Bohemian Benedictine Press, 1899-
NCWC News Service, issued by the press department, National Catholic Welfare Conference, Washington, D. C.
New York Times, The, New York, N. Y.
Rudé Právo. U'střední organ kommunistické strany československa (Organ of the Communist party), Praha, 1920-
Svobodné Slovo, list československé strany socialistické, Praha, 1944-

INDEX

Abbiamo Bisogno, 156
Absolutism
—enlightened, 92
—of People's Democratic Republic, 341
—policy of, 96
—reactionary, 93
Academic League, 215
Achilles, 20, 95
Acta Apostolicae Sedis, passim.
Acta Curiae, 283
Action Committees, 306
Action Committee of the National Front, 288 and *passim.*, X.
Adalbert, St., 65, 66, 158, 358
—celebrations of, 200
Adamček, Leopold, 408
Adamits, 86
Adler, Viktor, 105
Adolf of Auersperg, Count, 99
Agrarian
—party, 182, 186, 442
—reforms, 256
Agricultural Commission, 271
Albík of Uničov, 75, 76
Alexander V, Pope, 74
Alliance for Liberation and Freedom in Czechoslovakia, 442
American Army, 173
Andrej-Svorad, 65
Andrew, St., 39
Anglican Church, 47
Antichrist, 69 and *passim.*
Anti-Semitism, 105, 146
Antithesis
—Reformation—Counter-Reformation, 140 and *passim.*
Apocalypse, 10
Apocalyptists, 69
Apostasies of priests, 128 ff.
Apostolate of Sts. Cyril and Methodius, 131, 161
Apostles
—first council of the hierarchy, 53
—relationship with Peter, 38
—as teachers, 22, 23, *passim*
through Chapters I and II
Apostolic internuncio, 192
Aristotle, 112
Association of the Defenders of Freedom, 254
Association of Moravian Women, the, 215
Atheism, 11, 67
Athenaeum, 118
Atlantic Charter, 167
Augsburg,
—meeting, 91
—principle of, 11
Augustine, St., 19, 81, 145
Augustinians, 97
Authority
—a physical person, 31
—a corporation, 31
—definition, 32
Australia, 437
Austria, 106, 146
—monarchy of, 107 and *passim.*
Austrian-Hungarian Monarchy, 11, 12, 67, 105
"Away from Rome" movement, 67 and *passim*

Baar, Jindřich, 119
Baden, 104
Bach
—absolutism of, 99
Badeni, 105, 107, 112, 114
Balbín, Bohuslav, 93
Baltazar Cossa (Pope John XXIII), 75
Baltzer, 103
Baptist, 47
Barnas, Štefan, 327, 391
Baroque period, 67
Barrow, Isaac, 38
Barták, Stanislav, 377, 378
Bartoli, Paulo, 315
Basilians, 205
Basle, general council of, 43, 88, 90
Bavaria, 104
Beckovský, 93

Belák, Žoltan, 387
Belgium, occupation of, 154
Benedict XV, Pope, 16, 122, 123, 125, 134
Beneš, Eduard, 122, 134, 135, 143, 151, 152, 167, 168, 169, 171, 178, 191, 204, 215, 216, 227, 228, 241, 242, 243, 244
Beneš, Jaroslav, 189
Beňo, Michal, 387
Beran, Josef, Archbishop of Prague, 12, 152, 187, 195, 202, 203, 218, 220, 244, 245, 247, 251, 266, 280, 281, 282, 288, 301, 324, 326, 363, 364, 366, 372, 373, 406, 410
Beránek, Thomas, 395
Berchtesgaden, 151
Berlin Pact, 182
Bernolák, 94
Bethlehem Chapel in Prague, 73
Bertoli, Paulo, 376, 416
Beroun, 173
Beust, 99
Bielitz, 107
Billot, Ludovicus, 50
Bishops
—successors of the Apostles, 22, 33, 34, 55 and *passim.*
—defenders of Church rights, 56, 247, 228, 232, 332, 344, 407, 408, 412, 313, and passim.
Bismarck, 94, 104, 107, 121, 153, 155
Bláha, Oldřich, 203
Blahoslav, Jan, 89
Blesík, Jan, 377, 378
Boháč, 128
Bohemia, 86 and *passim.*
Bolshevism, 148, 186
Bolzano, Bernard, 97, 98
Boniface VIII, Pope, 23
Boniface, St., 104
Bonifatius Verein, the, 109
Bordeaux, 178
Borgongini-Duca, 135
Bosnia, annexation of, 121
Boukal, John, 392
Braito, Sylvester, 161, 377, 378
Bratislava, 404
Brauner, Francis, 99
Brentano, Franz, 111, 144
Breslau, 332
Briedon, Daniel, 366
British broadcasts, 170
British socialism, 183
British-Soviet alliance, 167
Brno, 87, 162, 187, 225, 261, 405
Broj, F., 187
Brynych, 115
Buchenwald, concentration camp of, 162
Buchta, Josef, 387
Budapest, 120, 411
Budějovice, 408
Bugar, Miloš, 187, 217, 222
Bukovina, 106
Bulletin of the Catholic Clergy, 267, 268
Burnham, James, 444
Burýšek, Josef, 375
Burzio, Josef, 143
Buzalka, Michael, 195, 211, 390, 394
Byzantium, 10

Čech, Frank, 408
Caesar, 10, 15
Caesarea Philippi, 36
Caesaro-papism, 10
Cairo, 169
Calvinists, 41, 48
Candidates, priests as political, 247
Canon law, 6, 8, *passim*
Čarnogurský, Pavol, 217
Caroloferdinandea Universitas, 91
Carpatho-Ruthenia, 152, 171, 189
Čarský, Josef, 131, 196, 255, 390, 410, 504
Casablanca, 169
Catechisms, supervised by Communists, 257
Catholic Action
—authentic, 57, 139, 110, 155, 161 and *passim*
—schismatic, sponsored by Communists, 271, 273, 277, 278, 285, 296, 305, 307, 308, 310, 405, and *passim*
Catholic Charities in Prague, 218, 302, 371
—national administration of, 304
Catholic Church
—and New Church Laws, 335
—and reforms, 80
—Church-State relationship, 5, 16, 96, 232, 234, 306, 349, and *passim*
—enslavement of, 316
—heroic stand, 151
—hierarchical society, 51 and *passim*

—historical institution, 4
—independent society, 23, 29
—in catacombs, 414
—legal society, 28, 29, 32
—marks of, 27
—necessity of, 26
—perfect society, 3, 4, 17, 20, 22, 24, 25, 29, 30, 31, 32, 33, 81, 286 and *passim*
—private society, 5, 11, 13
—society of public law, 5, 11, 13
—public society, 4, 9, 13, 27, 28, 34
—religious society, 26
—society of chosen people (Hus), 69
—subjugation to state by Communists, 341, 400, 259
—supernatural society, 37
—superior to state, 10
—visible society, 11, 21, 26, 27
Catholic Club, 161
Catholic Congress in Prague, 12, 140
Catholic Moderna, 119
Catholic organizations, disbanding of, 258
Catholic Press, suppression of, 279
Catholic priests,
—statistics in Nazi concentration camps, 163
Catholic publications, suppression of, 257
Catholic schools, suppression of, 277
Catholic youth, 131
Census, 127, 130
Central Action Committee, 227, 233, 266
—of the National Front, 249, 250, 259, 307, 332, 333, 342
—of the Communist party, 253 and *passim*
—of Catholic Action (schismatic), 297
Central Council of Lutherans in Slovakia, 217
Central Europe, 10, 106
Čepička, Alexej, 14, 232, 245, 247, 261, 288, 307, 315, 328, 341, 371, 372, 373, 375, 387 and *passim*
Černocký, Bohuslav, 282
Černý, Jan, 162
Černý, Josef, 225, 438
Cerreti, 134
České, Budějovice, 323
Český, Brod, 85
Chalice, as symbol of Hussites, 88
Chamberlain, 150, 152, 166
Charisms, 57, 59
Charles IV, King, 66, 70, 71, 73, 85, 91
Charles University in Prague, 68, 72
Chatel, Ferdinand, 103
Cheb, 87
Chelčický, Peter, 88, 89, 90, 143
Chiliasm, 86
Chlumčanský, Archbishop of Prague, 98
Christian
—democracy, 57
—Democratic party, 149, 212
—Social party, 117
—People's party, 222
—union, 444
Christian Brothers, 124
Chudoba, Bohdan, 187, 188, 215
Church-state, negotiations of, 312 and *passim*
Churchill, Winston, 166, 167, 178
Ciano, 154
Čihak, Josef, 391, 408
Čihost in Bohemia, Miracle at, 373
Cinek, Francis, 128, 162, 203
Ciriaci, Peter, 136, 138, 140
Civil Marriage, text of Bill of, 351
Clementis, Vlădŏ, 166, 398
Codex Encyclius, 10
Comenius, Jan Amos, 89, 92, 116, 143
Cominform
—religious program of, 273
—second meeting of, 273
Comintern, the, 166
Communion
—under both species, 77, 85, 87
Communism, materialistic and anti-Christian, 308
—relations with Catholic Church, 187
Compactata, 88
Comte, Auguste, 112
Concentration camps, 162, 163, 399, 436
Concordat, 94, 102
Conference
—of Czechoslovak hierarchy, 218
—for the restoration of Christian tradition in Czechoslovakia, 440
Confiscation of ecclesiastical property, 210, 214, 256, 258

Confraternity of St. Michael, 214
Congregation
—of the Council, decree of, 9
—of the Holy Office, condemning the Jednota, 126
Congregationalist, 47
Congress
—of Catholic Youth, 215
—of Labor Unions, 227
—of Peasants' Committees, 227
Congrua, 268, 269, 335, 351
Consistory
—Bishop's offices occupied by state commissioners, 300 and *passim*
"Conspiracy Against the Republic," 217, 362, 363
Constance, Council of, 41, 69, 71, 77, 79, 83, 85
Constantine, 9
Constitution of Czechoslovak Republic
—of Feb. 29, 1920, 132, 133, 240
—of May 9, 1948, 239, 318
Cooperation of state and Church, 416
Cordovani, Mariano, 286
Corpus Christi celebration, 282
Council of Free Czechoslovakia, 438, 439, 441, 444
Counter-Reformation, 11, 67, 91, 92, 93, and *passim*
Coup d'état, 220, 406, 410
Craftsmen, Middle Class party, 438
Croatians, 121
Cvinček, Andrej, 204, 213
Cyril and Methodius, Sts.
—association of, 117, 118
—league of, 158, 440, 444
—movement, 131
—regiment, 123
Czech Academic League, 131
Czech Brethren, 91, 92, 113, 163, 188, 189
Czech crown, 68, 92
Czech intelligentsia, 10
Czech nobles, protest against, 85
Czecho-Moravian Church, 158
Czechoslovak Army, mobilization of, 150, 151
Czechoslovak Catholic Bank, 162
Czechoslovak Church, 126, 127, 128, 129, 130, 144, 158, 227, 254 and *passim*
Czechoslovak Communists, 98, 166 and *passim*
Czechoslovak episcopate
—protest against *Bulletin of the Catholic Clergy,* 267
—letter *ad clerium,* 270
—letter against schismatic Catholic Action, 279
Czechoslovak exiles, 170, 436, 442, 445 and *passim*
Czechoslovakia,
68, 150, 225, 148, 152, 225, 154 and *passim*
Czechoslovak legions, 122
Czechoslovak National Catholic Church, 277
Czechoslovak National Church, 371
Czechoslovak refugees, statistics of, 436
Czechoslovak Republic, 37, 38, 39, 122, 132, 140, 221, 400
Czechoslovak schism, 126
Czechoslovak State, 67, 68
Czech Reformation, 10
Czokaš, Karol, 408

Dachau, concentration camp of, 162, 163, 288
Daladier, 151
Dalmatia, 106
Daluege, Kurt, Reichsprotector, 163
Darkness, Temno, 114 and *passim*
Dechet, John, 366, 367, 369, 371, 403
Decrees of the President of the Republic, the, 186
Defenders of Peace, 398
De Gaulle, Charles, 178
De Groot, 51
Deism, 21
De Lagarole, Paul, 109
De Liva, Ottavio, 373, 416
Democracy, 154, 399 and *passim*
Demonstration of Students, Nov. 17, 1939, 159
Denis, Ernest, 130
Descartes, 72
Deutschnationaler, Verein, 106
Děvin, 310
Devotio moderna, 70, 158
Dialectical materialism, 148 and *passim*
Didachus, 57
Diplomatic immunity of representative of Vatican, violation of, 315
District National Committee in Turnov, 321
Divini Illius Magistri, 251

Divini Redemptoris, 156
Dlouhý-Pokorný, 128
Dobner, Gelasius, 94
Dobrovský, Josef, 94, 97, 113, 116
Dobrovský Pastier, 412
Dobrý Pastier, 412
Documentation Catholique, 412
Doellinger, Ignatz, 103, 104
Doerner, Francis, arrest of, 280
Dohalský, 162
Dolanský, John, 136, 222
Dolek, Jan, 317, 318, 320
Dolní Smokovec, 260, 327, 328
Domažlice, 87
Dorost, 131
Dositej, Serbian bishop, 128
Dostál-Lutinov, Karl, 119
Dostojewski, 188
DP camps, 437
Draft of a bill concerning payment for personal and material needs of churches—of July 15, 1949; text of, 332-333
Drtílek, Otakar, 405
Drtina, Prokop, 186, 219, 221, 223, 229
Ducháček, Ivo, 438
Dudas, Cyril, 408
Durčanský, Ferdinand, 218, 442
Durich, Josef, 122
Duriš, Julius, 222, 256
Dvořák, Antonín, 395
Dvořák, Xavier, 119, 125, 128
Dvorník, Francis, 10
Dyk, Victor, 12, 119

Ecclesiastical hierarchy
—a divine institution, 47 and *passim*
Ecclesiastical property, confiscation of, 85, 184
Economic determinism, 148
Eden, Anthony, 169
Education, Ministry of, 301, 302
Einsenkolb, V., 105
Eliáš, General and Prime Minister, 163
Eltschkner, Antonín, 373, 386, 391, 409, 412
Emauzy monastery, 109
Emigration from Czechoslovakia, 437 ff.
Encyclicals
—*Firmissimam Constantiam*, 156
—*Ingruentium Malorum*, 424, 433
—*Mit Brennender Sorge*, 155
—*Orientales Ecclesias*, 424, 425
Enlightenment, the, 11, 93, 96, 97, 103
Epilogue, 447
Episcopal conferences replaced by conferences of patriotic priests, 404
Episcopalians, 47
Episcopal vicars
—statement opposing state commissioner in episcopal office, 320
Episcopate
—negotiations with government of 400 and *passim*
Ernest of Pardubice, 70
Ethiopia, 147
Eucharistic circles, 270, 292
Evangelischer Bund, 107
Evangelical Youth
—association of, 269
Excommunication of Communists
—decree of, 313, 309, 402

Falk, 104
Falkenauer, Frank, 405
Fanfrdla, Karel, 162
Farský, Dr., 128
Fascism, 147, 148, 155 and *passim*
Fascist anti-government plot, 217
Fathers Conventuals, 302
Febronianism, 11, 38, 103
Ferdinand II, 91, 92
Ferdinand Franz, Duke, 146
Ferdinand, King, 90
Fesl, Michael, 97
Feudalism, 347
Feudal system, 10
Feuerbach, Ludwig, 148
Fiala, Francis, 302, 303, 304, 305
Fierlinger, Zdeněk, 166, 174, 227, 228, 230, 310, 387, 398 and *passim*
Filipec, Kamil, 282
Finda, 162
Five Year Plan, the, 184
Forni, Raffaele, 190, 192
France, 229
Francis Joseph, Emperor, 99
Franěk, Dr., 223
Frankfurt, Council of, 94
Frank, K. H., State Secretary, 153
Franta, Peter, 405
Franz of Florencourt, 108
Frederick II, Emperor,

—law concerning heretics of, 49
Free Europe radio, 412
Freemasonry, 97
Fuerstenberg, Archbishop of Olomouc, 117
Fulda,
—conference of, 104

Gabriel, Francis, 408
Galicia, 106
Gallicanism, 11, 43, 103
Garaffe, Apostolic Legate, 91
Gautsch, Count, 114
Gazette of the Catholic Clergy, 298, 301, 355, 356, and *passim*
General elections
—May 26, 1946, 185, 186
—May 30, 1948, 244
Geneva
—conference of, 147
George of Poděbrady, King, 88, 89
George Schoenerer, 146
George VI, King of England, 168
German Army, 159
German Catholic Church, 103
German Empire, 162
German Red Cross, 160
Germans, 38, 68, 84, 89, 150, 153, 166 and *passim*
—expulsion of, 184
Germany
—arbitrary agreement of, 151
Germany,
—disarmament of, 147
Germany
—forced-labor camps in, 164
Germany
—neo-paganism of, 156
Gestapo, 153 and *passim*
Glogar, Josef, 404
Godfrey, W., Apostolic Delegate, 190, 191
Goebbels, Joseph, 153
Goering, Herman, 154
Gojdič, Pavol, Bishop, 205, 394, 395, 412
Gothic period, 84
—school, 84
Gottwald, Klement, 166, 219, 227, 228, 241, 244, 278, 312, 350, 373
Gratian, 10
Government Bureau for Church Affairs, 335 and *passim*
Graz, 109
Great Britain, 166, 229 and *passim*
Greece
—occupation of, 154
—government in exile of, 167
Greek Catholic Church, 205 and *passim*
Gregorian calendar
—introduction of, 205
Gregory XII, Pope, 74, 76, 77
Greguška, Josef, 408
Gross, Joseph, 110
Gunther, Anton, 104
Guntherians, 103
Gustav Adolf Verein, 107

Habáň, Methodius, 161, 189
Haberman, Minister of Education, 135
Hácha, Emil, Dr., 152, 153, 182
Hála, Francis, 222, 229
Hálek, Jiří, 441
Halle, 107
Hammarskjold, Dag, Secretary General of UN, 445
Hapsburgs
—dynasty of, 11, 90, 91, 92, 93,
—96, 105, 119, 144
—Empire, 97
Harnack, 58
Havelka, Rudolf, 405
Havlíček, Karel Borovský, 94, 98,
—*Kutna Hora* Epistles of, 102
Haynald, Archbishop of Kolscza, 103
Hegel,
—doctrine of, 97
—dialectical idealism, 148
Heidler, Alexander, 364
Heindrich, Arnošt, 219
Henlein, Konrad, 150
Henry VIII, 312
Herbart, 111
Herben, John, 114
Hergenrother, Joseph, Cardinal, 69
Herzegovina,
—annexation of, 121
Heydrich, Reinhard, Reichsprotector, 163, 164
Hierarchy
—a divine institution, 4, 47, 49, 412
—ordinals, 32, 33
—ordinis, 32, 33
—division of, 33
—definition of, 47
—necessity of, 50, 52, 59

—as intermediator of Christ's power, 50
—as a necessary requirement for the Church, 50
—suitability of, 52
and *passim*
Hilgenreiner, Karl, 115
Hille, 98
Historical materialism, 148
Hitler, Adolf, 141, 146, 150, 152, 153, 159, 167, 380
—Hitlerism, 157 and *passim*
Hlas Československa, 412
Hlasists, 120
Hlinka, Andrej, Msgr., 132
Hlouch, Josef, 195, 323, 391, 413, 408
Hluboká over the Moldau, 303, 304
Hobbes, 72
Hobza, Antonín, Dr., 4, 5, 6, 393
Hodonín, 202
Hodža, Milan, 151
Hohenzollerns, 105
Holland
—occupation of, 154
—government in exile of, 167
Holý, Prokop, 87, 143
Holy days, cancellation of, 215
Holy Father, the, 30 and *passim*
Holy Orders
—lower, 56
—higher, 56
Holy See, 214, 236, 402
Hopko, Basil, 391, 412
Horák, Alexander, 278, 404
Horský, Dr., 117
Horvath, Stephan, 212
Hostýn, 160
Houska, Miroslav, State Commissioner of Archbishop's Office, 280, 316 and *passim*
Hradčany Castle, 87, 228, 238
Hradec Kralové, 300, 301
—meeting of episcopal vicars in, 320
Hradil, Frank, 444
Hromádka, F. L., 188, 302
Hronek, Ladislaus, 387
Huber, 104
Hulín, 303
Humanism, 84
Human society
—definition of, 18
—four factors of, 18
—purpose of, 18, 19
—a perfect society, 18
—the moral power of, 31
—authority of, 31
—public welfare of, 18
—two perfect societies, 19
and *passim*
Hume, David, 72
—scepticism of, 112
Hungarians, 120, 121, 184, 188
Hurban-Vajanský, 120
Hurdálek, Bishop, 97
Hus, John, 10, 41, 49, 69, 70, 71, 72, 73, 74, 75, 76, 78, 80, 83, 84, 81, 86, 88, 95, 123, 131, 135
Hussites' anthem, 158
Hussites' drive against Rome, 85 and *passim*
Hussitism, 66, 70, 84, 86, 94, 123, 124, 144, 177, 238, 272 and *passim*
Huyn, Archbishop of Prague, 125
Hviezdoslav, 120
Hynek, Josef, 395

Iconoclasm, 9, 124
Ignatius of Antioch, 56
Impanation, 69
Individualism, 148
Indulgences, 76
Innsbruck, 109
Intellectualism, 72
Interdict, Prague, 76
International law, 6, 7, 9
International Refugee Organization (IRO), 457
International Student Day, 159
Internuncio, 6, 7
Internunciature of Prague, 315
Iron Curtain, 3, 13, 187, 401, 416, 433
Ius reformandi, 91

Jablonský, Father, 98
Jagellons, 89
Janduno, John, 69
Janota, Dr., 318, 319
Jansenists, 104
Jantausch, Pavol, 131, 196
Japan, 167
Jarolímek, Bohuslav, 201, 203, 281, 391
Jednota katolickeho duchovenstva
—origin of, 125, 127

—demands of, 125
—condemnation of, 126
—liquidation of, 131
Jednotný Svaz zemědelců
—association of farmers, 250
Jeremias, 36
Jerome of Prague, 72, 76, 78, 83
Jesuits
—introduction into Bohemia, 190
—expulsion of, 93
Jesus Christ,
—full jurisdiction, 22, 35, 36 and *passim* regarding references to Church.
Jewish priests, 23
Jews
—persecution of, 164, 165. See Anti-Semitism.
Jihlava, assembly at, 88
Jílek, Vojtěch, 160
Jirásek, Alois, 67, 93
Jirsík, Valerian, 98, 102, 117
Johaneum, 124
John of Jenštein, 70
John Nepomucene, St., 124, 158
—600 year anniversary, 197 *ff*.
John Očko of Vlaším, Cardinal, 70
John the Baptist, St., 36
John XXIII, Pope, 59, 74, 75, 77
Josephinism, 11, 13, 43, 96, 103
Joseph II, Emperor, 92
—reforms of, 93, 386
Julian calendar, 205
Jungman, Josef, 94
Jureček, Josef, 250
Jurisdiction
—definition of, 32
—object of, 33
—division of, 48
—of the Pope, 33, 34
—granted by canonical mission, 33 and *passim* with reference to Church, hierarchy, society.

Kaizel, 111
Kajpr, Adolf, 214, 377, 378
Kant, Immanuel, 72, 97, 112
Karlovy Vary (Karlsbad)
—meeting of Cominform in, 273
Kasan, 387
Kašpar, Karel, Cardinal, 155, 157, 162, 202
Katholiken Tage, 108, 110, 117
Katolická Akce, publication of, 278
Katolické Noviny, 215, 263, 279, 306, 397
Katolík, 215, 379
Kempný, Jan. 187, 212, 218, 221
Kirsch-Veit, 98
Klácel, Francis Matthew, 97
Klátil, Franta, 187
Klimek, Adolf, 229, 438
Klofáč, Václav, 115
Klokoty, 160
Kmeťko, Karol (Archbishop of Nitra), 195, 206, 207, 211, 219, 255
Kněžská Liga (Priests' League), 127
KNV Gottwaldov, 263
Kobylka, Deputy, 227
Kočvara, Štefan, 223
Kollár, John, 94, 120
Koněv, Marshal, 179
Konrad of Vechta, Archbishop of Prague, 75
Kopecký, Václav, 213, 215, 222, 381
Kopřiva, Ladislav, 273, 398
Kordač, Archbishop Francis of Prague, 115, 125, 130, 135, 140
Košice Program, 179, 182, 183, 202, 206, 315, 439
Kossuth, F. W., 102
Kotalík, Francis, 406
Kovač, Alfons, 395
Kovář, Dr., 189
Kozák, J. B., 189, 230
Koželuhová, Helena, 187, 229
Krajina, Dr., 229
Král, František, 442
Kramář, Karel, 111, 121, 122, 123, 132
Kratochvil, Josef, 162, 189
Krejčí, Francis, 130
Kremlin, the, 398, 399
Kristek, Josef, 387, 405
Krodt of Bonn, 103
Krofta, Kamil, 95, 136
Krojher, 127, 130
Kroměříž, 304
Krugner, Salesius, 97
Kruzlich, Immrich, 212
Kubáň, Methoděj, 387
Kubíček, Frank, 405
Kubík, Josef, 406
Kulač, Jaroslav, 391, 392, 408
Kulturkampf, 104, 107, 219
Kultusministerium of Vienna, 11, 12, 13
Kupecký, John, 92

Kupka, Josef, bishop, 162
Kutal, Francis, 373
Kutná Hora, 87
—agreement of, 90
—decree of, 73
Kuzmany, association of, 217

Labor unions (URO), 184, 185 and *passim*
Ladislav of Naples, 76
Land reforms, 184, 256, 257
Lateran agreement in Italy, 6
Lausanne, Conference of, 147
Laušman, Bohumil, 228, 230
Law of October 14, 1949
—economic security to churches and religious associations, text of, 338 *ff.*
—establishment of state office for church affairs, text of, 335 *ff.*
League of Nations, 147
Leibnitz, 72, 97
Leipzig
—council of, 103
—university of, 73
Lenin, 275, 386
Leningrad, 166
Leo XIII, Pope, 60, 104, 108, 330
Leo Verein, 109
Lettrich, Josef, 213
Liberalism, 11, 21, 93, 94, 117
Liberec, 201
Lichner, John, 223
Lidice
—annihilation of, 163
Lidová demokracie, 187, 231, 249
Lincoln, Abraham, 183
Linz, Program of, 105, 106
Lipany, 87, 88
Litoměřice, major seminary of, 97
Litomyšl, 201
Locarno, Agreement of, 147
Lochman, John, 162
Locke, 72
London, battle over, 153
Loreta, 160
Los von Rom movement, 11, 12, 68, 94, 96, 104, 106, 107, 109, 110, 119, 130, 144
Ludvík, King, 89
Lueger, Karl, Dr., 108
Luther, Martin, 11, 41, 89, 103
Luxemburg
—dynasty, 66
—occupation of, 154
Lysá over Elbe, 303

Maecenases, 188
Macháček, Pavol, 408
Machalka, Augustin, 377
Machula, Jaromír, 192
Mafia, 122
Magna Carta of March 16, 1939, 164
Majer, Salesius of Osek, 103
Majer, Václav, 438
Majestas, decree for freedom of religion, 91
Mandl, Antonín, 280, 392
Mara, Jan, 282
Marani, Marino, 309, 402
Marian sodalities, 269
Marie Theresa, Empress, 92
Maritain, Jacques, 9, 17, 44
Marmaggi, Francis, nuncio, 135, 136
Marrakesch, 167
Marshall Plan, 219, 220
Marsilius of Padua, 38, 59, 69
Martinů, 162
Marxists, 230, 437 and *passim*
—Marxist courses, 258
Marx, Karl, 116, 148, 149, 189, 386
Masaryk Democratic Federation, 437
Masaryk, Jan, 219, 221, 228, 230
Masaryk, Thomas Garrigue, 12, 66, 67, 79, 109, 110, 111, 112, 113, 114, 117, 118, 121, 122, 124, 140, 143, 145, 149, 186, 188, 189, 216
Mastilák, Jan, 377, 378
Matocha, Joseph Karel, 238, 255, 259, 310, 311, 313, 314, 327, 365, 413
Matoušek, Kajetán, 255, 391
Matyáš, Emperor, 91
Meixner, Arthur, 192, 377
Melanchthon, 38
Memel, occupation of, 154
Memorandum of the Clergy
—text of, concerning the projected law on financial guarantees by state, 334 *ff.*
Mendel, Gregor, 97
Metropolitan Chapter of St. Vitus,
—meeting of 406
Meyer, August, 38
Meyer, Ferdinand of Zwickau, 105
Micara, Clemens, 134
Michelis of Braunsberg, 103
Mikuláš of Litomyšl, 72
Mikulášek, Francis, 377, 378

Milíč of Kroměříž, 70
Minařík, Josef, 377
Mindszenty, Cardinal, 315, 411
Minister of Information, 213. See Kopecký
Minister of State Police, 398. See Kopřiva.
Mladá Boleslav, 201
Modernism, 11, 21, 47
Modus vivendi, 12, 134, 140, 190, 219, 255, 256, 258, 327, 328, 340, 400
—text of, 137, 138
Mogyprossy, Ladislav, 408
Mojzes, association of Catholic students, 258
Molde, 98
Moltke, 121
Moravian empire, 65
Moravian nobles, protest against Council of Constance, 85
Moscow, 166
—meeting in, 169
Moulino, 103
Mountain Blaník, knights of, 158
Mrtvý, Wenceslaus, 392
Munich, 152, 154, 205
—general congress of, 104
—conference of, 147, 148
Musealní Slovanská Společnost, 120
Mussolini, Benito, 147, 152, 154

Náboženská matica, 269
Na Hlubinu, 161, 378
Napp, E. F., 97
Našinec, 215
National Assembly, 215, 244, 335, 406
National Catholic Welfare Conference, 437 and *passim*
National Committee for a Free Europe, 441, 442
National Committees, 173, 182, 185, 241
National Council, 411
National Democratic party, 185, 438
National Front, 212, 438 and *passim* with reference to government and political party
Nationalism, 103, 118
Nationalization, 184
—of schools, 216
National Socialism, 149, 150
National Socialist party, 115, 184, 185, 186, 216, 221, 230, 332, 442, 437
Na vyboj, 187
Nazi occupation, 12, 171, 187
Nazis
—confiscation of Church property, 161
—evacuation of villages by, 164
—liquidation of diocesan consistories, 162
—prohibition of pilgrimages, 160
—end of tyranny, 170
Nazism, 147, 148, 150, 152, 155, 160, 167, 170
Necsey, Eduard, 195, 413
Nejedlý, Zdeněk, 166, 214, 236, 265, 278, 310 and *passim* with reference to school and Church.
Němec, Francis, 438
Neo-Catholics, 104
Neo-utraquists, 90, 91
Neopomucenum, 108, 131, 139
Nepustil, J., 139
Nermuť, Jindřich, 187
New Church Laws, approbation by National Assembly, 350
Nicea-Constantinople Synod, 27
Nicean Council, 128
Nicodemus, 447, 448
Nietzsche, Friedrich, 155
Ninth Congress of the Czechoslovak Communist Party, 284
Nobles, union of 452 Czech and Moravian, 85
Nominalism, 69, 70, 71, 72, 74
Nominalist, 72
Non-opportunists, 103
Nosek, Francis, 136
Nosek, Václav, 166, 215, 217, 221, 224, 260, 357, 375
Novák, Bishop of Czechoslovak Church, 189
Novák, Oswald, 406
Nová Ríše, concentration camps for priests, 405
Nové Obzory (New Horizons), 444
Nový, Vilém, 310
Nový Život, 376, 412
Nuncio, 6, 135
Nuremberg, meeting at, 103

Oath of allegiance to people's democratic regime, text of, 351
Obligatory civil marriage, bill of, 285
Obroda, 187
Obtulovič, Lutevít, 218
Obuch, Otto, 218

Occam, 69
Old Catholics, 104, 105, 109, 110, 117
Old Czech party, 111, 116
Oliva, Eduard, 203, 387, 406
Olomouc, 161, 221, 404
Onderek, Francis, 335, 391, 406
Ondrák, Ambrož Leo, 220, 422, 442, 444
Opasek, John, 391, 392
Opatrný, Theofil, 373, 406
—forced resignation of, 406
Opik, Ambrosius, 108
Oranienburg, concentration camp at, 159
Order
—definition of, 55
—natural, 18, 19
—supernatural, 18, 19
Ordinariate in Prague, vacancy of, 407
Orel, 123, 131, 161, 444
Orphans, 87. See Taborites
Orthodox Church, the, 13, 117, 118, 163, 189
Osservatore Romano, 250, 367, 392, 394

Pacelli, Eugenio, 155
Pácha, Wenceslaus, 395
Palacký, Francis, 73, 87, 94, 111, 145, 121
Páleč, Štěpán, 72, 76, 78
Pallier, Václav, 134
Pan-Germanism, 107, 109, 105, 121, 146, 150
Panico, 140
Pankrác Penitentiary, 350
Pan-Slavism, 13, 120
Pantheistic Realism, 69
Papal Bull of September 2, 1937, 140, 141, 191
Papal nuncio, as dean of diplomatic corps, 192
Parachutists, 163
Parity of parties, 183
Partisans, 171
Pašek, Bishop of Old Catholics, 104
Pastoral letter of August 26, 1948
—text of, 252
————of June 19, 1949
—text of, 283-86
———of November 17, 1949
—text of, 353-58
Pastoral power, 47 and *passim*
Patent of Tolerance, the, 93
Patková, Dr., 227
"Patriotic" priests, 48, 278, 302, 310, 341, 398, 405, 409, 416
Pavlík, Vilém, 187
Pax Romana, 215
Pearl Harbor, 167
Peasant unions, 185
Pekař, Josef, 79, 84, 92, 130, 146
People's Democratic Regime, 401 and passim with references to government
People's party, 107, 136, 184, 185, 216, 220, 249, 305, 444
Peřina, 93
Pernerstorfer, 105
Peroutka, Ferdinand, 244, 437
Pétain, Henri, 154
Peter, expelled master of Dresden, 77
Peter, St.
—authorization of, 35
—in Rome, 41
—pastoral power and *passim* with reference to Church, hierarchy, jurisdiction.
—primacy of, 37, 38, 39, 40
—vicar of Christ, 38, 40
—visible head of the Church, 34
Petr, Alois, 227, 230, 266, 278, 265
Pfeiffer, Benedict, 97
Photius, 38, 41
Pícha, Mořic, 255, 301, 302, 320, 327, 387, 391
Pietor, John, 223
Pilgrimages, 160
Pisa
—Council of, 43, 74
Pistorian Synod, 59
Pittsburgh
—agreement of, 132
Pius II, 88, 89
Pius VI, 59,
Pius IX, 99
Pius X, 119, 123
Pius XI, 16, 136, 137, 139, 155, 190, 331, 414
Pius XII, 192, 193, 196, 200, 201, 420, 424, 416, 419
Plato, 112
Plíhal, 406
Plojhar, Josef, 230, 247, 148, 251, 260, 278, 310, 388, 414
and *passim* with references of patriotic priests
Plzeň, 87, 173, 201

Pobožný, Robert, 255, 326, 364, 387, 391, 412, 415
Podlaha, Antonín, 131
Poland
—occupation of 154
—government in exile of 167
Polanský, Diónysius, 278
Poles, 68
Police Commander Dynybyl, 222
Police SNB, 225
Polish minority, 152
Politburo, 273
Pontiff of Rome
—Head of Catholic Church, 277
Pope, the
—dogma of infallibility, 103
—heroic stand, 158
—jurisdiction of, 4, 286
—letters to Czechoslovak bishops, *passim*
—primacy of, 38
—successor to St. Peter, 4
—supreme head of the Universal Church, 3, 298
Positivism, 112
Pösteny, Jan, 211
Pozdech, 204
Prager Tagblatt, 128
Pragmatic Sanction, 92
Pragmatism, 112
Prague, 221, 301
Prague Articles, 86, 88
Prague, Conference of bishops at, 344, 352
Prchala, 442
Prečan, Leopold, archbishop, 136
Predestinarianism, 69
Přerov, meeting of Catholic modernists at, 119
Priests
—public declaration of loyalty to bishops, text of, 323, 324
—statistics on arrests of, 399
Proces proti vatikánským agentům v Československu, 393
Procházka, Adolf, 186, 222, 229, 444
Procházka, Matěj, 111, 117
Procopius, St., 65
Progressive movement, 12, 157, 165, 309
Protection of the democratic people's regime, bill of, 255
Proctectorate of Bohemia and Moravia, 152, 161
Protestant Patent, 102
Protestants, liberal, 21
Protocol of Karlovy Vary, text of, 273 *ff*.
Proudhon, 148
Provisional National Assembly, 183, 215
Provincial National Committee for Bohemia, 223
Prussians, 104, 166
Przemyslide, 66
Pujman, 278

Quebec City, meeting at, 169

Rabas, Francis, 365
Rád, Catholic cultural review, 161
Radical realists, 72
Radimský, Vladimír, 139
Rajhrad, Benedictine monastery at, 162
Rakovník, 173, 229
Rádl, Emmanuel, 188
Rašín, Alois, 121
Rath, Ilja, 377
Rationalism 21, 72
Rauscher, Cardinal of Vienna, 103
Realism, 69, 70
Red Army, 173, 178, 179
Reformation, 11, 68, 79, 123
Reformists, 47
Reich codex, 269
Reichsprotector, 152, 157, 159
Reinkens, 103, 104
Reischl, Frederich of Munich, 103
Regional Action Committees, 253 and *passim* with reference to government and political parties.
Religious indifferentism, 308
Reparations, 147
Rerum Novarum, 108. See Leo XIII
Resistance movement, 173, 187 and *passim*
Rex-sacerdos, medieval idea of, 10
Richerianism, 43
Rieger, F. L., 99, 108, 111
Ripka, Hubert, 170, 171, 178, 220, 221, 437
Rittel, 104
Ritter, Saverio, 140, 143, 192, 194, 260
Robert Bellarmine, St., 26
Rokycana, 87
Rokycany, 173
Romža, Theodor, bishop, 205
Ronge, John, 103

Roosevelt, Franklin D., 167
Rosegger, Peter, 105, 106
Rožmital, Castle, 405
Rozsévač, 252
Royal Air Force of Great Britain, 153
Royal *placet,* 11
Rozehnal, Alois, 187
Rudé Právo, 303, 310, 311
Rudolf, Emperor, 91
Runciman, Lord, 150
Russia
—ally of Western powers, 166
—despotism of, 166
—non-aggression pact with Germany, 154
—occupation of, 154
—recognition *de jure,* 169
Russian Army, purge of, 168
Russian Orthodox Church, 258
Růžička, 102
Rykýr, Rudolf, 395
Ryška, Josef, 395

Sabol, Šebastian, 205
Sacred Congregation of the Holy Office,
—decree regarding schismatic Catholic Action, text of, 285, 286
—declaration concerning marriage of Communists, text of, 309
—decree of excommunication of Communists, text, of, 307, 308
—decree concerning consecration of a bishop without canonical provision, text of, 415
—a warning concerning youth, text of, 402
Sacred Congregation of Council of June 29, 1950
—concerning canonical institution and provision of ecclesiastical offices, text of, 403, 404
Sacred Consistorial Congregation,
—declaration about banishment of Archbishop Beran from his see, text of, 409, 410
Saint Vavřineček, 162
Šanda, Adalbert, 125, 409
Sázava, 310
Sborník Velehradský, 118
Schafer, Andreas, 387, 405
Schikora, Rudolf, 160
Schlatleiter, Albanus, 109
Schoenerer, George von, 105, 106, 107
School reforms, 216, 340
Schulte, 103, 104
Schultes, 51
Schulz, Karel, 161
Schwarzenberg, Cardinal of Prague, 103
Schwarzenberg, Francis, 192
Sdruženi demokratických uprchliku, (alliance of democratic refugees), 441
Sea of Tiberias, 39
Self-accusations, 411
Sensualism, 72
Serbs, 121
Sezimovo Usti, 243
Shrines, 160
Sidor, Karol, 442
Sigismund, Emperor, 77, 78, 85, 87, 88
Sigismund of Hohenvart, Count Karel, 99
Šilhan, Frant., 377
Simony, 174
Skoupý, Karel, 195, 204, 364, 405, 413, 416
Škrabík, Andrej, 366
Skrbenský, Cardinal, 131
Slanský, Rudolf, 306, 398
Slavíček, 375
Slavonic liturgy of SS. Cyril and Methodius, 13
Šling, Otto, 398
Slovak bishops, 211, 217 and *passim* with reference to Church and state.
Slovak commissioners, 404
Slovak Democratic party, 183, 213, 217, 221, 442
Slovakia
—autonomous government, 152
—independent state, 153
—religious situation in, 204
—special legislation concerning Church, 134 and *passim* with reference to political development.
Slovak National Council, 258
Slovak National Council (SNR)
—decree of nationalization of schools, 206
Slovak National uprising, 216
Slovak Parliament, 182
Slovak Party for Freedom, 213
Slovak Republic, 195, 202
Smetana, Augustin, 102

Šmídek, Karel, 117
Sobota, John, 387, 404
Sochorec, Rostislav, 222
Social Democratic party, 115, 116, 149, 184, 185
Socialism, 149, 184, 166, 316
Socialistic bloc, 185
Socialist program, 183
Socialists, 124, 128, 136, 167, 172, 216, 437, 439
Socrates, 112
Sokol, 127, 163
Soukup, Francis 115
Soviet-Czechoslovak agreement, 178
Soviet-Czechoslovak economic treaty, 220
Špilberg, prison of, 162
Soviet Union, 174, 225
Špilberg, prison of, 162
Spiritualia, 59
Spolok sv. Vojtěcha, 120, 211
Šrámek, John, 12, 115, 117, 130, 131, 136, 157, 186, 215, 222, 229, 444
Stalin, Josef, 166, 168, 219, 316
Stanislav of Znojmo, 71, 72
Stanovský, 162
Stará Boleslav, 160
Staré Město-Velehrad, 222
Stašek, Bohumil, 162
Šťástný, Alfons, 115
State Bureau of Church Affairs, 335, 348, 401
State censorship, 215, 292
State commissioners in ecclesiastical offices, 282, 346, 401, 404
State *patronat*, 347, 406
Štěfaník, Milan Rostislav, 122
Stehlík, Antonín, 406, 410
Stěhule, Dr., 128
Stepinac, Aloysius Cardinal, 196
Stockholm resolution for peace, 419
Stojan, Antonin Cyril, archbishop, 117, 121, 158
Strahov, Abbey of, 12, 281
Straka, Francis, 247
Stránecký, Vilém, 440
Streicher, Julius, 146
Stranský, Jaroslav, 218
Stříž, Antonin, 201
Strossmayer, bishop of Diakovar, 103
Student uprising against Nazis, 159
Štulc, Václav, 98, 117
Štúr, Ludovít, 94
Sudeten, 104 and *passim*
Sušil, Francis, 117, 158
Šusta, Josef, 130, 145
Svatá Hora, 160
Svatoš, Ludvík, 128
Svaz revoluce, 203
Švec, Otakar, 391, 392, 393, 408
Švehla Antonín, 115, 136
Šverma, 166
Svétlík, 162
Sv. Martin Declaration, 122
Svoboda, Ludvík, 224, 227, 228
Svobodné Slovo, 224, 225
Syrový, Jan, 151

Taaffe, 105
Tabach, 189
Tábor, 85, 86, 88, 116
Taborites, 87
Tachov, 87
Tajovský, Vít, 375, 377
Te Deum celebration in St. Vitus Cathedral, 245
Teheran, meeting in, 169
Tenora, 162
Terezín, concentration camp in, 163, 164
Tertullian, 55
Thirty Years' War, 92
Thomas, Aquinas St., 18, 20, 33, 40, 43, 52, 61, 72, 189
Tiso, Josef Dr., 153, 182, 195, 202, 204, 213
Titman, Alois, 408
Toufar, Joseph, 374
Toman, Josef, 405
Tomášek, Francis, 255
Totalitarian regimes, 154
Třebizký, 118
Treason of the Vatican and Bishops, the, 279
Trent, Council of, 59, 61, 90, 91
Trial of Religious in Prague, 377
Triple Alliance, 121
Trochta, Štépán, bishop, 195, 236, 245, 255, 259, 391, 395, 415
Trnava, 327, 408
Tuchačevsky, Marshal, 168
Tuleja, John, 387
Turnov, 201, 321
Tusar, Vlastimil, 132
Two Year Plan, 189
Tylínek, 162, 203
Tyl, Heřman, 395

Urban, Jan, 189, 201, 377, 378
Ubi Arcano Dei, 414

URO, 222, 234
Ursiny, Jan, 218
Ultraquists, 89, 90
Ultramontanism, 104
Uh. Hradiště, 202
Underground movement, 153
Union of Young People of the Czechoslovak Church, 269
Unitarians, 189
Unionism, 136 and *passim*
United Nations Assembly, 444
United Nations Assembly, text of memorandum, 445.
United States, 166, 167, 229
Unity of Czech Brethren, 89, 90, 93
Universal Declaration of Human Rights, 434

Valdes, 86
Valdštejn, 124
Vandalism, 86
Velehrad, 117, 160, 136, 306, 310
Veritas, 412
Verolino, Gennaro, 260, 315, 363, 376, 416
Versailles, Treaty of, 147, 148
Vestnik Katolického duchovenstva, 270
Verdier, John, Cardinal, 140
Vicarii forannei, 280
Vichy government, 154
Vienna
—Congress of, 1815, 192
—parliament of, 116
Vigorita, Peter, 308
Vilím, Blažej, 229
Vinařický, Karel Al., 98
Vishinsky, Andrei, 273
Višnovský, Nicolas, 404
Vitus, St., Cathedral, 281
Vladislav, King, 89
Vlček, Francis, 365
Vološín, A., 152
Vojtaššák, John, 200, 211, 327, 391, 394
von Papen, Franz, 147, 155
von Ribbentrop, 151
Vyšehrad, 87
Vatican
6, 7, 10, 134, 136, 158, 191, 213, 306, 315, 370, 373, 399, 400, 401
—Council of, 39, 42, 43, 59, 94, 103, 105
—diplomatic relations disrupted, 416
—radio, 300, 401, 412, 413

Word of God, free preaching of, 85
Waldeus, 69
Waldensians, 69, 77
Waldhauser, Konrad, 70
Warnsdorf, 104
Warsaw rebellion, 153
Washington, D. C., meeting in, 169
Weber, Antonin, bishop, 195
Weltanschauung, 249
Wenceslaus of Dubá, 358
Wenceslaus, St, 66, 67, 124, 158
Wenceslaus IV, King, 70, 73, 75, 85
Wenceslaus Square in Prague, 228
White Mountain, battle on, 91, 92
William I, Emperor, 106
William II, Emperor, 121
Willman, Otto, 110
Wilson, Woodrow, 122
Windthorst, Ludwig, 104
Winter, Edward, 97
World War I, 105
World War II, 147, 163, 172
Wyclifites, Czech, 72
Wyclif, John, 11, 41, 68, 69, 74, 75, 76

Yugoslovia
—government in exile of, 167
—occupation of, 159
Young Czechs, 111, 116
Young Men's Christian Association, 437

Zahradnik, Bohuslav, 125
Zahradník-Brodský, 128
Zápotocký, Antonín, 185, 215, 222, 227, 250, 278, 286, 287, 310, 315, 316
Zarecký, Stěfan, 408
Žatec, 87
Zbyněk Zajíc of Hassenburg, Archbishop, 72, 74, 75
Železný, Jan, bishop, 78
Zela, Stanislav, bishop, 9, 162, 391, 392, 393, 313
Zenkl, Peter, 222, 437
Zgarbik, Antonin, 214
Zionists, 277
Žižka, Jan of Trocnov, 85, 86, 87
Zlin, 306
Zmrzlik, Ludvík, 315
Zorin, Valerian Alexadrovic, 228
Zwingli, 11